United States Congress House

Report of the Committee on Banking and Currency

Together with Hearings there of, ..

United States Congress House

Report of the Committee on Banking and Currency
Together with Hearings there of, ..

ISBN/EAN: 9783337119560

Printed in Europe, USA, Canada, Australia, Japan

Cover: Foto ©Suzi / pixelio.de

More available books at **www.hansebooks.com**

REPORT

OF THE

COMMITTEE ON BANKING AND CURRENCY,

TOGETHER WITH

HEARINGS

THEREOF, ON

BILL H. R. 8149,

FIFTY-THIRD CONGRESS, THIRD SESSION.

1894.

WASHINGTON:
GOVERNMENT PRINTING OFFICE.
1894.

OMMITTEE ON BANKING AND CURRENCY, HOUSE OF REPRE SENTATIVES UNITED STATES.

FIFTY-THIRD CONGRESS.

WILLIAM M. SPRINGER, Illinois, *Chairman.*

EWIS SPERRY, Connecticut.
CHOLAS N. COX, Tennessee.
TH W. COBB, Missouri.
AVID B. CULBERSON, Texas.
ILLIAM T. ELLIS, Kentucky.
MES E. COBB, Alabama.
HN DE WITT WARNER, New York.
M L. JOHNSON, Ohio.
JAMES C. C. BLACK, Georgia.
URIEL S. HALL, Missouri.
JOSEPH H. WALKER, Massachusetts.
MARRIOTT BROSIUS, Pennsylvania.
THOMAS J. HENDERSON, Illinois.
CHALES A. RUSSELL, Connecticut.
NILS P. HAUGEN, Wisconsin.
HEN Y U. JOHNSON, Indiana.

FRED L. FISHBACK, *Clerk.*

p

NATIONAL BANKING ASSOCIATIONS.

DECEMBER 17, 1894.—Committed to the Committee of the Whole House on the state of the Union and ordered to be printed.

Mr. SPRINGER, from the Committee on Banking and Currency, submitted the following

REPORT:

[To accompany H. R. 8149.]

The Committee on Banking and Currency, to which was referred the bill (H. R. 8149) to amend the laws relative to national banking associations, to exempt the notes of said banks from taxation upon certain conditions, and for other purposes, having had the same under consideration, report the same back with the recommendation that it pass.

The laws of the United States heretofore passed authorizing national banking associations to issue circulating notes require that the banks issuing them shall deposit with the Secretary of the Treasury bonds of the United States as a security for the ultimate redemption of such notes. The amount of circulating notes can not exceed 90 per cent of the par value of the bonds. At the time the national banking act was passed a bond security of this kind was deemed necessary to secure the bill holders against possible loss.

THE SECURITY REQUIRED.

Your committee are of the opinion that a security to the full amount of the circulating notes issued is no longer necessary for the safety of the notes. The bill, the passage of which is recommended by your committee does not require the deposit of bonds of the United States, or of any other interest-bearing obligation, but in lieu of such security provides as follows:

First. A guaranty fund consisting of Treasury notes, including the notes issued under the act of Congress approved July 14, 1890, equal to 30 per cent of the circulating notes applied for.

Second. A safety fund, which will amount when it reaches its maximum to 5 per cent upon the total amount of national-bank notes outstanding.

Third. A first lien upon all the assets of the association issuing the same.

In case the guaranty and safety funds and the assets of the failed bank are not sufficient to redeem the notes of such bank, a pro rata assessment upon all the other banking, associations, according to the amount of their outstanding circulation, is to be made by the Treasury Department, and the banks so assessed shall have a first lien upon the assets of each failed bank for the amount properly chargeable to such bank on account of the redemption of its circulation. It is believed by your committee that the funds thus provided will be amply sufficient to secure the notes of failed banks.

AMOUNT OF THE SECURITY.

According to the report of the Comptroller of the Currency for the year ending October 31, 1894, it appears that there were at the close of that year in operation in the United States 3,756 national banks, with an authorized capital stock of $672,671,365. The bill reported by your committee limits the amount of circulating notes which any bank may issue to 75 per cent of its capital stock. If, under this bill, the national banks should take out the entire circulation to which they would be entitled, the aggregate of circulating notes would be $504,000,000. The 5 per cent safety fund upon this circulation would amount to $25,020,000. The guaranty fund required by the bill upon this circulation would amount to $151,000,000.

The resources of all the banks at that time amounted to $3,473,922,055. It thus appears that upon a possible circulation of $504,000,000 there would be a present available security of $151,000,000 guaranty and $25,000,000 of safety funds, and an ultimate fund upon which assessments could be made to the amount of $3,473,922,055. During the great financial crisis of 1893, 158 national banks suspended payment, having a capital stock of $30,350,000. If the national banks in the United States had taken out the full amount of circulation to which they were entitled at that time, under the proposed bill, if it had been in force at that time and if the suspended banks had taken out their maximum circulation, the notes of such banks would have amounted to $22,762,000. Thirty per cent of that amount would have been secured by the deposit of legal-tender notes. This would have left $13,934,000 of circulating notes for payment out of the safety fund, which, as before stated, would have amounted to $25,020,000.

These facts demonstrate conclusively that if the proposed bill had been in force during the crisis of 1893, if all the banks had theretofore taken out circulation to the maximum amount allowed by law, and if the failed banks had also taken out their maximum circulation, the guaranty and safety funds would have been ample for the payment of the entire circulation of the outstanding notes, and would have left a surplus of over $11,000,000 still in the safety fund without the necessity, even in a great crisis of that kind, of making any assessment on the resources of the other national banks. But of the 158 banks which suspended payment, 86 banks, with a capital stock of $18,205,000, resumed business within the year, and were able to pay all their liabilities, including their circulating notes. Only 65 banks, with a capital stock of $10,935,000, passed into the hands of receivers. If we assume that the notes of the 65 banks only were to be paid out of the safety and guaranty funds, there would have been only $8,200,000 of notes outstanding if all of the banks which passed into the hands of receivers had taken out notes to the maximum amount allowed.

The 30 per cent guaranty fund would have paid $2,460,000 of these notes, which would have left only $4,100,000 to have been paid out of the 5 per cent safety fund. But all of the failed banks had available assets which would have been applied to the payment of their outstanding notes. Their unavailable assets, which would have realized something in the end, and the amount which would be received on account of the personal liability of the stockholders, would further lessen the amount which would have to be paid out of the safety fund. If it should be assumed that all of the national banks which were in existence on the 31st of October, 1894, were organized under the proposed bill, and that all of them in a great financial crisis should fail, and if it should be assumed that all of them had taken out circulation to the maximum amount allowed by the proposed bill, the conditions would then be as follows:

The whole amount of circulation would be $504,000,000. The guaranty and safety funds in the Treasury would amount to $176,000,000. This would leave $328,000,000 in circulating notes, the payment of which would be secured by pro rata assessments upon all the national banks whose resources, as before stated, amounted, on the 31st of October, 1894, to $3,473,922,055. The amount of notes, it will be seen, would not equal 10 per cent of the resources out of which they could be paid. The resources of the national banks do not include the personal liability of the stockholders, which is equal to the whole amount of the stock, and this amount, which at that time, as before stated, was $672,000,000, is an additional security for the ultimate redemption of the circulating notes. In view of these facts, your committee are of the opinion that should the proposed bill become a law, the notes which would be issued under it would be absolutely safe under any and all possible business conditions.

JOINT LIABILITY FOR CIRCULATION.

Some doubt has been expressed as to whether banks would take out circulating notes under the proposed bill, in view of the remote and contingent joint liability of all the banks for the circulating notes of each. Your committee are of the opinion that this is not an unreasonable requirement. National banks enjoy valuable privileges and franchises. They owe something to the public, in consideration of the benefits which they receive from legislation. If they are regardful of their own interests and the interests of the note holders there can be no loss to them nor to the note holders by reason of this requirement. The tax of 1 per centum upon the circulating notes of national banks heretofore required is reduced by the proposed bill to one-half of 1 per cent per annum. The proceeds of this tax are intended to reimburse the United States for the expense of printing bills, in the first instance, and reprinting mutilated bills and expenses incident to the issuance and ministration of the currency bureau.

There is also a tax imposed of one-half of 1 per cent upon the amount of circulating notes to constitute the safety fund provided for in the bill, but when this tax accumulates to 5 per cent upon the amount of the circulating notes outstanding it is to cease, and will not be reimposed unless the safety fund be reduced in payment of the notes of failed banks. The Secretary of the Treasury is authorized by the proposed bill to invest any money belonging to the safety fund in United States bonds, and such bonds and the interest accruing thereon are to be held as a part of the safety fund.

REDEMPTION OF NOTES.

The proposed bill provides that each bank shall redeem its notes at par on presentation at its own office, or at its own office and at such agencies as may be designated by it for that purpose. Any bank may retire any portion of its circulation by forwarding its notes to the Comptroller of the Currency for cancellation, and thereupon 30 per cent of the amount of the canceled notes shall be returned to the bank. This permits the bank, when retiring its notes, to withdraw its portion of the 30 per cent guarantee fund, but it can not withdraw any amount of the 5 per cent safety fund. Any bank which desires to take out circulation after a portion of the safety fund has been contributed by other banks must pay its pro rata share into said fund before receiving notes.

DEFACED AND MUTILATED NOTES.

The same provisions of law as heretofore existed in regard to defaced and mutilated notes are provided in the proposed bill for notes issued under it.

TIME OF TAKING EFFECT.

Section 7 provides that national banks heretofore organized and having bonds on deposit to secure circulation shall, on or before the 1st day of July, 1895, withdraw such bonds, and deposit with the Treasurer of the United States a guarantee fund, consisting of legal-tender notes, including the notes issued under the act of July 14, 1890, equal to 30 per cent of its outstanding circulation at that time, thus bringing the existing banks under the provisions of the new law.

SECTIONS REPEALED.

Sections 9 and 12 of the act approved July 12, 1882, and section 31 of the act approved June 3, 1864, and all acts and parts of acts amendatory thereof are repealed by the proposed bill.

The sections repealed are as follows:

SEC. 9. That any national-banking association now organized, or hereafter organized, desiring to withdraw its circulating notes, upon a deposit of lawful money with the Treasurer of the United States, as provided in section four of the act of June twentieth, eighteen hundred and seventy-four, entitled "An act fixing the amount of United States notes, providing for a redistribution of national-bank currency, and for other purposes," or as provided in this act, is authorized to deposit lawful money and withdraw a proportionate amount of the bonds held as security for its circulating notes in the order of such deposits; and no national bank which makes any deposit of lawful money in order to withdraw its circulating notes shall be entitled to receive any increase of its circulation for the period of six months from the time it made such deposit of lawful money for the purpose aforesaid: *Provided*, That not more than three millions of dollars of lawful money shall be deposited during any calendar month for this purpose: *And provided further*, That the provisions of this section shall not apply to bonds called for redemption by the Secretary of the Treasury, nor to the withdrawal of circulating notes in consequence thereof.

The Secretary of the Treasury stated before the Committee on Banking and Currency that it might not be absolutely necessary to repeal section 9, above mentioned, for the reason that the proposed bill dispenses entirely with the deposit of bonds and with the payment of lawful money to redeem circulation, but the spirit of the section is, as stated by the Secretary, that the national banks shall not redeem in the aggregate more $3,000,000 of their circulation per month, and having retired any part of their circulation they shall not be permitted to increase it again until after six months. It is for this reason that the bill proposes to repeal that section.

Section 12 is as follows:

SEC. 12. That the Secretary of the Treasury is authorized and directed to receive deposits of gold coin with the Treasurer or assistant treasurers of the United States, in sums not less than twenty dollars, and to issue certificates therefor in denominations of not less than twenty dollars each, corresponding with the denominations of United States notes. The coin deposited for or representing the certificates of deposits shall be retained in the Treasury for the payment of the same on demand.

Said certificates shall be receivable for customs, taxes, and all public dues, and when so received may be reissued; and such certificates, as also silver certificates, when held by any national banking association, shall be counted as part of its lawful reserve; and no national banking association shall be a member of any clearing house in which such certificates shall not be receivable in the settlement of clearing house balances: *Provided*, That the Secretary of the Treasury shall suspend the issue of such gold certificates whenever the amount of gold coin and gold bullion in the Treasury reserved for the redemption of United States notes falls below one hundred millions of dollars; and the provisions of section fifty-two hundred and seven of the Revised Statutes shall be applicable to the certificates herein authorized and directed to be issued.

Section 5207 of the Revised Statutes, referred to in section 12, prohibits any national bank from depositing certain kinds of Government securities as collateral for obligations incurred by them, and that provision is made applicable by this section to the gold and silver certificates.

It is the opinion of the Secretary of the Treasury that if the right to deposit gold and obtain gold certificates is taken away a greater amount of gold will be paid into the Treasury of the United States for customs duties than heretofore.

Section 31, above mentioned, which is repealed by the proposed bill, requires each national bank in certain cities to keep a fixed reserve equal to 25 per cent of the amount of their deposits, and requires national banking associations in other cities to keep a fixed reserve of 15 per cent on their deposits.

That part of the section which required the computation to be made on the circulation of the bank as well as on the deposits has been repealed, so that as the law now stands these banks are required to keep this reserve on their deposits alone.

The repeal of section 31 is not an essential part of the currency system embraced in the proposed bill. The Secretary of the Treasury, in his report to Congress at the beginning of the present session, recommends this repeal, and gives the following reasons therefor:

It will be observed that the plan submitted proposes the repeal of all provisions of existing laws which require national banks to hold a fixed reserve against deposits, and, as this is a departure from the practice which has prevailed continuously for more than thirty years, it is proper to state, briefly, the reasons which have prompted me to make this suggestion. When the national banking system was originally authorized it was regarded by many as a doubtful experiment at best, and accordingly various precautionary restrictions and limitations were imposed for the security of the note holders and depositors which practical experience has since shown to be unnecessary and sometimes harmful. Among these are the requirements that bonds shall be deposited to secure 90 per cent of their par value in circulating notes and that a fixed reserve, which can not be lawfully diminished, shall be held on account of deposits. The consequence of this last requirement is that when a bank stands most in need of all its resources it can not use them without violating the law.

The necessity for holding a sufficient reserve against deposits is not questioned, and, in fact, the business of receiving deposits and discounting paper ought never to be conducted without it, but it should be held for actual use when the occasion arises, and not made legally inaccessible at the very time when it was theoretically supposed to be beneficial in sustaining the credit of the bank and affording relief to its customers. Under the present law, when a bank finds its reserve in danger of reduction below the legal requirement, on account of the demands of its depositors, it is compelled at once to call in its loans, thereby increasing the distrust and aggravating the situation, which a judicious use of the reserve would have relieved; and besides, at such times, in order to protect the reserve, which is then entirely useless for all practical purposes, clearing-house certificates, various forms of time checks and bills, and other devices of doubtful legality are habitually resorted to for the purpose of supplying circulation to take the place of lawful money lying idle in the vaults of the banks.

To provide for a reserve which can not be utilized, even at a time of the greatest stringency and distrust, without incurring the penalties of forfeiture, affords a most striking illustration of the impolicy of legislative interference with the natural laws of trade and finance. It is not the duty or province of the Government to control or regulate the private affairs of the people, except for certain well-defined purposes, and as the custody and use of funds belonging to depositors are matters which affect only the interests of the immediate parties they should be left to their own judgment and discretion. The duty of the Government, so far as it has any duty in the premises, is simply to provide that all the currency issued under its authority is sufficiently secured to prevent its loss or depreciation in the hands of the people, who are compelled to receive and pay it out in the transaction of business; but a bank is not dependent upon the Government for authority to receive deposits, and its use for that purpose by the public is as purely voluntary as the credit extended to any other corporation or to a private individual.

Every prudently managed bank, if left free to conduct its deposit and discount business in the manner most advantageous to its own interests and the interests of its patrons, will undoubtedly keep on hand a reasonable reserve to meet not only all the ordinary demands upon it, but to provide for such emergencies as are liable to occur in the community where it is located; but it ought not to be prohibited by law from using such reserve for the only purposes it was designed to accomplish. The average amount of reserve held by all the national banks does not usually exceed 17 or 18 per cent of their deposits, while the statistics show that the State banks doing a deposit and discount business, and which are not required by law to keep a fixed reserve, have generally kept on hand, in ordinary times, about 20 per cent of their deposits, a fact which conduces strongly to sustain the position that a regulation upon this subject is not really necessary in order to secure the safe management of banking institutions, and therefore ought not to be continued.

RETIREMENT OF LEGAL TENDERS.

Section 9 of the proposed bill provides that the Secretary of the Treasury may in his discretion use from time to time any surplus revenue in the redemption and retirement of United States legal-tender notes, but the amount of such retired notes shall not in the aggregate exceed an amount equal to 70 per cent of the additional circulation taken out by all of the banks under the proposed bill. This limitation upon the amount of legal tenders to be retired is for the purpose of preventing any forced contraction of the total volume of the circulating medium. Under the proposed bill an amount of legal-tender notes equal to 30 per cent of the circulation would be deposited in the Treasury and thus withdrawn from circulation. The net increase of circulation would be 70 per cent of the total circulation taken out. The amount which the Secretary might retire with the surplus revenues could not therefore contract the total volume.

The reasons for providing for the retirement of legal-tender notes may be briefly stated as follows:

First. The amount of such notes outstanding at this time is about $500,000,000, including the notes issued under the act of July 14, 1890. A gold reserve of $100,000,000 is required to be kept in the Treasury for the redemption of legal-tender notes on demand. In the settlement of foreign balances gold is required. A constant drain has been going on for several years in order to settle foreign demands. All persons desiring to ship gold abroad obtain it by applying to the Treasury of the United States. Those paying customs duties pay in silver certificates or legal-tender notes. The whole demand for foreign shipment of gold is upon the Treasury of the United States. When the gold reserve is reduced below what is deemed by him a safe limit the Secretary of the Treasury issues bonds to replenish it, and after it is replenished the drain continues, and the gold reserve is again brought below the limit. Another issue of bonds becomes necessary, and thus results a continuous repetition of bond issues.

Second. There is an apprehension in the minds of investors, both in this country and in Europe, that at some time the Government may fail to pay the legal-tender notes in gold on demand. This apprehension gives insecurity to investments and prolongs the financial depression. It is believed by your committee that if the volume of legal-tender notes could be gradually reduced by applying the surplus revenues for this purpose better financial conditions would prevail.

GOVERNMENT LIABILITY.

It should be stated in this connection that the proposed bill will exempt the Government of the United States from all liability for the redemption of national-bank notes and place the sole responsibility upon the banks themselves. The banks will be amply able to take care of their own issues, the Government will be released from any liability, and bill holders will be secured under the provisions of the proposed bill from any possible loss.

BANK PROFITS.

The Secretary of the Treasury submitted to your committee an estimate prepared in the office of the Comptroller of the Currency as to the probable profits of circulation by national banks under the proposed bill as compared with profits under the existing law. The statement of the Secretary of the Treasury upon this subject is as follows:

Under the plan proposed a national bank having a capital of $100,000, and being therefore entitled on a deposit of 30 per cent to take out a circulation of $75,000, would make profit for the first year and for all the years up until the point was reached where the safety fund of 5 per cent was complete of $1,972.93. The expenses that are charged to the bank are the annual cost of redemption of its whole circulation, the taxes, the express charges on the whole of its circulation, the cost of plates, and the agents' fees for redemption. Every item of expense has been deducted. The net profit on the $75,000 of currency for the first year is calculated at $1,972.93, and after the first year at $2,722.93.

A national bank doing business under the present law on a deposit of 2 per cent bonds would realize under the present system a profit of $434.28 after the same deductions have been made, and a national bank issuing circulation of $75,000 on 4 per cent bonds would have a profit of $611.50.

If a bank is issuing currency on a deposit of 5 per cent bonds its net profit on $75,000 circulation is $559.83; and if it is issuing its circulation on 6 per cent currency bonds (which are selling at a less premium, but pay a higher rate of interest) the profit on a circulation of $75,000 is $1,648.17.

Statement showing profit accruing to a bank issuing circulation upon the plan proposed by the Secretary of the Treasury.

[Under plan proposed by the Secretary.]

A bank with $100,000 capital could receive $75,000 in notes, but must deposit $22,500 in legal tenders.

$75,000 loaned at 6 per cent would yield		$4,500.00
Deduct expenses, etc., viz:		
Loss of interest on $22,500 invested in "legal tenders" deposited at 6 per cent	$1,350.00	
Annual cost of redemption of $75,000 circulation	37.50	
Express charges on $75,000 circulation	2.50	
Cost of plates for $75,000 circulation	6.25	
Agent's fees on $75,000 circulation	5.82	
This charge is based on cost of present plan of redemption.		
¼ of 1 per cent tax on $75,000 for "safety fund"	187.50	
¼ of 1 per cent tax on $75,000, Bureau expenses	187.50	
	1,777.07	
1 per cent tax on $75,000 for "safety fund" first year	750.00	
		2,527.07
Net profit on $75,000 first year		1,972.93
Net profit on $75,000 after first year		2,722.93

Statement showing profit accruing to a bank issuing circulation based upon a deposit of United States 2 per cent bonds October 31, 1894.

Amount of bonds necessary to secure $75,000 circulation		$86,805.55
Interest on $86,805.55 bonds (costing, at 90 per cent, $83,333.33) at 2 per cent		1,736.11
Interest on $75,000 circulation at 6 per cent		4,500.00
Gross profits		6,236.11
Deduct:		
1 per cent tax on $75,000 circulation	$750.00	
Annual cost of redemption	37.50	
Express charges	2.50	
Cost of plates for circulation	6.00	
Agent's fees	5.83	
		801.83
Net profits		5,434.28
$83,333⅓ (cost of bonds) would yield at 6 per cent		5,000.00
Net profit in favor of circulation		434.28

Statement showing profit accruing to a bank issuing circulation based upon a deposit of United States 4 per cent bonds, October 31, 1894.

Interest on $83,333.33 bonds (worth at 115 $95,833.33) at 4 per cent		$3,333.33
Interest on $75,000 circulation at 6 per cent		4,500.00
Gross profits		7,833.33
Deduct:		
1 per cent tax on $75,000 circulation	$750.00	
Annual cost of redemption	37.50	
Express charges	2.50	
Cost of plates for circulation	6.00	
Agent's fees	5.83	
Sinking fund (reinvested quarterly) to liquidate premium	670.00	
		1,471.83
Net profits		6,361.50
$95,833.33 (cost of bonds) would yield at 6 per cent		5,750.00
Net profit in favor of circulation		611.50

Statement showing profit accruing to a bank issuing circulation based upon a deposit of United States 5 per cent bonds, October 31, 1894.

Interest on $83,333.33 bonds (worth at 119 $99,166.66) at 5 per cent		$4,166.66
Interest on $75,000 circulation at 6 per cent		4,500.00
Gross profits		8,666.06
Deduct:		
1 per cent tax on $75,000 circulation	$750.00	
Annual cost of redemption	37.50	
Express charges	2.50	
Cost of plates for circulation	6.00	
Agent's fee	5.83	
Sinking fund (reinvested quarterly) to liquidate premium	1,355.00	
		2,156.83
Net profits		6,509.83
$99,166.66 (cost of bonds) would yield at 6 per cent		5,950.00
Net profit in favor of circulation		559.83

Statement showing profit accruing to a bank issuing circulation based upon a deposit of United States 6 per cent bonds, October 31, 1894.

Interest on $83,333.33 bonds (worth at 108 $90,000) at 6 per cent		$5,000.00
Interest on $75,000 circulation at 6 per cent		4,500.00
Gross profits		9,500.00
Deduct:		
1 per cent tax on $75,000 circulation	$750.00	
Annual cost of redemption	37.50	
Express charges	2.50	
Cost of plates for circulation	6.00	
Agent's fees	5.83	
Sinking fund (reinvested quarterly) to liquidate premium	1,650.00	
		2,451.83
Net profits		7,048.17
$90,000 (cost of bonds) would yield at 6 per cent		5,400.00
Net profit in favor of circulation		1,648.17

STATE BANKS.

Section 10 of the proposed bill provides for repealing the 10 per cent tax upon the circulating notes of State banks on conditions which are set forth in that section. These conditions are:

(1) That such bank has at no time had outstanding its circulating notes in excess of seventy-five per centum of its paid-up and unimpaired capital.

(2) That its stockholders are individually liable for the redemption of its circulating notes to the full extent of their ownership of stock; but this shall not be required in the case of persons holding stock as executors, administrators, guardians, or trustees, if the assets and funds in their hands are liable in like manner and to the same extent as the testator, intestate, ward, or person interested in such funds would be if living and competent to act and hold the stock in his own name.

(3) That the circulating notes constitute by law a first lien upon all the assets of the bank.

(4) That the bank has at all times kept on deposit with an official of the State authorized by law to receive and hold the same, a guaranty fund in United States legal-tender notes, including Treasury notes of eighteen hundred and ninety, equal to thirty per centum of its outstanding circulating notes; and

(5) That it has promptly redeemed its notes at par on demand at its principal office, or at one or more of its branch offices, if it has branches.

It will be seen that these conditions, if observed by the States, will throw around the State-bank circulation the most essential safeguards which are provided for the national currency. If they are not observed, the 10 per cent tax will be imposed, and the notes will thus be suppressed. It is true that some conditions required for national currency are not required for State-bank currency, but, in order that State-bank currency may be made equally safe, the States must provide the additional safeguards, if any, which may be necessary.

SUFFICIENCY AND FLEXIBILITY.

Your committee are of the opinion that if the proposed bill should become a law it will provide for a safe, sufficient, and flexible currency. One of the chief objections to the present currency system in this country is want of flexibility. The amount of paper currency in circulation in this country, except as to national-bank notes, is fixed by statute. The bond security required for national-bank notes makes flexibility very difficult, if not impossible. Such flexibility as is required by the conditions of trade and commerce is absolutely wanting. The proposed bill requires that the Secretary shall keep on hand blank notes, which can be issued at any time to any amount which may be required by business conditions, within the limit of the circulation permitted under the bill.

Thus provision is also made for retiring notes promptly when the banks may desire to do so, and as the outstanding notes will be taxed one-half of 1 per cent per annum, and as the banks taking them will be deprived of 30 per cent thereof in legal tender notes, there will be an inducement to retire the circulation when it is not needed, and at the same time an inducement to take out circulation when business conditions require it.

The extraordinary conditions which confront the Treasury Department have constrained the members of the majority of the committee, while not agreeing to all the provisions of the bill nor to all the reasoning employed in this report, to concur in reporting the measure to the House for its consideration, each reserving to himself the right to offer such amendments as he may deem proper and to vote on the bill finally as he may determine.

All of which is respectfully submitted.

VIEWS OF THE MINORITY.

The minority of the Committee on Banking and Currency, to which was referred bill 8149, "To amend the laws relating to national banking associations, to exempt the notes of State banks from taxation upon certain conditions, and for other purposes," having had the same under consideration, most heartily and enthusiastically join the Democratic majority of the committee in repudiating bill H. R. 8149, known as the Carlisle bill.

We find the Democratic majority using the following words:

> The extraordinary conditions which confront the Treasury Department have constrained the members of the majority of the committee, while not agreeing to all the provisions of the bill nor to all the reasoning employed in this report, to concur in reporting the measure to the House for its consideration, each reserving to himself the right to offer such amendments as he may deem proper and to vote on the bill finally as he may determine.

We submit the following statement of why we were shut up to a disapproval of the Carlisle bill, and this course only, much as we appreciate the pressing demand for wise and prompt action by Congress to relieve the strained financial condition of the whole country, and more especially the pressing necessities of the United States Treasury.

The whole action of the party majority of the committee was most extraordinary and not approved by its voting majority. Secretary Carlisle read a part of the bill on the first day of his address to the committee, saying he had not finished dictating it and would bring it in when he finished his address to the committee on the following day, which he did. It was not again read or in any manner considered in committee, and an opportunity to consider or amend it was refused to all members, Democrats and Republicans alike.

On Saturday at 4 p. m., immediately upon the close of the examination of Mr. St. John, of New York, a motion was made to close the hearing and go into executive session. Upon the attempt of a member of the minority to make a motion to take up the bill for consideration they were informed by the chairman, Mr. Springer, that the Democratic party majority had concluded not to submit the bill to the committee for any motion whatever, but to report it to the House on Monday, and that each member could offer what amendment he chose in the House. We, therefore, make no apology for neglecting to obey the House, as bound on our oaths to do, in reporting bills submitted to us, viz, to report them to the House in as perfect a draft as we can devise, in order to relieve the House from considering and perfecting imperfect and even crude bills designed to accomplish what it is the desire and duty of the House to do. This plain statement is due the Republican minority, who really represent the voting majority of the committee, in order to excuse us from a share of the just criticism which should fall upon those who, with unseemly haste precipitate upon the House a bill which, in our judgment, is as faulty in its text, as well as in important provisions, to accomplish the object it purports to attain as any bill any committee has ever reported to any Congress.

This criticism of the bill will not only be found to be eminently just, but far within the truth when the Carlisle bill is compared with the magnitude of interests that would be injuriously affected by its enactment into law as it is reported. It is the opinion of a number of the most clear-headed and eminent financiers in the country that if the Carlisle bill was enacted into law within twenty days that it would precipitate a panic far more severe than that of 1893, as it would compel the forced sale upon the market of nearly two hundred millions of United States bonds within six months.

This haste to report this bill is all the more inexplicable when it is remembered that Secretary Carlisle testified that this bill, which he had drafted himself for the relief of the Treasury, would not, in any event, relieve it materially for five years, and might not for twenty years, as follows:

Mr. WALKER. Have you thought of how long a time it would take to retire the greenbacks?

Secretary CARLISLE. It might be that it would take twenty years, and it might be done in five or six years.

Section I, line 3, repeals "all acts and parts of acts which require or authorize the deposit of United States bonds to secure circulating notes," etc., instead of "so much of all acts and parts of acts," etc. How many thousands may be seriously injured by such needlessly wholesale repeal of statutes, or whether the Supreme Court, after years of litigation, might by construction reenact some parts of such statute which Secretary Carlisle had repealed, no one can tell.

Section V, lines 11 to 14, provides that "each association hereafter organized, and each association applying for additional circulation, shall pay its pro rata share into the said fund before receiving notes," without defining how the total fund or each share shall be ascertained.

Lines 16 to 19 of the same paragraph provide that "when a national banking association becomes insolvent its guaranty fund held on deposit shall be transferred to the safety fund herein provided for and applied to the redemption of its outstanding notes." That is to say, it is merged in the safety fund, and again there is no provision in the bill for the use of the safety fund except by implication in the lines quoted.

Lines 19 to 24 of the same paragraph provide that "in case the said last-mentioned fund (safety fund) should at any time be impaired by the redemption of the notes of failed national banks, and the immediately available assets of said banks are not sufficient to reimburse it, said fund shall be at once restored by pro rata assessments upon all the other associations," and lines 25 to 28 read: "Associations so assessed shall have a first lien upon the assets of each failed bank for the amount properly chargeable to such bank on account of the redemption of its circulation," and these are all the provisions in the bill of how anyone is to proceed, and without defining who shall proceed to do it, or as to how the notes of failed banks shall be redeemed. That is, on the face of the Carlisle bill, when a bank fails its guaranty fund is to be paid into the safety fund. Then the notes of the failed bank are to be paid out of the safety fund. Then all of the national banks in the country are to be assessed to make up the safety fund, if depleted in the process, and then all the national banks of the country are to put in their claims to the receiver of the failed bank for the moneys they have paid on assessment for the payment of the notes of the failed bank.

Probably Secretary Carlisle intended to provide that the guaranty fund of the failed bank should be first expended in taking up the currency notes of the failed bank and that whatever additional sum was necessary should be taken out of the safety fund to complete their redemption, and the safety fund should be replenished out of the assets of the bank, and if there was a deficiency in the assets of the failed bank which was made up out of the safety fund, that all of the banks should be assessed to make good the safety fund.

These two oversights are accounted for, probably, by the haste with which the bill was drawn, for, as before stated, Mr. Carlisle informed the committee that he had dictated it very hastily to his stenographer, when it is the opinion of many that there is not a man in the country who can draw any bill to accomplish what the Secretary has attempted without spending nearer a month than a week in studying the far-reaching effects of its provisions, in order to make it safe to enter upon legislation affecting interests of such magnitude. But these things are of little consequence and belittle rather than enlarge the fatal and inexpressibly important objections to the bill as a whole.

Whatever legislation is had with reference to the finances of the country or banking in its effect upon national banks should be permissive and not mandatory as to national banks while their present charters continue. To provide, as in section 7, "that every national banking association heretofore organized and having bonds on deposit to secure circulation shall, on or before the first day of July, eighteen hundred and ninety-five, withdraw such bonds and deposit with the Treasurer of the United States a guaranty fund consisting of United States legal-tender notes, including Treasury notes," can not be justified upon any principle of safe legislation. As has been before stated, it could not fail to produce a panic, and the recklessness of such legislation would startle not only financiers in this country but of the world.

To pass over many most serious objections in minor details that the great and fundamental objections may not be obscured, the provisions of exemptions as to State banks, notwithstanding the many restrictions imposed upon them, would drive every existing national bank that desires to take out circulating notes into the State-bank system if the bill were enacted.

The taxation of national-bank notes is one-half per cent per annum in section 3 of the bill and one-half per cent per annum under section 5 of the bill, making a total of 1 per cent per annum, which would be a taxation of five million per annum upon the banks under the national system, which there is no reason to believe from any experience of the past would be imposed upon them under any State system. Furthermore, the States, even the most conservative among them, would be far more liberal than the United States will ever be or ought to be as regards bonds or any other security or redemption fund, for they require the deposit of no bonds whatever. We can not believe that it was the intention of the framers of the Carlisle bill to make the conditions under which national banks should issue currency any more onerous than those imposed or likely to be imposed upon State banks, or that it was the intention of Secretary Carlisle or of those who now enthusiastically support the Carlisle bill or will vote for it in Congress to force the national banks to operate under State charters, and yet frankness compels us to say that we feel assured from our examination of it, and from the testimony taken before the Banking and Currency Committee, that such would be the inevitable effect of the bill if it became a law in its present form.

Time has not been allowed us for a careful examination of the evidence or a more methodical and thorough analysis and formal objection to the various provisions of the bill, but we particularly desire to call the attention of the House to the fact that of the witnesses not more than one or two who appeared before the committee failed to seriously object to the Carlisle bill, and even those witnesses upon cross-examination repudiated many sections of it. The witnesses were not voluntary witnesses, whose most conservative and reasonable fears have been aroused lest the bill be enacted, but witnesses invited by the chairman of the committee, of his own motion, without consulting the committee. These gentlemen were eminent as financiers, and as unprejudiced as any men are likely to be, and yet there are scores of men in the country as eminent as they who would gladly have appeared before the committee and have spoken in tones that would have given pause to any such legislation as that proposed in the Carlisle bill.

The chairman, Mr. Springer, presented a letter to the committee, read it, and proposed to put it in the record, approving the Carlisle bill, from a western banker, and when asked if he had other letters from bankers concerning the bill he replied, "Yes; many—fifty," and when asked if they all approved of the bill, his reply was, "No; only this one."

The passage of the Carlisle bill may meet some political exigency, of which we do not know, but we do know that its passage will aggravate rather than relieve the perplexities of the financial situation, and especially that of the United States Treasury. The United States legal-tender notes withdrawn from circulation, did all existing national banks take out all the circulation permitted under the bill, would only be $151,000,000, still leaving $350,000,000 to vex the Treasury. This would not afford any substantial relief to the constant drain of gold from the Treasury.

It would make still more conspicuous and thus more urgent the demand made for gold upon the Treasury and the notes issued under the bill would make confusion worse confounded in the currency by adding from 1 to 45 more kinds of money to those already existing. Twice within a short time has the House declared its unalterable opposition to allowing State banks to issue currency notes, once on June 6, 1892, by a vote of 84 for to 118 against it, and again under the leadership against State banks of the gallant and versatile gentleman from Illinois, the Hon. William M. Springer, on June 6, 1894, by a vote to repeal the 10 per cent tax of 102 for to 172 against. Therefore, we protest against again consuming the time of the House in a profitless discussion of that objectionable section of the Carlisle bill.

Finally, we are of the opinion that it is not safe for the House to enter upon the line of legislation proposed until some bill is brought before it that has received far more attention than the Carlisle bill, and we recommend that it be indefinitely postponed.

Respectfully submitted.

J. H. WALKER,
M. BROSIUS,
THOS. J. HENDERSON,
CHARLES A. RUSSELL,
NILS P. HAUGEN,
HENRY U. JOHNSON.

WASHINGTON, *December 17, 1894.*

THE NATIONAL CURRENCY AND BANKING SYSTEM.

NOTES OF HEARINGS BEFORE THE COMMITTEE ON BANKING AND CURRENCY OF THE HOUSE OF REPRESENTATIVES.

WASHINGTON, D. C., *Monday, December 10, 1894.*

The committee met at 10 o'clock a. m. in the room of the Committee on Ways and Means.

Present: The chairman (Mr. Springer) and Messrs. Sperry, Cox, Cobb of Missouri, Culberson, Ellis, Cobb of Alabama, Warner, Johnson of Ohio, Black, Hall, Walker, Brosius, Henderson, Russell, Haugen, and Johnson of Indiana.

The CHAIRMAN. The committee has met at this time for the purpose of carrying out its order embraced in three resolutions, passed at the last meeting of the committee, as follows:

Resolved, That, beginning with Monday next at 10 a. m., this committee take up the recommendations of the President and the Secretary of the Treasury with reference to the currency, and that there be invited to appear before us the Secretary of the Treasury and the Comptroller of the Currency.

Resolved, That the chairman of this committee be authorized to invite such persons as he may think proper to appear before us in the same matter, and to arrange for hearing them, with a view to completing all hearings on or before the 15th instant, at which date all hearings shall be closed.

Resolved, That meetings of this committee for the purpose of these hearings may be called by the chairman at any time during the coming week, and that five members present shall be a quorum for the purposes of such hearings.

In pursuance of those resolutions, I have invited the Secretary of the Treasury to appear before the committee at this time and to make a statement in relation to the general banking system which he proposed in his annual report. I suggest that that part of Mr. Carlisle's report relating to the currency be incorporated in the minutes of this hearing.

The following is the portion of the annual report having reference to the subject of the currency and the banking system:

"In my last annual report I called attention to the unsatisfactory condition of our financial legislation, and especially to the issue and redemption of circulating notes by the Government, and the inability of the Secretary of the Treasury, under existing laws, to make prompt and adequate provision for the support of the public credit. The experience of the past year has confirmed and strengthened the opinions then expressed, and I therefore respectfully but most earnestly urge upon Congress the necessity for remedial legislation during its present session. The well-known defects in our financial system and the serious nature of the evils threatened by them have done more during the last two years to impair the credit of the Government and the people of the United

States, at home and abroad, and to check our industrial and commercial progress than all other things combined, and our first and plainest duty is to provide, if possible, some effective method for the prompt and permanent relief of the country from the consequences of the present unwise policy. A brief statement of the practical and unavoidable results of the existing legislation will demonstrate its injurious effects upon our financial affairs more clearly than any argument that could be submitted.

"After many fluctuations, the gold reserve held for the redemption of United States legal-tender notes was reduced on the 17th day of January, 1894, to the sum of $69,757,824, and the cash balance in the Treasury, excluding the current liabilities, but including the gold reserve and subsidiary and minor coin, was $83,961,402. The current ordinary expenses for the support of the Government were, and for some time had been, very considerably in excess of the current receipts, and, consequently, it was impossible to procure gold for the reserve without resorting to the issue and sale of bonds, under the authority conferred by the act of January 14, 1875, commonly known as the resumption act. Accordingly, bonds to the amount of $50,000,000, bearing interest at the rate of 5 per centum, and payable after ten years from date, being one of the three classes of bonds authorized by the act referred to, were issued and sold for the sum of $58,660,917.63, no bid having been accepted which would yield the purchaser more than 3 per centum upon his investment. On the 6th day of March, 1894, the free gold in the Treasury amounted to the sum of $107,446,802, which was the highest point that has been reached since March 25, 1893. The lowest point reached by the reserve since the resumption of specie payments was on the 7th day of August, 1894, when, by reason of withdrawals in the redemption of notes, it was reduced to $52,189,500. After that date it was slowly replenished by voluntary exchanges of gold coin for United States notes by the banks, and by small receipts of gold in the payment of dues to the Government, until the 14th day of November, 1894, when it reached the sum of $61,878,374.

"In the meantime, however, the frequent presentation of notes for redemption in gold by individuals and institutions not desiring it for export, clearly indicated the existence of a feeling of uneasiness in the public mind, while foreign exchange was almost constantly at or near a rate which made it more profitable to export gold than to purchase bills, and, consequently, withdrawals for shipment were daily threatened. In addition to these causes of anxiety, the vast accumulation of money at our financial centers and the general depression in business which prevailed in this country, had so reduced the rates of discount that the inducement to keep funds abroad, where better investments could be made, were much greater than in ordinary times, and this, together with the other facts stated, made it highly imprudent to neglect any precaution which appeared necessary to insure the safety of our financial position. In fact, some shipments of gold were actually made, and as the season was approaching when in the usual course of trade and financial operations large exportations nearly always occur, it was considered absolutely necessary for the maintenance of the public credit and the continued execution of the monetary policy declared by Congress in the act of July 14, 1890, and repeated in the act of November 1, 1893, to resort again to the issue of bonds. With a current revenue inadequate to defray the ordinary current expenses, and practically no receipts of gold from customs or other sources, it was evident that the Treasury would be unable to meet even the usual demands for export, which, however, would probably be very much augmented by the increased apprehension produced by the depleted condition of the reserve. Heretofore, when redemptions have been demanded to any considerable amount, they have commenced at a time when the reserve was sufficiently large to sustain the loss without seriously endangering the credit of the Government, or impairing the soundness of the currency; but with a reserve of only $61,878,374 to begin with, it would not have been possible at any time heretofore, and in my opinion would not be possible hereafter, to meet the obligations of the Government in the manner plainly required by the letter and spirit of the statutes enacted by Congress upon the subject.

"This was the condition of affairs when, on the 14th day of November, proposals were issued for the sale of additional United States 5 per cent ten-year bonds to the amount of $50,000,000, reserving in the official announcement the right to reject any or all bids, and requiring the payment of 20 per cent in gold coin, or gold certificates, at the time of the acceptance of each bid, and 20 per cent at the end of each ten days thereafter, but giving purchasers the option to pay the whole amount at once, or at the maturity of any one of the intervening installments. The result of this proposition was that 486 bids were received, amounting to $178,836,050, nearly all of which were at rates which would yield to the investor 3 per cent, or less, upon the sums proposed to be paid. One bid for the whole sum of $50,000,000, upon the basis of 2.878 per cent, and being the most advantageous offer for the Government that was made, either singly or by aggregating the separate bids, was accepted, and the proceeds of the sale, $58,538,500, have nearly all been paid into the Treasury according to the terms of the sale.

"This transaction justifies the opinion that a 2½ per cent bond, having a reasonable time to run, could probably have been sold at par, and certainly that a 3 per cent bond could have been disposed of at or above that rate. The fact that a bond bears so high a rate of interest and has so long a time to run that it must be sold at a large premium deters many from offering to purchase and detracts considerably from its investment and speculative value in the hands of the comparatively few who are willing to take the risk of future fluctuations in its price. The consequence is that the purchases are made almost exclusively by large moneyed institutions and capitalists who are familiar with such securities, and the people generally are precluded from investing their savings in the only form which is known to be perfectly good and always convertible into money. As the authority to issue and sell bonds already exists, and the present state of our financial legislation compels its occasional exercise, I repeat the recommendation made in my last annual report that, in the interest of the Government and people, power be conferred upon the Secretary of the Treasury to negotiate loans at a lower rate of interest and for a shorter time than are now allowed. The existence of such authority, instead of increasing the probabilities of a frequent resort to that means of raising money, would have the contrary effect, because, when it is known that the Secretary of tne Treasury is clothed with ample power and facilities to procure means for the maintenance of the reserve, public confidence in the ability of the Government to meet promptly all demands upon it will be much stronger than under present circumstances. Besides, the policy of limiting the Government to the sale of an antiquated bond, bearing a rate of interest wholly inconsistent with the existing state of the public credit and having a longer time to run than is apparently necessary at the date of its issue, can not be justified upon any grounds of expediency or principle. The only bonds which the Government now has authority to issue for any purpose are described in the refunding act of July 14, 1870, passed nearly a quarter of a century ago, and since then the credit and resources of the country have so greatly improved that the fiscal legislation of that period is wholly unsuited to the present situation.

"The law should be so amended as to conform to the conditions and requirements of the public credit and service at the present time, and I earnestly hope that Congress will take early and favorable action upon the subject.

"Had there been no statute or public policy requiring the Government to redeem in coin and reissue its own notes and to maintain the parity of two kinds of coin of unequal intrinsic value, there would never have been a time since the close of the war when the funds in the Treasury were not ample for all other purposes, and no issue of bonds could, therefore, have been necessary. But while the statutes referred to remain in force, and so long as there are in circulation under the authority of the Government two coins unequal in value, but equal in legal-tender qualities, every consideration of good faith and sound policy requires the prompt redemption of the notes on presentation in the kind of coin demanded by the holder and the constant observance of such administrative methods as may be necessary to preserve the purchasing power of the less valuable metal. This is essential to the continued circulation of our standard silver dollars and their paper representatives at par, and to abandon this policy, without substituting a better one in its place, would not only fail to cure many of the evils now existing, but would entail upon the people of the country additional and greater ones.

"If, however, the mandatory legislation which keeps a large volume of Government notes in circulation, notwithstanding their repeated redemptions in coin, and also imposes upon the Government an obligation to maintain the parity of the two metals in respect to their purchasing and debt-paying power, is perpetuated, it is evident that the Treasury must remain in a position which will compel it to procure and furnish gold to all who demand it, whether they be our own citizens or citizens or subjects of other countries. At the same time it will have no lawful or regular means of obtaining gold, except by the issue and sale of bonds, thus periodically increasing the interest-bearing public debt without either making permanent additions to its stock of this metal or diminishing to any extent its obligations on account of the notes redeemed. This situation is the necessary result of three features of our currency legislation, and it can not be permanently avoided, or even temporarily improved, without material changes in our laws relating to that subject. These features are:

"(1) The circulation of United States notes as currency and their current redemption in coin on demand.

"(2) The compulsory reissue of such notes after redemption.

"(3) The excessive accumulation and coinage of silver and the issue of notes and certificates against it upon a ratio which greatly overvalues that metal as compared with the standard unit of value in this and the other principal commercial countries.

"These features are the most prominent characteristics of our financial code and they constitute a monetary system unlike that of any other enlightened government in the world. One of their most obvious effects is to defeat all attempts of the Treasury Department to procure and keep constantly on hand a sufficient amount of gold to inspire entire confidence at home and abroad in the ability of the Government to preserve its own credit and maintain a sound currency for the use of the people. Frequent issues of bonds for the purpose of procuring gold, which can not be kept after it has been obtained, will certainly cause increased distrust among our own people as well as among the people of other countries, and not only swell the volume of our securities returning from abroad for sale or redemption, but increase the withdrawals of foreign capital heretofore invested in our domestic enterprises; and it must be admitted by all, no matter what opinions they may entertain upon current questions of finance, that such a condition of affairs can not permanently continue without still more serious consequences to the material interests of all our citizens than have heretofore been experienced.

"The result of all our commercial and financial transactions with the people of other countries has been to keep us almost constantly in the position of debtors, and, generally, to a very large amount. The prosperity of our people, therefore, depends largely upon their ability to sell their surplus products in foreign markets at remunerative prices in order to secure money or establish credit abroad with which to pay interest and dividends upon loans and other investments which our customers there have made here. Ordinarily, when there is no distrust of our currency or other discouraging influence, a considerable part of the interest and dividends earned by foreign capital in this country is annually or semiannually reinvested here, and this, together with the fact that under normal conditions the balance of trade is in our favor, enables our people to meet their obligations abroad without reducing their stock of money at home. But, when distrust arises, either as to our ability to pay or as to the value of the money with which we intend to pay the foreign capitalist not only ceases to reinvest, but proceeds to withdraw all his money by disposing of his American securities in order to protect both capital and income against threatened depreciation. There are but two ways in which this withdrawal can be effected; one is for our people to export and sell their commodities in foreign markets to a sufficient amount to create a balance of credit in their favor equal to the amount to be withdrawn, and the other is to ship gold, that being the only money recognized in the settlement of international balances. The extent to which these withdrawals have occurred during the last two years, and the manner in which they have been accomplished, are partially shown by the facts that, although our exports of merchandise, including silver bullion, exceeded our imports during the fiscal year 18 3 to the amount of $36,279,795, the net export of gold was $86,897,275, while during the fiscal year 1894 the net export of that metal was $4,172,665, notwithstanding the balance in our favor on account of merchandise and silver bullion sold abroad amounted to $264,314,663. It thus appears that our people were compelled to pay abroad in merchandise and gold during the time named at least $391,000,000 more than they received back, and this vast sum has been abstracted largely from the active business enterprises of the country, so affecting their growth and prosperity as to limit consumption, reduce prices, and discourage productive industry.

"But, independently of these considerations, our own people have a clear right to demand a sound and stable currency for use in the transaction of their business at home, while their purely commercial relations with the people of other countries, upon whom the producers of exportable commodities are compelled to rely for the consumption of their surplus, can not be profitably maintained unless they are always in a condition to pay for what they buy in as good money as they receive for what they sell. We can not, therefore, preserve our trade relations with the best customers for our surplus products unless we maintain a monetary system substantially in accord with theirs; and until they manifest a disposition to cooperate with us in effecting a change upon terms just and fair to all our interests, we ought to continue our adhesion to the gold standard of value with as large a use of silver as is consistent with the strict maintenance of that policy. But in order to insure the success of such a policy, it is necessary not only that the Government should be at all times prepared to redeem its direct obligations in the standard unit of value and preserve equality in the exchangeable value of all its legal-tender coins, but that its ability and determination to discharge this duty shall be so manifest as to command the entire confidence of the public.

"Since the resumption of specie payments, on the 1st day of January, 1879, United States legal-tender notes, and Treasury notes issued under the act of July 14, 1890, have been redeemed in gold to the amount of $260,000,000 and all the notes so redeemed have been reissued and are now outstanding. They are a constant menace to the gold reserve, and no scheme of financial reform can be complete or effectual which does not provide at least for their gradual elimination from our currency system. To retain them as a part of the currency of the people and refuse to redeem them in standard coin on demand would be repudiation in its most odious form, because the larger part of these notes were forced into the circulation by the Government at a time and under circumstances which justified the most implicit reliance upon its good faith. On the other hand, to continue their redemption and reissue under present conditions endangers the entire volume of our currency, discredits the obligations of the Government and people, increases the public debt, and seriously embarrasses the administration of our financial affairs.

"While no proposition should be entertained that will have a tendency to degrade the currency, or in any degree impair public confidence in its safety, I am convinced that the interests of the country require such changes in our legislation as will disconnect the Government entirely from the business of issuing or reissuing circulating notes and thus relieve its fiscal department from the periodical demands upon its resources which under the existing system must continue to disturb the financial and general business affairs of the people. In proposing such changes no consideration should be ignored which affects the industrial or commercial interests of any part of the country, for all the people are alike concerned in whatever promotes or retards the healthy development of our great national resources.

"It is not the capitalist alone whose interests are affected by the use, or threatened use, of a depreciated and fluctuating currency, and the consequent derangement and diminution of business. A paralysis of business, whatever may be its cause, strikes first the wage earner, then the man of moderate means, and lastly the capitalist who has accumulated a surplus store of goods or money. A sound and elastic currency, capable of adjusting its volume easily and rapidly to the actual demands of legitimate business, is what the common interests of all our people require, and no argument is necessary to show that such a currency is impossible under any system of compulsory issue, or reissue, of circulating notes. Arbitrary regulation of the volume of circulation to be kept outstanding is wholly inconsistent with the maintenance of a healthy financial condition and is the exercise of a function which does not properly belong to the Government of the United States, or any other public authority. Its effect is to force paper currency upon the people when it is not needed, and deprive them of it when it is needed, thus establishing and maintaining an improper and unwarranted connection between the Government and the private business affairs of its citizens, and making their successful prosecution largely dependent upon the judgment or caprice of a superior authority having no interest in the transactions except, perhaps, a partisan interest not in harmony with sound fiscal arrangements.

"Under our present currency system, so far as it consists of notes issued by the United States Government, the volume of circulation was intended to be, and is, in fact, unchangeable; it is unalterably fixed at a certain amount and, no matter how great the emergency may be, it can be neither enlarged nor diminished. The only part of the currency possessing in any degree the quality of elasticity is that issued by the national banking associations, and it is now generally conceded, I believe, that in this respect, at least, it has failed to meet the requirements of the situation at some of the most critical periods in the business affairs of the country. This failure is attributable, in my opinion, to three principal causes: First, the large volume of United States currency of various kinds kept constantly outstanding, making the contraction or expansion of the comparatively small national-bank circulation less effective than it would otherwise have been; secondly, the difficulty and delay in procuring, and to some extent in retiring, circulation; thirdly, and mainly, the provisions of the law which require the deposit of United States bonds to secure circulation, and restrict the issue of notes to 90 per cent of the par value of the bonds. With $900,000,000 in United States notes, Treasury notes of 1890, silver certificates, and gold certificates, besides about $625,000,000 in gold and silver coins, constantly outstanding, none of which can be lawfully retired by the Government without substituting other currency in its place, the national-bank notes, which amount to only $207,500,000, or about 12 per cent of the whole, can not exert a very effective influence upon the volume of outstanding currency at any time, and especially at times when large contractions or expansions are most needed. But the greatest difficulties are encountered, and the national-banking system, as now organized, is least effective, when the business of the country demands quick expansions of the currency to meet sudden emergencies. In the first place, in order to secure additional circulation the banks are required, at the very time when money is most difficult to procure, to deposit United States bonds, worth in the market much more than their face value, upon which they will receive notes only to the amount of 90 per cent upon the par value of the securities; and, in the second place, under the present laws, which do not authorize the Treasury Department to prepare and hold a reserve of blank national-bank notes ready for delivery immediately upon application, from thirty to sixty days must ordinarily elapse before the issue can be made, and in the meantime the emergency has probably passed. Thus, the inducement to take out circulation when business necessities are greatest is very small, if it exists at all, and even if applications are made the circulation will probably not be secured until too late to afford relief.

"In addition to these obstructions to the prompt increase and decrease of circulation, the ninth section of the act of July 12, 1882, which provides for the extension of the corporate existence of national banks, expressly prohibits them from retiring their notes to a greater amount than $3,000,000 in the aggregate per month, and enacts that no bank which has made a deposit of lawful money in order to withdraw its circulation shall be permitted to make any increase in its circulation for a period of six months thereafter. These provisions are so manifestly in conflict with the dictates of sound policy that they require no comment.

"In view of the foregoing considerations, and many others that might be urged in favor of a reorganization and reformation of our paper-currency system, I have prepared the outlines of a plan which, in my opinion, will relieve the Government to a great extent from the burdens now imposed upon it, secure within a reasonable time a safe and elastic national and State-bank currency, and result ultimately in the permanent retirement of United States legal-tender notes of both classes. It is, in brief, as follows:

"I. Repeal all laws requiring, or authorizing, the deposit of United States bonds as security for circulation.

"II. Permit national banks to issue notes to an amount not exceeding 75 per cent of their paid-up and unimpaired capital, but require each bank, before receiving notes, to deposit a guarantee fund, consisting of United States legal-tender notes, including Treasury notes of 1890, to the amount of 30 per cent upon the circulating notes applied for. This percentage of deposits upon the circulating notes outstanding to be maintained at all times, and whenever a bank retires its circulation, in whole or in part, its guarantee fund to be returned to it in proportion to the amount of notes retired.

"III. Retain the provision of the law making stockholders individually liable, and provide that the circulating notes shall constitute a first lien upon all the assets of the bank.

"IV. Impose a tax of one-half of 1 per cent per annum, payable semiannually, upon the average amount of notes in circulation, to defray the expenses of printing notes, official supervision, cancellation, etc.

"V. No national-bank note to be of less denomination than $10, and all notes of the same denomination to be uniform in design; but banks desiring to redeem their notes in gold may have them made payable in that coin. The Secretary of the Treasury to have authority to prepare and keep on hand, ready for issue upon application, a reserve of blank national-bank notes for each banking association having circulation.

"VI. Require each national-banking association to redeem its notes at its own office, or at its own office and at agencies to be designated by it.

"VII. To provide a safety fund for the immediate redemption of the circulating notes of failed banks, impose a tax of • per cent per annum upon the average circulation of each bank until the fund amounts to 5 per cent of the total circulation outstanding. Require each new bank, and each bank taking out additional circulation, to deposit its proper proportion of this fund before receiving notes. When a bank fails, its guarantee fund held on deposit to be paid into the safety fund and used in the redemption of its notes, and if this fund shall be impaired by the redemption of the notes of failed national banks, and the immediately available cash assets of such banks are insufficient to reestablish the fund, it shall at once be made good by pro rata assessment upon the other banks, according to the amounts of their outstanding circulation; but there shall be a first lien upon all the assets of the failed bank or banks to reimburse the contributing banks. The safety fund may be invested in outstanding United States bonds having the longest time to run, the bonds and the interest upon them to be held as part of the fund and sold when necessary to redeem notes of failed banks.

"VIII. Repeal the provisions of the reorganization and extension act of July 12, 1882, imposing limitations upon the reduction and increase of national-bank circulation.

"IX. Repeal all provisions of the law requiring banks to keep a reserve on account of deposits.

"X. The Secretary of the Treasury may, in his discretion, use any surplus revenue of the United States in the redemption and retirement of United States legal tender notes, but such redemptions shall not in the aggregate exceed an amount equal to 70 per cent of the additional circulation taken out by national and State banks under the system herein proposed.

"XI. Circulating notes issued by a banking corporation, duly organized under the laws of any State, and which transacts no other than a banking business, shall be exempt from taxation under the laws of the United States when it is shown to the satisfaction of the Secretary of the Treasury and the Comptroller of the Currency—

"(1) That such bank has at no time had outstanding its circulating notes in excess of 75 per cent of its paid-up and unimpaired capital.

"(2) That its stockholders are individually liable for the redemption of its circulating notes to the full extent of their ownership of stock.

"(3) That the circulating notes constitute by law a first lien upon all the assets of the bank.

"(4) That the bank has at all times kept a guaranty fund in United States legal-tender notes, including Treasury notes of 1890, equal to 30 per cent of its outsanding circulating notes; and

"(5) That it has promptly redeemed its notes on demand at its principal office, or at one or more of its branch offices, if it has branches.

"XII. The Secretary of the Treasury may, under proper rules and regulations to be established by him, permit State banks to procure and use in the preparation of their notes the distinctive paper used in printing United States securities; but no State bank shall print or engrave its notes in similitude of a United States note, or certificate, or national-bank note.

"Whatever may be the objections to the issue and circulation of United States legal-tender paper, upon either constitutional or financial grounds, it has become so incorporated into our currency system, and constitutes so large a part of our active circulation, that it could not be suddenly withdrawn without producing, in the present state of our laws, considerable disturbance in the fiscal operations of the Government as well as the business of the people, and, therefore, the plan now suggested provides for its gradual retirement, by the use of surplus revenues hereafter received, a process which will probably require several years for its completion. As these notes can not be retired until other forms of currency to an equal amount have taken their place, there will be neither a forced contraction nor expansion of the circulation on account of the change. In the meanwhile, for the double purpose of protecting the Treasury as far as possible under the circumstances from repeated presentations of notes for redemption in gold and establishing a safe basis for the national and State bank notes, the former are to be required to keep always on deposit and the latter to keep constantly on hand legal-tender paper to an amount equal at least to 30 per cent upon their outstanding circulation.

"If all the national and State banks now in existence should take out circulation to the full amount proposed to be authorized, the guaranty fund alone would absorb about $225,000,000 of legal-tender notes, and the national-bank safety fund, when raised to its full amount of 5 per cent upon outstanding circulation, might be made to absorb about $3,500,000 more.

"As the plan suggested proposes to exempt the Government of the United States from all liability for the redemption of national-bank notes and place the sole responsibility upon the banks themselves, a guaranty fund of not less than 30 per cent upon the outstanding circulation is regarded as a very proper and necessary feature of the system. A safety fund consisting of only 5 per cent upon the circulation, together with governmental liability for redemption in case the fund should at any time be insufficient, as proposed in one of the plans recently made public, would, of course, secure the note holder, but it would pledge the faith and credit of the United States in a business in which they have no pecuniary interest whatever, and for that reason alone, if there were no others, such a system would be quite objectionable and, in my opinion, not attainable.

"In the case of the State banks this guaranty fund will constitute a permanent reserve, which, together with the individual liability of stockholders and the first lien upon all the assets, will make its circulating notes entirely safe. In my opinion the imposition of a tax by the Federal Government upon the use of circulating notes, lawfully issued by State banks, is an unjustifiable, if not an unconstitutional, interference with the authority of the several States; but its validity has been judicially sustained, and as it does not appear to be practicable to repeal it absolutely at this time, it is proposed to avoid its prohibitory effect by exempting from taxation the notes of such banking institutions as may be organized and conducted under conditions which will amply protect the holders of their paper. While direct governmental supervision is not, and ought not to be provided for, the requirement that a bank, in order to secure exemption from taxation, must satisfy the Secretary of the Treasury and the Comptroller of the Currency that it has complied with all the conditions imposed will enable those officials to adopt such measures as may be necessary, in each case, to ascertain every material fact involved in the inquiry. The contingent liability to a heavy rate of taxation upon the whole amount of its circulating notes when paid out by itself, or by other banks, will constitute, it is believed, a sufficient incentive to secure sound and conservative management and to a great extent dispense with the necessity for such official supervision as is proposed to be retained over national banks.

"It will be observed that the plan submitted proposes the repeal of all provisions of existing laws which require national banks to hold a fixed reserve against deposits, and, as this is a departure from the practice which has prevailed continuously for more than thirty years, it is proper to state, briefly, the reasons which have prompted me to make this suggestion. When the national banking system was originally authorized it was regarded by many as a doubtful experiment at best, and accordingly various precautionary restrictions and limitations were imposed for the security of the note holders and depositors which practical experience has since shown to be unnecessary and sometimes harmful. Among these are the requirements that bonds shall be deposited to secure 90 per cent of their par value in circulating notes, and that a fixed reserve, which can not be lawfully diminished, shall be held on account of deposits. The consequence of this last requirement is that when a bank stands most in need of all its resources it can not use them without violating the law. The necessity for holding a sufficient reserve against deposits is not questioned, and, in fact, the business of receiving deposits and discounting paper ought never to be conducted without it, but it should be held for actual use when the occasion arises, and not made legally inaccessible at the very time when it was theoretically supposed to be beneficial in sustaining the credit of the bank and affording relief to its customers. Under the present law, when a bank finds its reserve in danger of reduction below the legal requirement, on account of the demands of its depositors, it is compelled at once to call in its loans, thereby increasing the distrust and aggravating the situation which a judicious use of the reserve would have relieved; and besides, at such times, in order to protect the reserve, which is then entirely useless for all practical purposes, clearing-house certificates, various forms of time checks and bills, and other devices of doubtful legality are habitually resorted to for the purpose of supplying circulation to take the place of lawful money lying idle in the vaults of the banks. To provide for a reserve which can not be utilized, even at a time of the greatest stringency and distrust, without incurring the penalties of forfeiture, affords a most striking illustration of the impolicy of legislative interference with the natural laws of trade and finance. It is not the duty or province of the Government to control or regulate the private affairs of the people, except for certain well-defined purposes, and as the custody and use of funds belonging to depositors are matters which affect only the interests of the immediate parties, they should be left to their own judgment and discretion. The duty of the Government, so far as it has any duty in the premises, is simply to provide that all the currency issued under its authority is sufficiently secured to prevent its loss or depreciation in the hands of the people, who are compelled to receive and pay it out in the transaction of business; but a bank is not dependent upon the Government for authority to receive deposits, and its use for that purpose by the public is as purely voluntary as the credit extended to any other corporation or to a private individual.

"Every prudently managed bank, if left free to conduct its deposit and discount business in the manner most advantageous to its own interests and the interests of its patrons, will undoubtedly keep on hand a reasonable reserve to meet not only all the ordinary demands upon it, but to provide for such emergencies as are liable to occur in the community where it is located; but it ought not to be prohibited by law from using such reserve for the only purposes it was designed to accomplish. The average amount of reserve held by all the national banks does not usually exceed 17 or 18 per cent of their deposits, while the statistics show that the State banks doing a deposit and discount business, and which are not required by law to keep a fixed reserve, have generally kept on hand, in ordinary times, about 20 per cent of their deposits, a fact which conduces strongly to sustain the position that a regulation upon this subject is not really necessary in order to secure the safe management of banking institutions and, therefore, ought not to be continued.

"A safety fund, consisting of 5 per cent upon the outstanding circulation of all the banks, to insure the prompt redemption of the notes of failed banks is believed to be a necessary feature of any plan which proposes to dispense with the deposit of bonds and exempt the Government from liability on account of the national-bank currency. That the Government should be exempt, and the entire responsibility for the redemption of their own notes assumed by the banks, is a proposition which, for many reasons, I think, will receive the approval of the general public and ought not to be opposed by any special interest. The requirement that the banks shall pay their own obligations imposes upon them no greater hardship than is imposed by law upon every other business and financial institution in the country, and the only argument that can be plausibly urged against it, in the case of the banks, is that, as the Government has undertaken through their agency to secure a sound circulating medium, it should pledge its credit to keep it good under all circumstances. The conclusive answer to this is that the Government has discharged its whole duty in the matter when it has by its legislation provided such safeguards as will, with honest and competent management, guarantee the safety of the notes issued by its authority; and this is one of the results which the proposed plan is intended to accomplish. The deposit of 30 per cent by each bank as a guarantee fund for the redemption of its own notes, and a deposit of 5 per cent by all the banks in a common safety fund for the redemption of the notes of failed banks, together with a first lien upon all the assets, individual liability of stockholders, official supervision, and the power to assess all banks to supply deficiencies, constitute the effective parts of a system which will afford to the note holder ample assurance against loss and at the same time leave a liberal margin for profit on the circulation.

"One beneficial effect of requiring each bank to redeem its own notes will be the promotion of more careful and conservative management of its affairs, thus avoiding to a large extent the causes which have produced a majority of the failures heretofore. Governmental responsibility for the redemption of any part of the obligations of the banks has a strong tendency to encourage speculative adventures and careless methods, which would not otherwise be permitted by the directing officials, and is, besides, inconsistent with the policy that the banking business, like all others, should be conducted upon the credit and at the risk of the parties most directly interested in its success.

"In order to provide a wider field for the active circulation of our silver coins and certificates, which now constitute about one-fifth of the entire volume of our currency, and to protect the Treasury as far as possible against the accumulation of certificates returned in payment of customs and other dues to the Government, it is proposed that no national-bank note of a less denomination than $10 shall be issued. The bank notes under that denomination now outstanding amount to $63,258,949, and there are also in circulation $64,418,831 in old United States legal-tender notes in denominations less than $10, $60,193,658 in Treasury notes of 1890, and $131,047,547 in silver certificates, making in the aggregate $318,618,985 in small notes, or only about $19,000,000 less than the entire issue of silver certificates.

"Attention was called to this subject in my last annual report, and the opinion was then expressed that it would be good policy to retire these small notes and replace them with larger ones of like character. Such a course would not subject the people to any inconvenience in the transacting of their ordinary business, and would keep permanently outstanding a much larger amount of silver coin and certificates than has heretofore been done, thus relieving the Treasury to a considerable extent from one of the difficulties which frequently embarrass its operations. The large notes would be used generally in conducting the more important transactions of the people and in the payment of dues to the Government, so that, while no denomination would be excluded from circulation, public and private interests would be alike subserved. These changes could be made gradually as the various kinds of notes are received into the Treasury, and with very little, if any, additional expense.

"The fact that our circulating medium is composed of so many different kinds of currency would seem to require the enactment of such legislation as will provide a place in which each can be safely and conveniently used, and as this can be done without discrimination against any of them, it ought not to be omitted from any plan which proposes permanent changes in the system. The policy of various other countries in this respect appears to have enabled them to avoid the difficulties encountered here in the attempt to keep the less valuable coins and their representatives in circulation, without derangement of the currency or disturbance of the public finances.

"Great Britain, with $550,000,000 in gold and only $112,000,000 in silver, none of which is full legal tender, authorizes the issue of no note of a less denomination than £5, equal to $24.33; France, Belgium, and Italy, with $976,000,000 in gold and $518,300,000 in legal-tender silver, issue no notes of a less denomination than 20 francs, or $3.86; Holland, with $27,600,000 in gold and $53,400,000 in legal-tender silver, issues no paper below 25 florins, equal to $10.05; Spain, with $40,000,000 in gold and $126,000,000 in legal-tender silver, issues nothing below 25 pesetas, or $4.72; Denmark, Sweden and Norway, with $28,000,000 in gold and $12,100,000 in limited legal-tender silver, have no paper under 10 crowns, or $2.68, and Austria-Hungary, with $130,-000,000 in gold and $81,000,000 in legal-tender silver, is gradually retiring all notes under 10 crowns, or $4.04. None of these countries have any paper based exclusively upon silver, as we have, and consequently all payments made in sums less than the denominations of notes mentioned must be made in actual coin, which would not be the case here if the recommendation now made should be complied with. Our stock of full legal-tender silver coins is larger in proportion to the stock of gold than in any of the countries named, except Holland, Belgium, and Spain, and yet we continue to obstruct their circulation by the issue of small United States notes and bank notes, which serve the purpose of the people in their daily transactions no better than the coins or certificates based upon them.

"The experience of this country under the act of February 28, 1878, which limited silver certificates to denominations of ten dollars and over, and under the act of August 4, 1886, which removed that restriction, justifies the belief that the change now proposed would result in a greatly increased use of silver coins and certificates, and that they would be much less likely to return to and remain in the Treasury than at present. At the time of the passage of the act last referred to, permitting the issue of silver certificates in denominations of one, two, and five dollars, standard silver dollars not represented by certificates had accumulated in the Treasury to the amount of $93,959,880, although the total coinage up to that date was only $235,643,286. Within four months after that date, although in the meantime the coinage was progressing at the usual rate, the amount of free silver held in the Treasury was reduced to $71,259,568, and it continued to decrease, on account of the demand for small certificates, until it became so reduced that further issues of certificates had to be limited, practically, to the current coinage of the dollars."

STATEMENT OF SECRETARY CARLISLE.

The CHAIRMAN. Mr. Carlisle is present, and the Chair requests that he will give to the committee a general explanation of the plan outlined in his annual message to Congress, and state what the practical working would be of a law of Congress that might be passed for the purpose of carrying his plan into effect.

Secretary CARLISLE. Mr. Chairman and gentlemen of the committee: I came here this morning in reply to a request received from the committee for the purpose, as I supposed, of answering such questions as might be propounded to me by the chairman or by members of the committee, and of making such explanation of the various provisions of the proposed plan as may be deemed necessary, but without the slightest expectation of entering upon anything like a general argument or statement in regard to the proposition as that has been done to a very considerable extent in my annual report.

I believe, Mr. Chairman, from my observation of what has taken place in the meetings of the various national bank associations, that there is a general opinion in the country now that the provision of the national banking law which requires the deposit of United States bonds to secure circulation is practically a failure, or rather that it is no longer applicable to the situation as it exists at present. It seems to be generally agreed that it is an obstacle to the elasticity of the currency, for the reason (among others) that at the very time when currency is most needed by the banks in order to secure additional circulation the banks must purchase, or at least must deposit, with the Treasurer of the United States, bonds that are worth from 114 to 115 cents on the dollar, in order to secure circulation to the extent of 90 per cent of the par value of the bonds. In other words, the banks are required to put on deposit a good deal more than they get out, and for that reason there is no sufficient inducement to increase the circulation.

The second provision of the plan which I propose is intended to make the notes entirely secure without a deposit of bonds, or rather the second provision, together with other provisions, is intended to do so. There will be the individual liability of stockholders. The notes of a failed bank will be a first lien on all the assets of the bank. There will be official supervision, and there will be a guarantee fund amounting to 30 per cent of the circulation. There will be a safety fund, as required by another provision of the proposed bill, amounting to 5 per cent on the aggregate outstanding circulation of all the national banks, which fund will be available for the redemption of the notes of any failed bank. And my opinion is that these various provisions are sufficient to make the notes perfectly safe in the hands of the people, without any deposit of United States bonds.

Under the existing law there are two other provisions, or, rather, one other provision and one omission, which prevent the rapid retirement or increase of circulation by national banks. One is the fact that the Secretary of the Treasury now has no authority to prepare and keep on hand a reserve of national-bank notes ready to be distributed whenever applied for. The other is the ninth section of the act of July 12, 1882, which permits national banks to retire not more than three millions per month of the aggregate of their circulation, and prohibits any national bank which has thus withdrawn any part of its circulation from increasing its circulation to any extent for six months thereafter.

The practical effect of the omission in the law to authorize the Secretary of the Treasury to keep on hand a reserve of national-bank notes was shown during the summer of 1883. It will be remembered by gentlemen of the committee that there was a period during that summer when currency was at a premium. At that time the national banks applied for additional circulation, amounting to somewhere about $40,000,000, and the Treasury Department proceeded, as rapidly as possible, to get out the notes, but before they could be got out and delivered to the banks the emergency had passed, and the consequence was that several millions of the notes came back to the Treasury Department for cancellation in the original packages in which they had been issued, the official seal never having been broken.

Now, it is evident that if the Secretary of the Treasury had possessed authority at that time to keep on hand a sufficient supply of notes, they could have been issued the next day after application was made for them; but the operation of the ninth section of the act of 1882 is very plain, and everybody can see that there may come a time when banks may want to make a reduction in circulation to the amount of many millions, or when the business of the country may require an immediate increase of circulation; but under the operation of that section it can not be done.

This plan proposes to repeal that section, in connection with other features, and to confer on the Secretary of the Treasury authority to keep on hand a reserve of national-bank notes. That reserve, however, should at no time, I think, exceed the difference between the amount of the particular bank's outstanding circulation and the 75 per cent on its capital which it would be authorized under this bill to take out. That is to say, if a bank with $100,000 capital had out $50,000 of circulation the reserve of its notes in the Treasury should not exceed $25,000. This would give to every bank all the circulation that it is entitled to have.

I would now be glad to answer any questions which members of the committee may desire to ask me.

The CHAIRMAN. Will the Secretary please explain in what manner this mode of securing circulation differs from what is known as the Baltimore plan?

Secretary CARLISLE. The Baltimore plan proposes to authorize the banks to issue circulation up to 50 per cent of their capital stock, without any actual deposit whatever in the Treasury, but with the provision that each bank shall be subject to a certain rate of taxation until a fund has been raised equal to 5 per cent of the total outstanding circulation of all the national banks.

This fund is to be a common fund, and is to be used for the purpose of redeeming the notes of failed national banks. In case the fund shall be insufficient at any time to redeem the notes of failed national banks (that is, shall be reduced below 5 per cent of the total outstanding circulation), then the Government of the United States is, out of its own funds, to redeem the notes and look to the assets of the failed bank for reimbursement.

The plan which I have proposed requires, in the first place, the deposit of a sum equal to 30 per cent of the amount of circulating notes applied for by the bank, this money to be held all the time and to constitute a separate fund belonging to the bank which makes the deposit. In addition to that, there is to be a safety fund raised by taxation on all the banks in the same way as is proposed in the Baltimore plan, out of which the notes of failed banks shall be redeemed; and if that fund shall prove insufficient (or if it be reduced below 5 per cent of the total amount of national bank circulation) and if the immediate available assets of the failed bank are not sufficient to redeem its notes, the Treasury Department is to assess all the other national banks pro rata, according to the amount of their circulation to reimburse this fund. The banks that pay this assessment are to have a first lien on all the assets of the failed national bank, and the Government is not to be in any way responsible.

When a bank fails this 30 per cent deposit which belongs to it will be paid at once into the safety fund and used for retiring the notes of the failed bank. If at any time a bank desires to retire its circulation while still continuing in business, it may do so by redeeming its notes and sending them to the Treasury Department and having them destroyed; and the proper proportion of the 30 per cent fund is to be returned to it.

Mr. HALL. The section of the act of July 12, 1882, to which you have just referred, was it put in the national banking law for the purpose of preventing an expansion or a contraction of the currency?

Secretary CARLISLE. That was supposed to be the purpose.

Mr. HALL. You know that there is, in some parts of the United States, a sentiment that it is dangerous to vest in bank corporations the great power of expanding and contracting the volume of currency, and that feeling had probably something to do with that ninth section. I wish to hear you as to whether you think there is any danger of putting that power of expanding and contracting the currency in the control of corporations and outside of Government control.

Secretary CARLISLE. I think it may be assumed, in the first place, that neither national banks nor any other banks would expand or contract the currency unless it was to their interest to do so; and certainly it will not be the interest of the banks to contract the currency at a time when the business of the country requires its expansion, nor to expand the currency at a time when the business of the country is not sufficient to employ all the circulation that is out.

In other words, I think that it will work automatically, and that when a bank finds that the business of the country is in such a condition as to demand more circulation, that increased circulation will be issued. If, on the other hand, a bank finds that the business of the country is so depressed that the outstanding circulation is superabundant, its interest will be to contract the currency. You will remember that the banks are to keep at least 30 per cent of the amount of their circulation with the Treasury Department, and that they are to pay a tax on their circulation.

In other words, I think that the commercial interests of the country will, all the time, determine, one way or the other, when a contraction or an expansion is needed, and that the banks will respond to that necessity. They will do so if they look to their own interests. On the other hand, if you are to have an absolute fixed amount of currency outstanding among the people I do not think that the business interests of the country are at all subserved by it.

Mr. JOHNSON, of Indiana. That is one of the objections to the issue of currency by the Government.

Secretary CARLISLE. Yes. The objection is that the Government now has outstanding a certain amount of money (silver, gold, and paper) not one dollar of which can be retired by any public authority without having another dollar put in its place.

Mr. HALL. You understand the general idea of the people on that question and you think that that idea was embodied in the ninth section of the act of 1882?

Secretary CARLISLE. There might be danger, when a panic strikes the country, that banks would improperly withdraw their circulation for the purpose of protecting themselves against their outstanding liabilities; and I think that provision was inserted in the act of 1882 on account of particular transactions that occurred in 1881 at a time when the refunding bill was pending before Congress, and when a certain section was put into the bill which required national banks thereafter taking out circulation to deposit 3 per cent United States bonds (not disturbing any bonds then on deposit). I think there was an impression through the country that the effect of the fifth section of that bill would be to compel national banks to take out of the hands of the United States Treasurer the bonds which they already had there, and to substitute for them 3 per cent bonds; and the consequence was that within thirteen days the banks withdrew $18,000,000. It was feared that there would be a serious crisis; but the President, Mr. Hayes, vetoed the bill, and the House failed to pass it over the veto. That was, I think, the cause of the insertion of that provision. It was an extraordinary case. It was the case of a clear misapprehension on the part of the banks.

Mr. JOHNSON, of Indiana. The fund provided for ultimate redemption in the Baltimore plan is, I understand, less than the fund provided in your plan.

Secretary CARLISLE. It is the same precisely.

Mr. JOHNSON, of Indiana. The same in amount?

Secretary CARLISLE. Precisely. The fund for the redemption of the notes of failed national banks is the same in the Baltimore plan and in my plan—the safety fund. That fund will be equal to 5 per cent on the total outstanding circulation of all the national banks. But, in addition to that, the plan submitted by me requires each bank to put up 30 per cent of its circulation.

Mr. JOHNSON, of Indiana. The amount of money in your plan is larger than that provided for in the Baltimore plan?

Secretary CARLISLE. It is larger in the case of each particular bank, which is to be required to deposit 30 per cent of its circulation.

Mr. JOHNSON, of Indiana. The advocates of the Baltimore plan claim, do they not, that the fund which that plan provides for is amply sufficient to pay the notes of all banks likely to be insolvent. What have you to say as to that?

Secretary CARLISLE. While the advocates of the Baltimore plan claim that the 5 per cent will be sufficient, yet they do not content themselves with that, because they provide for governmental liability.

Mr. JOHNSON, of Indiana. The difference between the two plans is that the Baltimore plan requires the Government to become liable for the notes of insolvent banks, whereas your plan does not require the Government to assume the liability?

Secretary CARLISLE. The plan which I have suggested proposes a safety fund of precisely the same amount as is proposed in the Baltimore plan, and then, instead of having governmental liability, as the Baltimore plan proposes, this plan proposes that the banks which contribute to the safety fund shall still remain liable for keeping the fund good.

Mr. JOHNSON, of Indiana. I understand that; but what I want to get at is this: The Baltimore plan proposes the ultimate liability of the Government for the redemption of the notes of insolvent banks?

Secretary CARLISLE. Yes.

Mr. JOHNSON, of Indiana. And your plan puts that liability on the banks?

Secretary CARLISLE. Entirely.

Mr. JOHNSON, of Indiana. And the Government is not to be liable at all?

Secretary CARLISLE. Not at all. The Government is not to be liable at all. This plan proposes that the banks, which are to be called on in the first place to create this fund, shall at all times keep it good for the purpose for which it is intended, and that if the fund be impaired by the redemption of the notes of failed banks, all the banks shall then be assessed pro rata, according to their circulation, to make the fund good again, and that each bank thus assessed shall have a lien on the assets of the failed bank for reimbursement. In other words, this plan makes the national banks liable for the redemption of the notes of failed banks, and protects the Government entirely from all responsibility except the printing of the notes and the holding of the guarantee and safety funds.

Mr. JOHNSON, of Indiana. The advocates of the Baltimore plan cite the statistics in the office of the Comptroller of the Currency to show that, if there had been no Government bonds deposited to secure the circulation of national-bank notes, the fund created by the tax on circulation would have been sufficient to pay all the notes of failed banks since the establishment of the national banking law, and would leave the Government $50,000,000 ahead?

Secretary CARLISLE. It does not occur to me that we are justified in concluding that because the losses by the failure of national banks did not exceed a certain amount when they had bonds on deposit, they would not have exceeded that amount if there had been no deposits of bonds. The fact that there was no greater loss may have been on account of the fact that there had been a deposit of bonds to secure circulation.

The present law, as amended in 1874 or 1875, requires every national bank to keep on deposit with the Treasurer of the United States a sum equal to 5 per cent on its outstanding circulation for the purpose of redeeming its notes; that is, for the current redemption of its notes. The outstanding circulation of national-bank notes now is about $207,500,000. Therefore that fund would be a little over $10,000,000. You will observe that this fund is only for the current redemption of notes—for the redemption of such notes as come in each day from the national banks—which have been previously deposited at the subtreasuries at New York, New Orleans, Philadelphia, or elsewhere. I had an investigation of that fund made some time ago, and found it scarcely ever had more than six or seven millions in it.

The CHAIRMAN. Please to explain whether there will be any time between the failure of a bank and its final winding up, through the operation of the courts, when its notes would be at a discount under your plan.

Secretary CARLISLE. I think not. Experience under the present law shows that bank notes are never all presented at once. When a bank fails its notes are all scattered throughout the country, and they come in gradually. It will be known that the notes are perfectly safe and that the receiver who has been appointed by the Comptroller of the Currency has in his hands the assets to pay the notes and there is no haste in having them redeemed. The notes will be good, because there is, in the first place, the safety fund of 5 per cent on the total bank circulation, the 30 per cent deposit on the circulation of each individual bank, individual liability of all the stockholders, a first lien on all the assets, and, if necessary, assessments upon all the banks, to make the fund good, and, unless all the banks fail, the notes will be paid. On the subject of current redemption I would like to say this: The plan now proposed disconnects the Government entirely from the business of redeeming national-bank notes, and places the responsibility for the current redemption of these notes, as well as for their final redemption, on the banks themselves. Under the operation of the present law the Treasury Department is put to very great inconvenience and the expense is greater than it ought to be.

If you look at the daily reports in the newspapers of the Government receipts, you will find from $300,000 to $500,000 a day for the redemption of national-bank notes. These are not mutilated and defaced notes, or notes otherwise unfit for circulation, but they are notes which are, perhaps, just as well fitted for circulation (a large part of them) as they were when they went out of the Treasury Department. The process is this: The New York banks, mainly (but also the banks in other places, to a certain extent), find themselves overloaded with national-bank notes issued by banks all over the United States, from Maine to California. The national-bank note is not receivable for customs dues in New York or anywhere else. It is receivable for other dues to the Government. Large payments of customs dues are made every day at New York, and the national-bank notes are not as useful to the banks of New York as other kinds of money are. The consequence is that the banks send them down to the subtreasury and have them redeemed in lawful money of the United States.

The statute says that they shall be redeemed in United States notes; but in actual practice they are redeemed in all kinds of lawful money. Sometimes they are redeemed by giving a check, and sometimes they are redeemed by transferring funds to Chicago or some other place. At any rate, the law provides that the Treasurer of the United States must redeem them. He does so, and he sends them to the Treasury Department. There they are counted and assorted, the notes of each separate bank being put by themselves, and then the banks whose notes have been redeemed are notified, through the Treasurer of the United States, that their notes, to a certain amount, have been redeemed, and that they must send forward the lawful money to reimburse the Government for what it has paid in redemption of them. It sometimes happens that we have many millions suspended in the air, if I may use that expression, because we have paid out lawful money to redeem these national-bank notes.

Mr. WALKER. As that lawful money belongs to the banks, its payment does not deplete the Treasury?

Secretary CARLISLE. No; it does not deplete the Treasury, but it keeps the fund down.

Mr. WALKER. That is the intention of the law, is it not?

Secretary CARLISLE. Yes; but the banks do not make the fund good sometimes for two or three weeks, and we are subject all the time to this trouble and annoyance of having to redeem the national-bank notes, probably to the amount of $300,000 or $400,000 every day in lawful money, and then have to correspond with all the banks to send it back.

Mr. WALKER. How do you propose to correct that?

Secretary CARLISLE. I propose that the banks shall redeem their own notes.

Mr. WALKER. Over their counter?

Secretary CARLISLE. Over their counter; or that they shall have agencies, if they desire to establish them, at other points. For instance, if a bank in Omaha desires an agent to redeem its notes in Philadelphia or New York it may provide such an agent, and then, if the notes are redeemed the bank will send them, if they are unfit for circulation, to the Treasury Department, and will have new notes issued for them. But the Government will be relieved from the obligation to provide for the current redemption of national-bank notes. You see, therefore, that as the law stands now any bank—or anybody else for that matter—wanting lawful money in exchange for national-bank notes may present the national-bank notes at a subtreasury of the United States and get lawful money for them, thereby taking away from us the very class of bills on which gold can be demanded at the Treasury. If this plan were adopted exactly the reverse of that would be the case. The United States Treasury would receive national-bank notes as it does now, and if the United States Treasury wanted lawful money it would send the notes to the banks and get lawful money for them.

Mr. WALKER. What trouble or risk does this redemption make to the Treasury of the United States which is not compensated for? In other words, is not all the trouble and risk on the banks except as to clerk hire?

Secretary CARLISLE. I do not think there is any loss sustained by the United States in that way. If we were to put a strict construction on the statute (which never has been done) I think that the national-bank note is redeemable only here in Washington, because the law says that presentation of the notes shall be to the Treasurer of the United States. But in practice, the different assistant treasurers all over the United States have been receiving those notes.

Mr. WALKER. That is for the accommodation of the people?

Secretary CARLISLE. Yes.

Mr. WALKER. And it cheapened the expense of money to the people. You do not object to that? You do not advocate changing that?

Secretary CARLISLE. Not if the present system remains in force, but I would change the system, and I would relieve the Government entirely from the redemption of national-bank notes.

Mr. JOHNSON, of Indiana. Aside from the principle of divorcing the Government from the redemption of national-bank notes, do you not think that the fact that the Government is ultimately liable for their payment would have a greater tendency to give the people confidence in them than the plan which you suggest of putting the ultimate redemption of those notes on the banks?

Secretary CARLISLE. That of course is a mere matter of opinion. I think that the fact that the Government stands behind the national-bank notes has a tendency of course to give greater confidence in the stability and safety of those notes; but I think that the people are perfectly satisfied with their soundness without that.

Mr. WALKER. You say that the 5 per cent safety fund would be available for notes of failed banks in the first place, and, in the second place, that the 30 per cent deposited by each bank would be also available, and then that the Government would have all the assets of the failed banks to pay the notes?

Secretary CARLISLE. Together with the assessment on all the surviving national banks to make good this safety fund.

Mr. WALKER. In the first place, the 5 per cent is available as an asset of the banks?

Secretary CARLISLE. Oh, no. The whole safety fund is available as an asset of the banks.

Mr. WALKER. And then the 30 per cent deposited for each bank?

Secretary CARLISLE. Yes.

Mr. WALKER. And before the safety fund would be trenched upon at all all the assets of the bank outside of it would be liable for the payment of the notes?

After the bank has gone into insolvency, and after those three items are exhausted, then you go further and say that the banks which make up the safety fund will have a lien upon all the remaining assets of the failed bank, as I understand you?

Secretary CARLISLE. Yes. If I understand you, you are simply supposing a case.

Mr. WALKER. No. I am taking no supposition. I am simply stating what you supposed.

Secretary CARLISLE. This is the plan: That the Government shall hold 30 per cent of the outstanding circulation of each bank. That fund belongs to the bank which deposits it. Then the Government shall hold a fund equal to 5 per cent of the total amount of circulation of all the national banks. That is to be a common fund, and to belong to all the national banks for the purpose of redeeming the notes of any of those that may fail.

Mr. WALKER. Furthermore, they are to have a prior claim on all the assets of the failed bank.

Secretary CARLISLE. I am coming to that. When the bank fails the 30 per cent which it has put on deposit is paid into the safety fund of 5 per cent and augmented to that extent.

Mr. WALKER. No; it is set over against the assets of the bank.

Secretary CARLISLE. It is paid into the safety fund and the notes of the failed national bank are to be paid out of that fund. The 30 per cent goes to augment that fund.

Mr. WALKER. Then the notes of the failed bank are paid?

Secretary CARLISLE. Then the notes of the failed bank are paid immediately out of this safety fund, augmented by the addition of the 30 per cent, and out of the immediately available assets of the failed bank, which are in the hands of the Government receiver and who can see exactly what they are. If they are sufficient to redeem all the outstanding notes of that failed bank without impairing the fund (that is to say, without bringing it down below 5 per cent) there is no assessment made on all the banks; but if it appears that this safety fund as thus augmented, and the immediately available assets of the failed bank that are in the hands of the receiver, are not sufficient to redeem the notes of the failed bank without bringing the safety fund down below the 5 per cent, then all the other banks are liable to make it good.

Mr. WALKER. It seems to me that the way a business man would state it would be this: If a bank fails the 30 per cent on deposit is put into the assets to increase the assets, and that first the circulating notes are paid.

Secretary CARLISLE. That is the effect of it.

Mr. WALKER. And if they are not sufficient to pay the circulating notes of the bank, then the safety fund is called upon to pay the deficiency, and the banks are all assessed to make up any depletion in the 5 per cent safety fund. Then you go on to say that still the banks have lien upon the failed bank to make the safety fund good.

Secretary CARLISLE. You assume, Mr. Walker, that we are not going to provide for redeeming the notes of a failed national bank until we have wound up its affairs. We go on immediately to redeem.

Mr. WALKER. I am taking the final result.

Secretary CARLISLE. It might happen, of course, that a bank would fail so badly that the 30 per cent and all its assets would not pay its notes. That, of course, would be one of those cases of total failure.

Mr. JOHNSON, of Indiana. Your plan requires the strong banks to be responsible for the weaker ones?

Secretary CARLISLE. That is it. That is taken from the Baltimore plan, which seemed to meet the approval of five or six hundred national banks.

Mr. JOHNSON, of Indiana. But not to the same extent as your plan. It requires only a certain fund to be paid in, and then the Government steps in and becomes responsible.

Secretary CARLISLE. You are mistaken in that.

Mr. JOHNSON, of Indiana. The Baltimore plan does not require the Government to be responsible for any deficit, and yours does.

Secretary CARLISLE. No; just the reverse.

Mr. JOHNSON, of Indiana. Well, then, would not your plan be more objectionable to the strong banks than the Baltimore plan?

Secretary CARLISLE. I think not.

Mr. JOHNSON, of Indiana. Why not? The strong banks would have to make good the losses of the failed banks?

Secretary CARLISLE. Of course in the case of so bad a failure as Mr. Walker has assumed, where the failed bank substantially leaves no assets at all.

Mr. WALKER. No; I have not assumed that. All the plans assume that a bank may fail. My only point was to find out what you meant by having the remaining assets of the failed bank available to reimburse the banks that are taxed to make up this 5 per cent safety fund, when there were not sufficient assets in the failed bank to pay its notes.

Secretary CARLISLE. That assumes that a bank has failed so badly that its assets will not pay its notes, which is a very rare occurrence indeed.

Mr. WALKER. I believe that only six banks have failed to that extent during the existence of the national banking law.

Mr. JOHNSON, of Indiana. Suppose that a bank does so fail, the Baltimore plan puts the ultimate responsibility on the Government?

Secretary CARLISLE. Yes; and to that I object.

Mr. JOHNSON, of Indiana. Then why should the banks of the country approve your plan which makes the strong banks responsible for the weak ones?

Secretary CARLISLE. They must decide that for themselves. I am looking at the interests of the Government and people, but with a due regard also to the interest of the banks.

Mr. WARNER. As I understand it, Mr. Secretary, under your plan the final responsibility in the case of a failed bank would be on all the national banks, whereas under the Baltimore plan the final responsibility would be on the Government?

Secretary CARLISLE. Exactly.

Mr. WARNER. In addition to that, under your plan you have the 30 per cent deposit of legal-tender notes. Do you regard that as necessary for reasonable safety, or is it out of superabundant caution that you require it as an experiment for the time being?

Secretary CARLISLE. I think I ought to say in reply to that question that I do not regard it as absolutely essential to the safety of the notes, but I think it is a wise precautionary measure, inasmuch as the Government is to be entirely exempt from liability for redemption. I think that it is a provision which will operate for the benefit of the Government.

Mr. WARNER. The 30 per cent which each bank has to deposit does not go into a common fund, but is to be retained for the redemption of the notes of that particular bank?

Secretary CARLISLE. Yes.

Mr. WARNER. Am I right, then, in my view that if the guarantee fund proposed at 5 per cent were raised, say, to 7 or 7½ per cent, that would afford the same or similar security for the redemption of all the notes of failed banks that would be afforded by your 5 per cent provision with the 30 per cent deposited of the particular bank? Under your plan 30 per cent of the entire outstanding circulation of each failed bank would be redeemed by its own deposit, and then there would be left 70 per cent of its circulation to be redeemed out of the 5 per cent guarantee fund. Would that insure any more prompt or certain redemption than if the redemption of whole outstanding circulation were provided for by a 7½ per cent guarantee fund?

Secretary CARLISLE. Of course, if your 7½ per cent fund would redeem the outstanding circulation, the redemption would be as prompt one way as the other.

Mr. WARNER. Seventy per cent of the outstanding notes of a failed bank, as I now understand you, are to be a lien on this 5 per cent guarantee fund?

Secretary CARLISLE. That is all.

Mr. WARNER. So that if 100 per cent of outstanding circulation had to be redeemed, that 100 per cent would be no greater strain upon the 7½ per cent guarantee fund than are the 70 per cent upon the 5 per cent fund?

Secretary CARLISLE. I understand that. The proportion is about the same.

Mr. WARNER. Then, if the banks object to the 30 per cent deposit and are willing to submit to a 50 per cent larger guarantee fund, would not that make the notes as secure in practice or even more secure than the plan which you propose?

Secretary CARLISLE. I think that with the 7½ per cent safety fund and the common liability of all the banks provided for the notes would be safe; but, in my opinion, the banks ought to be required to put up 30 per cent of the circulation to make their notes perfectly secure. That is my opinion.

Mr. COX. On the point by Mr. Warner, is there not another additional advantage in requiring the greenback deposit to be held in the Treasury; that so long as it is there it prevents the Treasury, to that extent, from having to pay gold on the greenbacks thus deposited. That advantage is to the Government?

Secretary CARLISLE. That advantage is to the Government.

Mr. JOHNSON, of Indiana. You provide for the ultimate taking up of these greenbacks?

Secretary CARLISLE. Hereafter.

Mr. JOHNSON, of Ohio. I understand that the great advantage which you claim for your plan is that it furnishes an elastic currency?

Secretary CARLISLE. That is one of its advantages.

Mr. JOHNSON, of Ohio. I can see very clearly the interest of the banks to go to the limit—to issue as much currency as they can. Under your plan I believe, if carried out, the banks would issue all the currency that they can. I wish you to explain what interest they would have in reducing their circulation at any time, and what ability they would have to meet the emergency after they reached the limit?

Secretary CARLISLE. I do not believe that the banks will immediately issue currency to the full extent. I believe that no bank will issue circulation on which it has to pay a tax unless the business of the country demands it and unless the bank can use it profitably. Whenever it can use it profitably it is an evidence that the business of the country does require additional circulation, and whenever it can not use it profitably the bank will retire it.

Mr. JOHNSON, of Ohio. The banks in the South and West that have use for money will go the entire limit.

Secretary CARLISLE. Probably they may, but I mean that the aggregate will not be beyond the demands of business. In any particular locality where money is in such demand that a bank is justified in issuing increased circulation, I think the bank will issue it, and it ought to issue it. On the contrary, when the interests of the locality do not demand it, the bank will withdraw its circulation rather than pay a tax upon it.

Mr. JOHNSON, of Ohio. That tax is a small one.

Secretary CARLISLE. Yes; but if the bank does not use its circulation it will retire it. Under the present system it is considerable trouble for a bank to withdraw its increased circulation. If a bank now desires to withdraw its circulation it must send in lawful money to the full amount of the circulation which it desires to retire.

Mr. JOHNSON, of Ohio. Will not banks have to do the same under your plan?

Secretary CARLISLE. No, sir. A bank must now send to the subtreasury of the United States the full amount of lawful money of the United States in order to withdraw its notes. Having done that, the bank is not allowed, under the operation of the law of 1882, to take out another dollar of circulation for six months. But under my plan a bank may retire its circulation to-day and take it out again to-morrow.

Mr. JOHNSON, of Ohio. How?

Secretary CARLISLE. All that it has to do is to send its notes to the Treasury Department when it wants to retire them, and redeposit 30 per cent when it wants to reissue them. I have heard an objection made to this plan on the ground that it will require a bank to keep on hand all the time a fund for the redemption of its own notes. Now, any gentleman acquainted with banking knows that a bank may redeem its notes and pay them out again immediately, so that its cash is not diminished.

Mr. JOHNSON, of Ohio. The German plan provides that banks can issue notes by the payment of 5 per cent.

Secretary CARLISLE. Yes; and that is one feature of the Baltimore plan—that the banks shall have a right to issue 50 per cent on a safety fund and then may issue an emergency circulation equal to 25 per cent of its capital. Under the German law the Bank of the Empire is permitted to issue 385,000,000 marks in what is called "uncovered money." If any bank in the country does not wish to take that uncovered money, the Bank of the Empire has the right to take it, and in case of emergency may issue additional notes by paying 5 per cent tax. I do not know whether any case has occurred where that bank has availed itselt of that privilege. Perhaps it has. But my objection to that plan is that at the very time when the people want this additional currency a tax is put upon it, which makes it harder to obtain, and that it makes a difference between the notes. Why not have all upon an equal footing?

Mr. JOHNSON, of Ohio. Because you must have elasticity.

Secretary CARLISLE. You will have elasticity if the business of the country fluctuates so as to demand more money or less money.

Mr. JOHNSON, of Ohio. Some banks will avail themselves of all their rights to issue circulation, and some will not.

Secretary CARLISLE. I suppose so.

Mr. JOHNSON, of Ohio. If it is an inducement for the banks to issue the money, they are likely to do it.

Secretary CARLISLE. Let me remark that the profit which a national bank makes out of its circulation is a very small item on its total profits.

Mr. JOHNSON, of Indiana. Your system of making the strong and well-managed banks responsible for the weak and ill-managed banks might have a tendency to induce banks to incorporate under some other system than the national banking system, some system which did not contain that provision.

Secretary CARLISLE. The national banking system might offer other advantages which the other system did not offer.

Mr. JOHNSON, of Indiana. Your plan provides for both national and State banking systems?

Secretary CARLISLE. No; my plan does not provide for any State banking system except that the circulating notes of State banks shall be exempt from taxation under certain conditions. It simply proposes to afford an opportunity for the organization of State banks of issue.

Mr. JOHNSON, of Indiana. Can the Government refuse to accept notes of a failed bank if your system be enacted into law?

Secretary CARLISLE. Not so long as the notes are in circulation.

Mr. WALKER. Have you drawn up a bill which embodies the provisions of your plan?

Secretary CARLISLE. No, sir; I have drawn one tentatively.

Mr. WALKER. Can you send such a bill to the committee?

Secretary CARLISLE. I can.

The CHAIRMAN. Mr. Ellis desires me to ask in what funds would the notes of the failed banks be redeemed?

Secretary CARLISLE. Just as they are now redeemed, in lawful money of the United States. I have here, Mr. Chairman, a bill which I have drafted tentatively, and if it is the pleasure of the committee it can have it while I am making these explanations.

Mr. HALL. You were speaking on the question of an elastic currency. Does not the question whether a currency is elastic or nonelastic depend on the demands for money?

Secretary CARLISLE. I think so.

Mr. HALL. No more money would be in circulation than the business interests of the community demand?

Secretary CARLISLE. It would not if left to natural laws.

Mr. WALKER. I ask that the hearing be suspended for a moment so that we may invite the Secretary to hand his bill to the committee.

Secretary CARLISLE. I would like before presenting the bill to have an opportunity to examine it a little more critically.

Mr. WALKER. I ask that the record of the hearing be printed each day.

The CHAIRMAN. The Chair will order that to be done.

Mr. BROSIUS. I understand that your plan contemplates an apportionment of the ultimate responsibility for the notes of failed banks between all the national banks of the country in the proportion of 30 to 70 or 3 to 7 in case there is a very bad break and there are no other assets of the bank. I was going to ask you what led your mind to adopt that particular ratio of responsibility? Why did you take 30 rather than 20 or 40?

Secretary CARLISLE. The idea of taking 30 per cent as the amount which should be deposited to secure circulation originated, I think, in my own mind, from the fact that under the old system of banking which prevailed in this country, and which has prevailed in other countries, about 30 per cent of specie was supposed to be necessary to secure the redemption of notes. It may be that it was arbitrary, but it was about the proportion. Thirty per cent is about the amount of specie held in the banks of France, England, and Germany for the payment of the notes. Neither of these banks has any specific piece of property, or any specific amount of money, pledged for the redemption of its notes, and neither of them is required to hold any reserve on account of deposits.

Now, as to this plan, it is proposed to impose a tax of one-half of 1 per cent per annum, payable semiannually upon the average amount of notes in circulation, to defray the expenses of printing notes, official supervision, cancellation, etc. The tax now is 1 per cent, but I think that one-half of 1 per cent will be amply sufficient for this purpose. It is proposed that in ascertaining the average amount of outstanding circulation there shall be included all the notes of each national bank that have been actually issued to it and which have not been redeemed and canceled.

I make that suggestion for this reason: There is a question now whether in assessing this tax upon the average amount of national-bank circulation we are to include any of the bank's own notes which it has in its own possession, although the notes are not canceled and are not in fact redeemed by the bank, but are held as part of its cash. It is known that the Attorney-General of the United States has given an opinion that they are to be excluded, and the consequence is that we shall, perhaps, have very large claims made against the Government for refunding this tax alleged to have been improperly collected for thirty years past.

Mr. WARNER. You mean upon the notes held by the banks as their till money?

Secretary CARLISLE. Yes, I think that when a national-bank note is paid into the bank by a depositor and is not received by the bank for the purpose of being canceled and is not canceled, it ought to be within the meaning of the law just as much in circulation as if it had been paid into any other national bank.

The CHAIRMAN. Now, in regard to the fifth proposition, which is that there shall be no national-bank note of a less denomination than $10. Will you please explain?

Secretary CARLISLE. The fifth proposition is that no national-bank note shall be of less denomination than $10, and that they shall be uniform in design, but that banks desiring to redeem their notes in gold may have them made payable in that coin. The first part of this provision, I think, ought to be adopted and put in any plan of currency reform that may be agreed to by Congress. There are now, as shown in my report, about 318,000,000 of United States legal-tender notes, Treasury notes under the law 1890, silver certificates and national-bank notes outstanding of less denomination than $10. There have been 337,000,000 of silver certificates issued. So it will be perceived that the field now occupied by small notes of various kinds affords an opportunity for the circulation of all the silver certificates outstanding except $19,000,000.

But these silver certificates are performing the work of the country to-day, according to my observation. Gentlemen will find that the money in their pockets consists largely of silver certificates. But if we are to have these various kinds of money in circulation, I am unable to see why it would not be a wise policy on the part of Congress to provide a safe place where the silver certificates can be used by the people, so as to keep them outstanding and prevent them from coming back into the Treasury. At some seasons of the year we are overloaded with silver certificates. Therefore, I propose to provide not only for the retirement of national-bank notes under the denomination of ten dollars, but all other notes as well.

Mr. HALL. Would that leave under the control of the Government money under the denomination of ten dollars?

Secretary CARLISLE. Certainly.

Mr. HALL. There is one clause in that fifth provision which worries me more than any clause in the bill; and that is, "But banks desiring to redeem their notes in gold may have them made payable in that coin." I would like to hear you upon that clause.

Mr. WARNER. But first as to the condition on which State banks may issue currency without the inhibition of the present tax. Do I understand that you would or that you would not require that the notes of the State banks should be of the denomination only of ten dollars and upward?

Secretary CARLISLE. I have not included that in my plan, although I have thought a good deal about it. I have not determined in my own mind as to whether or not (as these notes are to be substantially for local circulation) it would be a good policy to limit their denomination. That is one of the questions I would like the committee to consider and to decide for itself. I mean as to the notes of State banks.

Mr. WARNER. In case national-bank notes are limited to $10 and upward, would not the exemption of State banks from that limitation take away the benefit which you propose by limiting the denominations of national-bank notes?

Secretary CARLISLE. Undoubtedly, to some extent.

Mr. JOHNSON, of Indiana. It might give banks a greater inducement to organize under State law?

Secretary CARLISLE. It might. Those are considerations which have occurred to me, but which I have not decided in my own mind.

Mr. WALKER. You contemplate that the notes which would be issued by State banks would be practically local notes?

Secretary CARLISLE. Would be used for local circulation. Now, in reply to Mr. Hall's question, section 5185 of the Revised Statutes reads:

SEC. 5185. Associations may be organized in the manner prescribed by this Title for the purpose of issuing notes payable in gold; and upon the deposit of any United States bonds bearing interest payable in gold with the Treasurer of the United States, in the manner prescribed for other associations, it shall be lawful for the Comptroller of the Currency to issue to the association making the deposit circulating notes of different denominations, but none of them of less than five dollars, and not exceeding in amount eighty per centum of the par value of the bonds deposited, which shall express the promise of the association to pay them, upon presentation at the office at which they are issued, in gold coin of the United States, and shall be so redeemable. But no such association shall have a circulation of more than one million of dollars.

That last provision has been repealed. Section 5186 of the Revised Statutes reads:

SEC. 5186. Every association organized under the preceding section shall at all times keep on hand not less than twenty-five per centum of its outstanding circulation, in gold or silver coin of the United States; and shall receive at par in the payment of debts the gold-notes of every other such association which at the time of such payment is redeeming its circulating notes in gold coin of the United States, and shall be subject to all the provisions of this Title: *Provided*, That, in applying the same to associations organized for issuing gold-notes, the terms "lawful money" and "lawful money of the United States" shall be construed to mean gold or silver coin of the United States; and the circulation of such associations shall not be within the limitation of circulation mentioned in this Title.

On the Pacific Coast paper currency is not much in circulation, athough perhaps the gold banks are confined exclusively to the city of San Francisco. I thought that inasmuch as these banks are now authorized by law, and as they are in existence, and are required to keep on hand 25 per cent in gold or silver coin, in addition to their other security, I would not propose to disturb them.

Mr. HALL. You do not see any possible danger that may result from them to the rest of the United States?

Secretary CARLISLE. I can not see why if a national bank desires to bind itself to redeem its notes in gold it may not do so.

Mr. RUSSELL. Without that gold provision these banks would have the right to redeem their bills in lawful money?

Secretary CARLISLE. Yes, just as every other bank is required to redeem its bills in lawful money.

Mr. RUSSELL. You think that this new currency will be retained on a parity with gold, although it can be redeemed in silver?

Secretary CARLISLE. It can be redeemed in silver now. This will not change the law in the least. The national-banking law provides that the national banks shall redeem their notes in lawful money. The Government is now required to make the current redemption of bank notes in United States notes, but, as a matter of fact, we do not always do so.

Mr. RUSSELL. But if you take away this power will these new notes be on a parity with gold?

Secretary CARLISLE. So long as the Government keeps the whole volume of currency on a parity with gold silver will be as good as gold.

Mr. WALKER. It will not change the conditions an iota.

Mr. SPERRY. What class of money do you now redeem in gold?

Secretary CARLISLE. United States legal-tender notes of the old issue and the Treasury notes of 1890.

Mr. SPERRY. Popularly known as the Sherman Act?

Secretary CARLISLE. Yes.

Mr. SPERRY. No others? You do not redeem silver certificates in gold?

Secretary CARLISLE. No; we never have done so.

Mr. SPERRY. You do not redeem silver dollars in gold, either?

Secretary CARLISLE. Never.

Mr. SPERRY. Your plan contemplates the retirement of greenbacks?

Secretary CARLISLE. Ultimately.

Mr. SPERRY. Then ultimately there would be no paper money outstanding payable in gold?

Secretary CARLISLE. No money which the Government would be bound to redeem in gold except gold certificates.

Mr. SPERRY. If your plan should retire the greenbacks there would be no paper money on which the Government would have to pay gold?

Secretary CARLISLE. No, sir.

Mr. SPERRY. Then we would be on a silver basis?

Secretary CARLISLE. No.

Mr. SPERRY. On what basis would we be?

Secretary CARLISLE. On the same basis as now. The Government would continue to receive gold and silver, and gold and silver certificates for customs and for all other dues to the Government, and would receive national-bank notes for all dues to the Government except customs, and it would maintain the parity of the two metals in that way. We do not maintain the parity of the two metals by redeeming silver dollars or certificates in gold, but by the constant practice of receiving them in full satisfaction of every debt due to the Government, and paying the man to whom the Government owes money gold if he wants it. We make no distinction between gold and silver at the Treasury Department. If any creditor of the Government wants silver he gets it, and if he wants gold he gets it.

Mr. SPERRY. The Government now maintains parity by redeeming the Sherman notes and the greenbacks in gold. But after the Sherman notes and the greenbacks are all retired there would be no way of maintaining parity except as the Government receives either gold or silver in payment of duties.

Secretary CARLISLE. Yes; and of course the banks must maintain their credit by paying their customers gold if they demand it.

Mr. WARNER. Would not the working of your bill, by eliminating small denominations of notes, reduce the proportion of silver and increase the proportions of gold in the hands of the banks?

Secretary CARLISLE. That is my theory about it exactly. It makes a place for the silver.

Mr. WARNER. And you think there would be a greater tendency than there is now on the part of the banks to pay gold for notes?

Secretary CARLISLE. Undoubtedly.

Mr. JOHNSON, of Ohio. Do you provide for any other means of a demand to take out circulation? In other words, the present bank deposit is $225,000,000, of which the bulk is in greenbacks, and the banks hold these greenbacks, although they can have any other money.

Secretary CARLISLE. Undoubtedly. So they could hold all the gold of the country, if they had not the greenbacks.

Mr. JOHNSON, of Ohio. There are only 500,000,000 of these legal-tender notes, and the gold in the banks amounts to more than $500,000,000.

Secretary CARLISLE. There are not more than $500,000,000 gold outstanding outside of the United States Treasury. You may put these extreme cases that would defeat any plan. You can not legislate for all time to come. You must legislate for the present.

Mr. WALKER. Have you thought of how long a time it would take to retire the greenbacks?

Secretary CARLISLE. It might be that it would take twenty years, and it might be done in five or six years. If the proposed law had been in force during Mr. Cleveland's last administration, or during Mr. Harrison's administration, the greenbacks would have been retired.

Mr. SPERRY. Is there a discrimination made at present by the banks in favor of greenbacks?

Secretary CARLISLE. As a general rule the banks keep considerable amounts of them in their vaults. I think if you go into any bank you will find the silver certificates all on the top in the piles of money that they are using daily, and that the other notes are at the bottom.

Mr. SPERRY. If the time should come, what reason have you to suppose that the entire receipts of the Government would not be paid in silver?

Secretary CARLISLE. I do not think there would be silver enough to do it. Silver now constitutes only one-fifth of our entire circulation, and if my suggestions should be adopted to retire all the notes under the denomination of $10 and to leave that whole field to be occupied by silver, and by silver certificates, I think it would be so occupied. Dues to the Government are not paid, as a general rule, with small bills. They are inconvenient to handle in large amounts, and consequently dues to the Government are paid in large bills, so that silver bills of small denominations will not come back to the Treasury. The country must have small currency, as it is impossible to transact the daily business of the people without it.

Mr. WALKER. You mean small currency as distinguished from coin?

Secretary CARLISLE. I mean small paper currency or coin. The people must have some medium of a character which they can use in small transactions. That is what keeps our subsidiary coin out. It is not legal tender except up to the amount of $10, yet it is in circulation just like other money.

Mr. WALKER. Would it not be wise to make subsidiary coin legal tender for any amount, and for this reason: The people can not get it conveniently out of the banks now, because the banks do not hold it in large quantities. I am clearly of opinion that there should be no limit to the legal-tender quality of any money issued by the Government except nickel and copper coins. Do you think that subsidiary silver coin should be made legal tender to any amount?

Secretary CARLISLE. I would not like to express a very positive opinion on that single proposition. But it is very evident to my mind that our legislation in reference to subsidiary silver coins needs revision in some way to relieve the Government from the obligation which rests upon it all the time of redeeming it in lawful money. As you say, nearly everybody in this country (at least in towns and cities) keeps a bank account. They get this subsidiary coin into their possession, and they take it to the banks. The banks can not pay it out very well. They can not use subsidiary coin in the payment of checks except, perhaps, to the amount of 75 cents, and they can not keep it in their reserves. The result is that when it accumulates in the bank, the bank takes it to the subtreasury, and we find it hard to get out again into circulation. If it were made legal tender, perhaps that would cure the trouble, or if the Government were exempted from the responsibility of redeeming it in other lawful money it would not come back to us.

The CHAIRMAN. The Secretary will please explain the ninth section of his bill—the repeal of all provisions of law requiring banks to keep a reserve on account of deposits.

Secretary CARLISLE. On that subject I have said, perhaps, all that I can say in the report submitted to the House of Representatives. I am very decidedly of the opinion myself that the provisions of law which require banks to hold a certain fixed reserve against deposits is injurious rather than beneficial. I can imagine very well what would have been the condition of the Treasury Department a year ago last April if there had been a law on the statute books which provided expressly that the Secretary of the Treasury should not use any part of the gold reserve except on penalty of impeachment, or of fine and imprisonment.

That is the case of the banks now. Every bank is now required, whenever it infringes on its reserve, to make it good within thirty days, or take the risk of having the Comptroller of the Currency put it in the hands of a receiver. As a matter of fact, State banks which are not required by law to keep a fixed reserve, do keep it; if they are well managed, they keep an adequate reserve. In other words, if a bank is well managed it will always keep enough cash on hand to meet the demands of its depositors; and I do not see how a provision of law which prevents them from using that reserve for the purpose for which it was intended can be wise. But that is a matter in which the Government and the Secretary of the Treasury can have no special interest. But to say to a bank that it shall keep 15 or 25 per cent reserve against its deposits, and shall not use it at the time when it is needed, seems to me almost absurd.

Mr. WALKER. I agree with you fully in that.

Mr. HALL. The authority of the Government for instituting a system of guaranteeing the redemption of notes circulating as money is based upon the broad principle of the power of the Government to regulate matters in regard to finance. Where is there any authority in the Constitution or in the original formation of the Government for the United States Government to look into the question of deposits and discounts of banks?

Secretary CARLISLE. I have expressed my opinion about that in my report. Of course my opinion upon this subject is theoretical; but it is my opinion, nevertheless, that it is not the business of the Government to interfere with the private affairs of a bank with its depositors any more than it is its business to interfere with manufacturing or commercial corporations. The matter of depositing money in a bank is a matter between the bank and its customers, and nobody else. The bank does not acquire its right to receive deposits from any Government authority. I can receive deposits if anybody is willing to make them with me. It is entirely a matter of private concern between the parties. If the Government undertakes to superintend the issue of paper to circulate as currency then the Government does assume the duty of seeing that it is a safe currency.

Mr. HALL. Does not this reserve fund in itself tend to impair the elasticity of the currency?

Secretary CARLISLE. It does, and at the very time when currency is most needed. A bank should have the right to use all its resources for the benefit of the community in which it is located, and should not be compelled to disappoint people whose necessities compel them to borrow money. The great banks of Europe are not required to keep any reserve. The Bank of England has found itself six or seven times, in its history of two hundred years, with its reserve run down. Whenever the reserve runs down in England now, without any authority of law, but by the permission of the Government authorities, the banking department calls upon the issue department to let it have additional notes, and puts up security of some kind. In other words, the banking department purchases from the issue department a certain amount of notes, or the issue department purchases from the banking department a certain amount of securities, and pays for them in new notes.

Mr. WARNER. There is a question in my mind as to whether a repeal of all the provisions of law as to national banks requiring a reserve on account of deposits might not have the result of giving national banks an advantage over State banks in cases where the State chooses to provide that its institutions shall keep a reserve against deposits.

Secretary CARLISLE. Yes.

Mr. WARNER. So that it would practically prevent a State from enforcing, as a general principle, throughout its borders, the keeping of any reserve against deposits?

Secretary CARLISLE. It will be observed, however, that the reserve which is required to be kept by the national banking system, and which would be required to be kept by the State banking laws, does not consist of the money of the banks. It is not the bank's capital that is reserved; it is the depositors' money. It is the money which the depositors put in, and for the State to say to depositors they must not take out the money they had put in because the bank has made discounts down to or below 25 per cent of its deposits would not be exactly right.

Mr. WARNER. I agree with you entirely. How do you distinguish between money of the banks and money of the depositors as to the reserve?

Secretary CARLISLE. You can not say, of course, that any particular bill belongs to a bank or to a depositor; but if a bank has deposits to the amount of $500,000 the reserve simply diminishes its discount fund.

Mr. WALKER. It is admitted to be necessary for the safety of the bank that it shall keep a reserve, which experience has shown on, the whole, bears a certain proportion to its deposits. There is a bill before this committee to allow banks to make use of its reserve to any extent, provided it averages for thirty days the reserve required, and that if it does not that the bank shall pay interest to the Government on the average deficiency. Is it not better to preserve the present law, rather than to leave the banks at liberty to have no reserve, when nine-tenths of the banks get most of their knowledge of banking from the very act itself?

Secretary CARLISLE. I agree with you that no bank can be safely managed without having a reserve fund, and I think that if a bank did not keep something on hand to pay its depositors they would not continue business with it very long.

Mr. WALKER. Is not the reserve the safety fund for the depositors in the bank of the same character as the safety fund which you propose for the bill holders?

Secretary CARLISLE. The bill goes into the community. The people can not transact business well without using it, and they look to the banking act to see whether the bill is safe or not; but the dealings of depositors with banks is entirely voluntary on their part. It is a credit which they give to the banks.

Mr. WALKER. You say that it is entirely voluntary whether a man uses a bank or not. Legally that is so, but practically and morally no man can do business unless he uses a bank.

Secretary CARLISLE. Nor can he not do business without buying food and clothing but he determines for himself where he will purchase them.

Mr. WALKER. We are talking now about regulating banks, not about food or clothing. A majority of the depositors in a bank have no means of knowing anything about the bank, and do you not think that if we are regulating the banking system at all that we should regulate the reserve?

Secretary CARLISLE. There might be some way of relaxing it which would be satisfactory.

Mr. WALKER. Have you examined the way of relaxing it in the bill H. R. 171?

Secretary CARLISLE. No, sir; I have not.

Mr. WALKER. Do you hold that the Government owes no duty to the depositors in a bank?

Secretary CARLISLE. The Government is under no more obligation to bank depositors than to any other citizens.

Mr. WARNER. Would it be inconsistent in the plan you suggest if section 9 should be modified by providing that the States in which national banks are situated may require of national banks such a reserve on account of deposits not greater than the reserve required from their own State institutions.

Secretary CARLISLE. That would still leave them liable to have an inflexible rule put upon them.

Mr. WARNER. Would not your proposition practically prevent the State from enforcing, in regard to any banking institution, any provision for a reserve? And should not the States be left free to enforce such reserve in the case of national banks as they enforce in the case of their own banks—the question of deposit being one entirely for the States and not for the United States?

Secretary CARLISLE. That might have the effect of operating in favor of the national banks instead of in favor of State banks.

Mr. WARNER. Would it not entirely wipe out State banks as banks of deposit?

Secretary CARLISLE. If the States should require their banks to hold reserves against deposits, and the national banks in fact held none, the State banks would be safer and more attractive to depositors than the national banks. I do not think that a man capable of managing a bank would think that he could loan out, all the time, every dollar in the bank and have nothing to meet the demands of his depositors.

Mr. WARNER. Would not the ninth section be practically an inhibition against the States requiring banks to keep a reserve on account of deposits?

Secretary CARLISLE. It might have that effect.

The CHAIRMAN. Now, as to section 11 of your proposed bill.

Secretary CARLISLE. I have set out in this report the outlines of a plan for exempting the use of circulating notes issued by State banks from taxation on certain conditions, which embodies my views on the subject, as a practical question. Theoretically I do not believe that the Government of the United States should impose any tax upon notes lawfully issued by a State bank. But there is such a tax, and its validity has been declared by the Supreme Court of the United States; and it seems impossible, or at least impracticable, under the present circumstances, to repeal it absolutely; and it might not be good financial policy, even if it were practicable. My idea was that we would relax it so that it would not be absolutely prohibitory. I believe that a State-bank note issued under the conditions set out in this plan would be safe.

We are to have the individual liability of the stockholders. We would have the 30 per cent on the circulation always retained, and we would have all the other safeguards heretofore mentioned. I think we would have, I will not say, a perfectly safe bank note (perhaps that would be a little too strong an expression), but we would have a reasonably safe bank note for the use of the people. The third paragraph in this plan requiring a provision of law making stockholders individually liable I would amend by providing that it shall not apply in the case of administrators, guardians, trustees, etc., provided the estates and funds in their hands belonging to the cestui que trust are liable under the law. In other words, I would exempt from personal liability a trustee or administrator.

Mr. COX. After these limitations and conditions have been complied with by a State bank which desires to go into banking, who is to decide and settle the question as to whether the conditions and limitations under the act have been complied with? Where would you lodge that authority?

Secretary CARLISLE. This plan proposes that the notes of State banks shall be exempted from taxation when it is shown, to the satisfaction of the Secretary of the Treasury and of the Comptroller of the Currency, that all the conditions have been complied with. Under this plan no authority would be issued in advance to a State banking association to issue notes without taxation. But a State bank would organize itself under the law and proceed to issue its notes, and when the time came to collect the tax upon its notes it would simply be required to show to the Secretary and Comptroller that it had complied with all the conditions of the law, and therefore no tax would be assessed upon its notes.

Mr. COX. The bank, under that statement, would have to assume the responsibility that it had complied with the conditions of the law, and if the United States authorities decide that it had not, it would be subject to taxation on its notes.

Secretary CARLISLE. Yes; I think that would be sufficient to induce the bank to comply with the conditions of the law.

Mr. COX. I have no doubt that in that case the proper authorities would issue rules so as to instruct its subordinate officers how to proceed.

Secretary CARLISLE. The officer making the inquiry in regard to the taxation would have the right to take all reasonable steps to ascertain the facts. If necessary for him to see the books of the bank, he could see them. It is true that there would be no provision in the law compelling a State bank to submit to an examination of its affairs, but if the agent of the Treasury Department made a request to be permitted to see the books of the bank, and the bank declined, the agent's answer would be very brief. It would be, "Very well, you must pay the tax."

Mr. WARNER. What difference do you intend between the "deposit" or custody of the guarantee fund in United States legal-tender notes on the part of a State bank and the "keeping" guarantee fund of 30 per cent in the case of a national bank?

Secretary CARLISLE. I have thought about that a good deal, and have not come to any entirely satisfactory conclusion in my own mind as to whether the bank should be allowed to keep that deposit in its own vaults or whether it shall be required to keep it with some State authority.

Mr. JOHNSON, of Indiana. Why not with some national authority?

Secretary CARLISLE. Because I do not think that national authority has anything to do with it. I think that all the power which the United States has on this subject, if any, is the power to tax as laid down by the Supreme Court, and I think that you may tax upon conditions as well as tax absolutely. But I do not think that the Government of the United States has any authority to take hold of a State-bank system or to manage the affairs of a State bank except to the extent of saying that it will not tax State-bank notes under certain conditions.

The CHAIRMAN. Would you leave the reserve in the vaults of State banks and require national banks to put their reserve in the vaults of the National Treasury?

Secretary CARLISLE. The effect on the bank is just the same, but I am not clear in my own mind whether we should permit State banks to keep the 30 per cent reserve in their own vaults or require them to deposit it with some State official.

Mr. JOHNSON, of Indiana. Would not that offer superior inducements to the State bank instead of to the national bank?

Secretary CARLISLE. I do not think it would offer superior inducements. If a bank desires to withdraw any part of its reserve it can redeem its notes and withdraw part of its reserve. If a bank proposes to manage its affairs honestly, it makes no difference to it whether its reserve fund is in its own vaults or in the vault of some public official in the State or here.

Mr. JOHNSON, of Indiana. Would not the fact of the reserve being in their own vaults be an extra inducement to State banking?

Secretary CARLISLE. I think that depends altogether upon the purpose of the bank. If a bank desires to conduct its affairs honestly and faithfully, it does not make a particle of difference whether its guarantee fund is kept in its own vaults or anywhere else. If it wants to use its guarantee fund in violation of law, of course it would want to keep it in its own vaults.

Mr. WALKER. If you are going to put any conditions at all upon

State banks, why not put on the condition that 30 per cent of its circulation shall be in the custody of the United States? Do you not assume (in saying that this reserve fund may be left in the custody of the State banks) that you have more confidence in their integrity than you have in the integrity of the national banks?

Secretary CARLISLE. Not at all. If a bank puts its 30 per cent fund here the Secretary of the Treasury has to keep a strict account of every note issued by that bank.

Mr. WALKER. You have to do so in any case.

Secretary CARLISLE. Not at all. We would have to issue notes to the State banks, and we would have to take charge of its whole business substantially so as to know all the time what circulation each bank had out; and whenever it retired notes we would have to register and destroy them. This would send the entire issue business of the State banks to the Treasury Department of the United States.

Mr. WARNER. Just as much so as national banks.

Secretary CARLISLE. Exactly.

Mr. WALKER. If I understand your purpose in having State banks and national banks, it is that business men and bankers may elect whether they will take the State-bank note or the national-bank note. If that is your reason, ought not the appearance of the State-bank note be entirely dissimilar to that of a national-bank note?

Secretary CARLISLE. Certainly. That is provided for. "The Secretary of the Treasury may, under proper rules and regulations, to be established by him, permit State banks to procure and use in the preparation of their notes the distinctive paper used in printing United States securities; but no State bank shall print or engrave its notes in similitude of United States notes or certificates or national-bank notes."

Mr. WALKER. My point is this: That the note would be in the eye of the law, or after a critical examination, or even any examination, in the similitude of a United States note; and if it is printed on the same paper, I submit that in taking those notes in quantities, or singly, people could not at once determine or decide whether it was a State note or a United States note, although they might not desire to handle State notes. It seems to me that if you have a distinctively colored paper, the color of the paper ought to be such that the difference would be apparent at once and conspicuous, and that that provision of your bill does not reach to that extent.

Secretary CARLISLE. The provision goes only to the extent of providing that the State note shall not be in the similitude of a United States note. Of course every note issued by a State bank would have on it the name of the bank and the name of the State, and the note as a whole, as to ornamentation and style, would have to be different. I thought it would be necessary to have the distinctive paper, if possible, in order to guard against counterfeiting, but that is a matter of detail.

Mr. WALKER. It seems to me, Mr. Secretary, that the plan you have given us interferes with State banks.

Secretary CARLISLE. It does not interfere at all. The plan only permits them to do certain things if they want to do it.

Mr. WALKER. That it does interfere is the way it reaches my mind.

Secretary CARLISLE. I do not so regard it.

Mr. WALKER. I understand that, but you can see at once that it is furnishing the opportunity for a State-bank note to appear before the community in the dress and similitude of a United States note, because the color of the note and paper is the same. Where a man takes a note nowadays, in counting a hundred dollars, he takes very little notice of anything more than the denominations of the notes; he sees that they are similar in color. though different in portions of the engraving and the name; but, without a critical examination, such as a citizen ought not to be required to give a note in business transactions, he can not tell whether the note is a greenback, a silver certificate, or a national-bank note.

Secretary CARLISLE. They are notes, however, of different characters.

Mr. WALKER. But they are all equally good.

Mr. JOHNSON, of Indiana. Under your plan would not the State bank be to a limited extent under the control of the Federal Government?

Secretary CARLISLE. No.

Mr. JOHNSON, of Indiana. As I understand it, it must come under Federal supervision to some extent before it has any right to issue notes.

Secretary CARLISLE. I disclaim any authority on the part of the Government to control. They can be taxed, it is true, but this plan simply provides that if they comply with these conditions we will not tax their notes; we can not require them to comply.

Mr. JOHNSON, of Indiana. Do you not think, if you impose in your plan certain necessary conditions precedent before a State bank can issue notes, that that is, to a certain extent, subjecting it to national control?

Secretary CARLISLE. No; I think not. My own position would lead me logically to the absolute repeal of the tax.

Mr. JOHNSON, of Indiana. Were there not many charters under which State banks of issue issued paper before the war, which charters contained all of the limitations and restrictions on the powers of the banks that are found in your plan?

Secretary CARLISLE. I am not able to say, Mr. Johnson, how many of them, if any, contained those conditions.

Mr. JOHNSON, of Indiana. You do not know?

Secretary CARLISLE. No, sir.

Mr. JOHNSON, of Indiana. The safety of a note to the people consists not so much in the provisions of the charter as in the enforcement of those provisions; am I not right about that?

Secretary CARLISLE. You can not enforce a provision unless it is contained in the charter.

Mr. JOHNSON, of Indiana. But I say the safety of a note in the hands of the holder depends not so much upon the provisions of the charter of the bank as upon the rigid enforcement of the provisions of that charter.

Secretary CARLISLE. Certainly the bank must not violate, but if it does it must be held to the execution of the law in its charter.

Mr. JOHNSON, of Indiana. There is no power of visitation or examination, and nothing requiring reports at the hands of the State bank to the General Government in your plan, is there?

Secretary CARLISLE. No; but the State bank must satisfy the Secretary of the Treasury and Comptroller of the Currency that it has complied with these conditions, and must comply with whatever request those officials make of it, or it will be taxed.

Mr. JOHNSON, of Indiana. What preliminary power or authority do you give to the General Government to ascertain from time to time whether or not the State bank, under your plan, is complying with the limitations which you propose to impose?

Secretary CARLISLE. Do you mean the institution of an investigation, independently of the question of taxation?

Mr. JOHNSON, of Indiana. So that the Secretary and Comptroller can readily ascertain whether or not the conditions have been complied with.

Secretary CARLISLE. Every power that any intelligent man would consider necessary in such a case.

Mr. JOHNSON, of Indiana. Point out, if you please, what is reserved with reference to that particular point by your plan.

Secretary CARLISLE. We do not propose to do it at all. We do not believe that we ought to have the power to examine without the consent of the bank.

Mr. JOHNSON, of Indiana. Then there is no power in your plan, as I understand, which authorizes the General Government to visit these banks to inspect them, or to require reports of their condition from time to time, in order that the Government officials may see that they are complying with the law under which they are allowed to issue notes without the 10 per cent tax?

Secretary CARLISLE. No express authority is given to any officer, as a matter of right, to visit any State bank and inspect its books and accounts. But the Secretary of the Treasury and the Comptroller of the Currency have the right to require, and will require, the banks to furnish to them information necessary to enable them to decide whether the banks have complied with these conditions or not; in other words, the power to see that they are rightfully exempt from taxation.

Mr. JOHNSON, of Indiana. Suppose the bank complies with that requirement for a period of time, and then there arises a suspicion that it is not complying; what power has the Government, under your plan, to see that the bank is still acting in good faith, or otherwise?

Secretary CARLISLE. Every power that an intelligent man can possibly want to exercise, because we can say to the bank, "We will tax you unless you show to our entire satisfaction that you have complied, during the whole of this year, with the conditions imposed." The taxes will be payable every year. At the time when the tax becomes payable, a bank will apply for exemption, and will undertake to show to the Secretary of the Treasury and the Comptroller of the Currency that it is entitled to exemption because it has complied with all these conditions. The Secretary of the Treasury and the Comptroller of the Currency may then say to the bank, "The evidence you have furnished us upon this subject is not satisfactory; we want something further; we want to look at your books and accounts." I say such a case might arise. Suppose the bank declines; then all the power we have is to tax the notes.

Mr. COBB, of Alabama. And that will destroy the bank.

Secretary CARLISLE. Yes; but the bank can carry on business without making itself amenable to these requirements. In that case, however, you destroy it as a bank of issue.

Mr. COBB, of Alabama. It seems to me that it is a destruction of the bank.

Secretary CARLISLE. There is not only a tax of 10 per cent upon that bank itself for each one of the notes it has paid out, but there is a tax upon every other bank that has paid out those notes during the whole year.

Mr. JOHNSON, of Indiana. A tax on every dollar every time it is paid out?

Secretary CARLISLE. Every time.

Mr. JOHNSON, of Indiana. Suppose the bank presents what it deems sufficient evidence to the governmental authorities that it is exempt from taxation and they are not satisfied, but propose to tax the bank; what remedy has the bank when the evidence is not regarded as ample?

Secretary CARLISLE. If it has been compelled to pay an illegal tax, I suppose the bank would have the same remedy that anybody else would have under the same circumstances.

Mr. HALL. May I ask you a question right there?

Secretary CARLISLE. Yes.

Mr. HALL. On the same line that Mr. Walker and Mr. Johnson have questioned you, I want to know if the parties most vitally and deeply interested in the validity of the circulation and use of that currency are not the banks themselves?

Secretary CARLISLE. Yes.

Mr. HALL. If they fail to put forward a currency that would circulate as well as any other currency, are they not the persons who will be most injured thereby?

Secretary CARLISLE. I think so.

Mr. JOHNSON, of Indiana. And would not the doctrine of the "survival of the fittest" currency apply to the issue of State-bank currency, as well as to any other kind?

Secretary CARLISLE. I think so.

Mr. WARNER. As a matter of fact, Mr. Secretary, would not these examinations which would take place in fact, although not expressly provided for under your plan, probably be in the end the best advertisement that a bank of issue could have, just as in the case of examination of insurance corporations nine-tenths of their advertising consists of the publication of the results of examinations?

Secretary CARLISLE. Undoubtedly that would be the case with the banks.

Mr. JOHNSON, of Indiana. Was it not the case before the war that State bank notes which had so depreciated that they were at a discount continued to have currency, and that people were compelled to take them?

Secetary CARLISLE. Certainly. But I do not believe, gentlemen, that you can reestablish what was called the wild-cat banking system in the United States any more than you can reestablish the conditions out of which the system arose. Those conditions have all passed away, and you can not have a bank of issue that could sustain itself unless its notes are safe or reasonably safe. The education and experience of the people of the United States for the last thirty years have carried them a long way beyond the point of keeping in circulation any depreciated bank paper.

Mr. WALKER. Is not this the theory upon which all examinations of banks are now made: That a bank can at any time make its condition sound for a day or two or for three or five days; that if notifications are sent to the bank beforehand that the examiner is to appear, the examination is practically valueless; and that, therefore, the examiners are required to appear at unexpected times, and calls are made upon banks at unexpected times for report as to their condition; and does not your theory contemplate exactly the opposite of that, that of allowing the banks to make their own representations to the Department?

Secretary CARLISLE. You mean with respect to State banks?

Mr. WALKER. Yes. Does not your whole testimony here proceed upon exactly the opposite theory to that which I have stated?

Secretary CARLISLE. As to national banks——

Mr. WALKER. No; as to the State banks.

Secretary CARLISLE. I will come to that. As to the national banks, this plan proposes no change whatever in the method of reporting, which is required five times a year, or in the method of examination. The only penalty to which the State bank is proposed to be subjected for failure to comply with all these conditions and keeping all the time in the situation which the law requires is the payment of the 10 per cent tax upon its circulation. If that is not sufficient to induce the bank to comply with these conditions, then the plan as to the State bank will be a failure, and no State bank can issue notes, because it will be closed up at once. If it has not complied with the conditions, then it will have to pay the 10 per cent tax, and no bank can live under that tax, so that there will be no State bank of issue in existence thatdoes not comply with these conditions.

Mr. WALKER. Mr. Secretary, that does not reach the point at all, because that is in the line of the banks' declarations, assuming that they are honest and fair and wise and prudent. It assumes all those things. Now, the theory is, as I have said, that the national banks all need investigation, and they need investigation at times and occasions when they do not expect it. They are under constant temptation to increase their receipts, to enlarge their dividends, by practices that are not safe. That is the ground upon which irregular and unexpected visitations are made, and evidence procured by outside parties, namely, examiners, or anyone who may be employed. Your theory proceeds in exactly the opposite direction, that the banks are to report to you their condition, and that this condition is permanent and continuous, and I submit that it would take about as large a force, and investigation at unexpected times, to find out whether the bank has complied with your conditions. We know something about customhouse oaths, and so we may know something about bankers' oaths.

Secretary CARLISLE. Instead of assuming that all of the State banks, as a fundamental proposition upon which this plan is based, will be honest and faithful in the discharge of their duties under the law, you may assume just the contrary; you may assume that they will all be dishonest and unfaithful, and if so their circulation will be taxed out of existence.

Mr. WALKER. Then after the horse is stolen we will lock the stable door?

Mr. HALL. In answer to the question asked you by Mr. Walker in regard to the importance of having a careful guardianship over these banks, I want to know whether, referring to sections 19 and 20 of the act approved February 8, 1875, touching the issue of notes and putting the 10 per cent taxation on them—and it was in that act that the old sections were incorporated—there is not a provision in those sections that the 10 per cent tax applies not only to the issuance of notes, but to every time notes are paid out, so that the tax of 10 per cent applies to every time notes are paid out.

Secretary CARLISLE. It applies if the note is paid out by the bank of issue, or by any other bank, or by any individual.

Mr. HALL. Now, would not that make every other bank and every other individual especially and personally interested in seeing that the bank of issue had complied with the conditions precedent that exempted it, and would not that tend to create a constant surveillance over the bank which would be better in its effect even than the official examination of a national bank?

Secretary CARLISLE. That is what I said a few moments ago; that no bank or individual will take that note unless he is satisfied that it is a good note and that the bank issuing it has complied with the law.

Mr. BROSIUS. How long, under your plan, would a State bank issue circulation before being required to exhibit evidence to the Treasury Department that it has complied with the conditions specified in your plan?

Secretary CARLISLE. I believe the 10 per cent taxation upon the issues of State bank circulation is not made payable semiannually, as it is in the case of a national bank.

Mr. BROSIUS. It is made payable annually.

Secretary CARLISLE. Then a State bank could go on issuing notes until the time came for paying the tax.

Mr. BROSIUS. Under your plan a State bank could continue issuing its own notes for a period of one year before the Treasury Department would have any right to call upon it for any exhibition of its right to do so.

Mr. HALL. They can do that now.

Secretary CARLISLE. They can do that now just as well.

Mr. JOHNSON, of Indiana. In response to a question asked you awhile ago, you said the time had come when people could not be induced to take bad money. I suppose you meant knowingly induced to take bad money. Is it not true that under any system of banking that can be devised money might be taken by people under a misapprehension, thinking it to be good, when it should afterwards turn out to be bad in their hands?

Secretary CARLISLE. Oh, yes. What I intended to express was this: That the people would inform themselves before taking the notes; in other words, that if a State bank should be established in your town, for instance, the people of your town, of course, would know something about its condition, and they would not take its notes unless they were reasonably safe, because there are plenty of other notes to be had; nor would they make deposits in that bank unless the bank were reasonably safe. There are are national banks all over the country whose notes are now in circulation. But thirty to fifty years ago, when large parts of the South and West were comparatively unsettled, when they had no banking facilities, no easy and quick communication with financial centers, no easy methods of making exchanges, they had to have a currency of some kind, and they resorted to almost everything that looked like a bank bill, and banked upon mortgages upon real estate, and various kinds of securities. But I am satisfied that nothing of that sort can be done now.

Mr. JOHNSON, of Indiana. While I might be satisfied with a bank in my own State, I might want to pass some of those bills to somebody living outside of my State.

Secretary CARLISLE. All those arguments are legitimate and fair, Mr. Johnson, but they apply to the national banks just as well as to the State banks. My opinion is that the State-bank note, issued under those conditions, will be a good note.

Mr. COBB, of Alabama. Is not your proposed plan unfriendly to the State banks in this: That the conditions are so stringent that they can not circulate their notes?

Secretary CARLISLE. I do not know that it is unfriendly to State banks.

Mr. COBB, of Alabama. In this respect: That the conditions are so stringent as to make every individual who takes a circulating note of one of those banks, so highly responsible, that every intelligent citizen would be afraid to take hold of a State-bank note.

Secretary CARLISLE. That is what I said a few moments ago. I thought that was one of the guarantees that only good notes would circulate.

Mr. COBB, of Alabama. Is it not a guarantee that you could not, under your plan, have State banking at all?

Secretary CARLISLE. I do not think so. I think that if a State bank complies with the conditions imposed the people would take notes if they needed them. I confess, Judge Cobb, that I do not attach the same importance to this State-bank provision that perhaps some other gentlemen do. I do not know to what extent it would be utilized, even if it should be adopted. But still there seems to be a demand in some parts of the country for such a system, and I am willing to accede to that demand.

Mr. COBB, of Alabama. I would like to have the plan more liberal, because I am in favor of State-bank money, and the point I make is that under your plan it is impossible to have any State-bank currency.

Secretary CARLISLE. You can, if you have a good currency, I think.

Mr. COBB, of Alabama. How can any individual citizen know that it is good currency, so that he may know he is escaping the penalty of the law in circulating it?

Secretary CARLISLE. He has the assurance that the bank would not undertake to issue notes under this system, subject to the 10 per cent taxation, without complying with the conditions of the law; that the bank could not afford to put itself in that attitude.

Mr. COBB, of Alabama. And that is all the guarantee he has, is it not?

Secretary CARLISLE. No; he has the additional guarantee which every man has who takes a bank note. He has some faith, of course, in the people who conduct the bank, the general commercial credit and standing of the institution itself.

The CHAIRMAN. In order to avoid the objection, Mr. Secretary, that Mr. Cobb, of Alabama, has suggested, of discrimination against the State banks, would it be proper to remit the taxation upon such banks as complied completely with the provisions which you propose to apply to the national banks, and would not such provision secure a greater uniformity than is possible under the system which you propose?

Secretary CARLISLE. Do you mean, Mr. Chairman, to make a provision that they shall keep on deposit, say, with some official of the Government, or keep in their own hands, 30 per cent of their circulation and also a safety fund?

The CHAIRMAN. I mean, is there any objection to applying to the State banks, as a condition of being relieved from the taxation, the same provisions precisely, mutatis mutandis, which you apply to the national banks?

Secretary CARLISLE. Then I see no use whatever of providing for a State banking system; it would be all a national banking system then.

The CHAIRMAN. If you apply one condition, you may apply that as well as the other?

Secretary CARLISLE. If you undertake to impose conditions upon them in order to secure exemption from taxation, of course you can impose such conditions as you please. But if you are to impose upon them the same conditions as are imposed upon national banks, then of course we shall have to take supervision of them, because we now exercise supervision of the national banks.

Mr. JOHNSON, of Indiana. You dropped a remark a bit ago that gave me, as an individual, some encouragement, for I like very much some of the general features of your plan, though there is one element that I do not like. If it were possible to get through this Congress a bill revising our banking and currency system so that the Government may be divorced from banking, and retire all the Government issues, and dispense with the bond security, which prevent elasticity, and secure an elastic system of currency in order to meet the needs of the people, why is it necessary to insist upon a revival of the mistakes of the State banking system? Do you consider the State banking system as absolutely essential now to currency reform?

Secretary CARLISLE. I have just said that I attach less importance to the State banking system than many other gentlemen do, but that there seems to be a demand in certain parts of the country for State banks in order to supply them with the currency for local use at certain seasons of the year, issued upon some plan which would give it a sufficient amount of elasticity to enable the banks to put it out when it is wanted, and to take it in when it is not needed; and I said that in deference to that sentiment I had incorporated that feature into this plan.

I believe, in the first place—and I am giving you now only my individual opinion, I am not criticising the decision of any judicial tribunal—that the imposition of this tax upon State banks by the United States Government, for the purpose for which it was imposed, was an unconstitutional exercise of power. But the courts have said that it was constitutional. Therefore, my position, as I say, would lead me logically to the repeal of the whole law on that subject. That, however, can not be done, and, in deference to the demand which seems to exist in many parts of the country for a State banking system, this has been incorporated here upon such conditions as, in my opinion, would secure a sound circulating medium. That is my position.

Mr. JOHNSON, of Indiana. The point I make is this, Mr. Secretary, Will not your plan, with the State-bank system eliminated, give to the people of sparsely settled districts the elastic currency which you say is needed and reasonably meet all their requirements?

Secretary CARLISLE. I think it would. But at the same time, a part of this plan, and, in my opinion, the most valuable part of it, is that provision which authorizes the Secretary of the Treasury to use from time to time, in his discretion, the surplus revenue to enable him to retire the old legal-tender notes, the Treasury notes of 1890, to the extent of 70 per cent upon the amount of notes issued under this system. You understand that when a national bank takes out circulation under this system, or when a State bank takes out circulation under this system, it will increase the circulating medium nearly 70 per cent, because it is required to lock up 30 per cent.

In order to make a wider field for the exercise of this authority to redeem and cancel the old United States notes and the Treasury notes the State-bank circulation is as useful as the national-bank circulation, because this plan provides that the Secretary of the Treasury may retire these notes to the extent of 70 per cent of the national-bank circulation taken out or 70 per cent of the State-bank circulation taken out. In other words, it affords to the Secretary of the Treasury an opportunity to relieve the Government from the current redemption of gold paper to a larger extent than he would without the State banking system.

The national banks to day have about $672,000,000 capital, and the State banks have enough more to make about $1,000,000,000. Of course no one can tell in advance to what extent notes will be taken out under this system, but if notes were taken out to the full capacity of the banks, State and national, it would require the deposit of about $125,000,000 of these notes, to say nothing of what might go into the safety fund.

Mr. JOHNSON, of Ohio. Can not the undivided profits of the national banks be at once converted into capital? We have $300,000,000 under that head.

Secretary CARLISLE. Yes; that could be done, but I am considering the capital stock alone. That would dispose of $225,000,000 of outstanding notes, provided the whole amount were taken, which of course it will not be for a long time.

STATEMENT BY SECRETARY CARLISLE—Resumed.

Secretary CARLISLE. Mr. Chairman, I apologize to the committee for being late. I was compelled to go to my office, and found it impossible to get away in order to be here at the time agreed upon yesterday. As a great many questions are being asked in relation to the Baltimore plan, I think it would be very well to have it incorporated in my statement.

The CHAIRMAN. It has been already ordered to be incorporated in the proceedings of the committee.

Secretary CARLISLE. In accordance with the request of the committee made yesterday, I have prepared a bill which, with the permission of the committee, I will read, if it is thought desirable for me to do so.

The CHAIRMAN. Please to do so.

Secretary Carlisle read the bill prepared by him, as follows:

AN ACT to amend the laws relating to national-banking associations, to exempt the notes of State banks from taxation upon certain conditions, and for other purposes.

Be it enacted by the Senate and House of Representatives of the United States of America in Congress assembled, That all acts and parts of acts which require or authorize the deposit of United States bonds to secure circulating notes issued by national banking associations be, and the same are hereby, repealed, and such notes hereafter prepared shall not contain the statement that they are so secured.

SEC. 2. That any national-banking association organized as now provided by law, and any national-banking association hereafter organized, may take out circulating notes to an amount not exceeding 75 per cent of its paid-up and unimpaired capital upon depositing with the Treasurer of the United States United States legal-tender notes, including Treasury notes issued under the act approved July 14, 1890, entitled "An act directing the purchase of silver bullion and the issue of Treasury notes thereon, and for other purposes," as a guaranty fund equal to 30 per cent of the circulating notes applied for. The association making such deposit shall be entitled to receive from the Comptroller of the Currency circulating notes in denominations of $10 and multiples thereof in blank, registered and countersigned, as provided by law, and all such notes, together with the circulating notes of national-banking associations now outstanding, shall constitute, and are hereby declared to be, a first lien upon all the assets of the association issuing the same. All circulating notes hereafter furnished to national-banking associations shall be uniform in design, but any association desiring to redeem its circulating notes in gold may have them made payable in that coin; and the Secretary of the Treasury is hereby authorized and directed to have prepared and keep on hand ready for delivery on application a reserve of blank notes for each national-banking association having circulation, but such reserve for each bank shall at no time be in excess of the difference between the amount of its notes then outstanding and the total amount which it is by this act authorized to receive.

SEC. 3. That in lieu of all existing taxes each national-banking association shall pay to the Treasurer of the United States, in the months of January and July each year, a duty of one fourth of 1 per centum for each half year upon the average amount of its notes in circulation, and in computing such average all notes issued by such association and not actually retired from circulation in the manner hereinafter provided shall be included.

SEC. 4. That each national-banking association shall redeem its notes at par on presentation at its own office or at its own office and at such agencies as may be designated by it for that purpose, and whenever such association desires to retire the whole or any part of its circulation, the notes to be retired shall be forwarded to the Comptroller of the Currency for cancellation, and thereupon 30 per centum of the amount of such canceled notes shall be returned to the association. Defaced and mutilated notes, and notes otherwise unfit for circulation, which have been redeemed by any association, may be returned to the Comptroller of the Currency for destruction and reissue, as now provided by law.

SEC. 5. That in order to provide a safety fund for the prompt redemption of the circulating notes of failed national banking associations, each such association now organized, or hereafter organized, shall pay to the Treasurer of the United States, in the months of January and July in each year, a tax of one-fourth of 1 per centum for each half year upon the average amount of its circulating notes outstanding, to be computed as hereinbefore provided, until the said fund amounts to a sum equal to 5 per centum upon the total amount of national-bank notes outstanding, and thereafter said tax shall cease. Each association hereafter organized, and each association applying for additional circulation, shall pay its pro rata share into the said fund before receiving notes; but an association retiring or reducing its circulation shall not be entitled to withdraw any part of said fund. When a national banking association becomes insolvent, its guarantee fund held on deposit shall be transferred to the safety fund herein provided for and applied to the redemption of its outstanding notes, and in case the said last-mentioned fund should at any time be impaired by the redemptions of the notes of failed national banks, and the immediately available assets of said banks are not sufficient to reimburse it, said fund shall be at once restored by pro rata assessments upon all the other associations according to the amount of their outstanding circulation; and the associations so assessed shall have a first lien upon the assets of each failed bank for the amount properly chargeable to such bank on account of the redemption of its circulation.

SEC. 6. That the Secretary of the Treasury may from time to time invest any money belonging to the safety fund in United States bonds, and the bonds so purchased, and the interest accruing thereon, shall be held as part of the said fund. Such bonds may be sold when necessary and the proceeds used for the redemption of the circulating notes of failed national banks.

SEC. 7. That every national banking association heretofore organized and having bonds on deposit to secure circulation shall, on or before the first day of July, 1895, withdraw such bonds and deposit with the Treasurer of the United States a guarantee fund consisting of United States legal-tender notes, including the Treasury notes issued under the act of July 14, 1890, equal to 30 per cent of its outstanding circulation at the time of such withdrawal and deposit, and all laws and parts of laws requiring such association to deposit, or to keep on deposit, with the Treasurer of the United States bonds of the United States for any purpose other than as security for public moneys shall be, and are hereby, repealed from and after the said date.

SEC. 8. That sections 9 and 12 of the act approved July 12, 1882, entitled "An act to enable national banking associations to extend their corporate existence, and for other purposes," and section 31 of the act approved June 3, 1864, entitled "An act to provide a national currency secured by a pledge of United States bonds, and to provide for the circulation and redemption thereof," and all acts and parts of acts supplemental thereto or amendatory thereof be, and the same are hereby, repealed.

SEC. 9. That the Secretary of the Treasury may, in his discretion, use from time to time any surplus revenue of the United States in the redemption and retirement of United States legal-tender notes, but the amount of such notes retired shall not in the aggregate exceed an amount equal to 70 per cent of the additional circulation taken out by national banks and State banks under the provisions of this act; and hereafter no United States notes, or Treasury notes authorized by the act of July 14, 1890, entitled "An act directing the purchase of silver bullion and the issue of Treasury notes thereon, and for other purposes," of a less denomination than $10 shall be issued, and as rapidly as such notes of denomination less than $10 shall be received into the Treasury they shall be canceled and an equal amount of notes of like character, but in denominations of $10 or multiplies therof, shall be issued in their places; but nothing in this act shall be so construed as to repeal, or in any manner affect, the second section of the said act of July 14, 1890.

SEC. 10. That the use of circulating notes issued by a banking corporation, duly organized under the laws of any State, and which transacts no other than a banking business, shall be exempt from taxation under the laws of the United States, when it is shown to the satisfaction of the Secretary of the Treasury and Comptroller of the Currency—

(1) That such bank has at no time had outstanding its circulating notes in excess of 75 per centum of its paid-up and unimpaired capital.

(2) That its stockholders are individually liable for the redemption of its circulating notes to the full extent of their ownership of stock; but this shall not be required

in the case of persons holding stock, as executors, administrators, guardians, or trustees, if the assets and funds in their hands are liable in like manner and to the same extent as the testator, intestate, ward, or person interested in such funds would be if living and competent to act and hold the stock in his own name.

(3) That the circulating notes constitute by law a first lien upon all the assets of the bank.

(4) That the bank has at all times kept on deposit, with an official of the State authorized by law to receive and hold the same, a guarantee fund in United States legal-tender notes, including Treasury notes of 1890, equal to 30 per centum of its outstanding circulating notes; and

(5) That it has promptly redeemed its notes at par on demand at its principal office, or at one or more of its branch offices, if it has branches.

SEC. 11. That the Secretary of the Treasury may, under proper rules and regulations to be established by him, permit State banks to procure and use in the preparation of their notes the distinctive paper used in printing United States securities, but no State bank shall print or engrave its notes in similitude of a United States note, or certificate, or national-bank note.

It will be observed that section 8 of this bill repeals sections 9 and 12 of the act of July 12, 1882, which I had better read in order that they may go into the statement. Section 9 is:

That any national banking association now organized, or hereafter organized, desiring to withdraw its circulating notes, upon a deposit of lawful money with the Treasurer of the United States, as provided in section four of the act of June twentieth, eighteen hundred and seventy-four, entitled "An act fixing the amount of United States notes, providing for a redistribution of national-bank currency, and for other purposes," or as provided in this act, is authorized to deposit lawful money and withdraw a proportionate amount of the bonds held as security for its circulating notes in the order of such deposits; and no national bank which makes any deposit of lawful money in order to withdraw its circulating notes shall be entitled to receive any increase of its circulation for the period of six months from the time it made such deposit of lawful money for the purpose aforesaid: *Provided*, That not more than three millions of dollars of lawful money shall be deposited during any calendar month for this purpose: *And provided further*, That the provisions of this section shall not apply to bonds called for redemption by the Secretary of the Treasury, nor to the withdrawal of circulating notes in consequence thereof.

It might not be absolutely necessary to repeal that section of the statute if the plan now proposed should be adopted, because the proposed plan dispenses entirely with the deposit of bonds and with the payment of lawful money to redeem circulation. But still the spirit of the section is that the national banks shall not redeem in the aggregate more than $3,000,000 of their circulation per month, and that having retired any part of their circulation they shall not be permitted to increase it again for six months. Therefore I have included in the proposed bill a provision to repeal that section.

Section 12 is—and about this there will be room for considerable difference of opinion—

That the Secretary of the Treasury is authorized and directed to receive deposits of gold coin with the Treasurer or assistant treasurers of the United States, in sums not less than twenty dollars, and to issue certificates therefor in denominations of not less than twenty dollars each, corresponding with the denominations of United States notes. The coin deposited for or representing the certificates of deposits shall be retained in the Treasury for the payment of the same on demand. Said certificates shall be receivable for customs, taxes, and all public dues, and when so received may be reissued; and such certificates, as also silver certificates, when held by any national banking association, shall be counted as part of its lawful reserve; and no national banking association shall be a member of any clearing-house in which such certificates shall not be receivable in the settlement of clearing-house balances: *Provided*, That the Secretary of the Treasury shall suspend the issue of such gold certificates whenever the amount of gold coin and gold bullion in the Treasury reserved for the redemption of United States notes falls below one hundred millions of dollars; and the provisions of section fifty-two hundred and seven of the Revised Statutes shall be applicable to the certificates herein authorized and directed to be issued.

Section 5207 of the Revised Statutes, here referred to, prohibits any national bank from depositing certain kinds of Government securities as collateral for obligations incurred by them, and that provision is made applicable by this section to the gold certificates. There are now outstanding about 61,000,000 of gold certificates; or, rather, there are in existence about 61,000,000 of gold certificates, some 2,500,000 of which are held in the Treasury, the remainder being in circulation or held by the banks as part of their reserve.

My own opinion is that it is not good policy for the Government to establish a warehouse for the holding of gold, and issuing certificates against it to circulate, because I believe (looking at it purely from a Treasury Department standpoint) that this gold, or much the larger part of it, would come into the Treasury and stay there if certificates were not issued upon it, because the banks and the trust companies and other institutions (especially the banks) which desire circulation can not use their gold to circulate. The gold coin itself will not circulate to any considerable extent, because it is cumbersome to handle and the banks would not keep it in their vaults at their own risk. Therefore, if the gold certificates were not issued, this gold would come into the Treasury and the legal-tender notes or the Treasury notes of 1890 would be taken out and put into circulation or would be held by the banks as part of their reserve, just as they now hold the gold certificates.

The latter part of this section seems to have no connection whatever with the first part. It provides that the issue of gold certificates shall cease whenever the gold reserve is reduced to $100,000,000; and yet the section does not require the Secretary of the Treasury to issue gold certificates except when the gold is brought by the owners and deposited. There seems to be an incongruity in the section in that respect.

But, as I have said, the repeal of that section is not an essential part of a plan of currency reform, and the question as to whether it will be or not good policy to deprive the Secretary of the Treasury of the authority to issue these certificates, or whether to take off that mandatory provision which compels him to issue them, is one about which there may be a difference of opinion. My own view of it (looking at it entirely from an official standpoint) is that it would be beneficial to the Government not to issue these certificates, but to compel the persons who hold the gold to keep it at their own risk or to put it into the Treasury of the United States, and get out currency in lieu of it.

The next repeal is that of section 31 of the original banking act, which has been amended in some respects. It is the section which requires each national bank in certain cities to keep a fixed reserve equal to 25 per cent of the amount of their deposits and other capital stock, and requires national banking associations in other cities to keep a fixed reserve of 15 per cent on their deposits and capital stock. That part of the section which requires the computation to be made on the circulation of the banks, as well as on the deposits, has been repealed, so that as the law now stands these banks are required to keep this reserve on their deposits alone. I have already, in my official report and in my statement made to the committee yesterday, given the reasons which induce me to recommend the repeal of those provisions, and I suppose I need not go into it now further, unless some member of the committee desires to interrogate me on the subject.

It will be seen, Mr. Chairman, that among the conditions imposed upon State banks, in order to exempt them from taxation under the laws of the United States, they are required to keep on deposit with an official of the State authorized by law to reserve and hold the same a guaranty fund in United States legal-tender notes (including the Treasury notes of 1890) equal to 30 per cent on their outstanding circulation. Some criticism was made upon the proposed plan as printed in the report of the Secretary of the Treasury, on the ground that it made no provision for the custody of that 30 per cent, and a clause has been inserted in the bill which I have submitted to the committee to-day to meet that objection.

I think that it is met fully and fairly, because it deprives the State banks of all opportunity or power to touch this reserve except by retiring their circulation. Whenever a State bank retires its circulation or any part of it, a proper proportion of the guaranty fund will be returned to it by the State official.

The CHAIRMAN. Are not those conditions on which a State bank may issue circulating notes substantially the same as are imposed upon national banks?

Secretary CARLISLE. They are almost precisely the same so far as regards the guaranty fund, but there is no requirement here that the State banks shall keep a safety fund of 5 per cent. The safety of the State-bank notes is made to depend on the assets of the bank, on its commercial credit, on the individual liability of its stock-holders, and on the fact that it must deposit 30 per cent to secure its circulation. Its notes are a first lien upon its assets, and, as I said yesterday, if this does not make a reasonably safe note I am not able to devise a law that would do so.

Mr. COX. One of the points to which I desired to call your attention in making a State officer the holder of this 30 per cent guarantee fund has been remedied. Now, I desire to call your attention to another fact, which is as to the liability clause for the redemption of the circulating notes. If that fact appears in the charter of the bank it will be conclusive on that point?

Secretary CARLISLE. Of course.

Mr. COX. So I ask you if, in order to make it a little more definite, it would not be permissible that the stockholders' liability should appear in the charter of the bank. The fact that the bank has at all times kept its guarantee fund would appear from the statement of the officer who holds it. But ought not that provision also to appear in the charter of the bank?

Secretary CARLISLE. What provision?

Mr. COX. The provision which requires the 30 per cent guarantee fund to be deposited.

Secretary CARLISLE. The proposed bill says that the State officer shall be authorized by law to hold this deposit. I assume that every State which desires to have State-bank circulation will have a State-bank commissioner or some other officer authorized by law, so that it will not be necessary that the provision should appear in the charter of every State bank.

Mr. COX. And so with other facts as to the liability clause.

Secretary CARLISLE. The State may have a general law, and therefore it will not be necessary that it should appear in the charter of the bank.

Mr. BROSIUS. You have said, Mr. Secretary, that your plan, as explained, will secure a reasonably safe State-bank note. But as to that portion of the State-bank circulation which is not covered by the "safety" and "guarantee" fund?

Secretary CARLISLE. There is no safety fund in the case of State banks.

Mr. BROSIUS. I speak of the 30 per cent fund and the 5 per cent fund. That portion of the State-bank circulation not covered by those funds must depend for its redemption on the assets of the bank. That means, does it not, that it depends entirely on the solvency of the bank's creditors?

Secretary CARLISLE. It depends, in the first place, on the assets of the bank, and in the second place on the individual liability of each stockholder of the bank, and in the third place on the deposit of the 30 per cent guarantee fund.

Mr. BROSIUS. I am excluding all of the notes of the State bank except the additional 70 per cent. That depends for its security on the assets of the bank.

Secretary CARLISLE. And on the individual liability of the stockholders.

Mr. BROSIUS. It depends upon the solvency of the bank's debtors and upon the solvency of the stockholders. Is it not possible, in that view of the case, that a bank might be so badly broken that its notes will not be redeemed at all?

Secretary CARLISLE. All things are possible. I will not undertake to say what is not possible.

Mr. BROSIUS. You admit that that is possible?

Secretary CARLISLE. Oh, certainly.

Mr. BROSIUS. That possibility is in the nature of a residue of risk, and after all the security is attained which is attainable. My inquiry is, Would it not be better, under your bill, to put that residue of risk on the Government of the United States rather than on the note holders?

Secretary CARLISLE. Better for whom?

Mr. BROSIUS. Better for the people of the United States.

Secretary CARLISLE. I think not. My theory is that the Government of the United States should be disconnected entirely, if possible, from the banking business, and should not incur any liability in connection with that business except to see that it throws such safeguards around the issue of bank notes as to make them sound in the hands of the people.

Mr. BROSIUS. Is that objection of yours a constitutional one or a practical one?

Secretary CARLISLE. I think it both constitutional and practical. I think that when the Government embarks in a business that belongs to private corporations it is going into a business in which it is likely to suffer.

Mr. SPERRY. Your plan provides that no national bank shall issue bills of less denomination than ten dollars. Does the same apply to the State banks?

Secretary CARLISLE. No, sir. That is one of the questions about which I have, of course, thought very seriously, but it has not been incorporated into the bill, and the reason why (which may not be a very good one) was that the State-bank notes will probably circulate to a larger extent than the national-bank notes among the masses of the people in the locality or region where the State bank is located, and that perhaps it would not be wise to undertake to limit them to notes of ten dollars and upward.

Mr. SPERRY. Have you made any estimate of the probable profits of circulation of national banks under your system?

Secretary CARLISLE. Yes; an estimate was made in the office of the Comptroller of the Currency at my request, and although I have not had an opportunity to review the calculation submitted, I assume that they have been correctly made. Under the plan proposed a national bank having a capital of $100,000 and being therefore entitled on a deposit of 30 per cent to take out a circulation of $75,000, would make profit, for the first year and for all the years up until the point was reached where the safety fund of 5 per cent was complete of $1,972.93. The expenses that are charged to the bank are the annual cost of redemption of its whole circulation, the taxes, the express charges on rhe whole of its circulation, the cost of plates and the agents' fees for tedemption.

Every item of expense has been deducted The net profit on the $75,000 of currency for the first year is calculated at $1,972.93, and after the first year at $2,722.93. A national bank doing business on a deposit of 2 per cent bonds would realize under the present system a profit of $434.28 after the same deductions have been made, and a national bank issuing circulation of $75,000 on 4 per cent bonds would have a profit of $611.50.

Mr. WALKER. At the present price of bonds?

Secretary CARLISLE. Yes, taking everything exactly as it is. If a bank is issuing currency on a deposit of 5 per cent bonds, its net profit on $75,000 circulation is $559.83; and if it is issuing its circulation on 6 per cent currency bonds (which are selling at a less premium, but pay a higher rate of interest), the profit on a circulation of $75,000 is $1,648.17.

Mr. WARNER. At what rate of interest is it assumed that that money is loaned?

Secretary CARLISLE. At 6 per cent all the way through. It is well known, of course, that the profits of the circulation of a national bank constitute a very small item of the total profits of the institution, but I had those calculations made simply to show that at least it would not be a disadvantage to the banks to take out circulation under this bill.

Mr. JOHNSON, of Indiana. Have you made any calculation as to the amount to which circulation would be issued under your plan if all the banks amenable to it, both national banks and State banks, should take out circulation to the full extent of their right to do so?

Secretary CARLISLE. Yes.

Mr. JOHNSON, of Indiana. What would be the amount?

Secretary CARLISLE. $750,000,000 including what is now out. From that there must be deducted the 30 per cent that will be put up for a guarantee fund, which would amount to $225,000,000. That would be simply the immediate effect of the taking out of the full percentage of circulation by all the national banks and by all the State banks. The effect would be to make $750,000,000 less the $225,000,000 which would have to be put up as a guarantee fund.

Mr. JOHNSON, of Indiana. What amount of United States Treasury notes, and of the notes issued under the act of 1890, would be taken up in order to guarantee that issue?

Secretary CARLISLE. $225,000,000, to say nothing about the 5 per cent safety fund. If the same kind of notes should be put into and held in that fund, as of course the Secretary of the Treasury would have done if he could, it would add about $3,500,000 more.

Mr. JOHNSON, of Indiana. It would still leave a good many greenbacks out to vex the Government.

Secretary CARLISLE. Certainly, to be redeemed hereafter, because I do not think it practicable to secure any legislation now that would immediately retire United States notes and Treasury notes. In the first place, if it were practicable to secure the passage of a law which would authorize the Secretary of the Treasury to issue bonds bearing a low rate of interest, and use the proceeds for the immediate redemption of these notes, the result would be an immediate contraction of the currency to the extent of about $498,000,000, unless the national banks and the State banks should be allowed to conduct their business at the same time under a plan that would induce them to take out the same amount of circulation.

Mr. JOHNSON, of Indiana. Then your system is only a partial relief for the Treasury drainage of gold.

Secretary CARLISLE. That is all that I thought we were able to secure.

Mr. JOHNSON, of Indiana. The plan of Mr. Eckels, as stated here yesterday, provides for taking out less circulation, does it not?

Secretary CARLISLE. No; it provides for taking out circulation up to the full extent of the capital stock of each bank.

Mr JOHNSON, of Indiana. But it applies only to national banks, not to State banks.

Secretary CARLISLE. The State banks and the national banks together have a capital stock of about $1,000,000,000. Of this the national banks have $672,000,000. Under the plan proposed by the Comptroller of the Currency the national banks can take out circulation to the full amount of their stock, to wit, $672,000,000, but the State banks can take out none, I believe.

Mr. JOHNSON, of Indiana. By Mr. Eckels's plan a much larger amount of United States notes and of Treasury notes issued under the act of 1890 would be deposited with the Government than under your plan.

Secretary CARLISLE. Yes.

Mr. JOHNSON, of Indiana. And therefore there would be less of them out to drain the Treasury of its gold?

Secretary CARLISLE. If you will allow me, I will state what I understand Mr. Eckels's plan to be as stated in his report. He proposes that national banks shall be allowed to take out circulations to the amount of at least 50 per cent of their capital upon their assets or commercial credit, but to secure the redemption of the notes of failed banks, there shall be raised by taxation a safety fund equal to 5 per cent upon the outstanding circulation of all the banks. But if the banks take out this circulation, then they are to be compelled to deposit with the Treasurer, United States legal tender and treasury notes, to the full amount of the difference between this form of circulation and the total amount of their capital stock; and upon this deposit they are also to have notes equal to the amount of the deposit, thus compelling the banks to take out circulation equal to the whole amount of their capital, or take out none. I do not wish to criticise Mr. Eckels's plan; but, in my judgment, an obvious and fatal objection to it is that it requires national banks to take out and keep in circulation two different kinds of notes, one based on the deposit of national money, and the other based upon the commercial credit of the bank.

Mr. JOHNSON, of Indiana. One great object of every one of these bills is to save the Government from the necessity of current redemption of its paper whereby the Treasury is constantly subject to a drain. Is it not a fact that under Mr. Eckels's system the saving would be much greater than under yours, for the reason that he requires the hypothecating, so to speak, of a larger amount of Government paper than your plan requires?

Secretary CARLISLE. It would; but I do not think that the national banks would take out circulation if they could avoid it.

Mr. JOHNSON, of Indiana. Why should a national law of banking and currency make any different conditions for the issuing of currency by State banks than by national banks?

Secretary CARLISLE. I do not see the necessity of a national law making any conditions at all about State banks, except as to taxation.

Mr. JOHNSON, of Indiana. You put that upon constitutional grounds?

Secretary CARLISLE. Upon that and upon grounds of policy as well. This bill does not require a State bank to comply with any conditions whatever. It leaves the State banks in the condition of complying with them, if they choose, or of paying the tax on their circulation if they do not comply with them. The tax is already on their notes, and my proposition simply is that if a State bank desires to exempt itself from the payment of a tax which the Supreme Court of the United States has held to be a constitutional tax, it shall do so by complying with certain conditions. In other words, I recognize in that statute of the United States which puts a tax upon the issue of State banks no validity at all except as a revenue measure. I personally question the right of the Congress of the United States to prohibit directly or indirectly the issue of notes of a State bank when it is authorized to issue them by the law of the State. Therefore, if Congress has any power at all in the premises it is a revenue power—a power to raise money by taxation, and Congress may modify the exercise of that power in any way it pleases.

Mr. JOHNSON, of Indiana. But do not the provisions of your bill make it absolutely impossible for a State bank to become a bank of issue unless it complies with certain conditions?

Secretary CARLISLE. Under the law now it is prohibited entirely unless it pays the tax.

Mr. JOHNSON, of Indiana. While technically you may say that the Government does not undertake to prevent the issue of currency by State banks, does it not, as a matter of fact, do so?

Secretary CARLISLE. It retains to a limited extent the same restriction which the law has already imposed on State banks, and it simply provides that these banks may exempt themselves from those restrictions or limitations (in the form of a tax) by complying with certain conditions. So in the taxation of beer or distilled spirits or tobacco, Congress may modify the law so as to provide that in case they are manufactured in a certain way they shall not be subject to the tax.

Mr. JOHNSON, of Indiana. Do you think that that is not a governmental restriction?

Secretary CARLISLE. It is simply a modification of the authority already exercised by the Government over State banks. The effect is that if the bank does not comply with the conditions the present law would be enforced against it.

Mr. COBB, of Alabama. And you are willing to retain that modified control of State banks simply because you can not get rid of the control altogether?

Secretary CARLISLE. As a mere question of right, I would be in favor of repealing the tax upon the notes of State banks. I do not assert that it would be good financial policy to do so under the present circumstances. It might not be. But logically my position would lead me to advocate the unconditional repeal of the tax upon State-bank circulation. It can not be done, in my opinion, and perhaps it might not be good financial policy to do it under existing circumstances; and therefore I have proposed simply that the act shall be so modified that the State banks can issue a sound and safe note, and exempt itself from taxation.

Mr. HALL. The questions asked you by my colleague from Pennsylvania (Mr. Brosius) were based upon the idea that there was a hazard as to this currency issued by the national banks. I ask you if the 5 per cent safety fund does not always protect the issue of all money by national banks under your plan?

Secretary CARLISLE. It will, as long as there is any solvent national bank in existence.

Mr. HALL. Therefore, unless there is a total failure of all the national banks in the United States, the national banks are safe?

Secretary CARLISLE. Yes; or substantially that. So many of them might fail that the surviving banks would not be able to redeem the outstanding circulation.

Mr. HALL. In section 10 of your proposed bill you speak of the liability of stockholders in State institutions. You mean by that what we in the West call double liability?

Secretary CARLISLE. Yes; it is a liability for the redemption of the notes to the full extent of the stock held.

Mr. HALL. In the first organization of the bank the stockholders may pay in the full amount of stock, and yet they will be liable for as much more of the capital stock as if they had never paid in any of it at all.

Secretary CARLISLE. Yes; and that is dedicated first to the redemption of the notes as well as all other assets of the bank.

Mr. HALL. I would like to hear you upon a question mentioned by Mr. White a moment ago. I understood him to state that the elasticity of the currency was secured under the Baltimore plan, but that under your plan there would be practically no elasticity at all. I should like to know what difference of elasticity exists between the two plans.

Secretary CARLISLE. There is no difference in the elasticity; that is to say, there is no difference between the amount of circulation to be taken under the Baltimore plan and the amount to be taken out under the plan now proposed. But there is a difference as to the conditions under which it could be taken out. Under the Baltimore plan a bank is authorized to take out on the security of a 5 per cent safety-fund, with the ultimate liability of the Government behind it, a circulation to the amount of 50 per cent of its capital. Then it will be authorized to take out an additional amount of circulation equal to 25 per cent of its capital stock paid up and unimpaired, making a total circulation of 75 per cent of its capital stock, just as is proposed in this plan. But in order to get that 25 per cent additional, or emergency circulation as the Baltimore plan denominates it, the bank is required to pay a heavy rate of taxation. The plan does not state what the rate is. So, I repeat, there is no difference between the amount of circulation that can be taken out under the two plans, but the conditions are different.

Under the Baltimore plan if a stringency occurs in the financial affairs of the country, and the banks desire to add 25 per cent to the 50 per cent circulation they already have, they must pay some heavy rate of taxation, which, of course, would raise the rate of interest not only on that 25 per cent of circulation, but on the whole volume of currency. Now, I suppose that it is good banking when a stringency occurs in the community to increase the rate of discount to a certain extent, because the effect of that is to prevent the people who are really not in distress from borrowing money, and leaves it to be borrowed by those who are really in distress, and who need it in their business. But I do not think it good policy to require a bank by law to charge a high rate of interest on its currency. I think that should be left to the bank itself. This provision in the Baltimore plan, as I understand it, is taken from or suggested by the provisions of law in regard to the Bank of the

Empire in Germany. I am not aware of the fact (although it may be so) that that bank has ever availed itself of that provision.

The CHAIRMAN. It has on several occasions.

Secretary CARLISLE. Perhaps it has. I have not read anything on the subject for a good while. Mr. White thought that the present difficulty arises more from the fact that there has been a deficiency in the revenue than from any other cause. I am not able to agree with Mr. White about that. It is true that we did not have this trouble when we had a surplus revenue, because we were then able to redeem the United States notes and the Treasury notes in gold without touching the reserve. But even if we had had a surplus revenue during the last two or three years, the withdrawal of gold for shipment has been much greater than it was before. During the year 1893 the net exports of gold were nearly $87,000,000, an amount never equaled before in the history of the country. That was caused, I think, not by the fact of an insufficiency of revenue, but by the distrust which prevailed in financial circles not only here but abroad. Of course the fact that our revenue was insufficient was one of the features which aggravated the situation.

Mr. HALL. It has been stated by Mr. White in regard to your bill (not in the spirit of criticism, but probably drawn out by some question) that the effect of it would be to release 165,000,000 of greenbacks now covered under a bushel by the reserve and throw that amount on to the country as a drain upon the gold reserve.

Secretary CARLISLE. I do not think so. The banks, if judiciously managed, as I believe and hope they will be, would still hold their reserves. I do not think any banker would say that it was safe for him to conduct his banking business without a reserve, and he will always want to hold it in the best money, so that he can put his hand upon something that is always safe—something that he can go and get the gold for, and will naturally, without compulsion, hold it in legal-tender notes, Treasury notes, and gold certificates. As to another suggestion, that under this plan the national banks and individuals can hoard United States legal-tender notes and Treasury notes, and thereby prevent the organization of any more national banks, I think that any gentleman who looks for a moment into the matter will see that is not a sound objection, because in order to do that the banks would have to lose the interest on all that money. There are now 498,000,000 of such money outstanding, and there is no danger that the banks would undertake to hoard and keep it out of circulation.

Mr. JOHNSON, of Ohio. No circulation can be issued under your plan except by a deposit of some part of the 498,000,000 of legal-tender notes.

Secretary CARLISLE. Yes.

Mr. JOHNSON, of Ohio. Taking 23,000,000 of that as being possibly destroyed would leave still 475,000,000 available. If the national banks and the State banks took out circulation to the limit of their present capital that would require 225,000,000 of these legal-tender notes. The national banks could convert their surplus into capital and take out an additional amount of circulation; that is practicable, is it not?

Secretary CARLISLE. Yes.

Mr. JOHNSON, of Ohio. But assuming that they do not, without that risk and without the purchase and cancellation of these greenbacks, there would be left 250,000,000 of greenbacks outstanding. The 250,000,000 can be held in the reserve of the banks now without cost to them, so that there would be no available greenbacks for new banks to get circulation on unless they paid a premium for the greenbacks.

Is it not possible, therefore, that if it is profitable to these banks they can either require a profit on the greenbacks in order to allow new banks to take out currency, or can refuse to let them have the greenbacks and thus corner the business of the national bank note issue.

Secretary CARLISLE. As I said before, all things are possible; and if banks can find a way to make these greenbacks profitable to themselves, they might do so; but what would be the effect on the Treasury Department? It would be relieved at once of the difficulty under which we are now laboring. There would be no greenbacks out, and of course there would be no gold taken out of the Treasury. Whenever that time comes I presume we will have a Congress which will take such action as is necessary for relief. We can only legislate for the present time and provide as far as we can foresee for the future.

Mr. JOHNSON, of Ohio. Would not that have this result: Three or four national banks with 280,000 stockholders interested to prevent the changing of the law by which they have cornered the basis of the circulating medium.

Secretary CARLISLE. Yes; but that is a very small proportion of the American people.

Mr. JOHNSON, of Ohio. But it is the most powerful organization you can imagine. Your estimate of the additional profit that a bank with a circulation of $75,000 would have over its profits under the present law averaged, I think, about $2,000.

Secretary CARLISLE. About $1,500.

Mr. JOHNSON, of Ohio. In five years it will average $2,000 a year. That makes $750,000,000 of circulation, at a profit to the banks of $15,000,000.

Secretary CARLISLE. To the whole 4,000 banks. I have not made the calculation, but I suppose it to be correct. I do not object to national banks making all the profit they can legally, nor do I object to State banks doing the same thing.

Mr. JOHNSON, of Ohio. Would you not object if by that they prevented other banks from taking out currency?

Secretary CARLISLE. I would not want to give them a monopoly.

Mr. JOHNSON, of Ohio. You would not do so if you would allow them to deposit gold in order to take out currency.

Mr. WALKER. I wish to bring out as clearly as possible the difficulties under which the Treasury is laboring in regard to maintaining the gold standard which the law requires you to do. It has been said that the present difficulty is because the revenues of the Government are too small. Is it not a fact that no gold is now being paid into the Treasury, and that the habit of paying the Government's dues in something other than gold has been increasing for a long period, and that we have got to that point that even if our revenues were now increased so as to have a surplus the chances are that we should still have to sell bonds to get gold?

Secretary CARLISLE. I do not see the immediate prospect of the Treasury Department being in a position which will enable it to avoid the issue of bonds. I am sorry to say it, but that is the actual condition, provided we are to continue the redemption of these notes in gold (not in silver) and maintain the parity of the two metals.

Mr. WALKER. Is it not a fact that on the construction of the law, both on the part of the Treasury Department and on the part of the public, shows a consensus of opinion that the Treasury must buy gold and that, however large the revenues may be, if any gold be wanted for shipment or for the redemption of greenbacks the Treasury is at the mercy of any syndicate of bankers, foreign or domestic?

Secretary CARLISLE. There is no doubt about that.

Mr. WALKER. And the only relief is either to extinguish the greenbacks or to have their redemption put upon some other basis. That is the condition of things exactly, is it not?

Secretary CARLISLE. It is, and I am very much inclined to think that it would afford but little relief to the Treasury if we were to require one-half or perhaps even the whole of our customs dues to be paid in gold.

Mr. WALKER. Would not that send gold to a premium at once?

Secretary CARLISLE. Before the resumption of specie payments, when there was outstanding no paper which the banks or individuals could present to the Treasury and demand gold, the payment of customs duties in gold could be very well maintained, because when the Government got the gold it could hold it. But, under the present system, if the law required the customs duties to be paid in gold, the importer might simply come to the subtreasury and get the gold for greenbacks, and the same gold would remain there, substantially, all the time in the subtreasury, being turned over day after day. Now, if we had a surplus revenue, we could save some gold out of it, but having no surplus revenue, I doubt very much whether the legal requirement that customs should be paid in gold would be of any benefit to the Treasury Department. If we got all our customs duties paid in gold there might be an accumulation, and we might save the surplus.

Mr. HENDERSON. As long as there was a hundred millions of gold reserve kept in tact in the Treasury was there any alarm about the redemption of our outstanding Treasury notes and other obligations?

Secretary CARLISLE. I think there was not any general alarm. There may have been some individual opinion that the time would come when there would be a drain upon that reserve.

Mr. HENDERSON. Was it not when we began to increase the volume of currency under the Sherman law that the alarm was felt throughout the country?

Secretary CARLISLE. I have caused to be made out at the Bureau of Statistics a graphic statement which will show the movement of gold into this country and out of this country, from which the operations of the silver laws will be shown very clearly. Gold ceased to come in; our imports of gold ran down immediately on the passage of the Sherman law and continued to go down.

Mr. HENDERSON. We increased the volume of currency by the Sherman law to the amount of $140,000,000.

Secretary CARLISLE. To the amount of $156,000,000.

Mr. HENDERSON. And during the same time that amount of gold was shipped out of the country.

Secretary CARKISLE. A great deal more than that, I think. I would say roughly that the aggregate net exports of gold were more than that.

Mr. HENDERSON. Was it your opinion that the Sherman law was really the cause of the exportation of gold?

Secretary CARLISLE. I think it was one of the most potent causes. It was the threat pending over the financial world that we would get upon a silver basis by reason of our constant accumulations of silver.

Mr. HENDERSON. If we had increased the gold reserve over a hundred millions of dollars, instead of allowing it to be reduced, do you think that there would have been any trouble under the Sherman law?

Secretary CARLISLE. I think not. I think that these troubles are largely (if I may use the expression) sentimental, largely the result of scares.

Mr. HENDERSON. Naturally the people would have been alarmed by the large purchases of silver.

Secretary CARLISLE. They would not have been alarmed if they had seen the gold increasing instead of diminishing.

Mr. WARNER. Attention has been called to the question of the relative security of State-bank and national-bank currency as proposed by your bill. There is nothing in that bill, is there, which would prevent a State from imposing such additional safeguards on State banks as it might deem necessary to give the currency of State banks greater security.

Secretary CARLISLE. Nothing whatever.

Mr. WARNER. And there is every presumption that the States would do everything that was proper in that direction.

Secretary CARLISLE. I take it for granted that a State is competent to manage its own affairs.

Mr. WARNER. In your estimate as to the comparative profit of banks on their circulation under the present plan and under the plan proposed by yourself have you made any calculation as to whether under the present circumstances, in view of the low rates of discount, there would be any profit on bank circulation under either plan?

Secretary CARLISLE. I have not made any such calculation as that, and I do not know. I would have to assume some rate of interest, and it has been assumed at 6 per cent.

Mr. WARNER. In relation to the receipts of gold in the Treasury, is it not true that any development of business by which the demand for currency became greater would tend to increase the amount of gold paid into the Treasury?

Secretary CARLISLE. I think so.

Mr. WARNER. Is it not true that in 1893, for example, one of the results of the stringency then was to increase the amount of gold paid into the Treasury?

Secretary CARLISLE. Yes; it came in quite rapidly, so that we were able to build up the reserve. Then it was withdrawn for exportation, and we had to build it up again. The Treasury Department accumulated, I suppose, during that summer and fall a gross amount of $30,000,000 of gold, but it went out again.

Mr. WARNER. Is it not prossible that, under any currency system so elastic as to keep down the outstanding circulation to the amount required by the business of the country, the proportion of gold received in the Treasury would be much greater than it has been for the last few years?

Secretary CARLISLE. I think so.

Mr. WARNER. So that it might result, from proper elasticity alone, that Treasury receipts would be in gold to a much greater extent than of late?

Secretary CARLISLE. It might.

Thereupon, at 1.06 o'clock p. m., the committee took a recess until 2 o'clock p. m.

AFTER RECESS.

Hon. James H. Eckels, Comptroller of the Currency, appeared before the committee.

Mr. HALL. Before Mr. Eckels begins his remarks, I want to suggest, Mr. Chairman, that the members of the committee just allow Mr. Eckels to go ahead in his own way and make his own argument from beginning to end. Let us make notes as he goes along, and then at the close of his remarks we can ask him questions. I say this, because I know it embarrasses a man oftentimes, and sometimes disconcerts him, to be asking him questions at a time when he is making a logical and connected statement.

The CHAIRMAN. That suggestion will be adopted as the sense of the committee, if there be no objection.

Mr. Eckels, the Comptroller of the Currency, in pursuance of an invitation extended to him by the committee, is now present, and will address the committee.

The chair will suggest, as he has communicated to Congress already his annual report which refers in some portions of it to the currency, that he make any additional or further explanation of the plan which he has suggested to the committee that he may deem desirable or necessary.

STATEMENT OF HON. JAMES H. ECKELS, COMPTROLLER OF THE CURRENCY.

Mr. ECKELS. Mr. Chairman and gentlemen of the committee, I am not familiar with the methods in vogue in hearings before a Congressional committee, and therefore if I should state something that should be omitted, or if I should omit something that should be stated, I shall be very glad of any suggestions on the part of any member. After making the statement which occurs to me may be made I shall be very glad to answer any questions that the members of the committee may desire to put to me.

In submitting my report to Congress, in accordance with the provisions of the statute defining the duties of the Comptroller of the Currency, several things entered into consideration, leading me to make the suggestions which appear in detail in my report. I felt that the importance of the subject was so great that nothing ought to be undertaken in the way of national legislation unless the resultant effect should be more beneficial to the general public than is the present system.

The benefit which a bank confers upon a community arises from the fact that it represents, if I may use the term, the organization of capital. By that I do not mean the combination of capital as that term is understood, but it represents organized capital. A bank in every community gathers into it the idle money of such community and directs it into channels where it can be of benefit in the development of such enterprises as the community is interested in; and to that extent it is of sufficient importance to warrant a very careful consideration of everything in the way of legislation which trenches upon it.

After a bank is established the public is led to deposit in it the amount of money which they have no use for in the daily transactions of business, and therefore every dollar going into the bank becomes a means of supporting, instead of a single transaction, as would be the case where money is passed from hand to hand in each transaction, a great number of transactions.

The extent of the banking interest in this country—and I speak now simply in this instance of the national banks—is represented in capital alone to the extent of quite $680,000,000. The assets which the national banks hold are something over $3,400,000,000. The number of depositors in national banks alone approaches 2,000,000 people, and when you come to add to that the number of depositors in State and savings banks you find that there are almost 8,000,000 depositors, or one person in about every seven or eight of our total population.

Mr. JOHNSON, of Ohio. That may possibly represent the same man several times.

Mr. ECKELS. That may be, but the duplication is simply a small percentage.

This number of people, this amount of capital, and the amount of deposits represented have led me to think that anything undertaking a radical change from what is now in existence should be surrounded with such safeguards that it would, immediately upon going into operation, command the complete confidence of the people. Banks are largely built upon confidence, and that is especially so of a bank which issues notes. Confidence is something that can not be constructed as you construct a house. You can not construct credit. You can not build credit as you build a house, or as you construct any mechanical device. It is the result of growth. Just as a tree grows so credit grows, and you have to do, in dealings with banks, that which will make them immediately receive to themselves the confidence of the people, and make the instruments which they issue as instruments of credit entitled to the confidence of the people.

The national banking system is a system which might very aptly be said to be a national habit with the people, because the great majority of the people who are now in active business are people who know little or nothing of any other system of note issue; and even upon the side of deposits the general public, I think, has had thoroughly ingrained into it during the last thirty years the predominance of the national bank to such an extent that it may very justly be said that the dealing with them is an integral part of the business habits of the people.

Therefore, when it is undertaken to change something which has been so long in operation, and which is so intimate in all its relations with every business interest, and which affects them so largely and reaches so many people, it can not be done by any decided or rapid method.

Mr. WALKER. Any new method.

Mr. ECKELS. Any new method. Therefore, when I took up the national-bank act to make suggestions to Congress at this time it seemed to me nothing ought to be touched in it which could not be materially improved upon. I thought also that nothing ought to be touched which was not absolutely essential to the attainment of such reformations in the currency as would be promotive of the business interests of the people, and to that extent be a benefit to the Treasury Department of the Government.

The present system of banking in this country differs from that of any other country, except the countries of the English-speaking peoples. This is an important consideration which must be taken into account by this committee and by Congress in dealing with this question. In this country the note-issuing function of our banks is at present but the incident to banking. The deposit account is the principal. The Bank of France makes the note-issuing function everything. The French people keep their money in their individual possession, and use large amounts of it in their daily transactions, and do not trust the banks. So also the Germans and other Continental people. Therefore you must draw a distinction when you come to invent a system of issuing notes and come to consider the banking interests between this country and France. The same thing can be said of Germany. The same thing can be said of the banks in Russia. The only similarity between the banking interests of other countries and this is that which exists between the banking interests of England, Scotland, Ireland, Canada, and this country. Therefore when you undertake to devise for the United States a new system of issuing currency, you can not do it without taking into full account the fact that the use of the deposit feature is the principal thing, and anything which shall injuriously affect the deposit side of banking must be injurious to the whole system.

It is proposed, in the plan which is suggested in my report, to disturb as little as possible the present order of things. I think I state in that report that if you simply desire to devise a means of making a bank note absolutely and unquestionably secure, then the present system is as good as could possibly be devised, so long as the Government maintains its full faith and credit with its debtors through the payment of the bonds which it issues. If, however, you attempt to devise a system which would make the note holder just as safe, and at the same time meet the complaint which is constantly made of the present system, of requiring a deposit of bonds whose value in the markets fluctuates, while keeping always the same percentage of issue against such bond deposits, you must have some other system which will secure the note upon the one hand and on the other hand have such elasticity in the issuing power that it shall always be responsive to the varying wants of business.

You must, in order to make any bank note a proper currency and one which will command the complete confidence of the people, convertibility upon demand—not ultimate convertibility, but such convertibility that whenever a note holder wants the money for which he holds the promise of the bank to pay at that very instant the bank shall pay him the money which his note calls for. Therefore, of course, the convertibility of the note is a first consideration.

After this consideration comes the proper regulation of the issuance of the notes, and if a system can be devised whereby the convertibility of the note is made absolutely certain, in coin upon demand, and at the same time you can give to the bank the power, in times when a great amount of money is needed, to meet the then needs of business, you will secure a system which, to the extent that it gives such elasticity, will be a great improvement upon the present.

The plan suggested in my report requires of the bank to deposit with the Treasurer of the United States, so long as the bank shall be in existence, 50 per cent of its capital stock in legal tenders in exchange for which deposit, dollar for dollar, it shall receive bank notes which shall be untaxed, and be used as a part of the legal-tender reserve of the bank against deposits. To this extent, at least to the extent of 50 per cent, so long as the Government stands back of the legal tenders, 50 per cent of the notes are absolutely secure.

For doing this I would give the banks the privilege of issuing to the extent of the other 50 per cent of their capital notes against their assets, secured by a proper safety fund to be raised by a proper tax.

The question will undoubtedly occur to many people: Why should the banks be required to deposit this 50 per cent of legal tender—whether because it is necessary to make absolutely certain the redemption of the notes, or for some other purpose? Frankly, I do not believe that it is necessary for the security of the notes. I believe that with a proper safety fund, raised by a proper rate of taxation, the notes issued would be perfectly safe.

But the Treasury of the United States is confronted with a condition which grows out of the fact that under the exigencies of the war the law-making powers authorized the issuance of a currency which, in and of itself, never could have maintained itself if the Government had not endowed it with legal-tender qualities; and coupled with that was the provision that it should be exchangeable in amounts of $50 and multiples of $50 for a United States bond drawing a certain rate of interest. That promise to pay money, not money itself, was only agreed to, according to the debates in Congress at that time, because of the necessities of war; and according to the decision of Judge Strong in the legal-tender case, was held to be properly a legal tender only because of the exigencies of war. Afterwards these issues were no longer made exchangeable for bonds, and thus recognized distinctively as a debt of the Government to the people who held those promises to pay.

This change was for the reason, as Secretary Chase stated, that the bond which thereafter had to be issued could not be floated to such advantage as otherwise because of this exchangeable feature of the legal-tender act. But thereafter Congress still felt, and the idea was still entertained, that this issue of the Government was not money, but was simply the promise to pay money, for which, as had been stated in the debates prior to its issue, the Government, with all the property of the citizens, stood back of; and so, under Secretary McCulloch, it was permitted to be retired at the rate of $4,000,000 per month. Thereafter, as you all know, the retiring of them was done away with, and the amount fixed as to the extent to which the legal tenders should be an outstanding obligation. For the purpose of maintaining the credit of the Government these legal-tender issues, sanctioned by the courts, were always to be redeemed in coin, as was provided—no; it was not provided, but the practice of the Government was to maintain its credit, and so it proceeded to redeem them in coin, and the construction was that they were redeemable in gold.

For some time this condition of affairs did not work particularly to anyone's disadvantage, although I think the general consensus of those who have looked into the matter of the issue of promises to pay, not convertible on demand, but only ultimately convertible, is that it made the war a great deal more expensive than it otherwise would have been. These promises to pay, however, did not materially affect the Government, especially under the resumption act, until the Government found itself without surplus revenue. Therefore, not having a surplus revenue, it was unable, in order to maintain the credit of the Government, to currently redeem these notes except by borrowing money through the issue of bonds, which of late it has been compelled to do.

It is evident that the trouble with the Treasury upon that side is the source, to the greatest degree, of the disturbed business conditions of this country, and is the greatest source of danger to the maintenance of public credit, both at home and abroad. The imperfections of the banking system, which go simply to elasticity in the matter of the issue of the notes of banks, are but an inconvenience and a bar to domestic trade, simply compelling banks to resort to other credit devices instead of promises to pay in the form of bank notes.

The difficulty arising through the redemption currently and reissue of the evidences of indebtedness on the part of the General Government is that which depletes continually the gold reserve, and so long as they are reissued, so long as they are a source by which the gold can be taken out of the Treasury, and so long as a single one of them is out, just so long will it be impossible to keep there your gold reserve above $100,000,000 or $50,000,000. So long as people can get these greenbacks, then the issuance of bonds and the supplying of new gold is like pouring water into a hole—into an abyss which is fathomless.

The result of such state of affairs is that the confidence of not only our own people, in the ability of the General Government to maintain the parity of the two metals and keep faith with the public in the redemption of its indebtedness, is continually shaken, but confidence of other countries, who are dealing with us, in our ability to so do, is also shaken. You can not get away from the idea that in monetary affairs you can not legislate for the American people alone, unless by that same legislation you decree that the people of this country shall trade with no one except people who live within the domain of the Government of the United States. So long as the people of the United States in their business relations are brought so intimately close with people of other countries, just so long must the monetary laws of this country be regardful of other conditions than our own.

You can not have here a currency system, or rather a Government currency system, which disregards the fact that other countries dealing with us only use the metal, for international exchange, which, by the whole commercial world, is regarded as the one necessary metal for exchanges. Therefore, saying nothing about the maintenance of the value of our currency issues at home, you must maintain the public credit abroad so long as these business relations exist; and so long as so many American securities are held abroad as are at the present you must maintain the redemption of Government notes in gold coin.

Undoubtedly the manly thing to do, and the thing that ought long since to have been done, would be the redemption and the canceling of these notes in accordance with what was designed at the time of the enactment of the legal-tender act, followed by the authority given to Secretary McCulloch, but which was afterward repealed.

But the conditions which now exist are simply such that, without a surplus revenue or without the issuing of a bond funding the greenbacks and Sherman notes, you can do nothing unless some plan which is equitable and puts no hardship upon anyone can be devised.

Personally I am very frank to say that I do not think the Government ought to unload its proper duties upon its citizens. I do not think the Government has any more right to do a thing that is not exactly proper in itself than an individual has. But at the same time we have to take conditions as they are, and the conditions which exist now are such that there seems to be no probability and no possibility of having those notes immediately canceled by means of a surplus revenue; and I do not think that bond issues are very popular.

But it is proposed now to give the banks what, I think, is a valuable franchise, the right to issue notes against assets as against a deposit of bonds. For that franchise it seems to me that the banks ought to be willing to make a fair return.

I do not think the Government ought to be in the banking business. No government has ever successfully issued notes, made them legal tender, and escaped trouble from them. It is safe to say that the cause which produced one effect a hundred years ago in the same line of finance will produce the same effect now, and it does not make any difference whether it is the English or French Government, or the Government of the United States that undertakes it. To the extent of getting those notes out of the channel of current redemption, and to that extent relieving the Secretary of the Treasury, and thereby the business interests of the country, because they are affected by the continual disturbance in the Treasury Department, growing out of the effort to maintain the current redemption of these notes, for that purpose, and on the ground that it is giving the banks a franchise, which I think may prove to be a profitable one, I think the banks ought to be compelled, for the right given them of issuing a percentage of notes of their capital stock against their assets, to deposit with the Treasurer of the United States legal-tender notes and thus get them out of the way of current redemption. These notes, as I said before, would be returned dollar for dollar in bank notes.

Mr. WALKER. Treasury notes?

Mr. ECKELS. These Treasury notes would be received and returned dollar for dollar in bank notes. They would not be subject to any taxation, giving the bank the benefit of that. They would be permissible to be held to an equitable extent as a part of their legal reserve, if legal reserves are maintained.

And upon that point it is probably proper to say that at present, under the clause in the national-bank act which compels banks to keep a legal reserve against deposits, $165,000,000 of legal tenders are locked up in that way and gotten out of the way of current redemption.

The CHAIRMAN. Will you be kind enough to state that again?

Mr. ECKELS. I say it is proper to say at that point that under the present system requiring the banks to keep a legal reserve against their deposits, of 15 per cent in places that are not reserve cities and 25 per cent in cities that are reserve cities, $165,000,000 of legal tenders are locked up in the banks, and thus to that extent are removed from the channel of current redemption.

Mr. WALKER. To-day, you mean?

Mr. ECKELS. Yes; I refer to the figures obtained at the time of the last call, October 2.

The only change which this makes in existing laws is this: That under existing laws every bank, before it is permitted to do business as a national bank, is compelled to deposit so long as it exists one-fourth of the amount of its capital stock in United States bonds. It can take out, if it pleases, circulation on that one-fourth, or it can simply leave the bonds. But it must make the deposit whether or not it takes out any circulation. There are seven or eight banks which have deposited bonds but have never taken out circulation, because there was not enough profit in it to warrant the trouble.

Under this plan I suggest I would compel them to deposit $50 as security, giving them dollar for dollar for it, and $50 in addition against their assets, thus giving $100 against a deposit of $50 in legal tenders instead of, as under the present system, compelling them to deposit for that circulation 4 per cent bonds, $114 as security and receiving $90 in exchange.

The profits to the banks, of course, would be nothing upon the legal tenders which they exchange. A bank would have to look for its profits in the notes which, having deposited the legal tender, it was permitted to issue against its assets.

It is said that probably the banks could not keep out any more than the 50 per cent which they must keep in circulation for the legal-tender deposits, but I think an inquiry into the facts will show that this is not so. The deposit of legal tenders and the exchange dollar for dollar, it will be seen, does not in any wise lessen the volume of the circulating medium of the country, because for every dollar of greenbacks deposited is given out instead a dollar through the bank. So that, so far as that is concerned, the volume of the currency would remain the same.

Under the present capital stock of the banks they would deposit about $340,000,000 of legal tenders withthe Treasurer.

A MEMBER. What is the exact amount?

Mr. ECKELS. It is a half of $668,000,000. There are altogether $498,000,000 of legal-tender notes and notes issued under the law of 1890. If no other bank went into the system, if no bank increased its capital, if no bank capitalized its surplus, which could readily be done, and as soon as it might be taken out, or as soon as it could be put into operation with due regard to safety, there would be taken away about $334,000,000 of legal tenders which are now used for the purpose of getting gold out of the Treasury. That alone would not, as I said, either increase or expand the present volume of our currency.

Mr. HALL. Would it interrupt you, Mr. Eckels, for me to ask you a question about that $165,000,000?

Mr. ECKELS. No, sir.

Mr. JOHNSON, of Indiana. I think we had better adhere to our original plan.

The CHAIRMAN. Members of the committee are not supposed to interrupt Mr. Eckels.

Mr. HALL. I would say to the committee that Mr. Eckels and I were talking about this question during lunch.

A MEMBER. I object.

The CHAIRMAN. The gentleman from Missouri can put his question at Mr. Eckels's convenience.

Mr. ECKELS. As I said before, to that extent it would neither be a contraction nor expansion of the volume of the circulating medium, but simply a substitution of one thing for another.

Now, in addition to compelling the banks to deposit that amount of legal tender for the privilege of the issue against the balance of the 50 per cent of their capital stock against assets, I would say that they should provide a redemption fund to that extent in gold coin, making the banks themselves responsible for the redemption of their notes in gold coin, and ultimately the Government would have to redeem in gold coin either the legal tenders which were deposited or the notes of the banks to the percentage of the legal tenders. But currently I would compel the bank to redeem that percentage of its notes in gold coin, and the only responsibility which the Government should assume, so far as that percentage of notes is concerned, is the ultimate redemption of the legal tenders deposited or the percentage of notes issued against them when the bank went out of existence, either through voluntary or involuntary liquidation. My idea being that these notes should be kept with the Treasury, just as the 25 per cent of bonds is kept there, whether or not notes are issued against them permanently, because when the bank goes out of existence it is provided that the Government shall redeem and cancel the legal tenders which it had on deposit.

These are the burdens which are put on the banks. Unless there is a sufficient profit in circulation banks will not take out circulation. There is no sentiment in the thing at all. It is simply a matter of business, and banking people, like everybody else in business, are in it because of the profit there is, and if there is no profit in circulation under the present system, or very little, they will not continue in the note issuing business, which is such a trivial thing as compared with the deposit business of banks, but will go out of the national banking system, and to that extent will reduce the already present volume of national-bank issues.

The question as to whether or not the banks would continue to issue notes would turn entirely upon the question of profit, and that would depend entirely upon the number of their promises to pay in the shape of bank notes which they could keep in circulation. The complaint on the one hand is now that there is no profit in circulation because they are compelled to deposit $114 and only get $90 in return, thus locking up so much of their capital which they could more advantageously use in the immediate communities in which they are doing business. On the other hand, the complaint is that the profit on circulation is so slight under the present system that it is not worth while for banks to issue it because of the difficulty of getting their notes into circulation on account of the great volume of United States issues which circulate and crowd out the national-bank issues. They are, however, able to keep in circulation at present $207,000,000. I think in 1890 circulation was down to $120,000,000, but the banks found more use for notes, and possibly more profit, and so they have taken out more.

It is safe to say that if you did not change the volume of currency at all, but left it just as it is, the banks could keep out this $340,000,000 exchanged for their legal tenders, as that would simply fill up the vacuum by taking the issues away from the Government, and, in addition, could keep out as much national-bank circulation as they have at present, which would amount to $207,000,000. To the extent, therefore, that the $207,000,000 is issued against assets, they would make a considerable profit, and if they should, as they undoubtedly would, at seasons of the year when there was more demand for money, take out the balance of the issues due upon the 50 per cent of capital as against their assets, to that extent would their profits be enhanced. Just as you would have an actuary of a life insurance company figure out profits upon investing in the stock of a life insurance company, after taking the losses which are incident to the business, so you can take and figure out, from what you know of the present circulation and the present ability of the banks to use note issues as against bank deposits, what the profit would be if they were allowed to issue against a deposit of legal tender and against their assets.

Mr. WALKER. Plus what they issue themselves.

Mr. ECKELS. On what they issue themselves is where the whole profit would be. If they can make a profit by issuing $90 against an investment of $114, on $207,000,000 of currency it is safe to say that they can make a large profit on deposits of $50 and note issues of $100. I think that is simply a matter of figuring.

As to the question of elasticity: Of course there is no elasticity in the 50 per cent which is issued against legal tenders, because that is simply a fixed sum. But the elasticity in the issue would be within the percentage of notes to the extent of 50 per cent, the range of 50 per cent issued against the assets. I believe that within that range could be found the elasticity which the wants of business require. I believe that the question of elasticity is one which is governed by two things. It is governed by the needs of business, on the one hand, and it is governed, on the other hand, by the fact that the notes issued are made convertible into coin, not ultimately, but immediately; and that if you have out a large volume of currency, bank note or any other currency, that is redeemable, not theoretically, but redeemable in fact in coin, every dollar which is not needed for business will immediately return for redemption; that, in other words, you can not keep out and in circulation a redeemable dollar to the extent that that dollar is not needed; that the needs of business control; and that every dollar which is redeemable in coin upon demand and that is not needed for the daily transactions of business will, from the law of business itself, go right back to the issuing bank and be redeemed, and not be issued again until it is again needed. So that the question of elasticity depends upon these two things, or, in fact, upon the one thing.

Mr. WALKER. And to the interest of the bank?

Mr. ECKELS. And the interest of the bank; yes. It would not keep the money out, of course. unless there were a profit in it. So I think within the range of the 50 per cent of notes issued against the assets convertible upon demand would be such elasticity as is needed.

Mr. JOHNSON, of Ohio. Where would they be redeemable?

Mr. ECKELS. They would be redeemable, if you follow the present law, either at the banks themselves, or in Washington; or, if you change the present law, at the banks themselves or at such point of redemption as should either be named by the bank, with the approval of the Comptroller of the Currency, or, as might be provided by the Government, at such point as should be named by the bank. I think prior to the present system it was provided that the banks might name redemption agencies, with the approval of the Comptroller of the Currency. It would be just as under the old Suffolk system in Massachusetts, the notes of banks issued in New England which were convertible into coin and were not needed for business immediately went back for redemption, and there was never kept out a single dollar more than was needed by the people in their business.

I do not believe you can force into existence a single dollar more than is needed, if it is good money. The whole thing turns upon the goodness of the dollar so far as the redemption feature is concerned.

Therefore, I think the system which I have suggested would relieve the Treasury, to the extent which I have named, of the current redemption of the $340,000,000 of greenbacks. On the other hand, I think in the range of percentage which I have named would be found elasticity and profit to the bank.

Now, the other thing which must be considered in connection with issues against assets is whether or not the notes issued against the assets would be perfectly good. I think upon the question of note issues, whether State or National, the Government, ought to have something to say as to what banks should issue notes, and under what circumstances.

There are a great many things which Governments can not do them selves, but there are a great many things which Governments have an inherent right to regulate, just as municipal governments regulate the right as to where gunpowder shall be kept—as has been said by some authority, just as municipal governments regulate certain internal arrangements; just as the State government to-day regulates how savings banks shall be kept, how depositors or the other people interested in banks shall be protected; just as the Government of the United States regulates or undertakes to regulate the commerce between the States under the interstate-commerce act.

There is power which inheres in Government, but which it is not best for it to exercise. I think that, especially in the issuance of bank notes, the thing ought not to be done by Governments, because Governments have never yet been able to properly control the issues which come directly from them, through the fact that, in order to make their money circulate at all, they must attach to it a legal-tender quality and compel a man to take a thing which otherwise he would not. Somebody has very aptly said that the giving of a legal-tender quality to Government issues was all right so long as people believed in the divine right of kings, and believed that in a king's touch there was divine healing, but not now when we do not entertain such beliefs. So, on the same principle, Governments, because of the power in them, or which they assume to themselves, give these bank notes legal-tender quality, and therefore they circulate because of that fact.

Mr. JOHNSON, of Ohio. Would you receive these notes for public dues?

Mr. JOHNSON, of Indiana. I object to any interruption. I think the gentleman from Ohio had better let Mr. Eckels proceed.

Mr. ECKELS. I will come to that later, Mr. Johnson.

So that I think the Government ought to regulate these issues for the reasons which I have named.

The other question to be considered, I started to say, was whether or not these notes would be paid—the notes which are issued against assets. Of course, the only thing you can judge by in arriving at any conclusion as to a matter of that kind is something of a speculation. But very frequently you can take a certain set of facts and put them together and arrive at a correct conclusion on the theory that when a thing has been done or produced by certain causes, it is safe to say that the same causes will produce the same effect.

It is safe to say that the losses which have occurred under the national-bank system would not have occurred, nor would there have been any danger of loss if a single dollar of bonds had not been deposited, for the loss has not occurred because of the management of the banks and the supervision and care which have been exercised over them. It has not been because of a deposit of bonds.

Mr. WALKER. The failure has not occurred?

Mr. ECKELS. Yes; the failure has not occurred.

I venture the assertion that with the same set of men, following the same kind of banking, and under the same uniformity of the system and the same supervision as required by the public, by statements every so often, to make reports or statements every so often, prohibited from lending upon any asset which was not a quick asset, such as real estate, but carrying on a purely commercial business as the banks do, the same thing would have resulted if there had not been a single dollar of security deposited here. It has not been the security unused which produced these results, but it was because of the methods employed in banking, and because the men in control of the banking institutions of the country operating under the system, conducted them in such a manner that, instead of being a great source of loss, they have been a source of profit to them and a source of benefit to the people. Because, whoever may be the people who are engaged in banking, the fact is that since the present banking system the business of this country has been so facilitated that it is impossible to see how it could have been done otherwise than through the banks. The invention of instruments of credit, the transacting of business involving immense sums of money, has all been accomplished by banks.

Now, the elasticity of the Bank of England issues has been found upon every great occasion to be inadequate to meet the wants of the business interests of Great Britain at times of great financial disturbances. The Peele Act undertook to see how many dollars, not what percentage, but how many dollars, should be issued of what are known as uncovered notes, or notes which are not, dollar for dollar in gold, deposited in the basement of the Bank of England. It fixed the amount in 1844 under then existing conditions. In 1847 the defect of the attempts to fix any absolute volume of issue was found to be patent, and the result was that three years after the enactment of the

Peele Act, when it was supposed that the question of the issuance and control of circulation had been settled perfectly, the proper authorities had to give to those in charge of that branch of the banking of England the right to issue above the amount of uncovered notes fixed by the Peele Act; and by the notes thus issued, coupled with the further fact that the directors of the Bank of England at that time were induced to loan those who had proper security at a raised rate of interest, the panic was averted.

The same thing occurred in 1857, and the same method had to be resorted to on account of the lack of elasticity because of the fixing of the amount of uncovered notes which could be issued by a hard and fast line determined by the law; and the same thing in 1866.

Now, the elasticity of this system is to be found in the fact that, not, as was the case in the Peele Act, which controlled the Bank of England and by which the exact number of dollars of uncovered notes was fixed, but because the amount of notes which will be issued under it will depend entirely upon the banks themselves and upon the number of banks which come into the system. So, it is safe to say, that there will always be within the percentage of 50 per cent a sufficient range in elasticity.

The notes which have been issued by the Bank of England, under the permission given to issue over its uncovered notes—the increase over the uncovered notes has always been just as good as any other notes. Of course they are issued against securities, but it has been found that the best security which any bank can be possessed of, and the security which is the most rapidly convertible, is the good commercial business paper of a bank. If anybody doubts that, he has simply to look into the history of the last financial distress in this country, a year ago, when it was found that a bond was about the hardest thing there was to convert. But the quick commercial paper was found to be most readily convertible.

Therefore you would have here, for the issue of what you might term your uncovered notes, the rapidly convertible assets of a bank.

The Scotch notes have never failed of redemption. There never has been a discredited note issued by a bank in Scotland, and that is due, not to any other fact than that the people have confidence in the Scotch banker, and to the further fact that the Scotch banker has built up his credit and established confidence among the people by the fact that his notes are redeemable in coin upon demand. A Scotch note has never been discredited, has never been depreciated, and the note holder has never lost a dollar, except possibly in one or two instances, and I am not positive about those, nor have the stockholders ever been called upon to contribute anything to make good the losses on notes. I think when the failure of the Bank of Glasgow occurred, a number of years ago, other banks, for the sake of the credit of all the banks, came forward and took up the notes of that bank.

Mr. JOHNSON, of Indiana. There was an unlimited liability of the stockholders, however.

Mr. ECKELS. Yes; of course there was unlimited liability of the stockholders. There was that difference, of course.

The Canadian notes are issued simply against the assets of the bank, coupled with which is a safety redemption fund. The redemption fund is simply for the notes of failed banks. The amount of it is 5 per cent of the outstanding circulation. There never has been a Canadian bank note discredited, and never has one failed of redemption. In my report I have undertaken to figure out what percentage would be necessary.

Of course it is a matter of calculation, and I may have stated it too large or too small. What is necessary is to establish the principle. If the principle is correct, then the details are easily worked out.

You should have a banking system which will not place so much of a hardship upon the issue of the banks as to make them prefer the deposit side alone to the deposit and note issue combined. You should have a system which will get the Treasury out of its present difficulties until it can do what it ought to do, redeem and put away these notes. You should have a system which makes every note of a bank convertible on demand, such a system as assures note holders of failed banks that the notes which they hold shall be redeemed immediately, upon presentation, out of a fund to be held by the Government as agent only.

In this whole matter of redemptions I think the Government simply, if it has anything to do with it—and that is a question which is open for discussion, as to whether it ought to have anything to do with it or not—but if it has anything to do with it, ought only to stand in the position of agent, with supervisory control to see that the banks do redeem; and not leave it entirely to the banks themselves to ascertain, after a note has been discredited, whether the redemption is going on or not. But, if the Government has anything to do with the redemption of these notes issued against the assets of the bank, or, for that matter, anything to do with the redemption of notes issued against legal tenders, it ought to be simply in the relation of agent. I do not think the Government ought to lend its credit to banks except to the extent of taking such precautionary measures as will give the people to understand that somebody is looking after these promises to pay. I think it is generally understood that promises to pay do not take care of themselves without some sort of supervisory care of them.

Therefore, with the bank note made elastic and made perfectly safe, the Government relieved of its present embarrassments until it reaches the proper point where it can do as everybody else does—when he gets in debt, pay its creditors—I think the general good of the people would be promoted.

Upon the question of redemption the only thing that ought to be taken into consideration is as to whether or not the Government ought to have anything to do with it or not, or whether or not there should be a change of this system which is so embedded in the minds of the people, of having every dollar of notes issued secured by a deposit; whether or not you can get the people to immediately take the promises of the bank to pay without a deposit of security, unless the Government retains some sort of supervision over the redemption of them, not being responsible for the redemption, but exercising supervision to see that when a bank gets near, in its redemption fund, to a line, or gets below the line of the amount necessary for the current redemption, somebody connected with the Government notifies the banks of that fact.

You can calculate that in any change of system which does away with deposited security the people are going to be a little timid. It will take a long time to educate them up to it. They have got to learn some things, and they have got to unlearn some things. Whether or not you can accomplish so much, or whether it would be wise to undertake to accomplish so much at a single lesson, is a question for you to determine.

If you have a bad system you must cure the worst defect to start with. The other things are to be taken up in order. They may not be material. You must keep that in view. When you come to the matter of reserve against deposits, it, as the Secretary of the Treasury says, is a matter of discussion as to whether or not it would be wise to abolish it. I think everybody will recognize the truth of what he says, that it is a great embarrassment at times to the business interests that the banks can not loan money when down to the minimum percentage of reserve. I think that percentage is put at what might be termed, and what has been termed by writers upon these questions, the apprehension point, that point where people become a little uncertain as to whether or not a bank is solvent enough to redeem its demand obligations.

There is much that can be said upon the question as to whether or not there ought to be a fixed limit. I think criticism has been passed frequently upon the Bank of England that at times of great emergencies it has attempted, while there was no fixed law on the subject, to have a hard and fast line, and would not loan as much as it ought. Of course fixed reserves, as in 1893, sometimes work a hardship. But you can not entirely make your calculations from what occurred in 1893. I think the man who investigates all the phenomena of that year will see that it comes within the line, as has been stated by some prominent financial writer, I think Ricardo, that at times when everybody demands coin from a bank, when all the depositors demand coin, no banking system and no system of reserves can meet it. The sort of feeling which overtakes people when every man rushes to a bank and says: "I want my deposit; I want my checks cashed; I want my money," will break down any system.

It is impossible at such times to have enough money on hand to meet that demand, because the percentage of business done in this country is over 90 per cent of credit, and the balance is only done on a cash basis. Therefore the cash in all the banks, if every depositor wanted his money, would not be sufficient to meet the demand. Last year presented one of those conditions when there was a state of fear among the people that no banking system could have stood up under it; but the banks which had the largest reserves stood up the longest, and even they could not have stood up if they had not devised means to do it. You can always rely upon the business instincts of business men to devise means to meet just such emergencies. So I say you can not entirely judge from what occurred during that year as to this question of fixed reserves.

But this is to be remembered, taken in connection with what I have said about the deposit feature of banking in this country being the great feature, that you can not afford to scare the depositor upon the one side by making his deposit subject to a first lien for the notes issued by the bank and on the other taking away a reserve kept for the depositor's special benefit. On the other hand, it is worth while to take into consideration whether you will abolish a hard and fast line which at times does work possibly a hardship to the general business interests, although last year I do not think all the commercial failures occurred by not being able to get money. I think the surprising thing is that there were not more failures. The failures were not commercial failures, but manufacturers shut down because they could not get money.

But that 15 per cent and that 25 per cent is by law for the benefit of the depositor who contributes to the business interests of this country to-day, in the national banks alone, over $2,000,000,000. The law says that when the percentage of reserve is down to 15 per cent in what are known as places that are not reserve cities, and 25 per cent in reserve cities where there is a great and rapid demand for the deposits, while in the nonreserve cities, the agricultural communities, the people are in the habit of leaving their money longer, so that it is not necessary to keep the same amount on hand, it shall not be touched except for the depositor. But that sum is there for the benefit of the depositor. Now, if the depositor has money there subject to check, under the law he can get it; every dollar is to be paid to him. The law simply provides that when the bank gets to that point it shall not make any new loans or discounts except in taking up sight bills of exchange or such paper as is immediately convertible into money; and that below the 15 per cent and the 25 per cent the money shall be held for the benefit of the depositor. But if a man has a deposit he can come in and get it and put it into business or use it for any other purpose he may desire, drawing out the very last dollar of it if he so desires.

The law recognizes the fact that the banks will at times be compelled to make loans and discounts in order to meet the wants of their depositors. If loans and discounts are made by banks, even at a time when it is a technical violation of the law, the law gives the banks thirty days in which to make it up. Instead of making the provision mandatory upon the Comptroller of the Currency that he shall—upon the banks not making their reserve good in thirty days—the law says that he may, with the approval of the Secretary of the Treasury, put such banks in the hands of receivers and wind them up.

In the report for 1893, which I made to Congress, that matter is discussed; but, as the Secretary says, and as I say, it is a matter of discussion. I thought, however, that it was wise to bring it out in order that when you gentlemen fully consider the question you may take in consideration the views which have been suggested both for and against. I think simply taking the single year 1893 is not a fair guide, because that was unprecedented in all these respects. It was a time when we were suffering internally, and the aggravation was not only internal, but we were suffering externally from the fact that our difficulty was, on the one hand, that there was a foreign demand for exchanges for a great many American securities which were either sent here because the holders doubted our credit, or because they had to have money to make up losses in their own countries, and we were suffering internally because depositors in banks were so frightened within the period from May to October that they drew out more than $300,000,000.

Of course, to meet such state of affairs, the banks had to call in their loans and discounts, and the result was that they called in $358,000,000. But, in order to make the trouble as slight as possible upon the business interests, they took out $36,000,000 additional of bank-note currency, and they also added to their borrowings about $40,000,000. They gave their customers the benefit of the $36,000,000 additional of bank notes and the amount of their borrowings—a sum of money in the neighborhood of $50,000,000, and in addition thereto, under the stress of circumstances—and I think it was a thing that was perfectly commendable—they issued clearing-house certificates, making available for loaning purposes the amount of money which the clearing-house certificates covered.

Now, gentlemen, these are my views upon what I have said in my report, and upon the question of banking generally.

Mr. WALKER. Mr. Chairman, we have now been in session until 22 minutes to 4 o'clock. I move that we adjourn until 10 o'clock to-morrow, and at that time we continue the hearing of the Secretary.

Mr. ECKELS. There is just one other statement that, before the committee adjourns, I should like to make, in order to be fairly understood, and that is this: That while the Secretary of the Treasury and myself agree on general principles, we differ a little as to methods. I think that is perfectly fair to the Secretary and fair to myself.

Mr. JOHNSON, of Indiana. May I ask you one question?

Mr. ECKELS. Certainly.

The CHAIRMAN. I think it is necessary to conclude this hearing to-night.

Mr. JOHNSON, of Indiana. I simply desire to ask one question.

The CHAIRMAN. Other gentlemen have been invited to appear before the committee to-morrow. The chair thinks we can finish this hearing in a few minutes to-day, and therefore makes the suggestion that each member put one question to Mr. Eckels, so as to allow an opportunity to all the members to interrogate him. Mr. Johnson, you may now put your question.

Mr. JOHNSON, of Indiana. Your plan contemplates exclusive Federal control?

Mr. ECKELS. I did not go into that branch. It is not within my province. The question of the safety of the issue of notes by State banks would, to my mind, turn entirely upon the construction placed upon the right of investigation reserved by the Federal authorities of note-issuing State banks. I think a very important matter to consider in connection with all bank issues is that any scheme ought not to be devised simply for the purpose of increasing the volume of currency. So, in the matter of bank issues, national and State issues, or both, I think this ought to be taken into consideration. I repeat, the question of the safety of State-bank issues is a question which would depend entirely upon the construction given to the supervisory powers as contemplated by the Secretary of the Treasury in the plan which he has suggested. I believe, as the Secretary of the Treasury stated, the dangers incident to State-bank currency are not as a great many people seem to think, for the reason that a different state of affairs exists than did prior to the establishment of the national system. Business methods have improved in the interval and values have increased. But whether or not such issues would be safe is a matter I should prefer to leave entirely to the discretion of Congress.

I think, though, it ought to be remembered that whatever relief is to be given to the Treasury through deposit of legal tenders by banks, it will not do to count too much upon State banks, as there are certain States whose constitutions prohibit State-bank issues, and they are very important banking States, such as Texas, Missouri, Illinois, and others.

Mr. JOHNSON, of Indiana. I asked you the question because you had not said anything on that subject to the committee. Of course I am familiar with your report on this subject.

Mr. HALL. You spoke about there being $165,000,000 of greenbacks, these original Treasury notes, and the amount of notes issued under the Sherman law, held in reserve, and you said that by abolishing that reserve the amount will be thrown on the market, as we make use of the expression, and go to deplete the gold reserve.

Mr. ECKELS. They could be used for that.

Mr. HALL. Pardon me. What I wanted to ask is this: Could it not be used for that purpose now?

Mr. ECKELS. No; because the law requires that this reserve against deposits shall be kept in lawful money, and there is not enough lawful money in the banks, without taking in some of the legal tenders, to keep up the lawful reserve. There is lawful money reserve in bank as follows:

Gold coin	$125,020,290.92
Gold Treasury certificates	37,810,940.00
Gold clearing-house certificates	34,096,000.00
Silver dollars	6,116,354.00
Silver Treasury certificates	28,784,897.00
Silver fractional currency	5,422,172.58

In addition thereto there were on hand in order to make up the percentage that under the law the banks are compelled to have—legal-tender notes, $120,544,028, and United States certificates of deposit for legal-tender notes, $45,100,000.

Mr. WALKER. I think my motion is now in order, Mr. Chairman. I think we shall have time enough to hear Mr. Eckels without sitting so many hours. I move that we adjourn until to-morrow, when we can hear Secretary Carlisle. I think there is ample time this week to have these hearings.

The motion was rejected.

Mr. BROSIUS. State whether you think, in view of the great amount of money now in the banks of the country—more than our people can use, and very likely more than they will be able to use for years to come—there is any urgent need for a revision of our financial system at this time.

Mr. ECKELS. For the sake simply of getting out money, I say no; but for the sake of a proper bank system and for the purpose of relieving the embarrassment of the Treasury under which it labors, I say, emphatically, yes. There ought to be a revision.

Mr. WARNER. You mention the frequent examination and publication of statements of the condition of issuing banks as one of the safeguards which we now have. May I ask how comparatively important you consider it, whether very important or of comparatively little importance?

Mr. ECKELS. I think it is a matter of great importance, and I think if the Banking Committee were as familiar with the reports which come in as I am, and the number of times banks have been saved, and especially during 1893, by the action of bank examiners, they would agree with me that it is very important. And as showing the importance of it, I think most of the States now have their bank examiners and bank superintendents to look into State institutions.

Mr. WARNER. I have other questions, Mr. Chairman, but I will take my turn.

The CHAIRMAN. Mr. Cox desires to ask a question.

Mr. COX. There was so much noise, Mr. Eckels, that I did not just hear your statement; but as I understand the matter of disposing of the capital stock, 50 per cent of it shall be paid into the Treasury of the United States in greenbacks and legal-tender notes; that is the first part, and upon that the bank receives an equivalent amount of bank notes.

Mr. ECKELS. Yes.

Mr. COX. So he gets just dollar for dollar for that?

Mr. ECKELS. Yes.

Mr. COX. Upon the next proposition, the remaining 50 per cent of its capital stock, he may receive dollar for dollar for that?

Mr. ECKELS. If he desires it, yes.

Mr. COX. That 50 per cent is based upon the assets of the bank, as I understood?

Mr. ECKELS. Yes.

Mr. COX. There is nothing behind it to redeem it except the 50 per cent of assets, the capital stock?

Mr. ECKELS. And the safety fund, in case of a failed bank.

Mr. COX. The safety fund is suggested, I understand. Now, to come back to the Government issue one minute. That, I understand, is not to be redeemed in coin until the banks surrender their charters?

Mr. ECKELS. The percentage of notes against legal tenders is to be ultimately redeemed by the Government, but if any man wants current redemption of them in gold, the banks have to supply the gold for that redemption.

Mr. COX. Precisely. I am looking to the Government. There is no way to force the Government to redeem, is there?

Mr. ECKELS. Oh, no: as I say, I would entirely divorce the Government from the redemption feature, except that it might deem it wise to keep the Government as an agent. The Government, of course, would redeem in gold the legal tenders deposited when the bank ceased to do business, or sooner if it was deemed wise and the Government was financially able to so do.

Mr. COX. Our minds are evidently both on the same point. The greenbacks are placed in there—I call them greenbacks—for the redemption of bank notes when a bank goes into liquidation either voluntarily or involuntarily. Now, the bank has deposited that and has had its 50 per cent of these notes. Does the Government again surrender these greenbacks for the purpose of redeeming those bank notes?

Mr. ECKELS. No. My idea would be that the Government would then destroy these greenbacks after redeeming them in gold. The Government would simply substitute to the bank gold for these greenbacks and cancel the Government notes.

Mr. ELLIS. Is not the Government liable for the ultimate redemption of the notes?

Mr. ECKELS. The Government would be liable for the redemption of 50 per cent, because those were issued on promises to pay for which the Government is now liable. But the other 50 per cent would be redeemable to the extent of this safety fund.

Mr. COX. And the assets of the bank?

Mr. ECKELS. Yes.

Mr. ELLIS. The plan of the Secretary does not contemplate the ultimate cancellation of these greenbacks, while your plan does.

Mr. ECKELS. I think you are mistaken there. The Secretary contemplates the ultimate redemption of them, but through use of the surplus revenue of the Government. On the issuance of a certain number of bank notes a certain number of legal-tender notes shall be canceled.

A MEMBER. I want to know what the practical difference is.

Mr. ECKELS. The difference is that under the plan of the Secretary of the Treasury if a bank wants to reduce its circulation it can withdraw its legal tenders. My idea is that when legal tenders come in the bank could not take them out again. Whatever reduction a bank would make in circulation it would have to be of its safety fund.

A MEMBER. Do you not understand that the plan contemplated by the Secretary is that the bank shall then regain this 50 per cent when it liquidates?

Mr. ECKELS. Oh, certainly.

A MEMBER. His plan puts it back in circulation, while your plan destroys it, as I understand.

Mr. ECKELS. But upon the other hand, his expectation is that out of the reserve of the Government there shall be the notes taken for redemption and cancellation. You can not rush the plan into operation. Of course it will have to come into operation gradually. If the banks deposit the 50 per cent of legal tenders and take the bonds you would immediately lock up $340,000,000 out of $498,000,000, and if the reserve fund is kept, of course a certain percentage of legal tenders, though not so large as at present, will be kept in the reserve against deposits. On the other hand, I think the Secretary, in his report, figures that if all the national banks would take out circulation and the State banks——

Mr. WALKER. Give us the figures on national banks first.

Mr. ECKELS. If all the national banks would take out 75 per cent—75 per cent of $675,000,000 would be how much?

Mr. WALKER. About $515,000,000.

Mr. ECKELS. And take 30 per cent of that.

Mr. WALKER. That would be about $155,000,000.

Mr. ECKELS. About that in round numbers. But that would contemplate the keeping out all the time of 75 per cent of the capital in bank notes. You would have to keep it out continually. If sufficient bank capital were invested in taking out notes to absorb all the legal tenders, under the plan suggested by the Secretary, you would have to increase your currency and keep out all the time additional bank notes to the extent of about $875,000,000.

Mr. JOHNSON, of Ohio. I want to ask whether the plan proposed by the Secretary of the Treasury would, in your judgment, furnish a flexible currency?

Mr. ECKELS. Yes; I think it would furnish a flexible currency.

Mr. JOHNSON, of Ohio. What is the inducement?

Mr. ECKELS. As I have just told you, under the theory that if a bank note is immediately convertible into coin no dollar will stay out that can not be used in business. That gives it the flexibility.

Mr. JOHNSON, of Ohio. Is it not true that where there are 3,700 banks it would be difficult to get at the notes of any one bank to present it?

Mr. ECKELS. That, as the Secretary of the Treasury says, is a matter for discussion. I have just stated my views on the question. The whole question is whether the principle is correct. If that is correct, then there ought not to be much difficulty in working out the details.

Mr. SPERRY. I should like to inquire, Mr. Comptroller, what is the profit on circulation to a bank so as to induce it to put out circulation?

Mr. ECKELS. Please repeat your question.

Mr. SPERRY. I desire to get at your judgment as to the profits to the banks upon circulation so as to induce them to go into your scheme. You, as I understand, require $50, say, of legal tenders deposited with the Treasury. That having been done, you give the banks $50 more on their general assets.

Mr. ECKELS. Yes; I allow $100 of bank note issues for each $50 of Treasury issues deposited with the Treasurer.

Mr. SPERRY. How much would you consider a safe reserve for the redemption by the banks of the $100 outstanding?

Mr. ECKELS. I think 5 per cent is considered safe now for current redemption.

Mr. SPERRY. That would be carried in legal-tender money?

Mr. ECKELS. It would be part carried in gold coin.

Mr. SPERRY. Would you require gold coin as distinguished from other money?

Mr. ECKELS. Simply for this reason: Whenever you wanted to get money to pay trade balances with other countries you could get a certain percentage reserve in gold coin and make the banks furnish that instead of the Government. That is the whole idea. We have got to have so much gold coin in order to settle international exchanges.

Mr. SPERRY. Would you require banks to redeem their issue in gold coin, or any part of it?

Mr. ECKELS. Yes; I do not think that the bank note would circulate at all unless it were redeemable in gold coin.

Mr. JOHNSON, of Ohio. It might be redeemable in silver.

Mr. ECKELS. Of course if you maintain the parity between the two metals you can use silver or gold. It all turns on that question. But in the meantime you have got to have it redeemable in that which is regarded by the greatest number of people in the world as the best money for carrying on business.

Mr. SPERRY. We are speaking of the proposition as it may be crystallized in the form of a statute. Would you require banks to redeem their circulation, or any part of it, in gold coin?

Mr. ECKELS. I have stated that I would.

Mr. SPERRY. The whole of it?

Mr. ECKELS. As long as there was any lawful money you might require it to be redeemed in lawful money. Of course, under the policy of the Government to keep all of its issues on a parity, every issue is equivalent to gold, being convertible into gold on demand.

Mr. SPERRY. Would you require banks to redeem in lawful money, or would you limit them to redemption in gold coin?

Mr. ECKELS. As long as lawful money is out I would let them use part of it, and I would have part redeemed in gold coin.

Mr. SPERRY. What part?

Mr. ECKELS. I have stated that 50 per cent of their circulation should absolutely be redeemed in gold coin. This for international trade.

Mr. SPERRY. As a reserve to be held in the bank?

Mr. ECKELS. For redemption purposes; 50 per cent of the reserve for redemption purposes should be in gold coin for this reason: That under the practice of the Government these notes are redeemable in gold coin.

Mr. SPERRY. If you require the banks to redeem in gold coin they must just carry gold coin for the purposes of reserve. If you allow them to redeem 50 per cent in lawful money and the balance in gold coin, then it seems to me they would have need to carry a certain per cent in lawful money and a certain other per cent in gold coin. If you allow them to redeem in lawful money I do not see how the banks will be able to carry a gold-coin reserve unless you require them to redeem part of their outstanding circulation in gold.

Mr. ECKELS. That is what I have been trying to explain, that I would compel them to redeem a part of their bank notes which are issued against legal tenders in gold coin, and for the reason given, viz, to settle international balances which must be settled in gold coin. I would compel them to that extent to redeem in gold coin, and to that extent the banks should carry gold coin, for the reason that whenever you want to settle international exchanges the gold could be obtained.

Mr. SPERRY. I am looking at the matter as an implied contract between the note holder and the bank itself. Now, there is no distinction between the $50 which the bank gets into circulation, predicated upon a deposit, and the other $50 which it gets upon its own credit.

Mr. ECKELS. But every bank, for the maintenance of its own credit and protection, will give the note holder whatever kind of money he may want. It will be obliged to do this for self-protection; and if it does not do it, its neighbor will, and the result will be that the bank which does not thus maintain itself will be discredited. That will be regulated, I think, by competition.

Mr. SPERRY. Would you give the option to the national banks to carry a certain percentage to redeem in gold coin, or give the national banks the option of redeeming in lawful money?

Mr. ECKELS. I think the bank ought to be permitted to redeem in lawful money, except a certain percentage; but I think it is rather a distinction without a difference, because people know that they can take the lawful money and get the gold with that.

Mr. SPERRY. I know, but they can not always conveniently do that. I am speaking now as to the matter of the rights of the note holder as against the bank when you put those rights into the rigid form of a statute. What are the rights of a note holder, under your system, in relation to redemption?

Mr. ECKELS. The same rights that are now the rights of the holder of any legal tender who is dealing with the United States Government relative to the redemption of such Government issues.

Mr. SPERRY. Then the bank may redeem in silver, for instance?

Mr. ECKELS. If it does redeem in silver, and silver is not on a parity with gold, I do not think the bank would have very much business to transact afterwards.

Mr. SPERRY. All that I want to know is whether the note holder would have the right to demand a certain percentage redeemed in gold, or whether he would be obliged to allow his notes to be redeemed in lawful money to a certain percentage?

Mr. ECKELS. I think he could demand a certain percentage to be redeemed in gold.

Mr. SPERRY. Then on that point you distinguish between the different legal-tender moneys?

Mr. ECKELS. You might term it a distinction, but in practice you would find that all the banks would give to the note holders whatever sort of money the note holders wanted; and it would be on the ground of self-protection because if banks did not do so the issues of those banks would be discredited. I think it is safe to rely upon the banks looking out for themselves, and thus regulating this matter.

Mr. WALKER. I should like to ask the Comptroller if the banks, under his suggestion as to what the law should be, would not be placed in the same identical position that the United States Treasury has been in up to this time—that the banks and Government, by great commercial and economic laws, should pay what they agreed to pay.

Mr. ECKELS. Yes; I think so, with this difference: That the managers of banks would not be hampered by the same laws that do not give the Secretary of the Treasury necessary powers incident to what he is called upon to do. People in other lines of business are not hampered in that way.

Mr. WALKER. Let me ask this second question: Is it not a fact that when gold is taken out of the United States Treasury it goes into the possession of parties other than the Government, and many times into foreign countries, while in the case of a bank there is no inducement to draw it except for shipment. It is deposited in another bank at once, which places it again within the redemption circle, whereas, when it is taken out of the United States, it is gone forever, so far as the United States Treasury is concerned?

Mr. ECKELS. Yes; because people do not want gold coin. They prefer paper, as being more convenient. People really do not want to carry coin around with them. Therefore the whole thing turns upon the belief of those who are dealing with the bank, in the ability of the bank to maintain its credit and give them coin, if at any time they should desire to exchange the bank's paper promises to pay, for coin. It is just as if I were dealing with any one of you. I would not take your promise to pay unless I had a feeling that you would pay, and especially I would not take it payable on demand unless I felt that any day, whether to-morrow or a year from now, I could go to the one who had given me such note and receive from him the money due on the note. All these notes of banks are promises to pay on demand. That which will give them currency among the people is whether or not when demand is made the person who issues them, whether it be a corporation or an individual, will meet that demand.

Mr. JOHNSON, of Ohio. You promised to answer a question that I asked you awhile ago, but did not do it.

The CHAIRMAN. As to whether these notes should be receivable for Government dues.

Mr. ECKELS. I would arrange it by percentages, because at present the legal tenders, as I understand, are accepted for dues.

Mr. JOHNSON, of Ohio. So are national-bank notes.

Mr. ECKELS. No, not for customs dues.

Mr. JOHNSON, of Ohio. They are for internal revenue.

Mr. ECKELS. Oh, yes.

Mr. JOHNSON, of Ohio. Would you still do that?

Mr. ECKELS. Yes, and I would have a certain percentage, basing it upon the amount of legal-tender notes issued by the Government, accepted in payment of customs, because they would be equivalent to gold, being based on legal tenders or Treasury issues, which are on demand always redeemed in gold at the Treasury.

Mr. WARNER. I believe that you suggested, Mr. Comptroller, that the 50 per cent deposit of legal-tender notes was not, in your opinion, a necessary security to the currency?

Mr. ECKELS. I do not think it is necessary——

Mr. WARNER. It is an alternative between raising money by taxation to retire the greenbacks and——

Mr. ECKELS. Yes, and I think that——

Mr. WARNER. I have not come to the point yet, quite. Now, is not the requirement of that deposit of 50 per cent just so much of an obstruction to the free development of the currency and to just that extent a tax upon borrowers?

Mr. ECKELS. I hardly think so; but suppose you get dollar for dollar in exchange for it for loaning purposes?

Mr. WARNER. If you tie up just that amount of money as a condition to getting dollar for dollar, is not that just so much of a tax upon the money which you do get?

Mr. ECKELS. Yes; but the idea is with a great many people that these legal tenders ought not to be in circulation at all; that those evidences of debt ought to be gotten out of the way. Under the plan suggested there is no contraction or expansion in the present volume of currency. There is another consideration: I said it was perfectly safe. I have no doubt but that it would be perfectly safe. But as I have suggested, you must teach the people, all classes of people—you have 65,000,000 of people to deal with, scattered all over the country—and he majority of those who are in business have never known anything but a bank-note currency which is dollar for dollar secured. Now, the practical question is whether you can make so much of a change from the existing order of things and yet retain the confidence of the people in your notes. It is not a sentimental question, it is a practical question.

Mr. WARNER. Let me put it in another shape. Do I understand, then, that the alternative is to put a tax upon wealth to pay off the greenbacks, or a tax upon borrowers in order to carry them?

Mr. ECKELS. I think it would be a tax on borrowers, if your premises are correct. But I do not admit the correctness of the premises you state.

Mr. WARNER. Is that not the fact?

Mr. ECKELS. Possibly it is. I have no doubt that if the people could thoroughly appreciate the expense that is now incident to this system of things, as they will appreciate it if you issue an interest-bearing bond every four months to the extent of $50,000,000, they would see that the expense on that side is a great deal harder burden than whatever additional expense in the way of interest on this side would be.

Mr. WARNER. Instead of taxing wealth to pay the greenbacks we are taxing the borrowers to carry them?

Mr. ECKELS. Yes.

Mr. CULBERSON. I do not understand the proposition that way.

Mr. WARNER. I am perfectly willing, if I had the time, to explain it, but I do not wish to intrude on the time of the committee to explain it.

Mr. CULBERSON. I do not think the Comptroller has made that assertion.

Mr. ECKELS. There is one other thing. I hope the committee will pardon me if I make too many suggestions, but there is one thing which I think worthy of consideration in connection with the present system, and that is its uniformity of supervision. I am not saying anything now about the note issues, but simply about the uniformity of supervision. A great many people have a surplus of capital which they can not use to advantage in the communities in the East, and the Middle and the other States where the systems are older than in the Northwestern and in portions of the South. The result of that has been this: That, understanding this uniformity and the general method in banking, there has been invested in banking capital in the West and in the South, by these people who had a superabundance which they could not use profitably at home, a great amount of banking capital. That capital has been so much additional money to these places that needed it for the purpose of developing their natural resources. It has served the same purpose as if that amount of capital had been imported. In addition thereto, the establishment of such banks has educated the people of those communities up to the point of depositing in banks, thereby giving to such communities the benefit of an available capital which, but for the establishment of such banks, would have remained either in the pockets of the people or have been stored elsewhere. So that every dollar, as I stated before, is made to bear a great many transactions instead of but a single one.

I have made several investigations because I thought they would be important to the Committee on Banking and Currency. One was to ascertain the number of depositors in the country having in banks sums of $1,000, under $1,000, and over $1,000, etc., and I found there were almost two million depositors in national banks and four million depositors in savings banks; and adding the number of depositors in State banks would bring it up to about eight millions of depositors. Then I made an investigation also as to the amount of checks, etc., used in retail transactions, and I found that there was about 55 per cent of purchases from grocers, clothing men, and all that sort paid by credit instruments. Then I made an investigation, or looked up a former investigation that had been made, as to the amount of capital which had been invested in the banking interests in the South, the West, and Northwest in national banking.

Mr. BLACK. By whom?

Mr. ECKELS. By people in the North and East.

The evidence of the extent of this investment is found in the fact that in 1889 nearly one-third of the capital stock of 520 national banks in

Iowa, Minnesota, Missouri, Kansas, and Nebraska was contributed by Northern and Eastern stockholders, while in Dakota, Idaho, Montana, New Mexico, Utah, Washington, Wyoming, and Arizona more than one-half of the capital stock of 144 national banks was held by nonresident shareholders. In the States of Virginia, West Virginia, North Carolina, South Carolina, Georgia, Florida, Alabama, Mississippi, Louisiana, Texas, Arkansas, Kentucky, and Tennessee, of the shares of 410 national banks, a little more than one-sixth of the total was held by nonresident shareholders.

Simply to show to what extent capital has been brought into these places in order to develop them, I think this is an important consideration in dealing with the banking question.

The CHAIRMAN. One gentleman invited by the committee to present his views, Mr. Lackland, president of the Boatmen's Bank, of St. Louis, has sent a brief communication stating his views. If there be no objection the Chair will hand it to the reporter to be printed in lieu of reading.

Mr. JOHNSON, of Indiana. Why not have it read to-morrow?

The CHAIRMAN. It will be inserted in the proceedings if there be no objection.

There was no objection, and the letter referred to is as follows:

BOATMEN'S BANK,
St. Louis, December 8, 1894.

MY DEAR SIR: I have yours of 6th instant, and regret very much that I can not appear before your committee in Washington City. I have very decided views on the currency question, and will preface this by saying that I have been in active business since 1837, and have experienced all the ills of State-bank money.

I don't approve of any of Mr. Carlisle's bill for many reasons. The first is that I don't think any bank ought to be allowed to issue paper money. Why should a bank be allowed to put forth their bills payable as money any more than any other corporation or capitalist? In my opinion, it is giving an undue advantage to the banks. Nothing ought to be allowed to pass as money without the broad seal of the Government. It is a function that belongs exclusively to the Government and ought not to be delegated to any other source. They have all the machinery for protecting the people against counterfeiting; besides, are equipped with subtreasuries and strong boxes thief proof, which afford absolute security, besides the promise and ability of the Government to redeem all its pledges.

My idea of a perfect currency is very simple and could be easily accomplished. In the first place, have all the tariff revenue paid in gold; then Congress authorize the Government to issue one thousand millions of legal tender notes, no note under the denomination of five dollars. This issue to be legal-tender and payable in gold at any of the subtreasuries of the United States on demand. With this issue redeem all the outstanding silver certificates, gold certificates, legal tenders and national-bank notes, as to have but one currency, then have the Government accumulate $250,000,000 of gold, and this, together with the silver now in the subtreasury, to be held for redemption of this new issue. This, in my opinion, would be the very perfection and simplicity of the whole subject.

A good deal has been said in regard to the elasticity of currency. In my opinion this is a delusion. The object of this is when the cotton or other crops come to market that this expansion takes place to move the crops. Now the theory of this is when the crops are marketed that this currency will be returned to the banks and there lay idle six months until the crops are ready again for market. Now anybody conversant with banking business knows very well that a banker is never so unhappy as when he has a surplus of money on hand, consequently that money will be used, and when the crops come along they will be suffered to take care of themselves. My experience is that when the crops come forward the money will be found to move them. Another point in the elasticity of currency is made that it can be available in panics. No legislation can prevent panics. They come, I may say, as a necessity, to purify the commercial atmosphere, and are the accumulation of years of prosperity, and are one of the financial laws for the settlement and readjustment of things, and will occur, in the very nature of things, in spite of any proposed relief.

I have hurridly set forth my views, without any elaboration, and you can take them for what they are worth; but in my opinion they are worth consideration, for

I regard this as one of the most important subjects now agitating the public mind. To adopt Mr. Carlisle's theory of banking would be a step backward, and I would regard it as one of the greatest calamities that could befall this country.

Very truly, yours,

R. I. LACKLAND.

Mr. S. W. COBB, M. C.,
Washington, D. C.

Mr. Parsons is out of the city, and I can not find any other banking gentleman that can spare the time to go to Washington City.

The CHAIRMAN. There being no other business before the committee this evening, the committee will now adjourn, to meet at 10 o'clock to-morrow morning, for the purpose of continuing this hearing.

Thereupon, at 4.12 o'clock p. m., the committee adjourned.

WASHINGTON, D. C., *Tuesday, December 11, 1894.*

The committee met at 10 a. m.

Present—The chairman (Mr. SPRINGER), Cobb of Missouri, Ellis, Cobb of Alabama, Warner, Johnson of Ohio, Black, Hall, Walker, Brosius, Henderson, Russell, Haugen, and Johnson of Indiana.

The CHAIRMAN: Gentlemen of the committee, we had expected that the Secretary of the Treasury would be here at this time, but as it is a little late and time is passing rapidly, I suggest that we shall proceed. I have asked Mr. Horace White, of New York, to address the committee. In pursuance of authority conferred on the Chair, I addressed a letter to Mr. White, and he has kindly accepted the invitation, and is now here. After he has concluded his remarks Mr. Hepburn and Mr. Horner will address the committee.

Mr. HALL. Will the same plan be followed to-day as was followed yesterday with reference to Mr. Eckels?

The CHAIRMAN. The Chair was going to suggest that we follow the same plan as we did yesterday, allowing gentlemen who address the committee to proceed in their own way without interruption. After they are through, any member of the committee can submit questions.

The Baltimore convention, at which a plan was adopted last October, has had its proceedings printed; and, if there be no objection, it will be printed in the record of these proceedings.

The Baltimore plan and the plan outlined in Secretary Carlisle's report are here printed in parallel columns:

THE BALTIMORE PLAN.

SECTION 1. The provision of the national banking act requiring the deposit of bonds to secure circulating notes hereafter issued shall be repealed.

SEC. 2. Allow the banks to issue circulating notes to the amount of 50 per centum of their paid-up, unimpaired capital, subject to a tax of one-half of 1 per centum per annum upon the average amount of circulation outstanding for the year, and an additional circulation of 25 per centum of their paid-up, unimpaired capital, subject both to the tax of one-half of 1 per centum per annum and to an additional heavy tax per annum upon the average amount of such circulation outstanding for the year; said additional 25 per centum to be known as "emergency circulation."

SECRETARY CARLISLE'S PLAN.

I.

Repeal all laws requiring, or authorizing, the deposit of United States bonds as security for circulation.

II.

Permit national banks to issue notes to an amount not exceeding seventy five per centum of their paid-up and unimpaired capital, but require each bank before receiving notes to deposit a guarantee fund, consisting of United States legal-tender notes, including Treasury notes of 1890, to the amount of thirty per centum upon the circulating notes applied for. This percentage of deposits upon the circulating notes outstanding to be

SEC. 3. The tax of one-half of 1 per centum per annum upon the average amount of circulation outstanding shall be paid to the Treasurer of the United States as a means of revenue, out of which the expenses of the office of the Comptroller of the Currency, the printing of circulating notes, &c., shall be defrayed.

The excess over one-half of 1 per centum of the tax imposed upon the "emergency circulation" shall be paid into the "guarantee fund" referred to in section 6.

SEC. 4. The banks issuing circulation shall deposit and maintain with the Treasurer of the United States a "redemption fund" equal to 5 per centum of their average outstanding circulation, as provided for under the existing law.

SEC. 5. The redemption of the notes of all banks, solvent or insolvent, to be made as provided for by the existing law.

SEC. 6. Create a "guarantee fund" through the deposit by each bank of 2 per centum upon the amount of circulation received the first year. Thereafter impose a tax of one-half of 1 per centum upon the average amount of outstanding circulation, the same to be paid into this fund until it shall equal 5 per centum of the entire circulation outstanding, when the collection of such tax shall be suspended, to be resumed whenever the Comptroller of the Currency shall deem it necessary.

The notes of insolvent banks shall be redeemed by the Treasurer of the United States out of the guarantee fund, if it shall be sufficient, and if not sufficient, then out of any money in the Treasury, the same to be reimbursed to the Treasury out of the "guarantee fund" when replenished, either from the assets of the failed banks or from the tax aforesaid.

National banking associations organized after this plan shall have gone into operation may receive circulation from the Comptroller of the Currency upon paying into the "guarantee fund" a sum bearing the ratio to the circulation applied for and allowed that the "guarantee fund" bears to the total circulation outstanding, and to be subject to the tax of one-half of 1 per centum per annum, as called for by the Treasurer of the United States for the creation and maintenance of this fund.

No association or individual shall have any claim upon any part of the money in said "guarantee fund" except for the redemption of the circulating notes of any insolvent national banking association. Any surplus or residue of said "guarantee fund" which may be hereafter ascertained or determined by law shall inure to the benefit of the United States.

SEC. 7. The Government shall have a prior lien upon the assets of each failed maintained at all times, and whenever a bank retires its circulation, in whole or in part, its guarantee fund to be returned to it in proportion to the amount of notes retired.

III.

Retain the provision of the law making stockholders individually liable, and provide that the circulating notes shall constitute a first lien upon all the assets of the bank.

IV.

Impose a tax of one-half of one per centum per annum, payable semiannually, upon the average amount of notes in circulation to defray the expenses of printing notes, official supervision, cancellation, etc.

V.

No national-bank note to be of less denomination than ten dollars, and all notes of the same denomination to be uniform in design; but banks desiring to redeem their notes in gold may have them made payable in that coin. The Secretary of the Treasury to have authority to prepare and keep on hand ready for issue upon application a reserve of blank national-bank notes for each banking association having circulation.

VI.

Require each national-banking association to redeem its notes at its own office, or at its own office and at agencies to be designated by it.

VII.

To provide a safety fund for the immediate redemption of the circulating notes of failed banks, impose a tax of per centum per annum upon the average circulation of each bank until the fund amounts to five per centum of the total circulation outstanding. Require each new bank, and each bank taking out additional circulation, to deposit its proper proportion of this fund before receiving notes. When a bank fails, its guarantee fund held on deposit to be paid into the safety fund and used in the redemption of its notes, and if this fund shall be impaired by the redemption of the notes of failed national banks, and the immediately available cash assets of such banks are insufficient to reestablish the fund, it shall at once be made good by pro rata assessments upon the other banks, according to the amounts of their outstanding circulation; but there shall be a first lien upon all the assets of the failed bank, or banks, to reimburse the contributing banks. The safety fund bank and upon the liability of shareholders for the purpose of restoring the amount withdrawn from the "guarantee fund" for the redemption of its circulation, not to exceed, however, the amount of the failed bank's outstanding circulation after deducting the sum to its credit in the "redemption fund" (section 4) already in the hands of the Treasurer of the United States.

SEC. 8. Circulation can be retired by a bank at any time upon depositing with the Treasurer of the United States lawful money in amount equal to the sum desired to be withdrawn, and immediately upon such deposit the tax indicated in sections 2, 3, and 6 shall cease upon the circulation so retired.

SEC. 9. In the event of the winding up of the business of a bank by reason of insolvency, or otherwise, the Treasurer of the United States, with the concurrence of the Comptroller of the Currency, may, on the application of the directors, or of the liquidator, receiver, assignee, or other proper official, and, upon being satisfied that proper arrangements have been made for the payment of the notes of the bank and any tax due thereon, pay over to such directors, liquidator, receiver, assignee, or other proper official, the amount to the credit of the bank in the "redemption fund" indicated in section 4.

may be invested in outstanding United States bonds having the longest time to run, the bonds and the interest upon them to be held as part of the fund and sold when necessary to redeem notes of failed banks.

VIII.

Repeal the provisions of the reorganization and extension act of July 12, 1882, imposing limitations upon the reduction and increase of national-bank circulation.

IX.

Repeal all provisions of the law requiring banks to keep a reserve on account of deposits.

X.

The Secretary of the Treasury may, in his discretion, use any surplus revenue of the United States in the redemption and retirement of United States legal-tender notes, but such redemption shall not in the aggregate exceed an amount equal to seventy per cent of the additional circulation taken out by national and State banks under the system herein proposed.

XI.

Circulating notes issued by a banking corporation, duly organized under the laws of any State, and which transacts no other than a banking business, shall be exempt from taxation under the laws of the United States, when it is shown to the satisfaction of the Secretary of the Treasury and the Comptroller of the Currency—

(1) That such bank has at no time had outstanding its circulating notes in excess of seventy-five per centum of its paid-up and unimpaired capital.

(2) That its stockholders are individually liable for the redemption of its circulating notes to the full extent of their ownership of stock.

(3) That the circulating notes constitute by law a first lien upon all the assets of the bank.

(4) That the bank has at all times kept a guarantee fund in United States legal-tender notes, including Treasury notes of 1890, equal to thirty per centum of its outstanding circulating notes; and

(5) That it has promptly redeemed its notes on demand at its principal office, or at one or more of its branch offices, if it has branches.

XII.

The Secretary of the Treasury may, under proper rules and regulations to be established by him, permit State banks to procure and use in the preparation of their notes the distinctive paper used in printing United States securities; but no State bank shall print or engrave its notes in similitude of a United States note, or certificate, or national-bank note.

STATEMENT OF MR. HORACE WHITE.

Mr. HORACE WHITE, of New York, proceeded to address the committee. He said:

After I had the honor of an invitation to appear before the committee last Sunday I put my views on the subject of the Baltimore plan in writing, and I will take the liberty of reading them to you. I will remark beforehand that the paper is only twenty-five minutes long, so that nobody need be dismayed at its possible length.

Mr. WALKER. I desire to ask Mr. White whether he has, in form, the draft of any bill which he approves, whether it includes the Baltimore plan or not. If he has I wish he would hand a copy of it to the committee.

I understand that Mr. White, or some other member of the Baltimore convention committee, has formulated a bill including the Baltimore plan. If so, I should like to have copies of it presented now so that we may use it in our questions.

The CHAIRMAN. Mr. White can state how that is.

Mr. WHITE. I have drawn a bill which embodies my ideas of the Baltimore plan, but it has not been adopted by the Baltimore committee, which consists of eight or ten gentlemen living in different parts of the country, and if I were to submit it now it would be only a presentation of my own views.

Mr. WALKER. I would like to have it. It may include the Baltimore plan or it may not, but it is Mr. White's views put into a bill.

Mr. WHITE. There are two other members of the Baltimore committee here now, and I should like to act in cooperation with them in a matter of this kind.

The CHAIRMAN. Mr. White may hand in his plan and it will be printed in the proceedings of the committee.

Mr. WALKER. Do we not want to see the plan while Mr. White is here?

The CHAIRMAN. Mr. White says that he desires to consult with his associates.

Mr. WHITE. I will consult with them immediately after I get through with my remarks; and we shall save time in that way. Gentlemen, the Baltimore plan deals with only one part of the banking business—that of issuing circulating notes. It is often said that the issuing of notes is not a necessary function of a bank. It is true that a bank may exist without it, but a banking system without note issues comes far short of rendering to the community all the service that it is capable of.

As money is an instrument of exchange, a bank is a machine of exchange. It consists of a guarantee fund called capital stock, and of the earnings of the community called deposits, which, together, form a body of assets. These assets are kept in a liquid state, or state of solvency, so that anybody having a claim against the bank can at any time draw it out in the form of money or realize it in the form of goods by giving his check. The condition that a bank must be in so that its assets shall always be "solvent" is determined by experience. Three banks still existing were started before the Federal Constitution was adopted. From that time to this the banks and the people have been learning by experience what things promote solvency and what things imperil it. The science of banking consists of all the means devised to preserve and maintain solvency. These are to be found in the history of banking and in the laws regulating it, which have been passed, amended, or repealed from time to time.

At common law any man may issue his promissory notes and circulate them as money if people are willing to take them. But this is like the right to make or keep gunpowder or to sell liquor. It is the paramount right and duty of the State to provide for the safety of the community. Hence it may prescribe the regulations under which circulating notes shall be issued, or gunpowder be stored, or liquor be sold. It is not bound to give equal privileges to all persons to exercise these functions. It may authorize one bank of issue, or one powder mill, and no more.

The evolution of banking in Massachusetts is one of the most interesting chapters in the history of the science. Little by little, from generation to generation, the stones were laid of the edifice which is known as the Suffolk system.

The wit of man from the earliest ages has been engaged (for the most part unconsciously) in finding means to exchange goods and services with the least expenditure of labor and capital. Since the precious metals are capital, and since the moving of them hither and thither requires labor, the system which reduces the use of them to the lowest terms consistent with safety is the best system. Under the Suffolk system anybody of good character who was engaged in a legitimate business could exchange his promissory note, running sixty or ninety days, for the notes of a bank payable on demand, and these notes would pay the wages of his employees or they would buy the raw materials of his trade anywhere in the United States or Canada. The notes were redeemed by the Suffolk Bank in Boston from day to day as fast as the course of trade took them thither. How were they redeemed? They were redeemed by the bills receivable of the issuing bank. The man who gave his sixty or ninety day note had by this time sold his products or had received payment for a previous lot in a draft on Boston and had paid his note with the draft, and the bank was thus enabled to keep its balance good at the Suffolk. There was no limit to the work that the system would do. All years and all seasons were alike to it.

The Suffolk Bank was a clearing house for country bank notes. Its managers originally conceived that a profit could be made by persuading country banks to deposit money with it for redeeming their notes at par in Boston. As the country banks did not see any profit to themselves in such an arrangement they refused. Then the Suffolk began to send their notes home for redemption. It secured the cooperation of five other Boston banks. The country banks had hitherto monopolized the field of circulation even in Boston. Their notes being at a discount more or less according to the distance and difficulty of reaching their place of issue, and not being received on deposit at par by the Boston banks, they would be paid out by everybody for purchases and thus kept in circulation. The Boston notes, on the other hand, would be promptly returned to the issuing banks as deposits or in payment of debts due to them.

The six banks, headed by the Suffolk, soon began to make it hot for their country cousins by incessant calls for specie. The latter made a great outcry. They called the Suffolk syndicate "The six-tailed Bashaw" and other opprobrious names, but the run continued remorselessly until they began to come in and make the deposits required for a redemption fund. When they had once done so they found their credit so much improved that their notes had a wider circulation than ever and would stay out longer than before, because their circulation had a greater range. At the time when the Suffolk system was at its best I lived in Chicago. The notes of Massachusetts banks were in great request there. They were considered the best currency going and they bore a premium over the notes of Illinois and Wisconsin banks.

The Suffolk system of redemption was not made compulsory by law. It was voluntary, like the clearing-house system in general. It subjected the goodness of all bank notes in the range of its influence to a daily test. All the banks in the system were washed every day. This was very good for their health, but daily washing does not always prevent disease. A bank might become rotten while keeping up its redemption fund at the Suffolk, just as a bank may now become gradually unsound while maintaining its position at the clearing house. Nevertheless, the Massachusetts system, taken altogether, realized the ideal of bank-note issues, in the sense of supplying machinery for swapping the goods and products of the country with the least expenditure of labor and capital.

Notwithstanding its abounding merits and great success, New York has exercised a wider influence on banking than Massachusetts or any other State. This has been due to two essentially different and even contradictory methods of note issues, known as the safety-fund system and the free-banking system. The former began in 1829 and continued till about 1860. The latter began in 1838 and still survives in the national banking act. The main question now before the country is. Which of the two shall prevail hereafter? Both systems aim to secure note holders, and both are adequate to that end. The question that ought to engage attention is, which one corresponds most nearly in other respects the ideal of banking which was so nearly realized in Massachusetts? That is to say, which one best answers the purpose of a machine for swapping goods and services with ease and regularity and with the minimum of expense?

The safety-fund system was the invention of Josiah Forman, of Onondaga County, N. Y., who, in presenting it to Martin Van Buren, governor of the State, said that he had taken the idea from the organization known as the Hong merchants of Canton, China, all of whom were liable for the debts of each, and who had attained an incomparable credit by that means, no such thing as the failure of a Hong merchant being known. He did not propose, however, that all the banks should be liable for the debts of each, but merely that they should all contribute something to a common fund to provide for the redemption of the notes of failed banks. The contribution to the fund was to be one-half of 1 per cent annually on the capital of the participating banks until 3 per cent should be accumulated.

The plan was adopted, but by a mistake in the framing of the law the safety fund was not limited to the redemption of the circulating notes, but was made applicable to all the debts of the failed banks. This accidental error led to mischievous consequences and brought the system into disrepute. Elderly bankers, who were in business while the safety fund was in vogue, have assured me that the system was a total failure, but when I have asked them for particulars they could not give any. They only spoke from general recollection that the fund was inadequate to meet the claims made upon it. That is true, but it means not that the annual contribution of one-half of 1 per cent was insufficient to redeem all the notes of failed banks, but that it was insufficient to pay all the depositors as well. The fact is that it would have been sufficient to pay the notes of all the failed banks during the time the system lasted, with a considerable surplus over, if it had not been diverted to other uses.

Another mistake in the safety-fund law was that it did not provide that the notes should be registered and countersigned by any public officer. The result of this omission was that there were over issues of notes, so that $700,000 of fraudulent ones came upon the fund and were redeemed out of it. Both of these mistakes were rectified by subsequent legislation, but not until the system had been subjected to a severe strain and to unmerited obloquy. The upshot of the whole matter is that the safety-fund principle, apart from such infantile disorders, was a grand success, and although it was buried thirty years ago, at the place of its birth, is alive and in high esteem in a neighboring country, and is now showing signs of revival at home. The system was adopted in Canada in 1890 in order to secure the prompt redemption of the notes of failed banks, i. e., to avoid a discount on the notes of such banks pending liquidation.

Under the Canadian system the circulating notes are the first lien on the assets, and it is believed that the assets will always suffice to redeem the notes, but the delay in converting them into cash, prior to the establishment of the safety fund, had led to a temporary discount on such notes. There is now in the Canadian bank circulation redemption fund $1,800,000, and it is believed to be sufficient to meet all casualties of this kind. Under the Canadian law the Government is not responsible for the notes of failed banks, but such notes draw interest at 6 per cent. The maximum amount of the fund is 5 per cent of the outstanding circulation of all the Canadian banks, and it must be kept up to this maximum, the minister of finance having power to call on the banks for additional contributions, when necessary, not exceeding 1 per cent in any year. When the assets of failed banks are paid in, however, refunds may be made to the contributing banks of the excess over 5 per cent.

Under the New York safety-fund system all the capital of the banks was applicable to the banking business strictly. This raises the question, What is the banking business? It is the business of working a machine of exchange, and thus dispensing with the use of the precious metals, as far as possible, substituting credit therefor. Bank credit is a general belief that what a bank promises to do it is able to do. When this belief becomes fixed, it is a great advantage all around to dispense with the use of the precious metals as media of exchange, and to keep on hand only sufficient to serve as a touchstone of the paper instruments; in other words, to keep the standard of value at hand merely for purposes of comparison. How much gold is required for this purpose? That is a question to be answered by experience in different cities, States, and nations. I would not undertake to say how much is required in New York, or in Chicago, or in the United States as a whole, but I should say that we need a less percentage than the countries of Europe, because we are not exposed to the alarms of war, which are very disturbing to credit.

I said that under the New York safety-fund system all the capital of the banks was applicable strictly to the banking business. It was not so under the free-banking system. That system had its origin in a political upheaval which began in 1835. Prior to this time the history of banking in New York had been largely a narrative of bribery, corruption, and favoritism in the granting of bank charters. You will find all the details in Hammond's History of Political Parties in that State. I should like to give you some of them now, but it would take too much time. The long and short of it is, that there was a revolt in the Democratic party against these abuses, just as there was a revolt against Tammany Hall the other day. The revolt of 1835 was also against Tammany, and the seceders were called Locofocos. They are now called "Anti-snappers."

The Locofocos began by fighting against bank corruption and monopoly. As they progressed and gained strength, they enlarged their plan of campaign and attempted to reform the earth, and I honor them for it. They set the ball rolling for free trade, and whatever measure of success that doctrine gained in the North before the war was due chiefly to their impulse. They unhorsed the Democratic party in New York City, and although they did not get into the saddle themselves they produced so much alarm that the party took up the subject of bank reform seriously and passed a law to make banking free to everybody. In fact they rather overdid their job, for they allowed individuals as well as banks to issue circulating notes, and that law stands on the statute book of New York to-day.

Now, bear in mind that the uppermost thought of the people in 1838 was not good banking but equal rights, and the wit of the legislature was exercised in devising a system which should meet a political rather than a financial exigency. The plan adopted was brought forward by Mr. Abijah Mann. It provided that circulating notes might be delivered by certain State officers to banks or individuals who should deposit with said officers certain securities, worth at the time of deposit something more than the par value of the notes. The system thus inaugurated had a checkered career, which it would take too much time to narrate. It harmonized so nicely with the American idea of equal rights and "a fair chance for everybody" that it spread like wildfire, and its effects in that part of the country where the chairman of this committee and myself lived in our younger days were very much like those of wildfire. They taught me the lesson that in securing equal rights in banking it is necessary to give some attention to the principles of banking. These were for the most part overlooked in the New York law, and they were wholly overlooked in the Illinois, Indiana, and Wisconsin imitations of it.

The principle of credit, which is the vital principle of banking, was expunged from bank-note issues. What was substituted for it? Simply this: That if a bank would drop a dollar and ten cents into a slot, a dollar would drop out, which the bank could then lend to its customers. In other words, the bank's usefulness was paralyzed, on its note-issuing side, at the start. But, you say, security for the note holder was gained in this way. Not exactly. Your chairman and I, who saw the notes of the free banks of Illinois sold at a discount of 60 per cent, and hardly any of them at a less discount than 10 per cent, know better than that.

The testimony of Azariah Flagg, comptroller of New York, shows that the safety-fund system, with its little tax of one-half per cent per annum, furnished as much protection to note holders as did the 110 per cent of deposited security under the free-banking system. Why was this? Simply because under the former system the bank had the 110 cents in its own vaults, i. e., employed in the discount of commercial paper, instead of being lodged in the State treasurer's vaults at Albany. The true fund for the redemption of circulating notes is the sum total of the liquid assets of the bank, including its bills receivable. It is the same fund exactly as that out of which it pays the checks drawn upon it from day to day.

The Baltimore plan provides for a guarantee fund of the same percentage as under the Canadian law, and it makes the circulating notes a first lien on the assets of the bank. There is an outcry against this last feature from some people, who say that the poor depositors will suffer. But what is the condition of the poor depositors now? Are not the notes a first lien on the assets? Are not the security bonds a part of the assets? Can any depositor get any part of this fund until the notes are paid in full? And, supposing that the bonds should ever fall short of paying the notes, could the depositor get any part of the remaining assets until the par value of the notes was deducted? Of course not. This outcry about the poor depositors is loudest in Boston, and it comes from persons who are probably not aware that the law of Massachusetts now, and from the earliest times, has made circulating notes a first lien on the assets of banks. This law was reenacted by Massachusetts in her last revision, that of 1880. I venture to say that if the 10 per cent tax on State-bank notes were repealed, Massachusetts would cling to this provision more tenaciously than ever, as she ought to. The same provision exists in the State constitution of New York.

I see no objection to the repeal of the 10 per cent tax on State-bank notes, provided the State banks comply with all the requirements of the national banking law, and provided the means of enforcing these requirements are lodged with the Comptroller of the Currency. But a mere power of observation, without the power of enforcement, I should consider unwise, unsafe, and sure to cause embarrassment and to end in disaster.

The Baltimore plan contemplates that the Government shall continue, as now, responsible for the redemption of bank notes. I consider this very desirable, although not indispensable. It is a provision in the interest of the public, not of the banks. The redemption clause of the present law was prompted by bitter experience of the losses incurred by delay in the redemption of failed-bank notes, even in cases where the security bonds were good and where redemption at par was reasonably certain. Of course the Government takes care that it shall lose nothing by the operation. It has the security bonds and the 5 per cent redemption fund in its hands, in addition to which it holds a first lien on the assets and on the shareholder's liability to recoup itself for any possible deficiency.

The redemption clause applies only to failed bank notes. It is no advantage to a failed bank to have the Government redeem its notes and then recoup itself out of the bank's property. The only beneficiaries of the provision are the people of the United States, since all of them are holders, more or less, of the national-bank currency. It may be said that the redemption clause is an advantage to the banks, because it gives a wider and more lasting credit to their notes than they would otherwise enjoy. This is true, but this, too, is for the public advantage. It is an inestimable advantage that the public are not put to any trouble in deciding whether a bank note is good or bad. The whole *raison d'être* of a good banking system is a high state of credit—the higher the better. If this credit is promoted by Government redemption of the notes and without pecuniary loss to the Government that fact constitutes its sufficient justification.

The Baltimore plan simply takes the law as it finds it. It adds nothing to it in this respect. It makes a change in the manner of reimbursing the Government for the redemption of failed notes. The only question is whether the suggested change puts the Government to any greater risk. This is a question of mathematics. It is to be answered by the tables of bank mortality in the past thirty-one years.

It has been said that there is no more reason why the Government should guarantee the notes of a bank than those of a merchant, a manufacturer, or a farmer. This would be true if the notes of the merchant, the manufacturer, and the farmer were allowed to circulate as money, but not otherwise.

The analogy fails because the latter do not pass from hand to hand, all over the country, with the express authority of the Government. The right to issue circulating notes has generally been under governmental control, and ought always to be so. It is a corollary from this proposition that the Government ought not to allow anything to circulate which is bad or doubtful. The steps which the Government takes to insure the goodness of the circulating medium are strictly in the public interest, and not in any private and corporate interest. To prove this it is only necessary to ask what would be the condition of affairs if it took no such steps. The history of the first half century of the Republic is full of mournful examples of unregulated or half-regulated banking.

It may be said that the Government ought to reap the profit of the paper circulating medium. Conceding this to be true, the question remains, how can this profit be best secured? Experience has shown that Government profits are best obtained by means of a tax, not by entering into business competition with citizens. There is no objection to a tax on bank notes for purposes of revenue purely. We have always had such a tax. Nobody would desire to impose an excessive tax. It would be absurd to create a new system and kill it by the same act. It is submitted that all the advantages in the way of revenue that can be gained by Government issues can be gained equally by taxing bank notes, while the disadvantages under which we now labor will be avoided. The disadvantages are found mainly in the inflexibility of Government issues. These are a fixed sum. We can not make it greater without paving the way to indefinite expansion, dependent upon political majorities solely.

Moreover, the existence of Government issues has thrown upon the Treasury the ungrateful task of maintaining the ultimate gold reserve of the country, and it has taught the people to look to the Government for relief in every case of monetary stringency. These evils are inseparable from Government note issues, and they are certain to increase as time goes on, since there will soon be nobody on the stage of action who has known any other system.

The retirement of the legal-tender notes was not included in the Baltimore plan. It was probably deemed best not to ask for too many things at once, but I am decidedly in favor of their retirement. When I say retirement, I mean cancellation and extinction, not temporary withdrawal.

Of course, cancellation implies either surplus revenue or funding into bonds; that is to say, it must be possible to meet the public expenses without paying out the legal tenders as they come in for taxes, or there must be authority to fund them as the floating debt of a railroad company is funded. I should prefer the latter course, because it is the most certain and expeditious. I do not perceive the wisdom of hiding them away for a longer or shorter time, and thus giving occasion for a demand to pull them out of their hiding places and put them in circulation again. My reason for desiring the extinction of the legal-tender notes is that they are a constant menace to business interests.

Business men are in a chronic state of alarm lest the Government should not be able to redeem them in gold, or lest a political party should come into power on a platform of not redeeming them at all. You can not have any real business stability while such apprehensions exist.

Moreover, the greenbacks teach people to believe lies. They create the belief that the Government can make money, than which a more damaging lie never gained lodgment in the human brain. They have kept political parties in hot water for thirty years and have obstructed the pathway for all other reforms. They are an obstacle to the national progress, and ought to be put out of their misery without further delay.

I thank you, gentlemen, for your kind attention. Now, if any gentlemen wishes to ask me any questions, I will answer them if I can.

Mr. WALKER. I ask again that copies of Mr. White's bill be distributed if Mr. White has them.

The CHAIRMAN (to Mr. White). When would it suit your convenience to submit the bill which you have prepared?

Mr. WHITE. Probably now, if Mr. Hepburn and Mr. Homer agree.

Mr. HOMER (a member of the Baltimore committee). I would like to state, in explanation of this matter, that at the meeting of the American bankers' convention, at which the Baltimore plan was acted upon, a committee was appointed for the purpose of having prepared a bill carrying with it the underlying principles of the Baltimore plan. The activity of this committee (the committee on banking and currency), and of the country, generally, on the question of currency, was, I must confess, rather a surprise to us, and it has caught us in the position of not being prepared, to-day, to present to you a bill in such form, and embodying those principles, properly worked out, such as the entire committee would like to submit. We are engaged in the preparation of such a bill.

I can see no objection to Mr. White's handing in to you now the measure which he has taken the pains to prepare. What my own judgment would be, that, with the existing multiplicity of bills and ideas on this subject, those bills that carry out only in part the general Baltimore plan and the indorsed idea of the entire committee appointed by the American Bankers' Association, might only add to the existing confusion. I have not the remotest objection to the scrutiny of Mr. White's bill, but it will be handed in by him as his individual bill, and not as the bill of the American Bankers' Association.

Mr. WHITE. That is all right.

The CHAIRMAN. The chair is of opinion that the members of the Baltimore committee having the matter in charge should submit their formulated plan in their own way. There is plenty of time. Mr. White can submit the formulated plan at any time.

Mr. WHITE (handing several copies of his bill to members of the committee). I submit this as an embodiment of my individual views.

Mr. White's bill is as follows:

A BILL to amend the National Bank Act.

SECTION 1. From and after the passage of this Act, no banking association shall be required to deposit with the Treasurer of the United States any United States bonds, either as preliminary to the commencement of the banking business, or for the security of circulating notes to be hereafter issued.

SEC. 2. In lieu of the deposit of bonds as security for circulating notes hereafter to be issued, each national banking association shall be entitled to receive circulating notes from the Comptroller to the amount of fifty per centum of its paid-up unimpaired capital, as determined by the Comptroller of the Currency, upon paying to the Treasurer of the United States lawful money to the amount of two per centum of such circulating notes and thereafter a tax at the rate of one-half of one per centum per annum upon the average amount of its circulation outstanding for the year, which tax shall be additional to all other taxes whatsoever on bank notes. Said tax shall be collected in the month of January. The said two per centum and the proceeds of said tax shall constitute a guarantee fund for the redemption of the notes of insolvent national banks, and the tax shall be collected until the fund amounts to not less than five per centum of the entire circulation issued under the provisions of this act. This fund shall be in addition to the five per cent redemption fund now provided by law. No association or individual shall have any claim upon any part of the money in said guarantee fund, except for the redemption of the circulating notes of any insolvent national banking association. Any surplus or residue of said guarantee fund which may be hereafter ascertained or determined by law shall inure to the benefit of the United States.

SEC. 3. In addition to the amount of circulating notes provided for in the foregoing section, each association shall be entitled to receive from the Comptroller circulating notes to the amount of twenty-five per centum of its paid-up unimpaired capital, upon paying to the Treasurer of the United States lawful money to the amount of two per centum of such additional circulation and a tax of one-half of one per centum per annum upon the average amount of the same outstanding for the year, payable as provided in section two, and an additional tax at the rate of four per centum per annum upon the average amount of such additional circulation outstanding for the year, all of which sums shall be a part of the guarantee fund aforesaid: *Provided, however*, That any excess in said guarantee fund over the five per centum aforesaid, resulting from the tax on said additional circulation, shall belong to the United States.

SEC. 4. The average amount of circulation outstanding, upon which the tax herein provided for shall be imposed, shall be the average amount of notes issued to the association and not held by, or in possession of, itself; and the highest amount outstanding in any month shall be taken in computing the average for the year.

SEC. 5. When the guarantee fund shall be equal to five per centum of the entire circulation of all the banks outstanding, the collection of the tax of one-half of one per centum per annum shall be suspended, but the same shall be resumed whenever the guarantee fund shall fall below five per centum, and it shall be continued until that amount is again accumulated. Said tax shall be collected in the manner now provided by law for the collection of the tax on the circulating notes of national banking associations.

SEC. 6. Whenever the insolvency of any national-banking association shall be ascertained in the manner provided by law, its outstanding circulating notes shall be redeemed by the Treasurer of the United States out of said guarantee fund, if the same shall be sufficient, and if not sufficient, then out of any money in the Treasury. As the proceeds of its assets, including the personal liabilities of shareholders, are paid into the Treasury by the receiver, in the manner now directed by law, before any dividend shall be paid to depositors or any other creditors of the bank, the guarantee fund shall receive a sum equal to the outstanding circulation of such insolvent national bank as far as the proceeds of such assets permit. And the United States shall be first paid out of said guarantee fund, when replenished, for all advances made in pursuance of this section.

SEC. 7. Associations applying for circulation after the first payments into the guarantee fund shall have been made may receive circulating notes from the Comptroller of the Currency upon paying into said fund a sum bearing the ratio to the circulation applied for and allowed which the guarantee fund bears to the total circulation outstanding, and shall be subject to the tax of one-half of one per centum per annum, as called for by the Treasurer of the United States for the creation and maintenance of this fund.

SEC. 8. The annual report of the Comptroller of the Currency to Congress shall embrace a statement showing the aggregate amount of money in the guarantee fund, the payments made into it during the year, the payments made out of it during the year, and the amounts, if any, advanced by the United States for the redemption of the notes of insolvent banking associations and the repayment thereof. It shall be the duty of the Treasurer of the United States to furnish the Comptroller such information as he may request, in writing, from time to time, for the purpose of preparing said statement.

SEC. 9. Whenever and so often as bank notes are issued to any association under the provisions of this act it shall be the duty of the Secretary of the Treasury to retire and cancel legal-tender United States notes and Treasury notes, to the amount of eighty per centum of the sum of bank notes so issued, as said legal-tender notes are received into the Treasury. And for this purpose he is authorized to use any surplus revenues from time to time in the Treasury not otherwise appropriated. If at any time the surplus revenues are not sufficient to enable the Secretary to carry out the provisions of this section, he shall resume the cancellation as soon as possible and continue it until the said eighty per centum of United States notes shall have been extinguished. If at any time the amount of legal-tender notes in the Treasury shall not be sufficient to enable the Secretary to carry out the provisione of this act, he shall so report to Congress, and shall resume the cancellation in ths ratio aforesaid as soon as practicable.

SEC. 10. Any association may retire its circulation, or any part thereof, at any time upon depositing with the Treasurer of the United States lawful money in amount equal to the sum desired to be withdrawn, and immediately upon such deposit all taxes shall cease upon the circulation so retired.

SEC. 11. In the event of the winding up of the business of an association by reason of insolvency, or otherwise, the Treasurer of the United States, with the concurrence of the Comptroller of the Currency, may, on the application of the directors, or of the liquidator, receiver, assignee, or other official, and upon being satisfied that proper arrangements have been made for the payment of the notes of the bank and any tax due thereon, pay over to such directors, liquidator, receiver, assignee, or other proper official the amount at the credit of the bank in the five per centum redemption fund.

SEC. 12. Section nine of the act of July twelfth, eighteen hundred and eighty two, entitled "An act to enable national banking associations to extend their corporate existence, and for other purposes" is hereby repealed. Any association heretofore organized, desiring to withdraw its circulating notes, in whole or in part, may do so under the provisions of section four of the act of June twentieth, eighteen hundred and seventy-four, entitled "An act fixing the amount of United States notes, providing for a redistribution of national-bank currency, and for other purposes;" but the clause of section four of said last-mentioned act, which provides "that the amount of the bonds on deposit for circulation shall not be reduced below fifty thousand dollars," is hereby repealed.

Mr. JOHNSON, of Ohio (to Mr. White). Are you familiar with Secretary Carlisle's plan?

Mr. WHITE. In a general way. I believe I have a copy of it in my pocket.

Mr. JOHNSON, of Ohio. Under that plan, limiting the circulation by a deposit of legal-tender notes, is it not a practicable thing to have the issuing power absolutely monopolized by the present national banks—that is, if $225,000,000 of greenbacks are deposited for the present amount of their notes?

Mr. WHITE. The greenbacks are put under a bushel, as I said.

Mr. JOHNSON, of Ohio. Yes, put under a bushel. This reserve of $225,000,000 or $250,000,000 could be held by the national banks without expense, so that new banks would be debarred from getting hold of legal-tender notes for the purpose of issuing circulation thereon. Could not the national banks thus, under the Secretary's plan, monopolize without any expense the issuing of national-bank currency—I mean the present banks with their present capital and present reserve?

Mr. WHITE. I suppose that new banks that desired to obtain currency could get gold and deposit it.

Mr. JOHNSON, of Ohio. The Secretary's plan does not provide for a reserve in gold.

Mr. WHITE. But the new banks could buy legal-tender notes with gold.

Mr. JOHNSON, of Ohio. But the old banks could absolutely refuse to dispose of their greenbacks.

Mr. WHITE. That is hardly supposable.

Mr. JOHNSON, of Ohio. My point was not whether it is likely, but whether it is not, in your judgment, a possible thing for the present banks to get hold of all the greenbacks and prevent new banks from getting currency?

Mr. WHITE. I think it may be physically possible.

Mr. JOHNSON, of Ohio. Do you believe that Mr. Carlisle's plan would furnish a flexible currency—an elastic currency—so that there would be an incentive to enlarge the currency when business interests so required and to contract it when business interests so required?

Mr. WHITE. No, sir; emphatically I do not. His plan requires the deposit of $30 for every $75 of national-bank notes.

Mr. JOHNSON, of Ohio. The incentive to enlarge the circulation is there, but there is no incentive to reduce it.

Mr. WHITE. My idea is that the lack of elasticity would result from the fact that a bank would be obliged to put up $30 every time that it issued $75 in bank notes. I do not think that there would be any elasticity in that way. As to the returning of the notes that is another question. I should say that the notes would return to the issuing banks when they were no longer needed.

Mr. JOHNSON, of Ohio. But an elastic currency is one which will accommodate itself to the needs of business.

Mr. WHITE. A currency which will expand and contract, according to business requirements, is an elastic currency.

Mr. JOHNSON, of Ohio. You do not think that the Secretary's plan furnishes such an elastic currency?

Mr. WHITE. I do not.

Mr. SPERRY. In what form of money does the Baltimore plan contemplate the redemption of notes?

Mr. WHITE. In the same way as now.

Mr. SPERRY. In any legal-tender money?

Mr. WHITE. Certainly, in any legal-tender money. The Baltimore plan is not an attempt to meddle with the legal-tender laws.

Mr. SPERRY. In your judgment, would it be best to have the redemption required in coin?

Mr. WHITE. Not until the Government money is all retired. I am opposed to any scheme for creating a premium on gold while your legal-tender money exists.

Mr. SPERRY. You think that the tendency of requiring coin redemption of national-bank notes would be to put a premium on gold?

Mr. WHITE. Yes. The minute that the Government makes a distinction between different kinds of money the public will do the same.

Mr. SPERRY. Would the notes issued under the Baltimore plan supply the place of other paper money?

Mr. WHITE. Only to the extent that there is a demand for them, over the Government issues. The Government issues are forced issues, and when there is a demand for more than the Government issues, the banks, under the Baltimore plan, will supply it.

Mr. SPERRY. Do you think that there is a tendency for every bank to inflate its own bills?

Mr. WHITE. It could not do it; it never could. I have studied that matter up from the bottom, beginning with the history of the Government, and I am convinced that a bank has no power to inflate with its own notes if it redeems them in specie.

Mr. SPERRY. You think, then, that the bills of all the national banks would circulate under the Baltimore plan the same as now?

Mr. WHITE. Yes; unless you change the law. The present law requires that all the banks receive the notes of every other bank.

Mr. SPERRY. Is that provided for under the Baltimore plan?

Mr. WHITE. The Baltimore plan does not disturb existing law in that particular.

Mr. SPERRY. It gives the legal-tender quality to bank notes.

Mr. WHITE. It makes them receivable for public dues, of course. They are not receivable for customs duties.

Mr. SPERRY. Supposing you took from the notes under the Baltimore plan that quality of legal tender, so that every bank would be compelled to receive the notes of every other bank?

Mr. WHITE. Then the notes would probably flow in for redemption faster than they do now, and the banks would be put to more expense in keeping their redemption fund full.

Mr. SPERRY. You mean the redemption fund in Washington?

Mr. WHITE. Yes.

Mr. SPERRY. But the bills would circulate just as widely as they do now, would they not?

Mr. WHITE. Yes, I think so; just as the Canadian bills do in their own country. The Canadian law requires that every bank shall have one redemption agency in every province of the Dominion.

Mr. SPERRY. If the banks were required to carry a coin reserve instead of a legal-tender reserve, would not the tendency be to drive the greenbacks into the country?

Mr. WHITE. I do not see why it should. The greenbacks are as good as gold.

Mr. SPERRY. If the Baltimore plan should require the national-bank notes to be redeemed in coin the banks would be required to keep a coin reserve?

Mr. WHITE. Yes.

Mr. SPERRY. But as they now redeem in greenbacks they are compelled to keep a greenback reserve?

Mr. WHITE. Yes.

Mr. SPERRY. If the national-bank currency were to be redeemed in coin would not the tendency of that be to drive greenbacks back into the Treasury?

Mr. WHITE. The Treasury is required to put them out again immediately.

Mr. SPERRY. But the banks would carry a coin reserve instead of a greenback reserve?

Mr. WHITE. Yes.

Mr. SPERRY. If the banks were to substitute coin as their reserve the $165,000,000 of greenbacks now held as a reserve would find their way back into the Treasury?

Mr. WHITE. They can only find their way back there by being taken in for taxes, and then the Government has got to spend them the next day for its expenses. I do not see the point of the inquiry.

Mr. SPERRY. The point of the inquiry was, that the greenbacks are now used as a reserve fund, and my suggestion was whether or not under the Baltimore plan national-bank notes would not take the place of the greenbacks as a circulating medium to a large extent, provided they were redeemable in coin instead of greenbacks?

Mr. WHITE. I do not think so, because silver certificates circulate everywhere, and they are not receivable for customs duties. There is a legal discrimination there, and yet the silver certificates go everywhere with perfect ease, so that I do not see why the greenbacks should not continue to do so.

Mr. WALKER. As I understand you, this bill which you have presented to the committee is submitted as your individual suggestion, to be acted on by the banking committee.

Mr. WHITE. It is a bill which I drew up as embodying my ideas of the Baltimore plan.

Mr. WALKER. If that bill were enacted into law would it, in your judgment, correct the financial and banking troubles of the country?

Mr. WHITE. I think it would have that tendency.

Mr. WALKER. It is not a question of tendencies, but I want to have your idea as to whether it would do so or not?

Mr. WHITE. I do not claim to be omniscient.

Mr. WALKER. I did not ask you to be omniscient, but I ask you whether it is your belief that it would do so?

Mr. WHITE. Yes.

Mr. WALKER. It is your belief that this bill would correct the financial troubles of the country?

Mr. WHITE. My belief is that it would create an elastic currency, but I do not undertake to say that it would cure all the ills of our financial system. I think it would tend to promote an elastic currency, and that is what the Baltimore plan aimed to do.

Mr. WALKER. Is that all that it aimed to do?

Mr. WHITE. I think so.

Mr. WALKER. Was that all the purpose of the bankers who met in Baltimore and formed the Baltimore plan—the purpose to create an elasticity of currency?

Mr. WHITE. That is my idea.

Mr. WALKER. Then it appears that the American bankers who met in Baltimore made no attempt to formulate any system which would correct the acknowledged evils of the financial system of this country?

Mr. WHITE. Except to create an elastic currency.

Mr. COBB, of Alabama. Without abandoning the element of uniformity and safety, of course?

Mr. WHITE. Yes.

The chairman suggested that questions by members of the committee should be made as pointed and brief as possible, the object being, he said, to obtain the views of gentlemen addressing the committee and not the views of members of the committee. But this remark, he said, did not apply, of course, to Mr. Walker.

Mr. WALKER (to Mr. White). I suppose that paper money, in order to be good money, must have the implicit confidence of the banking and commercial classes of the country, and the confidence of the people of the country and of the world that it shall be redeemed in coin?

Mr. WHITE. Yes; that is my idea.

Mr. WALKER. And the trouble to-day is that that is not the view entertained of our paper money?

Mr. WHITE. I said in my discourse that the business community was under the apprehension that the time might come when the Government would not be able to redeem its paper money in coin.

Mr. WALKER. And that is the feeling to-day?

Mr. WHITE. Yes; I think it is the feeling in this country and abroad—more especially abroad.

Mr. WALKER. Are you not absolutely of opinion that nothing can give this country a sound financial system that does not practically retire the greenbacks?

Mr. WHITE. Yes, sir; thoroughly.

Mr. WALKER. Does your bill demand that?

Mr. WHITE. Yes.

Mr. WALKER. Point out the section.

Mr. WHITE (reading). "Whenever, and as often as, bank notes are issued, it shall be the duty of the Secretary of the Treasury to retire and cancel legal-tender United States notes and Treasury notes to the amount of 80 per cent." That is copied from the resumption act of 1875.

Mr. WALKER. How is he going to do it?

Mr. WHITE. I will go on and read. (Reading.) "For that purpose he is authorized to use any surplus from time to time, * * * and if, at any time, the amount of legal-tender notes in the Treasury is not sufficient to enable the Secretary to carry out this act he is to report to Congress and to resume the cancellation as soon as possible."

Mr. WALKER. That proposition is based, of course, on the existing condition of the revenue laws and of the Treasury?

Mr. WHITE. Yes.

Mr. WALKER. And when we are having a deficiency every month of several millions of dollars? There is no immediate relief proposed in your bill?

Mr. WHITE. No, there is not.

Mr. WALKER. Then it is not complete for that reason. That is to say, there is no practical provision in your bill for the retirement of greenbacks and Treasury notes?

Mr. WHITE. No. I said in my discourse that I was in favor of having the greenbacks funded into bonds. I did not put that into the bill because I thought it quite improbable that any political party would agree to it at the present time.

Mr. WALKER. If no political party would agree to it, no political party will agree to take any substantial and effective steps to correct the existing evils of the currency.

Mr. WHITE. I am not so certain as to that. I think that if a bill were before the public to redeem greenbacks out of the revenues the public would be more likely to swallow that bill than one for issuing bonds.

Mr. WALKER. Is not the exigency such that when this committee met, and when your banking association met, the whole country rose and said they wanted the matter corrected at once?

Mr. WHITE. The emergency is no greater now than it has been for sixteen years past, but public opinion is more pressing.

Mr. WALKER. Do you not think that the exigency is greater than it has been, and that this matter is culminating?

Mr. WHITE. No, sir; I think that the exigency culminated by reason of your revenues being less than your expenditures. I think that that is what brought the misery on the Treasury.

Mr. WALKER. If there is no immediate prospect of, and if your bill does not provide for, immediate work in correcting this evil by retiring, practically, greenbacks and Treasury notes, do you not think that the bill which should be passed by this Congress ought to make it for the interest of the banks to assume the current redemption of the greenbacks and Treasury notes until such time as they can be retired?

Mr. WHITE. If you could make it for the interest of the banks to do it I suppose it would be desirable.

Mr. WALKER. If a plan could be reduced to law by which the banks could make more money than they do now in issuing currency notes, and also in assuming the current redemption of the greenbacks, is it your opinion that that plan ought to be adopted, and adopted at once?

Mr. WHITE. I do not know what currency notes are.

Mr. WALKER. Do you know what bank notes are?

Mr. WHITE. Yes; but you use two phrases, currency notes and bank notes, and that makes a distinction between them.

Mr. WALKER. My point is this: If a system could be devised under which the banks could make more money in issuing bank-note currency (promissory notes), plus their assuming the current redemption of greenbacks and the Treasury notes, do you not think that that plan ought to be adopted by Congress, if it is practicable and can be done?

Mr. WHITE. I would have to ask you what is meant by the banks redeeming greenbacks.

Mr. WALKER. I have not asked you that question.

Mr. WHITE. You spoke of the banks assuming the redemption of greenbacks.

Mr. WALKER. Yes; I mean if the banks could be induced to pay them in coin as they do a bank note. That is what I understand by current redemption. If it could be made to the interest of the banks so that they could issue notes against their own assets, and at the same time currently redeem all the existing Treasury notes and legal-tender notes—if that could be done, and if it could be made more profitable for the banks to do that than it is under the present system, do you not think that Congress should adopt that policy now?

Mr. WHITE. Not unless the greenbacks are to be canceled. If they are to be paid out again every day I would not be in favor of it.

Mr. WALKER. My idea is that greenbacks are canceled every time that they are redeemed in coin.

Mr. WHITE. I do not understand cancellation to be redeeming a note to-day and paying it out to-morrow.

Mr. WALKER. When a bank note is paid into a bank and redeemed in coin the practical effect of that is the same as if that bank note were burned up and another bank note issued in its place.

Mr. WHITE. Yes; I understand that; the bank not being responsible.

Mr. WALKER. But my idea is that the bank should be responsible, and that the greenbacks and Treasury notes which are assigned to each particular bank should be marked with the name for each bank.

Mr. WHITE. That would make such a complicated plan that I would not undertake to give an off hand opinion about it.

Mr. WALKER. Is it complicated if a bank takes from the Government $50,000 in bank notes, which it itself must redeem (precisely as it redeems them now), and at the same time is obliged to deposit $50,000 in lawful money, and it is stamped on the back of these notes with red ink that the bank agrees to redeem those bills so marked? That is very simple and very practical, and these notes are just as easily identified as the notes of the bank. Now, if it were made to the interest of the banks, so that the banks would make more money by disposing of all the greenbacks and Treasury notes, would you not think it advisable?

Mr. WHITE. No; I would not.

The CHAIRMAN. The chair requests that members will confine their questions as far as possible to the matter immediately before the committee.

Mr. WALKER. As that is a criticism on my questions——

The CHAIRMAN. Not at all.

Mr. WALKER. My point was to show the defects of the Baltimore plan and the excellences of it.

Mr. HALL (to Mr. White). I understood you to make the statement that under the plan suggested by the Secretary of the Treasury there was no elasticity of the currency provided for.

Mr. WHITE. I did not say quite that. I said that I thought that a requirement to put $30 of greenbacks under a bushel every time that $75 of notes are issued was not consistent with elasticity. I say it would be more elastic than it would be to require $114 to be put up for every $100 taken out. It would be more elastic by the difference between $30 and $114. That is all that I meant to say.

Mr. HALL. The provisions in the Baltimore plan look to the issue of circulating notes to the amount of 50 per cent of the paid-up and unimpaired stock of a bank. The plan advocated by the Secretary of the Treasury provides for the issue of bank notes not to exceed 75 per cent of the capital stock of a bank, and requires a deposit of 30 per cent in greenbacks or in the Treasury notes of 1890. What is the difference between these two plans on the point of elasticity.

Mr. WHITE. Just this: A bank is disabled to the amount of $30 which it put up for exercising the right of issuing notes to the amount of $75.

Mr. HALL. You take the position that it is very important, on account of the gold being drained out of the Treasury by the bucket chain process now going on, to get the greenbacks where they can no longer be drained out of the Treasury. Under the Baltimore plan, as set forth in the circular issued from Baltimore, is there any way to stop that flow from the Treasury?

Mr. WHITE. No, sir; there is not.

Mr. HALL. Is it not better, in the present condition of things, to adopt the plan of the Secretary which, as you express it, puts the greenbacks under a bushel—covers up 30 per cent of them—and prevents them from being used as a drain on the Treasury for its gold?

Mr. WHITE. I ought to have stated perhaps (and my idea of the drain on the Treasury is this) that it is caused by a deficiency of revenue and not by the redemption and re-redemption of greenbacks, because that system has been going on for sixteen years and we never found any difficulty about it until the revenues of the Government fell below its expenditures.

Mr. HALL. I understood you to say that so long as the greenbacks were outstanding they were a menace, and tended to impair the public credit?

Mr. WHITE. Yes; by acting on the imaginations of men; not otherwise.

Mr. HALL. Would it not be well to put that menace under a bushel instead of leaving it, as you do in the Baltimore plan, out in the public gaze?

Mr. WHITE. Of the two methods I should prefer that most which would produce a surplus in the Treasury. That would very largely remove the menace which now acts on the imaginations of men. They see a deficit of $69,000,000 in one year and the draining of the gold reserve in consequence of that. That condition of things must necessarily act on the imagination of the public and lead many to apprehend disaster.

Mr. WARNER. You mentioned the subject of a tax on State-bank circulation. Does not any tax on bank circulation tend to restrict the elasticity of the currency and increase the rate of interest?

Mr. WHITE. Just the same as a tax on any business does. England levies a tax on Bank of England notes.

Mr. WARNER. Would not the requirement to put up 30 per cent or any other percentage of greenbacks or of any other securities, in order to issue national-bank notes, have the same effect? That is to say, that it would be a practical tax on circulation, and would increase the rate of interest and result in a loss of elasticity?

Mr. WHITE. Yes; I think so.

Mr. WARNER. Then, as compared with your own suggestion—of funding the greenbacks into Government obligations, to be paid either now or some time by taxation—does not any plan which involves the depositing of Treasury notes as a condition of circulation involve a tax on the borrower in the shape of an increase of interest?

Mr. WHITE. Yes; indirectly that would be the effect of it.

Mr. WARNER. You referred to the fact that if similar requirements were put on State-bank circulation that are put on national-bank circulation the notes of State banks would be made equally safe. What did you mean by that?

Mr. WHITE. There is a clause in the national banking law which allows any State bank to come into the national banking system to-morrow and avail itself of all the privileges of the national banking law.

Mr. WARNER. By becoming a national bank?

Mr. WHITE. Yes. I do not think it possible to have the State banks and national banks subject to two jurisdictions at the same time. What is going to happen when a State bank goes into insolvency? Can the Comptroller of the Currency do anything about it? He can only sit back and observe what somebody else does, but the moment he attempts to do anything himself he comes in conflict with State laws.

Mr. WARNER. As we have just made a treaty with Japan recognizing that its laws are those of a civilized nation, we might recognize that the laws of a State are on the same parity. As to the question whether, under the Secretary's plan, it would be possible for the present national banks to monopolize the circulation without any expense to themselves, I ask you is it not true that the suggestion of a premium on greenbacks would involve an expense to those banks if they did not sell their greenbacks and take advantage of the premium?

Mr. WHITE. I should think so.

Mr. WARNER. Is it true that it would allow them to monopolize the circulation without expense to themselves?

Mr. WHITE. All that I can say is that it might do so. That is one of those rather complicated questions in finance which can only be determined satisfactorily by experiment.

Mr. WARNER. If the banks held the greenbacks, and still continued to hold them after they were at a premium, would not that involve expense to them?

Mr. WHITE. Yes; of course.

Mr. WARNER. And could not any other party enjoy the same advantages that the banks had by taking greenbacks at par?

Mr. BROSIUS. I understand that you think that if there is a necessity for getting rid of the entire issue of greenbacks the preferable way to do it would be to issue low-rate bonds, for the purpose of redeeming them and getting rid of them in that way, rather than putting them under a bushel?

Mr. WHITE. Decidedly.

Mr. BROSIUS. Do you think that the chief difficulties which now afflict our people arise from a Treasury deficit, rather than from any imperfection in our existing banking system?

Mr. WHITE. I think that the immediate trouble lies in the Treasury deficit; but the chronic trouble lies in the other direction.

Mr. BROSIUS. Then does your system or the Baltimore system relieve the difficulties which proceed from a Treasury deficit?

Mr. WHITE. The Baltimore plan attempts to cure the chronic trouble, not the immediate trouble.

Mr. BROSIUS. The Secretary of the Treasury, in his report, in stating the conditions which now afflict the country classifies them as follows: First, the frequent presentation for redemption in gold by individuals and institutions; second, the foreign exchange being at the rate which makes it more profitable to export gold than to purchase bills of exchange, and thirdly, the vast accumulation at our financial centers and the general depression of business. I want to know whether the Baltimore plan, or your plan, or any other plan that you have cognizance of, is calculated to mitigate the evils arising from that condition of things so distinctly stated by the Secretary?

Mr. WHITE. I think not.

Mr. BROSIUS. After you have attained all the safety and security possible for making the assets of the bank liable for the redemption of its notes, is there not still a residue of risk which must follow somewhere of the bank note not being redeemed at all?

Mr. WHITE. Yes.

Mr. BROSIUS. Do you not think that it promotes the efficiency of the bank notes and the public good by satisfying the public mind of the safety of bank notes to have the Government of the United States take that possible or speculative risk rather than to let it fall on the note holder himself?

Mr. WHITE. Certainly I do, and I stated that most emphatically in my discourse.

Mr. COX. Speaking of the State-bank system, if you were to put the same restrictions, limitations, and requirements on the State banks as are put on the national banks there would be no necessity for State banks at all?

Mr. WHITE. No; there would not be.

Mr. COX. But suppose you say, by proper legislation, that unless the State banks do certain things they shall be subject to the tax, but that in case they do the things required of them the tax will be released; and suppose you confer jurisdiction upon the Government of the United States to collect the tax if the banks do not comply with the requirements, but that if they do comply with the requirements the Government of the United States has got nothing to do with them; what would be the objection to that?

Mr. WHITE. The difficulty is this. A bank complies with the requirements to day; the Comptroller of the Currency looks over the papers and says, "Yes; you have complied with those requirements;" but the bank does not comply with them to-morrow. What, then, is the Comptroller to do? You say he is to tax the bank, but the bank, in the meantime, may have gone to pot.

Mr. COX. If a State bank issues its notes to-day it is subject to the tax, but does the Government go every day to collect the tax?

Mr. WHITE. No.

Mr. COX. Would not the banks be subject to the enforcement of the tax if they violated the requirements, just like any other tax imposed upon any privilege or right?

Mr. WHITE. Yes.

Mr. JOHNSON, of Indiana. I understand your position to be this: That if the currency and banking system is to be revised, it is simpler and safer to have one uniform system under Federal control than to undertake the experiment of two systems, one under Federal control and one under State control.

Mr. WHITE. I am in favor of one system. The second system would be really forty-five systems.

The committee took a recess till 2 p. m.

AFTER RECESS.

The CHAIRMAN. Mr. Ellis, of Kentucky, desires the chair to recall Mr. White, as he desires to submit a question to him.

Mr. WALKER. Mr. White had not concluded his testimony. He simply stood aside so that Mr. Carlisle might go on. I suppose there are a number of gentlemen here who would like to further interrogate Mr. White.

The CHAIRMAN. The chair understood that Mr. White had concluded his statement, but if gentlemen desire to interrogate him further they can do so.

Mr. ELLIS. Mr. White, I understood you to state this morning that you had examined the plan proposed by the Secretary of the Treasury?

Mr. WHITE. Yes; I have in a cursory way.

Mr. ELLIS. I wish to call your attention to one view of that plan, and ask your opinion upon it. It is section 5 of the bill, I believe, as he has prepared it. His plan proposes that notes may be issued by national banks to the amount of 75 per cent of their paid-up and unimpaired capital, but before issuing such notes they will be required to put up 30 per cent. The bill also provides for a safety fund which shall amount to as much, perhaps, as 5 per cent. Then, in the case of a failed bank, it is provided that this guaranty fund, this 30 per cent, shall be transferred to the safety fund, and that out of that the notes of failed banks shall be paid; if that is not sufficient to satisfy the notes of failed banks, then the deficiency shall be made up by assessment upon all of the banks that have entered into the scheme. Now, the question which I wish to ask you is this: What, in your opinion, would be the effect of such provision as that? If every national bank is to be the guarantor of the notes of any other national bank in the country, would this system be acceptable? Would it be profitable, or would it be practicable, in your judgment?

Mr. WHITE. I think most of the banks would at first decline to enter into the system; but I think also that the wiser ones would immediately see that the redemption fund there would be far in excess of any amount that would ever be called for, and, therefore, probably they would come in gradually. But still I think their inclination at first would be to stay out.

Mr. ELLIS. There would be, you think, a disposition on the part of the banks to refuse to become guarantors of the notes of other banks.

Mr. WHITE. Yes; I think so. The Canadian system provides that the banks may be assessed for the deficiencies of failed banks, but not in excess of 1 per cent in any one year. An arrangement of that kind would be, I think, very satisfactory in this country. People would see the amount of loss in any year, and they would look at the assets and see that the fund applicable to the payment of the notes of failed banks would probably be in excess of the demands made upon it and they would come in. But if it were required that they should be responsible for the whole amount in every case, then I think there would be more hesitation.

Mr. WALKER. At once responsible, I suppose you mean?

Mr. ELLIS. Yes; that is the provision of this bill, that they become at once responsible. (To Mr. White): Is it your opinion that if such a provision were incorporated into a banking system it would be a success?

Mr. WHITE. I should be very doubtful about it.

STATEMENT OF CHARLES C. HOMER.

Mr. Charles C. Homer, of Baltimore, was introduced by the chairman to the committee, and made the following statement:

Mr. Chairman, I might preface my remarks by stating that I did not know what might be required of me here; and that, consequently, I have not prepared any special or set address to deliver before you. I inferred that the object of my citation was to explain to you, as far as lay within my power, the features of the Baltimore plan.

I would say to you that the projectors of the Baltimore plan have had no intention of formulating a general financial scheme which would grapple with all of the confusing elements that now exist in our national finances. It was simply our intention to create a plan which would cure, or tend to cure, the chronic conditions that have arisen in our country in the past, and with which we will no doubt be met in the future; and, for the purpose of so improving and so perfecting the national banking system by providing it with amendments that this system, which is, I think, universally acknowledged as the best system that any country has ever had, may be able to grapple with those difficulties which it has been only partially able to meet in the past.

The first requisite of a bank note is that it be secure. We have in our plan made the assertion that a bank note may be secure without a bond deposited for its guarantor. We have established this fact by statistics, and the arguments produced have been so convincing that the reception of this innovation upon the national banking system has been a matter of great gratification and satisfaction to its projectors.

For nearly thirty years we have lived under the impression that no note could be absolutely secure unless there were held a Government bond of equal or more value, or some other bond of a like comparative value, as its sponsor. This idea has been removed, and the plan carries with it not only the indorsement and the assent of the leading advanced thinkers upon matters of finance, but it has, to our gratification and pleasure, received the indorsement of the highest financial executive officers of our Government.

The second requisite for a good bank note is uniformity. It must have for its basis of credit a uniform system of safeguards, of legal protections thrown around it, of uniform examinations looking to the assets upon which its credit is based, and a uniform supervision by the Department as to the compliance of the officers of the institutions with the requirements imposed by law; and, above everything else, in my judgment, one head to give uniform interpretations to the laws as constructed, in order that the same condition of affairs, the same decisions, the same rulings, the same determinations may meet each and every institution in whatever part of our country it may be located. We feel, no matter if the same universal law be applied to all of the States, that the interpretation of that law in forty-four or more different States will not have the same uniform effect and will not provide us with the same uniform safeguard that the one positive interpretation of that law by the Comptroller of the Currency would have.

It was, furthermore, our intention to so amend and to so broaden the national banking act that its doors would be open to each and every individual, to each and every corporation, which felt that the requirements of his or its locality, or self-interest through profit, made it necessary to have circulation.

We have endeavored to obliterate the feeling that has existed with reference to the national banks as enjoying advantages over State banking institutions, and I think, from the correspondence that I have had upon this subject with gentlemen at the head of leading State institutions of our country, that among the thinking classes where they have intelligently investigated the trend of our amendments, they see that the barrier, or the jealousy, or whatever it may be termed, between State banks and national banks, under our suggestion, is purely imaginative and will disappear.

If it be the wish of the committee I will hurriedly take up the leading sections of the Baltimore plan. I repeat that I have not prepared any notes, and if I should grow tiresome upon any portion of it I will esteem it a favor if I am promptly stopped.

Section 1 is the provision for repealing the requirement of a deposit of bonds. It has been demonstrated beyond question that the best asset a bank can have for the redemption of circulation is its bills receivable maturing daily and being paid daily, furnishing the ready means more quickly perhaps for the purpose of redeeming its notes than would be offered by the possession of bonds seeking an uncertain market.

Section 2 provides for the issue of 50 per cent of circulation under ordinary conditions, with a proviso for an increase of 25 per cent when emergencies justifying shall arise. Our statistical research demonstrated the fact that a certain part of a good bank-note circulation is in a constant condition of absorption by the public; that there is a certain portion of that circulation to which the term of elasticity or nonelasticity is hardly applicable. It is in daily, in constant use. It is deposited in bank and is only a temporary withdrawal from the uses of commerce. It comes in to-day, it goes out to-morrow. The manufacturer deposits with us to-day a large sum. His pay day being to-morrow, he withdraws it again for his business purposes. We are simply the custodians of it. It has not served its entire usefulness, and the simple fact of its redeposit in bank does not establish the fact that it is no longer needed by the community.

We have felt that the elasticity of this part of our currency would be supplied by ordinary redemptions, constantly going on from day to day. As the Secretary of the Treasury stated in his remarks yesterday, they aggregate millions of dollars daily—we will say a million a day. We think this withdrawal would provide the elasticity desired or that might be required for that portion of our currency (the 50 per cent issue) which we permit under a nominal tax.

We have felt, furthermore, drinking experience largely from the panics of 1873, 1883, and 1893, that the clearing-house certificate performs an effective service in staying the damaging effects of panics. We have placed that portion of our circulation under a heavy tax for the simple purpose that each and every bank, urged by the payment of this tax, would adopt the promptest means for so shaping the affairs of its customers and those dependent upon it, as well as its own condition, as to secure a prompt withdrawal of this circulation after it had served its purposes.

There was a considerable difference of opinion at one time with reference to the matter of taxation, and I think, borrowing an idea which appeared in the plan of the chairman of this committee, we considered the question of a graduated tax for the matter of emergency circulation. It was finally determined that the line of departure between the ordinary and the emergency circulation should be very sharply marked, in order that the conditions might be restored to their normal state as promptly as possible. A graduated tax for a part of the use of this extraordinary circulation would not be so effective, in our judgment, as a sharp and severe tax the moment we entered into an unnatural condition of affairs, and that it would be the aim and object of each and everyone to get back to the normal condition as promptly as possible.

It has been stated that this large tax which we proposed to impose upon the emergency circulation would have to be borne by the unfortunate whose condition compelled him to borrow this money of the banks. I can only speak in this respect for our own city. I do not know of a single case, of my own knowledge, in Baltimore where more than 6 per cent was exacted from any customer by a bank during the year 1893. The tax of the clearing-house certificates, which was 6 per cent in Baltimore, was cheerfully borne by the bank availing itself of their use for the purpose of tiding the distressed depositor over his difficulties.

The next section simply refers to the tax for the purpose of defraying the expenses. A subclause of that section states that the excess over one-half of 1 per cent of the tax imposed upon the emergency circulation shall be paid into the guarantee fund referred to in section 6. The object of inserting this was that, of course, in such times and with such an increase of circulation, the risk to which the guarantee fund which we have provided was set out against would be increased naturally, and that whatever might arise from the extra tax imposed upon this circulation should be turned into the guarantee fund as an extra insurance risk, in order to offset the extraordinary demands that might arise against it through any failures during such critical periods.

The banks issuing circulation shall continue the 5 per cent redemption fund as we have at present. I think I am correct in stating that the experience of the national banking system has demonstrated the fact that 5 per cent upon the circulation outstanding, deposited in the hands of the Treasurer, has always proved more than ample to meet the redemption of national-bank bills. I believe that there has always been a large idle fund in the hands of the Government for the purposes of making these redemptions, and that the provision of 5 per cent which we have retained is ample for the purpose for which it was created.

The fifth section states that the redemption of the notes of all banks, solvent or insolvent, is to be made as provided for in the existing law, i. e., Government redemption. We have felt, that in order to establish a strictly uniform currency, and a currency in which the note holder might have the very fullest confidence, the redemption of all national-bank notes should be continued as at present by the Secretary of the Treasury. To protect the Treasury upon this score we, in section 6, create a guarantee fund, by which we require the deposit the first year of 2 per cent, and then an annual tax of one-half of 1 per cent, to be continued until this guarantee fund shall reach 5 per cent upon the outstanding circulation; to be then suspended, to be resumed, however, when impaired through the redemption of the notes of any failed banks.

Taking the national-bank capital of to-day to be in round numbers $700,000,000, the average national-bank circulation outstanding (50 per cent) would be $350,000,000. A guarantee fund (5 per cent upon that amount) would be $17,500,000. Investing this sum, as suggested by the Secretary of the Treasury this morning, at 3 per cent would yield an annual income to that fund of $525,000.

The records of the Comptroller's Department show that in the first thirty years of the history of the national banks the entire loss that would have befallen this fund, had there been no bond for the protection of the note holder, would have amounted to $953,000, a little more than $30,000 per annum.

With an income, after investing, of $525,000 and with a liability only averaging $30,000 per annum, it strikes me that there can be no question as to the sufficiency of the guarantee fund which we have established.

Mr. WALKER. How much is the guarantee fund?

Mr. HOMER. $17,500,000 invested at 3 per cent would yield $525,000 per annum.

The next clause of that section provides for the redemption of the notes of failed banks by the Treasurer of the United States out of the guarantee fund, if it shall be sufficient, and if not sufficient, then out of any money in the Treasury, the same to be reimbursed to the Treasury out of the guarantee fund when replenished, either from the assets of the failed banks or from the tax aforesaid.

I think I have demonstrated with sufficient clearness that there can hardly ever arise a condition of affairs whereby the Government will be called upon to use any other funds in the redemption of the notes of failed banks than that which the banks themselves have provided in the creation of the guarantee fund.

The next section provides, with reference to the contribution of national-bank organizations started after this plan shall have been in operation—that is so equitable that it requires no explanation and no argument—they shall pay into the guarantee fund a sum bearing the ratio to the circulation applied for and allowed that the guarantee fund bears to the circulation outstanding, and shall then be subject to the tax of one-half of 1 per cent per annum, as called for by the Treasurer of the United States, for the creation and maintenance of this fund.

The next clause, which the Secretary of the Treasury has adopted in his plan, is that no association or individual shall have any claim upon any part of the money in said guarantee fund except for the redemption of the circulating notes of any insolvent national banking association, and that any surplus or residue of any such guarantee fund shall enure to the benefit of the United States.

Our purpose in providing that section was to prevent any bank from carrying upon its books as an asset its interest in this guarantee fund, and we were led still more into the adoption of this plan because after the dismemberment of the New York State guarantee fund there was endless litigation among the banks and with the State as to the ownership and the interest of the fund. So it was a question that we wished to set at once and forever at rest. It was a contribution to a fund for a specific purpose, and after that purpose had been accomplished it should no longer be a part of an asset of any bank, but should enure to the Government and belong to the Government absolutely and beyond question.

The next section is the one covering the prior lien upon the assets. It has been very fully discussed here.

The next section refers to the retirement of its circulating notes by a bank, at any time, upon depositing with the Treasurer of the United States lawful money equal in amount to the sum desired to be withdrawn. That is the existing law, without any change.

The ninth section refers to the winding up of a bank, and is taken verbatim from the Canadian law. It says that in the event of the winding up of the business of a bank by reason of insolvency or otherwise, the Treasurer of the United States, with the concurrence of the Comptroller of the Currency, may, on the application of the directors, or of the liquidator, receiver, assignee, or other proper official, and upon being satisfied that a proper arrangement has been made for the payment of the notes of the bank and any tax due thereon, pay over to such directors, liquidator, receiver, assignee, or other proper officials the amount to the credit of the bank in the redemption fund indicated in section 4.

This refers only to the redemption fund, not to the guarantee fund.

I think I have now given you a hurried review of the various sections of the Baltimore plan.

I approach the plan of the Secretary of the Treasury with a great deal of hesitancy and diffidence, because he is the highest financial officer of our Government. But there are some features of it that my own experience and observation as a bank man can hardly permit me to assent to.

He requires a deposit of 30 per cent in the guarantee fund, in addition to the 5 per cent established by the Baltimore plan.

I can not find that this demand is anywhere warranted by past experience. Of course we know the motive. It is to relieve the Government from the responsibility of the redemption of a large portion of its own notes. I feel that the manly course of the Government, as it is of the individual, is to redeem its paper when it is looked at shyly, in order to retain its credit.

Section 5 states that no national bank shall issue notes of a less denomination than $10. Per se, this is not objectionable, but it forces upon the people, in their interchange through business, an unnecessary burden, as anyone who has carried around with him a pocketful of silver can testify to as well as I can.

In section 6 the Secretary suggests that each national bank redeem its notes at its office or through its agencies designated by it. I believe the central redemption of national-bank notes, as it has been in vogue for the past thirty years, has given us ample proof that this is a perfectly businesslike and proper method for the redemption of national-bank circulation.

If the Secretary is correctly reported in his discourse before you yesterday, he made the statement that the redemption by the Government of the circulation of national banks was a tying up of money. Upon this head I can not agree with him. On the contrary, there is no tying up of money, but there is an untying of money, because the very money with which the Secretary redeems the circulation of bank notes has already been deposited and placed in his hands for that special and specific purpose, in the 5 per cent redemption fund. A constant redemption of national-bank notes over the counter of each and every bank, or through its agency, would be a much more serious tying up of the circulating medium of our country than the redemption arrangement in existence to-day. Our currency would be locked up in the express offices. As it is now, we carry it to the subtreasury, or to the Treasury, and we receive at once for it a medium to take the place of that which we have deposited.

Another feature that might be stated in objection to this is, Would it not be a hardship to first require the banks to deposit 30 per cent of lawful money as a guarantee fund for the payment and redemption of their paper, depriving them of so much of a ready and available asset, and then compel them, in addition to that, to redeem their notes over their own counter or through their agencies? We are stripping them of a part of the very thing which now insures prompt redemption of a bank note the moment it is presented at a bank counter.

With reference to the assumption by the banks of the circulation ultimately of all national banks, I would state that I fear any such provision in the law might lead to hesitancy on the part of the most conservatively managed institution. The clause practically establishes a copartnership of one bank with the other, without any voice in the management or control of the institution whose paper it is bound to pay. No wise business man would enter into such a copartnership with an unlimited liability.

It is one of the features that we have built upon, in the redemption of the notes by the Secretary of the Treasury, that the interest of the Government in the final redemption of the bank bill, although it is only a technical responsibility, is of such a character as to insure, on the part of the Comptroller of the Currency, a very rigid supervision and control over the banks which enjoy the benefit of the circulation. We have in the Comptroller of the Currency a strong ally for the protection of each and every one of us who has entered and who will enter into that copartnership. But to permit the bank to issue the circulation (without any desire to reflect) through mismanagement, through bad judgment on the part of the Comptroller in the selection of his staff of examiners and assistants, would rob this plan of one of the chief safeguards upon which we have relied in establishing the guarantee fund. I feel that under proper management, under proper supervision, the safety fund which we have created is so much more ample to protect the Government from any loss whatever in the redemption, and in the responsibility for redemption, of failed notes, that there is only a naked risk depending upon that guarantee.

With reference to the Secretary's provisions for State bank circulation, I have always felt that if we surrounded and required of the State bank desiring circulation the same safeguards, the same compliance with the law, the same deposit and securities, the same supervision, examination, and publication of reports, etc., there would be practically nothing left of the State bank except the shell; that it would be a national bank in all of its features; and if we can so frame the national-bank law that the currency of this country will be uniform, we shall have accomplished a great step forward and shall have supplied a currency that will be, as it has been in the past, good everywhere within the boundary and beyond the boundary of our country. If we do not exact from the State banks all of these safeguards and conditions we at once establish two kinds of currency, and I think that the education of our people in the matter of bank notes during the past thirty years has been such that they will hardly sanction retrogression. It is not necessary now to scrutinize any bill that we may receive. We know that it is good, and it is accepted without question.

With reference to the exemption from taxation, etc., to be granted on State bank circulation, of course it is a discrimination. I do not wish to discuss that point.

With that, gentlemen, I think I have finished.

Mr. WARNER. You suggest that the banks would shrink from the unlimited liability, which you compared to that of a copartnership, for circulation. Why, then, should not the Government shrink from it?

Mr. HOMER. Because the Government has the active control and supervision over those banks. Without that rigid scrutiny on the part of the Government the field is open for the creation of banks for questionable purposes, for the issuance of circulation upon which the entire national banking system would at once become responsible.

Mr. WARNER. Would it be proper to sum up your suggestion in this way: That in your belief the Comptroller of the Currency would exercise a sharper and more effective supervision if the Government were ultimately liable than if the banks were ultimately liable?

Mr. HOMER. It would.

Mr. WARNER. That is your position?

Mr. HOMER. Yes.

Mr. WARNER. Then the only extent to which the liability of the banks, from which they would, as you believe, shrink, and the liability of the Government, which you suggest it should assume, is the difference between the extent and the effectiveness of the supervision which the Comptroller of the Currency would be apt to exercise in the one case, as compared with the other?

Mr. HOMER. That is my view.

Mr. JOHNSON, of Indiana. Public confidence in this matter is absolutely vital?

Mr. HOMER. It is.

Mr. JOHNSON, of Indiana. Is it not more likely that the public will have confidence in this matter if it thinks the Government is ultimately liable than if the public feels that the Government is simply a mere custodian of the bank assets for the payment of these notes?

Mr. HOMER. It is.

Mr. WARNER. Upon the question of redemption, do I understand that it is your idea that the normal redemption, under the system you propose, shall be through the Bureau here at Washington, as it is now?

Mr. HOMER. Well, at Washington and the subtreasuries throughout the country.

Mr. WARNER. Practically as it is now?

Mr. HOMER. Practically as it is now. There is no change suggested.

Mr. WARNER. Is it not the case, however, that, as compared with what you might call normal redemption—if each bank were required to redeem its bills over its own counter, without any obligation on any other bank to receive any bills other than its own—the system you propose would be very much less effective, and that redemption would be very much less prompt in case of a lack of demand on the part of the business of the country?

Mr. HOMER. The currency drifts to the financial centers. The financial centers relieve themselves by depositing their national-bank notes with the subtreasury. That at once calls for the deposit of lawful money by the banks whose currency has been redeemed by the Secretary of the Treasury, and the notes are retired from circulation. If they can be used again in that locality, well and good; otherwise, they remain in the vaults of the banks.

Mr. WARNER. As a matter of fact, however, are not the amounts of redemptions and the rate of redemption very small under the present system, as compared with what they were and would be under any system leaving each bank simply to redeem its own currency? In your opinion, is not redemption very small under the present system, as compared to what it used to be under the Suffolk system?

Mr. HOMER. Yes; it is small. There was this feature under the Suffolk system: The Suffolk system required the daily redemption of notes. It prohibited the issuance, by any bank, of any note except its own. Applying this locally, it might prove very effective and beneficial. Spreading it out, however, throughout the entire country, would, in a very short time, create a currency famine such as has been unheard of in this country. The currency would be found in express offices, in transit from one point of the country to another, and we would have for use simply a few of our own notes that might come to us over our own counter. There would be, in my judgment, a vast tying up of currency for exchange medium by requiring the whole country to submit to the daily redemption of its circulation.

Mr. WARNER. In other words, if I understand you correctly, the Suffolk bank system, or the natural redemption system, would leave currency much more elastic, but in your view it might bring about a famine which would more than make up for the advantages?

Mr. HOMER. Yes.

Mr. WARNER. But the system which you propose is defective, so far as the one point of elasticity is concerned, when compared with the other system.

Mr. HOMER. Of course there is not the same elasticity about a note that is redeemed only at the central bureau without the requirement of a daily redemption.

Mr. WARNER. Your system is less elastic in that particular than the natural system of redemption?

Mr. HOMER. The point, I think, is stated in the explanation of the various clauses of the Baltimore plan, that a certain part of the circulation is in constant absorbtion—that is, in use—and does not require the elasticity or inelasticity to be applied to its whole volume, but only a certain portion of it.

Mr. JOHNSON, of Indiana. Your plan contemplates that the existing national bank law shall continue intact, except as it is altered or repealed by it.

Mr HOMER. It is a continuation of the national banking act, with the substitution of a lien upon assets for bond deposit.

Mr. JOHNSON, of Indiana. Therefore, each bank under your system would receive the notes of other banks?

Mr. HOMER. Oh, yes.

Mr. WALKER. I understand, from what was said by Mr. White, that the only item in what is known as the Baltimore plan that would affect the general finances of the country, aside from what the banks have looked out for in their own interests, is the provision that the surplus revenues shall be used to retire the Treasury notes?

Mr. HOMER. No, sir; we have not entered into any question with reference to national finances at all. Our aim has been to cure and correct the defects in the national banking system. We have not grappled with that problem of finances.

Mr. WALKER. So that this convention of the bankers of the country has considered nothing except their own immediate banking business and what would benefit that business?

Mr. HOMER. Yes; we had no discussions, no conferences.

Mr. WALKER. Your deliberations were confined wholly to those provisions of existing law, and the provisions that you would like to have exist in the law, which would benefit the banking interests of the country?

Mr. HOMER. No; there were other things we should like to have had.

Mr. WALKER. Not what you would like to have had, but what your scheme embraces.

Mr. HOMER. Well, we felt——

Mr. WALKER. No; not what you felt, but what you desired to get out of the scheme.

Mr. JOHNSON, of Ohio. I submit, Mr. Chairman, that it is unfair to interrupt the gentleman when he is answering.

Mr. HOMER. The scheme simply embraces the perfection of the national banking system.

Mr. WALKER. The perfection of the national banking system with reference to the interest of the banks?

Mr. HOMER. The interest of the banks is the interest of the public.

Mr. WALKER. The interest of the public was secondary, but the interest of the banks, as they desired, was primary.

Mr. HOMER. That may be the feeling in some sections, but I do not think that it is so in ours. We are very closely allied in Baltimore; the banks and the depositors are stanch friends and allies.

Mr. WALKER. You have said that you did not grapple with any of the evils of the present financial conditions.

Mr. HOMER. Yes.

Mr. WALKER. That you did not grapple or attempt to grapple with any of them except this one.

Mr. HOMER. We confined ourselves to the national banking act.

Mr. WALKER. Do you think the difficulties connected with the national-bank act as such were what caused or aggravated the panic of 1893?

Mr. HOMER. No, sir; but the national-banking act, as it now is, is so constructed that it was not able to grapple with the extraordinary demands that were hurled upon it by the events of 1893.

Mr. WALKER. What was the source of those demands?

Mr. HOMER. It was the panicky feeling of the country.

Mr. WALKER. What did that arise from?

Mr. HOMER. It arose largely from the fear, in my judgment, that the Government would not be able to maintain its gold redemption of all its obligations.

Mr. WALKER. Then it comes to this: That we cannot have a safe currency system, a safe monetary system, until there is a correction of this relation of the affairs of the Treasury to the finances and banking of the country.

Mr. HOMER. I think that is very necessary.

Mr. WALKER. Do you not think that the very primary thing that these bankers ought to grapple with in this case, they being trained men, should have been the whole question of the finances of the country?

Mr. HOMER. We should have met with very little encouragement, perhaps, if we had attempted the solution of the entire question.

Mr. WALKER. Do you think there is any body of men in all the country better qualified to do so than they?

Mr. HOMER. I should not like to say that there is not.

Mr. WALKER. Is it presumable that there is a body of men better qualified?

Mr. HOMER. Hardly.

Mr. WALKER. It seems that your organization looked, first, to the requisite of a bank note that should be secure.

Mr. HOMER. Yes.

Mr. WALKER. Do you think that you have added to the security of the circulating bank notes of the country as to their ultimate redemption, by your system, over the present system of using United States bonds?

Mr. HOMER. No; but I think we have established a security just as good.

Mr. WALKER. But you have not improved it?

Mr. HOMER. No; it can not be improved, unless you say there can be something better than our Government bonds.

Mr. WALKER. In the second place, have you made any progress toward making the currency of the country any more uniform than the national-bank currency now is?

Mr. HOMER. No; we have not undertaken to do that. We have not attempted to disturb that factor of the existing law.

Mr. WALKER. Then you have made no progress at all in the scheme you propose?

Mr. HOMER. I do not think the existing uniformity of the bank-note currency can be improved upon.

Mr. WALKER. Then you have proposed a scheme which you want adopted that will not make a note any more secure, and will not make it any more uniform, have you?

Mr. HOMER. No; but we have done this: We have increased the

functions, the ability to serve, the ability to help, through the national-bank system, by the substitution of the difference between the cost of the bond and the circulation that we have received.

Mr. WALKER. That would increase the profit of the bank on circulation.

Mr. HOMER. There has been very little in that respect, and an increase would not be harmful.

Mr. WALKER. I amnot talking about that. Would you increase it?

Mr. HOMER. Slightly.

Mr. WALKER. Do you think you could get money any more quickly than you could by depositing those bonds and taking out bills if they were already printed?

Mr. HOMER. If I am obliged to deposit $114,000 and get only $90,000 in return, I am worse off.

Mr. WALKER. That comes back to the interest of the bank instead of the interest of the public?

Mr. HOMER. Not entirely, sir. Suppose I have here a customer who desires to make a loan of $10,000, and that such a plan would enable me to lend that amount to him, whereas the other plan would only enable me to give him a part, the ability to lend is certainly in the interest of the public.

Mr. WALKER. Are you aware of any jealousy that exists between State and national banks to an extent that injures the financial interests of the country?

Mr. HOMER. I am not; though I confess that there is a feeling between them.

Mr. WALKER. Do you think that feeling is injurious to the finances of the people?

Mr. HOMER. Its influence might go to this extent, that it might create a currency which, traveling with the national-bank currency, would give us two classes of circulation medium.

Mr. WALKER. I am not talking about that at all. You are entirely off the subject. I ask you if you have any knowledge whether the bankers assembled at that convention considered that the finances of the country to-day were being injured by the jealousy that existed between the State banks and national banks?

Mr. HOMER. No, sir.

Mr. WALKER. Then you went to work to devise a system that would remove that jealousy?

Mr. HOMER. There was a feeling, not on the part of the bankers, but so far as it came within my knowledge there has been a feeling in communities, in sections of the country, against the national banking system.

Mr. WALKER. That is another subject. What you testified to was that you thought that your scheme would remove the jealously between the State banks and the national banks.

Mr. HOMER. It is the general feeling that exists with reference to the national banks and their desirability.

The CHAIRMAN pro tempore (Mr. Sperry). Mr. Hepburn is here, and can give us about an hour, but desires to take the 4 o'clock train away from the city.

Mr. WALKER. If this gentleman is willing to remain over after to-day I have no objection to his now leaving the stand to allow Mr. Hepburn to make his statement. But the committee have invited this gentleman here to tell us what the bankers have done and what they have not done.

The CHAIRMAN pro tempore. The committee will perhaps put some limit, so that we can hear these different gentlemen.

Mr. WALKER. I do not propose to pursue these inquiries with anybody except this gentleman. But my point is this: Here is an organization of the national bankers of this country that met in Baltimore——

Mr. HOMER. It is not an organization of national bankers. There were State bankers as well as national. It is known as the American Bankers' Association.

Mr. WALKER. Both State and national?

Mr. HOMER. Yes.

Mr. WALKER. I supposed it was national. They met, after the great crisis of 1893, in the present condition of the finances of the country and the present condition of the Treasury, and have brought before this committee a scheme that would make confusion worse confounded and ask us to adopt that scheme, and I thought I would like to propound some questions that would develop the fact that they have paid no attention to the interests and wants of the country, or to relieving the Treasury, but were simply looking out for their own interests in these times. It looked to me a good deal like fiddling while Rome burns. I will, however, withdraw any further questions if it is the desire of the other gentlemen of the committee.

Mr. WARNER. I should like to ask one question.

The CHAIRMAN pro tempore. If the committee would like to hear Mr. Hepburn for three-quarters of an hour, they now have an opportunity, otherwise he can not be heard at present, for he has to leave the city.

Mr. WALKER. I am perfectly willing to give way. I believe other members of the committee would like to ask questions of this gentleman.

Mr. HEPBURN. I suggest that the committee proceed with the examination of this gentleman, who is one of the most competent bankers of the country.

The CHAIRMAN pro tempore. The Chair feels that he would like to take the sense of the committee on this question. There may be a majority of the committee who would rather hear Mr. Hepburn than to continue the hearing of this gentleman.

Mr. HOMER. I am sure they would.

The CHAIRMAN pro tempore. Without any motion having been made, the Chair will take the sense of the committee on that point.

Mr. BLACK. That is an unfortunate way to put it, it seems to me. We do not want to discriminate against this gentleman.

Mr. HOMER. Let me say that I wish the committee would excuse me. I have a sick cashier at home, and it was only with difficulty that I got away at all.

Mr. WALKER. I want to enter my most serious protest against being cut off. I have a few questions that are very vital as to the development of this Baltimore scheme, and this is the first witness we have had on this subject. I do not desire to interrogate Mr. Hepburn upon these same points at all. I think I shall avail myself of my right in the committee to ask some questions of this gentleman, for I have the floor.

The CHAIRMAN pro tempore. Without limit?

Mr. WALKER. I think I will be reasonable in limit, but I should like to ask a few more questions. (To Mr. Homer:) If I understand you, the banks of Baltimore that availed themselves of the use of the certificates of the Baltimore clearing house paid for the use of those certificates 6 per cent?

Mr. HOMER. Yes, sir.

Mr. WALKER. You say that your scheme would collect in the Treasury a fund of $17,500,000?

Mr. HOMER. Yes; if all the national banks enter the scheme, and taking $700,000,000 as a round sum for national banking capital to-day.

Mr. WALKER. That the income upon that at 3 per cent would be $525,000 per year?

Mr. HOMER. Yes, sir.

Mr. WALKER. And that the losses, as shown by the history of banks of the last thirty years, would be only $30,000 per year?

Mr. HOMER. $953,000 for the thirty years would be a little over $30,000 per annum.

Mr. WALKER. Then you would collect interest on this, but you say nothing about that being seventeen and one-half times as much as the statistics show would be necessary.

Mr. HOMER. Yes, sir.

Mr. WALKER. You have not any doubt but that any tax upon the banks is a tax upon the people of the country in the increased cost of the money to them and the increased cost of goods and everything else, have you?

Mr. HOMER. We would be simply paying under this plan the same tax that we are paying under existing law.

Mr. WALKER. I knew that from the law. I understood that myself; but my point was, whether all these taxes do not ultimately come out of the people, and how you can justify yourself in imposing a tax of seventeen and one-half times as large as is necessary.

Mr. HOMER. The first motive or incentive for that was to furnish a fund absolutely secure, about which there could be no question.

Mr. WALKER. Is there any fire-insurance, life-insurance, or any other kind of company in the world that takes seventeen and one-half times as much taxation as is necessary to secure it?

Mr. HOMER. It is the provision in force under the Canadian system. It is based upon precedent.

Mr. WALKER. You said that in your direct examination. But my question is direct: How could you be justified in taking a tax seventeen and one-half times more than would be necessary in order to make every bill issued by the banks absolutely secure?

Mr. HOMER. Whether they would be justified in taking that?

Mr. WALKER. In taking that tax and taking it out of the people who use the money, and out of the banks from which they borrow the money. I am not putting it on the ground of taxing people for the support of the Government; that is another thing.

Mr. HOMER. It is an excessive fund; we have too much security.

Mr. WALKER. That is all I want on that point. The issue of bank notes, under your system, is limited entirely by capital?

Mr. HOMER. Yes.

Mr. WALKER. Without any reference to the surplus that the bank may have?

Mr. HOMER. Yes.

Mr. WALKER. I should say not the surplus, but the reserve, without any reference to the reserve.

Mr. HOMER. There has never been any reserve for circulation.

Mr. WALKER. Here is a bank, we will say, that has $100,000 capital and $500,000 of deposits. That bank can issue $50.000 circulation, and there are hundreds of instances of that sort in the banking system. Here is another bank that has $100,000 capital that has only $50,000 of deposits, and that bank issues $50,000 of circulation on its assets. So it turns out that in the one case the one bank has $50,000 of circulation, or one-third of its assets, and in the other case it has only one-sixth, even if that. What is the point of making so unequal an arrangement as regards putting the circulation at so low a point with the assets of the bank, the surplus fund, the reserve fund, etc., when the bank might safely issue three or four times as much?

Mr. HOMER. By making it 50 per cent?

Mr. WALKER. Why that?

Mr. HOMER. Baltimore conservatism dictated an absolutely safe plan for note issue.

Mr. WALKER. Do you not think it is just as safe to issue $100,000 where you have six times that amount of assets, as to issue $50,000 where you have three times that amount of assets?

Mr. HOMER. Do you rely on the deposits as an absolute asset to meet the circulation of the bank?

Mr. WALKER. I should say that when the whole of the assets of the bank are liable for its bills, so far as the bills are concerned, they become assets because nothing can be paid out of those deposits until the bills are paid.

Mr. HOMER. Yes, that is very true; but is it not right to say that the best security for bank notes should be the bank's own money and not its depositors? If I have $100,000 on deposit I am handling $50,000 of my own money, and I do not feel that I have any absolute right to issue circulation as against deposit money intrusted to the bank by other people; I have only the right to hazzard the actual money of the bank represented by its capital.

Mr. WALKER. Then you make a distinction between capital and assets; but what the bank has with which to pay its circulating notes is its assets over its liabilities?

Mr. HOMER. Yes, sir.

Mr. WALKER. A bank to-day is holding one-sixth more than the reserve the law requires; the law would require a reserve, which is the bank's, without any reference to its capital of $125,000, and it can issue $100,000, while under the system you suggest the reserve held by the bank to pay its notes would be $12,500 for $50,000. That is all I have to say about it.

Mr. JOHNSON, of Indiana. With reference to bank profits on circulation it is impossible to have a circulation without profit to the bank, is it not?

Mr. HOMER. Well, the existing circulation is largely compulsory. I know of very few banks in the country who have to-day the maximum amount of their circulation.

Mr. JOHNSON, of Indiana. The trouble is that the profit is too small?

Mr. HOMER. The profit is too small. I think the Baltimore banks, with but few exceptions, have the minimum amount.

Mr. JOHNSON, of Indiana. The profit of the banks on circulation does not necessarily amount to an oppression of the interests of the people?

Mr. HOMER. No.

Mr. JOHNSON, of Indiana. The banks might make a profit and the people receive a benefit at the same time?

Mr. HOMER. Yes.

Mr. WALKER. Your plan does not relieve the Treasury in any way, and is not intended for that purpose?

Mr. HOMER. No, sir.

Mr. WALKER. You still leave the Treasury as it is now, subject to the constant watchfulness of the people here and abroad, with the probabilities that the bills will be put in for redemption and gold taken out?

Mr. HOMER. Certainly.

Mr. WALKER. And your plan is not intended to meet anything of that kind at all?

Mr. HOMER. No, sir; it is simply a perfection of the national banking law.

Mr. BROSIUS. You have said that the experience in the past has established the fact that the best security a note circulation can have is the bills receivable of the banks in the aggregate?

Mr. HOMER. Yes.

Mr. BROSIUS. I have no doubt of the truth of that; but in an individual instance may not a bank be so badly managed, may not such poor judgment be exercised in effecting its loans that those bills receivable might not be a security at all for its circulating notes?

Mr. HOMER. Undoubtedly.

Mr. BROSIUS. If, in a given year, there should be a half dozen banks of the United States so conducted that their bills receivable would not turn out to be a security for their circulation, would not every holder of bank notes of those particular banks feel that the danger of loss from holding such notes might fall upon him unless there were some other security?

Mr. HOMER. Do I catch your question clearly—that the holder of a note of an insolvent bank might fear loss under this plan?

Mr. BROSIUS. Yes; that is, if the responsibility for the entire security is the bills receivable of that bank.

Mr. HOMER. Under the Baltimore plan?

Mr. BROSIUS. My point is whether there should not be some other security for the circulation of every bank note than the assets of the bank itself.

Mr. HOMER. We have given you that, Mr. Brosius, in the guarantee fund.

Mr. BROSIUS. I know you have, and you have given to us, in the ultimate responsibility, the guarantee of the United States Government.

Mr. HOMER. Yes.

Mr. BROSIUS. And I quite agree with you in that particular. But I wanted to direct your attention to what you said about the safety of the bills receivable of the banks as a security for their circulation. Suppose each bank stood upon its own bottom, and you can easily imagine a case where the bills receivable of a particular bank would not be any security at all.

Mr. HOMER. That is true.

Mr. BROSIUS. Then in order to make the holder of a bank note entirely secure there must be some other security than that of the assets of the particular bank?

Mr. HOMER. Yes.

Mr. BROSIUS. You meet that contingency by your reserve fund?

Mr. HOMER. By our guarantee fund.

Mr. BROSIUS. And you meet any residue of risk that may remain after the assets are exhausted, whether they are good or bad, and the 5 per cent, by having the ultimate responsibility of the Government of the United States to give every man who holds a note satisfaction and peace of mind?

Mr. HOMER. That is correct, sir.

Mr. SPERRY. I should like to inquire whether you have made any calculation of the profit on circulation under the Baltimere plan or under the Carlisle plan?

Mr. HOMER. No, sir; I have not.

Mr. SPERRY. You would not be able to say whether the profits are such under the Secretary's plan as to insure the banks making a profit?

Mr. HOMER. The profit would be somewhat larger under the Baltimore plan than under the Secretary's plan, because while the Secretary gives us 75 per cent of our circulation he exacts from us a deposit of 35, which would leave 40 per cent of circulation. The Baltimore plan gives 50 per cent with a deposit of 5 per cent for the guarantee fund. The difference would be but slight, however.

Mr. SPERRY. Are there any features, aside from deposits of 30 per cent under the Secretary's plan, which under your plan would be so objectionable to the banks as to prevent them from adopting it?

Mr. HOMER. Outside of that general guarantee?

Mr. SPERRY. Outside of the $30 legal-tender deposit on the $100.

Mr. HOMER. I am hardly prepared to answer that question, Mr. Sperry. The deposit of money for the circulating notes is more advantageous to the banks than a deposit of Government bonds, because the amount of currency issued against the same amount in dollars invested is larger.

Mr. COBB, of Alabama. Is it the premium on United States bonds which alone gives the profit in circulation?

Mr. HOMER. No, sir; but that is one of the features.

Mr. COBB, of Alabama. Is it the main feature?

Mr. HOMER. If the premium is larger than the difference between the par and the amount allowed, the premium would be the main element; but the feature is this: That on an investment of $114,000 we receive circulation to the extent of $90,000.

Mr. COBB, of Alabama. But you get interest on the $100,000?

Mr. HOMER. That is true; but we have staring us in the face a premium account subject to fluctuations, which in a year like 1893, with much depreciation in the market value even of our Government bonds, would very materially impair the profits of the bank.

Mr. COBB, of Alabama. That is the reason I asked the question. I simply wanted to know whether that premium was the real and sole cause or the prime cause.

Mr. HOMER. No, sir; it is not; it is the fluctuations in premiums to some extent.

Mr. COBB, of Alabama. When not above par the profit of the banks would be greater?

Mr. HOMER. It would be greater; it would require the investment of less capital.

Mr. COBB, of Alabama. Then you would not have cause to complain of this want of profit, except for such loss of profit as comes from ordinary causes?

Mr. HOMER. There has been no complaint as to the profit under the Baltimore plan, and was none in the deliberations of the American Bankers' Convention. Our aim was to establish an elastic currency, and we kept in view the idea of creating elasticity and avoiding the other feature, which ties up more money than you receive, and which prevents elasticity in bank circulation.

Mr. COBB, of Alabama. You regard elasticity as a necessary element of profit?

Mr. HOMER. Not only as a necessary element of profit, but as a necessary requirement of the conditions of trade.

Mr. WARNER. Is it true that the less a currency system is obstructed the lower will be the interest?

Mr. HOMER. Yes, sir.

Mr. WARNER. And when obstructed, to that precise extent you simply pass on that charge, or the burden of that obstruction, to those to whom you lend money?

Mr. HOMER. Yes; that would naturally be the case.

Mr. WARNER. And the less obstruction to you in getting currency the lower will be the interest?

Mr. HOMER. To a certain extent that is true, and it would perhaps be a general rule.

Mr. WARNER. And that is a corresponding benefit to the country, which accompanies the benefit to the banks in being able to get out currency easily?

Mr. HOMER. Yes.

Mr. WALKER. That applies just as well to excessive taxation.

Mr. HOMER. Upon the emergency——

Mr. WALKER. I do not mean that; I mean upon the $17,000,000; if the taxation is excessive, that is a tax on the system.

Mr. HOMER. I have explained here that the purpose of this plan was to create an absolutely safe currency without a bond deposit. Now, if this committee or this Congress should feel that the banks have been too liberal in the creation of a guarantee fund, I am sure there will be no argument advanced against a reduction of that amount.

Mr. WALKER. But you present this to us as the ultimate result of a careful——

Mr. HOMER. Of a conservative action.

Mr. WALKER. Of a careful and conservative action by a bankers' convention, the members of which know more about finances than all of us know, and, as one of your men said, more than we do, for he said that we were entirely incompetent to deal with the question, or, in fact, to deal with much of anything else. So long as you take that position I do not know that I care to interrogate you further about it.

Mr. COBB, of Alabama. Do you think your plan gives us the cheapest currency consistent with safety?

Mr. HOMER. I think it does.

Mr. SPERRY. I have heard some criticism of the Baltimore plan by reason of the fact that the Government is made ultimately liable for the redemption of the bills. Would it be possible to modify the Baltimore plan and leave that responsibility of the Government out of the question, and administer it through the safety fund only?

Mr. HOMER. I believe, as I stated, Mr. Sperry, that it would be absolutely safe under the rigid supervision of the Comptroller. I feel that the responsibility in this matter is small and technical only, and that, while it is technical, it is of sufficient force to assure the careful supervision and control of the banks issuing currency.

Mr. SPERRY. Then your judgment is, to put the question another way, that under the supervision of Federal control and the safety fund you would regard the currency as being safe?

Mr. HOMER. I believe it would be a safe currency.

Mr. SPERRY. Would it be as satisfactory to the people, in your judgment?

Mr. HOMER. I think not.

Mr. SPERRY. Do you mean it would be so unsatisfactory that the bill would not pass readily?

Mr. HOMER. No, sir; I would not hazard that, because it would be a good and safe note, in my judgment.

Mr. SPERRY. A note that all the banks would accept?

Mr. HOMER. Yes, sir.

Mr. SPERRY. Then the people would accept it?

Mr. HOMER. There would be no question at all about it, but I feel that a country as enlightened and as commercially active as our own ought to have the best circulation which can be created.

Mr. BROSIUS. Do you think it is right for the government of any country to authorize the issue of any bank note for general circulation without guaranteeing the redemption of it?

Mr. HOMER. I am not an advocate of State-bank circulation.

Mr. BROSIUS. Neither am I.

Mr. HOMER. I believe in having a good note; a note that will pass from hand to hand without the least question or doubt as to its bringing the amount for which it was issued.

Mr. SPERRY. A note under the Canadian system does not carry any Government warrant?

Mr. HOMER. No, sir.

Mr. SPERRY. A note issued under this system would be just as good as a Canadian note, would it not?

Mr. HOMER. I think so.

The CHAIRMAN. Mr. Hepburn, who was to address the committee at this time, has informed the Chair that, owing to a previous engagement, he has been obliged to go to New York on the 4 o'clock train, and that he can not appear again before Thursday of this week. For that reason, and there being no other gentleman to appear before the committee at this time, if there be no objection, the committee will stand adjourned until 10 o'clock to-morrow morning.

The committee adjourned at 3.22 o'clock p. m.

WASHINGTON, D. C., *Wednesday, December 12, 1894.*

The committee met at 10 a. m.

Present: the chairman (Mr. Springer) and Messrs. Sperry, Cox, Cobb of Missouri, Ellis, Cobb of Alabama, Warner, Johnson of Ohio, Black, Hall, Walker, Brosius, Henderson, Russell, Haugen, and Johnson of Indiana.

On motion of Mr. Warner it was ordered that 250 preliminary copies of the report of the proceedings of the committee be furnished daily for the use of members of the committee.

Mr. Johnson, of Indiana, and Mr. Cox pointed out certain inaccuracies in the report, and were informed by the chairman that the matter was open for revision and correction, and that the corrected report only would pass into a permanent form and be presented to the House; and the chairman invited members of the committee to make all necessary corrections and hand them to the clerk.

LETTER OF MR. LYMAN J. GAGE.

The chairman stated that he had addressed a letter to Mr. Lyman J. Gage, president of the First National Bank of Chicago, requesting him to appear before the committee, and had received a telegram in reply stating that it was impossible for Mr. Gage to appear before the committee, but that he would communicate his views in writing. The chairman had received a letter from Mr. Gage this morning; and, as that gentleman was a very eminent authority on the subject of banking and currency, his letter would be printed in the report of the proceedings.

Mr. Gage's letter was thereupon read by the chairman, and is as follows:

FIRST NATIONAL BANK OF CHICAGO,
Chicago, December 10, 1894.

DEAR SIR: I am honored by receipt of your request to appear before your committee on Saturday next, or on some day prior thereto, in re the recommendations of the President and the Secretary of the Treasury concerning the currency.

The notice is so short that I can not arrange to be present in person, but beg very briefly to state here the conclusions at which I have arrived.

Agreeing with the criticisms made by these officers of the Government as to the present weakness of our situation, and the great desirability of separating the Government from the direct responsibility of currency issues, I am persuaded that the country is not ready to accept their recommendations as to the methods proposed. In making any change the method should be so simple that all can comprehend it, and it should be seen that the incidental effects would not be in any direction disturbing to trade, commerce, or industry. I believe that the "Baltimore plan" carries the true principles of a credit currency, but we cannot reach it by any one step, and years may intervene before it could be realized. In the meantime, the way for the Government to step out of the currency business and place the burden of redemption upon the banks is plain.

Authorize the issue of $250,000,000 of 2½ per cent bonds, payable at such time as Congress may elect (twenty-five years desirable), to be offered to subscribers at par. Accept in payment United States legal-tender notes or Treasury notes, the same to be canceled.

Amend the national-bank act so that banks can obtain note issue to the face value of bonds deposited as security for circulation. Reduce the tax on circulating notes to one-half of 1 per cent.

This done, national-bank notes would make good the vacuum caused by the retirement of Government notes; in fact, there would be some expansion under it, to be followed later by some contraction through forced redemption of bank issues, if it be true, as some claim, that the volume of circulating media in the United States is larger than can be maintained, and that the outflow of gold is nature's method of equalizing things. If this be so, if contraction through the exportation of gold, or by the retirement of a portion of the paper money, be a logical sequence of our situation, then, in that case, the Government being safe from demands, the banks with circulation outstanding would be obliged to bring their issues within narrower limits; but all this would work itself out, and need not be dwelt upon at length now.

The problem is this: To take the Government out of the note-issuing business—

(1) Without contracting the currency in the process.
(2) Without inviting to expansion.

Secretary Carlisle's plan is subject to the danger involved under the last suggestion.

Yours, very truly, LYMAN J. GAGE.

Hon. W. M. SPRINGER,
Chairman Banking and Currency Committee,
Washington, D. C.

P. S.—Were the above suggestions to receive serious consideration, there are some features of the national-bank act that would require amendment in order to give note holders easier and cheaper access to the point of redemption than now exists. Redemption agents in cities should be restores, but these are details which I will pass by.

LETTER OF MR. EDWARD N. GIBBS.

The chairman stated that he had also addressed a letter to Mr. Edward N. Gibbs, treasurer of the New York Life Insurance Company, requesting him to appear before the committee. Mr. Gibbs had sent his regrets that he could not come, but had forwarded a brief statement of his views. This letter was likewise read by the chairman, and is as follows:

NEW YORK LIFE INSURANCE COMPANY,
New York, December 11, 1894.

MY DEAR SIR: In view of your courteous invitation, and my inability to appear before your committee, I venture to express, in much fewer words than I should be able to do if present, views I entertain respecting the banking and currency question as it exists to day. I should like to say—

First. That, in my judgment, the legal-tender notes are the greatest danger our existing financial system has to contend with.

Second. With some slight modifications, born of experience, our national banking system is, or can be made, the best in the world.

Third. If the Government would retire from the banking business; that is to say, that portion thereof forced upon it by the exigencies of the last war, refunding—with such deliberation as would prevent unnatural contraction of the currency—the outstanding legal-tender notes into a long time low rate of interest bond, available for banking purposes, the result upon the business of the country could be only helpful.

Fourth. In this connection, such restrictions as experience has demonstrated as unnecessary, might wisely be removed from the national banking act, so that, based upon the new bonds, there should be sufficient profit to the national banks, South, West, North, and East, to provide, as is their legitimate function, the paper money of the country. This would imply removal of existing tax on circulation and proper requirements for prompt redemption of circulation.

Yours, truly,

EDWARD N. GIBBS, *Treasurer.*

Hon. WM. M. SPRINGER,
Chairman Committee of Banking and Currency,
Washington, D. C.

The chairman also stated that he had sent an invitation to Mr. Enoch Pratt, of Baltimore, president of the board of trade of that city, and who was one of the gentlemen present at the convention of the American Bankers' Association at Baltimore. Mr. Pratt regretted his inability to attend, but had sent no statement of his views. Mr. George A. Butler, president of the National Tradesmen's Bank, of New Haven, Conn., the author of a pamphlet on the subject, copies of which were on the table, was present, and would address the committee.

REPORT OF THE COMPTROLLER OF THE CURRENCY.

Mr. JOHNSON, of Indiana, moved to have incorporated in the proceedings that portion of the report of the Comptroller of the Currency which relates to amendments to banking laws, and it was so ordered.

The portion referred to is as follows:

"AMENDMENTS RECOMMENDED.

"The act enumerating the duties of the Comptroller of the Currency specifically requires that in his annual report to Congress at the commencement of its sessions he shall suggest "any amendment to the laws relative to banking by which the system may be improved and the security of the holders of its notes and other creditors may be increased."

"In compliance with the foregoing there were submitted at the last session of Congress certain recommendations looking to the amendment of existing laws. As yet the suggestions then made remain unacted upon, and therefore they are resubmitted. It is unnecessary to here set them forth in detail or again give the reasons then assigned in support of them. In a general way it may, however, be stated they cover the following points:

"That associations, if the present law is not changed as to a bond deposit, be authorized to issue circulating notes equal to the par value of the bonds deposited; that the semiannual duty on circulation be so reduced as to equal one-fourth of 1 per cent per annum; that the Comptroller, with the approval of the Secretary of the Treasury, be empowered to remove officers and directors of national banks for violations of law; that loans of any bank to its executive officers or employees be restricted; that the assistant cashier under certain conditions be authorized to sign circulating notes; that some class of public officers be empowered to administer the general oaths required by the national-bank act; that bank examiners be required to take an oath of office; that the Comptroller be empowered to fix their compensation, and that provision be made for supervising examiners.

"It is believed the taking of proper legislative action upon these proposed amendments would be for the betterment of the system and promotive of the public good.

"The amendments thus suggested, however, affect in the largest degree only the administrative features of the present national-bank act, and are of less relative importance than the remedying of any defects which may exist in the note-issuing power vested by it in the banks. No section of the law should be disturbed which can not be materially improved upon and no amendment engrafted unless such amendment will work out better results than flow from the existing order of things.

"The present law, it must be conceded, has been successful in every material feature, excepting in the matter of bank-note issue, and here the failure has been but a partial one. The notes issued by the banks under governmental supervision have been uniform in appearance and under any and all circumstances of the full face value which they purport to carry. They have possessed the first requisite of a good bank-note issue—immediate convertibility in coin upon presentation.

"It is probable that there could be no better plan for simply insuring the note holder against loss than the present requirement of a deposit of bonds to secure a bank's circulation, but it is equally certain, however, that a method could be devised not less safe in this respect and in addition thereto possessing that which is as essential and is now wholly wanting—elasticity of issue. The complaint therefore made against the present system is that, lacking in elasticity of issue, it fails to meet as fully as it ought the varying wants of the country's trade and commerce. This defect must attach to every scheme for currency issued by the banks against a deposit of bonds, the market value of which fluctuates while the percentage of issue, less than the value of the bonds granted the banks, remains unchanged. It must also be wanting in such a method because of the delay, in the face of a pressing need, occasioned by a tight money market or other reason, in securing and depositing the bonds required and taking out the circulation thereon.

"But serious as is this fault, and retardful as it is to the business interests of the country, any attempt to remedy it which should lose sight of or in anywise make less certain the present unquestioned credit and convertibility of the bank issues of the country could not be justified. It is a duty of Governments to see that the currency which circulates among the people ought always to be of the very highest character, and the soundness of which should never be a subject of inquiry. For thirty years the American people have had such a bank currency, and having seen the value of it, both here and abroad, they will not be content to have any innovation made unless such new departure insures not only equal but better results.

"It is respectfully suggested that not only as good but better results would be obtained if the present banking act were amended by repealing the provision thereof requiring each, bank as a prerequisite to entering the system and issuing bank-note currency, to deposit Government bonds.

"In lieu of such provision should be substituted one permitting the banks to issue circulating notes against their assets to an amount equal to at least 50 per cent of their paid-up unimpaired capital. In order to guarantee the note holder against loss on account of the issue of any insolvent bank, a safety fund should be provided by graduated taxation upon the outstanding circulation of the banks until the same should equal not less than 5 per cent of the total of such outstanding circulation, such fund to be held by the Government as an agent only and for the purpose of immediately redeeming the notes of such insolvent bank. It should be as speedily as possible replenished by a first and a paramount lien out of the assets of the bank and the shareholders' double liability. The redemption of such notes should be immediate upon presentation. Whatever other changes, if any, it would be necessary to make in the present system relative to current redemption of bank notes, and the Government's position relative to the same and kindred matters, it is unnecessary to here set forth. If the recommendation here made, together with that which will follow, should receive consideration at the hands of Congress, a bill drawn after careful study and investigation of the whole subject would necessarily embody all the details incident to a change from a bond to a safety fund security as a basis for bank circulation.

"Before presenting what seems to the Comptroller to be as important a phase of the question under discussion, and one which, if properly worked out, would be of great benefit to the General Government, it is pertinent to state that the change in the form of security for bank-note issues proposed was sanctioned not only by the American Bankers' Association, which recently met in Baltimore, but is indorsed by many of the leading financiers and students of political economy in this and other countries. It is embodied in the Canadian bank system, and in part, at least, in the Scotch, English, and German systems. It is safe to say that a note-issuing bank's best assets are its good business notes falling due and paid each day, and that the loss attendant upon notes issued and circulated against such assets under systems permitting it has been comparatively nothing. Only by issuing against them instead of against a bond security can any degree of elasticity in the note-issuing function be attained. It certainly can not be reached in the present hard and fast line fixed by existing law.

"As an aid in arriving at the proper per cent of taxation necessary to raise a fund sufficient to redeem the notes of failed banks and the expense incident to the conduct of the office of the Comptroller of the Currency the following, taken from official records, is submitted:

Average annual circulation of national banks, 1864 to 1894	$282, 801, 252
Outstanding circulation of failed banks	17, 819, 541
Cost to General Government on account of national banks, as shown by the books of the Comptroller's Office	7, 610, 169
Additional estimated cost	7, 732, 914
	15, 343, 083
Tax of one-fourth of 1 per cent for thirty-one years	21, 917, 073
Tax of one-fifth of 1 per cent for thirty-one years	17, 533, 674

"It will thus be seen that a tax on national banking circulation of one-fifth of 1 per cent would have repaid the cost of the national banks to the General Government, and also that a tax of one-fourth of 1 per cent would have redeemed the notes of all failed national banks; in fact, a tax of two-fifths of 1 per cent would have been ample to meet both the cost of that system and the redemption of the notes of failed national banks. Under the existing laws, the Government standing responsible for the redemption of the circulation of failed national banks, up to January 1 last, had there been no bond deposit whatever, the loss to it would have been but $1,139,253, and of this amount $958,247 represents the loss by banks whose trusts are still open and will pay further dividends, thus reducing the amount last named.

"In considering the question of the benefits to the public of a bond deposit on the part of the banks it is well to remember that the comparatively few failures on the part of national banks have not been because of any security given by them for their circulation, but because of prudent and honest management on the part of those in charge of them, and the careful supervision and examination of them by the officers of the Government. Under the same character of management and the same superintendency and watchfulness on the part of the Government, failures would not be more numerous under a change in the respect named, and therefore the deductions made from the facts of the past are a safe basis for calculations as to the future.

"The changes thus outlined will, upon investigation, it is believed, prove to be safe in affording complete security to the note holder and give to the business interests of the country a note issue responsive to their needs. Within the measure of percentage of issue against assets granted the banks will be such range as will enable them to keep out sufficient currency to meet the ordinary demands of business and to speedily take out whatever extra amount is necessary to meet extraordinary occasions. It will not permit of an overissue if the notes issued under such system are convertible in coin on demand and the proper and speedy redemption of them is afforded. The business world will use just such amount of them as is necessary to carry on trade, and the remaining ones, it being unprofitable to have them in circulation, will at once return for redemption.

"The profit upon the issue of circulation to the banks by such change would be so augmented that it is giving to them a franchise for which it is suggested they should be called upon to make proper return to the

General Government. This return should not, however, be of such a character as to defeat the ends sought in the privilege given.

"For a long time the chief source of embarrassment to the General Government and the cause of so great uncertainty in the business conditions of the country is the continual danger threatened by the use made of the currency issues of the Government, and the inability, when the revenues of the Government are inadequate, to maintain, except through bond issues, such a reserve of gold coin as is required by law. The current redemption of the legal-tender issues and the Treasury issues under the Sherman Act of 1890, and the reissuing instead of cancellation of the same, must always create distrust of the Government's credit abroad and at home, so long as the laws now upon the statute book remain unchanged.

"The General Gevernment ought to be wholly free from direct issuing and redeeming of notes to pass as money among the people. No country yet has ever successfully engaged in so doing, and the experience of the Government of the United States has proven no exception to the rule. The general cost and loss entailed upon the Government, the repeated periods of uncertainty as to its credit, and the stability of our monetary system have been so great as to make the legal-tender and Treasury issues of 1890 one of the extraordinary burdens placed upon the people. The relief given in increasing the volume of the circulating medium has been as nothing compared with the expense incident to maintaining the reserve in gold at all hazards necessary to keep intact the Government's credit and provide for their current redemption.

"These issues ought to be redeemed and canceled, and the Government thus enabled to retire from the banking business—a business for which it is so poorly adapted and equipped. The intention of those who first authorized the legal-tender issues was that it should so do at the earliest practicable moment, and the discussion then carried on in Congress is replete with such protestations. The first Congressional enactment signed by President Grant after his inauguration as Chief Executive was one reasserting the determination of the Government to preserve unquestioned the public faith, and the closing clause of it was "And the United States also solemnly pledges its faith to make provision at the earliest practicable period for the redemption of the United States notes in coin."

"In the light of the present condition of the Government's finances, that which ought to have been done when there was a surplus in the Treasury can not now be undertaken, and the same conditions must continue to weaken the country's credit and plague the lines of business unless a means is devised for removing these issues from the channel of current redemption until such time as the Government finds itself in such a position to do that which at first was the intent of all—gradually redeem and cancel them.

"If the franchise is granted the banks of issuing circulating notes against their assets instead of against a bond security, it is suggested that the banks in return should recompense the Government by relieving the Treasury Department of the current redemption in coin of the present Treasury issues. The ultimate redemption, of course, must fall upon the Government, but the embarrassment does not arise from their ultimate redemption but from their current.

"It is therefore suggested that if Congress shall repeal the provisions of the present act requiring the national banks to make a deposit of Government bonds in order to secure circulating notes, and substitute therefor a provision giving them instead the right to issue the same against their assets, it incorporates therein and as a part thereof that as a prerequisite to so doing the banks be compelled to deposit with the Treasurer of the United States legal-tender issues, or issues under the Sherman act of 1890, equal in amount to the difference between the percentage of their capital stock of issues granted against their assets and the total of such capital stock. The deposit thus made ought to remain with the Treasurer until the bank ceased either through voluntary or involuntary liquidation to do business, and in either case the Government ought to then redeem and cancel such Treasury issues deposited. It is only by such permanent deposit during the life of the bank that the issues named can be removed from current presentation for redemption.

"As against this deposit of legal tenders and Sherman notes so made there should be issued to the banks dollar for dollar of national bank notes, either of the same or different design, as might be deemed best, that thus fixed the volume of the currency, as it is now contributed to by the issues of the Government, would not be contracted so long at least as the banks making such deposits are in existence. The percentage of the bank notes issued against this deposit should be free from any taxtion imposed upon circulation, and ought to be such percentage as is deemed equitable, to be used as a part of the banks' legal reserve held against deposits.

"The law should make it incumbent upon the banks to deposit with the Treasury for the current redemption of such notes gold coin to an amount necessary to make sure the current redemption of them. The Government should not undertake or in anywise become responsible for the current redemption of these notes. Its responsibility should end with its redemption of the notes deposited to secure such circulation when the bank ceased to exist. At present a current redemption fund of 5 per cent of the outstanding circulation is found sufficient, and it is probable that in the future no greater amount would be required.

"As already suggested, it is not deemed necessary to here enter into a discussion of details. The principle, if correct, can be incorporated into a law framed in such a manner as to meet any objections, be just and equitable to all concerned, and while placing upon the banks a daily burden now borne by the Government, give them just compensation in making circulation a source of legitimate and fair profit instead of loss. The elasticity of issue in national-bank circulation will be found in the percentage of issue against assets, subject to the necessary rate of taxation and secured by an adequate safety fund to guarantee the note holder against loss on account of the notes of insolvent banks and in a current redemption fund maintained for daily redemption. The Government will be aided, the bank given in exchange a dollar for every dollar deposited, and thus relieved of the loss incident to depositing an amount of its capital stock in excess of the return in notes granted it. No violent contraction of the currency would follow such a course, but whenever contraction would occur it would be not less gradual than would at other times the expansion incident thereto.

"It is respectfully suggested that as a necessary element to the securing of proper elasticity of issue in our bank-note currency, section 9 of the act of July 12, 1882, regulating the retirement and issuing of circulation to banks within a fixed period of time, should be repealed, and also that such amendment should be made to the law as will necessitate the banks keeping in the office of the Comptroller of the Currency a sufficient amount of blank notes as will enable them to secure circulation at once, instead of after a period of delay, frequently of sufficient duration as to make the issue unavailable to relieve the pressure existing at the time of ordering the same.

"It has been suggested from many eminent financial sources that the whole question of a banking and currency system ought to be referred by Congress to a commission, created by the proper act, appointed by the President, and clothed with proper authority. A commission, non-partisan in its character, composed of men of eminent abilities, could unquestionably devise a currency system sound in every part and one which would commend itself to every interest of the country. It could largely take the question out of politics and have it considered simply in its business aspects and upon merit alone; but if the present Congress is to enact a law upon the subject the appointment of a commission could avail nothing. If, however, nothing more definite can be accomplished, the question of the creation of such commission ought to be considered and acted upon."

STATEMENT OF MR. GEORGE A. BUTLER.

Mr. George A. Butler, president of the National Tradesmen's Bank, of New Haven, Conn., addressed the committee. He said:

Mr. Chairman and gentlemen of the committee: I shall labor under some embarrassment, from the fact that I am not accustomed to this kind of business. My habits of mind are those of the library rather than of the committee room or platform. I have been ill, and left a sick room to come to Washington, and I have not come prepared to make a set speech of any kind, and I take it for granted that none of you would care to listen to an academic essay on the history and principles of money. I take for granted that you prefer to take up the existing condition of things, and if I think that there are any evils underlying them to be eradicated, to point them out; and if I have any ideas that remedies can be applied to them, to express such ideas. I assume that it is rather on that line that you would prefer me to speak.

It is very difficult for me to know just what to say and just where to leave off. I will be brief. I hastily threw together yesterday afternoon, in a very rough form, a few thoughts to outline the situation, which seem to me necessary in discussing any plan of currency. The first thought which comes to my mind is this: That if the condition of the country to-day is not perilous it certainly is very serious, and to my mind it is one which naturally and deservedly causes a great deal of anxiety.

I verily believe that the one great cause of the retardation of business improvement in the country to-day is the uneasiness which people throughout the country feel in relation to our national finances. We have a great many different kinds of money, and none of them complies with any strict economical principle of currency. There is not a single one of them (except gold) that is not in direct violation in some respect of well-known and well-accepted fundamental principles of currency.

The situation to-day is very peculiar. There seem to be a redundancy of the currency, and then, again, there seems to be a scarcity of the currency. That situation is a peculiar one in any country, and, I think, a dangerous one. Now, what evidence have we of any redundancy in the currency? The one test which all nations at all times apply to currency matters is the movement of specie. If my memory does not play me false (for I brought no memorandum with me, and have to rely on my memory for everything), within the past four years the net export of gold, together with the gold used in the arts and business, have been just about twice the amount of the production of our mines. Now, that may take place from two causes—from a redundant currency and from profound distrust abroad, which leads foreign nations to send home our securities, which they held in large amounts.

If the outflow of gold, which has been going on so heavily for the past four years, is the result of a redundant currency, it will not cease until it has eliminated the surplus currency from our circulation; and in that process it will be the best part of our circulation which leaves us. If the outflow of gold is one wholly or in part the result of fear abroad and of the sending home of our securities, the outflow will soon cease if it be dependent on that cause alone. But, while it is merely a matter of opinion, Mr. Chairman and gentlemen, I do not think it can be demonstrated. But as a somewhat careful student and watcher of current events, I will venture the opinion that a large part of the gold has gone abroad as a result of economical causes flowing out of a redundant currency. Redundancy, of course, always operates to create a higher range of prices in the country until it increases imports and checks exports, and until gold goes out of the country. You are all familiar with the operation of this rule. Now, I have no doubt that there is a certain element of redundancy, which of itself, perhaps, is of no great importance except from a point of economy, which is growing out of the fact that none of our currency conforms to the movements of commerce and trade (not even our national-bank notes).

There is not even a method of redemption, worthy of the name, by which activity can be given to the circulation. The redemption bureau is located in this city, removed from and out of the lines of travel of the great commercial and financial cities, making the redemption of the notes cumbersome and expensive to the banks. So far as I know of the custom of the banks in this matter, they only return to Washington the soiled and badly mutilated notes. All the other notes they send to their correspondents in New York. With a central redemption (I mean a bureau of redemption in the financial center of the country, and with branches in the other semi-financial centers) the system might be made effective in the highest degree. Under the Suffolk bank system that redundancy and that sluggishness in the movement of currency was never known, because all the other banks rushed their notes to the Suffolk bank, and the Suffolk bank sent them home twice a week. I think myself that there is a limit of redundancy. We have first the legal-tender notes and silver and silver certificates, which are limited strictly to a fixed amount. There is no system or way by which there can be any contraction or lessening of these amounts. The small amount of national-bank notes in circulation is too small in proportion to the whole of our circulation to have any effect on it in this respect, even although redemption were more effective than it is. By removing the bureau of redemption from Washington to New York, the redemption of notes would be so much more frequent and effective that it would give more activity and flexibility, or elasticity, to the currency than the present method of redemption.

I need not tell you, gentlemen, that there are times in the year when the country needs a very much larger amount of circulation than it needs at other times. I hardly need to say that there is no possible way of getting another system of currency in this country to-day. The fatal defect of our Government currency lies in the fact that it has no connection whatever with the commerce, the industry, or the trade of the country. It can be put in circulation only in one way. It can be withdrawn from circulation only in one way. The Government can put it in circulation only in paying its debts. The Government can withdraw it from circulation only by raising it from dues. But there is no contraction following out of that. There is no flexibility following out of that, because it is simply a transaction between one or a dozen individuals and the Government.

Again, the Government has no legal means of maintaining any reserve against the notes that it may have in circulation. It has no assets. We have heard a great deal about faith, but faith does not butter bread nor parsnips. Neither does it redeem nor give flexibility or virtue to any currency. Confidence, of course, is necessary in all business. But, as I say, the Government has no legal way of maintaining any reserve which it must have now or must have in the future. I see no legal way now, because, while it is legal for the Government to sell bonds to make up its deficit, it is illegal for the Government, under the present circumstances, to sell bonds to make good the reserve. At the same time that course is unnecessary, unscientific, and extremely expensive. I do not see why the selling of bonds might not be continued indefinitely. It seems very much like pouring water into a sieve and catching it in another sieve. One million of legal-tender notes deliberately worked could take one hundred millions of gold out of the Treasury of the United States in any one year. Ten millions of legal-tender notes, worked to the full capacity that they might be worked, could withdraw a thousand millions of gold from the Treasury.

I will not go into the process of it. You all understand that well enough. This process may go on, and it will not in any way affect any of the economical conditions bearing either on the currency or the trade of the country. It can not, in any degree whatever, affect the outflow of gold. That is independent of Government transactions; it is purely economical. It is a question of exchange brought about by various causes. For instance, it is estimated that Americans spend abroad every year $90,000,000. Another $60,000,000 goes abroad for interest on various investments in this country held abroad. That is $150,000,000. Add to that $25,000,000 or $30,000,000 paid out for foreign freight and $10,000,000 for insurance and sundries, making in all $195,000,000. Say that we receive $40,000,000 from immigrants who come into this country. There would be still left $135,000,000 in the nature of maturing obligations against the country, independent of any commercial transactions.

Now, Mr. Chairman, there are only two ways by which that immense amount of maturing obligations can be paid by this country—that is, by the product of its soil and industry, or by its gold and silver. Of course, gold and silver produced from our mines in excess of our own local needs are as legitimate an article of export as cotton, wheat, or petroleum. But we are met by this fact: If our exports exceed our imports by $100,000,000 year after year there is still a variable balance of trade. Now, the Government does not occupy any position by which it can come in and arrest that tendency and that outflow of the precious metals. It is purely a question of commerce and trade, and to commerce and trade it must be left. The Government is as powerless in the matter as a 10-year-old child. Selling bonds will have no effect upon it. And I will inject this remark just here: It has been frequently urged on the Government to sell its bonds abroad and import gold. You can bring the mountains of Switzerland here just as well as you can do that. So long as these conditions exist gold will leave the country, and the question which forces itself to-day on every reasonable man's mind is this, How long will that continue and the country remain on a sound financial basis?

I am not an alarmist. I have been in the banking business all my life, from a boy up. I have been through all the panics, but I will confess that I have never seen the time when I felt more uneasiness in regard to the future of the country than I do at this hour. The question, gentlemen, is, How can this outflow of gold be arrested and the danger to our national finances be overcome? There is but one single way by which any country can arrest any undue exportation of its precious metals. That thing comes (whether voluntarily or otherwise) through an adverse condition of exchange which demands exportation of the precious metals, and which reacts on the banking interests of the country, causing the banks to contract their loans. That process ends in forcing down prices, so that in the country which the gold is leaving and in the other countries to which it is flowing prices will be at par, making allowance, of course, for the cost of transportation, interest, etc. That is the only method by which it can be corrected.

If, Mr. Chairman, this difficulty is the result of distrust, and if it has grown out of the fact that foreigners have sent home our securities in large amounts, the trouble will probably pass away during the coming winter and spring. Congress can do much to relieve all this distrust. Nay, it can do enough to build up confidence and bring tens and tens of millions of dollars of foreign capital into this country, and then certainly this movement of gold would be arrested and the country would have nothing to further fear. But if this outflow of gold is the result of economic causes independent of any purely financial strife, gold will continue to go until it has eliminated the surplus currency of our circulation—until it has gone in such quantities as will put a pressure on all the financial institutions of the nation. It will continue to go until the people, who are even now crying about low prices, will be very glad to sell their products (I am very sorry to say it, it seems so cold and cruel) at lower prices than they sell now. I am afraid that prices will go even lower before the arrest of gold can be made.

Mr. Chairman, there have been immense changes in the natural relations between the United States and other countries in relation to this country during the past four or five years. Some years ago I warned Western and Southern men against the probability of low wheat and low cotton. I told them (that which has now become a fact) about Russia extending her railways into Western Asia, about Egypt raising wheat, and about India drawing from London £91,000,000 every year for seven articles of raw material—wheat, cotton, opium, rice, etc. To day the United States stands confronted with a competition which it never had dreamed of, and which apparently very few people in the country to-day seem to know anything about. It has western Asia, with Russian railways to bring its products to market. It has Egypt, it has India, and it has South America in its sweep. It is hard, dreadfully hard, on the farmers of the United States. But those who stand nearest to the soil have, from the foundation of the world to this hour, always had a struggle for a very moderate existence. I see no reason to believe that there will be any change in the future, but I see many reasons to believe that all the wheat and cotton producers of this country have got before them a long competition, and they must suffer mercilessly from countries where labor is cheap and where the government does all it can to bring the products of the country into market.

These questions, gentlemen, all affect the finances of the nation, because they all act to produce an adverse condition of exchange. I need not say to so intelligent a body of men that if we send abroad less cotton, less wheat, less corn, less petroleum, something else must go to take their place. I can see but one remedy, and that is brains. Brains in everything, in farming as well as in banking and manufacturing. Farmers must produce as cheaply as possible, and the country must (and it will) enlarge its lines of exports, and so, perhaps, arrest or retard the outflow of gold.

But, Mr. Chairman, to bring this question right down before us. The question of the hour is what methods Congress can adopt that would put it in the power of the country to arrest in a natural way this outflow of gold and to relieve the impending danger which hangs like a pall over our whole land. Congress must do that which should have been done, in my judgment, a quarter of a century ago, relieve the interference of the Government with the commerce and trade of the individual. I speak with positiveness, because that is my way, and I cannot stop to pick out fine words. Just so long as the Government of the country stands between the manufacturer, the merchant, and the banker in every transaction there can be no certainty in the results of the labors of any of them.

Mr. Chairman, I stand here to-day before you gentlemen of a wide experience and versed in the study of legislation, and I must say that while I speak with confidence, I wish also not to be charged with a lack of respect and of modesty. But these things are not new. History repeats and repeats itself. I will venture to say that any gentleman in this land may bring forward the most original financial thought that has been expressed in this country in the last thirty years and I will agree to duplicate everyone of those thoughts and show them to be a hundred or two hundred or four hundred years old. The merchant has suffered for generations and generations from the claims of kings, ministers, parliaments, and legislative bodies. He has suffered from a lack of their comprehensive knowledge of the principle of currency. And, therefore, while I do not intend to pass censure or even criticism on the great legislative body of this country, I do want to speak with such earnestness as, if possible, to impress you gentlemen with the immense responsibility that rests upon you. This country can not escape disaster unless something is done, and done quickly. I did not hesitate in 1880 to say that the resumption of specie payments did not settle a single financial question, and that every one of them would come up against us. I was also bold enough to say that if financial laws were not changed this country would pass through one of the most severe panics and periods of commercial disaster ever known; but I was only applying a little part of history to it.

Now I will bring the question down to practical propositions and practical legislation. How can the Government get out of this matter? It seems to me that the method is simple. Let Congress pass a good banking and currency act. Make a part of this act (and you can not, in my judgment, have a good banking and currency unless you do so) the gradual withdrawal and destruction of the legal-tender notes. Much as the old State banks have been censured and maligned, the country never suffered the annual depression, the severe constrictions in moving crops which it has suffered under our present financial system. With a circulation that never exceeded, at its highest point, $200,000,000, there never was any difficulty then in moving cotton, corn, and wheat to market. The notes of the State banks expanded. The wheat, cotton, and corn came to market, and the notes followed and went into the banks and remained there until another occasion of a similar character occurred.

Can we, with our present currency, to-day do that work which the old State-bank currency did so well? As a little matter of history, I want to say that I do not believe that Connecticut could have equipped her soldiers for the field in the late war had it not been for the old State-bank circulation. The greenbacks had not become plentiful enough, nor the national-bank notes. In my own institution we never, up to the time of the war, had been able, with the capital of $300,000, to get out $225,000 of circulation. Under every effort we made to keep it out it remained about $125,000, and even then we used to send it to Ohio, Illinois, and Indiana. But the work of preparing our soldiers for the field demanded more money, and ran our circulation up to $230,000. We practically violated the law to that extent, but the State got its funds, and, if it had not been for that, Connecticut would have been very much embarrassed in preparing her soldiers for the field.

After twenty-five years of study and thinking about banking matters I want to state right here frankly that I do not come before you as a novice presenting ideas which have dawned upon my brain during the last twelve months. If such was the case, and if I had not given the subject exhaustive study, I would have had no right to appear before you, nor would I have a right, in my judgment, to put a single thought forward for the consideration of others.

But any man who has given a special study to any subject, however humble and modest his mental capacity may be, is justified, I think, as the result of those years of study, in trying to impress his views upon others. Of course, others need not take them unless they choose to do so. I did not intend to bring forward any plan of my own in reference to the currency question, for the simple reason that I did not personally wish to do anything which might make me considered as in any degree antagonistic to what is called the Baltimore plan. That is the first concerted action on the part of bankers to obtain any legislation in regard to banking and currency. But it is not in every respect just what I want, and I hope that in the final draft of the bill it will be somewhat modified.

I have refused to make my own views public until a few days ago for just that reason, but when I saw in the papers that the Secretary of the Treasury would recommend a bill to Congress I felt that there was no need of my keeping back, because I know that any views which I may express would not be considered antagonistic to the Baltimore gentlemen. I want to say that in justice to myself, and also in justice to the Baltimore people and the Baltimore plan.

The bankers in Baltimore have done something which I have never known banking men to do before in all my experience. Bankers are the worst kind of people for combining, and I want to pay to the Baltimore people my unqualified approbation in that respect. If Congress will pass the Baltimore plan I have nothing to say; but if this committee is going to prepare, as it probably will, a measure for considering the Baltimore plan and the Comptroller of the Currency plan and the plan of the Secretary of the Treasury, then I do not know why I might not come forward and put in my little plan.

I differ somewhat from either of the other plans, not in their fundamental features. None of these other plans provides for redemption in a large city like New York. Now, I think that a redemption bureau located in the city of New York is vital to any system of paper money. There is no reason in the world why such a bureau should be located in Washington. It is not a governmental office. It has no connection with the Cabinet. The Comptroller of the Currency has nothing to do with the President and has very rarely to consult with the Secretary of the Treasury. His business is thoroughly a financial banking business. His office is the head office of the national banking system, and it should be located in the greatest financial center of the United States. That will make redemption so effective that there need not be fear of any inflation.

I want to lay stress on that particular feature, and I also want to lay all the stress that I possibly can on the ninth section of the plan which I submit, and that is that for every $100,000 of bank notes put into circulation there shall be $75,000 of legal-tender notes retired. The amendment which I have sketched out would require a reserve of 25 per cent in specie, so that if a bank issues $100,000 of currency and keeps $25,000 in specie that will leave the currency in precisely the same amount as before.

But it may be said that this will not operate to prevent a redundant currency; but such is not the case. Put the redemption agency in New York and I will guarantee that no bank will hold on to the notes of other banks. Every banker will be against every other banker in the country, and will send the notes of other banks home just about as fast as they are received, so as to make space for his own notes. That will have a tendency to localize the circulation: that is, the circulation of each bank will have a radius around its own institution, instead of spreading all over the country, and it will relieve any superabundant currency that may be in circulation.

I will not say that there may not be a little element of inflation from any paper money convertible into specie on demand, but I say that if the plan which I have sketched shall become law that inflation can never be any but a very slight one. It never can be so great as to jeopardize the solvency of the institution or the permanency of specie payment. I have no hesitation in saying, gentlemen, from an experience of thirty years as a banker, and as a man who, although young at the time, took a great interest and prepared very elaborate tables of the circulation of Connecticut banks and of redemption through the Suffolk bank system—I have no hesitation in saying, I repeat, that if Congress will adopt any one of the bills before you, giving a little larger scope to the Baltimore plan and putting this redemption feature into the plan of the Secretary of the Treasury, this country will have the best system of banking and currency which the world has ever known. I am not afraid to stand before you gentlemen and stake my reputation upon it, and I would even go farther if this were a monarchy, and would stake my life upon it and not fear taking any risk.

Just one word more and I am done. The question comes, How shall we deal with the State banks?

The CHAIRMAN. I suggest that you read a brief synopsis of your plan.

Mr. BUTLER. I formulated my ideas very briefly into the draft of a bill as follows:

AMENDMENT TO THE NATIONAL BANKING ACT.

First. All sections and parts of sections relating to the deposit of United States bonds to secure the circulation of the banks, and in any way relating to such bonds, are hereby repealed.

Second. Banks organized under the national banking act, or that may be organized under said act, may receive from the Comptroller of the Currency circulating notes to the amount of 75 per cent of their paid up and unimpaired capital.

Third. Notes of the denomination of less than $10 are hereby prohibited.

Fourth. Each bank shall keep a reserve in specie equal to 25 per cent of its average outstanding circulation.

Fifth. On the second Tuesday of January and July of each year the banks shall pay to the Treasurer of the United States a tax of 1 per cent upon the average circulation for the six months preceding, and ending December 31 and June 30 of each six months, until such tax shall have formed a fund to the amount of $3,000,000, after paying therefrom such charges as shall hereinafter be provided; then, thereafter, the said semiannual tax shall be one-half per cent upon the average circulation for each six months thereafter, until the said fund shall amount to $10,000,000; then, thereafter, the semiannual tax shall be one-fourth per cent for each six months until said fund shall amount to the sum of $20,000,000.

Whenever said fund shall amount to the sum of $20,000,000, the Comptroller of the Currency shall assess the banks such per cent upon their average circulation as may be necessary to defray all of the expenses of the department of the Comptroller of the Currency, and to keep unimpaired said fund of $20,000,000: *Provided*, That the Comptroller of the Currency shall not assess the banks at a rate greater than 1 per cent upon the average circulation for each six months of each year. The Treasurer of the United States shall keep said fund, created and maintained by said semiannual tax on the circulation, separate and apart from any and all of the general funds of the Government. It shall not be counted as any part of the general fund, nor shall it be entered into any statement of the resources and liabilities of the United States.

Sixth. The Treasurer of the United States shall provide a vault for the safe-keeping of said fund, which vault shall be known as the national-banks' vault, and shall be used for no other purpose than that of the banks.

The said fund shall be designated and known as the guaranty fund of the national banks. The Treasurer shall provide books, which shall be kept and used for said fund only. The Treasurer shall pay out of said fund the cost of providing vaults and safe-keeping thereof, and shall pay out of said fund the cost of preparing plates from which the notes of the banks shall be printed, together with all expenses of printing and delivering the notes to the banks, and every expense of the department of the Comptroller of the Currency, and for a suitable building for said department, as hereafter provided, and the balance of said fund shall be kept for the sole purpose of redeeming all notes of insolvent banks that may not have assets sufficient to pay all the debts of such insolvent banks.

The department of the Comptroller of the Currency shall be located in the city of New York, and the 25 per cent reserve shall be kept at the department of the Comptroller of the Currency. The Secretary of the Treasury of the United States shall buy a suitable lot in the city of New York, and shall cause to be erected thereon a building such as may be needed for the department of the Comptroller of the Currency, and shall cause to be erected in said building ample and safe vaults for the safe-keeping of the reserve on the circulation of the banks. There shall be a board of control, consisting of not less than five presidents of banks, to be selected by the clearing house of the city of New York. The Comptroller of the Currency shall be chairman of said board of control.

Said board of control shall have charge and custody of the reserve, and shall make such regulations for the safe-keeping of the reserve as they may deem best.

One-fifth of the reserve shall be under the immediate control of the Comptroller of the Currency, for the prompt redemption of all notes that may be presented for redemption.

Four-fifths of the reserve shall be kept in a separate vault, which shall be so constructed and arranged, and provided with locks, that the vault can be opened only by the joint action of a majority of the board of control.

Whenever the Comptroller of the Currency shall have redeemed notes of any one bank to the amount of $1,000 he shall return them to the issuing banks, which shall immediately reimburse the Comptroller for such notes. The lot, building, vaults, etc., shall be paid for out of the guaranty fund.

All banks that shall come under the provision of the national banking act, after said buildings, vaults, etc., shall have been paid for, shall pay the same semiannual tax as was paid by other banks and for the same period of time that all banks may contribute their just share to the expense of establishing this system of currency.

The title to said lot, building, etc., shall be in the Secretary of the Treasury of the United States in trust for the banks.

In the event of any change in the national banking act, or in the event of its repeal, which shall make this property no longer necessary for the purpose for which it was provided, it shall be sold at public auction to the highest bidder, unless sold at private sale by the board of control, who shall have the power to do so, and the proceeds of such sale shall be divided among the banks in proportion to their contribution to the same.

Seventh. Any bank organized under the laws of the State in which it is located may receive circulating notes from the Comptroller of the Currency to the amount of 75 per cent of its paid-up and unimpaired capital, upon a vote two-thirds of its stockholders, making the word "national" a part of the legal title of the bank, and accepting all of the provisions and conditions of the national banking act.

Eighth. The banks may freely use their reserve in time of panic, or in time of great and unusual apprehension and alarm, and such use of the reserve shall not be to their prejudice in any manner whatsoever, but shall be deemed the wise and proper use of a fund created by law to be kept through all ordinary times, to provide a fund to be used in an emergency. But the banks shall restore their reserves to their normal amounts whenever the Comptroller of the Currency shall determine that the emergency warranting its use no longer prevails.

Ninth. For every $100,000 of bank notes put into circulation $75,000 of the legal-tender notes shall be redeemed and destroyed. The Secretary of the Treasury may sell bonds of the United States in such amounts as may be necessary to carry this out. Said bonds shall be for such length of time, rate of interest, and all other conditions and regulations as the Secretary of the Treasury may deem best. Previous acts and laws in regard to the sale of bonds of the United States are not to be considered as in any way relating to this act, or in any way restricting the Secretary of the Treasury in the issue and sale of such bonds as may be necessary to give force and virtue to this act.

Tenth. Before issuing a certificate authorizing a bank to begin business, the Comptroller of the Currency shall cause careful inquiry to be made as to the character and reputation of those proposing to organize a bank, and if they are not found to be of good character and reputation he shall not give the certificate.

Any section or part of a section of the national banking act conflicting with any of these amendments thereto are hereby repealed.

The question often arises as to how the State banks are going to do. It is a very simple matter. We should maintain, in my judgment, the unity of the currency. It should be the same all over the country, and therefore any bank issuing currency should issue it as a national currency. The word "national" should appear upon it and it should be a part of the legal title of the bank. The simple process of two-thirds of the stockholders of a State bank voting that it shall be a State national bank and that they accept the provisions of the national bank act is all that is necessary. There is no use in preparing a different kind of note for State banks. That would be a cumbersome and embarrassing business.

Now, Mr. Chairman, I thank you and the gentlemen of the committee for giving me your attention, and I will answer such questions as any member of the committee may choose to put to me.

Mr. JOHNSON, of Indiana. The mode that you suggest for State banks coming in under the proposed system really makes them national banks, does it not?

Mr. BUTLER. Certainly.

The CHAIRMAN. So far as the currency is concerned?

Mr. BUTLER. I do not know why they should not come in under the national banking act the same as other banks. If they do not, let them not have any currency issued to them. They are national banks under the same conditions.

The CHAIRMAN. You do not require that the State banks shall give up their local charters in which they may have special privileges?

Mr. BUTLER. If they have some special privileges, they can maintain their charter by complying with the stipulations of the national-bank act.

The CHAIRMAN. In view of your own experience as a banker, do you think there should be two kinds of currency in circulation in the United States, one kind State currency and the other national currency? What would be the effect in practical dealings if one of these kinds of currency should be deemed a little better than the other even without producing a nominal discount?

Mr. BUTLER. I think there would be a preference given to the notes which carried the word "national" on them.

The CHAIRMAN. Then what would be the effect upon the other notes?

Mr. BUTLER. It would tend to limit their circulation very materially.

Mr. WARNER. They would be sent home for redemption more promptly?

Mr. BUTLER. Yes.

Mr. WARNER. As to that matter of redemption, you are familiar with the Suffolk plan by actual experience?

Mr. BUTLER. Yes. Let me say one word as to that. After this large expansion of the notes of our national bank to fit our soldiers for the field, our excess of currency came back inside of ninety days and we never could put it in circulation again. That is the important part of the whole thing.

Mr. WARNER. In your mind the elasticity of circulation results first from a lack of obstruction in putting it out, and then from a lack of obstruction to paying it in by those who hold it?

Mr. BUTLER. Not wholly. Banks must have in their possession an amount of notes in excess of what they keep out.

Mr. WARNER. You mean till-money?

Mr. BUTLER. Yes.

Mr. WARNER. But with that exception, that will be the case?

Mr. BUTLER. Yes.

Mr. WARNER. Your suggestion is that the present redemption facilities should be added to by having such facilities for redemption at one great city like New York, or at several centers, so as to bring in the notes more promptly for redemption when they are not needed for business?

Mr. BUTLER. I would have the main redemption bureau in the city of New York.

Mr. WARNER. With the object of bringing in the notes more promptly when they are not needed for business?

Mr. BUTLER. With that sole object; for a speedy, prompt and forcible redemption.

Mr. WARNER. Somewhat in the manner, and with the intention of having a similar effect, to that which we experienced under the Suffolk bank system?

Mr. BUTLER. Yes.

Mr. WARNER. Yesterday a distinguished banker expressed a fear that if that extraordinarily prompt redemption which used to be attained by the Suffolk bank system should be applied to all the currency of the country we would be in danger of a terrible currency famine. Have you any such apprehension?

Mr. BUTLER. It could not possibly happen.

Mr. WARNER. You have no apprehension of that at all?

Mr. BUTLER. It could not happen.

Mr. WARNER. Your idea is that the greater facilities there are for redemption the better?

Mr. BUTLER. The greater and sharper the redemption facilities of the country are the greater work the currency will perform. I make the prediction that if you carry out any of the plans before you (whether the Baltimore plan or the plan of the Secretary of the Treasury or my own plan) and put a redemption bureau in the city of New York the business of the country could be carried on better with $200,000,000 less currency than there is out to-day through the effectiveness of redemption and through the activity of circulation.

Mr. WARNER. The amount of circulation would thus adjust itself automatically to the business needs of the country?

Mr. BUTLER. Undoubtedly, unquestionably.

Mr. WARNER. And that is desirable?

Mr. BUTLER. It is the most desirable thing.

Mr. WARNER. And you do not believe there would be any danger in it?

Mr. BUTLER. I think there could not be. I will go further and say that that is the one great dominant virtue—that the redemption system would act as a financial barometer to every bank in the country, notifying them of danger. Whenever there is a little disturbance in business there would be an increased redemption of the notes of the bank, and the moment their notes came back to them in a little larger quantities they would know that there was a little overtrading and that there was danger ahead.

Mr. WARNER. If the Suffolk bank system were so perfect in its operation would it not be fair to assume that if the Government repudiated all responsibility for the redemption of notes the banks would arrange a volunteer plan very much better than the present plan?

Mr. BUTLER. The Suffolk bank system was only local. It was a New England institution. Bankers are a pretty good kind of men, but you can not trust them in everything.

Mr. WARNER. Did we not have a pretty good system in New York at that time?

Mr. BUTLER. Yes.

Mr. WARNER. And, in fact, was there not a pretty good system in every part of the country where finance was well developed?

Mr. BUTLER. The notes of our bank were sought in almost every State in the Union.

Mr. WARNER. And they came back for redemption?

Mr. BUTLER. They did, and we always took care of them. I have talked with a good deal of confidence before you, and now I want to give you one little bit of personal reminiscence and history which I hope will help to give what I have said a little more weight than it perhaps would otherwise have had. The institution which I have the honor of representing, beginning with the panic of 1873, had never failed to cash any note presented to it. It had never failed to furnish cash for the pay rolls of its manufacturing customers. It had never refused a dollar of discount to any of its customers up to the maximum which it had promised to supply; and it never has borrowed a dollar. But I do not hesitate to antagonize the interest of bankers in large cities, and in my own city, and I say that a reserve of 25 per cent in New York, Philadelphia, Boston, and Chicago is not enough. It has been proved over and over again that it is not enough, because, let the New York bankers say what they will, they do suspend in every panic and we do not. The New York Clearing House is simply a cash suspension.

Mr. WARNER. The other bankers have their deposits in the New York banks.

Mr. BUTLER. Yes; and the draft upon them on that account is larger.

Mr. WARNER. They—the New York banks—have to carry the outside bankers in this fashion. That is the trouble.

Mr. BUTLER. Yes. I said just now that bankers are a good class of men, but you can not trust them entirely. The desire to make money is too strong. Now, the problem of a large reserve and yet a flexible reserve is a very delicate one. In my pamphlet I have attempted to deal with it, and I think quite successfully. That is, that the banking act should compel the banks in the large cities to keep a reserve of 33⅓ per cent. In cities of over ten thousand inhabitants I am inclined to think that there should be an average reserve of 25 per cent, and in smaller towns a reserve of 15 per cent.

Mr. WARNER. And they should not be allowed to deposit the greater part of it in the city banks?

Mr. BUTLER. They should keep a part of it at home. We never go along ourselves with a reserve less than 25 per cent. Our statements to the Comptroller of the Currency will show that our average reserve is larger than 25 per cent. Of course we could not go through the panics as we did if we did not keep a larger reserve than 15 per cent. Now, I come here as a banker and I antagonize my own business and I say make it expensive for the banks to issue too much currency. If you give them the right to issue currency, make it expensive enough on them to make the currency good. Give the country as good a currency as it can get. If the banks do not wish to pay the expense of this good currency they are not obliged to take out. There are other banks that will take it out, and the man who wants to growl about it, let him growl.

As to the guarantee fund, I made some figures embracing twenty-nine years of the national banking system. Take all the national banks that have failed within that twenty-nine years and if you had not only made the notes payable out of this guarantee fund, but the deposits also, that fund would have paid every dollar lost by depositors as well as every dollar of notes, and there would have been more than two and a half times the amount left in the Treasury. In other words, in the twenty-nine years the banks have paid into the Government seventy-nine millions as a tax on their circulation, and if that had been applied to paying the depositors in failed banks as well as the notes of failed banks, it would have paid every dollar of it and still left fifty-two millions in the Treasury. Now, an experience of twenty-nine years that leaves such a result as that gives no ground to any fair-minded man to complain that the currency of this country is not safe as it can possibly be. There is no more possibility of a man losing a dollar now under the Baltimore plan or under my own than there is of his being translated.

Mr. WARNER. Is there any danger under the Secretary's plan?

Mr. BUTLER. I do not think so.

Mr. COX. I want to draw your mind back to the State-bank system. You made the remark that when these State banks were in existence there was no difficulty in moving the crops and that they were a great aid in that purpose. Now, if the State banks should make their notes as safe as the notes of the national banks can there be any objection of their issuing bank notes?

Mr. BUTLER. In some respects I am very much in sympathy with your question, for the reason that I have never believed that, strictly speaking, the Government of the United States has any business at all in reference to banks.

Mr. COX. I agree with you there.

Mr. BUTLER. And certainly has no business to make a note legal tender. Anybody who studies the Constitution and reads the decision of the Supreme Court of the United States in relation to legal tender is perfectly confounded. The Government has one power over banks, and that is the power of taxation. It can tax us out of existence, but it can not tax us into existence. But, as the country has settled down to the idea of a national banking system, and has become so imbued with the beauties of the unity of circulation, and as I no longer believe that it is worth while to struggle against the unconstitutional decisions of the Supreme Court (at least what I consider such) it has become a matter of general acceptance, and there is so much value in a unity of circulation that I think the State banks ought to be willing to give way to it.

The value of having all the currency throughout the country of the same kind is very great, and nobody is contending to-day, and never will contend against the right of the General Government to pass a national banking law. That power is conceded, and bowed down to (though with very stiff knees on my part). If Congress has any right to do anything with the currency at all except to coin gold and regulate the value of coins, I think that the banking system should be made one which applies to the country as a whole, and that any bank which wishes to issue notes should come in under the national banking system.

Mr. Cox. You have put your answer entirely on the ground of unity of system?

Mr. Butler. Yes.

Mr. Cox. Is it not now the case in this country, and is it not well known in all financial centers that, in certain places in the country, there is more money than there is any use for, and that in other places (especially in the South) there is hardly enough money to transact business? Do you not find that state of affairs now?

Mr. Butler. That we can not remedy. Money goes where the accumulation of wealth is. I was passing through Alabama and Louisiana some years ago in an observation car with several Southern bankers, and one of them said to me: "What we want, Mr. Butler, in the South is more money." I said, "What for?" I said, "If you draw a check upon a bank for $1,000 and you have an account there to that amount have you any trouble in getting the money?" "No." "If you sell 100 bales of cotton to a responsible man have you any trouble in getting the money for it?" "No." "If a responsible man owes you $1,000, have you any trouble in getting paid?" "No." "Then," said I, "what do you want more money for?" He said, "To develop the country." "Oh," said I, "what you want is more capital." "Now," I said, "I can not conceive how under heaven the Government can put the money in circulation at all; but suppose the Government can do just as a great many people in the South and West want it to do, give us more money, what will be the result? Perhaps 10 per cent of it," I said, "will stay with you because it will cause a slight rise in prices. The 90 per cent will go to New York and New England banks because those States hold the accumulated capital of the country, and money goes where capital is. By this inflation you would have created a condition of things where you would want 10 per cent more circulating capital for business, but you have not created anything from that capital and you have put yourself in a tighter box than before." That is the operation of inflation, and it must be so. Yet the people who do not make a study of this thing do not understand it, and a great many people can not comprehend the subject anyway.

Mr. Cox. Your idea was that there is no necessity for any State institution in the way of banking, but the ground you put it on a moment ago is that we must have a unity of currency. My first question assumed the issue by State banks of notes absolutely good. It is not a question for us to decide whether the people need those notes or not. Can it be possible to pass any note except it is absolutely good over the counter of a bank under the present condition of things?

Mr. Butler. In answer to that I will say that while I am only giving my own personal preferences, if a bill were prepared giving to State banks a little peculiar advantage in regard to that, I would not be antagonistic. I do not think it vital, but I prefer the other way. That is all a matter of preference.

Mr. COX. Always assuming that the currency of State banks is good, you see no objection to its issue?

Mr. BUTLER. No.

Mr. JOHNSON, of Indiana. Aside from the question as to the constitutionality of the law taxing State-bank issues, are you not of opinion that soundness and uniformity in the currency is much more likely to be secured and maintained by one system of note issue under direct Federal control, than by leaving each State to devise a system of State-bank issue for itself?

Mr. BUTLER. There can be no question about that.

Mr. JOHNSON, of Indiana. Is it not your opinion that a change in the existing currency system, along the line of the Baltimore plan, which will dispense with rigid bank security for circulating notes and supply a flexible currency, obtained under what is known as the safety system, will meet, as far as possible in the nature of things, this complaint of lack of money in the rural and sparsely settled districts where money is wanted at some time to move the crops and is not so much needed at other times?

Mr. BUTLER. I recognize that there are a good many places where there are small banks and where the need of facilities for circulation is just the same. A local bank, though small, will be able to give you all the local circulation you want, in my judgment.

Mr. JOHNSON, of Indiana. You were asked if you thought it possible that bad State-bank notes could be paid out over the counter of a bank. Now, is it not a fact that under what is known as the old State-bank régime which prevailed in this country before the war that was often done?

Mr. BUTLER. Yes; that was often done.

Mr. JOHNSON, of Indiana. Also, that the trouble with bad currency consists in the fact that it gets into circulation under the impression that it is good, whereas in point of fact (owing to some defect in the law or to some administration of the bank) the bank is not sound, and immense loss is occasioned to the public?

Mr. BUTLER. Under any system that we are contemplating now, the provision which admits any State bank presupposes that the Comptroller of the Currency sees that it complies with all the conditions required of the national banks.

Mr. JOHNSON, of Indiana. Does that not make it a national bank?

Mr. BUTLER. Practically, but the State banks maintain their separate charters all the same.

Mr. JOHNSON, of Indiana. Is it not a fact that during that old régime bank notes circulated right along at a discount, and that the necessities of some men and that the exegencies of trade required people to take these bad notes at a discount?

Mr. BUTLER. There were bad notes in circulation, and considerable evil was caused by them.

Mr. JOHNSON, of Indiana. Is it not also a fact that bad bank-issuing systems in this country were maintained in some States right along, notwithstanding better examples afforded by good banking systems in other States?

Mr. BUTLER. The banks in some States were very much better than in others. I do not want to say that any were bad, but some of them were rather defective.

Mr. JOHNSON, of Indiana. In your opinion are there not more opportunities for failure from having a number of systems of note issues than from having one simple system?

Mr. BUTLER. I think that that is possible. I would not wish to call it probable, but it is possible.

Mr. COBB, of Alabama. Do you believe that there would be any material danger in repealing absolutely the 10 per cent tax on State banks?

Mr. BUTLER. Yes; very probably there would be.

Mr. COBB, of Alabama. With the condition of the country so varying from what it was in former days?

Mr. BUTLER. I would not do it. I want it distinctly understood that I would not favor any paper money of any kind except by the withdrawal of some other, unless it were to meet a certain political emergency.

Mr. COBB, of Alabama. Is there to-day existing a condition of things under which wild-catting is possible?

Mr. BUTLER. There is very little wild-catting now. Banking has become more widely known and banking men have become better known to each other. Any bank that would attempt anything of that kind would be crushed out very quickly, almost before it got started.

Mr. HAUGEN. How crushed out—by legislation or by public opinion?

Mr. BUTLER. If I thought that there was wild-catting going on, I would sit down and write to the Comptroller of the Currency that he had better investigate it.

Mr. HAUGEN. If the State-bank tax were repealed, there would be no jurisdiction over State banks on the part of the Comptroller of the Currency.

Mr. RUSSELL. Under the Secretary's plan, the Comptroller of the Currency would have no right to make that investigation.

Mr. BUTLER. I believe, as things are to-day, that we should confine ourselves to one kind of currency.

Mr. COBB, of Alabama. Have you any such provisions by the banks themselves?

Mr. BUTLER. We have between ourselves.

Mr. HAUGEN. In Wisconsin we have a State banking law under which wild-catting was done before the war, and the only thing which has kept the banks there from operating under that system is the imposition of the 10 per cent tax. The State law never has been changed. It remains now upon the statute books.

Mr. BUTLER. I am not in favor of an unconditional repeal of that tax.

Mr. COBB, of Alabama. Do you believe that the condition of banking in this country now, and the condition of the country generally, does not make it impossible for a State bank to issue and circulate money that is not secured?

Mr. BUTLER. I think that such circulation would be very small.

Mr. BROSIUS. Does your plan contemplate the ultimate responsibility of the Government for the notes issued?

Mr. BUTLER. No, it does not. I do not think, myself, that a Government guarantee is necessary.

Mr. BROSIUS. Your plan contemplates a specie reserve of 25 per cent, does it not?

Mr. BUTLER. Yes.

Mr. BROSIUS. And that reserve shall be put under the custody of the Comptroller of the Currency—a certain percentage of it—and that the remainder of it is to be under the control of the board of control.

Then I find in another section of your plan that the banks are permitted to use a portion of that reserve. If a bank is permitted to use a portion of that reserve which is locked up under the control of the board of control, how does the bank get the reserve for use?

Mr. BUTLER. I meant to have inserted a word there. I am referring in that clause to the reserve on deposits, not to the reserve on circulation. I want to put in the word "deposit" there, as it escaped my mind.

Mr. BROSIUS. Then that reserve, as I now understand you, is not available as security for the circulating notes?

Mr. BUTLER. The 25 per cent specie reserve is.

Mr. BROSIUS. Where does that remain?

Mr. BUTLER. In the department in New York, if the department were removed there. I for one would keep banking as free from Government as I could; so I selected that board of control to be located in the monetary center of the country.

Mr. BROSIUS. You have stated that the present banking system lacks elasticity. Have the kindness to hear this statement:

> The estimated circulation on July 1, 1893, was $1,593,700,000. This increased in three months to $1,700,000,000, and by February of this year reached in round numbers $1,740,000,000. From July to May it declined to $1,690,000,000. In other words, the past ten months have witnessed an expansion of our circulation of nearly $150,000,000, followed by a contraction of about $50,000,000, leaving the present volume about $100,000,000 more than that of July 1, 1893.

Now, my inquiry is, whether that does not exhibit a considerable degree of elasticity in the present system of banking.

Mr. BUTLER. To some extent it does, but not in the way in which I use the word "elasticity" or in the way in which Mr. White used it. But expansion and contraction in the case you have read are arbitrary. They have not grown out of any industrial or commercial transactions. What I mean, and what Mr. White means, by an elastic currency is this: A currency with which the banks will have at all times notes in excess of what they can keep in circulation throughout the year, and that they will have idle notes in their vaults which they can use at the time of the moving of the great crops. The low interest paid on our Government bonds and the high market price for them prevent the banks from taking out a single dollar of circulation except such as they can keep out at all times. Therefore, there is no expansion and there is no contraction there. These are not the contraction and expansion which affect commercial transactions. The expansion is merely that which follows legislation in regard to coining and printing money on the one side, and on the other side the contraction comes from banks which find it more profitable to surrender their circulation than to take in their bonds.

Mr. BROSIUS. The secret of elasticity consists, does it not, in having the notes to put out when they are needed and in taking them back when they are not needed?

Mr. BUTLER. I could not put it any better.

Mr. BROSIUS. What idea did you intend to convey to the committee when you said that the Government should be prevented from interfering between merchants, manufacturers, and bankers in their transactions with each other?

Mr. BUTLER. That is one of those cases where my words were perhaps not so felicitous as they would be if I had sat down and thought them over carefully. I did not mean any direct interference, but I meant the fact that the Government was so involved in the whole system that there was a general interference, not an individual and personal interference, but one inherent in the system.

Mr. BROSIUS. Do you mean to say that that interference inheres in the system of issuing Government paper?

Mr. BUTLER. Yes, and in the arbitrary coinage of silver.

The CHAIRMAN. A portion of the flexibility to which Mr. Brosius refers was caused, was it not, by the purchase of 4,500,000 ounces of silver a month under the Sherman act? That caused the elasticity.

Mr. BUTLER. No, that is expansion; it is not elasticity.

Mr. WARNER. In regard to the withdrawal of greenbacks, I understand that you are very much in favor of the withdrawal of the greenback circulation?

Mr. BUTLER. Yes, I am.

Mr. WARNER. What is the method which, in your opinion, should be adopted for that withdrawal?

Mr. BUTLER. I would have any withdrawal of greenbacks by the Government made very carefully, so that it would not in any way produce any contraction or jar on the finances of the country, and I do not know any better way than to have that withdrawal follow the issue of bank notes.

Mr. WARNER. You would have the withdrawal or the circulation of the greenback currency made a condition precedent to the issue of new currency?—or would you provide for it by some separate provision?

Mr. BUTLER. I would make it a part of the bill.

Mr. WARNER. It would be one way to meet your views if, by a separate section, the bill shall provide that the Treasury should have the right to fund a certain amount of greenbacks in proportion to the new currency to be issued.

Mr. BUTLER. That I have in my proposed bill.

Mr. WARNER. It would also come within your general statement if it were provided (as it is in Secretary Carlisle's plan) that on the issue of more currency a certain amount of greenbacks should be sequestrated, as it were?

Mr. BUTLER. Yes; I think it very desirable.

Mr. WARNER. In the first case the withdrawal of greenbacks would not be a tax on the new currency?

Mr. BUTLER. I do not know that I quite catch your idea.

Mr. WARNER. If it is made a condition of issuing new currency that the bank issuing it shall sequester a certain amount of greenbacks, is not that a practical tax on the issue of new currency?

Mr. BUTLER. I did not mean that. The Comptroller of the Currency issues to a bank $100,000 in notes, and immediately turns over to the Treasurer of the United States or the Treasury of the United States and immediately gets possession of $75,000 in greenbacks. If he has not the cash in the Treasury authority is to be given to sell bonds.

Mr. WARNER. A plan has been prepared by which, as a condition of getting out currency, the bank that is permitted to issue it shall attend to the sequestering of a certain proportion of that amount in greenbacks. The result of that is, is it not, a practical obstruction to the issue of currency to the extent of the interest that is lost on the greenbacks so sequestrated?

Mr. BUTLER. Do I understand you to mean that the banks are to become possessed of a certain amount of greenbacks and to destroy them?

Mr. WARNER. No; but to lock them up; to put them in the Treasury.

Mr. BUTLER. And ultimately the Government has to redeem them?

Mr. WARNER. I suppose that ultimately the Government will have to redeem them.

Mr. BUTLER. It seems to me that Secretary Carlisle injected a political element into his bill. It seems to me that he thought that that would be a method by which some parties might be induced to retire the legal-tender notes, by the banks issuing them as a part of their reserve, and in that way getting them out of the way and putting the Government in the position to pay them. I take that to be rather the object of getting these greenbacks out of circulation, but it does not produce any economic effect.

Mr. WARNER. Is it not an obstruction to the issue of currency to the extent of the loss of interest on these greenbacks?

Mr. BUTLER. Certainly.

Mr. WARNER. And does it not tend to raise the rate of interest?

Mr. BUTLER. No; that is a mistake. It will add to the cost of doing business. Suppose after I get home I should find that the board of directors had voted to double my salary, that would add something to the expense of the bank, but it would not add anything to the rate of interest charged to its customers.

Mr. WARNER. Suppose there is a demand for money to move the crops. If it costs more to issue currency will you not charge your customers more for the use of the money?

Mr. BUTLER. That is governed entirely by the money market. It is like the case of a farmer. If he has 1,000 bushels of potatoes and has to sell them, and they are only worth 25 cents a bushel, he must sell them.

Mr. WARNER. But in that case will the farmer raise potatoes?

Mr. BUTLER. Not next year.

Mr. WARNER. Will you, as a banker, issue currency unless it pays you a profit?

Mr. BUTLER. Of course not.

Mr. WARNER. Will you not charge that rate of interest which will make it pay you a profit?

Mr. BUTLER. I will if I can get it.

Mr. WARNER. Will you not, as a condition of issuing more currency, exact enough interest to pay you a profit?

Mr. BUTLER. Under any of these systems the banks will have some additional loaning facilities, and in my judgment that will have some tendency to make a lower rate of interest.

Mr. WARNER. The more facilities the banks will have the lower the rate of interest will be?

Mr. BUTLER. Of course; I think it will have that general tendency

Mr. WARNER. In regard to branch banks, have you given that subject any consideration?

Mr. BUTLER. I would not be a good authority on that subject, though I presume I am familiar enough with it to answer your questions

Mr. WARNER. Do you think that the question of branch banking—that of permitting banking to be done by a single institution in a large number of localities—is one which is or may be of very great importance in settling any system that may be proposed?

Mr. BUTLER. I do not see any objection whatever in having branch banks; but it is rather non-American in its idea.

Mr. WARNER. How does it work where it is practiced?

Mr. BUTLER. No better, I think, than where they do not have it.

Mr. WARNER. Your opinion, then, would be rather against the advisability of branch banks?

Mr. BUTLER. Yes; it is extending a man's care over a larger field than he can well attend to.

Mr. WARNER. We had branch banks in this country before the war

Mr. BUTLER. Yes; and they have them now in Canada, and Scotland, and France, and Germany, and they seem to work well; but after all, with the dash and the rush of American people, I do not think I would like to have branch banks.

Mr. SPERRY. What would be the effect on Secretary Carlisle's plan if the requirement of a 30 per cent reserve were eliminated?

Mr. BUTLER. He puts that in there to take the place of where I have a 25 per cent specie reserve. He calls it a guarantee, but I should call it a reserve, only he is in favor of reserving greenbacks, not specie.

Mr. SPERRY. His plan would tend, of course, to get so much greenbacks out of the field?

Mr. BUTLER. Yes; that is why I said that there was a little political idea in it.

Mr. SPERRY. Under the Suffolk banking system did the banks pay out their own notes exclusively or did they pay out the notes of other banks?

Mr. BUTLER. Their own notes almost exclusively. We always had an abundance of our own notes on hand. There was hardly a time when our institution did not have thirty or forty thousand dollars of its own notes in its vaults.

Mr. SPERRY. Do you think that under the Baltimore plan banks would pay out their own notes exclusively?

Mr. BUTLER. There is no doubt about that.

Mr. SPERRY. So that the effect would be that each bank would circulate its own notes?

Mr. BUTLER. Yes.

Mr. SPERRY. And to that extent it would have a localizing effect?

Mr. BUTLER. Decidedly.

Mr. WARNER. And you would depend upon that for elasticity?

Mr. BUTLER. Yes.

Mr. SPERRY. You prefer a note redeemable in coin, I take it?

Mr. BUTLER. Yes, I do.

Mr. SPERRY. If you have a note redeemable in coin immediately on demand, do you think there is any danger of expansion or inflation of the currency where every bank is obliged to take up its own notes?

Mr. BUTLER. There would be a little danger. Ricardo said a good many years ago that if it were possible not one dollar of gold from Australia or California would have got into the market. The banks would only take out just that amount of bank notes which they could keep in circulation, but that would come far short of what the law would allow them to take out. I doubt whether the banks would average more than 30 or 20 per cent of the circulation which the law would allow them.

Mr. SPERRY. Would the inflation be such as to approach the danger point?

Mr. BUTLER. With this specie reserve it would not be, and that is why I prefer the specie reserve to the legal-tender note reserve. I would have a large reserve anyhow. Canada, I think, is very lax in all its reserv elegislation. The German law requires a reserve of 33⅓ per cent for the Imperial bank and for all other banks that issue notes. Any circulation in excess of about ninety-four millions must be either fully covered by coin or must have a tax of 5 per cent paid upon it. There is no doubt but that Germany intended to form a currency system after England. The features of the two systems are very much the same.

I found some time ago that the paper money circulation of Germany was was twice what the law allowed under what they call "uncovered." There was twice that amount of money in circulation.

Mr. SPERRY. If the banks under either of these proposed systems would put out their own bills only, do you think that the tendency would be to retire greenbacks from circulation?

Mr. BUTLER. Of course if greenbacks were paid in to us the only way for us to do would be to send them on. We would not pay out other bank notes.

Mr. ELLIS. I presume that you have examined the bill submitted by the Secretary of the Treasury?

Mr. BUTLER. Yes.

Mr. ELLIS. I would like to have your opinion, as a practical banker, with reference to section 5, which provides that the banks organizing under the plan proposed should be responsible ultimately and immediately for the notes of any bank in the system which might fail.

Mr. BUTLER. I would not make that a sweeping obligation. I do not like that feature at all.

Mr. ELLIS. I would like to have your opinion, as a banker, as to whether or not the present national banks would accept this system and organize under it.

Mr. BUTLER. I do not believe they would organize under that provision. It is a responsibility which bankers shrink from.

Mr. ELLIS. This provision would make your bank in Connecticut responsible for the conduct of a bank out in the State of Washington?

Mr. BUTLER. I think the banks would not come in under it. I think they would rather do without the notes. I think that provision of the law would practically nullify the act.

Mr. ELLIS. State what modification of the Carlisle plan would make it acceptable to the bankers of the country.

Mr. BUTLER. That central redemption in New York, with branches, and the elimination of that feature which you spoke of would, I think, make it a pretty fair banking act. I should rather have the Baltimore plan with the central redemption than the other.

Mr. ELLIS. Would you eliminate the State-bank system altogether from any plan?

Mr. BUTLER. That is not a thing which I would insist on against any great pressure, but I do think its elimination is very desirable.

Mr. ELLIS. Would the notes which might be issued under the plan which you propose (which does not provide that the Government should ultimately guarantee their redemption) be as satisfactory to the public as the present national banking system?

Mr. BUTLER. Of course the Government guarantee carries a great deal of weight with the public, but I believe that when a system is in operation and the strength of it is seen the people would forget that there was any such thing as Government, so far as bank notes were concerned.

Mr. ELLIS. If those banks were organized and the Government had no responsibility either for the immediate or the ultimate redemption of the notes, and if a large number of large banks in the country should fail, would not that be calculated to produce a panic, and would not the holders throughout the country want to redeem their notes at once?

Mr BUTLER. No; I think not. The thing which causes almost all panics and all runs on banks is not so much the solvency or insolvency of a bank as it is the fear of the people that they will not be able to get their money when they want it. That is the largest element in all panics.

Mr. ELLIS. What is your objection to using United States Treasury notes as a reserve fund?

Mr. BUTLER. That is a mere sentiment. Gold is awfully pretty.

Mr. WALKER. Have you read the testimony of Mr. Carlisle?

Mr. BUTLER. Yes, in part; but I do not know how much of it has stuck to my memory.

Mr. WALKER. Mr. Carlisle testified that the 30 per cent to be deposited was to be a fixed sum beyond the control of the banks, except as they withdrew their notes. Now, the reserve fund, as we understand it in banking, is a reserve that may be used by the bank at any moment and for any purpose. He having said that this is a note reserve fund, by what authority do you say that it is equivalent to what we understand as a bank reserve?

Mr. BUTLER. I have no authority for it; it is only a supposition.

Mr. WALKER. Mr. Carlisle says it is a note reserve fund to make the notes secure, and, furthermore, it is deposited with the Government entirely. Now, is not that thoroughly inconsistent, and is it not even impossible of supposition that it is a bank-reserve fund as you and I understand a bank reserve?

Mr. BUTLER. Certainly, if it could not be used.

Mr. WALKER. It could not be used by the bank.

Mr. BUTLER. If it could not be used by the Comptroller of the Currency for redemption of notes we might just as well not have it.

Mr. WALKER. It can not be.

Mr. BUTLER. Then we might just as well not have it.

The CHAIRMAN. I think that the Secretary of the Treasury distinctly stated, as part of the plan, that the law should not require a fund for the redemption of deposits.

Mr. WALKER. He distinctly stated that his bill did not require any deposit reserve at all to be carried, and that this was left entirely to the good judgment of the banks. His 30 per cent fund is entirely eliminated from the reserve which the bank carries.

Mr. BUTLER. When I read his testimony I noticed that, but it went out of my mind.

Mr. COBB, of Alabama. You stated that you objected very strenuously to making all the banks responsible for a failed bank. Suppose that responsibility were limited to 1 per cent, would it be a very serious objection?

Mr. BUTLER. I have got it in my plan at 2 per cent.

Mr. WALKER. The idea is that no bank or individual is ever willing to assume an unknown liability?

Mr. BUTLER. That is it.

Mr. WALKER. If there is a known liability—

Mr. BUTLER. There would not be so much objection to it.

Mr. HALL. In reply to a question by Mr. Johnson, of Indiana, you interjected the remark that the Secretary of the Treasury had injected a political element into his plan. You referred to the requirement of the deposit of 30 per cent in legal-tender notes as a guarantee fund. That was the political element you referred to. Now I ask you if, under the provisions of your plan, you have any method of retiring legal-tender notes?

Mr. BUTLER. Yes; I make the provision that for every $100,000 of bank notes put into circulation the Secretary of the Treasury is to retire $75,000 of legal-tender notes and issue bonds.

Mr. HALL. Is there any such provision in the Baltimore plan?

Mr. BUTLER. I have forgotten.

Mr. HORACE WHITE. There is nothing in the Baltimore plan on that subject. I introduced it in my plan which I submitted yesterday.

Mr. HALL (to Mr. Butler). Do you not regard the present financial condition by which these legal tender Treasury notes are used for the purpose of exhausting the gold reserve as a dangerous and critical condition?

Mr. BUTLER. I do not see how any man can have two opinions on that subject.

Mr. HALL. You think that it is a dangerous and critical condition?

Mr. BUTLER. Yes; I do.

Mr. HALL. But this so-called political element which you spoke of in Secretary Carlisle's plan is simply an element which tends to relieve a very embarrassed condition?

Mr. BUTLER. Yes; to some extent. When I used the word "political" I did not mean it as a matter of party politics, but as a general term.

Mr. HALL. In answer to a question of Mr. Ellis's, referring to the fifth section of Secretary Carlisle's plan, you said that no banks would come in under its operation so long as the fifth section remained in that plan.

Mr. BUTLER. With unlimited responsibility for other people's actions, I suppose they would not. I do not believe that any bank would accept unknown liabilities.

Mr. HALL. Did you ever read section 5 of Mr. Carlisle's bill?

Mr. BUTLER. I have read it, but I do not recollect exactly now how it is worded. I have been quite ill, and I am quite weak yet.

Mr. HALL. Section 5 reads:

SEC. 5. That in order to provide a safety fund for the prompt redemption of the circulating notes of failed national banking associations, each such association now organized, or hereafter organized, shall pay to the Treasurer of the United States, in the months of January and July in each year, a tax of one-fourth of one per centum for each half year upon the average amount of its circulating notes outstanding, to be computed as hereinbefore provided, until the said fund amounts to a sum equal to five per centum upon the total amount of national-bank notes outstanding, and thereafter said tax shall cease. Each association hereafter organized, and each association applying for additional circulation, shall pay its pro rata share into the said fund before receiving notes; but an association retiring or reducing its circulation shall not be entitled to withdraw any part of said fund. When a national banking association becomes insolvent its guaranty fund held on deposit shall be transferred to the safety fund herein provided for, and applied to the redemption of its outstanding notes; and in case the said last-mentioned fund should at any time be impaired by the redemption of the notes of failed banks, and the immediately available assets of said banks are not sufficient to reimburse it, said fund shall be at once restored by pro rata assessments upon all the other associations according to the amount of their outstanding circulation, and the associations so assessed shall have a first lien upon the assets of each failed bank for the amount properly chargeable to such bank on account of the redemption of its circulation.

Now, the liability is to this 5 per cent safety fund. The banks are to keep that up, and when a bank fails the 30 per cent guarantee deposited by that failed bank is transferred at once to the 5 per cent safety fund, and the banks that keep up this 5 per cent have an immediate lien on the assets of the defunct bank. Do you think that an increased hazard?

Mr. BUTLER. I would not consider it any risk to the bank at all, but yet I do not think that the average board of directors of a bank would vote for it.

Mr. HALL. In view of your mind being refreshed as to the provisions of section 5 of Mr. Carlisle's bill, would you then say that, if it was a law, the national banks or the banks in the United States would not take out circulation or come under the conditions of the law simply on account of the provisions of section 5?

Mr. BUTLER. I think it very problematical—very.

Mr. HALL. I should like to know what your statement is based on.

Mr. BUTLER. No reasonable man likes to bind himself to an absolutely unknown responsibility.

Mr. HALL. Is there an unknown responsibility in the provisions of that section?

Mr. BUTLER. Yes; the banks do not know just what it is. It is not a definite responsibility. But I do not believe there is any risk in it. I may be entirely wrong. It is a mere matter of opinion, and I may be wrong in that while I may be right in everything else.

Mr. COX. In your opinion as a banker, if the guarantee fund is made up of the 5 per cent safety fund and the 30 per cent deposit of the failed bank added to it, do you think there is any danger of the banks having to pay anything in the case of a failed bank?

Mr. BUTLER. Not a bit.

Mr. COX. So the unknown liability lies in a myth at last?

Mr. BUTLER. Yes, it does.

Mr. ELLIS. With reference to the matter you were just talking about in answer to questions propounded by Mr. Hall the Secretary of the Treasury has testified, and has explained the difference between his bill and the Baltimore plan. I wish to read you the interpretation which he puts on section 5. He says on page 15 of the testimony:

> The plan which I have proposed requires, in the first place, the deposit of a sum equal to 30 per cent of the amount of circulating notes applied for by the bank, this money to be held all the time and to constitute a separate fund belonging to the bank which makes the deposit. In addition to that, there is to be a safety fund raised by taxation on all the banks in the same way as is proposed in the Baltimore plan, out of which the notes of failed banks shall be redeemed. And if that fund shall prove insufficient (or if it be reduced below 5 per cent of the total amount of national-bank circulation), and if the immediate available assets of the failed bank are not sufficient to redeem its notes, the Treasury Department is to assess all the other national banks pro rata, according to the amount of their circulation, to bring this fund up. And the banks that pay this assessment are to have a first lien on all the assets of the failed national bank, and the Government is not to be in any way responsible.

With that interpretation of this section by the author of it, and with that fact known to national bankers and directors, I repeat my question: Would they organize under it?

Mr. BUTLER. I think it would interfere very greatly with our organizing under it. If I were personally committing my own money I would have no fear of a loss, and yet I would not commit our institution to it, because I am handling other people's property.

Mr. JOHNSON, of Indiana. In your opinion what would be the effect on the national banks issuing circulating notes under the enactment by Congress of a national-banking law which would impose pretty rigid conditions on them and which at the same time would permit banking by State banks under very lax conditions?

Mr. BUTLER. That ought not to be done.

Mr. JOHNSON, of Indiana. What would be the effect on national banks of such a discrimination?

Mr. BUTLER. I do not know that it would have any effect on the national banks at all, because every bank stands alone and every community stands alone.

Mr. JOHNSON, of Indiana. Would it not have a tendency to induce banks to incorporate under State laws?

Mr. BUTLER. I do not know. The word "national" is considered as being of as much advantage as that would be a disadvantage.

Mr. JOHNSON, of Indiana. But if a national banking law imposed rigid conditions would the effect not probably be that the national banks would incorporate under State laws?

Mr. BUTLER. I think they would.

Mr. JOHNSON, of Indiana. As banks of issue?

Mr. BUTLER. I think they would.

Mr. JOHNSON, of Indiana. If permitted by a national banking law?

Mr. BUTLER. I think they would.

Mr. JOHNSON, of Indiana. As I take it, you feel that there is no danger of loss to whosoever assumes the ultimate liability of these circulating notes under this safety fund system?

Mr. BUTLER. I do not believe that there is a possibility of loss.

Mr. JOHNSON, of Indiana. Therefore, whether it fall upon the banks or upon the Government will really not make much difference so far as actual loss is concerned, will it?

Mr. BUTLER. No.

Mr. JOHNSON, of Indiana. Is it not very important for the success of a bank currency that the people shall have faith in its soundness?

Mr. BUTLER. Yes; there is no question about that.

Mr. JOHNSON, of Indiana. Do you not think that they would be much more liable to have more faith in it if they felt that the Government was ultimately liable for the payment of the notes than if the ultimate liability rested elsewhere?

Mr. BUTLER. Yes; I think that that would add to the confidence, undoubtedly.

Mr. JOHNSON, of Indiana. Then would you not favor ultimate Government liability to the note holder under the safety-fund system?

Mr. BUTLER. I do not think it necessary at all; and I am so constitutionally opposed to the Government having anything to do with the banking business that my own tendency is to cut clear of the Government.

Mr. JOHNSON, of Indiana. Laying aside the constitutional scruples and looking at it as a practical business man, do you not think that the people would have more confidence in any system of circulating notes that carried with it its ultimate redemption by the General Government?

Mr. BUTLER. There can not be any question at all about that.

Mr. WALKER. When you speak of the confidence of the people, is not the confidence of the people, so far as currency is concerned, a synonym with the confidence of bankers?

Mr. BUTLER. It comes practically to that, to a large extent.

Mr. WALKER. When you say that there is no risk under this 5 per cent guarantee, I suppose you mean by that that there is no risk after all the banks of the country have gone into the system. You do not mean to say that there would be no risk if there were only ten banks in it?

Mr. BUTLER. At the first start there would be, perhaps, an element of risk.

Mr. WALKER. There would be a serious risk if there were only ten banks in it?

Mr. BUTLER. The risk would not be worth considering.

Mr. WALKER. Would it not be worth considering for the first year, supposing there were only ten banks in it with a capital of $100,000 each?

Mr. BUTLER. I think not.

Mr. RUSSELL. If your opinion as a banker is correct, that the national banks generally would fail to organize under Secretary Carlisle's plan, with the contingent liability of section five in it, then the practical result of the Secretary's plan would be to give this country a State-bank currency, would it not?

Mr. BUTLER. I think you are right about that, but I had not thought about it.

Mr. WARNER. You spoke of every bank standing on its own bottom and on its own credit in the confidence of the community in which it does business. During the last panic, for example, your depositors did not institute a run upon you, as a consequence of knowing that banks were breaking in Wisconsin, Colorado, and other States. In case however, that they had knowledge that your bank was responsible with others, for the circulation of banks which (they heard) were breaking on every side, would that not have produced a very grave feeling of apprehension among the people?

Mr. BUTLER. That panic was not a note panic at all. It was a depositors' panic.

Mr. WARNER. I was referring to the effect of this clause of section 5. At present your bank is not responsible for the currency of any other bank.

Mr. BUTLER. No.

Mr. WARNER. Nor for its business?

Mr. BUTLER. No.

Mr. WARNER. So, when your depositors hear of banks breaking in Washington, Colorado, and other States, that fact does not, of itself, cause them to worry about the soundness of your bank?

Mr. BUTLER. No.

Mr. WARNER. In case, however, a plan involving section 5 went into effect, and the depositors in your bank knew that your bank was responsible as an ultimate guarantor, for the circulation of the numerous banks throughout the country, which, the newspapers told them, were breaking; would not that cause them to have some apprehension as to your bank?

Mr. BUTLER. They would not have the same confidence.

Mr. WARNER. And would not that tend to bring about a run on your bank?

Mr. BUTLER. Undoubtedly.

Mr. WARNER. And is not that a serious objection to the unlimited responsibility provided for in section 10?

Mr. BUTLER. Very serious.

The committee here took a recess till 2 p. m.

AFTER RECESS.

The chairman stated to the committee that he had received a telegram from Mr. Cornwell, dated Buffalo, N. Y., December 11, and announcing that he would be in this city at noon to-day, but that he had not yet appeared.

Mr. ELLIS. Mr. Chairman, I should like to interrogate Mr. Butler again.

ADDITIONAL STATEMENT OF MR. GEORGE A. BUTLER.

Mr. ELLIS. In your statement before recess you stated that prices of farm products, such as cotton and wheat, had been constantly declining for a number of years. I do not think I understood the reason which you gave for that decline and should be glad to have you state it now.

Mr. BUTLER. I intended to state that the building of railways by Russia in western Asia and the opening up of a large wheat and cotton region in Asia, and also the fact that the attention of Egypt had been given to cotton and wheat, together with the large supplies from the Argentine Republic, had created a competition that the United States had never heretofore had for our wheat and cotton. That is the statement I meant to make.

Mr. ELLIS. Is it your opinion, then, that the cause, or one of the causes, of this reduction in prices grows out of overproduction and increased competition?

Mr. BUTLER. Largely, yes. I do not quite like the use of the word "overproduction;" it is rather unscientific from the political economist's point of view. I would rather say that the cause has been new and sharp competition.

Mr. ELLIS. Does the plan which you have suggested propose to deal with conditions like that? And what, in your judgment, would be the effect upon the agricultural interests of the country if your plan were adopted and enacted into law?

Mr. BUTLER. Whether my plan or any similar plan should be adopted, it will simply place the banks and currency of the country in a natural condition, making the movement of currency natural and easy, and one that will adjust itself to any industrial conditions. That is all I claim for the plan.

Mr. ELLIS. Your plan, then, would not, if I. understand, either necessarily or probably result in a revival of the agricultural interests of the country?

Mr. BUTLER. It would not necessarily affect the prices in any way. Banking of itself does not operate in that way. But what I would say is this, that the better the banking and the better the currency, the better will all the agricultural and other interests of the country be.

Mr. WALKER. Is it not a fact that the cheaper the exchange and the less number of middlemen you have between consumer and producer, the better will be the prices to the producer?

Mr. BUTLER. Unquestionably.

Mr. COBB, of Missouri. But that will not increase the demand for breadstuffs.

Mr. BUTLER. That will depend on the number of mouths in the world.

Mr. COBB, of Missouri. If we raise more than we can ourselves consume, that necessarily is overproduction?

Mr. BUTLER. That is a question that a banker can not deal with; that is a local question.

Mr. BLACK. What are your rates of interest?

Mr. BUTLER. With us varying from 5 to 6 per cent; but with us we never charge over 6 per cent in a panic, no matter how severe the panic.

Mr. BLACK. I mean under normal conditions.

Mr. BUTLER. Call it 6 per cent.

Mr. BLACK. Can you suggest any remedy for this condition of things: Take my city, for instance, where there is a bank whose stock is worth $150 a share; I can not go into that bank with its own stock, or with any other security, even United States bonds, and get money for a less rate than 8 per cent.

Mr. BUTLER. What city are you from?

Mr. BLACK. Augusta, Ga.

Mr. BUTLER. The rates are higher in the South and West than with us.

Mr. BLACK. Can you suggest any remedy for that, if there is any?

Mr. BUTLER. Either of these plans before you will enable the bank in your city to extend its loans, and therefore give larger facilities, because just in proportion that they can keep their notes in circulation do they add to their loaning capacity.

Mr. BLACK. But that bank has no notes.

Mr. BUTLER. I mean under one of the new systems proposed.

Mr. BLACK. They have to send to New York to get money. You bankers of the East lend money to them at 6 per cent; of course it costs something to get the money there, and costs something to handle it after it gets there, so that the result is that the farmer has to pay anywhere from 8 to 10 per cent for the use of it when he gets it.

Mr. BUTLER. I think no section of the country will be more greatly benefited by the adoption of any one of these plans than the South.

Mr. BLACK. When you say "any one" do you include the plan of the Secretary of the Treasury?

Mr. BUTLER. Yes; because that provides for an increase of the note issue. If that plan be adopted and the people organize under it they will get the benefit. It depends on that, of course.

Mr. COBB, of Missouri. You said this morning that you thought they would not organize.

Mr. BUTLER. I said if they did: I did not think of that.

Mr. WALKER. Will you please say what bills are before the committee? Is there any before the committee except the Carlisle plan and the Baltimore plan?

Mr. BUTLER. I should eliminate the Carlisle bill, because that one particular feature slips my mind all the time. I will say that if either the Baltimore plan or mine were adopted—I will limit it to those two—it would help the South more than any plan I know of.

Mr. BLACK. Explain how.

Mr. BUTLER. Because under the national-bank act a bank of, say, $100,000 capital pays out $114,000 to get $100,000 of bonds; it then takes out $90,000 circulation, and has to keep a 5 per cent reserve against that, which brings it down to $85,000, so the national banking system has taken $29,000 out of the capacity of that bank to lend money to you. Wipe out the national system entirely and put it under the State without any circulation at all, and it adds $29,000 to its loanable capital. If you take the Baltimore plan or mine you will see that it keeps out $50,000 of circulating notes. That $50,000 adds so much to the loanable force of the bank.

Mr. BLACK. In your opinion it would help by increasing the circulation of national banks?

Mr. BUTLER. It would also increase the loanable ability of the banks.

Mr. WALKER. You mean the local national banks?

Mr. BUTLER. Yes, sir.

Mr. BLACK. I should like to ask you one more question. It does not seem to come within the scope of the scheme suggested by the bankers, but it seems to me that there are two classes, if I may so speak, one looking after the banks and the other the Secretary of the Treasury, who is largely looking to the Treasury Department. It does not come within the scope of your scheme, but you are a gentleman of large experience and have given much thought to this subject. What do you say to the suggestion, so often made, that the Treasury may be relieved of requiring customs to be paid in gold?

Mr. BUTLER. I do not know. That question does not begin and end there. I do not know but that would send gold to a premium in the present condition of things. I think it would.

Mr. BLACK. I will ask you even a broader question than that. I should like to get your opinion as to the effect of the Government establishing the policy, as to redeeming this paper currency, of exercising its own option whether it would pay in silver or gold, rather than to let the holder decide that question for himself.

Mr. BUTLER. I can not answer that any better than to say this: The very hour that I am convinced that the Government will do it I will sell every dollar's worth of personal property I have on earth and invest it in real estate.

Mr. ELLIS. Why?

Mr. BUTLER. Because that brings the country to a silver basis and eliminates more than half the value of personal property in the form of stocks, bonds, mortgages, and everything of that sort.

Mr. HALL. Would it not affect real estate in the same way as personal property would be affected?

Mr. BUTLER. No; because in the case of real estate you can put up the rents in proportion. Before the last election I was intending to do this, and, indeed, commenced, but then the election occurred, which was not so favorable to the silver men, and I thought better of it and stopped.

Mr. BLACK. It appears to me that you gentlemen who represent the banks all seem very much in favor of a continual issue of United States bonds, and I have heard the expression used two or three times about the "manly way of doing this thing."

Mr. BUTLER. You have not heard any such expression from me.

Mr. BLACK. I do not recall that I have heard it from you, but I certainly have heard other gentlemen here who have used that very expression. They say the Government ought to be honest and manly, as an individual should be, and that the manly way for the Government to do would be to issue bonds and redeem these notes in gold.

Mr. BUTLER. If my remarks this morning were not absolutely free from everything that might sound like an imputation or criticism or reflection, then I was not able to keep control of my remarks, because I never allow myself to deal in any such language when speaking or writing on any public question.

Mr. BLACK. I was not criticising you at all; I did not mean to do that.

Mr. BUTLER. I understand. Let me say that I am not here in the interest of the banks at all. My little institution can live, and so can I, without Government notes, without Government bonds, or without any action whatever by Congress, and live very handsomely. But I am here purely in the interest of a sound currency. I have no other object in appearing before this committee.

The CHAIRMAN. The Chair desires to state that Mr. Butler's appearance before the committee was not at all in any way in consequence of any request emanating from him.

Mr. BLACK. I do not think it is necessary for the Chair to make that statement.

The CHAIRMAN. The Chair states that in justice to Mr. Butler himself.

Mr. BLACK. I do not understand that any of these gentlemen have appeared before the committee by their own invitation, but by the request of the committee.

The CHAIRMAN. That is right.

Mr. BUTLER. I do not understand that anything is imputed to me, but I should like to say that I am not used to speaking as I did this morning. I do not speak in this way once in three years, nor have I during my life, so that this has been an unusual experience for me.

Mr. HAUGEN. It is sometimes said that it is in the interest of the banks to contract the currency. I have heard that assertion in discussions on the floor of the House. What have you to say about that?

Mr. BUTLER. Simply that those who made the assertion did not understand the question. There is nothing further from the interest of the banks than to do anything of the kind. Such a course would be absolutely inimical to the banks, from every point of view. Such a thing has never been done in the history of the country.

Mr. WALKER. That is it exactly.

Mr. HAUGEN. The bank makes its principal profit out of deposits, and when money is plentiful the bank has more deposits and therefore more profit than when money is scarce, of course.

Mr. BUTLER. We have $50,000 of circulation under the national-bank act; it is not worth one stiver to us. If you do not pass a banking law, but will pass a law allowing me to retain the word "national" in the title of the bank, without requiring me to keep any bonds, the very first thing after that that we would do would be to sell all our bonds and surrender our circulation.

Mr. ELLIS. That would happen in every community where the interest is low, would it not?

Mr. BUTLER. Yes, sir.

Mr. HALL. Let me ask you one question, suggested by what has been drawn out by my friend from Kentucky (Mr. Ellis).

Mr. WALKER. I think Mr. Butler misunderstood at one point. I understood him to say that it would help the banks when interest was low and still more when it was high.

Mr. ELLIS. No. I asked him if they would not want to sell their bonds in every community where the interest was low, and to that he answered yes.

Mr. WALKER. It would be to the interest of a community, also, where the rate of interest was high.

Mr. BUTLER. Yes; the higher the interest the more inducement I have to get circulation.

Mr. HALL. With reference to the interest of the agricultural classes in matters of this kind, I want to know if, under the operation of what is generally known in the literature of political economy as the Gresham law—that poor money will always drive out good money—the agricultural and laboring classes of the United States, or of any government, are not more deeply and vitally interested in a safe and sound currency than any other class of people?

Mr. BUTLER. There is no question about it.

Mr. HALL. Can not the bankers and business men look after the question of getting good currency for themselves, and are not the laboring classes the ones who are liable to have the bad money left on their hands?

Mr. BUTLER. Bankers, capitalists, and speculators can always take care of themselves. It does not make any difference what the laws are, we can always take care of ourselves. It requires men of ability to occupy those places, if I do say so.

Mr. JOHNSON, of Ohio. Mr. Hall, of Missouri, has called your attention to the Gresham law. Suppose there are two kinds of currency in the country—national bank currency, which is receivable, at least in part, for public dues, and a State currency that has not the guarantee of anything except of the banks of issue, and is not receivable for any part of Government dues—would the Gresham law operate to drive out the good money?

Mr. BUTLER. That is a very well enunciated doctrine; there is no doubt about that; but it is sometimes misunderstood. In the case you suggest, with the two kinds of paper money in circulation, it would not drive out the good money, because of economic conditions. To drive out the good money there must be economic conditions affecting exchanges between two or more countries. There must be a circulation between at least two countries in order to make that law operative.

Mr. JOHNSON, of Ohio. Then, in your opinion, the Gresham law does not apply to the two kinds of paper described?

Mr. BUTLER. Our paper money has no circulation in other countries, and, therefore, it does not apply.

Mr. JOHNSON, of Ohio. Where paper money is not a legal tender for anything it is not, strictly speaking, money?

Mr. BUTLER. No.

Mr. JOHNSON, of Ohio. Where the Gresham law operates is where you can force a man to take a certain kind of money in payment of a debt. Where you can not do that, then the Gresham law does not operate?

Mr. BUTLER. It does not operate under those conditions.

Mr. WARNER. Where there is freedom of choice and freedom of redemption the Gresham law does not operate?

Mr. BUTLER. The question arises with reference to the operation of the Gresham law where there is a difference in the different kinds of money used in two different countries. Where there is a metallic currency, or any currency inferior to the best metallic currency, used in one country, there, in the course of time, the inferior currency will drive the best money out of circulation.

Am I taking up too much time? It will take two or three minutes to answer that question.

The CHAIRMAN. You are not taking up too much time at all.

Mr. BUTLER. A great many wise people make a mistake by not taking into consideration sufficient time to prove that law. For instance, my friend, George S. Coe, made an error in regard to the Bland bill; he thought it would produce immediate disaster. I told him he was wrong; that it would take fifteen or twenty years for the Bland bill to produce disaster under the Gresham law. Why? Simply because it would take from fifteen to twenty years to coin enough money under that law to practically fill the channels of circulation and crowd out gold.

Mr. WARNER. My question is slightly different. If there are two currencies, such as my friend from Ohio (Mr. Johnson) has suggested, afloat in the same community, neither being a legal tender, and every holder has the opportunity to force redemption of either, then, as I understand, the Gresham law will not work.

Mr. BUTLER. People will keep the best money and send home the poorest.

Mr. WARNER. And the Gresham law will not operate?

Mr. BUTLER. It is not operative in such case.

Mr. WARNER. Exactly.

Mr. BROSIUS. I desire to bring into more distinctive view your thought upon the real nature of the difficulty of inelasticity in our present banking currency. If I understand you, the chief difficulty is that, in order to have an elastic paper currency, the banks must be able to keep on hand at times a greater amount than is needed, in order to have it to use at other times when the need is greater.

Mr. BUTLER. Yes, sir.

Mr. BROSIUS. The portion of the currency which the banks are required to hold idle must not cost them too much. Under the present system you say it costs the bank too much to hold any amount of idle notes for issue when the need increases.

Mr. BUTLER. That is correct.

Mr. BROSIUS. That is the idea, is it?

Mr. BUTLER. Yes, sir.

Mr. BROSIUS. Then in order to have the volume of currency sufficiently elastic the banks must get that currency gratuitously; they can not afford to pay anything for it. Is that the idea?

Mr. BUTLER. They can not afford to pay very much for it.

Mr. BROSIUS. When the banks issue the notes themselves, as proposed in your plan, that costs them nothing?

Mr. BUTLER. No.

Mr. BROSIUS. And when the notes are required to lie idle in the bank, that is no expenditure to the bank?

Mr. BUTLER. That is correct.

Mr. BROSIUS. But they have to spend a part of their capital for the bonds to secure their notes, and that costs them too much; is that the idea?

Mr. BUTLER. That is correct.

Mr. BROSIUS. Now, suppose the bonds of the Government were sufficiently abundant to be obtainable with ease, and that they paid a sufficient interest, so that the banks could afford to hold in their vaults at all times a sufficient amount of this currency to use when the need increased—you understand me?

Mr. BUTLER. Yes, sir.

Mr. BROSIUS (continuing). Without any loss to the bank; then the elasticity would not be diminished, because the currency would be based upon Government bonds as security.

Mr. BUTLER. On the condition that the bonds carried the rate of interest that the bank must make on its loans, and only on that condition.

Mr. BROSIUS. Now what should you think of this proposition: Take the national banking system now in existence; refund the present bonded indebtedness with long time bonds at a certain rate of interest——

Mr. HALL. What rate?

Mr. BROSIUS. We will say 2½ or 3 per cent, whatever may be determined upon; then use those bonds and also such similar bonds as may be issued to pay off the greenbacks if such shall be issued as a basis for our national banking currency for years to come, there being then enough of them to be easily obtainable, and yielding interest enough to make it somewhat profitable to the banks. Would not the national banking system, as it is now in vogue, under those conditions supply this country with a sufficiently safe and adequately elastic currency for many years to come?

Mr. BUTLER. It would not.

Mr. BROSIUS. Why not?

Mr. BUTLER. Because the difference between $2\frac{1}{2}$ and 5 per cent interest, we will say, is so great that the banks would not keep any more circulation than they could keep out at all times.

MR. BROSIUS. Then the reason is that it would be too expensive to the banks?

Mr. BUTLER. That is it.

Mr. HALL. I think that we owe you a vote of thanks.

Mr. BUTLER. If I have succeeded in giving the committee satisfaction it is a great pleasure to me.

The CHAIRMAN. Are there any further questions to put to Mr. Butler?

The chair is informed that Mr. Cornwall is in the city, at his hotel, and will be here soon.

Mr. BUTLER. I congratulate you, gentlemen, on that, for Mr. Cornwall is a very bright man.

ADDITIONAL STATEMENT OF MR. WHITE.

The CHAIRMAN. A member of the committee desires to ask Mr. White to make a statement in regard to the Gresham law, which has been referred to.

Mr. WHITE. My understanding about the Gresham law is this: At the time Gresham lived there was no paper money. Therefore Mr. Butler is right in saying that Mr. Gresham's idea applied only to metallic money.

The question was propounded to Gresham by some public authority, Why is it that we have nothing but old, worn, and clipped silver money in circulation? (Silver was then the principal money in circulation in Great Britain.) Gresham replied truly that so long as a person was obliged to take a crown piece of short weight and could not help himself, of course he would use that money to pay debts with, and that when he had a good piece in his pocket he would sell it to somebody who would melt it and send it abroad.

From that proposition of Mr. Gresham, which was perfectly true, the Gresham law came into the literature of political economy, although the principle was not entirely new to Mr. Gresham. It has been traced in earlier history.

The CHAIRMAN. How far back in history is that?

Mr. WHITE. I think that the law applies equally to paper money, and that it is universally true, for I do remember that in Illinois there were, before the war, three or four different kinds of paper money in circulation, and that banks and individuals always used to pay out that which was a little the worst and keep what was the best. The New England bank notes, New York bank notes, and the notes of the State bank of Indiana, and of the State bank of Ohio, which were always at par and could always be used to make exchanges in New York at a very low discount, were kept by individuals and by banks for the purpose of making exchanges in New York and Boston, and they put out always the notes of Illinois, Wisconsin, and Georgia banks, which were at $1\frac{1}{2}$ per cent discount. There was a case where paper money was not a legal tender, and yet custom required people to take an inferior kind of money.

I can give you another illustration: The Confederate notes during the war were not a legal tender, and the bank notes of the South were not legal tender; but the custom required people—public opinion required the people to take the Confederate notes, notwithstanding they were not legal tender. The result was that the Confederate treasury notes crowded out the bank notes, which were a little better. People instinctively knew that bank notes were better than Confederate notes, though neither was legal tender. The Gresham law operated there, and gave the whole field of circulation to the Confederate notes.

Mr. ELLIS. I should like to ask you if the Gresham law operated at all, in your opinion, during the existence of what is known as the Bland-Allison law. Did we feel the effects of the Gresham law then, or did it have any effect upon the currency of the country?

Mr. WHITE. I do not think it had, because all the different kinds of money were absolutely at par with each other.

Mr. ELLIS. Is it not a fact that during the existence of the Bland-Allison Act the accumulations of gold in this country increased several hundred million dollars, until the time that law was repealed, over and above what the amount of gold was when that law went into effect?

Mr. WHITE. There was a great importation of gold in the years 1880 and 1881, amounting to about $140,000,000 or $160,000,000, due to trade conditions, I think, and to high prices of grain here and bad crops in Europe. After the year 1881, and for several years, I think the imports and exports of gold just about balanced each other.

Mr. JOHNSON, of Indiana. Notwithstanding the Gresham law, two kinds of paper money may circulate side by side, the one being inferior to the other.

Mr. WALKER. He did not say that.

Mr. WHITE. I said this: That if public opinion required two kinds of money to be taken, the inferior money will circulate and the superior money will be put to other uses and be hoarded.

Mr. JOHNSON, of Indiana. As I understand, you have given us an illustration occurring during the old State-bank times, where two kinds of money circulated, one being at a discount and the other not. In other words, the bad paper did not drive the other out, but those whose necessities required it were obliged to accept the inferior money.

Mr. WHITE. At the time the bad money drove the good money out under the Gresham law the field of circulation was taken by the inferior money, even though its inferiority was measured by only a very small fraction.

Mr. JOHNSON, of Indiana. You think it is not a desirable condition to have two kinds of paper money in circulation, one being good and the other inferior?

Mr. WHITE. Most undesirable.

Mr. JOHNSON, of Indiana. And that this is one danger with the State bank system of issuing paper money?

Mr. WHITE. Yes, sir; in my opinion.

Mr. JOHNSON, of Indiana. In fact, it is true of any system which has two or three different kinds of currency, whether paper or not?

Mr. WHITE. I remarked that there were three or four different kinds of money circulating in Illinois before the war, as the chairman of this committee remembers, and the bad money had the field of circulation.

Mr. JOHNSON, of Indiana. Is it not a fallacy to say that bad money will not circulate?

Mr. WHITE. Generally it is. I would not say that there may not be cases where bad money may not be driven out. The Suffolk bank, of Boston, managed, you know, to drive out inferior money.

Mr. JOHNSON, of Indiana. But that system was limited in operation; it did not extend over a vast country with a population like ours.

Mr. WHITE. No.

Mr. WALKER. No money but New England money circulated in Massachusetts or New England. There was no circulation whatever in New England for the poor money.

Mr. WHITE. That is so, and they had a law prohibiting the banks from paying out any notes but their own.

Mr. COX. There is a great diversity of opinion about this matter. I want to put this proposition to you squarely. My friend from Indiana (Mr. Johnson) starts with the supposition that State bank money would be inferior money.

Mr. JOHNSON, of Indiana. Oh, no; I did not start with that supposition.

Mr. COX. Your argument was that way, anyhow.

Mr. JOHNSON, of Indiana. I believe it to be true.

Mr. COX. We never had any State-bank money in our history that came in competition with national-bank paper money.

Mr. WHITE. No.

Mr. COX. Suppose you organize a State bank in a State where there is a national bank already in operation, with its circulating notes out. If the State-bank note is in the least degree in value below the national-bank note, would it not be absolutely impossible to pass the State-bank note over the counter? How could the bank get it out if it were not equivalent in value and not the representative of the same confidence by the people as in the case of the national-bank note?

Mr. WHITE. It would be a question between the banker and his customer. He would pass it over the counter, and then if the customer said he would not take it, he would not.

Mr. COX. Suppose the banker pays over the counter to you, say, $1,000. Then your object would be to pay it to me for $1,000. When you reach me and offer me the $1,000 of the State-bank money, I decline to take it. Your next step would be to carry it back to the bank, would it not?

Mr. WHITE. That is true.

Mr. COX. When you carried it back to the bank and asked the banker to give you credit for it on his books, and he declined to put it in that shape, but would only take it as a special deposit, then you would demand redemption, would you not?

Mr. WHITE. Yes; that is exactly the way I think it would work.

Mr. COX. If the State-bank note is well secured, and the issue is protected, so that it is as good as the note of the national bank and as well protected—assuming those facts—would it not be a great help in communities as a local currency in the transaction of business?

Mr. WHITE. Yes, sir.

Mr. COX. Assuming those facts to be true—because I do not want anything to do with it unless the assumption is good—then would it not operate in another direction, that is, become an active competitor with other bank notes, both national and State?

Mr. WHITE. Yes; all banks are competitors with each other.

Mr. COX. Assuming the facts as I have stated, and assuming those conclusions to be true, as you have answered me, tell me what real objection there can be to having a State bank.

Mr. HALL. A sound one.

Mr. COX. Assume that.

Mr. WHITE. There is the objection that Mr. Butler mentioned this morning, that they introduced heterogeneousness in currency, which is a bad thing.

Mr. Cox. Pardon me a moment. Would it not be an additional benefit if that currency, like our friend Mr. Butler said about the local currency, would have a tendency to circulate nearer home, assuming all the time that it is good?

Mr. White. It would be desirable that it should circulate at home, but it is a question whether it would circulate at home.

Mr. Cox. It would circulate if it were as good as the other.

Mr. White. The question where it will circulate will depend very much upon its goodness.

Mr. Cox. It would all depend on that.

Mr. White. And the credit it enjoys. It might circulate as far away from home as New York City, if it were perfectly good.

Mr. Cox. Let me call your attention to one part of our country. I know what the general remark is about capital, that we need more capital. I want to call your attention particularly to this fact in the condition of our State securities. Our railroad and municipal securities, as a rule, are all held away from home. Real estate is not a security in the national banks. Our bonds and stocks are away from home. The difficulty with us is in offering the security required by the national banking law. Now, assuming the same facts as before stated by me, that we make the security perfectly good, under proper limitations and restrictions, would not a system of that kind in the agricultural parts of the country, where they have no stocks or bonds of that character to use as collateral, be of great benefit?

Mr. White. A great benefit to them?

Mr. Cox. Yes.

Mr. Walker. To use real estate securities?

Mr. White. I use such securties as I have.

Mr. Cox. That makes it as good as the national-bank notes. Suppose you use real estate security?

Mr. White. Do you mean real estate notes?

Mr. Cox. No.

Mr. Warner. You mean short-time paper for current discount?

Mr. Cox. Certainly; the point being all the time that we must make it, under proper limitations and restrictions, as good as its sister paper at the next door, which you call a national-bank bill. Now, I ask you the question, if we do that would not that be of great value to a part of the country that has been deprived by misfortune—I will not speak of that—of its stocks and its bonds and the ready security upon which you can get money in the East and North?

Mr. White. Any community which has a perfectly sound bank is in better shape than it was before. That is a complete answer, I think. I say that any community which has a perfectly sound bank is in a better shape than it was before it had the bank.

Mr. Cox. That is true.

Mr. White. That is true whether the bank has circulating notes or not.

Mr. Cox. So it all comes back to the point that we make it absolutely good?

Mr. White. Yes.

Mr. Cox. That is where it all hinges at last.

Mr. White. So the community understands it is good and so it maintains a high credit.

Now, I want to say one thing more which this question has called up: I think any bank which lends money on mortgage security will not last very long.

Mr. Cox. I agree with you on that. I do not desire to follow that up, but I think the question is pertinent. Take the State of Tennessee, my own State. Her bonds are above par. Our interest all goes away from us. Now, I want to get an inducement to bring them back. A Tennessee bond to-day does not bear quite so high a premium as a United States bond, but it is absolutely good. Now, if we want to bank upon the Tennessee bonds, with the whole State bound for their payment—and other States are in the same condition—and with these restrictions, would it not be a great benefit to our citizens if our securities could be brought back home where the interest on them would be paid at home?

Mr. White. You see I do not believe in banking on bond security at all, and so I am not prepared to reply to that question in the affirmative.

Mr. Cox. I assume that that makes the issue good. I do not care whether it is commercial paper or bonds. But can there be any harm in permitting the State bank to issue its notes or promises to pay money if it be settled that they are absolutely good?

Mr. White. Well, I answered before that the only objection is that of heterogeneousness. That is an objection that applies to the nation at large.

Mr. Walker. Give a definition of good money. What is good money? You have been talking about good money.

Mr. Johnson, of Indiana. I want to ask a question.

The Chairman. The Chair will recognize the gentleman from Indiana in a moment.

Mr. White. I was about to say one thing more, led up to by Mr. Cox's question. I have been looking up the banking laws of some of the Southern States, as well as some of the Northern States, as those laws now exist, and I say that if either the Baltimore plan or the Secretary's plan should be adopted, to allow banks to issue on the safety-fund system, neither Virginia, North Carolina, Georgia, New York, nor Massachusetts could ever issue any notes in competition, because it would cost too much. They all require bond security to-day. Even Massachusetts has abandoned her old Suffolk system.

Mr. Cox. I did not intend, of course, to discuss the question of the different characters of securities, and I want to say to you that I am heartily in favor of the two systems. I think each one would be a benefit, and that both together would be of much more benefit to the people.

The Chairman. Did I understand you to say that your knowledge of the laws with regard to banking, in force in the States you name, leads you to say that the system proposed by Mr. Carlisle, or that in the Baltimore plan, would be more favorable to a locality for the taking out of circulation than would be the stocks of that locality?

Mr. White. No; I meant to say that if the Baltimore plan or any safety-fund system were adopted, discarding bond security, the national banks in those very States would occupy the field of circulation, to the exclusion of State-bank notes, because it would cost the State banks too much.

The Chairman. And therefore they could do better to adopt the national system?

Mr. White. Yes.

Mr. Black. I want to call your attention, in this connection, to the fact that the legislature of Georgia is now in session, and there has been a bill introduced in that legislature authorizing the State to bank under Mr. Carlisle's system. Do you not think that the States would change their laws where they do not now permit banking?

Mr. WHITE. They might do that. Some of the States have constitutional provisions against it.

Mr. JOHNSON, of Indiana. What local need would this State-bank paper, which Mr. Cox has assumed in his questions to be sound, supply which could not be as well supplied by a sound national-bank note?

Mr. WHITE. Not any.

Mr. JOHNSON, of Indiana. Is it not a fact that the German Government has, within a few years last past, taken away from the various States composing that nation the right to issue paper money, and substituted therefor a national currency?

Mr. WHITE. That I do not know. I have not examined that subject sufficiently to answer.

Mr. WALKER. Have you in mind the amount of gold in the United States at the time that we resumed specie payments, or at the close of the period of premiums on gold?

Mr. WHITE. I have not, and I do not know anybody that has. That is wholly a matter of conjecture.

Mr. WALKER. It was about $300,000,000, I think.

Mr. WHITE. I do not know. I say it is purely a conjectural matter.

Mr. WALKER. I do not mean all gold. I should have said the visible gold.

Mr. WHITE. I think the Treasury had $100,000,000 of its own gold, and that there was about $50,000,000 of other gold in the Treasury, represented by gold certificates. I do not think there was very much other visible gold.

Mr. WALKER. Can you tell us what the visible gold is in England, the gold of commerce? I think it is all in the Bank of England.

Mr. WHITE. I think it is about £24,000,000.

Mr. WALKER. That is the average sum. Have you in your mind the statistics with reference to the gold held in India, China, and Mexico used in commerce?

Mr. WHITE. No, I have not; the importations of gold into India in the last fifteen years have been very large, but the figures I do not know anything about.

Mr. WALKER. The point I want to get at is this: That international commerce, without regard to national laws, makes it to the interest of those engaged in commerce, of whom the banks are part in all countries, to maintain the gold necessary for their business, irrespective of laws. Is not that true?

Mr. WHITE. Oh, yes.

Mr. WALKER. Is it not true that the United States, England, India, China, Mexico, and in fact every country, has held about the same proportion of all visible gold for the purposes of international commerce?

Mr. WHITE. Yes, that is my opinion.

Mr. RUSSELL. I should like to ask Mr. White if, in his opinion, the provision of section 5 of the Secretary's bill is a serious obstacle to the organization of national banks for circulation.

Mr. WHITE. That is the provision which makes them all responsible?

Mr. RUSSELL. Makes them responsible for contingent liability.

Mr. WHITE. I think it is an obstacle. As Mr. Butler said this morning, I think the board of directors would shy at it.

Mr. RUSSELL. In your opinion, the provision remaining as it is now drafted in that bill would result in few national banks, if any, organizing for circulation?

Mr. WHITE. That is my opinion.

Mr. HALL. You are speaking of section 5, Mr. Russell?

Mr. RUSSELL. Yes.

Mr. HALL. I think Mr. White and Mr. Butler have unwittingly done injustice to Mr. Carlisle's plan. Have you carefully read that section, Mr. White?

Mr. WHITE. I heard you read it carefully this morning. I should like to hear it again.

Mr. HALL. I will state the substance.

It provides, in the first place, that each bank shall be required to deposit what the Secretary calls a guarantee fund of 30 per cent in greenbacks. Then a safety fund is created of 5 per cent by taxing all the banks. This safety fund is for the purpose of redeeming the notes of failed national banks. The minute a national bank fails, its guarantee fund held on deposit shall be transferred to the safety fund. That in and of itself will go a long way toward redeeming these notes. Then the notes themselves are made a first lien upon all of the assets of the bank, besides which there is a double liability clause with reference to the stockholders, and I should think that ninety-nine times out of a hundred that would certainly satisfy and pay all the notes of failed national banks. But in the event that it does not it is provided that there shall be an assessment upon all the national banks of the United States just for the purpose of bringing up this safety fund to its 5 per cent, out of which the notes of failed national banks are paid. Then give the national banks that contribute this a first lien upon all the assets, and a double liability clause against the stockholders, to reimburse them for the money they have expended for the benefit of that bank. Do you mean to say that that little contingent liability would have a tendency that in and of itself would prevent men from taking out charters under this plan?

Mr. WHITE. I agree with Mr. Butler exactly on that. To my mind it would not weigh a feather, because I say that the notes would be absolutely secure; and yet I think the average board of directors would shy at it; that they would say "that is an indefinite sum."

The CHAIRMAN. In that connection Mr. Carlisle, on page 15 of his report to Congress, states the total resources of the 3,755 national banks at $3,473,000,000, while the capital stock of all the national banks is only $672,000,000. If banks are restricted to the 75 per cent of their capital stock they will only be permitted to issue to the present number of banks on their capital stock $504,000,000 of currency. If every bank failed this is all they would be required to pay, and there would be a fund estimated at $3,473,000,000 with which to pay it. Are you of opinion, Mr. White, that the $3,473,000,000 would be ample security for $504,000,000, if all the banks were to fail?

Mr. WHITE. Yes. sir.

Mr. HENDERSON. Is that the resources of all the banks?

The CHAIRMAN. National banks only.

Mr. HENDERSON. Do they assess this 5 per cent on all their resources?

The CHAIRMAN. No; but all the resources are held liable to the bill holders for the payment of the circulating notes, and, in addition, there is a personal liability of the stockholders equal to the whole amount of the stock. I do not see here any estimate of that.

Mr. HALL. It is 5 per cent of the circulation.

Mr. RUSSELL. One question more, Mr. White. I understood you to say that, in your opinion, under the provisions of section 5 of the Secretary's bill, the directors of a national bank would shy at this proposition. Do I understand that you think if a bank desires to become a bank of circulation it would much prefer to be a bank of circulation organized as a State bank, rather than as a national bank, with the provisions of that section 5 remaining as they are?

Mr. WHITE. Yes; I should think so. I should think that the bank would take that method of circulating notes, if the door were open involving less liability.

Mr. BROSIUS. Apropos of your suggestion a moment ago, about the difficulty in some States of organizing State banks under the Secretary's plan, the constitution of the State of Pennsylvania provides that no note shall be issued by any bank organized in the State until the bank has filed with the auditor-general security equal to the amount of notes for their protection. Under such a constitutional provision the State could not organize any banks of issue under the Carlisle plan, could it?

Mr. WHITE. No; it could not.

Mr. BROSIUS. Why not?

Mr. WHITE. It would cost too much.

Mr. BROSIUS. Would it not make very expensive circulation?

Mr. WARNER. Not unless your securities were above par.

Mr. BROSIUS. It would depend upon the amount of interest, of course; but under ordinary circumstances I want to know your opinion about it.

Mr. WHITE. I do not think, as I said, that they could organize any banks of issue under the Carlisle plan in that State.

Mr. BROSIUS. In addition to investing its capital in these securities it would have to invest 30 per cent of its circulation, and then it would have 130 per cent of its circulation invested and tied up?

Mr. WHITE. Yes.

Mr. Warner asked Mr. Homer a question last evening, which was very proper and rather a pregnant one, and that was, If the banks would hesitate to guarantee each other how could it be safe for the Government to guarantee all the banks? I think there are two or three answers to that question. One is that the Government can do it on account of its bigness. I should not want to insure Mr. Warner's life, nor would he want to insure mine, but a life insurance company would be very willing to make such a contract. That is one answer. Another answer is that the Government has the power to tax all these banks, and it can recoup itself by taxation. The amount of failures of banks at any time can be ascertained, and the Government is able, if required, to pay out its own money, and then is able to recoup by making the other banks pay up.

Mr. WARNER. Can it do so except as a matter of the future?

Mr. WHITE. No.

Mr. WARNER. Then, as a matter of actual fact, would it not have to meet the responsibility from the Treasury—with the only resource left to tax other banks that were not responsible for the immediate exigency which caused it to lose money?

Mr. JOHNSON, of Indiana. That is the whole Baltimore plan. Might it not be possible that the Government officials would be a little more alert to examine banks if they knew that by the failure of banks the Government would have to redeem their notes from its own funds?

Mr. WHITE. Yes; not only more alert, but they have the power to take a bank by the collar and force it to make good the loss.

Mr. WARNER. Do you think it necessary for the security of the notes that the Government should assume that responsibility?

Mr. WHITE. I do not. I think it is desirable but not necessary. I think it is desirable, because it gives unlimited credit to the bank note, and that is understood by the public.

Mr. WARNER. As a matter of fact, after one or two years' experience, would not that plan, which was suggested by Mr. Butler, of people being used to taking money without loss upon it so work that people would become utterly indifferent as to the Government guarantee?

Mr. WHITE. Yes; there would be a constant tendency that way, just as there is in Canada. The Government there is not responsible, but the banks have unlimited credit.

Mr. WARNER. Which could not be added to by any Government guarantee, could it?

Mr. WHITE. In Canada?

Mr. WARNER. In Canada.

Mr. WHITE. That I do not know, whether it could be added to or not, but I say that their credit is unlimited.

Mr. WARNER. If it is unlimited there is nothing to add.

Mr. WHITE. Yes; the credit is sufficient at all events.

Mr. WARNER. Is there not this danger if, by legislation, the Government is put absolutely behind every bank note which it permits to circulate, that however carefully we may safeguard the issue by present law, there would be constantly left the temptation, in times of stress or whenever a part of our people thought they wanted more money, to take away one after another of those safeguards in order to enable currency to be issued more freely, and thus to bring about—gradually perhaps, but almost surely—a lessening of the dependence upon the guarantee and the increase of the dependence upon the Government fiat?

Mr. WHITE. A tendency in Congress to do that?

Mr. WARNER. Yes.

Mr. WHITE. Of course Congress could remove the safeguard, and there would be that tendency, but I do not think it would be dangerous. You can hardly conceive of a condition of things where there would be more demand for money than there was last July and August. Congress was in session at that time, but Congress did not take any steps to make any more money.

Mr. WARNER. But has there been a Congress elected for the last ten years in which, if it had been known that the amount of currency could be increased by not in any way decreasing its safety so far as the absolute Government guarantee was concerned, there would not have been a very strong movement to take away the safeguards which obstructed the increase of the currency?

Mr. WHITE. That is altogether a matter of opinion upon a political question, but I should not consider that condition a dangerous one.

Mr. JOHNSON, of Indiana. "White man is very uncertain" as to what he will do?

Mr. WHITE. Yes.

Mr. BROSIUS. Unless the Canadian system has been recently changed, I understand that there are three kinds of notes there—the usual bank notes and what they call the Dominion notes. I understand that there is an issue of $20,000,000 of Dominion notes; that these are guaranteed by the Government of England. Am I right?

Mr. WHITE. I am not aware of that.

Mr. ELLIS. He said the contrary of that.

M. BROSIUS. I say this Dominion issue of $20,000,000 is secured by Government securities?

Mr. WHITE. The Dominion issues are just like our own greenbacks; they are Government notes.

Mr. BROSIUS. They are based upon securities, are they not?

Mr. WHITE. The Government that issues them is itself the security.

Mr. BROSIUS. Then there are no Government securities at all used in Canada as a basis for circulation?

Mr. WHITE. Not that I am aware of.

Mr. BROSIUS. I have always understood—and I am sure I did not evolve it out of my own consciousness, because I must have got the information from reading books on the subject—that the Dominion issue of $20,000,000 is actually guaranteed by securities in the nature of our bonds. I may be mistaken, but I have the idea, and I must have acquired it from my reading, that not only is that so, but that the English Government in some way guarantees those Dominion notes. Are you aware of anything of the kind?

Mr. WHITE. I never heard of such a thing.

Mr. BROSIUS. That leaves only about $35,000,000 of notes in Canada which are based upon credit alone. Do you think you can safely reason by analogy between our country and a country that does not do any more business, probably, take it altogether, or very little more, than one of the big dry goods houses in the city of New York, and which only has at best about $35,000,000 of notes in circulation? Can you reason from the monetary system of such a country as that to the monetary system or the banking system of a country like the United States, where we have over a thousand millions of circulating paper?

Mr. WHITE. If the system is reasonable in itself, then the fact that it has the guarantee of a neighboring country adds force to the argument. I do not think that this Baltimore plan depends on the question of what the system is in Canada at all. The Baltimore plan must depend on human reason. The question of the system in Canada is simply an additional argument in support of the Baltimore plan.

Mr. BROSIUS. The principle being sound, might it not work much better in practice in a small country like Canada, with so limited an amount of circulation, and yet not work at all well in practice in a great country like ours?

Mr. WHITE. I do not see it that way. It is a matter of opinion, of course.

Mr. WARNER. I am just informed, from a very trustworthy source, that Mr. Brosius is correct, and that the Dominion $20,000,000 issues are secured partly by coin and partly by British securities.

Mr. BROSIUS. I thought I was right.

Mr. WHITE. I simply said I had never heard of it, and I never have.

Mr. JOHNSON, of Indiana. Mr. Warner asked you if you did not think that after a couple of years or so the people would acquire great faith in paper currency, even though the Government were not liable for its ultimate redemption. I will ask you if it is not of primary importance that the popular faith should attach to the currency from the very inception of its issue?

Mr. WHITE. I think so, decidedly.

Mr. JOHNSON, of Indiana. Whether that is not the important thing, and that there shall be no experiments making results doubtful?

Mr. WHITE. I think it is very desirable.

Mr. HALL. Is it not the fact that it was some years after the national-bank act was passed before that sort of currency became popular?

Mr. WHITE. I do not think there was ever any lack of faith in the national bank currency.

Mr. HALL. That it was not popular for several years after its first issue?

Mr. WHITE. I do not remember about that. You see in the original national banking law the Government was responsible for it. The national banking law was passed in 1863, and how could the notes be lacking in confidence when the Government was behind them?

Mr. HALL. They were looked on with disfavor on account of the repeal of certain State-bank laws.

Mr. WHITE. I know.

Mr. JOHNSON, of Ohio. Was there not a time, before the 10 per cent tax was enacted, when the State-bank money and the national-bank money circulated together?

Mr. WHITE. Oh, yes. That is true.

Mr. JOHNSON, of Ohio. I am entirely ignorant as to what the condition was at that time. How were they paid? Which issue did the people prefer?

Mr. WHITE. The tax did not go into effect until August 1, 1866.

Mr. JOHNSON, of Ohio. Before the tax went into effect, how did the national-bank currency and that of State banks operate together?

Mr. WHITE. They circulated side by side, and that is all I can say. I simply say that after the legal-tender act passed the State-bank notes became immediately redeemable in legal tender notes, and therefore there could be no difference between them, because the Government was behind both.

Mr. WALKER. Is it not a fact that the first national banking act was so drawn as to make it more profitable for the banks to remain under their State bank charters, not to abandon their State charters, and that the national currency was very limited in circulation until the 10 per cent tax went into operation?

Mr. WHITE. Yes, sir.

Mr. JOHNSON, of Indiana. I want to say that the question of confidence of the people in this currency was very different in 1863 from what it is now, because in the interval the people have been educated to rely upon national-bank notes, for the reason that they have entire faith now in the Government as their ultimate redeemer.

Mr. COBB, of Alabama. Did you intend to say that the Gresham law operates on paper currency in the same way in contracting that currency as on the metallic money?

Mr. WHITE. I did not say anything about contracting currency. I said that the Gresham law operated on paper currency in the same way as on metallic currency if it had either a legal-tender law behind it or public opinion behind it sufficient to force both kinds into circulation.

Mr. COBB, of Alabama. Is it not true that the operation of the Gresham law on metallic money is to drive it from the country, but that its operation on paper money is to make it slower of circulation without altogether driving it out?

Mr. WHITE. Yes, that is it.

Mr. COBB, of Alabama. Then the same consequences do not follow in the application of the Gresham law to paper money as to metallic?

Mr. WHITE. You can not drive paper money out of the country.

Mr. COBB, of Alabama. Nor out of circulation.

Mr. WHITE. No, not entirely, because there are certain things that the superior currency will do that the inferior will not. The inferior currency will have the field of general circulation, and the superior currency will have the field of circulation to the extent that it will pay certain debts and make exchanges in distant places when the other will not.

Mr. COBB, of Alabama. Then does it not follow that that law does not properly operate upon paper currency to its full extent as it does upon metallic money?

Mr. WHITE. If the paper currency is a legal tender, then I think it does operate to its full extent, except that you can not drive it out of the country.

Mr. COBB, of Alabama. Nor hide it away. It is still in circulation for the time being, is it not? The law only causes it to be withdrawn temporarily, does it not?

Mr. WHITE. Yes.

Mr. COBB, of Alabama. Whereas, upon metallic money the effect of the law is to drive it entirely out of circulation?

Mr. WHITE. It drives the matallic money to foreign countries.

Mr. WALKER. I want Mr. White to be correct on the record. It is a fact, I believe, that the gold of this country increased during the period of suspension of specie payments and was larger just before resumption than prior to that time. Now, my point is that you did not intend to say that the Gresham law would drive gold out of the country, but out of circulation.

Mr. WHITE. Oh, yes; there was a great deal of gold in existence in New York during the war.

Gentlemen, my train time has come, and I must ask to be excused. I am much obliged to you.

The CHAIRMAN. The chair desires to state that Mr. Cornwall has not arrived, at least has not appeared before the committee, although he is in the city. The chair will therefore suggest that, if there is no other gentleman present who desires to be heard, the committee adjourn, after an executive session, to meet at 10 o'clock to-morrow morning in this room.

The chair desires that the members of the committee will remain in the room for some executive business.

Thereupon, at 3.30 o'clock p. m., the committee went into executive session, and shortly afterwards adjourned.

WASHINGTON, D. C., *Thursday, December 13, 1894.*

The committee met at 10 a. m. Present: The chairman (Mr. Springer) and Messrs. Sperry, Cox, Cobb of Missouri, Ellis, Cobb of Alabama, Warner, Johnson of Ohio, Black, Hall, Walker, Brosius, Henderson, Russell, Haugen, and Johnson of Indiana.

LETTER OF MR. R. B. FERRIS.

Mr. Warner presented a letter which he had received from Mr. R. B. Ferris, vice-president of the Bank of New York.

The letter was ordered to be printed and is as follows:

THE BANK OF NEW YORK,
New York, December 12, 1894.

Hon. J. DEWITT WARNER.

DEAR SIR: As we have this morning the text of Secretary Carlisle's currency bill, I take occasion to make a few remarks. There seems to be no good reason why existing national banks who have United States bonds on deposit with the Comptroller of the Currency should not be allowed to continue as they are, either until their charters expire or the deposited bonds are paid off. Section 7 seems like forcing the banks to do what they have not been consulted about, and, in consideration of what the national banks have done for the Treasury, is a little inconsiderate.

The remark we so often hear, that a circulation based on deposit of bonds can not be elastic, is not strictly true. The reason the circulation of the national banks is not more elastic is the present method of redemption by the Department at Washington; it is a little slow. I do not mean to disparage the Department; the amount of work it does is immense, but the trouble is that only mutilated notes unfit for use are returned to the Department for redemption. This would be obviated by the establishing of central redemption agencies, say, one in this city for the State of New York, then when banks hold a plethora of money it would be an easy matter to sort out the New York State notes (by their backs) and return them to the redemption agent. The issuing bank, on receipt of them, sorts out those unfit for use, sends them to Washington for new notes, and stows away the others in its vault until time of need.

The notes being "on hand" reduces the amount of its tax and the bonds on deposit are earning interest. Now, when a bank finds there is a plethora of money, it makes a deposit of the United States notes with the Treasury, gets back its bonds, possibly sells them, and when the time of emergency comes, has to send on new bonds and wait the time when new notes can be printed, signed, and prepared for use; then the emergency may be passed. The fault is partly with the banks and partly with the system of redemption. Give the national banks par for their bonds and let them continue as they are, if they wish to.

Section 10, providing for the issue of notes by State banks, without the provision of a sinking fund, as provided in section 5 for national banks, makes the bill simply an inflation measure, modified by the deposit of 30 per cent in legal-tender notes and the provision (section 9) to cancel United States notes to the extent of 70 per cent of new circulation, issued when the Treasury has the means to do it.

As a bill to substitute national-bank notes for United States issues, it will be a failure, as it presents no inducements to solid banks to become insurers of the circulation of mushroom institutions, and the stimulant to organize State banks, not subject to United States inspection, is questionable.

Very respectfully, R. B. FERRIS.

Hon. J. DEWITT WARNER.

You are privileged to use my communications as you think proper.

LETTER OF WILLIAM B. DANA.

The chairman said that he had received a letter from Mr. William B. Dana, of the Commercial and Financial Chronicle. Mr. Dana was one of those gentlemen who had been invited to appear before the committee, and he stated his inability to do so.

The letter was ordered to be printed in the proceedings of the committee, and is as follows:

THE COMMERCIAL AND FINANCIAL CHRONICLE.

New York, December 12, 1894.

MY DEAR SIR: I thank you for your request to appear before your committee on the 15th instant for the purpose of attempting to give information with reference to banking and currency matters. My engagements are such at this period of the year as to render it impossible for me to be present. Excuse me if I add that industrial interests would no doubt be greatly benefited if Congress could pass a bank-note measure and at the same time provide some method for gradually getting rid of the legal-tender notes as the bank notes were issued. Mr. Carlisle's plan has this double purpose in view.

Thanking you again for your invitation, I remain,

Very truly yours,

WILLIAM B. DANA.

Hon. WILLIAM M. SPRINGER,
Chairman Banking and Currency Committee,
Washington, D. C.

STATEMENT OF MR. WILLIAM C. CORNWELL.

The chairman stated to the committee that Mr. Cornwell, president of the City Bank of Buffalo and president of the State Bankers' Association of the State of New York, had been notified to appear before the committee and was now present. The committee would be pleased to have Mr. Cornwell make any statement he might desire, and after that members of the committee might desire to put some questions to him.

Mr. CORNWELL said: Mr. Chairman and gentlemen, I want to make, if you please, three very brief suggestions, which, in the order that they are made, seem to me to be the most important in the situation as regards the finances of the United States.

First and most important, in my opinion, is that the greenbacks and Treasury notes shall be redeemed and canceled.

The real business of a Government, as regards money, is to stamp on gold and silver its fineness and weight. If a Government stops there it seems to me that it has done its greatest duty, and almost its entire duty in the premises. The Government has no right to issue paper with nothing back of it, and to make that paper legal tender. It has no right to create a currency, and by acts of law to force the people to take it at full value without regard to its intrinsic worth. I say it has no right, because all such issues up to date have ended in trouble. History proves that the greenbacks and Treasury notes are of that character.

They are the Government's notes to the extent of $500,000,000, payable on demand and payable in gold. They have caused trouble enough already. They are a constant menace to the gold reserve. They should be paid off.

My second suggestion is that the vacancy created by the retirement of the legal-tender notes should be filled with bank notes.

The best currency of the best nations to-day is mainly bank notes, which are a first lien on the assets of the bank. These assets are commercial possessions, representing the product of the brain and muscle of millions of people. They are the wealth of the nation. What better basis for circulation can there be than that—the actual wealth of the nation?

To fill the vacancy created by the retirement of legal-tender notes, and as fast as they are retired automatically national banks should be allowed to issue notes to a percentage of their capital without bond security, the notes to be a first lien on the assets of the bank, including the double liability of stockholders, with a guarantee fund made up by all the banks, the Government continuing to redeem and guarantee all notes. This, with a provision for an emergency issue, is practically the Baltimore plan. It is sufficiently good as far as it goes, and it goes far enough for the present. I think we could very well stop here and go on for a good many years without any other improvement.

But I believe in a thorough investigation based upon experience as to what should be done, and for that reason, and to perfect the system further and to work out the complicated and delicate problems attending it, an impartial expert commission should be appointed.

I recapitulate:

First. Retire legal-tender notes.

Second. Let the national banks take out notes under the Baltimore plan to replace them.

Third. Appoint an impartial expert commission to perfect the currency system.

Mr. WARNER. What would be your plan for the retirement of greenbacks and Treasury notes?

Mr. CORNWELL. The only way now open would be by the issue of low-rate bonds to redeem them with.

Mr. WARNER. You heard Secretary Carlisle's plan?

Mr. CORNWELL. Yes.

Mr. WARNER. That would provide for a quasi retirement of this greenback circulation for the time being?

Mr. CORNWELL. Yes.

Mr. WARNER. What do you think of that plan?

Mr. CORNWELL. As to the part which relates to the retirement of the greenbacks? I feel about it that it is not definite enough. The greenbacks are put away, but there is nothing to prevent their getting back again.

Mr. WARNER. To what extent do you regard as an obstruction to the issue of currency under that plan the requirement of the 30 per cent deposit? Is that an immaterial or a serious obstruction?

Mr. CORNWELL. No; I do not think it is an obstruction.

Mr. WARNER. Do you think that the deposit of 30 per cent in greenbacks under the Secretary's plan is necessary to the safety of the currency proposed to be issued under that plan?

Mr. CORNWELL. No; I do not.

Mr. WARNER. You think that it is quite safe without it?

Mr. CORNWELL. I would limit the issue of bank notes to 50 per cent of their capital instead of 75 per cent.

Mr. WARNER. Then you would limit the bank-note circulation of the country to a maximum of 50 per cent of the banking capital?

Mr. CORNWELL. Yes, at present, with the exception of an emergency circulation, which can only come into use in very serious times.

Mr. WARNER. You are in favor of that feature of the Baltimore plan?

Mr. CORNWELL. Yes; it is a simple way of meeting that point for the present.

Mr. WARNER. You would not lock up the greenbacks as a feature of your currency system?

Mr. CORNWELL. No; but before doing anything with the currency I would construct a plan to retire the greenbacks.

Mr. WARNER. As a separate measure?

Mr. CORNWELL. Either separately or with, but *first*.

Mr. WARNER. And having no necessary connection with the issue of currency?

Mr. CORNWELL. Except that with retirement of greenbacks there would be contraction, and something must fill the place for a while at least.

Mr. WARNER. No connection except affording a broader field to the new circulation?

Mr. CORNWELL. That is it.

Mr. WARNER. If, under the Secretary's plan, you deposited 30 per cent of greenbacks of the face value of the notes that you are to issue, that is an equivalent to a tax on the note circulation equal to the loss of interest on the 30 per cent of greenbacks deposited, is it not?

Mr. CORNWELL. The banks would take out that 30 per cent in their own notes, would they not, and instead of using greenbacks as currency they would use their own notes?

Mr. WARNER. Taking the net gain of circulation (whatever it is), the deposit of the greenbacks as a condition for securing them is equivalent to the loss of interest on that 30 per cent deposited, is it not?

Mr. CORNWELL. Do I understand that you assume that Secretary Carlisle's plan involves the deposit of 30 per cent in any case?

Mr. WARNER. Thirty per cent of the circulation. Now, to the extent of the inability of the banks to get out a large part of the circulation which they are entitled to they would be hampered by nonprofit on that 30 per cent.

Mr. CORNWELL. To the extent to which it was hampered that would increase the obstruction to getting out currency.

Mr. WARNER. You think that it would act in that way?

Mr. CORNWELL. Yes.

Mr. WARNER. And would have a tendency to increase the interest charged to borrowers from the bank, would it not?

Mr. CORNWELL. If you start from where we are now, with practically no profitable circulation——

Mr. WARNER. I mean, as compared with any plan which did not involve that obstruction.

Mr. CORNWELL. Yes; I think it would add to the expense of the banks. Of course, competition comes in to take care of the borrower.

Mr. WARNER. Does not competition, in view of reasonable profit, come in to regulate the amount of currency to be taken out?

Mr. CORNWELL. That may have its effect.

Mr. WARNER. And would not interest be higher with the additional tax or with the obstruction arising from this 30 per cent deposit than if the 30 per cent was not required?

Mr. CORNWELL. I think that would have its effect in regulating the rate of interest, though the effect would be very small.

Mr. WARNER. The effect, if any, however, would be to raise the rate of interest?

Mr. CORNWELL. Yes; rather to raise it than to depress it.

Mr. WARNER. In other words, bankers are going to do business at a profit if they do business at all?

Mr. CORNWELL. That is what they like to do.

Mr. WARNER. Your plan, however, would be to retire greenbacks by a bond issue?

Mr. CORNWELL. I think that would be the only way to do it now.

Mr. WARNER. In reference to branch banks, that subject has been casually referred to here once or twice. In your opinion, is the question of any considerable importance in determining our currency system?

Mr. CORNWELL. I think not now. It is a very important feature, but I do not think we ought to consider it now.

Mr. ELLIS. If I understood you, you stated that you believed the Government had no right to issue money with nothing back of it. I do not think that that was really what you meant to say, perhaps. Do you think that the Government has the power to issue money of any kind beyond the power given to it to coin money and to regulate the value of foreign coins?

Mr. CORNWELL. That is practically where the Government authority should end.

Mr. ELLIS. You also advocate the issue of bonds and taking up of greenbacks, and you think that the vacuum occasioned by that would be filled by the banks which would issue bank notes in lieu of the greenbacks?

Mr. CORNWELL. Should be filled.

Mr. ELLIS. Do you believe that if the greenbacks and Treasury notes were all redeemed and taken in by the Treasury, the banks would issue circulation in lieu of them?

Mr. CORNWELL. I think that in order to avoid contraction the issue of bank notes and the retirement of legal-tender notes should be coincident and automatic.

Mr. ELLIS. Do you mean to say by that that you would advise a provision requiring the national banks or the banks organized under this system you propose, to take out circulating notes to an amount equal to the amount of Government notes taken in?

Mr. CORNWELL. Either that or that the Government should be required to call in and cancel greenbacks as the national-bank notes are taken out.

Mr. ELLIS. I do not think I quite understand your objection to the plan suggested by the Secretary of the Treasury of depositing legal-tender notes to secure bank circulation. What do I understand your objection to that to be?

Mr. CORNWELL. That would be a temporary retirement of that amount of greenbacks. The Secretary's bill further provides for an optional retirement by the Secretary. What I say is that before we begin to issue bank notes we ought to get rid of the legal-tender notes, and that there should be a definite arrangement by which as the bank notes go out the legal-tender notes come in and be canceled.

Mr. ELLIS. What do you think of that provision in the plan proposed by the Secretary of the Treasury which requires every bank which goes into this scheme to become the guarantor of the liabilities of other banks?

Mr. CORNWELL. That practically is a provision in the Baltimore plan, though I think that in the talk on this subject before the committee that has not been brought out. It seems to me that section 6 of the Baltimore plan states that when the fund has reached 5 per cent the tax shall be suspended, and that when it goes below 5 per cent it shall be resumed. Now, if the 5 per cent fund is exhausted and the Comptroller of the Currency deems it necessary to replenish it, he does it by a tax on the banks of one-half of 1 per cent, so that eventually the Baltimore plan throws the entire responsibility onto the banks, although the Government has the responsibility at the start, has it at the time of the failed bank, and has it at taking up the notes of the failed bank, but eventually gets it back.

Mr. ELLIS. What in your opinion would be the effect of any system which requires every bank to become the guarantor of the notes issued by all the other banks of the country?

Mr. CORNWELL. As a practical piece of business it should not be done. But the currency is a little higher than and apart from ordinary commercial business. It has got to be protected and to be made absolutely secure, and in my opinion that is the only way to do it.

Mr. ELLIS. Do you believe that banks would be organized under a system of this sort if they understood in advance that ultimately their assets could be assessed and made liable for the notes of all failed banks throughout the country?

Mr. CORNWELL. Under the protection of the national-banking system as perfected at present and guarded in every way, I do.

Mr. ELLIS. I understand from that that you confine the system to a national-bank system exclusively?

Mr. CORNWELL. I would, because the national banking system has been in operation thirty years or more, and during all that period everything has been done to perfect it as far as possible. I believe that a man who has been in business thirty-one years successfully is a better man to take charge of a great interest than a man who is just starting.

Mr. ELLIS. What is your opinion as to the feature of the plan proposed by the Secretary of the Treasury, which proposes to exempt State banks from taxation on certain conditions?

Mr. CORNWELL. I feel that the introduction of the State-bank feature in the Secretary's plan is the weak part of the whole plan. I think that the Secretary himself thinks so, because on pages 41 and 42 of your proceedings he says that he regards that as entirely a side issue and does not give much importance to it. May I quote?

Mr. ELLIS. Yes.

Mr. CORNWELL. The Secretary says:

> Secretary CARLISLE. I confess, Judge Cobb, that I do not attach the same importance to this State-bank provision that perhaps some other gentlemen do. I do not know to what extent it would be utilized, even if it should be adopted. But still there seems to be a demand in some parts of the country for such a system, and I am willing to accede to that demand.

Further on the Secretary says:

> I attach less importance to the State-banking system than many other gentlemen do; but there seems to be a demand in certain parts of the country for State banks.

And in other places the Secretary expresses himself still more indifferently.

Mr. ELLIS. If that feature of the plan suggested by the Secretary of the Treasury is adopted, would it in your opinion increase or diminish, or what effect would it have on the circulation that might be issued? Would it tend to give a larger circulation than the national-bank system if that system were simply adhered to?

Mr. CORNWELL. There are just four things which we ought to have in the currency. First, security; second, convertibility; third, uniformity; and last, elasticity. Now, we have got the first three. We have got them in magnificent shape. We have got absolute security. We have got convertibility. We have got uniformity. Now, the introduction of a State-bank arrangement would wipe out uniformity, the thing for which, with the other two, the United States are celebrated all over the world. These three conditions of the national-bank notes were so brilliant that about fifteen years ago there was an element in the Canadian Parliament so infatuated with our national-bank note system that it was pressed very strongly that the Canadians should give up their system and adopt our national banking system simply because these three qualities of a first-class currency—security, convertibility, and uniformity—were predominant. Now, if we go into this State-bank arrangement we are going to wipe out one brilliant feature of the national currency, and that is uniformity.

Mr. COX. Do not the same features attach to the Canadian notes?

Mr. CORNWELL. Well, they do now under the Canadian bank bill of 1890. The only feature which the Canadians did not have was uniformity in this way, that their bills were subject to a discount under certain conditions. The bills of failed banks and bills of a distant province were subject to a discount. That was remedied by establishing central redemption agencies in all the large cities in Canada, from Ontario to Manitoba; and further, by making the notes of failed banks to begin drawing interest at once at 6 per cent. If a bank fails in Canada its notes begin to draw interest at 6 per cent, and therefore they are eagerly sought after by investors. There is no danger of their going to a discount and they might go to a premium.

Mr. WARNER. The Canadian banks are entirely independent of each other, are they not?

Mr. CORNWELL. Yes.

Mr. WARNER. So that in that particular they are just as independent essentially as would be the banks of one State of the banks of another State?

Mr. CORNWELL. Yes.

Mr. WARNER. Now, supposing that State-bank currency was permitted under such or similar safeguards as have been provided by the Canadian banking act, would, in your opinion, the currency lack that measure of uniformity and security which you consider so desirable?

Mr. CORNWELL. I fear it would, in this way. The banks in Canada are only 38 in number. Their capital is all very heavy. The Bank of Montreal has twelve millions of capital and is one of the great bulwarks of the nation. The banks are very few in number, are largely capitalized, and are hedged about by the most perfect education of employés, and inspectors and managers, and in that way they are very much safer than we can possibly suppose our State banks can be made at once. The limit of the capital of banks of issue is at least $500,000 with $250,000 paid in. My own opinion is that there should be a limit of capital to banks issuing notes; that is, that no small bank shall issue notes. My own feeling is that a bank should have $500,000 capital in order to be allowed to issue notes—simply as a matter of safety and as a matter of fostering large capital, which, I think, is a very great need in this country.

Mr. WARNER. Would it be proper to say, so far as you can suggest, the objections to a State-bank currency, under limitations similar to those prescribed by the Canadian act, that our State bank system would lack, at least at the start, the effect of the great branch-bank system of Canada; and that our State-bank currency would be based upon banks, the capital of which would be, in your opinion, on the average, too small; and that they would be handled by legislators or people, who, in your opinion, have not had the banking experience and education of those of Canada? In other words, so far as the main provisions of the law are concerned, our State-bank system would not lack that uniformity, which you consider desirable, if they were subjected to provisions similar to those prescribed by the Canadian banking act?

Mr. CORNWELL. All the banks of Canada are under the government of the Dominion, whereas our State banks would be under forty-four different governments.

Mr. WARNER. But if they were all brought under the same safeguards so far as note issues are concerned, that would produce no different effect, would it?

Mr. CORNWELL. No; and that is what has been done in the national banking system, and I can not myself see why any bank should want to be a State bank if there is any profit for it in going into the national-bank system. My own bank is a State bank because that is a very respectable thing to be in the State of New York, and because there is no profit in the national-bank system; but I will say frankly that if there were more profit in the national banking system we would change our institution without any feeling of patriotic sentiment, because I do not think it is a thing where that sentiment finds place.

Mr. WARNER. My question was as to whether under these restrictions the State-bank currency would not have the uniformity which you suggest is so desirable?

Mr. CORNWELL. Under one management I think it would.

Mr. WARNER. So far as the requisites for circulation are concerned, would not the circulation have that extent of uniformity which you consider desirable?

Mr. CORNWELL. You would have to adopt toward the State banks the provision of inspection.

Mr. WARNER. With that provision do you think it would have uniformity?

Mr. CORNWELL. Yes; that system of inspection is provided for in Canada.

Mr. WARNER. May I ask whether there is any other safeguard that occurs to you beyond the provisions that the notes of failed banks shall pay 6 per cent interest, and beyond the provision for inspection, that is not practically included in Mr. Carlisle's plan? He provides for the double liability of stockholders, for the first lien upon the assets of the bank, and for a limitation of the amount of notes to be taken out by a bank not to exceed 75 per cent of its capital. That, I believe, is more stringent than the Canadian provision.

Mr. CORNWELL. Do you mean as regards national banks?

Mr. WARNER. No; I mean as regards State banks. Suppose there were added to Mr. Carlisle's plan definite provisions for inspection, and also that the notes of failed banks should bear interest from the time of their dishonoring by the parent bank at 6 per cent so as to add to the inducement which you suggest of their being taken up and not being a burden upon the circulation. Then add provision for a redemption fund and for a safety fund. With those provisions, is there any reason why the State-bank currency would not have that uniformity which you consider so desirable?

Mr. CORNWELL. And what penalty would you provide for the nonobservance of those conditions?

Mr. WARNER. The collection of the 10 per cent tax.

Mr. CORNWELL. One thing would have to be provided—that their bills should be under one management.

Mr. WARNER. Suppose that their bills were printed and registered by the Comptroller of the Currency?

Mr. WALKER. Suppose they were national-bank notes?

Mr. CORNWELL. Let me tell you one thing about counterfeiting. That business has been reduced to a minimum. How? By the Secret Service of the Government, which has concentrated its energies in following up counterfeiters. With the State banks that feature could not be arranged, I fear; at any rate, not for a long time, because the thing must be concentrated under one head. Counterfeiting would be carried on simply because there would not be a service which goes after these fellows around the world and puts them into State prisons, as is done with those who counterfeit national-bank notes.

Mr. WARNER. Suppose the banking law is so amended as to make the counterfeiting of State-bank notes a Federal offense, too?

Mr. CORNWELL. If you do that, all right.

Mr. WARNER. I want to show that there is no inherent difficulty, outside of purely administrative features, in allowing State banks to issue currency under conditions which would insure the reasonable uniformity on which you would insist and which you consider so desirable.

Mr. HENDERSON. When you establish these conditions, I suppose you contemplate that the National Government shall do it.

Mr. HALL. Have you read section 5 of Secretary Carlisle's bill carefully? I mean the one providing for the guarantee fund and the safety fund and the redemption of the bank notes where a bank fails.

Mr. CORNWELL. I have.

Mr. HALL. Do you believe that there is anything in that section which would tend to prevent or would prevent banks from taking out charters under the provisions of this law?

Mr. CORNWELL. I do not.

Mr. JOHNSON, of Indiana. You said early in your statement something about the creation of a commission on this banking and currency matter. I wish you would elaborate your ideas a little more fully on that subject.

Mr. CORNWELL. That is a matter to which I do not attach a great deal of importance, for the reason that if my first suggestions are carried out the work of this commission would be simply to deliberate, and might extend over a good many years. It would be simply in the direction of being advisory with the banks for perfecting the system as thus changed.

Mr. JOHNSON, of Indiana. I thought you had reference, possibly, to the establishment of a commission, with a view to investigating defects and suggesting remedies and reporting at some subsequent session of Congress, with the view of framing and passing a complete currency system at that time.

Mr. CORNWELL. That might be done, but it should be done with the utmost deliberation, for the reason that the need of such a commission, in my opinion, would not be pressing after the legal-tender notes were retired and the Baltimore plan adopted.

Mr. JOHNSON, of Indiana. What I want to get at is this: Would you think it advisable to have a commission of the kind established to make a report before Congress attempts currency revision?

Mr. CORNWELL. No, sir; not until these two things are done.

Mr. JOHNSON, of Indiana. You think there is a necessity for immediate legislation?

Mr. CORNWELL. I think so.

Mr. JOHNSON, of Indiana. Do you think that proper and wise legislation can be obtained at once?

Mr. CORNWELL. I do.

Mr. JOHNSON, of Indiana. I understood you to say to Mr. Warner that the 30 per cent guarantee required to be paid up by the banks under Mr. Carlisle's plan would not render the circulation of bank notes unprofitable?

Mr. CORNWELL. No; I did not say that.

Mr. JOHNSON, of Indiana. Do you consider that phase of the plan as being objectionable on the ground that it would deprive the circulation of necessary profit to the banks?

Mr. CORNWELL. No; that was not my objection to it. My objection to it was that it seemed to me unnecessary and that it did not retire the greenbacks permanently.

Mr. JOHNSON, of Indiana. Would you consider it objectionable on the ground that it would interfere with the profits which the banks would make on their circulation?

Mr. CORNWELL. No, not on that ground. It deprives them of a certain amount of profit, but as the banks have been deprived for a good many years of any profit whatever, it is a question of getting as much as they can.

Mr. JOHNSON, of Indiana. One of Mr. Carlisle's purposes in requiring the deposit in the Treasury of greenbacks and Treasury notes issued under the act of 1890, when circulating bank notes are taken out, is to relieve the Treasury from the drain of gold caused by the presentation of those greenbacks and Treasury notes. Do you think that any plan which falls short of the absolute and immediate taking up and cancellation of all the United States Treasury notes and the notes issued under the act of 1890 will accomplish that purpose?

Mr. CORNWELL. I think that that is the best way to accomplish it. I do think, as a compromise only, that if it can be arranged very gradually and absolutely, so that the retirement is going on and will go on, that will probably help matters materially.

Mr. JOHNSON, of Indiana. If Mr. Carlisle's plan, for instance, would only retire about one half of these Government issues, would not the other half be utilized to draw gold out of the Treasury just as expeditiously and just as effectively as though they were all in circulation?

Mr. CORNWELL. Yes, sir. Whatever plan may be adopted must involve their entire retirement; that is, the retirement of the whole issue.

Mr. JOHNSON, of Indiana. The leaving of part of them off deposit would simply result in that part being used more frequently than though the whole were left out, with which to drain the Treasury of its gold, would it not?

Mr. CORNWELL. I think it would.

Mr. JOHNSON, of Indiana. Are you in favor of the Government being ultimately responsible for the final redemption of bank notes in any plan that may be devised by Congress?

Mr. CORNWELL. No.

Mr. JOHNSON, of Indiana. That is, however, a provision in the Baltimore plan, is it not?

Mr. CORNWELL. No, sir. The Baltimore plan provides for a continuation of the assessment under the 5 per cent redemption fund whenever the Comptroller of the Currency deems it necessary.

Mr. JOHNSON, of Indiana. You differ from my conception of the Baltimore plan and from that given by the other gentlemen who have appeared here in advocacy of it in your answer to my last question.

Mr. CORNWELL. I know, but I can not read section 6 in any other way (reading):

SEC. 6. Create a "guarantee fund" through the deposit by each bank of two per centum upon the amount of circulation received the first year. Thereafter impose a tax of one-half of one per centum upon the average amount of outstanding circulation, the same to be paid into this fund until it shall equal five per centum of the entire circulation outstanding, when the collection of such tax shall be suspended, to be resumed whenever the Comptroller of the Currency shall deem it necessary.

Mr. JOHNSON, of Indiana. But suppose the other fund out of which the Government is to recoup itself is exhausted, then the payment of these notes of failed banks would be an ultimate liability on the Government?

Mr. CORNWELL. Which it provides for by replenishment of the guarantee fund.

Mr. ELLIS. For what purpose?

Mr. CORNWELL. Whenever the Comptroller of the Currency deems it necessary, and I can not but think that he would deem it necessary if the fund was gone.

Mr. ELLIS. The Government would not have any authority to satisfy itself out of the fund thus assessed and made good, would it?

Mr. CORNWELL. I think it would. The plan may not, in so many words, provide for it, but it seems absolutely to follow what is done under section 6. The Government pays the notes of all failed banks out of this fund. Now, if the fund is depleted one-half the Comptroller of the Currency begins to assess the banks again until the 5 per cent fund is made up.

Mr. ELLIS. But would the Government have a right to recoup itself out of that fund?

Mr. CORNWELL. Certainly, because the Government makes an advance only.

Mr. JOHNSON, of Indiana. Laying aside the question as to the proper consideration of the Baltimore plan, what is your individual opinion as to whether or not the Government should become ultimately liable to the note holder for the payment of the notes of failed banks?

Mr. CORNWELL. I do not think it should.

Mr. JOHNSON, of Indiana. Would not the knowledge on the part of the people that the Government was ultimately liable have a very strong tendency to give that popular confidence in the money which is essential to its success?

Mr. CORNWELL. Not any more than the Government's guarantee, which is involved in this matter. If it is provided that the Government shall pay these notes, the Government guarantees them.

Mr. JOHNSON, of Indiana. That amounts, then, to ultimate Government liability, does it not?

Mr. CORNWELL. It may, but the Government gets its money back. The Government acts merely as a creditor, advancing money with the intention of taking up the notes.

Mr. JOHNSON, of Indiana. But suppose the Government does not get its money back?

Mr. CORNWELL. The only condition under which the Government does not get it back would be the failure of every bank in the United States without assets enough to pay the outstanding circulation.

Mr. JOHNSON, of Indiana. Do you take into consideration in establishing a sound currency the fact that the public impression as to the safety of the currency ought to be taken into account?

Mr. CORNWELL. I do, and for that reason I am more lenient in the matter of Government gurantee than I would otherwise be. The people of the United States are used to a currency, as far as the national banks are concerned, which is good in a week or a month or a year, and they never look at the character of a bill.

Mr. JOHNSON, of Indiana. They have faith in them because they feel that the Government is ultimately liable?

Mr. CORNWELL. Yes.

Mr. JOHNSON, of Indiana. Than you would have a Government guarantee so strong as to be equivalent to ultimate Government liability?

Mr. CORNWELL. It would amount to the same thing. I advocate that now because I do not believe in radical changes in the present condition as to security.

Mr. JOHNSON, of Indiana. Is there any danger that undue inflation would come from this system which you have advocated, and if so how would you guard against it?

Mr. CORNWELL. If the retirement of the greenbacks and the outgoing of the new national-bank notes were automatic there could not be inflation beyond what there is at present.

Mr. JOHNSON, of Indiana. But would the plan contemplate that more money might be taken out by the banks than the amount of the greenbacks retired?

Mr. CORNWELL. No, not yet.

Mr. JOHNSON, of Indiana. That would be the case under Mr. Carlisle's plan, would it not?

Mr. CORNWELL. I think it would.

Mr. JOHNSON, of Indiana. Then what have you to say, if anything, as to the danger of inflation under Mr. Carlisle's plan?

Mr. CORNWELL. I say that the retirement of the greenbacks should be automatic with the issue of the new bank notes, and that the issue of new bank notes at present should not go beyond the amount of greenbacks retired.

Mr. JOHNSON, of Indiana. Therefore, you disapprove of that feature of Mr. Carlisle's plan?

Mr. CORNWELL. Yes.

Mr. JOHNSON, of Indiana. Why would you have the Government guarantee continued?

Mr. CORNWELL. On the ground that the people are used to it. I would keep up the redemption of national notes in the Treasury and subtreasury in lawful money just as at present.

Mr. JOHNSON, of Indiana. Is this Canadian system national in its character, and under one central governmental control?

Mr. CORNWELL. Yes, sir.

Mr. JOHNSON, of Indiana. And the provisions of the charters of each of the banks are precisely the same?

Mr. CORNWELL. There are some one or two old banks in Canada under special charters, and have been for fifty years or more. These are not changed materially, except as to the regulation of currency issue.

Mr. JOHNSON, of Indiana. These charters are from——

Mr. CORNWELL. From the Royal Government of England, and the charters of the other banks are from the Dominion of Canada.

Mr. WARNER. When you speak of the charters of one or two banks in Canada, that may refer to forty or fifty bank branches, may it not?

Mr. CORNWELL. Yes.

Mr. WARNER. So as to be a considerable portion of the banking of the Dominion?

Mr. JOHNSON, of Indiana. There are no such things as State or provincial banks in the Canadian system, are there?

Mr. CORNWELL. No, sir.

Mr. JOHNSON, of Indiana. Nothing akin to what a State bank system would be in our Government?

Mr. CORNWELL. Nothing of the kind.

Mr. JOHNSON, of Indiana. Which do you think would be the safest and best adapted to the needs of our people, a single system under national control, or a system under State control?

Mr. CORNWELL. A single system under national control.

Mr. JOHNSON, of Indiana. Which do you think would be the safest and best, a single system under national control or a system under State control except as to certain specific conditions imposed by national authority?

Mr. CORNWELL. A single system under national control without any mixture.

Mr. JOHNSON, of Indiana. If you would undertake to authorize State banks to issue currency under certain conditions and restrictions would you not deem it necessary to impose conditions and restrictions upon these banks to the extent that it would virtually make them national banks?

Mr. CORNWELL. I would.

Mr. WARNER. With respect to their currency issue?

Mr. CORNWELL. With respect to their currency issue and to inspection and to penalties for violation of the conditions.

Mr. JOHNSON, of Indiana. Multiplicity in systems of issuing paper money would almost necessarily beget some system that would be considered safer than others, would it not?

Mr. CORNWELL. Yes.

Mr. JOHNSON, of Indiana. And would not that very fact have a tendency to beget preferences in money?

Mr. CORNWELL. Certainly.

Mr. JOHNSON, of Indiana. And would not that have a tendency to disturb the uniformity of the currency?

Mr. CORNWELL. It would.

Mr. JOHNSON, of Indiana. And would it not be disastrous in its effects?

Mr. CORNWELL. It would make trouble, and would be very undesirable.

Mr. JOHNSON, of Indiana. Are you familiar with the action of the German Government in taking up the paper money of the various German states and substituting therefor one system under national control?

Mr. CORNWELL. I have not followed it up particularly. Of course I am aware of it.

Mr. JOHNSON, of Indiana. That was done not long ago, was it not?

Mr. CORNWELL. Yes.

Mr. WARNER. The provisions of Mr. Carlisle's plan dispensing with the necessity of a reserve in the case of national banks—do you consider that as an important modification?

Mr. CORNWELL. I consider it right.

Mr. WARNER. As to the $10 limit below which the denomination of currency to be issued shall not go—what is your opinion upon that?

Mr. CORNWELL. I do not consider that so very important. I think that a $5 limit would be better. Of course the idea is to allow the circulation of silver, which is a thing to be desired—subsidiarily.

Mr. WARNER. Now, as to new banks coming in under the Baltimore plan. After it has been in operation four or five years a new bank, as a condition of taking out currency, would have to deposit the whole 5 per cent guarantee fund.

Mr Cornwell. It would have to pay in as much as if it had started in the beginning.

Mr. Warner. In other words, practically 5 per cent.

Mr. Cornwell. Practically the whole 5 per cent.

Mr. Warner. Would not that be an almost imperative obstruction against new banks coming in under the Baltimore plan after it had been running four or five years?

Mr. Cornwell. I do not think so. Everyone wishing to join a club or institution would pay an initiation fee and that would be in the shape of an initiation fee for a privilege. The privilege would be valuable. The bank might pay 5 per cent into safety fund and not make anything on its circulation the first year, but the next year it would begin to make a profit.

Mr. Warner. Your idea is that the Baltimore plan would make such a desirable club of banks that the initiation fee would be gladly paid to get into it.

Mr. Cornwell. Perhaps I had better not say any thing about that.

Mr. Warner. But you think the franchise would be so valuable in a few years that new banks would be glad to pay the initiation fee to get into it.

Mr. Cornwell. I think that it is not good judgment to induce people to go into the banking business too rapidly.

Mr. Warner. And this would keep them from doing it?

Mr. Cornwell. This would tend to make them consider whether it was worth their while.

Mr. Warner. To pay the 5 per cent?

Mr. Cornwell. To pay the 5 per cent. That is, whether they are going to make all the money the first year or whether they will make the money afterwards.

Mr. Warner. And risk the 5 per cent the first year?

Mr. Cornwell. Yes.

Mr. Warner. As to redemption, would you suggest broader facilities for redemption than those suggested by the Baltimore plan? Are you familiar with it?

Mr. Cornwell. I am familiar with it. I would not now, but I would ultimately.

Mr. Warner. You think that ultimately a more liberal plan should be adopted?

Mr. Cornwell. Ultimately.

Mr. Warner. As to the charters of Canadian banks, have they not been issued under successive governments, first under the British Government and then under the Canadian Government?

Mr. Cornwell. Yes. There are two or three banks under old charters.

Mr. Warner. How old?

Mr. Cornwell. Fifty years or more. The Bank of British North America, the Bank of British Columbia, and the Merchants' Bank of Prince Edward Island are three banks under old charters.

Mr. Warner. But there have been modifications in the banking law of Canada from time to time since, have there not?

Mr. Cornwell. Yes. These banks are nearly all banks that have been continued from time to time.

Mr. Warner. So that when you come to take the number of branches that each bank may have, there is a great variety, not in conditions for the issue of currency, but in the other parts of the charters of Canadian banks?

Mr. CORNWELL. Their charters were held when they came in under the Dominion laws, just as our State banks at the beginning of the war came in under the national banking law. The charters of our State banks were changed very little when they came into the national system. The Bank of North America, in Philadelphia, which has survived one change of dynasty, is an example of that. It is now a national bank.

Mr. WARNER. But the uniformity provided by Canadian law with reference to currency does not enforce uniformity in the other provisions of the charters of the several banks.

Mr. CORNWELL. No.

Mr. HALL. Do you believe that the greenbacks ought to be retired by funding?

Mr. CORNWELL. I believe that they ought to be retired, and that the only feasible way to retire them at present is to fund them.

Mr. HALL. Have you any system other than funding by which you would retire them under the Baltimore plan?

Mr. CORNWELL. There is no provision in the Baltimore plan for retiring greenbacks.

Mr. HALL. The funding of the greenbacks would furnish a basis for a continuation of the national-banking system in the United States for an indefinite time in the future, would it not?

Mr. CORNWELL. Yes.

Mr. HALL. It would furnish about four hundred and ninety millions of additional bonds which national banks could continue to bank upon?

Mr. CORNWELL. Yes.

Mr. HALL. Do you believe that the greenbacks are now creating any of this financial trouble?

Mr. CORNWELL. I do.

Mr. HALL. By draining the gold from the Treasury?

Mr. CORNWELL. Again and again.

Mr. HALL. Under Mr. Carlisle's plan there is a provision for placing 30 per cent of bank circulation in greenbacks, so that they can not be used for draining the gold from the Treasury.

Mr. CORNWELL. Yes.

Mr. JOHNSON, of Ohio. I asked you the question whether if the Carlisle plan left out any part of the greenbacks it would not be just as bad as if they had been all left out, and I understood your answer to be "yes." Now, let me ask you this question: If one-half or more of the greenbacks were temporarily put where they could not be used as a bucket to dip the gold out of the Treasury, would not that tend to put the rest of the greenbacks at a premium as a basis for banking, so as to keep them from being used as a means of draining the Treasury of its gold?

Mr. CORNWELL. I do not think that the foreign investor would look at it in that way.

Mr. JOHNSON, of Indiana. Under the provisions of the Carlisle plan nothing but greenbacks and Treasury notes of 1890 can be used as a basis for banking?

Mr. CORNWELL. Yes.

Mr. JOHNSON, of Indiana. Would not that fact tend to put greenbacks at such a premium that they would not be used as an instrument of draining the gold from the Treasury?

Mr. CORNWELL. It might have that temporary effect; but if a thing is bad and wrong, I do not believe in having anything to do with it.

Mr. JOHNSON, of Ohio. Do you not as a practical man have to recognize the feelings of the people of the United States on an important matter of this kind?

Mr. CORNWELL. As regards that sentiment, I do not believe that the business men of the United States (and these are the men who control legislation when it comes to ultimate control) have any such affection for the greenbacks as some people seem to think. I think that they hardly ever look to see whether the notes in their pockets are greenbacks or not. The greenback has been good for many years because of the magnificent resources of the country. If a very rich man has some notes out, everybody is willing to take them, because they know that he is very rich. But I do not believe that business men, when they come to look into this question carefully as they are going to do, will have any such affection for the greenback.

Mr. BROSIUS. In your judgment, is the redemption and cancellation of the greenbacks and Treasury notes of sufficient importance at this time to justify the imposition on the people of the United States of the burden which the issue of bonds for that purpose would entail upon them?

Mr. CORNWELL. In my opinion it is of the very first importance, and the amount of interest which the Government would have to pay on this forced loan, on which it is now paying no interest, would be a mere trifle compared with the good which it would do, and compared with the bad which has been done. The few millions which the Government would pay in interest by funding the greenbacks has been wiped out by hundreds of millions lost by the business men of the country because the Government was in that position.

Mr. BROSIUS. The injury which the greenbacks and the Treasury notes are now doing to the country is in the way of affording means of draining the gold reserve?

Mr. CORNWELL. Yes.

Mr. BROSIUS. Did we have any difficulty of that kind in this country when we had a Treasury surplus instead of a deficit?

Mr. CORNWELL. No, sir.

Mr. BROSIUS. If the present Treasury deficit was converted into a Treasury surplus, would not the difficulty cease at once, or to a large extent?

Mr. CORNWELL. It would cease until the tide was turned again, and then the drain would go on once more.

Mr. BROSIUS. Tell me why you think that the existence of the greenbacks and Treasury notes to the extent of $500,000,000 is incompatible with an elastic system of bank currency.

Mr. CORNWELL. I do not think it has anything to do with the elasticity directly.

Mr. BROSIUS. You have said that the only respect in which our banking system lacks practical perfection is the quality of elasticity.

Mr. CORNWELL. I am talking now about the national-bank system; yes.

Mr. BROSIUS. I am speaking of that, too.

Mr. CORNWELL. I did not know but that you included all Government banking.

Mr. BROSIUS. And you think that the only respect in which it lacks practical perfection is in the quality of elasticity?

Mr. CORNWELL. Yes.

Mr. BROSIUS. That consists in having notes at all times ready to pay out when there is a demand for them, does it not?

Mr. CORNWELL. When there is a legitimate demand by commerce.

Mr. BROSIUS. Exactly; that is the demand I refer to.

Mr. CORNWELL. And further than that, that they must retire when that demand ceases.

Mr. BROSIUS. Would they not do that anyhow?

Mr. CORNWELL. Not anyhow. They do not do it now.

Mr. BROSIUS. Let me direct your attention to the fact that at the time of the recent stringency, or at least in the early portion of that stringency, the national banks did not issue notes to within something over $7,000,000 of the limit of their right to issue them. Why did they not do that?

Mr. CORNWELL. Because there was no profit in it.

Mr. BROSIUS. This $7,000,000 would have cost them nothing. Why did they not take them out and use them if there was a demand for them? I am directing your attention to the fact (although I did not state it) that you have already intimated that if the bank currency was issued against the credit of the banks it would cost the banks nothing. They could keep the notes idle when they were not in demand and have them ready to issue to meet an increased demand when it should arise. I understand from you, as well as others, that the difficulty now is that the notes secured by Government bonds are so expensive that the banks can not afford to keep them ready for use when an increased demand arises. Am I stating it correctly?

Mr. CORNWELL. The inducement to issue bank notes is the inducement of profit.

Mr. BROSIUS. After you have deposited a certain amount of Government bonds you are entitled to an issue of 90 per cent of currency. And yet during the stringency of 1893 the national banks did not issue within seven millions of the amount which they were entitled to draw on their bonds, an amount of currency which would have cost them nothing at all. Now, if they would not issue these notes when it cost them nothing, what reasons have you for stating that they would issue notes under the same circumstances if they were issued against the credit of the bank, because in both cases they were equally inexpensive?

Mr. CORNWELL. I do not know about that seven millions; but will you tell me why they did not?

Mr. BROSIUS. I have given my views on that question on another occasion, but the committee does not care to hear me under these circumstances on that subject.

Mr. CORNWELL. Have you any statistics on that point?

Mr. BROSIUS. I think that the fact is shown in numerous forms. I do not think that any gentleman acquainted with the history of 1893 will question my statement.

The chairman remarked that the matter under discussion was not one brought up by the witness himself, and that therefore it should not be continued further.

Mr. CORNWELL. I recognize the questions of Mr. Brosius as being simply in the direction of gaining information, but I would like to ask him whether the nonissue of $7,000,000 was not due to the same reason that the $32,000,000, which have been asked for by the banks, were not issued, because the notes were not ready and printed in the Department?

Mr. BROSIUS. That may be so, but will you have the kindness to answer this inquiry, Why did not the banks, being sensible of the situation at the time, have these seven millions of notes in their vaults ready for use? Was the default in the Government or in the banks?

Mr. CORNWELL. The condition of the issue of national-bank notes has been such a water-logged sort of an affair for so many years that I have no doubt that the banks thought that there could be no relief from that, and instead of seeking that relief they got out clearing-house certificates, which they could use instantly. They issued these and saved the country.

Mr. BROSIUS. Do you conceive it possible to devise a banking system for the United States that will combine the four elements you have named—safety, uniformity, convertibility, and elasticity—by any means that will enable the banks themselves (each bank for itself and not jointly for all) to provide collaterals to protect the Government against its ultimate liability to the note holders for the redemption of the notes?

Mr. CORNWELL. I do not believe there can be any elasticity of currency which has for its basis special security of any kind whatever. The basis of all elasticity is a general security against the general assets of the bank. With special security there can be no elasticity. and the reason of that is that there must be two forces operating as to elasticity—one force to throw the notes out (to circulate them) and the other force to retire them when they are not needed. With a special security circulation the notes will go out when there is profit in their issue, and they will disappear when there is no profit. Under a general security the notes will go out when the community needs them and when the banks can push them out, but they will come back when that demand ceases.

Mr. BROSIUS. That is all very true; but it is not on the point of my inquiry. Do you mean that statement to be a negative answer to my inquiry—that you can not establish a banking system in the United States which will combine the four elements, safety, uniformity, convertibility, and elasticity, and at the same time to require each bank to furnish collaterals to protect the Government against its liability to the note holders?

Mr. CORNWELL. Kindly tell me what you mean by collaterals?

Mr. BROSIUS. Any kind of security—money, greenbacks, stocks, or bonds.

Mr. CORNWELL. Do you mean a pledge of general assets or a general guarantee by the officers of the bank?

Mr. BROSIUS. I mean a guarantee by the bank.

Mr. CORNWELL. You can not have this kind of a system by a pledge of special security, if you mean that?

Mr. BROSIUS. I do. Then, it is not possible to devise a banking system in which the security for the circulating notes will be dollar for dollar?

Mr. CORNWELL. No; not an elastic system.

Mr. WALKER. Do you think it possible for a Government to issue the currency of the people under any system that will be elastic—that is to say, that the currency can be had when opportunity demands it and go back automatically when it is not needed?

Mr. CORNWELL. No, sir.

Mr. WALKER. You are aware of the fact that there is no gold now being paid into the Treasury and has not been for quite a long time, it having come to that point that the people, being suspicious of the currency and of the financial system, have ceased to pay duties in gold; do you think that if it should develop that the receipts of the Government exceed the expenditures that habit would be changed and gold would be paid in?

Mr. CORNWELL. It might gradually have that effect; but it would not be permanent. It would be simply temporary as it has been heretofore.

Mr. WALKER. Would they not continue to pay the customs in Treasury notes and greenbacks? In other words, would not the Treasury still have to sell bonds for gold?

Mr. CORNWELL. Yes; for quite a while.

Mr. WALKER. For two or three years?

Mr. CORNWELL. Probably.

Mr. WALKER. Is it not a fact that the very pressing necessity now, and the thing which is essential to affect the financial condition of the country (which this committee is interested in), is that something shall be done to retire the greenbacks either absolutely or so that the Treasury will not be called upon for their redemption?

Mr. CORNWELL. Yes; that is very thoroughly my opinion.

Mr. WALKER. Can you tell us of any other system than that in the United States where banks are required to furnish bonds to secure their circulation?

Mr. CORNWELL. I do not know of any now.

Mr. WALKER. Is it not the opinion of bankers that bonds have no place in the currency system?

Mr. CORNWELL. Yes; I think that has been demonstrated.

Mr. WALKER. You have said that the Baltimore plan goes far enough for the present. You have said that several times, have you not?

Mr. CORNWELL. Yes.

Mr. WALKER. But the American bankers who met at Baltimore took no cognizance of the financial condition of the country, but simply of the questions of the banks issuing currency.

Mr. CORNWELL. Yes; I think that is all they covered.

Mr. WALKER. That is, their own collective interest in the money—to make money out of the circulation?

Mr. CORNWELL. No; I do not think it was with reference to the profits of the banks at all. I do not think that was the stimulating motive with any of the bankers who considered the question. Their motive was to get the system into the best possible shape for the people. I consider the profits which a bank makes on its currency a very small part of its business. The use which a bank is to the business men and to the community is the most important part of its whole business.

Mr. WALKER. We understand that the banks are a part of the international and individual exchanges, and as much a part of trade and transportation as railways; but my point is this: You do not claim that the Baltimore meeting took the financial condition of the country and of the United States Treasury into consideration in any way in this plan. Will you point out anything in the Baltimore plan which indicates that the bankers there took into consideration the financial condition of the country?

Mr. CORNWELL. It is not involved in the section that I read, but I think the intention was to make it possible to retire the greenbacks without contraction.

Mr. WALKER. That does not appear in the plan?

Mr. CORNWELL. If you retire the greenbacks without providing something else in lieu of them you cause contraction.

Mr. WALKER. Can you point out anything in the Baltimore plan which squints at the retirement of greenbacks?

Mr. CORNWELL. No; there is nothing of that kind there, but Mr. White has a proposition of that kind.

Mr. WALKER. Mr. White was acting for himself.

Mr. CORNWELL. My plan involves first the retirement of the greenbacks and then the adoption of the Baltimore plan.

Mr. WALKER. As a legislator, you being a legislator, and feeling that something must be done to retire these greenbacks, and that Congress can not be brought to enact a bill that will, do you not think that it is the duty of those responsible for legislation to find some way to prevent their being presented at the Treasury to drain gold? Do you not think that the first step?

Mr. CORNWELL. I am tired of compromise. I suppose it is a hard thing to get around, but I think we ought to find out what the right thing is and fight for it.

Mr. WALKER. But in the meantime if you were drowning you would not fight for a principle, but would fight to save your life. Now, the financial condition of the country is such that if anything can be devised to prevent greenbacks being constantly presented for redemption, do you not think it ought to be done?

Mr. CORNWELL. It is a question whether it is not time to face this thing.

Mr. WALKER. You are begging my question. I agree that it is always time to face things, and I am quite apt to do so. But here is a condition where the people will not be faced down or back, according to your ideas. Now, if it can be made to the interest of the banks to take out more currency by changing the present system and by the banks assuming the current redemption of the greenbacks proportionately, do you not think that that ought to be done?

Mr. CORNWELL. In other words, the question is whether we shall continue to borrow money to buy gold. I think I would keep on borrowing gold.

Mr. WALKER. That is to say, we would finally get out of the trouble quicker to let the disease go on until it can be wholly cured?

Mr. CORNWELL. I think so.

Mr. WALKER. Will you not tell us whether the Carlisle plan, in any financial or economic sense, retires the greenbacks?

Mr. CORNWELL. I do not think it does. It puts them into the Treasury to the extent of 30 per cent of the bank circulation taken out.

Mr. WALKER. Is it understood in the parlance of finance that putting a thing up for security retires it?

Mr. CORNWELL. No, sir.

Mr. WALKER. Then, you do not think that this plan in any sense retires the greenbacks?

Mr. CORNWELL. No, sir.

Mr. WALKER. Tell us how, in your opinion of the Baltimore plan, you can get any money whatever into circulation when we already have $1,200,000,000, and it is being stored in the banks, showing that there is no demand for money, and that the banks do not know what to do with the money they have? How could the Baltimore plan operate provided it was enacted into law?

Mr. CORNWELL. Of course a plan of currency operates only as the trade requires it.

Mr. WALKER. Then, you admit that it is simply——

Mr. CORNWELL. Simply getting ready for the future.

Mr. WALKER. And would have no immediate effect?

Mr. CORNWELL. No immediate effect, probably. I do not think we need any immediate effect with bank notes, except to retire some or to replace legal tenders if they are retired.

Mr. WALKER. So that really the Baltimore plan (which you have said, and others have said repeatedly, is all that need be done for the present) would have no effect whatever for the present. You do not want to assume that position?

Mr. CORNWELL. My statement was begun with the first and most important declaration; first, retire the Government legal-tender notes whether you adopt the Baltimore plan or any other plan, or leave the thing as it is; second, adopt the Baltimore plan in order to provide bank notes to take the place of the legal tenders.

Mr. WALKER. Then, your Baltimore plan was prepared as a secondary step?

Mr. CORNWELL. The Baltimore plan provided that the banks would do their part in the matter while the Government got ready to do its part.

Mr. WALKER. That was something to take effect in the future, not in the present.

Mr. CORNWELL. After the Government had done its part.

Mr. WALKER. You have intimated that the business of banking, as it is conducted under the State system, would divide up the business of the supervision of the banks, including the detection of counterfeiting, into 44 pieces, each one being so small that it could not afford to maintain an effective supervision and protection against counterfeiting.

Mr. CORNWELL. I did not say exactly "being so small." My idea is this: There are 44 different supervisions of State banks, while the effective supervision of counterfeiting is brought about by one supervision—the secret service of the United States. Now to get these 44 supervisions together under one system, in order to eliminate counterfeiting, would be a very difficult thing. We are trying to do it in the State bank association of New York. We are trying to join with other State associations to establish a detective bureau to operate all over the United States to keep out fraud, but it is going to be a difficult thing to do, and it will take a long time to do it.

Mr. WALKER. You have said that you think the $5 limitation for bank notes would be better than the $10 limitation. Why have a $5 limitation? For what purpose? Why should not the limit be $1 or $2? Is the sole and only reason for a $5 limit the fact that we have silver, and that the Government should provide for its use?

Mr. CORNWELL. Yes, sir; that is the only reason.

Mr. WALKER. If we had no forced silver coinage you would not be for a $5 limit?

Mr. CORNWELL. Not necessarily, as a matter of convenience. I think, however, that silver should be circulated now—in a subsidiary way.

Mr. JOHNSON, of Ohio. What effect, in your judgment, would it have on the price of gold if the Government were to redeem the greenbacks and Treasury notes in silver coin?

Mr. CORNWELL. You mean what premium gold would go to?

Mr. JOHNSON, of Ohio. Would it go to a premium?

Mr. CORNWELL. I would not dare to say to what premium it would go.

Mr. JOHNSON, of Ohio. You think it would go to a premium?

Mr. CORNWELL. Oh, certainly; at once.

Mr. JOHNSON, of Ohio. In the national-bank currency contemplated, I believe that the redemption of it by the banks is to be in lawful money?

Mr. CORNWELL. Yes.

Mr. JOHNSON, of Ohio. And that gives the banks an option of paying it in silver?

Mr. CORNWELL. Yes.

Mr. JOHNSON, of Ohio. And if the banks paid these notes in silver, would not that have the same effect and force gold to a premium?

Mr. CORNWELL. I do not think so.

Mr. JOHNSON, of Ohio. You think that if the Government paid its notes in silver, gold would go to a premium, but that if the banks paid their notes in silver, gold would go to a premium?

Mr. CORNWELL. I think it would not.

Mr. JOHNSON, of Ohio. Why?

Mr. CORNWELL. Because we are on a gold basis?

Mr. JOHNSON, of Ohio. Do you think that that quite answers the question? You say that in the one case gold would go to a premium?

Mr. CORNWELL. It would be sure to do so.

Mr. JOHNSON, of Ohio. But you say that if the banks should exercise the option which some people claim the Government has, and pay their notes in silver, gold would not in that case go to a premium.

Mr. CORNWELL. The currency of the country is at this time on a gold standard. If there were no demand for gold at the Treasury the gold would certainly remain there.

Mr. JOHNSON, of Ohio. But it is the difference in the two conditions which I wish you to explain.

Mr. CORNWELL. The difference is that the action of the Government in paying its notes in silver would establish a silver standard at once.

Mr. JOHNSON, of Ohio. And the same action by the banks would not?

Mr. CORNWELL. It would not.

Mr. WALKER. Because the Government is the final redeemer?

Mr. CORNWELL. Yes.

Mr. JOHNSON, of Ohio. The banks that exercised the privilege of redeeming bank notes in lawful money and redeemed them in silver, would they not force their notes to a discount as compared with gold?

Mr. CORNWELL. The exercise of the option would not have that effect, but if they insisted upon paying out silver when the note holder demanded gold their notes would be disliked in the community and would go to a discount.

Mr. JOHNSON, of Ohio. You think that if that were done by the banks it would have no effect on gold?

Mr. CORNWELL. It would have no effect whatever. The final redemption is by the Government.

Mr. JOHNSON, of Ohio. But not of the national-bank notes. They are supposed to be paid by the banks. Now, if a bank is presented with its own notes and exercises the right to redeem them in silver, you say that that will not force gold to a premium nor force the notes to a discount?

Mr. CORNWELL. No; because the Government is the agent of final redemption, and it is the declared intention of the Government to maintain the two metals on a parity.

Mr. JOHNSON, of Ohio. Then it is because silver is maintained on a parity with gold that the banks can exercise that privilege?

Mr. CORNWELL. Yes; if it were not they could not.

Mr. SPERRY. Do you know whether the banks that have failed recently in Newfoundland were under the Canadian system, or were they provincial banks?

Mr. CORNWELL. I think they were under the Canadian system. I am not sure about that.

Mr. BLACK. It seems to be assumed by all of these gentlemen that if State banks of issue were allowed there would be forty-four different systems; does that follow?

Mr. CORNWELL. It seems to me that, if they are under the supervision of the various State legislatures, it does.

Mr. BLACK. It does not follow that you would have, but that you could have.

Mr. CORNWELL. But still there are State banks in each one of the forty-four States.

Mr. HALL. No, sir; there are not.

Mr. BLACK. Is it not true that in a great many States such banks are prohibited by provisions of the State constitution?

Mr. CORNWELL. Yes; the number 44 was used inadvertently.

Mr. HALL. I think that you treated the Secretary's bill unjustly when you said that there was no provision in it for retiring greenbacks under any circumstances. Read section 9 again and see.

Mr. CORNWELL. I think I stated, in the early part of the interview, that their retirement was optional with the Secretary. He may provide for their retirement if he feels like it.

Mr. JOHNSON, of Indiana. It is claimed that there are certain seasons of the year—the crop-moving seasons—when in the sparsely-settled and agricultural parts of the country currency is scarce and high. What is your opinion as to the cause of it, and can there be a remedy devised for it? If so, what remedy would you suggest?

Mr. CORNWELL. The United States and Canada are the two countries that are subject to a squeeze in the fall. That is a reason why we want an elastic currency. The cause of the squeeze is the very large harvestry of crops at that time of the year. There is such a demand for money all at once to move crops that Canada demands for that purpose quite 20 per cent of its whole circulation. The banks of Canada respond to that demand immediately. Not so in the United States, there being no elasticity in the currency, which is owing to the fact that currency is based on a bond security. On that account the rates for money are high, very high sometimes.

Mr. JOHNSON, of Indiana. Is it your opinion that an elastic currency, such as suggested by you here, would remedy this disadvantage and enable those sections of the country to get money at reasonable rates of interest in crop-moving time?

Mr. CORNWELL. Without any doubt whatever.

Mr. JOHNSON, of Indiana. What benefit could the people in those various States have from the State-bank system of currency which they could not just as well receive from a national system of currency properly devised?

Mr. CORNWELL. None whatever, in my opinion.

STATEMENT OF MR. WILLIAM DODSWORTH.

The chairman stated that Mr. Dodsworth, editor of the Journal of Commerce, had been invited and was now present; and he called on Mr. Dodsworth to present his views to the committee.

Mr. Dodsworth thereupon addressed the committee. He said:

Mr. Chairman and gentlemen: In what I may respectfully submit relating to the question now occupying the attention of your committee I shall, for brevity's sake, take it as granted by the preponderant sentiment of the country, and therefore needing for legislative purposes no demonstration, that the present currency arrangements of the United States are radically defective.

In respect to our five hundred millions of full legal-tender paper I shall assume that it is derived from an illegitimate exercise of the legislative power of the Government; that it is inadequately guaranteed, inasmuch as it rests solely on the Federal power to tax or to borrow, and not on an equivalent of pledged assets; that it stands directly exposed to fluctuations in purchasing power, arising from political catastrophes or from fiscal emergencies; that its issue was governed mainly by necessities of war finance and not by sound economic laws; that its volume is entirely irresponsive to the fluctuating requirements of business, and that it has at last become tainted with distrust for which reasons it is lacking in the first essentials of a really sound and efficient form of currency.

In respect to silver money I assume that, though the policy of increasing or diminishing its volume is still a seething question, yet it does not specifically concern the problem immediately before your committee.

As to the system of note issues provided under the national banking laws, I shall take it for granted—as I think I safely may—that among economists, practical bankers, and intelligent students of monetary questions it is the largely preponderant conviction that the system has outlived any adaptation it may have originally possessed for satisfying the currency wants of the country, the main grounds for that conclusion being,—

(1) That the bond form of guarantee has been found incompatible with elasticity of issue.

(2) That said guarantee leaves no sufficient margin of profit to the issuer, and consequently prevents issuing.

(3) That the bonds themselves must, in a few years, mature and be retired.

(4) That the Government's engagement to pay the notes is an illegitimate exercise of Federal power.

(5) That, owing to obstructive restraints, the volume of notes can not be readily augmented to meet public emergencies.

(6) That the arrangements for insuring current redemptions of the notes fail of their purpose, thereby keeping the volume rigidly inflexible at the seasons when it should automatically contract or expand; and

(7) That, for these reasons, the national-bank circulation has shrunk to one-half its former volume, while the public requirements for money have been increasing.

I take it that the very general agreement of intelligent public opinion on these assumed propositions constitutes the occasion for this legislative inquest, and with your permission, therefore, I will confine my attention to the inquiry—how our bank currency system may best be placed upon a sounder basis, and how equipped with more elastic and automatic adaptations for satisfying the ever-increasing and yet ever-oscillating wants of the country.

In dealing with this question, it is manifestly desirable to adopt a course least calculated to disturb existing banking arrangements that need no change; and, with that purpose in view, it may be deemed proper to enact the new conditions relating to note issues in the form of amendments to the national-banking act. At the same time, upon every ground of right and equity, the power of issuing notes should be conceded to the banks operating under State laws, conditioned only upon the stipulation that they shall conform in all respects to the terms of issue imposed upon the national banks, thereby securing from all banks a uniform circulation. Any course short of this would, I conceive, be not only a political injustice, but an unwarrantable discrimination against a class of banks in every way deserving the privilege, and upon whose operations the business interests of the country are largely dependent.

As nearly as may be estimated in the absence of complete official data, the State banks of the United States have a total capital of about $275,000,000, and are the custodians of $750,000,000 of the people's deposits. Their capital bears a ratio of 36 per cent to their loans, while in the case of the national banks the proportion is only 33 per cent. Their ratio of capital to deposits is 37 per cent, which is identical with that of the national institutions. In 1892 their cash resources were in the ratio of 20 per cent of their deposits, while the nationals showed 19 per cent. Upon the true tests of relative strength and of soundness of methods, it is thus evident that the State banks have a slight advantage over the national.

The magnitude and solidity of this interest demand that it shall be denied no privilege conceded to any other class of banks. Thirty years of deprivation of the right of issue should suffice, and emancipation from the bonds of a prohibitory tax is surely now due. There is also a weighty practical reason for the recognition of this right. If the privilege of issue is withheld from this class of banks, the people are thereby deprived of the large benefits that would accrue to them from the use of their notes. Exclusion would not only be odious, as establishing a monopoly of an important function, but equally a wrong and an injury to the country at large, as an arbitrary restriction upon the needful supply of currency.

It seems incredible that the country would ever become reconciled to an exclusion of banking rights that would curtail the issuing ability of the banks to the extent of probably over $200,000,000, and ultimately more than that sum. The true principle to be followed in this branch of the question, I would therefore submit, is: The same rights, upon the same terms, to both classes of incorporated banks.

The present geographical distribution of the State banks deserves some consideration in determining this question, if equity toward all sections is to be maintained. In the New England and Middle States combined the amount of State bank capital is only 20 per cent of the total for the United States, while those States own about 54 per cent of the entire national bank capital. The distribution of the remaining 80 per cent of State bank capital is: In the Southern States 20 per cent; in the Western States 37 per cent: and in the Pacific States 23.7 per cent. Could it be considered just to deprive the South, the West, and the Pacific coast, which depend so largely upon State banks, of the valuable rights of issue so liberally vouchsafed to other sections?

In determining the maximum of circulation to be permitted to each bank, the safest and most equitable method seems to be that of establishing a uniform ratio as between the permissible amount of issues and the unimpaired paid-up capital, or the paid-up capital and surplus combined. The latter of these alternative standards has some important advantages over the former: inasmuch as it better represents the real resources of the bank; and, in the event of an impairment of surplus, would involve a curtailment of the permissible circulation. To that extent, the capital and surplus combined would be a more conservative measure of issue than the amount of capital alone.

In fixing the maximum of issue, it is important to keep in view the fact that from motives of prudence and reputation, banks of issue ordinarily keep their circulation materially within the authorized limit, whether that limit may be high or low. The maximum, therefore, should not be adjusted to what may be supposed to be a normal experience or a normal requirement, but should allow a somewhat liberal margin for expansion of volume in periods of unusual business activity, or under the accidental emergencies to which business is always liable. My individual judgment would be that a limit equivalent to 75 per cent of the capital of the bank would be entirely safe; and in this I am confirmed by the almost uniform opinion of many practical bankers with whom I have consulted on the matter.

As the present capital of the national banks is, in round numbers, $700,000,000, and that of the State banks may be estimated at about $275,000,000, this ratio would permit a maximum issue by the national and State banks of, say, $730,000,000 of notes. Were the capital and surplus combined to be chosen as the standard, the ratio might be reduced. In such case, as the combined capital and surplus of the national and State banks amount to about $1,410,000,000, a ratio of 50 per cent would afford an issuing capacity nearly equal to 75 per cent on capital alone. These estimates of the possible issue of new notes presuppose the retirement of some $200,000,000 of now existing national-bank notes, so that the net possible increase of note circulation (upon the present amount of national and State bank capital) would be $530,000,000. The actual increase might and probably would be a very different matter.

Should no steps be taken for retiring the outstanding Government notes, this capacity of issue might easily exceed the existing requirements of business. How far that might tend to induce an unhealthy inflation of the circulating medium would depend almost entirely upon the nature of the provision made for the redemption of the notes. Under such arrangements as are provided by the existing Treasury redemption agency such a result would inevitably follow; for that system obstructs, more than facilitates, redemptions. But with such provisions for enforcing redemption as might be devised, to which I shall later refer, no serious inflation need be feared. If, however, Congress should decree the withdrawal of the five hundred millions of Treasury paper, the new supply of bank notes would be none too much to fill the vacuum; and for such increases of currency as might be called for by the growth of population and trade, we should have to depend upon an expansion of banking capital, which, with the inducements arising from the profits on the new circulation, would doubtless be forthcoming.

Assuming the withdrawal of the bond form of guarantee against circulation, the question arises, What other form of protection of the notes should be provided? There seems to be but one really eligible substitute, namely, to constitute the notes a first lien upon the entire assets of the bank, and also upon the liability of the stockholders to assessment up to the full amount of their capital stock. There can be no possible question about the sufficiency of such a guarantee; the doubt would rather be whether it would not be largely excessive. Assuming the improbability that the failed bank had outstanding an amount of notes equal to the suggested maximum, namely, 75 per cent of capital, even then the guarantee afforded by the shareholder alone would exceed by one-third the amount payable to the note holders, and the assets of the bank would be so much further surplus over the note liabilities.

With the combined guarantee from assets and stockholders, the protection would be much more ample than that afforded by the existing deposit of bonds; the only difference being that, under the new method, the notes might not be redeemed with the same degree of promptness as they are under the now existing arrangements. Considering, however, that there could be no question about the ultimate full payment of the notes, there would be no reason why they should not continue to circulate until the holders were notified by the receiver to present them for redemption.

This amplitude of guarantee is suggested not because there would be any commensurate risk attending the notes, but because the public are excessively sensitive about the safety of bank currency, and it is necessary to guard against all possibility of such distrust by providing a protection which makes depreciation of the notes impossible. The guarantors need not object to the excess of guarantee, for it does not affect the amount of their actual liability, which really is, on the whole, a very small affair. During the unprecedented bank panic of last year, the failures of national banks represented only four-tenths of 1 per cent of the entire capital of those institutions. The experience of the national banks affords data from which the risks on bank circulation may be fairly estimated.

For the last thirty years, covering two great panics and two minor ones, the amount of the capital of banks which went into the hands of receivers averaged $1,463,000 per year. The average amount of the capital of all the national banks during that period was about $400,000,000. The proportion of the capital on which failures occurred to the total capital of all the banks was therefore a little over one-third of 1 per cent. There is no apparent reason why this ratio should not be maintained in the future. Upon the present $1,000,000,000 of national and State capital, the yearly failures might, according to this rule of experience, be expected to cover about $3,600,000 of capital.

Assuming that the banks were permitted to issue notes to the extent of 75 per cent of their capital, but kept out only 60 per cent—which I take to be a reasonable estimate—we should then have an annual crop of about $2,160,000 of insolvent notes, which would be equivalent to a fraction over one-fifth of 1 per cent of the whole banking capital. Against this would stand a total of $4,240,000,000 of bank assets and a stockholders' pledge of $1,000,000,000, in all $5,240,000,000, upon which the note holders would have a first lien. It therefore hardly seems necessary that either stockholders, depositors, or note holders should feel any serious concern about the risks attending note issues, or the nature or sufficiency of this proposed guarantee. If stockholders or depositors should desire to protect themselves against the guarantee given to the note holders, it would probably be found that the risk could be covered, from year to year, for a surprisingly small consideration.

Notwithstanding, there are those who think the entire assets and the duplicate liability of stockholders an insufficient protection, and suggest that, in addition, the issuing banks shall deposit legal tenders with the Treasury, to the amount of 30 per cent of their outstanding notes, and that a "safety fund," equal to 5 per cent of the circulation, shall be placed in the custody of the Treasury. As already shown, the 30 per cent deposit certainly could not be defended on the ground of guarantee necessities. What other purposes may have been contemplated in the proposal have not been explained. It has, however, this very serious objection, that for each million of expansion of note issues it necessitates a contraction of $300,000 in another form of currency.

If it be supposed that this proposal is intended to indirectly effect the withdrawal of Government notes from circulation, it would seem to be a sufficient answer that a more certain way of getting rid of that monetary excrescence would be to repeal the legal-tender act and to provide for the final liquidation of the notes, with such speed as may not disturb the monetary equilibrium. At this point may I be permitted to express my approval, in principal, of the provisions suggested for the retirement of the Treasury notes in section 9 of Secretary Carlisle's form of bill submitted to your committee? Considering the supreme necessity for the action contemplated, it would seem urgent, however, that the provisions be made mandatory, rather than dependent upon the uncertain discretion of the Secretary of the Treasury.

I would also suggest, in connection with this clause of the bill, that, when there is no surplus revenue devotable to the redemption, the Secretary of the Treasury shall be required to borrow on low-rate bonds, payable at the pleasure of the Government, an amount sufficient to provide for the note liquidations required under said section 9. Also, there seems to be some material incompatibility between the Secretary's proposal to retire the legal tenders and his further proposition that those notes shall be permanently deposited against bank-note issues to the amount of 30 per cent of the bank notes outstanding. For if the legal tenders are to be finally retired, what becomes of those deposited against bank circulation? That deposit fund would then be extinguished.

On the other hand, if the notes deposited against circulation are not to be withdrawn, then nearly two hundred millions of the Treasury notes might remain in existence for an indefinite and possibly very long period. In any event, a point would be reached in the process of retiring United States notes when, from lack of supply, the 30 per cent deposit could be no longer complied with, owing to the lack of legal tenders, and further issues by the banks would then be barred. Under these circumstances, as well as for other reasons, I would suggest that the 30 per cent deposit could be well dispensed with.

The suggested 5 per cent "safety fund" seems to lack any real occasion, except that it would provide a resource out of which the notes of a failed bank could be immediately redeemed, instead of waiting until the receiver had realized sufficient funds to liquidate the circulation. As a means for that object it seems to merit favorable consideration. The suggestion that this fund be accumulated through moderate periodic contributions also seems entirely unobjectionable.

I trust it may not be deemed obtrusive, on this occasion, to briefly consider the proposal of the Secretary of the Treasury that "all provisions of law requiring banks to keep a reserve on account of deposits" be repealed. It is undeniably true that the national banks usually keep a handsome surplus of reserve above the legal minimum, and this applies especially to the country banks, on which the law imposes a very light ratio of cash reserve; and this course being voluntary and the result of a conservative spirit, it carries a large measure of warrant that the banks may be safely trusted to regulate their reserves according to their own judgment.

It is equally true that, when the banks are pressed by emergencies, they have more respect for their own interests and those of their customers than for the mandate of the law, and therefore do not hesitate to disregard the statute and its penalties, which means that in practice the reserve law fails of its purpose. And it is further true that at the banking centers, pending critical conditions, the legal limitation of the reserve stands out as the "dead line," beyond which lies confusion and panic. The natural reluctance of the banks to cross the line until the last moment causes a contraction of loans, which intensifies distrust and increases the pressure for accommodation, and the result is that when the banks have resolved to disregard the law the crisis is found to have passed beyond their control, and apprehension is consummated in panic.

There can be no question that, while all our panics have been seriously aggravated through the operation of a compulsory reserve, some might have been wholly averted had the banks been free to use their lawful money resources according to their individual discretion. In theory, the legal regulation is designed to protect the banks; in practice, it imperils both them and their customers. It is difficult to specify any advantages accruing from this restriction that at all offset these serious disadvantages. There might be some reasonable justification of necessity if the banks were recklessly managed and regularly kept their reserves at a low point, but such is not the fact.

There would be some apology for the law if the reserves were made available under emergencies; but, on the contrary, while holding the means of remedy, the relief is withheld under penalty of corporate death. Such incongruity would be ridiculous were it not so serious. Nor would it much mend the matter, if discretion were given to the Secretary of the Treasury, or to the clearing houses, to relax the operation of the law when necessity seemed to call for such elasticity. Experience shows that such discretions are never used until the danger has gone well nigh beyond control; and the uncertain waiting for the intervention is one of the most demoralizing forms of suspense.

I can therefore regard the legal regulation of bank reserves against deposits only as an effete remnant of methods adapted for times when bank management was less intelligent and less conservative than in these days. The principle is venerable for its antiquity, and, to minds living more in the past than in the present, it may seem shocking to abandon this highly prestiged retraint; but, for myself, I can only conclude that the Secretary is as wise as he is courageous in urging the abolition of legal regulation of the reserves.

To my view public opinion, and I may say banking opinion also, has so far greatly underrated the practical importance of redemption arrangements. The things dependent upon a redemption system are no less important than these: The regulation of the volume of notes; their natural and equitable geographical distribution; the checking of undue issues by any individual bank; the restraining of unhealthy expansions of banking operations; the prevention of unwholesome redundancies of currency; the checking of financial and commercial speculations resting purely upon a superabundance of money facilities.

It is to be conceded that the propo ed enlargement of the freedom of issue might easily run into an excessive supply of circulation and an illegitimate expansion of bank credits. That possibility is so obvious that a measure which failed to provide protection against such a result would be radically defective, and after brief trial would bring upon itself the condemnation of the conservative sentiment of the country. The only safe means of preventing such a failure is to provide arrangements which would allow the utmost facilities of dispatch and economy for forwarding the notes for redemption. In devising such arrangements it is important to keep in mind who are the parties to use them.

The general public have no interest in redemptions, for they have no reason for desiring to change one form of money for another. The redemption agency is purely a banker's institution. The notes flow into the banks in the way of deposits, and it is to the interest of the bank receiving them to exchange them as soon as possible for "lawful money." In so doing, the bank makes the more room for paying out its own notes, and at the same time strengthens its own lawful money reserves. There is a constant competition between the banks to occupy the field of circulation, each one seeking to get out and keep out its own notes and using the redemption agency as a means of pushing into retirement the issues of its competitors.

This competition is the truest possible regulator of a bank-note circulation. It permits expansion of the volume when an increase is needed; it compels contraction when the outstanding volume is excessive. Under such a machinery there can be neither scarcity nor redundance. The regulating force is the self-interest of each bank checked by that of all others. If the bank is suspected of matters affecting its credit, that fact operates as a special inducement for sending its notes for redemption; and that discrimination puts its circulation under the severest regulation. It will thus be seen that the note clearing house, or redemption agency, becomes the very salt and conservation of a bank-note system, protecting the quality of the notes and assuring a healthy adjustment of their volume and their geographical distribution.

Not any or every form of agency, however, will insure these advantages. It is essential that the agency shall not be so far from the point of issue as to impose obstacles of time and expense in transmission. It is necessary that the charges for redemption service shall be nominal, and that the proceeds of the conversions be instantly remitted. None of these requisites are afforded by the existing redemption agency of the national banks. That institution has been a lamentable failure from the beginning; nor is there any possibility of so modifying it as to make it properly effective. Under that system the redemptions proper, excluding those connected with failed banks, and banks withdrawing their circulation, and also those connected with worn out notes, appear to amount to about forty million a year for the whole United States, or one-fifth of the outstanding volume.

What this amounts to, as compared with what is needed under a really healthy and competitive note system, may be inferred from the fact that in 1857 the Suffolk Bank of Boston, acting as redemption agent for the New England banks, effected $400,000,000 of redemptions; in other words, New England, with its financial dimensions of thirty-seven years ago, had tenfold the amount of redemptions now effected at Washington for the whole United States. That is the difference in results between an efficient and an inefficient redemption agency. The services of the Suffolk Bank were rendered at a cost of 10 cents per $1,000, while those of the national bureau cost 70 cents per $1,000.

With such an immense geographical area as our banks cover, it is an absolute impossibility that any single institution could afford effective redemption service. If redemption is to constitute the live and ever-active regulator that the protection of a bank currency imperatively demands, the points of redemption must not be one, but many. Failing that, the redemptions must be few; there will be no elasticity of issues, and the banks will be tempted to use their privilege to the maximum limit, because they will be comparatively secure against the return of their notes for liquidation.

With a view to keeping the agency near the point of issue, and thereby facilitating conversions, I would respectfully suggest that the

Washington agency be discontinued, and that in its place the law shall establish six redemption districts, and confer upon the Comptroller of the Currency authority to designate some one bank, situated at a point central to each district, which shall act as redeeming agent for all the banks in such district. Perhaps some such geographical determination of the respective districts as the following might be most equal and most convenient:

Redemption districts.	Groups of States.	Present capital.
No. 1	New England States	$187,000,000
No. 2	New York, New Jersey, Pennsylvania, Delaware, Maryland, District of Columbia.	197,700,000
No. 3	Southern States	71,500,000
No. 4	Ohio, Indiana, Illinois, Michigan, Wisconsin, West Virginia	124,500,000
No. 5	Iowa, Minnesota, Missouri, Kansas, Nebraska	76,500,000
No. 6	Pacific States and other Western States and Territories	41,000,000
	Total capital	678,200,000

Each of these divisions would include an amount of bank capital sufficient to warrant its having an agency of its own. Each of the agencies should be required to redeem not only notes issued within its district, but also any presented that may have been issued in some other district, recouping itself by forwarding such notes to the agency for the district in which they were issued. Such extra-limit redemptions, however, would probably be found unimportant in volume.

The importance of redemption is so vital that it seems necessary that the arrangements for facilitating it should be made imperative by law, rather than left to the voluntary action of the banks. And, for the same reason, it would seem prudent that the choice of agents should be left to the Federal Comptroller, as a disinterested dispenser of a function for which there might be troublesome competition, and which the banks have no organization to deal with.

The Suffolk Bank system affords the best model for the form of organization. It grew out of a banking necessity, and its development over a period of thirty years brought its machinery to a state of virtual perfection. Following that precedent, each bank in a given district should be required to deposit with its redemption agency an amount of "lawful money" equal to, say, 2 per cent of its outstanding circulation, and to keep that deposit at all times good. That deposit would, to a valuable extent, afford to the agent bank a resource for loans; and the use of that resource would be a sufficient compensation for the services rendered by the agent. This was the basis of compensation ultimately reached by the Suffolk Bank, and it was found so remunerative as to bring out active competition for the service from other banks.

Mr. HENDERSON. Are your suggestions intended to apply to State banks of issue as well as to the national banks?

Mr. DODSWORTH. They do contemplate providing for State bank issues as well as for national banks.

Mr. HENDERSON. The question I want to ask you is whether you propose that the State banks of issue should be under national control in any way?

Mr. DODSWORTH. So far as respects the issue of their notes; and entirely so far as the issue of their notes is concerned I think that there should be no distinction whatever.

Mr. HENDERSON. If they are to be under national control, why not have them as national banks instead of State banks?

Mr. DODSWORTH. That is a question which I presume each bank

would have its own reasons for answering. I do not see that that is a question which Federal legislation should concern itself about.

Mr. HENDERSON. Have you thought of the question as to how far (if we admit State banks of issue) the National Government would have any power or control over them, or would you admit them quite free from any Federal control in any way?

Mr. DODSWORTH. I scarcely understand your question.

Mr. HENDERSON. Have you thought of the question whether (if you admit State banks of issue) there is any power under our form of government for the General Government to exercise any supervision or control over them?

Mr. DODSWORTH. I conceive that if the General Government were to provide the conditions under which notes should be issued by State banks and should prescribe the limitations under which the issue should be operated (including inspection and all minor provisions for protection) it will be simply a matter whether the banks now organized under State laws would undertake to conform to those conditions. They would probably find it difficult, as a rule, at any rate at first, and I conclude that as a consequence the legislatures of the several States would find themselves under the pressure of public opinion (especially of banking opinion) to reconstruct their banking laws so as to include the very provisions which would be included in this proposed legislation as to national banks.

Mr. HENDERSON. Do you not think it very desirable that whatever system of currency we may adopt it should be a uniform currency that would be receivable and pass current in all the States of the Union?

Mr. DODSWORTH. That would be most essential, and I conceive that under such an arrangement as that, every note being issued (whether by a State bank or a national bank) under the same conditions of current efficiency and redemption, they would be identical with each other.

Mr. HENDERSON. You assume, then, that every one of the States that would legislate on the question of State banks would naturally follow on and adopt a uniform system?

Mr. DODSWORTH. They would have to adopt the forms prescribed by the new law, and in that case there would be no difference in the currency. There might be differences as to other matters—matters regulating loans and deposits—but as to currency, every note issued, whether of a national bank or a State bank, would be under the same conditions.

Mr. HENDERSON. Then, you would not dispense entirely with some sort of national control over State banks?

Mr. DODSWORTH. Matters outside of the circulation of State banks should be undoubtedly left independent of national legislation.

Mr. HENDERSON. I mean as to circulation. You do not intend to dispense with national control and national supervision over the currency issued by State banks?

Mr. DODSWORTH. No, sir.

Mr. JOHNSON, of Indiana. Do you think that we can so separate the functions of a bank of issue from the functions of a bank of discount and deposit that the issue function could be subject to one jurisdiction and the discount and deposit function be subject to another jurisdiction without inviting conflicting claims of jurisdiction between the United States and State authorities, and without bringing about a jarring of the system?

Mr. DODSWORTH. I think so.

Mr. JOHNSON, of Indiana. It does not suggest any such difficulties to your mind whatever?

Mr. DODSWORTH. It does not. In the case of national banks there can be no jar between the issue department and the discount branch of the business. And if it were found by any State that in order to have its banks avail themselves of the privilege of issuing notes the conditions would conflict with some existing law relating to deposits or redemption, or whatever it might be, outside of note circulation, the State legislatures would change their laws so as to produce a smoothly working condition as between the issue business of the banks and the discount or other branches of the bank.

Mr. JOHNSON, of Indiana. You would expect, then, that the conditions imposed by the national authorities would take precedence over any inconsistent provisions in the State charters, would you?

Mr. DODSWORTH. I am not sure whether I understand your question.

Mr. JOHNSON, of Indiana. You would expect that all of the conditions imposed in this proposed system by the Federal authorities on the banks should have precedence over any inconsistent provisions imposed by the charters from the State, whether those inconsistent provisions referred to issue or to deposits, or whether they were inconsistent directly or only as a matter of inference?

Mr. DODSWORTH. Precisely.

Mr. JOHNSON, of Indiana. You would subject the State banks of issue to every one of the provisions of the national-banking law?

Mr. DODSWORTH. So far as those provisions relate to the issue of bank notes, but no further.

Mr. JOHNSON, of Indiana. You would supervise the visitations prescribed by the Federal authorities for national banks over State banks also, including the right of examination by experts, and including compulsory reports under oath by the bank officials?

Mr. DODSWORTH. With reference to these police provisions (if I may so call them), if it were possible for the Comptroller of the Currency to get his knowledge through methods less offensive it would be preferable, I think; but if not, and if the present regulations should be a necessity, why I think they ought to be enforced.

Mr. JOHNSON, of Indiana. Suppose a State bank should become insolvent, to whom would you intrust the appointment of a receiver?

Mr. DODSWORTH. To the Comptroller of the Currency at Washington.

Mr. JOHNSON, of Indiana. It has never occurred to you that there would be any lack of simplicity or harmony in the system which you suggest?

Mr. DODSWORTH. There is some complexity, I concede. It might be better if we could avoid a system which from the beginning embarrassed the whole country, but the conditions of the country were not such as to admit of their being dispensed with. But we have got to have established methods, and to observe them as we find them, and it seems to me that we must conform ourselves to them.

Mr. JOHNSON, of Indiana. The established conditions that you refer to have simply limited the issuing of notes under the national banking law to national banks, have they not?

Mr. DODSWORTH. Yes.

Mr. JOHNSON, of Indiana. What would you consider safer and better for the people of the country, a system of note issue that was exclusively under national control or one that was exclusively under the control of the States?

Mr. DODSWORTH. I favor the largest possible method of freedom in all such matters. But at the same time, in the matter of providing a circulating medium, you have got to insist on everything which is conducive to the safety of the public as holders of the notes to be issued by the banks. That is, and necessarily should be, to some extent, regarded as a supersedure of the liberty of the bank.

Mr. JOHNSON, of Indiana. That is an inferential answer. Can you answer my question more directly?

Mr. DODSWORTH. If there is anything more specific in the question I shall be glad to answer it.

Mr. JOHNSON, of Indiana. The question I asked you was this: Which do you consider safest and best for the interests of all our people, a bank system of issue entirely under national control or a bank system of issue under the control of the several States, each State to devise its own system?

Mr. DODSWORTH. As an abstract principle I concede that the issuing of currency is an essentially different function from any other function exercised by the banks, and that whatever provisions should be made in regard to the exercise of that function it should be provided by the Federal power, on the same grounds that the Federal Government is intrusted with the power of issuing coin, and for the same reasons of public safety. But I do not say that, in securing that uniformity and safety of issue, it is necessary that there should go along with it an entire uniformity of banking methods generally. And it appears to me that, in order to provide for a more natural and fair and altogether more elastic system of general banking, there should be a freedom for different methods of banking operations as respects, for instance, the diversity of banking institutions which we have among our several States. I conceive that it is better that we should have freedom and an absence of central restraint over those functions of banking.

Mr. JOHNSON, of Indiana. You intend that answer to be taken in connection with what you said about State banks?

Mr. DODSWORTH. I do.

The committee here took a recess until 2 o'clock P. M.

After the recess Mr. Dodsworth continued his statement as follows:

Mr. COX. Mr. Dodsworth, as I got your idea in regard to the State banks, it was that the great thing to be desired was that their circulation, if they put out circulation, should be as good as any other paper currency; that is the point we are working to?

Mr. DODSWORTH. Yes.

Mr. COX. When we do that, as I understand your theory about it, then the Federal Government should have control of that matter of issues, and no further?

Mr. DODSWORTH. That the Federal Government should have control over currency matters alone.

Mr. COX. I mean over the banks issuing paper money.

Mr. DODSWORTH. Yes.

Mr. COX. So you would limit the Federal Government to the point of issue of paper alone?

Mr. DODSWORTH. You refer to Federal law?

Mr. COX. Yes; I refer to the Government and the laws that would control the issue of State-bank paper.

Mr. DODSWORTH. Yes, sir.

Mr. COX. And when that point was reached you would stop there and leave the States to control the other matters?

Mr. DODSWORTH. Precisely.

Mr. COX. That is the proposition?

Mr. DODSWORTH. Yes, sir.

Mr. Cox. To make the issue perfectly good—and that is the point to be reached, not to be doubted—if the Government requires of the State bank to deposit 30 per cent of its capital stock in the hands of a public officer, then makes the assets of the bank liable, in the first instance, for this issue, and then makes the stockholders liable to the extent of their stock, can there be any doubt about the validity of these notes, do you think?

Mr. DODSWORTH. The sufficiency of the guarantee afforded, I suppose you mean?

Mr. Cox. Yes.

Mr. DODSWORTH. I think it would be a superabundant guarantee, and, so far as respects the 30 per cent, needlessly injurious to the guarantor.

Mr. Cox. So that when you put 30 per cent of the capital stock of a State bank in the hands of an officer—I assume the character of the officer to be good—you give a first lien on the assets of the bank, and then the liability against the stockholders. Is it possible that paper based upon such conditions would be anything else except good?

Mr. DODSWORTH. I suppose it would be the largest credit ever given against an obligation.

Mr. Cox. Is not that especially so when the circulation is limited to the 70 per cent?

Mr. DODSWORTH. I agree to it.

Mr. Cox. Could there be any doubt about its being good?

Mr. DODSWORTH. No question about that. It is needlessly superabundant.

Mr. Cox. Is it not something more than practice and experience have demonstrated was ever required?

Mr. DODSWORTH. I know of no such guarantee in existence in any form.

Mr. Cox. Leaving that point, if the State bank is required to pay in 30 per cent of its capital stock, then required to give a first lien upon its assets, then required to make the stockholders liable to the extent of their stock, and then is limited to 70 cents on the dollar of its capital stock, do you know of any institution in this or any other country that makes it safer than that?

Mr. DODSWORTH. No, sir.

Mr. Cox. Let me turn your attention to the fact that in certain localities of this country, especially the agricultural part—and I am more familiar with the South than any other section—the public securities, such as bonds, stocks, and that character of liabilities, have substantially left us in the South, on account of our misfortunes—not stopping to speak about that. If a State bank organizes and makes its issue upon the security we have just discussed, do you not think that would be a great benefit to the people of the South?

Mr. DODSWORTH. The largest benefit possible.

Mr. Cox. Is it possible to confer any more than that in the way of banking?

Mr. DODSWORTH. No, sir.

Mr. Cox. In discussing what has been called the safety fund of 5 per cent, and making all of the national banks in one sense liable for all of it, let me ask your opinion upon this idea of that clause, the fifth clause, I think, in the Secretary's bill, providing that each bank stands for all the rest.

Mr. RUSSELL. The contingent liability clause.

Mr. Cox. Contingent liability.

Mr. WARNER. Mutual guarantee.

Mr. COX. Mutual guarantee; no matter what you call it, so you get what is in my mind. Can you see any objection to this? The objection, of course, in that lies in the fact of one bank going security for another that it knows nothing about. Suppose you require, instead of that, that the national bank, before it declares any dividends on its profits shall charge off, something like the premium account that we have had for a number of years, until it reaches the sum of 5 per cent upon its circulation, and holds that sum (5 per cent) unimpaired. Would not that be as good a security, so far as that individual bank were concerned, and would it not be better than to become security for the other banks?

Mr. DODSWORTH. I think so. Moreover, I think it is wholly an unsound principle of banking, for banks to redeem in this way a note under special emergency, to guarantee each other's obligations. In this case it is entirely unnecessary to make that guarantee. The 5 per cent fund, which is proposed to provide that amount for the redemption of notes in case of failures, would very much exceed any probable amount of failures within a given time. We will say $750,000,000 would be the necessary amount of bank circulation in the event of withdrawing the greenbacks. Then $500,000,000 would be required to compensate for that withdrawal of legal tenders; and, in addition to that, you would have a certain amount of bank circulation outstanding, $200,000,000, more or less, which would make the bank circulation in that event $700,000,000. Five per cent upon that amounts to $35,000,000 withdrawal, in the first place, from the current circulation of the country, and so far injurious, and so far a waste of credit.

The actual amount involved in failures, as demonstrated in the experience of the national banks since they began, has been for that period of thirty years, as I have already stated, about $1,400,000. Suppose the bank issues to exceed the past average twofold, which would give you a circulation outstanding of about $800,000,000 bank notes, in that case. At the ratio of risk which actually exists upon bank notes you would have a possible annual crop of failures to an amount that would involve some $2,500,000 to $3,000,000 of bank notes that would be necessary to provide for; and for that you would, under this 5 per cent provision, have $35,000,000 held. It seems to me to be a total waste of guarantee, unjustifiable by experience, and not sound banking. It seems to me that a 2 or 2½ per cent fund, instead of a 5 per cent fund, would correspond in a very much more conservative way to the actual requirements; and beyond that I am not satisfied in my own mind that there is any necessity for a fund of that character.

Mr. COX. I agree with you exactly. I do not think there is any necessity for it, but I am trying to follow this up so that there will be no doubt about it. Let me suggest this idea: By the national-banking system proposed by the plan of the Secretary of the Treasury there is the 30 per cent of greenback deposit, then there is the liability clause, then there is the first lien on the assets, and then there is that safety fund, as he calls it. Now, if that safety fund can be charged off by the banks for each individual bank, you see it becomes assets again of the bank, though it is charged off before you reach the profits. Would it not be better for each individual bank to proceed in that way than for the banks to become guarantors for each other?

Mr. DODSWORTH. I think so, decidedly.

Mr. COX. The object of the investigation of national banks by the Federal Government is to reach the point where the issue is absolutely safe, and when you come to the details of it it is only for the purpose of accomplishing and reaching the point where the issue is perfectly safe.

Mr. DODSWORTH. Precisely.

Mr. COX. So, if the Secretary or the Comptroller of the Currency be satisfied, under proper regulations and rules, that the State bank has paid in its capital stock, that it has deposited the 30 per cent of that in United States Treasury notes, that its charter has the liability clause, or the general law—I call it a charter—provides for a first lien on the assets of the bank, would you have any doubt about the solvency of the notes issued?

Mr. DODSWORTH. I should regard that as affording as strong a guarantee for the safety of the notes as the application of the same principle to national banks would.

Mr. COX. You would regard such notes as that as safe as if issued under the national-bank system?

Mr. DODSWORTH. Yes.

Mr. BROSIUS. I understand your statement to be that there is no better security for a bank circulation than the assets of the bank itself. The assets of the bank are affected in value by the ability of the bank to make its creditors sure of its solvency; is not that so?

Mr. DODSWORTH. Yes.

Mr. BROSIUS. The paper of an insolvent bank is not of much value, is it?

Mr. DODSWORTH. It is not.

Mr. BROSIUS. You say that the assets of the banks constitute the best security for their circulation that can be provided. Do you mean that statement to refer to the aggregate, that is, to the assets of all the banks, comparing the aggregate risk with the aggregate security, or do you mean to make the statement to cover also particular and independent banks, every bank?

Mr. DODSWORTH. I have not stated that, I think; if I did so it was through inadvertency. I have not stated that the assets alone were the best security.

Mr. BROSIUS. I include the double liability of the stockholders.

Mr. DODSWORTH. In that case I say that the guarantee is largely superabundant, not merely as applied to the banks taken as a whole, but as taken in the case of individual banks.

Mr. BROSIUS. Let me give you a case: Suppose a bank has a capital stock of $100,000. It deposits 30 per cent of its proposed circulation. That takes out 75 per cent of its capital stock. There remains then in the custody of the bank for its use 70 per cent of its capital stock and 75 per cent of circulation, making, both together, 145 per cent of its capital stock. Suppose the management of the bank turns out to be bad; that its officers are rascals, and a number of its stockholders become insolvent, so that their liability is not a factor in the security. What becomes of the notes of that bank when the break comes?

Mr DODSWORTH. In the first place, you have assumed——

Mr. BROSIUS. I have assumed a bad case.

Mr. DODSWORTH. You have assumed the 30 per cent deposit, and that is a thing I would not favor.

Mr. BROSIUS. I thought you did.

Mr. DODSWORTH. In the first place, there is 30 per cent of the amount of notes provided for. That would leave, say, $450,000 out of the $1.000,000 capital.

Mr. BROSIUS. I am only speaking of a single bank having a capital stock of $100,000. There is 45 per cent of the circulation still unprotected.

Mr. DODSWORTH. The 30 per cent is 30 per cent of 75 per cent?

Mr. BROSIUS. Thirty per cent of its circulation; yes.

Mr. DODSWORTH. You would have, in the first place, that 30 per cent of cash deposit. That would leave you, say, 75 per cent to be provided. That would have to be called for from the stockholders.

Mr. BROSIUS. Now, suppose the stockholders were insolvent.

Mr. DODSWORTH. I can only say to all this that it is, of course, quite a possibility to draw a picture of that character, and one even more dark; but at the same time I conceive that such a case would not represent a natural occurrence probably once in ten years, and it does appear to me that a law should be made to provide for probabilities as to actual events, and not for extreme improbabilities.

Mr. BROSIUS. Do you not provide for that very contingency when you provide a guarantee fund to be made up by all the banks to secure the liability of each and every bank? And, if there were no liability at all of this character, no possibility of such a case as I have described, when the assets of a particular bank would fall short of perfect security, would you ever require any additional guarantee of any kind except that all the assets and stockholders of each particular bank for itself and not jointly with others?

Mr. DODSWORTH. I concede that the 5 per cent deposit might suffice, and undoubtedly would suffice to provide against such an extreme improbability as you have supposed, but I do not conceive it to be good banking or wise legislation to make such an extreme provision for such an extreme improbability.

Mr. BROSIUS. I want your opinion, if you will have the kindness to give it to me, upon one other point: Is it possible or practicable to establish a banking system that will furnish a safe currency, and at the same time an adequately elastic currency for each bank, and supply collaterals or security enough to protect the Government in case it should have the ultimate liability in case of loss—to protect it against that liability, dollar for dollar?

Mr. DODSWORTH. It is possible to create such a scheme in the form of a statute, but I do not think you could ever get it worked out into actual operation.

Mr. BROSIUS. Would it be sufficiently profitable to work out in practice?

Mr. DODSWORTH. No, sir; it is inconceivable.

Mr. BROSIUS. The State of Pennsylvania—if you will pardon me for directing your attention to it—provides that before a bank of issue can be established, securities must be deposited with the auditor-general equal to the amount of circulation: that is, dollar for dollar. Now, in your judgment, under the constitution of Pennsylvania we could not, could we, establish a banking system that would work out in practice?

Mr. DODSWORTH. That would give you a satisfactory currency system?

Mr. BROSIUS. Yes; and work out in practice.

Mr. DODSWORTH. That is my judgment, most decidedly.

Mr. SPERRY. In banking on the safety fund principle, what would you consider a safe minimum capitalization for a bank permitted to issue circulation?

Mr. DODSWORTH. What would I consider a safe ratio of issues to capital?

Mr. SPERRY. No; not that at all. The Canadian safety-fund system, for instance, provides for a minimum capitalization of $500,000, as has been stated here, of which one-half must be paid up before they can do business. In attempting to establish the safety-fund principle in our system of banking, what would you consider the safe minimum capitalization for a bank in order to be permitted to issue circulation? Do you get the idea of my question?

Mr. DODSWORTH. Yes; I think so. I do not see why there should be any limitation upon the capital of the bank; that so long as the ratio was the same in all cases, it seems to me that the safety or the risk would be the same in all cases.

Mr. SPERRY. It occurred to me that a large bank might get the services of more conservative and better bankers, and take less risk, or stand the pressure better, than would be the case with small banks. I wanted to know if that would be your judgment?

Mr. DODSWORTH. That is my judgment.

Mr. SPERRY. If it is your judgment, you would still think that the bank with a small capital could just as safely issue circulation without resulting in a tax on the large banks through the safety fund?

Mr. DODSWORTH. Yes, sir.

Mr. RUSSELL. Referring to the suggestion of Mr. Cox to section 5 of the plan as proposed by the Secretary of the Treasury, that suggestion, as I understand it, being that the contingent liability of that section be substituted by what he designated as a 5 per cent reserve or safety fund; if that suggestion were adopted, does it not create an additional requirement, though not necessarily so, for national-bank circulation over and above the requirement of State-bank circulation?

Mr. DODSWORTH. Do you ask as to whether that is the implication of the Secretary's way of making it?

Mr. RUSSELL. No; I refer to the Secretary's plan, as represented in the bill which we have before us in section 5, which relates to the creation of a safety fund, and provides for a pro rata contingent liability, if necessary, upon all national banking establishments to maintain that safety fund. Mr. Cox's suggestion, if I understood it, was to substitute for that contingent liability a 5 per cent reserve, which each bank should maintain. Now, if that suggestion were substituted for the contingent liability (the 5 per cent reserve), would there not then be in that 5 per cent reserve an additional requirement—I will not say a necessary requirement—for the safety of the circulation for national. bank circulation over and above any requirement for State-bank circulation, as provided for in this same bill?

Mr. DODSWORTH. I presume that would be the case. I have not read the bill.

Mr. SPERRY. In other words, your presumption being correct so far, it would be a discrimination favorable to the State-bank circulation over national-bank circulation?

Mr. DODSWORTH. Yes.

Mr. COX. The bank assumes for itself to protect its own circulation, which is 5 per cent; that is not held as a reserve—not technically as a reserve—but before it can divide the profits of a bank it charges off, just exactly like you do with a premium account, and then it is an asset of the bank, and the bank has the use of it?

Mr. RUSSELL. Yes; but that is a requirement for national-bank circulation.

Mr. COX. I assume your point for the present, but the point I want to call attention to is that when the bank takes its profits, and out of those profits first reserves this 5 per cent, it is not set aside and locked up in its vaults at all, but becomes an active asset of the bank, so that a dollar of stock would be worth $1.05, which makes that additional plan for redemption in the nature of a surplus. But that does not cut the bank off from using it. In the crisis or panic that we have gone through in this country—this trouble, whatever you may call it—you give in your paper that you read this morning the losses that were sustained by the depositors in national banks. Now, I ask you in regard to State banks. In this crisis has not that depositor lost less in the State banks than he has in the national banks?

Mr. WALKER. In proportion to the capital, do you mean?

Mr. COX. In proportion to the capital?

Mr. DODSWORTH. I should have to refer you to the Comptroller's report for that.

The CHAIRMAN. That is all in the Comptroller's report.

Mr. COX. I understand that, but we want it in the evidence, too.

Mr. DODSWORTH. I think the actual loss incurred by State banks was somewhat larger than in the case of national banks, but the number of failures was smaller. The significance of that difference might depend very much upon the geographical distribution and upon the severity of the panic in different sections. The State banks are distributed principally throughout the Western, Southern, and Pacific States, a very large proportion of their entire capital, about 80 per cent of the State banks, being distributed over those sections south and west of this point. That has got to be taken into consideration in estimating the exact significance of the fact that the failures were larger under the State system than under the national.

Mr. COX. The national failures were larger than the State failures, taking it all together?

Mr. DODSWORTH. The State failures were larger in amount, but the number of bank failures was less in the case of national banks than in the case of State banks.

Mr. HALL. Mr. Dodsworth, under section 5 of the plan suggested by the Secretary of the Treasury, there is a provision that an assessment be made of one-fourth of 1 per cent for each half year on the amount of the circulating notes outstanding, until a sum amounting to 5 per cent of the total circulation of the national banks outstanding is secured, which is called a safety fund. In addition to that there is what the Secretary calls a guarantee fund, which is the deposit of 30 per cent of the circulating notes in greenbacks. Now, section 5 of his plan further provides that immediately upon the failure of a national bank to pay its notes the 30 per cent guarantee fund payable in greenbacks is turned over into the safety fund, and the notes of the failed bank are at once paid out of that 5 per cent safety fund.

After that the Government makes an assessment, if there is not enough in that 5 per cent safety fund to pay the notes, and keeps that up to 5 per cent; but any bank that pays the assessment to keep up this 5 per cent safety fund then has a lien upon all the assets, and there is also the double liability clause with reference to stockholders of failed banks to reimburse it. Do you believe that that creates any hazard or contingent liability upon the other banks that would tend to prevent them from going into business under this law? Is not the liability so remote that there would be no danger of banks refusing to organize under a law of this kind?

Mr. DODSWORTH. Certainly I should not consider it a sufficient inducement for a bank proposing to organize to refuse to organize.

Mr. HALL. There is nothing in that that would scare them out, in your opinion?

Mr. DODSWORTH. No, sir.

Mr. WALKER. You proposed in your paper, if I remember rightly, to divide the territory of the United States into six redemption districts. You advise that?

Mr. DODSWORTH. Yes.

Mr. WALKER. You thought that it was a proper scheme to provide redemption agencies. I want to ask you if you propose that each bank in the territory designated should be required to send notes which it desired to be redeemed to the agency for that district?

Mr. DODSWORTH. Yes, sir.

Mr. WALKER. That that should be a fixed obligation upon each one of these banks?

Mr. DODSWORTH. In case of its wishing——

Mr. WALKER. That is to say, that if a bank sent notes for redemption anywhere it choose, they should go to the redemption agency for that district?

Mr. DODSWORTH. It is a provision enabling the bank receiving the notes of another bank to get those notes redeemed. But when you ask whether it is an obligation on the bank to get the notes so redeemed at all——

Mr. WALKER. That is not my question at all. I will ask my questions so that they will not need an amendment.

Mr. DODSWORTH. I think I understand you. That is the purpose of the provision, to enable the bank receiving the notes of another bank to get those notes redeemed.

Mr. WALKER. That is a pretty big answer to a small question, and I will repeat the question. You advise dividing the country into six parts, with a redemption agency in each part. Is it your purpose that each bank in that territory shall be required to send its notes for redemption to the redemption agency for that territory?

Mr. DODSWORTH. Yes, sir.

Mr. WALKER. That answers the question, and that is all I want on that point.

Mr. DODSWORTH. Allow me to qualify that answer somewhat.

Mr. WALKER. In any way you choose, certainly.

Mr. DODSWORTH. If a bank within a given redemption agency——

Mr. WALKER. No; territory.

Mr. DODSWORTH. Territory; I beg your pardon. If a bank within a given territory has notes issued by some bank outside of its particular territory, it would likewise be empowered to forward that to the agent or agency in its own territory.

Mr. WALKER. To forward that where?

Mr. DODSWORTH. Forward that to the agency in its own district. That agency would be expected to forward it to the agent of the district in which the notes were issued.

Mr. WALKER. I assumed that you had that in your mind. I certainly had it in mine. Is it not a fact that, other things being equal, a firm or a bank; or anything else, is sound or unsound, is deserving of credit or not deserving of credit, in proportion as its liabilities are to its assets, whether large or small? That is true, is it not?

Mr. DODSWORTH. Yes, sir.

Mr. WALKER. Why, then, in outlying agricultural districts, where they want a bank quite as much as they do in a city, and where they can not usually aggregate a capital of more than $50,000 or $100,000, would you prohibit them from issuing circulating notes in proportion to their capital stock paid up and unimpaired? Why not allow the bank with a capital of $50,000 to issue $25,000 currency just as readily as you allow the bank of $500,000 to issue $250,000 of currency?

Mr. DODSWORTH. Certainly I would.

Mr. WALKER. I did not know that you took that position; I thought you contradicted it. I have nothing further to say.

Mr. DODSWORTH. I answered that to the gentleman at the other end of the table.

Mr. SPERRY. I will ask you to state whether, in your opinion, there is any reform needed in our present system of primary money.

Mr. WALKER. What is primary money?

Mr. SPERRY. Money of ultimate redemption—coin, gold and silver. Whether any reform is needed, in your opinion, along that line? If so, I shall be glad to hear what you have to say on that subject.

Mr. DODSWORTH. That touches upon a question that I presume is not included within the present inquiry.

Mr. SPERRY. Yes; I think it is.

Mr. DODSWORTH. It touches upon the silver question, and I should be glad not to answer any question upon that.

Mr. WALKER. I think he ought to be allowed to go into that.

The CHAIRMAN. The chair thinks we had better not. That is a subject not before the committee.

Mr. SPERRY. It might be, and I would like to have the gentleman's opinion.

Mr. DODSWORTH. I think the providing of a bank-currency system does not necessarily involve any consideration of what your coinage shall be.

Mr. SPERRY. Is it not so intimately connected with it that the one affects the other?

Mr. DODSWORTH. It does affect it, undoubtedly,

Mr. SPERRY. And from that point of view I want your opinion.

Mr. DODSWORTH. Of course all bank currency, in the event of our going upon a silver basis, would become payable in silver inevitably. It seems to me that, in all provisions relating to redemptions or payments of any kind, the kind of payment contemplated should be designated as lawful money, which would cover whatever might be lawful money at the time the obligation became payable.

LETTER FROM HON. A. B. HEPBURN.

The CHAIRMAN. Gentlemen of the committee, Mr. Dodsworth will be here in a moment, and in the meantime the chair desires to state that he has received a letter from Mr. A. B. Hepburn, formerly Comptroller of the Currency. Mr. Hepburn was invited to appear before the committee, and came and was here one day, and then was obliged to leave, on account of a prior engagement, to return to New York on the 4 o'clock train, and was not able to be put on the stand. He has written the chairman of this committee, submitting his views in regard to the question before us, and if there be no objection the chair will hand it to the reporter to be printed.

Mr. HALL. Let us have it read.

The chairman read the letter, as follows:

THE THIRD NATIONAL BANK OF THE CITY OF NEW YORK,
New York, December 12, 1894.

MY DEAR SIR: I am very doubtful about my ability to appear before the Committee on Banking and Currency on Thursday, and in view of all the circumstances I think, perhaps, no material good would be accomplished by my returning to Washington.

I therefore take the liberty of calling your attention to some features of Mr. Carlisle's bill which have undoubtedly occurred to you, but which I trust you will call to the attention of your committee, in executive session, after your hearings are closed and while you are engaged in the preparation of a bill.

Of course Mr. Carlisle's provisions requiring banks taking out circulation to deposit greenbacks or Treasury notes is made in the interest of relieving the Government, and not for the benefit of the currency issue. I do not know that I have any objection to that. I should like to see any safe course pursued which would relieve even temporarily the Government from present embarrassments. It should be borne in mind, however, that responsibilities and obligations to furnish gold that are transferred from the shoulders of the Government immediately fall upon the shoulders of the banks, and this currency proposition should be made in some form attractive, and not hedged about by too stringent provisions lest the banks will hesitate, if not decline to take out circulation.

It is by no means an unmixed blessing to the banks, the retirement of the Government from the banking business. While it would benefit the Government and the people as a whole, it would certainly put added responsibilities upon the banks. Now, in times of panic, they have only their depositors to take care of; then, they would have both depositors to supply with funds and the circulation of the country to redeem in coin upon presentation.

I am strongly opposed to the proposition to do away with the requirements that banks keep reserve, and my understanding of the law does not tally with that of the Secretary. The law, when it was drafted, as I understand it, was based upon the experience of prudent and well-managed banks, and the reserve was fixed at a point where prudent and well-managed banks carried their reserve. It was sought to fix a limit so that a well-managed bank would as often be over as under its reserve in the regular course of business.

This law is made not for the nine banks who would observe it without any legal provision, but for the tenth one that, either through incompetent, speculative, or unsafe management might fail to keep a proper reserve and to keep itself in a sufficiently strong position to meet the demands that might be made upon it. The requirement of the law is not rigid and inflexible, as named by the Secretary. The reserve is there to be used, and a bank is obliged to pay its obligations even if it takes the last dollar of its reserve, and the statute contemplates that it will do so. It is required, whenever below its reserve, to take proper measures to recover the same, which is wise and right. It is also provided that if a bank is below its reserve the Comptroller may notify them to make it good, and if the bank fails to do so for a period of thirty days after notification he may appoint a receiver.

There is sufficient flexibility in this provision to admit of banks using their reserve at all proper times and under all proper circumstances. That they do do it in times of panic is well known, and that the Comptroller has never at such a juncture required them to make good their reserve is equally well known, nor would any competent officer do so. The statement which the Secretary makes, that the State banks keep 20 per cent reserve whereas the national banks keep only 18, I do not think is well founded. I know it is not true as to the banks in this State, and so far as I have any statistical knowledge upon the subject, I do not think it is true anywhere, certainly not on the average of the country.

In section 10 the Secretary provides under certain conditions for the repeal of the 10 per cent tax He repeals the 10 per cent tax on State-bank circulation absolutely, while leaving a tax of one-half of 1 per cent upon the circulation of national-bank notes. Here is a discrimination at once which would place the national-bank circulation at a disadvantage to that extent. Should not the one-half per cent tax be retained on State-bank circulation in order to preserve the equity of treatment?

Again, he forbids national banks to issue notes in denominations under $10. No such restriction is imposed upon the State-bank circulation. There should be parity here also.

Again, he provides for a safety fund contributed by the national banks for the payment of the circulating notes of all national banks with unlimited liability. Should not the State banks be required to provide a safety fund in the custody of some State officer, of the same character and upon the same terms, in order, so far as possible, to preserve the equality between the two kinds of circulation? I think so.

Then, instead of doing away with the present reserve required of national banks, State banks taking out circulation should be required to keep the same reserve, and the Secretary and the Comptroller should be "satisfied" that they maintained their reserve, had issued no notes of less denomination than $10, had provided and maintained their safety fund the same as national banks are required to do, in addition to the other points mentioned in section 10 in regard to which the Secretary and the Comptroller must be satisfied.

Then the tax, instead of being repealed, should be reduced to one-half of 1 per cent.

Now, as to section 10. It provides that State banks may take out circulation, and in case they satisfy the Secretary and Comptroller on certain points it shall be exempt from taxation. Now, suppose they do not satisfy the Secretary and Comptroller. Suppose they fail to comply with these provisions, that the bank has been badly managed and the appointment of a receiver is necessary; then, in that case, having allowed this circulation to be placed in the hands of the people, the Government comes forward and exacts its 10 per cent tax, thus aggravating the situation and impairing what security there may be left for the benefit of the note holders and the depositors.

It seems to me that this is wrong. It is locking the barn after the horse is stolen. Instead of ascertaining in advance that the banks are entitled to issue circulation and allowing them to do so, they have this roundabout, cumbersome, unsatisfactory way of final adjustment. What is there to prevent a thoroughly bad State bank from taking out circulation, exploiting all they can, and then, when the period is up and the time arrived when they must satisfy the Secretary and the Comptroller, going to smash. They have utilized this tentative period in which to do all the harm they could possibly do.

On the other hand, a thoroughly well-managed State bank may hesitate to take out circulation with a possible 10 per cent tax hanging over them. Suppose a thoroughly well-managed State bank takes out circulation to the amount of 75 per cent of its unimpaired capital, and some time in the course of a year or six months, before the time for satisfying the Comptroller and the Secretary has arrived, the bank is burglarized, and they lose $50,000 or $100,000 through no fault of their management, thereby impairing their capital so that the circulating notes of the previous year have exceeded 75 per cent of their unimpaired capital. Under those circumstances they would have this 10 per cent tax to pay. Thus, again, the Government comes to the front to aggravate the sufferings of the people.

Now, I do not know just what would satisfy the Comptroller and the Secretary, but in my judgment nothing less ought to satisfy them than five verified reports of condition, published locally and filed with the Comptroller, and as many special reports as the Comptroller chooses to call for, and also the regular annual examination by an expert examiner, and as many special examinations as the condition of the bank and the judgment of the Comptroller may dictate. The law and practice require all that now of a national bank in order to "satisfy" the Comptroller and the Secretary of their condition. Could they, as responsible Government officers, accept any less conclusive evidence on the part of State banks, and if they do this, as it seems to me they inevitably must do under the terms of this bill, they make these State institutions in all respects national except as to name; therefore, it is wiser and better that State banks desiring to take out circulation become national banks in fact.

If circulation is to continue based upon Government bonds there is no reason in the world why State banks should not be allowed to take it out precisely the same as a national bank, but if it is to be based upon the assets of the bank I believe that every consideration of public safety and public propriety requires that these institutions should be under one central control with uniform laws, uniform requirements, and uniform usage.

The Secretary's discussion of the financial question in general I most cordially approve, and the conclusions he reaches I believe are wise and sound; but the details of the bill he has submitted, in my judgment, are open to very serious criticism.

Very respectfully, A. B. HEPBURN.

Hon. WILLIAM M. SPRINGER,
Chairman Committee on Banking and Currency,
Washington, D. C.

STATEMENT OF MR. GEORGE GUNTON.

Mr. GEORGE GUNTON, of New York, appeared before the committee, and made the following statement:

The CHAIRMAN. State your occupation, Mr. Gunton.

Mr. GUNTON. I am president of the School of Economics, and therefore what I shall have to say will be said more from the point of view of an economist than that of a banker interested in the machinery and profits of banking.

While listening to the testimony here and watching the committee, I have wondered that the committee have as much patience as they have. It seems to me that it would wear you out. I do not see how you are able to stay day after day and carry on questions and keep connected in your minds all the views that are presented.

Mr. JOHNSON, of Indiana. We do not.

Mr. GUNTON. If you do not, then you are human. I shall try to be as brief and direct as I can, having learned that in that way more will be drawn out, if there is anything in a statement, than if there is nothing in it.

I conceive the matter of banking as a business rather than as a political institution. It is to my mind an economical instrumentality for supplying a social want, very much as a factory is for supplying shoes or any other product. But money differs from shoes, in that it has to keep going all the time, whereas shoes worn on one pair of feet are liable to be worn out. For that reason it seems to be necessary that there should be as large an amount of security as possible, compatible with the solvency of those who issue the money—a little larger, possibly, than in the case of those who issue shoes.

In all the bills and arguments that have been presented before this committee, I have noticed, almost with rejoicing, a tendency to look toward an improvement or a remodeling of our banking and currency system so that it shall be more elastic, more free, more economical, and less political. Whatever may be the variations in the particular schemes brought before the committee, at least they all seem to point in that direction, and what I shall have to say will be along the same lines.

There seem to be three or four conditions that are needed in banking and money. One of those is flexibility, another is redemption, another is cheapness, and another is freedom—freedom in the going into the business and conducting it.

The schemes of the Baltimore bankers and of the Secretary of the Treasury seem to me to fall short of that, in that they neither provide coin redemption nor for eliminating the political element from banking.

I agree with the gentleman who spoke first this morning, that we can never have quick coin redemption unless we get the Government issue out of the way, and I believe that the first thing is simply to discharge the Government so far as the issue of money is concerned, and that means the entire retirement of Government notes. When that is done the issue of money falls upon the banker; then it is in the hands of business.

The question then arises as to the safety, and here nearly all the questions I notice from the members of the committee, addressed to the various persons who have been on the stand here, were as to what amount of reserve will furnish safety to the notes, how much issue there should be in circulation to capital, and about the 30 per cent reserve that Mr. Carlisle asks.

Now, it seems to me that the people in the business know and would find out very much better what is necessary to secure the circulation than any committee that sits around this table, or any number of men, with all due respect to all of you who meet in the two Houses. If it is a business, and if there is sufficient responsibility so that those who do the business pay the penalty for any mistakes of the business, they will find out better where the line of reserve will be and what the amount of issue should be relatively to the capital than can possibly be done by any persons like us, certainly like myself, not in the business.

Now, in the first place, it seems to me in reference to security, the large aggregate is always safer than the small unit.

The gentleman from Pennsylvania (Mr. Brosius) asked a question a little while ago as to what would happen if a number of the officers of banks were rogues, and the number of their stockholders were insolvent. Well, in a single bank it might be that the whole thing would go down, but in the movement of society I suppose there never was a community made up like that. If so, there would be no community. The law of averages and business interests and civilization, the survival of existence, makes it that in the large body there is but a small proportion of that kind. So that it seems to me that in the security of the circulation, the wider the ground, or the area upon which it rests, the safer it will be; and that as the money must be national—that is, it must circulate through the community—the banking system should be interrelated, so interrelated throughout the whole community that the banking capital, and the banking reputation, and the banking interests are combined with banking circulation.

Now, that being the general proposition, it being a business resting on economy and profit, every unnecessary insistence upon a reserve causes an increase in the cost of the production of bank notes, or, if you like, the cost of running a bank. Every increase in the cost of running a bank affects an increase, necessarily and ultimately, in the rate of interest. You can not help it. The rate of interest is the pay the bankers get for going into banking, and the reason why national banks do not issue is because there is no profit in it, as you have been told. Therefore, it is necessary that banking may be done as cheaply as possible in order that people who want money may get money at as low a rate of interest as possible.

Another point that seems to me to be found in this situation is that the people who need money most, and need it very badly at special times of the year, are the country people, and unless they can have it, unless the machinery of banking will supply it to them as cheaply as the central banks will, they are at a positive disadvantage. That is the case to-day. Of course the great banks in the cities do not need to issue notes. The Chemical Bank of New York does not issue notes. It depends upon its large line of deposits. But the country banks have no deposits, or very few, and their money has to come from the center. So that they have to pay more than double the interest that is paid by the city people.

Now, that seems to me to be one of the legitimate complaints that is behind the Populistic movement, namely, that the money is dear in the sense that it costs them a great deal to get it.

The banking system, if it is to be radically reorganized, ought to be so reorganized that it can supply notes, supply money, on the elastic plan nearly as cheaply, if not quite, at the extreme parts of the country as in the center; and that can only come by the possibility of banks being able to practically furnish what I call costless notes. If the banks can issue their own notes to their own people in their own localities, with as little cost as possible in the banking machinery, then the rate of interest of course will be low. I believe the rate of interest is subject to exactly the same economic influences as is the price of any commodity supplied to the community.

A gentleman of the committee yesterday morning asked whether the cost of the 30 per cent fund provided for by Mr. Carlisle's bill would not increase the rate of interest. The gentleman who was on the stand at the time said he thought not; that the rate of interest was governed by the law of supply and demand. If you will permit me just to put a pin in there, I think that is an entire heresy; that the law of supply and demand only acts upon that matter down to the point of the cost of doing the thing. I think that the dearest bank will be the bank which at the greatest disadvantage can supply its notes; that it will have to charge enough interest to pay its working expenses, or else it will not operate. And what it can get the others will get in the general tendency to uniformity in the rate of interest.

Therefore, if you, to-day, by unnecessary reserves or limitations of issue to capital, or any other way, add to the amount necessarily invested in the business done, you increase the cost of doing the business, and if you increase the cost of doing the business there is not power enough in all the laws and all the forces of society to make a bank go on without changing the rate of interest sufficiently to cover the cost, no matter what the bank may be. So that when we give the people a low rate of interest we must give them the minimum amount of burden on banking machinery.

Now, I submit for that reason, that the minimum amount of the burden which would be involved in the cost of banking machinery is that which the experience of the bankers themselves will discover, and not what any body of legislators can arbitrarily fix at this line or that; and for that reason I am not satisfied with Mr. Carlisle's plan, because it does not require the redemption of Government greenbacks, and until they are redeemed there can be no coin redemption. To say that the Secretary of the Treasury may retire them at his option is to say that they will never be retired. I do not think it is worth one straw to leave it to the option of the Secretary of the Treasury to retire the Government greenbacks when there is a surplus.

You know, gentlemen, that when there is a surplus there would be some political cry that there should be a reduction of the tariff, or something else to eat up the surplus, or to reduce the revenues in some way; and, if there was any little movement toward the greenback business, you would all be so weak you would not dare to talk about retiring Government greenbacks, because you would be afraid you would lose some votes in the States where the greenback issue was up. You are all human, and that is what would be sure to happen.

The state of mind of the public to-day is better toward this question than perhaps it has ever been before. The educational experience we have had in the last year or two is such that the public mind is now ready for some overhauling of our monetary system, and I think their experience and education have been sufficient to permit you to make the very best bill you are able. I believe there never was a time when you were less called upon to compromise and sort of catch at straws about this sentiment or that sentiment. So far as certain conditions that have recently obtained are concerned, I simply believe, Mr. Chairman, that we can afford at this time to do what is right, and do the best we can. That you can not always do. The public mind is such that sometimes, perhaps, no legislative committee can possibly do the best it knows how, because public sentiment is in a state that would simply kill it. That is sometimes the case, and legislators have a harder time, I know, than people like myself think when we stand off all the time criticising you.

Compromising and tacking are no doubt necessary modes of existence at times, but I believe there is less of it to-day than ever before, and I believe that you gentlemen can afford to go right straight at your work and do the best you know how.

Mr. Carlisle said that the Government greenbacks ought to be withdrawn, and the Baltimore plan says that the Government greenbacks ought to be withdrawn. Then withdraw them. I anticipate that some one will ask me the question, and so I say the way to withdraw them would be for the Government simply to issue bonds for that purpose, as has been suggested, say at 3 per cent, and let the banks issue on these notes just as they are taken up. In other words, that they be funded. I do not believe there is any reason for not doing that.

I have no objections, myself, to this 5 per cent fund. I do not know whether it would be enough or too much, and I do not believe that anybody else does. I think the estimate that Mr. Dodsworth has given, and that the banks have given, namely, that it would be ample, based upon the calculation of the number of failed banks to the national-bank system, is utterly fallacious, because they propose to withdraw the bond basis for the banking circulation. They are making their calculation on future failures. In other words, they are making their estimate upon a foundation that they propose to remove, and therefore the calculation that the future failures would be what they have been in the past, after they have taken that away, I do not think is worth one straw, simply because the basis of calculation is withdrawn.

However, whatever the fund might be, I have no objections to it, but I think the safe way, the better way altogether, would be on the redemption plan, rather than to have the limiting of the issues of banks to a certain proportion of the capital, as I observe the Baltimore plan provides 50 per cent, and the Secretary's plan 75 per cent, and Mr. Walker's plan 100 per cent. Of these plans I think the 100 per cent is the best of the three. But I do not know why it should be put there. I think it should be put on the basis of redemption, not on the specific notion of any fund there is there.

The coin redemption is the real test for the safety of the currency. It is the test of any of your notes. Just so long as the assets of the bank are such that redemption goes on, there is no reason for saying that the issue shall be limited here or there. That is the way it seems to me.

I therefore, Mr. Chairman and gentlemen, without taking up very much more of your time, suggest a somewhat different plan from anything that has been suggested, though parts of it have been suggested by almost everybody who has spoken. There is nothing new under the sun, probably, that is worth much, and I do not claim to have anything new. But the idea that I would suggest is that the banking system be organized under some confederated plan of the banks; in other words, that there be redemption agencies, as has been suggested, perhaps, the chief one in New York City, or at some great banking center, wherever that is, and I suppose it would be New York City; but that there be throughout the country—I do not know how many; Mr. Dodsworth has suggested a number, and he is probably right as to the number—a greater or less number of redemption agencies, as the emergency requires, or in other words, banks that are part of the central, having financial relations with it, and all the local banks redeeming in these central agencies, and that they be part of it; that there be a connection in the ownership of the stock, and therefore a supervision of issues by the higher banks over the lower, and that they redeem the notes of the local banks as they come; and whenever the amount kept with the banks above the local banks is sufficient for the notes to be redeemed, let the amount of issue go on; there should be no limit to it, except the limit of safety, and that the banks above, in other words, the capital and the general interests involved, shall decree.

And I would have, as a check upon what might be called a fraudulent effort, or an injudicious effort, to issue notes out of all proportion to the safety of the situation, that the notes of the local banks shall have upon them the signature of one officer of the bank above, that is the redeeming agency, so that they will know exactly how much issue there is being made relatively to the assets, etc.; and if they have any proof as to inordinate issue, they will at once have the matter looked up and refuse to put their names on their notes. In that way the circulating notes of the smaller banks in the country would be directly supervised by the banks of larger capital in the cities.

I observe that there has been some objection raised several times to any idea of banks assuming a responsibility other than their own. It should be true that while banks are business concerns, they are not quite private concerns. They are so social in their character that society has a right—and the very fact that you are going to legislate upon them presumes that right—to insist that the business shall secure its own solvency, and that the Government shall not be called upon, nor shall it call upon the Government. In that way will be obviated what is really the objectionable element, namely, the arbitrary regulations by which the whole banking capital must be held responsible to redeem the notes.

Mr. Carlisle's idea of collecting a tax, and collecting it more and more to enable the Government to redeem the notes of solvent banks, seems to cover that. The Baltimore plan seems to suggest just the 5 per cent, and then if there is not enough in this fund the Government shall foot the bill, so as to make the Government a part, and in some degree a sort of sponsor for the solvency of the banking system, which I think ought not to be the case. The banking capital of the Government ought to be responsible for the solvency of its own business, and it seems to me that if that were the case the very self-interest of the large capital interested would be such that through the interrelation of the central banks and redeeming agencies with the banks of issue—and the banks of issue, you know, are all country banks, not the city banks—the interrelation of the two will give them sufficient supervision, knowing their responsibility, to stop wide of inflation, knowing that they will have to pay the penalty themselves if it goes too far.

I think under this plan you will have at least the possibility of economy in expenses, with no tax on the circulation other than the business necessities of the working of the thing demand, just as is the case with the manufacturer in running his factory. If there is a penny to be saved anywhere by a new method to be adopted, then those who are running the factory have an interest in stopping the expense, and every such economy will tell, of course, upon the cheapness with which the money can be supplied and upon the rate of interest.

Now, it seems to me there can really be no doubt about the fact that under such an arrangement the country bank could issue its notes at as low a rate of interest practically as the bank that simply loans its deposits, because it would loan its own notes, and it would loan them on the title to property in its own neighborhood and cancel them when they came in, so that the only cost to them would be the cost of running the machinery; and the limit to the amount would be checked by the self-interest of those who have still more at stake than those below.

Issuing only up to 50 per cent of your capital, when you could profitably loan twice that much, and having in addition to that 30 per cent on deposit of your circulation, is just adding to the cost of every dollar that goes out unnecessarily, and adding, therefore, necessarily to the interest that must be collected for the work done.

There was one question asked yesterday morning, and I will anticipate it now. Somebody said, Do you think the national banks would organize under a plan under which they were jointly held responsible for the circulation? I think it was Mr. Butler said he did not believe they would. He finally said he did not think there was any risk about it, but he would not advise his bank to do it.

I also think Mr. Horace White rather thought that the banks would not organize under it. Now, the attitude that I think we ought to take upon that is to say, "Look here, banks, you get privileges over the community; we will make you organize under it, if you are going to do this business at all; you can not simply ask all the privileges and object to do that which is necessary to give efficiency to this system throughout the country." If we are clear—and of course that is the first thing to fix—if we are clear that that would be an advantage to those who really need the money and that it would certainly give a better opportunity for profit in issuing money, if it is clear that that would be a more efficient and more strictly business-like method of banking than having a few banks that do not need to issue money at all, and who simply say, "We do not need to issue; we have deposits enough, and we decline to come in," then let us simply say, "Gentlemen, you are in no such position, and we won't have any such nonsense about that; if you want to come in on the pure idea of getting all and lose nothing, stand all the chances but refuse responsibility, you must go into the railroad business or the shoe business or into the business of making steel rails."

Mr. JOHNSON, of Ohio. Where you have no chance to lose?

Mr. GUNTON. The money business is very strikingly a societary affair, and therefore I should say I would tax, and although the constitutionality of taxing banks may be disputed, we are doing it and seem to have the power to do it; and therefore I say I would put a tax of 10 per cent on the circulation of all banks that refuse to come in.

Mr. WARNER. Refuse to have any circulation?

Mr. GUNTON. Yes; and that ends that. I would put a tax of 1 per cent on their deposits and 1 per cent on their loans on their deposits. That would make them come in.

Now, I do not believe that there is anything illegitimate in that. I say if it is a scheme that is advantageous to the whole community and enables the small banks, the country banks, to really do a safe and elastic business, and can really discharge the Government in its relations—and I think that is the most important feature of the whole thing to me, to get the Government out of the business—I would simply say to them: "You can not do a banking business unless you com into this affair;" and as to the State banks I would say just the same. I would not make a particle of difference; all banks should be under that general condition.

Now, one other suggestion I have to make, and then I shall close. The suggestion that I have to make depends upon the question of the gentleman who asked Mr. Dodsworth about silver. It is with reference to coin redemption and the use of silver in coin redemption. I believe that that is a part of the banking system.

Mr. SPERRY. I shall be glad to hear what you have to say on that.

Mr. GUNTON. Since I am not a member of the committee, I believe I shall not be ruled out, Mr. Chairman, on that. Of course redemption should be in coin, silver and gold.

Now, we ought, in any way we can, to give as liberal a use to silver as possible, consistent with safety again. Safety should be the first thing in every movement, of course.

After I received the letter of the chairman of this committee inviting me to come here, I wrote down a very rough minute or skeleton that I thought I would publish in our magazine, and would leave it in the hands of the committee so that they can do with it what they may desire. In that I have suggested this: That the banks should be permitted to use silver in coin redemption, and that they should be permitted to use silver at 10 per cent below bullion value. Now, gentlemen, I want to call your attention to this. There you have the privilege of issuing silver coin at 10 per cent below the bullion value, such coin, of course, to bear the name and the number to be emitted by the Government, as all notes should be emitted by the Government; the number of grains and fineness to be furnished, of course; and the name of the bank, and, to distinguish it from the standard coin, the word "free" should be on; that such coin should be given in redemption at the option of the holder; and that such silver coin should be redeemable in gold whenever required, in just the same way as the bills.

Now, my idea is this: That it would give the banks 10 per cent advantage, and therefore furnish a motive for sending out silver. I believe that what we need is a motive for sending out silver, and then it will go out. If you will give capitalists a motive of a percent or two they will always work, and they won't work without it. They will let you drown or starve; if they can't make a cent out of you they will desert you.

Now, if it were said that that 10 per cent upon experiment might prove too much, I answer that it is merely the idea I want to suggest rather than the fixed amount; that this silver, of course, would be ultimately redeemable, and that the banks issuing it would be responsible for its redemption in exactly the same way that they now redeem their notes, only instead of being all fiat there is only 10 per cent of it.

If silver should decline, of course it would come in for redemption; if it should not come in it will go into the pot; and if it goes into the pot we will make more from it. There is no trouble about it. If it comes back for redemption it will be redeemed in gold, and no matter how much it should decline the banks would only be where they were when they were not allowed to issue a dollar; and every dollar's worth of silver that can go out in that way as so much property gives so much freedom to the use of silver and has behind it just as strict a guarantee of safety, or protection, or security, whatever you like to call it, as the notes have.

I do not pretend to have gone into it and worked out all the little proportions and everything; nothing of the kind. I do not pretend to know just what, any more than I believe any of you know just what, the reserve of a bank should be; none of you know that; nothing of the kind. You do not know that any more than you know just how many shoes you will have to issue, or ought to issue, in 1900, if you are shoemakers. Experience will have to determine that. I do not pretend to know where these particular lines should be drawn, but what I want to urge is that the general system of monetary affairs and banking should be reorganized on some confederated plan by which all the different points at issue should be integrated, one with the other, in some such general way as we have in our political institutions; that the monetary institutions of the country should at least follow the general lines of our political institutions, with interdependence of the local upon the larger center, and the larger center upon the still larger center, so that in the last analysis, in the same way that the United States Government stands behind the freedom of every American, no matter where he is, the United States banking system should stand behind every note that circulates in the United States, wherever it is, and that it should be governed by judgment and experience, and the penalty paid by the losses of those engaged in the business, and not by the Government, and not by the note holders.

Mr. JOHNSON, of Ohio. Your plan involves, first, the funding of the greenbacks?

Mr. GUNTON. Yes.

Mr. JOHNSON, of Ohio. And then you propose to turn over to the banks, national and State, I presume from what you say, the power to organize and form themselves into a pool or trust, or whatever you choose to call it?

Mr. GUNTON. Yes; call it the most objectionable name you can.

Mr. JOHNSON, of Ohio. And except as to the question of printing the notes and prescribing some general rule as to how they shall be paid, the Government is to have absolutely nothing to do with it?

Mr. GUNTON. That is it, Mr. Johnson, exactly.

Mr. JOHNSON, of Ohio. Now, with reference to silver coin, you propose, you say, that the customer is not required, on final redemption, to take it unless he wants it?

Mr. GUNTON. He has to stand in the same relation to it that he does to his note. He can turn it in for redemption and get gold.

Mr. JOHNSON, of Ohio. But must he, in the first place, take it if the bank offers it to him?

Mr. GUNTON. No.

Mr. JOHNSON, of Ohio. Then it is not a redemption; it is a mere bargain as to whether the man takes it or not.

Mr. GUNTON. So it is with the note; it is not legal tender any more than a bank note.

Mr. JOHNSON, of Ohio. But gold is.

Mr. GUNTON. Yes; and gold is the only thing that is.

Mr. JOHNSON, of Ohio. Do I understand you to describe the silver currency as wealth, consumable or otherwise?

Mr. GUNTON. Certainly it is wealth.

Mr. JOHNSON, of Ohio. What kind of wealth is it?

Mr. GUNTON. Oh, it is productive wealth, of course.

Mr. JOHNSON, of Ohio. Not consumable wealth?

Mr. GUNTON. No.

Mr. JOHNSON, of Ohio. A bank note is what?

Mr. GUNTON. The same thing.

Mr. JOHNSON, of Ohio. Productive wealth?

Mr. GUNTON. Certainly.

Mr. WARNER. Do I understand that you would have the large banks in each city prescribe, as it were, the amount of silver currency for the banks in the rural districts?

Mr. GUNTON. The redemption centers?

Mr. WARNER. Yes; it would depend upon their judgment as to how much the other banks should be allowed to issue. Is that your idea?

Mr. GUNTON. Yes; that is, that would be some check upon it, but not beyond the point of safety.

Mr. WARNER. You would have the few large banks at the centers deciding how much currency should be issued by the other banks of the country?

Mr. GUNTON. No; only in this sense, that their signatures are required on the notes issued by the smaller banks, which would act in such a way as to absolutely inform the officers of the larger banks how much the issue is, and give them an opportunity to look them up and keep a cautionary eye on them.

Mr. WARNER. You would leave them—the larger banks—to do what they thought best?

Mr. GUNTON. Yes; certainly.

Mr. WARNER. Have you any arrangement to keep a bank alive to-day when the silver is brought in?

Mr. GUNTON. No; no more than to keep it alive with reference to bank notes.

Mr. WARNER. Suppose the price of silver should come down, as it has in the last ten years, would you keep the bank alive by redeeming the outstanding silver?

Mr. GUNTON. No; the redemption of the silver would be carried on on the same basis as the redemption of paper. If a bank feels that its silver is a part of its assets as its notes would have to be paid, so silver would have to be paid in the same way.

Mr. WARNER. Then silver is the same as so many silver notes out?

Mr. GUNTON. Yes; only it is 10 per cent instead of 100 fiat.

Mr. WARNER. They are silver notes instead of paper notes?

Mr. GUNTON. If you like, only they have 90 cents' worth of wealth right in them.

Mr. WARNER. They are silver instead of paper.

Mr. GUNTON. Yes; only they are not silver notes.

Mr. HAUGEN. I understood you to say, at the conclusion of your remarks, that you wanted the Government to stand behind every note issued.

Mr. GUNTON. Not the Government to stand behind at all. I said what I wanted was that the banking system should be organized on a somewhat dependent relation of the weakest to the strongest, as compared with our political institutions. I made that illustration simply that the United States Government is behind the freedom of each individual citizen, and I said it should be behind all the banking capital in the same way.

Mr. HAUGEN. But you would have no Government supervision?

Mr. GUNTON. Yes; I would. I think the supervision that is provided for in the other bill.

Mr. HAUGEN. Somewhat similar to the present supervision?

Mr. GUNTON. Certainly. I do not think there is any need of taking off a particle of supervision—that is, let the Government do all the policeman work in the thing, but not invest any money, not issue any notes.

Mr. BROSIUS. I understand that your conception of a sound banking system is that it shall be in the nature of an organism?

Mr. GUNTON. Yes.

Mr. BROSIUS. You use the words "societary institution."

Mr. GUNTON. Yes.

Mr. BROSIUS. I use the word organism to refer to that in which all the parts, good or bad, mutually and reciprocally support each other.

Mr. GUNTON. Yes.

Mr. BROSIUS. How would you start an organism of that kind, supposing you were at the beginning of the banking system, and you had but one bank? Could you apply just the same principles to a single bank that you do to an aggregation of banks which could not be your organism?

Mr. GUNTON. Not to a single bank; a single bank would have the disadvantage in that a little misjudgment or a little fraud may circu late over such a small area that it may kill the unit.

Mr. BROSIUS. Then your principle is only applicable after the organism is fully developed and consists of an aggregation of parts which can mutually support each other?

Mr. GUNTON. Yes; and the present banks will constitute the machinery for just that organization right away.

Mr. BROSIUS. Then, it does not make any difference how many of these banks turn out badly, or how many rogues and rascals they are composed of, as long as there is enough of soundness in the entire organism, in the aggregation of parts, to meet all the losses perpetrated by any number of parts your system stands, does it not?

Mr. GUNTON. Certainly; only it does make some difference how many rotten ones there are, because the larger the number of bad ones the poorer will be the whole aggregation and the more the whole will have to suffer; and therefore that will be an incentive to scrutiny and care all the way down to see that there shall not be so many rogues.

Following is Mr. Gunton's proposed bill, referred to in the foregoing statement:

BILL RELATING TO BANKING AND CURRENCY.

TITLE: "To retire the Government's noninterest paying debt, to federalize and unify the note-issuing banks of the United States, to create a national fiscal institution for insuring coin redemption on notes passing as money, and to promote the free coinage of silver.

Be it enacted, etc. 1. That from and after the first day of March, eighteen hundred and ninety-five, no note of the United States shall be legal tender in payment of any debt, public or private, but that all debts, public and private, shall be thereafter paid in gold coin for all sums in excess of five dollars, and in silver coin for those below five dollars.

2. Until March first, eighteen hundred and ninety-five, legal-tender notes shall be fundable at par in sums of one hundred dollars and upward in multiples of one hundred dollars into United States interminable bonds bearing three per centum interest per annum, which the Secretary is hereby authorized to issue, for that purpose only, in the sum (of three hundred and forty-six million dollars) corresponding in amount to the sum of legal-tender notes outstanding; and national-bank notes shall be fundable at par into bank notes authorized by this act.

3. An annual Federal tax of ten per centum shall be collected by the collectors of internal revenue on circulating notes issued by any banker or bank, and an annual tax of one-fourth of one per centum on all deposits of any bank, and a further annual tax of one-fourth of one per centum on all loans made and commercial paper bought by any bank which shall fail to organize as a branch of the Federal Union of Associated Banks of the United States herein provided for.

4. The Federal Union of Associated Banks shall consist of four grades of institutions for banking, namely, local, metropolitan, State and a bank of the American union. Local banks shall consist of such as have a capital of not less than fifty thousand dollars nor more than two hundred and fifty thousand dollars, but every local bank shall be a branch of some metropolitan bank. Metropolitan banks shall consist of such as have a capital of not less than two hundred and fifty thousand dollars, but every metropolitan bank shall be a branch either of some State bank or of the bank of the American Union. A State bank shall have a capital of one million five hundred thousand dollars or more, and shall be a branch of the bank of the American Union.

The Bank of the American Union shall have a capital of one hundred million dollars, of which one-fifth shall be paid in gold coin and four-fifths in national bonds of the United States at par, in British consols at par, or in bonds of American cities having more than one million population, and shall be composed of such metropolitan and State banks as shall become stockholders in it and shall be represented in its board of directors, and of such other persons and corporations, public or private, as shall subscribe to its stock. It shall be the chief depository of the Government moneys. But so far as Government convenience may require other depositories they may be the State and the metropolitan banks.

5. Each branch bank shall become a member of the bank next above it in grade by investing one-fifth of its capital in the stock of such bank of higher grade, and its president shall be entitled to be one director therein: *Provided*, That all the stocks held by branch banks in any bank of higher grade shall not exceed a third of the total stock of such higher bank and shall be abated in the degree required to keep the aggregate at one third, and every bank of higher grade shall subscribe for and own reciprocally a block of stock in the bank of lower grade equal in par value to the stock which the latter owns in the former.

6. A third of the directors of the Bank of the American Union shall be presidents of the State and of the metropolitan banks.

7. The Bank of the American Union shall redeem, in coin, the notes of all State, metropolitan, and local banks, and each bank of higher grade shall redeem, in coin, on demand, all notes of lower banks, which are its branches. To protect each in such work of redemption it may require its branch bank to maintain with it a satisfactory deposit, and on failure of such lower bank to protect such work of redemption the prosecuting bank may have a receiver appointed therefor by the Federal court and press its claim for reimbursement in coin for past redemptions to liquidation

and the dissolution of such delinquent. But this right is not to preclude any note holder or the Comptroller of the Currency from employing the like remedy.

8. All customs duties shall be paid in gold only, but internal revenue taxes shall be receivable in bank notes of solvent banks.

9. All acts and parts of acts providing for bond security for note redemption are hereby repealed, but the visitatorial power of the Comptroller of the Currency, heretofore exercised under the national-banking law, is continued as to notes designed to circulate as currency under this act. In States which authorize a State banking department, such department shall be deemed and assumed to have concurrent jurisdiction with the Comptroller of the Currency in all that relates to the investments and securities which constitute the capital stock of the banks located in such State, and the deposits, loans, discounts, rates of interest, and liabilities to depositors in the same.

10. When three hundred and forty-six million dollars of the aforesaid interminable bonds shall have been purchased by the associated banks of the United States, and one hundred million dollars of capital in the Bank of the American Union shall have been subscribed by existing banks, or by banks organized to avail themselves of this act, and when all the Government notes presented to the Federal Union of Associated Banks for substitution by their own bank notes shall have been surrendered to the Treasury of the United States to be canceled, and the banks authorized by this act shall have issued their own bank notes in lieu thereof, the Comptroller of the Currency shall issue a circular letter declaring the system of associated banking herein provided for to be in full operation, and thereupon all bonds and securities heretofore deposited with such Comptroller to secure the redemption of national-bank notes in coin shall be returned to the respective banks owning them, and the notes thereupon issued by such banks, so far as the same have been returned to them, shall be surrendered to the Comptroller and destroyed.

11. Each State, metropolitan, and local bank organizing under this act shall be deemed ready to issue notes under the same when it shall have purchased and deposited with the Comptroller of the Currency for cancellation a sum in legal-tender notes bearing the same proportion to the volume of legal tenders now issued as the capital of such bank bears to the total capital of all the banks required or designed to be confederated under this system, to be certified by the Comptroller of the Currency; and shall be ready to receive and loan deposits under the same when both the Comptroller of the Currency and the chief officer of the State banking department of the State in which such bank is located shall certify that it has paid in and invested in securities satisfactory to both such departments the capital on which it proposes to be based, pursuant to the laws of such State relative to the investment of securities constituting the capital.

12. The Bank of the American Union shall have power to deal in foreign exchange, to issue drafts to and receive deposits from residents and governments of foreign countries, and to establish branches and offices in foreign ports, with capital of their own, of which a part shall be subscribed by the resident banks and merchants of the countries in which such foreign branches shall be located or with which they do business.

13. The Government of the United States, through its Comptroller of the Currency, shall have charge of the printing and distribution of all bank notes to be issued under this system, and its Comptroller of the Currency shall deliver the notes at a cost to be determined by the cost of engraving only, to the officers of all banks, with proper spaces prepared for the signatures of at least two of the officers of the bank issuing it, and of one officer of the higher grade of banks of which it is a branch, all of whom shall sign it before it shall become the note of the bank; and shall report such signing on the same day, with the denominations and quantities of notes signed, to the Comptroller of the Currency.

14. The Comptroller of the Currency shall publish daily and be prepared to respond by telegraph momently during business hours of each day to any inquiries from any bank as to the volume of duly signed notes issued to any other bank for loaning.

15. The bank notes authorized by this act shall be of different basic colors calculated to distinguish at sight, whether the note is issued by the Bank of the American Union or by some State, metropolitan, or local bank, to wit:

The basic color of the notes of the Bank of the American Union shall be gold or yellow.

The basic color of the notes of State banks shall be pale green.

The basic color of the notes of metropolitan banks shall be pink, violet, or purple.

The basic color of the notes of local banks shall be silver or white.

Every note so issued shall be the promise of the bank issuing it to pay the sum of   dollars, in coin of gold or silver, according to its denomination, to the bearer on demand—to be printed in clear and conspicuous language, unobscured by ornament.

16. All silver coin, which shall be hereafter issuable by the United States mints

at the option of any bank which is the holder of silver bullion, shall have stamped upon it, at the cost and with the mechanism furnished or paid for by such bank, the name of the bank which procures its coinage and the number of grains of standard silver (assayed by the mint) which it contains.

17. Every such coin, whether dollar, half dollar, quarter, or dime, shall be distinguished from the present standard and subsidiary coin, of which it is the freely coined counterpart by the legal designation "free," while the present coinage shall retain its designation "standard" or "subsidiary," as the fact may be.

18. Every free silver dollar shall contain ninety per cent of the quantity of silver bullion, as nearly as may be, which the standard gold dollar would buy in open market on the day of its issue, and subsidiary coins in the same proportion.

19. Every bank issuing free silver coins shall be held to redeem the free silver coin bearing its imprint in gold coin when presented in sums of five dollars and upward.

20. Any bank issuing notes of denominations less than five dollars may redeem them in free silver coins when presented for redemption in sums not exceeding five dollars.

Mr. WALKER. If this gentleman has finished and Mr. Rothwell can come to-morrow morning, I shall move that we adjourn.

The CHAIRMAN. That is a matter for the committee to determine.

Mr. WALKER. I move that the committee adjourn. I understand that he can come just as well to-morrow morning.

Mr. ROTHWELL. I will be in town to-morrow and I can come to-morrow.

The Chairman put the question upon Mr. Walker's motion, and declared that the noes seemed to have it.

Mr. WALKER. I call for the yeas and nays.

The yeas and nays were ordered, and upon being taken resulted—yeas 6, nays 7, as follows:

Yeas—Hall, Walker, Brosius, Russell, Haugen, Johnson of Indiana.

Nays—Springer, Sperry, Cox, Cobb of Missouri, Warner, Johnson of Ohio, Black.

So the motion to adjourn was rejected.

STATEMENT OF RICHARD P. ROTHWELL.

Mr. Richard P. Rothwell appeared before the committee and made the following statement:

The CHAIRMAN. You may please state your occupation.

Mr. ROTHWELL. I am mining engineer, and editor of the Engineering and Mining Journal, New York.

I desire to call the attention of the committee to a few points which seem to me to be important in the propositions that have been made in the Baltimore plan and in Secretary Carlisle's proposed bill, and which may not have attracted much attention. I do not wish to go into the details which are properly the function of bankers, and to be considered by them from their experience, for I am not a banker, but I am simply a student of finance and a business man.

The first point that I want to make in regard to the plan of Secretary Carlisle is that it is a measure of large inflation. I have jotted down a few notes here that I will give as explanatory.

OUR PAPER MONEY REDUNDANT.

The cause of the persistent gold exports draining the gold reserve is redundance in the volume of paper money.

The criterion of the state of the paper currency is the character of the customs payments at the port of New York.

The force of financial gravitation attracts any surplus of funds from the interior to the banks of New York. Ever since specie payments were resumed, January 1, 1879, the New York banks have made customs payments in the form of money they held in superabundance. Consequently, when their currency holdings are unduly large, customs payments are made in paper, and, since our people prefer paper to gold in general use, when business calls for the use of all the paper, the customs duties are paid in gold.

For the four years immediately preceding the passage of the Sherman Act, in July, 1890, the issues of paper money under the Bland Act of 1878, minimized, as they were by continuous contraction of the national-bank note circulation, were well within the demands of the country for paper money. The result was that more than 80 per cent of the customs duties at New York were paid in gold. In the fiscal year ending June 30, 1890, the proportion of gold in the customs receipts ranged between 85.7 per cent in July, 1889, and 95.8 per cent in March, 1890.

Mr. WALKER. Is it his position that paper is preferred to gold by the people?

Mr. ROTHWELL. In general use, where the two kinds are interchangeable.

The gold revenue thus received protected the Treasury gold reserve, which rose from $186,711,560 on June 30, 1889, to $190,232,405 on June 30, 1890 During these four years paper money was, in fact, more valuable to the banks than gold, as they paid out the gold to the Government and retained the currency for the use of their customers.

The operation of the Sherman Act quickly brought about a reversal of this condition. The percentage of gold in the customs declined at once. The way the notes were rejected from the channels of circulation is well illustrated by the following statement of customs receipts at New York in the month of August, 1890, 1891, and 1892:

Year.	Percentage of gold.	Percentage of Sherman Act notes.
1890	91.8	3.5
1891	12.8	31.5
1892	12.1	51.9

It will be seen that the issues of notes under the Sherman Act were larger than the country could absorb in the channels of circulation with the result that they displaced gold as the medium of customs payments.

As the Sherman Act made the currency redundant and inspired apprehensions as to our ability to maintain gold payments, the effect was to encourage exports of gold.

NET EXPORTS OF GOLD.

Years ending June 30—	
1891	$68,130,087
1892	495,873
1893	87,506,463
	156,132,423
Sherman Act notes outstanding June 30, 1893	146,341,386

It will be noticed that the country's loss in gold was substantially the amount of the issues under the Sherman law.

As the gold had disappeared from the customs receipts the weight of the export movement fell upon the Treasury gold reserve, which declined from $190,232,405 on June 30, 1890, to $95,485,414 on June 30, 1893.

The Sherman Act was repealed and inflation of the currency stopped, but the phenomena which preceded the repeal—that is to say, payment of customs duties in paper instead of gold and exports of that metal—exist to-day simply because the contraction in business resulting from the panic and the foreign doubts about the wisdom of our financial policy has lessened the demand for currency, leaving the volume still redundant.

The remedy is to retire the superfluity. If this were done customs duties would again be paid in gold, and in all probability gold exports would be within very moderate limits, if they would not cease entirely.

INFLATION UNDER THE PROPOSED PLAN.

The possibilities of immediate inflation under Mr. Carlisle's currency plan can be judged from the reports of the national banks to the Comptroller, October 2, 1894.

CURRENT LIABILITIES OF BANKS.

Due to depositors	$1,742,000,000
Due to banks	527,000,000
Other	30,000,000
	$2,299,000,000

CASH HOLDINGS.

Gold coin and certificates	197,000,000
Silver coin and certificates	40,000,000
Legals	166,000,000
	403,000,000
National bank notes	19,000,000
	422,000,000

Thus the cash holdings were 18.4 per cent of the current liabilities.

As Mr. Carlisle proposes to abolish the compulsory reserve against deposits 25 per cent, the whole of this 422 millions of cash holdings will be legally released, except a sum equal to 30 per cent upon the new circulation.

The capital stock of the existing national banks aggregates 669 millions.

The scheme will permit the issue of 75 per cent thereof, being 501 million of notes upon deposit of 30 per cent of these, or 150 millions in legal tenders.

POSSIBILITY OF SYSTEM WITH EXISTING BANKS.

INCREASE OF CIRCULATION BY NATIONAL BANKS.

Bank notes authorized		$501,000,000
Assuming no reserve were held by the national banks, deduct:		
National-bank notes to-day	$172,000,000	
30 per cent guarantee fund in legal tenders	150,000,000	
		322,000,000
Possible net inflation		179,000,000

It is fair to assume that the banks will use their own notes to meet their depositors' calls, holding specie and legal tenders sufficient only for current redemptions.

The business of the country centers in the banks, enabling them to dictate the character of the circulating medium in daily use. Self-interest will induce them to keep their own notes out, sending the Government paper to its creator through the custom-house and sub-treasury. As the channels of circulation are already full to overflowing, it would be only as the Government paper was forced out of circulation by the banks that the new bank notes would find room to circulate and the banks begin to profit.

The helpless condition of the Treasury under these circumstances is apparent.

LEGAL TENDERS OUTSTANDING SEPTEMBER 30, 1894.

Greenbacks	$346, 681, 016
Sherman Act notes	151, 609, 267
	598, 290, 283
Deduct possible deposits in guaranty fund (say)	150, 000, 000
In Treasury and afloat	448, 290, 283

Mr. JOHNSON, of Indiana. That is, you mean after deducting that which Mr. Carlisle provides?

Mr. ROTHWELL. Yes; assuming that the circulation is taken out by the national banks, not State banks, it would deposit $150,000,000 in the Treasury for the security of the circulation of the national banks and would leave $448,000,000 of Government paper afloat.

The possible inflation of national-bank circulation being 179,000,000, the probability is that a large part of these 448,000,000 of legal tenders would in time be forced back into the Treasury, making their cancellation imperative.

The 166,000,000 of legals now held by the national banks will permit the issue immediately of the maximum of authorized circulation.

The foregoing covers only the national banks, while Mr. Carlisle contemplates in addition the issue of notes by State banks.

The "Baltimore plan," if similarly analyzed, will be found to be like wise currency expansion measures, and this at a time when each dollar of new paper money must displace a dollar of the existing Government paper.

To make either system successful the legal tenders must get out of the way.

THE FIELD FOR THE SILVER CERTIFICATE.

Mr. Carlisle provides that no national-bank note shall be of less denomination than $10. If this limitation be also placed on State-bank issues, the field for the silver certificate will be quite broad enough.

Silver certificates outstanding September 30, 1894		$339, 676, 504
Small denominations of paper money:		
One-dollar	$39, 988, 823	
Two-dollar	28, 966, 529	
Five-dollar	249, 164, 409	
		317, 119, 461
Excess		22, 457, 143

These 22½ millions are a very moderate sum that a few years of prosperity will enable the country to absorb, and, once absorbed, would thereafter be always retained in circulation.

The question that arises from this showing is that the banks, under the Baltimore plan, or under Secretary Carlisle's plan, will have an inducement to issue their own notes and keep their own notes in circulation. Otherwise they would gain nothing, if they have no circulation of their own notes. In order to keep them out they will necessarily force the Government paper in. At present there is a superabundance of paper. That is the reason gold has gone out and that we get no gold through the custom-house. The amount of gold is down now to a mere nominal sum, it is all paper that is coming in, and as long as the business of the community does not require so much money as we now have afloat that condition of affairs will continue. The gold will not be deposited, it will be exported, owing largely to the fears of the foreigners that we are going to lose our standard currency and to fears of our general financial schemes, and owing also to the fact that the banks will take in what they deem of least value.

The Treasury is in this position: That it is authorizing an inflation, when its troubles are already due to a superabundance of paper money, and it will either have to make provision in the law allowing banks to issue circulating notes, a provision that would oblige the banks to keep the Government paper out right away—if such a provision can be put in the law—that will oblige the banks to keep Government paper out, which at the present time would mean that they could not issue any of their own; or the Government must fund its paper before the banks can issue any circulating notes at the present time. There does not appear to be any way around it; and, judging from the present condition of things. the surest index which we have of that is the receipts at the custom-house.

There is, of course, the very important question to my mind as to the ultimate redemption of notes. The Government is bound to redeem its notes in gold. We all know that. The banks would have to redeem their notes in gold, either directly or by some roundabout process—better directly—otherwise their notes will be at a disadvantage as compared with Government notes, and they could not get them out until the business of the country grew up to a requirement for a circulating medium better than now exists and which would absorb this superabundance of money that we now have.

Mr. JOHNSON, of Indiana. That is the difference between 75 per cent and 30 per cent?

Mr. ROTHWELL. Yes; that difference is inflation.

Mr. JOHNSON, of Indiana. The point you make is that there is no necessity, no use for that money?

Mr. ROTHWELL. There is no use for it now. Paper money is lying idle now, and we have too much for the condition of our business. If business increased and improved we would use the notes that we have, and gold would come into the Treasury through the custom-house. But as long as gold is not coming in there, it is an absolute demonstration that there is more paper than we require in business; and every bank in New York will tell you the same thing, that they are loaded down with paper that they can not use. This measure would simply add to that, and add to the difficulties of the Treasury, provided this money that is proposed to be issued were secured in such a way that it would be equally good with Government money. I take it that the law would require such conditions for security, and that the money that the banks would be authorized to issue would be as safe money as Government money. In that condition it would aggravate the condition of the Treasury. It would oblige the Treasury to redeem its own paper by loans unless it could force the banks issuing to give precedence, and then the banks would have to wait for their own circulation until the banks of the country grew up to the amount of money we have.

The question of the ultimate redemption in gold is becoming a more and more serious question, for the demand for gold is constantly increasing, and it is harder and harder to get.

Mr. WALKER. I understand, then, that you come to this conclusion: That the effect of Mr. Carlisle's scheme, if it works, would be to force the Treasury notes and the legal-tender notes back on the Treasury for redemption, and that it would require the selling of more and more bonds to meet the demand.

Mr. ROTHWELL. It certainly will if the bank notes can be made equal in value as security; that is, if the people would take them, for it is to the interest of a bank to force its own notes into circulation and to send home for redemption the notes of everybody else, and primarily, the Government notes would be sent in for redemption.

There is one question I desire to refer to, and that is the ability to get gold with which to redeem.

Mr. BLACK. Let us hear you on that.

Mr. ROTHWELL. I do not think that it would be possible for the Government to-day to get enough gold to redeem all its outstanding notes. The demand for gold is increasing all over the world. Since the condition amounting to full legal tender silver has been discontinued, the demand for gold has grown and there has been a constantly increasing demand for it. It is true that the increasing demand and the appreciation it has brought have induced a great many to go into the business of gold mining, and that the production of gold is increasing because the value of gold is greater than it was. But there is not nearly enough increase in the production of gold, when counted up for a long time, to compensate for the destruction of so much of the money as was represented by silver when there was a concurrent use of silver and gold.

On the question of the ultimate redemption of our Government obligations, our paper, our notes, as to what can be paid, if we go to work to increase this demand, that has already appreciated the value of gold, by asking for two or three hundred millions more of it, there is no saying where the value of gold will go to. That means that everything else which is now measured by gold as a sole standard will depreciate, and you can have no general prosperity on a constantly falling market.

Mr. WALKER. I submit that this question is not on the question before us.

Mr. ELLIS. He is talking very sensibly.

Mr. ROTHWELL. It is a question of the ultimate redemption of our notes. What are we going to redeem them in?

The CHAIRMAN. The Chair thinks the gentleman is in the line of the statements of the gentlemen who have heretofore spoken to us.

Mr. ROTHWELL. The question then is as to the rehabilitation of silver. I am a bimetallist; I am not a free-coinage advocate. By bimetallism I mean the full interchangeability of the metals. A concurrent circulation of the two metals can only be secured by an international agreement among the principal nations, which would afford a market under that agreement for all the silver and all the gold that might be offered, at whatever ratio that may be agreed upon among themselves.

This question, of course, brings up the question of bimetallism, which may not be within the domain of your commission, but the question of the ultimate redemption of paper circulation is.

As I have said, I believe in bimetallism, because it is the only means that we have of checking the appreciation of the standard of measurement. But I am thoroughly convinced that bimetallism can not be secured in any other way than by international cooperation, with a ratio to be adopted.

My own suggestion has been to make the ratio flexible, to put it under the control of such a commission as would necessarily have to be brought together under an international agreement—call it the international monetary clearing-house—and put the control of the ratio between the metals in the hands of this commission, which would from time to time, and slowly and by small degrees, so adapt the ratio to the conditions of production as would regulate production; for it is certain that the metal that it pays people the best to produce, people are going to produce most of; and that is, if the value of gold is increasing, the people will go into producing gold, and that is why we see more gold coming out now.

As to the value of silver now, there is no market for it. Its price has gone down so much that the production has enormously decreased. By regulating the ratio you could bring about an absolute stability of production. If there were ultimately too much of one metal produced to make it possible in the future to redeem it by the other, by changing the ratio somewhat, a very little of production would change it, and the more abundant would become less abundant, and the less abundant would become more abundant. So that the control of the ratio is an absolute condition of permanent bimetallism, and with that permanent bimetallism I do not see how we are going to redeem our notes, or how we are going to have a prosperous future with a constantly decreasing value for everything we produce.

Mr. WALKER. You understand that bank notes have a practically instant redemption to-day, so that a bank knows exactly what to do with its bank notes. They are redeemed by the Government, if not redeemed by the bank that issued them. That practically displaces them from circulation.

Mr. ROTHWELL. As long as the Government has something to redeem them with.

Mr. WALKER. That is not my point. The present law requires the bank to have something with which to redeem them, so that is no answer to the question. The point is that bank notes to-day have an instant redemption out of the redemption fund that the bank keeps here at the seat of Government.

Mr. ROTHWELL. Yes.

Mr. WALKER. Your next proposition is that the Government notes, the greenbacks and the Treasury notes, have but one redemption, and that is gold, and then the banker can do nothing practically with that gold but ship it abroad, because the banks all have as much gold as they want?

Mr. ROTHWELL. I do not know that, sir. They can not ship it abroad until it is wanted there.

Mr. WALKER. They will not take it out of the Treasury until it is wanted abroad, because they had as lief hold Government notes upon which they can get the gold ultimately?

Mr. ROTHWELL. But if a superabundance of notes are offered they will certainly redeem some of them. I do not hear any of the banks complaining of any excess of gold.

Mr. WALKER. You do not quite apprehend my question. There is a legal and compulsory redemption of bank notes. If there is any redundancy those notes must come back to the bank of issue, and if their customers are willing to take notes rather than to draw out their deposits from the banks on checks, then the bank can use those notes again. If the customers do not want those notes, they have got to lie idle in the bank, and that is retirement. That is clear, is it not?

Mr. ROTHWELL. Yes.

Mr. WALKER. But if a bank has either the silver certificates, gold certificates, or currency certificates, the only thing it can do with them is to send them down here to the seat of government, and as long as there is no advantage to them in that they can not ship abroad the silver dollars; they are limited to the gold, because they can sell the gold the world over. That is true, is it not?

Mr. ROTHWELL. The Government can reissue them.

Mr. WALKER. I am not talking about what the Government can do. When banks find that they have more money than they know what to do with, the tendency is to get gold, because that has a price the world, over and that increases the embarrassment of the Treasury by every dollar of currency that is issued.

Mr. ROTHWELL. Exactly.

Mr. WALKER. So that the Carlisle scheme, or any other scheme that increases circulation without providing for some method of retirement of the certificates, creates the difficulty under which silver labors?

Mr. ROTHWELL. Yes, sir; so long as the business of the country does not require the circulation, that is true.

Mr. JOHNSON, of Indiana. If the banks could use the 30 per cent they could just as well use any circulation of bank notes that are issued to that extent?

Mr. ROTHWELL. Yes; it would allow them to put those out, and they would come back to the Treasury.

Mr. JOHNSON, of Indiana. My point is, with reference to your statement, that there would be an excessive issue of notes, far beyond the needs of the community at this time. You state, the margin between 75 per cent and 30 per cent would be inflation of currency.

Mr. ROTHWELL. Yes.

Mr. JOHNSON, of Indiana. That would lie idle in the vaults of the banks until the expanding business required it; it would not cost them anything in the meantime to keep it, would it?

Mr. ROTHWELL. I assume they would keep it, and force the Government to hoard it.

Mr. JOHNSON, of Indiana. You said they could not use it because of the lack of business requirements.

Mr. ROTHWELL. It would take the place of Government money that is now doing business.

Mr. JOHNSON, of Indiana. It would more than take the place, would it not?

Mr. ROTHWELL. So much of it would; an equal amount of it would take the place of the Government money.

Mr. JOHNSON, of Indiana. You mean in the business of the country?

Mr. ROTHWELL. Yes.

Mr. JOHNSON, of Indiana. And the margin would lie idle until called for by business needs?

Mr. ROTHWELL. Yes. It is to the interest of the bank to get its own money out, and if the business of the country does not require any more money than is now existing, something will have to come in when it goes out, and it is the Government money that will come in.

Mr. RUSSELL. It will come back for redemption?

Mr. ROTHWELL. It will come back for redemption.

Mr. SPERRY. By what process of reasoning do you arrive at the conclusion that gold has appreciated?

Mr. ROTHWELL. As measured by the average values of commodities. It is true that this is a very complicated question, for the values of commodities depend largely upon other things as well. But statisticians who have tabulated these matters have come to that conclusion. Take our own Aldrich report, and you will see in that the average values of commodities. Take the Sauerbach's Index of Values Abroad, and you will find that there has been a steady appreciation in the value of gold; that it has bought more and more of everything. Take the value of the amount of reduction in cost, and there still remains a quantity which is attributed to appreciation in gold. The fact that people can get more for their gold is, I assume, the principal reason why people have gone into the business of gold mining more than they did sometime ago.

Mr. SPERRY. What period of time would you put as the time in which gold has appreciated?

Mr. ROTHWELL. As a commencement of this appreciation?

Mr. SPERRY. Yes.

Mr. ROTHWELL. It has been going on for some years. It has been going on since the curtailment of the use of silver as money of equal redemption. The demand for silver has declined since 1872 or thereabouts—since the Germans began to unload their silver. That has lessened the demand for silver, and increased the demand for gold.

Mr. SPERRY. Do you understand that wages, for instance, have declined since?

Mr. ROTHWELL. No; they have increased. They are an exception to to all the other commodities.

Mr. SPERRY. Then, in exchange for labor, gold has depreciated, has it not?

Mr. ROTHWELL. Yes, as to labor. Labor is not the only one, but it is almost the only one, of a very long list of commodities.

Mr. SPERRY. Are there any articles in the line which you have in your mind, the reduced price of which could not be sufficiently accounted for by other things than by the appreciation of gold?

Mr. ROTHWELL. Yes; articles of manufacture—all kinds of manufacture. They have pretty generally gone down.

Mr. SPERRY. As processes of production have cheapened?

Mr. ROTHWELL. Yes.

Mr. SPERRY. Does that account, in your judgment, for the depreciation?

Mr. ROTHWELL. No; the improvement in manufacture and the lessened cost to them would account for part of the depreciation in the gold value of the commodities, but not for all.

Mr. SPERRY. Take our great staples, cotton and wheat. Do you regard the price of them as due to the appreciation in the value of gold?

Mr. ROTHWELL. No; I do not. It is very possible that the appreciation in gold has its part in it, but the improvement in the means of transportation have had more to do with it than anything else.

Mr. SPERRY. Take cotton, for instance, which, I suppose, during the last three or four years has fallen perhaps 25 per cent in value, and even more than that.

Mr. ROTHWELL. Yes.

Mr. SPERRY. Do you imagine that gold has appreciated 25 per cent in the last ten years?

Mr. ROTHWELL. No; I do not for a moment suppose that the appreciation of gold measures the value of the depreciation of any kind of commodities.

Mr. SPERRY. If gold, in your judgment, has appreciated in value, how do you account for the fact that the earning capacity of gold, measured by interest, has depreciated, so to speak? A gold loan would be perhaps much cheaper than ever before. If gold has appreciated, how is it that its earning capacity has depreciated?

Mr. ROTHWELL. Under uniform conditions, not always clear, the question of outside conditions comes in there, just as it does in the value of commodities.

Mr. SPERRY. But if you confine your thought to gold alone in a series of years, I can not imagine any outside conditions that enter into the question. Take all the loans of different nations of twenty years past, and the earning capacity of gold has been declining, has it not?

Mr. ROTHWELL. That has been largely due to the greater stability of Governments and the more certainty there is in their repaying their loans.

Mr. SPERRY. I mean the interest-earning capacity.

Mr. ROTHWELL. The interest is lessening, because you have a greater certainty of getting your money back than you formerly had.

Mr. WARNER. And there is less insurance?

Mr. ROTHWELL. Yes. When you tabulate a whole series of articles you will find, after making proper allowance for all the elements, so far as we can measure them, that there still remains a certain amount of depreciation in the value of other things that is due to appreciation in gold; at least we know no other reason; and the practical proof of it is that everybody is going into gold mining. Why? Not, certainly, because gold is not worth any more than it was, but because it pays them better to go into it. It is worth more. You can buy more with it.

Mr. SPERRY. That has occurred within the last year, I suppose?

Mr. ROTHWELL. No; it has been going on for a great many years. The increase of investment and the increase in output have been going on for a number of years, but the increase of investment and searching for mines has been going on. Take the great house of the Rothschilds; for years they have been investing in gold mines, but they do not invest in silver mines.

Mr. SPERRY. If gold is appreciating and growing scarce, relative to the demand——

Mr. ROTHWELL. It is growing relatively scarcer, but the output is increasing from year to year, and therefore it is absolutely increasing in quantity. But it is, relatively, compared with the duty that is put upon it, decreasing.

Mr. SPERRY. Still it is so abundant, relatively, that it can be borrowed now cheaper than ever before, and it is more freely offered to borrowers.

Mr. ROTHWELL. No, you have to give a proper factor due to increased civilization and probity in that. Those are elements in the value of the rate of interest.

Mr. SPERRY. Now, another suggestion you made was that you think gold is not sufficient in quantity to meet the exchanges of the world; is that correct?

Mr. ROTHWELL. That it is not alone sufficient to meet the demand; that there is a greater demand than there is a supply?

Mr. SPERRY. Regarded as a single money metal there is not a sufficient amount necessary for the purposes of money?

Mr. ROTHWELL. You could, perhaps, get along without any gold at all, if you had the machinery arranged for that; but at the present time the demand for gold is greater than its supply.

Mr. SPERRY. Do you mean by that that the gold is so scarce that the Government can not afford to redeem the greenbacks with gold at the present time?

Mr. ROTHWELL. I think if you ask for $400,000,000 that is necessary for putting away $150,·00,000, the security for this issue that they are proposing, I feel very certain that the price of gold would go up and the prices of eveything else would come down.

Mr. SPERRY. Would you have all paper money redeemed by the Government all at once, in one day?

Mr. ROTHWLLL. I say if you wanted to redeem it in gold now?

Mr. SPERRY. That is, all in one day, when they will have to have three or four hundred millions to do it.

Mr. ROTHWELL. Yes; and that demand would enormously increase the profits of gold.

Mr. SPERRY. It has been suggested by one of the witnesses that $10,000 of greenbacks will take $100,000 of gold out of the Treasury. Now, would not that same process result in gold being in the condition that, if the Government redeems the $10,000 of greenbacks and puts out gold, in a short time the Government will receive that gold back again through the custom-house, and will have it in hand to redeem another $10,000 with?

Mr. ROTHWELL. I do not understand your question.

Mr. SPERRY. The Government receives dues through the custom-house?

Mr. ROTHWELL. Yes.

Mr. SPERRY. If, in the redemption of these greenbacks, it reduces the redundancy of paper currency, it again receives the gold the same as before?

Mr. ROTHWELL. Certainly; it will just as soon as it reaches that point where there is no redundancy; where there is a demand for the paper that is true; but I say, assuming that the banks put out an amount equal to the Government issues, and that there was no demand for that amount, or for almost that, the Government issues would come back.

Mr. SPERRY. Are you assuming that the bank issues would be receivable at the Treasury for customs?

Mr. ROTHWELL. No; I think it would be to the interest of the banks to put the Government paper in through the custom-house and have it redeemed.

Mr. SPERRY. The Government receives, perhaps, $200,000,000 a year through the custom-house, and you gave figures for the year 1889, I think, of 85 per cent as being received in gold.

Mr. ROTHWELL. Yes.

Mr. SPERRY. Now, If you could place our monetary situation in the position in which it was in 1889, the Government would receive $85,000,000 a year in gold?

Mr. ROTHWELL. Yes.

Mr. SPERRY. And, if it had that much surplus, it could redeem $85,000,000 of greenbacks every year?

Mr. ROTHWELL. If it had that surplus; yes.

Mr. SPERRY. So that it would not require very much actual gold to redeem the paper money, would it?

Mr. ROTHWELL. If you always had a surplus; but the point is that it does not ever keep enough to make these redemptions; it is just the other way.

Mr. SPERRY. The quantity of gold, I mean, depends more upon the reserves in the Treasury, does it not, than it does upon the outstanding paper currency?

Mr. ROTHWELL. I beg pardon.

Mr. SPERRY. The amount of gold depends more upon the surplus in the Treasury than it does upon the actual amount of paper outstanding?

Mr. ROTHWELL. I assume that if there is a superabundance of paper outstanding the Government will not have a surplus of gold in the Treasury, but with paper one could secure gold until there is no superabundance of paper.

Mr. SPERRY. But when you stated that there is a scarcity of gold you seem to carry to the committee the idea that the Government could not redeem its outstanding circulation because of the scarcity of gold; that, perhaps, $400,000,000 would be required.

Mr. ROTHWELL. Yes, if it had to do it at first.

Mr. SPERRY. Is not this true: That the Government could redeem on a very small amount of gold, carrying the redemption over a period of two or three years, provided the custom-house receipts were paid in gold instead of paper?

Mr. ROTHWELL. And that they exceeded its requirements?

Mr. SPERRY. Exactly.

Mr. ROTHWELL. Certainly; but those are conditions that do not exist with a redundant currency.

Mr. SPERRY. Those were the conditions that existed in 1889, according to your testimony.

Mr. WARNER. Was the currency redundant in 1889?

Mr. ROTHWELL. No; it did not become redundant until 1890—until after the operation of the Sherman Act.

Mr. SPERRY. When did the scarcity of gold become apparent?

Mr. ROTHWELL. In 1891. The receipts through the custom-house began to be made in paper, in Sherman bills, not in gold; then it ran down from 80 or 90 per cent to 12 per cent.

Mr. SPERRY. Your view is that gold became scarce in 1890; is that correct?

Mr. ROTHWELL. In the custom-house, yes.

Mr. SPERRY. I was speaking of the scarcity of gold as a general proposition.

Mr. ROTHWELL. No; it was elsewhere, but the people will always give the money that they think is of the least value, and they were afraid that the paper money out would be redeemed in silver, and so they preferred to keep gold and pay in paper money.

Mr. COX. I want to come back to the proposition about banking. Your argument against the Secretary's bill I should like to have in a nutshell, if I can get it. As I understand it, your theory or reasoning is that it puts out more paper money?

Mr. ROTHWELL. Assuming that the banks make their issues.

Mr. COX. It puts out more money. Assuming that it is taken out under the plan suggested, then you come to the conclusion that if the banks have not taken out that additional money they will have more paper money than they can use. Then they take the legal-tender notes and convert them into gold to hold. Is that the theory?

Mr. ROTHWELL. They will return the legal-tender notes to the Treasury, and they will circulate their own notes instead.

Mr. COX. The idea is to return the legal-tender notes and get rid of them, to make a place to get out their own?

Mr. ROTHWELL. Yes; otherwise they can make no money.

Mr. COX. In that view of the case, you think, by returning the legal-tender notes, so as to make a place for their own, it will increase the demand on the Treasury for gold?

Mr. ROTHWELL. Exactly.

Mr. COX. That is the idea?

Mr. ROTHWELL. That is it exactly.

Mr. Johnson, of Indiana, moved that to-morrow (Friday) evening, December 14, at 7.30 o'clock, the committee meet in executive session.

Mr. Russell moved to amend by making it Saturday evening instead of Friday.

Mr. Cox accepted the amendment.

The motion as amended was agreed to.

Thereupon, at 4.52 o'clock p. m., the committee adjourned until 10 o'clock to-morrow morning.

COMMITTEE ON BANKING AND CURRENCY,
Friday, December 14, 1894.

The Committee met at 10 a. m.

Present: The chairman (Mr. Springer) and Messrs. Sperry, Cox, Cobb of Missouri, Culberson, Ellis, Cobb of Alabama, Warner, Johnson of Ohio, Black, Hall, Walker, Brosius, Henderson, Russell, Haugen, and Johnson of Indiana.

The roll was called.

The CHAIRMAN. Mr. Pratt, of Baltimore, who was expected——

Mr. WALKER. Before Mr. Pratt comes before us I wish to have the record of the last meeting read; I mean of the meeting last evening. I was absent, but I understand that the committee held a meeting after the hearing adjourned; that there was a meeting of the Banking and Currency Committee and some action was taken. I get from the Post of this morning the following:

> The programme of the committee was decided upon at an executive session held after the hearing had been concluded. The Democratic members will meet to-night to discuss the reporting of the Carlisle bill, and it is expected that the measure will be agreed upon in its entirety. This action will be reported to a meeting of the full committee, to be held to-morrow evening, and then the bill will be submitted to the House on Monday. The Republicans have been notified to prepare their minority report by that time.

Now, I would like the record read which shows that.

The CHAIRMAN. The Chair will state what occurred.

Mr. WALKER. I prefer to have it from the record, if the committee has taken any action.

The CHAIRMAN. The record is upstairs, but I will state what it was.

Mr. WALKER. Very well.

The CHAIRMAN. A motion was made that the committee meet in executive session to-morrow night, Saturday night, at half-past 7 o'clock, and I gave notice to the minority members that the Democratic members would meet at half-past 7 in this room for consultation. That was all that was done.

Mr. COX. I want to get this exactly right. I made a motion that we meet at half past 7 and proceed with this matter to-morrow night; thereupon the gentleman from Connecticut (Mr. Russell) moved that the regular meeting of the committee be on Saturday night at half-past 7, skipping over to-night.

Mr. WALKER. Then your motion was for to-night?

Mr. COX. Yes, sir; it was that we should meet night after night, and Sunday, too, if necessary. That motion was made by Mr. Russell, and thereupon the chairman, after the committee was discharged, requested the Democratic members to meet here.

Mr. WALKER. Do you mean to say there was no vote taken?

Mr. COX. No; that was a caucus, or you may call it what you please. Mr. Johnson was here, and we tried to get him to come in to-night with your folks, and he said no, and then I said we would meet to-night.

The CHAIRMAN. The only action of the committee is that there would be an executive session to-morrow night.

Mr. JOHNSON, of Indiana. That grew out of the fact that you gentlemen had agreed in your minds what to do and our presence here would not have helped the thing any.

Mr. COX. I will say I did not name it to a single gentleman on the committee until I made the motion.

Mr. JOHNSON, of Indiana. I simply suggested that that would accelerate the thing on Saturday night, as the majority would be prepared to report to the full committee.

Mr. COX. I hope the gentleman is correct, and we will be able to agree.

Mr. WALKER. I want to move that that vote passed be reconsidered.

Mr. COX. I raise the point of order on that. There is no notice of it at all.

Mr. WALKER. But it is open to reconsideration. I ask the Chair if I am in order?

The CHAIRMAN. You are in order. The gentleman was not present to vote upon the subject and has voted neither way, but we will waive that.

Mr. WALKER. I believe that if I did not vote in the affirmative I have the right to make the motion. I want to say that this committee has been in session for eight or ten months. The exigencies to-day are not increased one iota from what they have been every day during the eight months. In fact, the situation is not as serious to-day, for we have over $100,000,000 in the reserve fund in the Treasury.

The Secretary has testified that the bill will not practically affect the Treasury Department of this Government for five years, and may not for twenty, and now this haste in action upon a bill reported here by the Secretary, which, upon his own testimony, he had spent no time in preparing or considering, I mean the actual drafting of the bill, saying that he had dictated a part of it to his stenographer the morning he came here, and it was handed in to us afterwards as a bill that ought to be most thoroughly and seriously considered; and I submit that this committee, if it proposes to report a bill to the House on as great a matter as this, such a bill ought to be one that can be enacted as it is reported, and we have no right to report a bill that we ourselves think should be amended in any respect.

It ought to be complete. That is what this committee is for—to draw a complete bill, and draw it as carefully as possible, and have it as complete as possible, and it can not be done in less than a week. I submit that there is not a man living in this country, I care not who or where he is, who can start originally, as the Secretary of the Treasury testified here he started, and draw a bill under the present circumstances and conditions of the finances of the Treasury and the currency of the country, and draw it in a week, so it is fit even to present to this committee so that the members of this committee can take it up and perfect it. I am not going to talk against time, or endeavor to cause any delay. I lay the whole case——

Mr. COX. I want to call your mind to the proposition that there is no information that I know anything of—I mean such as comes officially from the committee—as to what will be done with the bill.

Mr. WALKER. I will get to that in a moment. I wish to call the attention of the Chair to a point, and then I am done. I shall not detain the committee, or interfere with it or obstruct it, or talk against time, or anything else. I say that the committee ought to enter upon the consideration of any bill whatever without any limit as to time, and proceed as rapidly as they well can and perfect it: and when it is perfected, which will take over a week, or, as every gentleman on this committee knows, however seriously and expeditiously we may determine to act, that it is not becoming, that it does not compliment the legislators, it does not compliment Congress, of which we are a part, to have this undue and unseemly haste.

The CHAIRMAN. The question is upon the motion of the gentleman from Massachusetts to reconsider the vote by which the committee determined to have an executive session to-morrow night.

Mr. WALKER. I ask that the vote be taken by names.

The roll was called and there were—yeas, 3; noes, 7.

So the motion was not carried.

Mr. JOHNSON, of Indiana. I want to say right here, so there will not be any misunderstanding in regard to this matter, that the suggestion made by myself last evening, that the majority of the committee should meet on Friday night, and that if they desired after that we should have a general meeting on Saturday night, at which we should consider such a plan as they might agree upon, was predicated, as I stated then, upon what I saw to be the very great desire for haste upon the part of the majority of the committee, and upon the theory that I supposed, from what I had seen and heard, they had virtually agreed in their own minds upon a bill, and probably would be disposed to report it on Saturday night if they had a meeting on Friday night. In other words, I was not hastening the consideration of this bill. I was simply submitting to a necessity. It is my own opinion these hearings should be continued still longer and this subject should be considered carefully. I think it is a great mistake to report in this way, and I do not want to be put in the attitude of accelerating the hearing.

The CHAIRMAN. The Chair desires to state that Mr. Enoch Pratt, who is a gentleman of some years, was invited to be here this morning, but has not appeared before the committee, and the Hon. A. J. Warner, of Ohio, addressed a letter to the chairman, in which he requested the privilege of appearing before the committee as a representative of the American Bimetallic League, to enter his objections against the passage of any of the proposed bills. Mr. Warner is now present, and if it is the pleasure of the committee I will introduce him at this time. If there be no objection, Mr. Warner will take the stand.

Mr. WARNER, of New York. Before Mr. Warner, of Ohio, takes the stand, in behalf of my colleague, Mr. Tracey, I hand the chairman the following letter, which I suggest be made a part of our minutes:

NATIONAL COMMERCIAL BANK,
Albany, N. Y., December 8, 1894.

DEAR GENERAL TRACEY: Noting Mr. Carlisle's plan for national-bank notes, I desire to make a suggestion.

His plan limits the issue to a percentage on the capital stock, ignoring the surplus. My suggestion is, why not permit an issue upon the capital and surplus under certain conditions, as, for instance, that the bank should be restricted from disposing of its surplus while it had notes issued against it, thus making the surplus of the same value as the capital stock for this purpose.

If you could obtain Mr. Carlisle's attention I think this suggestion would be worthy of his consideration, and would secure the support of the strongest banks, which, of course, are those which have the largest surplus.

Yours, very truly,

ROBERT C. PRUYN, *President.*

Hon. CHARLES TRACEY,
House of Representatives, Washington, D. C.

The CHAIRMAN. I have also, if Mr. Warner will pardon me a moment, a communication from the Honorable Charles S. Fairchild, in which he states:

NEW YORK, *December 12, 1894.*

DEAR SIR: I telegraphed you to-day that I should not be able to meet your committee to-morrow.

I have been partially laid up with a cold for several days, and yesterday was kept in bed all day with it. In any event I should not be able to leave before the midnight train to-night, and as my cold still persists, I do not think it prudent to run the risk of exposure.

I thank you very much for the invitation, and greatly regret that I can not meet the committee.

I fear, however, that I could add nothing to what you already have heard which would be worth taking your time.

Very truly, yours, CHARLES S. FAIRCHILD.

Hon. WM. M. SPRINGER,
Chairman, etc., House of Representatives, Washington, D. C.

The CHAIRMAN. I have also a letter from the Honorable Henry W. Cannon, formerly Comptroller of the Currency, who was invited to appear before the committee, in which he says:

THE CHASE NATIONAL BANK,
New York, December 13, 1894.

DEAR SIR: Referring to your request of the 7th instant, asking me to appear before your committee to-day for the purpose of giving such information as I might be able to furnish in reference to banking and currency, and our telegraphic correspondence relating thereto, I regret to inform you that I now find it impossible to go to Washington either to-day or to-morrow, and inasmuch as I have no particular suggestions to make, I presume my presence will not be essential to the work of your committee.

I am, yours, very respectfully,

HENRY W. CANNON.

Hon. WILLIAM M. SPRINGER,
Chairman Committee on Banking and Currency, Washington, D. C.

The CHAIRMAN. I have also received a telegram from Mr. John R. Walsh, president of the Chicago National Bank, who was invited to appear before the committee, in which he states he had communicated his views on the subject to Comptroller Eckels, and requests that these be taken in lieu of his presence, as he is not able to appear at this time. This is a very short communication, and I will just ask that it be incorporated in the hearings.

CHICAGO, ILL., *December 10, 1894.*

Am much obliged for your suggestion, but it will be impossible for me to leave Chicago this week. You will find my views expressed in a letter to Comptroller Eckels, written a few [days] ago. May I ask you to be kind enough to look it over?

JOHN R. WALSH.

WM. M. SPRINGER,
House of Representatives, Washington, D. C.

NOVEMBER 17, 1894.

I am opposed to the so-called Baltimore plan for a new system of national currency, first, because it does not provide adequate security for the notes; second, because it throws on the Treasury of the United States the burden of redeeming notes of failed banks when the security for that purpose is insufficient; third, because I believe our people will never accept the notes of any bank not properly secured. This Baltimore plan is nothing but a revival of the old New York State safety-fund plan, a system which was abandoned long before the organization of any national banks. Without the assurance that the United States Treasury would redeem the notes of failed banks the proposed currency would not be taken at par in all sections of the country.

Notes of well-known banks in New York, Chicago, St. Louis, and other financial centers would be received, but the notes of small banks in the far West and out of the way places in the East would only be taken at a discount, thus restoring the old system of stump-tail currency. I do not see why the Treasury of the United States should guarantee the notes of any bank. It may be said that the Treasury would never be called upon to make this guarantee good. Possibly this might be true in prosperous times, but if the guarantee exists you may depend upon it that the amount of security provided to be used before the Treasury was called upon would be exhausted in hard times, thus making the Government practically a creditor of a lot of failed banks.

In my opinion the proper way to deal with the currency is for the Government to issue an irredeemable $2\frac{1}{2}$ per cent bond which could be made the basis of circulation for national banks up to the amount of their capital. As this currency is taken out the greenbacks could be withdrawn. This would put the Government out of the banking business at once and provide a currency that would be at par everywhere. I believe that the Government should fund all its obligations in bonds of the kind mentioned, but this is another question. You may depend on it that no matter what theorists tell you the so-called Baltimore plan will never pass Congress, and even if it should, it would not accomplish what its well-meaning friends have in view. It would not work.

Yours, truly,

JOHN R. WALSH.

Mr. JAMES H. ECKELS,
Comptroller of the Currency, Washington, D. C.

Mr. WARNER, of Ohio, will now make his statement before the committee.

STATEMENT OF MR. A. J. WARNER, OF OHIO.

Mr. WARNER said:

Mr. Chairman and gentlemen of the committee: A proposition like that now before this committee, which contemplates a radical change in the monetary system of the country, necessarily attracts a deep interest on the part of the whole people. I can not begin what I have to say in any better way than to read a single sentence from the speech of Sir Robert Peel, when he brought before Parliament the act of 1844. He said:

> There is no contract, public or private—no engagement, national or individual, which is unaffected by it. The enterprises of commerce, the profits of trade, the arrangements made in all the domestic relations of society, the wages of labor, pecuniary transactions of the highest amounts and of the lowest, the payment of the national debt, the provision for the national expenditure, the command which the coin of the smallest denomination has over the necessaries of life, are all affected by the decision to which we may come on that great question which I am about to submit to the consideration of the committee.

The act which Sir Robert Peel at that time presented to the Parliament of Great Britain was the celebrated act of 1844, the purpose of which was to separate the issue and regulation of currency from the business of banking, and to place the control over currency under one single department, to be regulated in accordance with established principles and subject in every particular to strict regulations of law. Mr. Chairman, probably no question in which the public is concerned ever underwent so thorough a discussion as this question of the regulation of currency, not only in this country, but particularly in Great Britain from 1810 down to 1857.

Every phase of the question was discussed over and over again. Parliamentary commission after commission was established to consider every proposition presented. First came the celebrated bullion report of 1810, then the report of the secret commission of 1819, then the commission of 1826, that of 1840, and finally of 1857, in which was summed up, in my judgment, the wisdom of the entire discussion, and to the discussion which then took place, so far as I know, nothing really has been added since that time. I believe that the general conclusions then reached have been accepted by all writers of distinction from that day down to this. Of course, they differ somewhat as to the proper methods of regulating the currency, but as to the principles then established I know of no disagreement among competent authorities, either on this side or on the other side of the ocean.

As members of the commission of 1857, besides Sir Robert Peel, then chancellor of the exchequer, there were such men as Disraeli, Gladstone, Sir James Graham, Sir James Willson, Mr. Wenglin, for forty or fifty years connected with the Bank of England, and a number of others scarcely less distinguished. There appeared before that commission such men as George Ward Norman, who was for thirty years governor or director of the Bank of England; John Stuart Mill, Lord Overstone, and others distinguished as great bankers and men of large experience in business.

In fact, the principles of currency regulation laid down in the report of 1840, have since been adopted in the main by every civilized nation on the earth, the United States being the only country now, as far as I know, among nations claiming to be enlightened that proposes to reverse the conclusion then arrived at, principles as well established in currency as the law of gravity in physics, and to return to a principle of regulation of currency that has been condemned by every writer of distinction for fifty years, as well as by the experience of every country that has tried it. The principle of regulation, as laid down by Sir Robert Peel on the recommendation of Lord Overstone, was that the currency, in order to maintain its value, must be made to vary, both as to time and amount, as a purely metallic currency would vary; that in no other way could it be kept at the same value as the standard.

In 1874 Germany adopted substantially the same principle with a modification which I think was a very great improvement. Under the act of 1875 of the Reichstag, the Imperial Bank of Germany was established and a unification of the currency undertaken by withdrawing the currency of the several states of the federation and substituting for it the currency of the Empire. By this law the Imperial Bank of Germany is permitted to issue a certain fixed amount of uncovered paper, just as the Bank of England was permitted to continue in circulation a certain fixed amount of notes without security, and so are the country banks, but that amount can not be increased as to the country banks, and only by the Bank of England by absorbing a part of the currency surrendered by the country banks.

The Bank of England is permitted to issue additional currency only upon the deposit in the issue department of coin or bullion for all the notes issued. That is the distinction between notes covered and notes uncovered. The Imperial Bank of Germany may issue notes in time of stress or panic in excess of the uncovered notes, upon condition of paying 5 per cent interest to the State. The purpose of that is to force the retirement of notes as soon as the exigency that called them out is over. For all notes issued beyond a fixed amount specified in the act coin or bullion must be deposited. That principle in the main governs all the countries of Europe.

The Bank of France, it is true, is governed somewhat differently, but it is a State institution with officers appointed by the Government, as is the Bank of Berlin, the chancellor of the exchequer being president of the bank. So that the issue and regulation of currency in all the countries of Europe is now made in accordance with certain fixed principles, and in that way, and in that way alone, can proper regulation of a note currency be secured. I believe this to be the united voice of all the economists and financial authorities of Europe. That in that way, and in that way alone, can the value of a note currency be maintained at all times at par with gold. The first objection, then, to this bill is that it departs entirely from that principle and that it establishes no certain principle of regulation whereby the value of the currency is to be secured.

Mr. COBB, of Missouri. What bill do you mean?

Mr. WARNER. I mean the bill submitted by the Secretary of the Treasury; and the same objection applies to the Baltimore plan, and every other plan which proposes to turn over the issuing and regulation of the money of the people to institutions organized for private gain. The primary object of the act of 1844, I say, was to separate the banking business from the duty of issuing and regulating currency, creating money, and on that question, after a discussion of fifty years, there was almost no division of opinion in England. The concurrent judgment of nearly everybody was that the business of banking is necessarily distinct and separate from that of currency creation, and that the two can not be blended without doing mischief. On that point I beg to quote from a few of the authorities of that day, and I will not take up much time in doing so, but I am sure it will not be without interest.

The one great question before the commission of 1857 was whether the right to issue circulating notes should be kept under the control of the Government, or whether the banks or the Bank of England should be permitted to issue notes to circulate as money.

On page 328 of this report Lord Overstone, who, as Samuel Jones Loyd, was one of the most distinguished and successful bankers and writers on the currency question, and, in fact, the real author of the act of 1844, was asked:

Do you consider the separation of the issue and the banking departments of the Bank of England to be founded upon the principle that the business of issue and the business of banking are in their nature distinct?—A. Undoubtedly; it is impossible to entertain any other view of the matter.

Further on in his testimony he says: "I certainly think it quite essential that the issue of paper money should be kept entirely separate and distinct from everything connected with the banking business. Again, on page 328: "The supply of the current coin—that is, the money of the realm—ought to be entirely separated from the banking business, which is simply trading in money, borrowing at a lower rate and lending at a higher rate. * * * Notes and certificates ought to be issued as the money, whether copper, silver, or gold is coined, under strict provisions of law, and by an authority, such as the mint, established by law and subject to strict regulations laid down in that law." And again: "The sole privilege of coining money, whether copper, silver, gold, or paper, ought to be vested in one institution, established for that exclusive purpose and subject to strict regulations of law; no share of such privilege ought to be conceded in any form to banks or to private individuals."

And again, on page 329, he says: "Perfect freedom of competition should be established in the business of banking, correctly understood, and effectually distinguished from the functions of coinage or from that of issuing paper tokens or representatives of coin—that is, bank notes, which, in fact, is coining under a form peculiarly susceptible of abuse—because the undue issue of paper notes is not restricted by that intrinsic value which effectually regulates the issue of metallic money." Lord Overstone then quotes from Daniel Webster, I think from his subtreasury speech of 1838, as follows: "The circulation of paper tends to displace coin; it may banish it altogether. At this very moment it has banished it." Asking the committee to mark well that fact, he says: "A distinct statement by so great an authority of that as Webster, that the coin of the United States had been banished entirely by paper money, by currency payable to the bearer on demand and issued in obedience to what was deemed to be the wants of the public." He continues then his quotation from Webster as follows:

If others may drive out the coin and fill the country with paper which does not represent coin, of what use is that exclusive power over coins and coinage which is given to Congress by the Constitution? Wherever paper is to circulate as subsidiary coin, or as performing in a greater or less degree the functions of coin, its regulation naturally belongs to the hands which hold the power over coinage. This is an admitted maxim by all writers; it has been admitted and acted upon on all necessary occasions by our own Government throughout its whole history.

He then quotes Took as saying, "the privilege of issuing paper money is a delegation of that which is universally considered as a privilege residing in the State."

Mr. George Ward Norman, so long connected with the Bank of England, referring in his testimony before the commission of 1857 to the bank act of 1844, said:

I conceive the ground of the act to have been that the issue of paper money is a perfectly distinct operation from the ordinary business of banking, and that you can not mix up together the issue of paper money and ordinary banking business without doing mischief.

Again, on the same page, 273, he says:

I consider bank notes as money, and I think that you do mischief when you place the issue of money in the hands of persons who carry on ordinary banking business. * * * I consider that the issue of money should be regulated by the State, and when the money is issued then that bankers should be allowed to deal with it as they pleased, * * * the principle of competition can not be introduced into the issue of paper money without doing mischief.

Again, on page 276, he says:

A bank has to deal with the money of the country which exists, but it has properly nothing to do with the issue of money.

Alexander Hamilton said, referring to the old State banks:

There is now no check to the creation of these money mints; anybody and everybody, with or without character, has a right to enter the field of competition. * * * The superintendence of a power of such immense and vital consequence to the integrity, stability, and permanent interests of the public as that of money-making ought not, in the very nature of its operation, to be legislatively lodged in the hands of individuals.

Mr. HENDERSON. Do you know when he said that?

Mr. WARNER. I think in 1839. It was immediately after the panic of 1837.

The value of no man's property, much less that of a community, should be placed at the capricious will of private cupidity and speculation.

I quote again from one of Webster's subtreasury speeches, in which he says:

Whenever paper is to circulate as subsidiary to coin or as performing in a greater or less degree the functions of coin, its regulation naturally belongs to the hands that held the power over the coinage.

Acting upon this principle, the business of banking and the creation of money are so distinct and separate in their nature that they can not be safely blended.

I say that all enlightened nations have abandoned the practice of turning over the issue and regulation of currency to an indefinite number of banks. It was stated yesterday before the committee that the three things necessary to a sound currency were, first, security; second, convertibility as a means of regulation, and third, elasticity. Now, I wish to refer to these three principles briefly in their order. First, security. One of the earliest Secretaries of the Treasury, Crawford, I think, and I have not had time to look that up, said that the security of final payment of notes was no such regulation of quantity as would secure stability in the value of the currency. That saying was quite extensively quoted in the British discussions on that question as being a clear statement of a perfectly sound doctrine.

Mr. Cobb, of Alabama. Please state that over again.

Mr. Warner. That the security of final payment of notes, or their redemption, is no such regulation of the quantity of money as will insure stability of value, and the reason for that is very apparent. The United States might now issue $500,000,000 of 5 per cent bonds, and if it would allow banks to take these bonds at par, is there any doubt but that the national banks would issue $500,000,000 of currency, or as much as they are allowed by law to issue? The ultimate payment of the notes would be amply secured—there would be no question about that, none whatever—but the quantity of the currency would be so increased that its value would become immediately depreciated.

At first the depreciation would extend not only to the paper part but to the coin as well, involving the entire currency of the country as compared with the currency of other countries; hence the principle of ultimate security was abandoned sixty years ago as a principle upon which the regulation of the currency could be safely founded. If security of note circulation is a safe principle, then security by a pledge of land ought to be as good as a pledge of bonds. John Law said: "Any goods that have the qualities necessary in money may be made money equal to their value."

Mirabeau said of the French assignats: "They represent real property, the most secure of all possessions, the land on which we tread." The fundamental error in this principle lies in the attempt to hold a thing as property and at the same time to coin it into money. At bottom the principle of basing the currency on bonds is just as vicious as basing it on land. There is no limit to the amount of bonds that may be issued any more than for the land that may be pledged, nor as much; but the principle itself is wrong for the reason that security of final payment affords no proper regulation of quantity upon which the value of each unit depends.

Richardo, in his evidence before the secret committee of the House of Commons in 1819, says:

Plans for an improved system of currency are frequently laid before the public, which rest entirely upon this fallacy. The exclusive object of these systems is to obtain for the paper currency to be issued under them a greater degree of security than that which is supposed to attach at present to the notes of the Bank of England. This end the authors of these schemes generally propose to accomplish by contrivances which they deem to be extremely ingenious, but which always resolve themselves into the simple plan of making property of some kind or other the basis of the circulation. Sometimes the plan suggested proposes to issue a paper currency against the security of land, sometimes against the security of the public debt, and sometimes against merchandise in the docks; but, having provided for the security of the notes, the plan generally terminates at this point: the projector apparently conceiving that he has satisfied all the desiderata of a good paper currency, although he has introduced no specific measure for regulating the amount of that currency and maintaining its value relatively to the currencies of the other countries of the world.

The second principle, as a means of regulation, is convertibility. In the bullion report of 1810 the doctrine seemed to be conceded that, if a currency was convertible—although the report stoutly contended against the doctrine that ultimate security was a safe principle at all times—that then it never could fall below the value of metallic money, or of the metallic standard; and that doctrine was held and acted upon, almost without dissent, I believe, until 1826. But the experience in England, after resumption in 1819, up to 1826, was such as to lead to a very careful reexamination of that principle, and although the directors of the Bank of England had, prior to that time, acted upon that principle and considered it perfectly safe, they were obliged, as Mr. Norman admitted, to abandon that principle.

It was during this period, from 1819 to 1826 and on to 1844, that the question underwent such a thorough discussion, when everything was thoroughly threshed out. Every suggestion and every claim was ground to powder and all errors sifted out and the truth finally established, and one of the conclusions reached was that even convertibility could be relied upon as a safe principle for the regulation of the amount of currency.

There were those even before 1826 who had opposed the doctrine that either security or convertibility could alone be relied upon to properly regulate the currency. Mr. Horner, in the Bullion Report of 1810, says:

An increase in the quantity of the local currency of a particular country, will raise prices in that country exactly in the same manner as an increase in the general supply of precious metals raises prices all over the world. By means of the increase of quantity the value of a given portion of that circulating medium in exchange for other commodities is lowered; in other words, the money prices of all other commodities are raised, and that of bullion with the rest. In this manner, an excess of the local currency of a particular country will occasion the rise of the market price of gold above its mint price. It is no less evident that, in the event of the prices of commodities being raised in one country by an augmentation of its circulating medium, while no similar augmentation in the circulating medium of a neighboring country has led to a similar rise of prices, the currencies of those two countries will no longer continue to bear the same relative value to each other as before. The intrinsic value of a given portion of the one currency being lessened, while that of the other remains unaltered, the exchange will be computed between those two countries to the disadvantage of the former.

Richardo says (see High Price of Bullion):

It would be readily admitted that whilst there is any great portion of coin circulation, every increase of bank notes, though it will for a short time lower the value of the whole currency, paper as well as gold, yet that such depression will not be permanent, because the redundant and cheap currency will lower the exchange, and will occasion the exportation of a portion of the coin, which will cease as soon as the remainder of the currency shall have regained its value and restored the exchange to par.

Webster said, in his speech on the subtreasury bill, March, 1838:

I contend even that convertibility, though itself indispensible, is not a certain and unfailing ground of reliance. There is a liability to excessive issues of paper, even while paper is convertible at will; of this there can be no doubt. Where, then, shall a regulator be found? What principle of prevention may we rely upon?

J. R. McCullough says:

When the currency of any particular country, as of England, consists partly of the precious metals and partly of paper converted into them * * * the excess of paper is not indicated by depreciation or fall in the value of paper, as compared with gold, but by a depreciation of value in the whole currency, gold as well as paper, as compared with other States.

Lord Overstone said, in his testimony before the commission of 1875, page 408:

Convertible notes may be issued, continually depreciating the currency, until the metallic portion of the currency has been entirely banished from the country.

On the following page he says:

The changes in the amount and value of the paper currency of the United States have been greater than in any other country, and it has produced an unprecedented amount of bankruptcy and ruin.

And again, page 41, he says:

It is undoubtedly true that convertibility is an ultimate security against a permanent excess of the currency, and fixes a limit beyond which such irregularity in its management can not be carried. But this principle only comes into operation through the medium of prices. If the currency be in excess, prices of all articles are affected in a corresponding degree; hence the balance of trade is disturbed, the exchanges are consequently affected, and a tendency is produced to export gold. * * * Convertibility will not by itself prove a sufficient protection against excess in a paper currency. The rule which requires that the amount of the circulation shall be made to vary with the amount of the bullion is of essential importance, and no system of paper currency can be secure which does not contain this as a self-rectifying principle.

And in his pamphlet on the management of the circulation previous to 1839, he says:

It is not sufficient merely to ordain, as Peel's bill did, the convertibility of the notes; it is further necessary to see that effectual means are provided for that end. It is now discovered that there is a liability to excessive issues of paper, even while that paper is convertible at will; and that to preserve the value of a paper circulation, not only must that paper be convertible into metallic money, but the whole of its oscillations must be made to correspond exactly, both in time and amount, with what would be the oscillations of a metallic currency, as indicated by the state of the bullion. Such a system, therefore, for the management of the circulation must be constructed as shall secure that due and steady regulation of the amount of the issues, through which alone any permanent security for their convertibility can be obtained.

The next principle is that of elasticity. They say we must have an elastic currency. The Secretary of the Treasury says:

A sound and elastic currency, capable of adjusting its volume easily and rapidly to the actual demands of legitimate business, is what the common interest of all our people requires.

I say to the Secretary of the Treasury that perpetual motion is a great deal easier to obtain than that kind of elasticity. It never did exist in the world and it never can. There is absolutely no such relation between the supply of paper money and the uses for money as admit of automatic regulation, and for a single reason. If paper money was issued only to meet the demands of business arising out of an increased number of transactions—that, is increased purchases and sales of goods—then such a principle might be possible; but the fact is the effect of an excessive currency is immediately to raise prices, and as prices rise the demand for money increases pari passu with the rise of prices, and when prices are doubled the demand for $2 in every transaction is just as great as the demand for $1 was before.

Mr. HALL. Does that principle apply to bank currency?

Mr. WARNER. Certainly, to bank currency as well as to any other, as I will show you a little further on; it applies to any currency that is issued in excess, I care not what kind of currency it is. It would apply to the precious metals if there was, at any time, such a production of the precious metals as would greatly increase the proportion of metallic money to commodities to be bought and sold or to be circulated by money, then the rise of prices that would follow would create an enlarged demand for money. Rising prices never take up and give back. They take up and hold. The experience of the whole world is against the idea that business takes up money and gives it back automatically.

Our experience under the old bank-note system is enough to set that at rest. One single fact is enough. Between 1830 and 1837 the notes of the banks of this country increased from $61,000,000 to $149,000,000, and then they went down until in 1843 there were only $53,000,000 of them. That was the way an elastic currency worked then, and it is the way it always worked. It is the way it worked in England when they had much more rigid restrictions than we have ever had in this country.

An elastic currency! It is a delusion. By what principle are banks governed, or will they be governed if we turn over to them the issue and regulation of the currency? I ask that question. Banks are institutions organized for private gains. They are controlled by one principle alone—their own interest. If they can derive a profit by putting out more currency, they will put it out. There is no limit to the quantity of money they would put out or that the country would take.

If you give to the national banks as now organized $1,000,000,000 of bonds at 5 per cent they would issue nine hundred millions of currency as fast as they could put it out, regardless of consequences. Simply because they could make money by putting it out. What did they do from 1864 to 1867 and 1868 and 1869, when there was already a full volume of other currency in the country. Prices were already inflated, but they kept on increasing the circulation. Why? Because it was to their interest to do it.

Now, I ask you gentlemen if the whole business of the world, or if the business interests of 70,000,000 of people in this country, the value of all their property, the wages of labor, the relation of property to debts, the prices of all products are to be subjected to the variations of a currency which may be increased or decreased as the interests of those engaged in the banking business may dictate.

It was admitted yesterday—and it was admitted by the Comptroller of the Currency and by the Secretary of the Treasury, which, to use a slang phrase, was a dead give away of everything—that the reason why the banks contracted currency was that it was to their interest to do so. That is, they contracted it when it was their interest to do so and expanded it when it was their interest to expand it. But what was the interest of the great majority of the people or of the business men of the country? You have only to make it to their interest and you can have as large a volume of money as you want.

Make it their interest to contract and they will contract it. But what a principle of regulation of that which determines the prices of all commodities and the value in money of everything!

On this question of elasticity let me read from the bullion report.

Mr. HALL. What bullion report?

Mr. WARNER. Of 1810, the Horner report, the famous bullion report.

As far back as the Bullion Report of 1810, Mr. Whitmore, then late governor of the Bank of England, stated the rule of the bank then to be "to govern its issues by the amounts of good paper offered for discount, on the principle that the public will never call for more than is absolutely necessary for their wants." This is what the Secretary of the Treasury seems now to think a safe principle; that is, business will not call for any more money than it wants, and banks will not put out any more than business calls for. But, referring to this principle, the Bullion Report says:

That this doctrine is a very fallacious one your, committee can not entertain a doubt. The fallacy upon which it is founded lies in not distinguishing between an advance of capital to merchants and an additional supply of currency to the general mass of circulating medium. (Bullion Report, p. 55.)

Lord Overstone, in his testimony before the commission of 1857, says, page 364, "the public will call for and take money to any extent"—there is no fear of that; and again, on page 365:

I have no hesitation in saying that the Bank of England can put out any quantity of its notes that it thinks proper; that the effects of that will be to drive gold out of the country; that the notes will take the place of gold in the circulation, and that will go on until the whole of the gold has been driven out of the country.

Sir Charles Wood said, discussing the act of 1844:

It was held in the bank parlor, as it is by many even now, that to issue paper on good commercial security was all that was necessary to insure the proper amount of paper being in circulation.

That idea, however, long ago was abandoned in England, but it seems ill to hold a place in this country.

Mr. WARNER. As Mr. Weguelin said, the wealth of the world is offered against money. A distinction must be drawn between borrowing money and buying money. Money on the one hand stands offered against everything, and everything on the other hand stands offered against money. Money will go out and continue to go out as prices rise, and as prices rise and confidence increases the demand for money increases and there is no principle of elasticity which operates until the point of explosion is reached. This is reached when gold begins to go out, or so much of it goes that confidence is destroyed; then panic follows and there must be a contraction all along the line. It is a contraction, however, after the explosion, and that is the way such a currency is regulated and always has been.

The experience of every country, I think, has been the same; that is, first an expansion, then a sudden, violent, and ruinous contraction. That is the necessary consequence of a currency the issue of which is left to the discretion of those issuing it or to their interest. It was shown in report of 1857 of the commission that even the 205 country banks of England could not be intrusted with the responsibility of issuing circulating notes. Sir Robert Peel said on that point:

It appears to me that we have, from reasoning, from experience, from the admissions made by the issuers of paper money, abundant ground for the conclusion that under a system of unlimited competition, although it be controlled by convertibility into coin, there is not an adequate security against the excessive issue of promissory notes.

Now, unless the issuers of paper conform to certain principles, unless they vigilantly observe the causes of influx or efflux and regulate their issues of paper accordingly, there is danger that the value of the paper will not correspond with the value of the coin. The difference may not be immediately perceived, nay, the first effect of underissue, by increasing prices, may be to encourage further issue, and as each issuer, where there is unlimited competition, feels the inutility of individual efforts of contraction, the evil proceeds until the disparity between gold and paper becomes manifest, confidence in the paper is shaken, and it becomes necessary to restore its value by sudden and violent reduction in its amount, spreading ruin among the issuers of the paper, and deranging the whole monetary transactions of the country.

If we admit the principle of a metallic standard and admit that the paper currency ought to be regulated by immediate reference to the foreign exchanges—that there ought to be early contractions of paper on the efflux of gold—we might, I think, infer from reasoning, without the aid of experience, that an unlimited competition in respect to issue will not afford a security for the proper regulation of the paper currency.

He then quotes what Mr. Hobhouse said when asked, "With the rise of prices would there be an increased paper issue by country bankers?"

He answered, "Yes; there will be an increase in the local circulation when prices rise."

Again he was asked, "Does it not often happen that your circulation is increased in the beginning of a drain of gold?" and he answered, "Yes; we do not pretend that our circulation is at all governed by it."

Now, take the ten thousand banks in the United States, and delegate the power to all of them to issue notes, and entrust to them the duty of regulating the currency of the country. What will be the result? When will they begin contracting? Not until the issue of money ceases to be profitable to themselves. The drain of gold will fall first, of course, upon the banks of the seaboard, the great cities. They may check their issues, but the country banks will pay no attention to that. Inflation will go on long after the gold begins to leave the country. Why, the idea of maintaining a gold standard under a system of currency of that kind is so at variance, not only with the experience of every nation in the world but of reason, that I am astonished that such a proposition as this should be brought forward at all.

Gentlemen, there is only one way to maintain the gold standard in the United States in my judgment, absolutely but one, and that is to restrict the circulation, reduce bank credits, bring down prices until our creditors abroad will choose to take of us commodities rather than gold for what we owe them. There is no other way. We are a debtor nation, and no debtor nation can maintain as large a volume of currency as a creditor country. Our people owe the people of other countries not less than $250,000,000 a year, certainly not less than that, annually. This must be paid in gold or commodities. It can be paid in commodities on one condition only, and that is that we will sell commodities as low as any other nation in the world, or sell them enough lower to induce our creditors to take of us goods and leave the gold here.

Now I say, gentlemen, that any measure which tends to raise prices in the United States will expel gold, I care not whether it be tariff or anything else. A tariff which operates to check imports may so far reduce the total sums to be liquidated abroad, but any tariff measure which raises prices will operate to expel gold. The expansion of the currency will have the same effect; we can not have currency expansion and a gold standard at the same time in this country. It is impossible. All this talk about a sound currency and an abundance of sound money is sheer nonsense. What is usually meant by sound money is dear money, and money can be made dear only by making it scarce, and, as Senator Jones says it is equivalent to saying they are in favor of scarce money, but plenty of it. The two things do not go together.

I make this exception, Mr. Chairman, to what I have said about the gold standard. Between 1879 (after specie resumption in this country) and 1892 we increased our indebtedness abroad by more than $200,000,000 a year on the average. That is, we increased our debt 2,500 million in the short period of twelve years. Thus, instead of paying the interest on what we owed abroad, instead of paying balances with exports or with gold, we gave new notes; that is, we sold securities. We sold bonds of one kind and another. But in 1892 they stopped taking securities. We were enabled during that period to maintain a higher level of prices in the United States than the level of other countries.

When our creditors stopped taking securities then the demand for gold came. Now, if the Government will issue $250,000,000 of bonds a year for the next five or ten years, undoubtedly we can pay our interest with new bonds—that is, give new notes for it—and then we can expand the currency, or we can by tariff legislation raise prices and still save our gold, but the end of that policy, of course, is national bankruptcy and ruin. It is the policy of "after us the deluge." But there is no way by which we can maintain the gold standard here but by restricting the currency, and not expanding it. We can not at the same time narrow the foundation of primary money, standard money, and then increase the superstructure of credit upon it and make it safe or secure. That is impossible. Our currency must be regulated with reference to the foreign exchanges, with reference to maintaining an equilibrium of prices between this and other countries, if we would maintain the single gold standard. I submit there is no answer to that proposition.

I beg to refer in this connection to the question of deposits and the extent of inflation possible under the proposed bill. Now, paper currency is not the only means by which prices may be raised, or by which we may have inflation. Indeed, the greatest inflation comes through bank credits—bank credits under the name of deposits. The report of the Comptroller of the Currency shows that the total deposits of all the banks reporting for October 2, 1894, was, in round numbers, $4,700,000,000 and some odd. Now, what does that represent? Why, it represents really a form of currency, but, instead of being represented by notes, it is a credit on the books of the banks against which the depositor can check.

The old way, when banks were first started, and before this modern system of bank credits was known, and when banks had the right to issue notes, if one borrowed a thousand dollars from a bank and gave his note for it the bank would issue to him its own notes, and he would take them and use them. The only inflation then, if there was any, was simply the notes of the bank. Now the bank gives the borrower a credit on his book and on the bank's books of a thousand dollars, which is called a deposit, although not a dollar has been placed in the bank by the borrower. The borrower then issues his own check on that. That credit has the same effect, so far as it goes, of so much currency.

Let me group this together and state it, as I think I can, in a way by which my meaning may be easily understood. We have in the United States, say, sixteen hundred millions of currency, gold, silver, and paper. Now, that is divided in this way: A little over a thousand millions are in the tills of merchants and in the hands of the people doing the every-day work of retail trade, paying the wages of labor, carrying on all the smaller transactions of the country. It is at work every day in the week; it is never idle. Five hundred and fifty millions of that volume of money is in the banks, taking all the banks of the United States.

Now, upon that $550,000,000 as a basis, the banks have erected a superstructure of bank credits of four thousand seven hundred millions, but not quite all of that is subject to check. Some of it is only subject to check on notice, but that is the total. This five hundred and fifty millions has been thus expanded into four thousand seven hundred millions. Now deduct from the four thousand seven hundred millions the five hundred and fifty millions, and in round numbers we have four thousand millions of bank credits, and some over $1,000,000,000 in the hands of the people. Now I submit it is through these two agencies, the money in the hands of the people and this credit currency in the bank, that all the transactions of every nature and of every description are carried on. Everything is liquidated by means of the one or the other of these two forms of currency, and the claim that 90 or 95 per cent of all business is done on credit, or by credit instruments, is a fallacy. It is all done out of this volume of currency and bank credits, the proportion being about four to one. The efficiency, however, is not as four to one.

The efficiency of the actual money is at any rate twice that of the bank deposits; but it is right there, in the expansion of bank credits under the name of deposits, that every panic that has ever taken place in this country originated. That is the storm center. Now, in the panic of 1893, there were $500,000,000 in the banks and four thousand millions of credits. Those who had in the banks the $500,000,000 of actual money became alarmed, but the other people who had deposits there did not become alarmed. They owed the banks, and they did not get alarmed by the panic. If they were alarmed it was because they were fearful they would be called upon to pay before they wanted to pay. Those who had actual money in the banks became alarmed, and began to draw it out. When they drew out about half of it, as they did, then this volume of credit currency must be reduced, in one way or the other, or the proportion between the money and the pure credit would be destroyed. The credit could not be reduced to that extent at once, of course.

Suppose that the $500,000,000 of currency had all been drawn out of the banks. Then, for the time being, this credit currency would have been absolutely extinguished, and in some places it was, pretty nearly. That is where the contraction and expansion come in. There is the elasticity of credit, and that is the thing which is dangerous, and it is not easily controlled. Now, add to that the increase of bank paper, and let me show here how much it can increase. Under the bill before the committee or under the proposition before the committee, the banks may issue up to 75 per cent of their capital, but as effective circulation this volume will be reduced by a reserve deposit of 30 per cent, leaving the effective per cent of capital in the form of currency 52½ per cent. That is, the real limit to bank currency is 52½ per cent of the capital. The plan of the Comptroller provides for 50 per cent, so that so far they practically agree. The capital of all the banks that may now issue currency is $1,060,000,000. Upon this $795,000,000 may be issued under existing law by the banks already in existence. From 15 to 25 per cent must now be held as reserves against deposits and 5 per cent against circulation.

Under the proposed law no reserves are required against deposits; only 30 per cent against circulation. Assuming that the proposed law will require a reserve altogether of 10 per cent more than is required under the present system against circulation and deposits, and it will cut down the volume of effective bank currency under the proposed law, say, to $715,000,000. If from this amount the present national-bank currency of $171,000,000 be deducted it leaves $544,000,000 as the possible inflation of the currency by existing banks, with no limit to the increase in the number of banks nor in the capital of existing banks.

It will be seen that the proportion of bank credits to reserves of actual money is more than 6 to 1 and it often rises much above that proportion. Should as large a part of the new currency go into banks to be made the basis of bank credits it would increase this fund by $200,000,000, upon which a superstructure of bank credits of $1,200,000,000 would in time be erected. Was ever a scheme so wild, uncertain, and unstable as this ever seriously proffered to a people before? Surely, there is nothing like it in the history of money. No land-money scheme, no bond-security scheme ever proposed came up to this scheme to coin credit into money.

Compare this with the restriction system of England, Germany, and other European countries. What other country would even for a moment entertain a proposition to turn over the issue and regulation of currency to 10,000 banks? Indeed, it is a proposition too monstrous for anybody to consider and maintain mental equanimity. If the author of this scheme had ever read the discussion on the subject of the regulation of currency which took place from 1810 to 1857 in England, or if he had ever read the Report of the Parliamentary Commission of 1857 he would never have connected his name with a scheme that can be compared with no other ever proposed, except that once undertaken by John Low.

Any proposition that turns over the regulation of currency to institutions organized for private gain is at bottom wrong. Unless it is to their interest to furnish the business world with money they will not do it, and the business world must suffer the consequences. There is the fatal defect in this proposition, and which in my judgment is enough to condemn it utterly.

Mr. Chairman, I will not take up the time of the committee any longer, but will simply say I am very much obliged to you, and that I would like to add to my statement a few quotations which I have not had time to read.

Mr. COBB, of Alabama. Can you give us something as a substitute? You have been tearing down, but you are not building up anything?

Mr. WARNER. I would do this: I would do exactly as is recommended in the report of 1857. There is but one way by which the currency can be automatically regulated. The world has never found but one, and that is through the production of the metals. Subject the supply of money to the same laws that govern the supply of everything else. Then if the production of metallic money should be unduly increased, it would, of course, become depreciated, as would be made manifest by rise in prices; but the point would very soon be reached where it would be easier to obtain a dollar, or where a dollar could be obtained with less labor and energy by producing something else to exchange for it than digging it from the ground; then the production of the metals would in that way be checked. I say that is the only automatic way the world has ever devised or ever known for regulating money.

In addition to that, all money that supplements the metals should be rigidly limited to some proportion between population and business, the one purpose being to maintain stability—the greatest possible stability. Again, another objection to the kind of currency proposed in this bill is, that it is not a legal tender. All money ought to be a legal tender. If it pretends to be money, it should be money when you pay it out as well as when it is paid to you. Nothing should be allowed to circulate as money that is not money.

Mr. JOHNSON, of Indiana. Do you think it proper the money should be issued by the Government?

Mr. WARNER. Either by the Government or by an institution under the control of the Government, and the issue of currency should be in accordance with fixed principles, subject to rigid regulation of law, and not left to the discretion of anyone or made subject to the interests of any private parties.

Mr. JOHNSON, of Indiana. You do not favor a bank issue?

Mr. WARNER. I separate the bank business from issues. Issue of money is a separate and a distinct thing from banking.

Mr. ELLIS. Mr. Warner, you did not elaborate on a suggestion made during your remarks, and I will ask you now to give us your view as to how the currency can always be maintained at par with the metals, the precious metals?

Mr. WARNER. The old rule laid down by Albert Gallatin, and generally accepted in the discussions in England, was this: That a paper currency must not exceed what the volume of the metallic currency would be if there was no paper. That is the old principle, but I think that is too rigid. It does not take into account the existence of any other currency in the world but metallic money. That would be a strictly correct principle if the world's money everywhere else was limited to the precious metals except in the country issuing the paper.

But the true rule I believe to be this. It is admitted as a general principle, first, that if there was nothing but metallic money in the world, it would distribute itself among the different commercial nations, in proportion to their trade, under the circumstances under which trade is carried on in the various countries, each having what is called its distributive share, or what would fall to it as necessary to maintain an equilibrium in the general level of prices. Now, if a paper currency never exceeds this amount, it can not fall below the value of the metals.

The law of distribution of money is just as true, however, of money composed partly of coin and partly of paper, if the paper is convertible into coin. Then the world's supply of money of that kind will be distributed in the same way that a metallic currency would distribute itself, only that the metallic part would pass from country to country in the settlement of balances or in maintaining the general equilibrium of prices.

I believe it to be a thoroughly sound principle that if our paper money never exceeds our distributive share of the world's money (that is, never exceeds what is necessary to maintain a level of prices here at the international level of prices) it can not be depreciated. That is the doctrine of Ricardo and of economists generally, I believe.

If the paper money is any less than our distributive share the metals (gold now) will come here to supplement it. Therefore, in laying down the rule for the regulation of paper currency you must draw the line of uncovered issues of paper far enough within what would constitute our distributive share of the world's money to always require some part of the coin of the world to supplement it, in order to maintain a general level of prices.

That is the doctrine acted upon in the bank act of 1844. They drew the line at the lowest point which the currency of Great Britain had reached for a long time and took that as perfectly safe for uncovered issues.

Mr. ELLIS. You have expressed an opinion that the right to issue currency ought to be taken from the banks. What would you substitute in lieu of that?

Mr. A. J. WARNER. I would establish a department of issue to be under control of the Government absolutely, and conform the issue by that department to certain principles under established regulations of law—the principles to be laid down in the law.

Mr. ELLIS. Would you make that issue legal tender?

Mr. A. J. WARNER. Always. I would have nothing in circulation as money that was not legal tender.

Mr. ELLIS. How would you have them redeemed?

Mr. A. J. WARNER. If you will sufficiently limit the amount of the paper redemption is immaterial, because it never will fall below the coin level. In 1848 the Bank of France was permitted to issue 350,000,000 of francs in irredeemable notes. At first, but for a brief period, these notes did depreciate, but they immediately recovered and were never below par in coin afterwards.

Mr. ELLIS. You stated in your address to the committee that the national banks would, in your opinion, if bonds were issued and they were permitted to get currency on them, take out currency up to the full amount, and that they would flood the country with money. Explain why it is that, under the power they have had under the existing law, they have not availed themselves to the full extent, and have not issued the currency which they were entitled to issue?

Mr. A. J. WARNER. I stated that if they could get bonds bearing a rate of interest high enough to make it profitable for them to issue currency they would do it. And that is the reason why they did issue so rapidly early under the national banking act. It was because they could get bonds at par bearing 5 and 6 per cent interest, and then they put out the currency as fast as they could.

But now the bonds are at such a high premium and the interest so high that it is not profitable for the banks to issue currency. In other words, if you make it profitable for them they will put out all the currency they can get out, and there is no limit to that.

The CHAIRMAN. State why it is that those banks, which have already put up their bonds to a certain amount, have not taken out the full amount of the currency to which they are entitled. Banks, in organizing, are required to put up a certain amount of bonds. Why do they not issue currency to the full amount of these bonds?

Mr. A. J. WARNER. They do, generally, unless they are holding the bonds for some other purpose.

The CHAIRMAN. The bonds are in the Treasury of the United States.

Mr. A. J. WARNER. They perhaps prefer to hold the bonds where they can dispose of them.

The CHAIRMAN. The law requires them to keep them in the Treasury in order to maintain their organization.

Mr. ELLIS. Where the banks have put up the minimum of bonds they have not taken out the circulation to which they are entitled and which they can have without further expense to themselves. Why have they not taken out the circulation?

Mr. A. J. WARNER. I know of no reason why, except that they prefer to hold the bonds for immediate sale or for use in some other way.

Mr. ELLIS. They can not use them. They are in the Treasury.

Mr. A. J. WARNER. I can see no reason why they did not issue that amount of currency.

Mr. COX. These banks had to put up the bonds in the Treasury under their charter. They are generally 4 per cent bonds and the interest on them is paid quarterly. Does it not often occur that the bank realizes quite as much in taking its interest on those bonds without any risk as it would by taking out the currency?

Mr. A. J. WARNER. I did not understand at first just what bonds were referred to. At times like this when prices are falling and the rate of interest is very low and security is uncertain, there is no object in the banks taking out more currency, as they can not even lend the currency they have. Always at times when prices are falling it is unprofitable to invest money in property of any kind. It is more profitable to hold the money, because that is rising in value all the time, and the banks had better hold it in their vaults, had better bury it than to invest it in property which is going down.

Mr. COX. Is not that the same rule that applies when they are hoard ing gold?

Mr. A. J. WARNER. Precisely the same.

Mr. ELLIS. You have examined the Baltimore plan and the Secretary of the Treasury's plan; state whether if either of those plans were adopted it would increase the volume of currency in the country.

Mr. A. J. WARNER. I think either of them would increase the volume materially, after time enough had been given to let it get into full operation.

Mr. ELLIS. What would be the effect on agricultural products if that happened?

Mr. A. J. WARREN. There would be a general rise in prices, except in products which depend for their market mainly on foreign demand, such as cotton or wheat, the surplus of which goes abroad. These would be affected only to the extent that the entire currency of the country became depreciated under the influence of an augmentation of volume. Other things, however, pretty generally, such as lands, houses, and everything not exportable and not dependent on foreign demand or on gold prices abroad, would rise.

Mr. ELLIS. What would be the effect on the price of gold if either one of those systems were enacted into law?

Mr. A. J. WARNER. The first effect would be, as stated by Mr. McCulloch and by Ricardo, a depreciation of the entire circulation as compared with the currency of other countries. That would involve gold along with paper, as stated by Webster; and that would be manifested by a general rise of prices here.

But gold would immediately begin to go out; and from a debtor nation it would go out fast. As soon as gold goes abroad (whether drawn from the Treasury or drawn from the banks) confidence would be shaken in the stability of the currency, and undoubtedly after a time gold would go to a premium, and there would almost certainly be a rush and a panic right there.

The CHAIRMAN. Do we understand that you are of the opinion that the volume of money in any country regulates the prices of commodities in that country and fixes them?

Mr. A. J. WARNER. Always. The prices are determined by the proportion of commodities to things to be bought and sold.

The CHAIRMAN. What is the per capita circulation in France?

Mr. A. J. WARNER. About $42, I believe.

The CHAIRMAN. And what is it in England?

Mr. A. J. WARNER. From $18 to $22—dependent on the estimate of the coin in circulation, which is not acurately known.

The CHAIRMAN. Is there that disparity between prices in England and France?

Mr. A. J. WARNER. No, sir; there is not that disparity. Nevertheless, prices depend on the proportion of the volume of money in a country as compared with commodities. In France the currency is supplemented by less than two thousand millions of bank credits.

In England, however, the circulation is supplemented by more than four thousand millions of bank credits, and when you put together the total currency (that is, the currency which operates on prices) you have at all times a very close approximate to an equilibrium; that is, the currency of England plus its bank credits (which does work as money) equals almost exactly the currency of France, plus the bank credits of France.

The CHAIRMAN. I understand you to mean by bank credits the whole amount of deposits in banks subject to check?

Mr. A. J. WARNER. Yes; that is right.

The CHAIRMAN. Have you ever estimated what would be the per capita circulation in this country if you include in it the bank credits?

Mr. A. J. WARNER. We have about four thousand millions in bank credits, one thousand millions in actual money in the hands of the people, and $550,000,000 in the banks.

The CHAIRMAN. What would be the per capita in this country?

Mr. A. J. WARNER. Divide the five thousand millions by 70,000,000 of population and it will leave the per capita about $70, which is less than that of England, including bank credits. But the relative efficiency of bank credits and currency are not the same. They are not equal. So that I usually count that it takes $2 in bank credits to do the work of $1 in actual currency.

The CHAIRMAN. The amount of bank credits in the country depends upon each individual making deposits in banks rather than keeping the money in his pocket.

Mr. A. J. WARNER. Deposits in money represent only an average of 20 per cent. The remainder consists of credit. But it affects prices, as I will show you by a paper I have here (after a search). I find that I do not have the paper I thought I had, in which I have given the proportion of currency to bank credits, attempting to equalize them as to their efficiency, but it is practically as I have stated. Instead of 90 or 95 per cent of business being done with credit, we have about four times as much bank credit as currency in actual circulation.

Its efficiency, however, is only about one-half an equal amount of currency. And that is true of the bank credits of other countries, but possibly not in same degree. You must take into account the conditions that exist in each country in comparing the currency of one country with the currency of another.

The CHAIRMAN. You have stated that bank credits affect prices as well as currency itself.

Mr. A. J. WARNER. Yes, sir. They operate, as Mr. McLeod says, almost the same as the old bank notes; and they no doubt do take the place, in a large measure, of the old bank-note issue.

The CHAIRMAN. If there was no tariff system between England and France, and no customs duties, would there be any difference between prices of ordinary commodities in England and France except the freight interest and charges?

Mr. A. J. WARNER. That is all.

The CHAIRMAN. Then what has this volume of currency in each country to do with it?

Mr. A. J. WARNER. The volume of currency determines the price level in both countries.

The CHAIRMAN. But the per capita circulation is $40 in one and only $18 in the other.

Mr. A. J. WARNER. That is qualified by the bank credits of the one as offset by the bank credits of the other. John Locke stated that law—that when the same quantity of money is passing up and down, the king in trade, then the variation in the prices of things, one with another, is in the things themselves under the law of supply and demand. But when you change the quantity of money that operates on prices, then you change the general level of prices.

The CHAIRMAN. Is it not a fact that at this time there is in the United

States a redundancy of currency compared with the business wants of the country?

Mr. A. J. WARNER. When prices are falling, and the volume of currency is being contracted money always accumulates in money centers. There are 5,000 persons each day added to the population, or a million and a half in a year, and there is no increase in the money volume.

Prices must go down. They are not low enough in this country to enable us to pay our debts abroad with goods, and therefore we are paying them in gold. Every business man who looks ahead knows that prices must go lower, that there is no possibility of a rise in prices under present conditions, and therefore he knows that he can not afford to borrow money to invest in property or business. He holds his money because that is the thing which is increasing in value, and under that condition of things nobody wants to borrow money.

The CHAIRMAN. Why does not the redundant currency inflate prices?

Mr. A. J. WARNER. Because the money itself is increasing in purchasing power all the time. It is the most profitable thing to hold. If a man has money now he had better bury it. It is the buried talent that is now increasing, not the talent that is being used. Always when prices are falling money will gather in hoards.

The CHAIRMAN. You stated that if we issued a thousand millions of 5 per cent bonds the banks would take them up and issue nine hundred millions of a circulating medium.

Mr. A. J. WARNER. I have no doubt of it.

The CHAIRMAN. If that were the case, would it inflate prices?

Mr. A. J. WARNER. It would not.

The CHAIRMAN. Why not?

Mr. A. J. WARNER. Prices are not inflated now because all of the wealth of the country is offered against money. All the property that I have is offered against money, but I can get little or nothing for it because prices are falling and money rising. Those who have money will not give it for property. They will lend money, but there is a great difference between lending money and paying it out for property. But this would all change when inflation began and prices began to rise.

The CHAIRMAN. If there is sixty millions of currency in the vaults of the banks which no one will borrow now, would anybody borrow if there was nine hundred millions more in the vaults of the banks?

Mr. A. J. WARNER. Just as soon as prices begin to rise and it became profitable to invest money, then everybody would want money, and property of all kinds would begin to advance. If this bill should pass property would begin to rise immediately. Investments would go from one thing to another; people would buy pig iron, and land, and everything else, because they would know that prices were going up.

The CHAIRMAN. You mean Mr. Carlisle's bill?

Mr. A. J. WARNER. Yes.

The CHAIRMAN. Then you ought to be in favor of it.

Mr. A. J. WARNER. I am in favor of a stable currency, not of inflation one year and stringency the next.

Mr. WARNER. You do not believe in the elasticity of currency?

Mr. A. J. WARNER. Elasticity in currency is a dream; it is a delusion. I might almost say that I think it is a modern fad. But there is a time when there ought to be provision made for the issue of more currency.

Mr. WALKER. You mean the temporary issue of currency?

Mr. A. J. WARNER. Yes; its temporary issue, and that in time of panic. The expansion of currency goes on as long as prices rise and confidence is kept up. Then everybody is willing to take money, because he can use it profitably. When the limit is reached, gold goes out of the country, and then explosion comes. Confidence is destroyed, people with money in the banks draw it out, and at such time there is no danger of having too much real money.

I think that the thing we need now is a provision for an issue of currency at that moment when credit currency in the banks is gone or is impaired, and when credit generally is destroyed. There ought to be a provision for issuing currency at such a time on securities; and that can be done through a department of the Government provided for the issue of currency.

It ought to be an issue without limitation, but on securities, with the condition that those getting it shall pay a rate of interest for it, says, from 2 or 3 per cent up, increasing as the quantity increases. That would operate to force the money back when the emergency that called it out passed. That is the wise provision of the Imperial Bank of Germany. The German Government allows an issue above the fixed limit, by paying to the Government a tax of 5 per cent.

Mr. BLACK. What security would you require for the issue of this money?

Mr. A. J. WARNER. I would let the banks deposit securities in the Government bureau and take out currency on which they should pay to the Government an interest of from 2 to 5 per cent, or higher, if needed. With such an interest on it they would only use the money as long as it was necessary to supply the demands.

Mr. BLACK. Would that not embark the Government in the banking business?

Mr. A. J. WARNER. The furnishing of currency is entirely different and separate from banking. It is like providing coin. And I hold that you might as well turn over the coining of money to the goldsmiths as the issuing of paper money to the banks.

Mr. BLACK. Why did not the framers of the Constitution, when forming that provision which dealt with money, go a little further and borrow your idea?

Mr. A. J. WARNER. They provided for coining money and regulating its value. But that was over one hundred years ago, when the modern system of commerce had hardly arisen.

Mr. BLACK. Can the modern system of commerce carry us beyond the fundamental provisions of the Constitution in that connection?

Mr. A. J. WARNER. I think that the decision of the Supreme Court that the Government has the right to issue notes settles that point, and if the Government may do it directly, it may do it through an agency. It may provide an agency adapted to that end. I remember that in a speech made in 1881 by the present Secretary of the Treasury different opinions were expressed by him from those expressed in his late report. He quotes the decision of the Supreme Court on that point.

Mr. BLACK. You say that the Government may do this through its agents?

Mr. A. J. WARNER. Yes.

Mr. BLACK. Is not the bank a very good agency of the Government?

Mr. A. J. WARNER. It would not be practicable to let every single bank in the United States issue money under this emergency plan, and then the demand for it will come mainly from the great centers of commerce—from New York, Boston, and Baltimore; and if you provide for an increase of temporary currency to stay panics in those centers it will be effectual for the whole country, and I think that it ought to be done immediately.

Mr. WARNER. Your idea is that panic culminates when the banks will not or can not lend money on securities which people have to offer?

Mr. A. J. WARNER. The explosion will not come until the banks have pretty nearly reached the limit. Then the currency increases and prices rise and gold goes out, and the panic comes and the public is made to suffer.

Mr. WARNER. The banks either will not or can not lend money on securities, and the people who have taken their money out of the banks can not. And your idea is that Government should not lend money on securities so long as anybody else will take those securities, but that when the securities are such that nobody else will take them, the Government ought to take them and lend money on them?

Mr. A. J. WARNER. Issue it to the banks.

Mr. WARNER. That is, whenever nobody else will lend money on securities we ought to provide that a person holding those securities may take them to the Government and get money on them?

Mr. A. J. WARNER. Nobody else can. The only power strong enough to come in and do that is the Government itself, and I hold it to be the duty of the Government to supply currency to the country.

Mr. WARNER. In other words, when nobody else will or can lend money on securities, the Government ought to do it?

Mr. A. J. WARNER. Yes; and do it on securities. It is simply providing currency when currency is greatly needed.

Mr. WARNER. How long would the credit of the Government last in that case?

Mr. A. J. WARNER. It would not be impaired at all. The credit of the Government would not be impaired if it should put out at such a time one or two or three hundred millions of currency, just as the Imperial Bank of Germany may do and as it has done. By taxing this currency, it will come back very rapidly as soon as the panic is over.

Mr. WARNER. In 1893 we had something like three thousand millions of different classes of gold and securities on which banks could ordinarily get money without any trouble. Would you have the Government issue currency against all of them?

Mr. WARNER. You do not require bullion as a security?

Mr. A. J. WARNER. No.

Mr. WARNER. Then ultimate redemption means what the securities might sell for?

Mr. A. J. WARNER. It is seldom that bank notes fail to be redeemed. Even under our old system of wildcat banking the notes were almost always redeemed after a time.

Mr. WARNER. Did the redemption of the notes the next year help in the panic?

Mr. A. J. WARNER. No; it did not, although the banks often went on issuing notes even after the bank had suspended. That was done in 1837. But let the Government, through a department, issue notes that would circulate as money at this time and under conditions that would force them back after the exigency was over. The Bank of England three times, in 1847, 1857, and 1866, had the limitation on its issue suspended, and the bank was allowed to issue notes without limit. But it has never had to avail itself of that very much, and I think that by depositing securities for currency, to be issued by the Government, there never would be a great amount of such issue, and as to credit, the Government could secure itself from ultimate loss.

Mr. WARNER. Then your idea is to let the Government issue money on securities on which banks would not issue the money?

Mr. A. J. WARNER. I have not laid down the principle of the Government issuing money on securities at any time, except in times of panic.

Mr. WARNER. And you would have the Government lend money on securities as long as securities could be furnished, and then, if the wants of the community demanded more money, you would have the Government issue it without security, as the Bank of England did?

Mr. A. J. WARNER. No; I simply argue that we ought to follow the plan of the Imperial Bank of Germany. I think that the safest, the soundest, and the best system.

Mr. WARNER. That is, you would have the quasi security of a high rate of interest on the money issued.

Mr. A. J. WARNER. Yes; a rate of interest that would force the notes back when the panic was over.

Mr. WARNER. Would you have any limit to the advance of money at that rate?

Mr. A. J. WARNER. I would make no limit but the security. When credit is destroyed there is no danger of an overissue of money.

Mr. BLACK. As I understand, your apprehension is that Mr. Carlisle's plan, if enacted into law, would drive gold out of the country?

Mr. A. J. WARNER. I have no doubt but it would.

Mr. BLACK. And you think that that would be very disastrous?

Mr. A. J. WARNER. As long as we are attempting to maintain the gold standard it would undoubtedly be very disastrous to have that broken.

Mr. BLACK. Is that the only reason for it?

Mr. WALKER. That includes all others.

Mr. A. J. WARNER. It includes many others. I do not want to be understood, however, as saying here that I think the fact of gold going to a premium would be detrimental (if it went there and stayed there) permanently to the United States. Indeed, I go a step further and say that I do not believe that any debtor nation on this earth can long maintain the gold standard, the United States not excepted. No debtor nation has done it. Every one that has tried it has failed, and the United States, as a debtor nation, must fail.

Mr. BLACK. You mean that if we expand our paper currency as long as we are on a gold standard, it is like adding to a superstructure without strengthening the foundation?

Mr. A. J. WARNER. That is it exactly.

Mr. BLACK. You have given us the principle which you say ought to control the issue of paper money. According to that principle have we enough paper money now, or too much, or how is it?

Mr. A. J. WARNER. I do not think we have too much.

Mr. BLACK. Have we enough?

Mr. A. J. WARNER. That depends altogether on the range of prices that you wish to maintain. If you wish to maintain the present low range of prices, yes. If you think that prices ought to be advanced, no. I think it more important to maintain stability than it is to have any given range of prices. However, I think that prices are altogether too low, relatively, to debts now.

Mr. BLACK. With that opinion, have we too much currency, or too little, or enough?

Mr. A. J. WARNER. Too little.

Mr. BLACK. How much more do you think we ought to have?

Mr. A. J. WARNER. I think we ought to restore at once the bimetallic standard of money, subjecting the money supply to the production of the mines, as through all the ages of civilization. I think that instead of narrowing the foundation of primary money to gold alone, while increasing the superstructure of credit, we ought to broaden the foundation of primary money, and make or increase our currency in that way. I think we ought to have more money, but it should be solid money—standard money.

Mr. COX. What ratio between the two metals would you suggest?

Mr. A. J. WARNER. I should restore the bimetallic standard at the ratio which has always existed. Then, after you have given monetary use to silver, if it is found that its value is not the same as gold, and if it is impossible to maintain parity of the coins of the two metals, there would be more reason to talk of a change of ratio. But remember, however, that the value of gold or silver depends mainly on its monetary use. We have taken the monetary use away from silver and doubled it up on gold.

Mr. JOHNSON, of Indiana. Do you think that parity would be maintained under the ratio you have suggested?

Mr. A. J. WARNER. Let me finish my statement, please. The chief value of the gold comes from its monetary use. The chief value of silver formerly came from its monetary use, and it is impossible that the value of silver bullion can now be the same as that of gold at the old ratio, with the monetary use doubled up on one and denied the other.

Mr. BLACK. You say that the value of the metal depends on its use as money?

Mr. A. J. WARNER. Yes; largely or mainly.

Mr. BLACK. Its use by whom?

Mr. A. J. WARNER. By the world; by everybody.

Mr. BLACK. When the use of silver has been discontinued by the rest of the world besides this country, how can we restore its use alone by ourselves?

Mr. A. J. WARNER. That brings me back to the question which was asked by the gentleman from Indiana (Mr. Johnson), can the United States maintains the parity of the two metals. I will give what I conceive to be the conditions under which the parity would be broken, and it would not be broken until that time, provided you allow no increase of the paper currency of the country. Our distributive share of the world's money now is about $1,600,000,000 under the conditions in which money is used and trade carried on in this country. That is, it takes about $1,600,000,000 to maintain the equilibrium of prices between the United States and other countries.

That being the case, if we added less than $1,600,000,000 (say that we were reduced to $1,200,000,000) prices here would fall below the international level, and gold would come here to make up the deficiency and to restore the equilibrium. The Secretary of the Treasury gives $625,000,000 as our gold, but I think that it is entirely an overestimate. If we restored the coinage of silver immediately and did not increase the paper currency at all, gold would go to a premium and leave the country only when we had provided ourselves with a volume of money by the coinage of silver equal to our distributive share of the world's money without gold, and when we had reached that limit gold would be gone and the parity broken. Now, how long would it take to provide the country with a form of money large enough to constitute our distributive share of the world's money without gold? That is the problem.

Mr. BROSIUS. Do you include bank notes as money?

Mr. A. J. WARNER. I do.

Mr. HALL. My mind is all deformed by your use of the term "money." I want to see if I can clear myself up a little bit. Do you use the term money to include checks, drafts, and bank credits?

Mr. A. J. WARNER. I do not.

Mr. HALL. When you are speaking about any increase of the forms of money in connection with prices, do you mean that to apply to bank credits and checks and drafts and clearing-house receipts and bank notes?

Mr. A. J. WARNER. I do not. Checks and drafts are never money, and are never classed as money. Bank credits are not classed as money for this reason: That the form of bank credits will vary with the supply of currency and with business demands for discounts. Money embraces gold and silver and bank notes intended to circulate as money—indeed all forms of paper money.

Mr. HALL. I understood you to say that any increase in bank currency (or what is known as bank notes) increases the prices of commodities?

Mr. A. J. WARNER. Bank notes do, certainly.

Mr. HALL. I would like to read this statement to you:

An issue of notes, smaller than what the public could employ and keep out in circulation, means only an inconvenience really trifling. Checks and bills would be more freely used, and that would be the whole of the matter. A little more gold coin would perhaps be employed, but the quantity would be trifling, and the value of gold is determined, not in England, but in Europe generally, or rather over the whole world.

A diminution of bank notes does not make this spare capital smaller; it only places less of it at the disposal of the issuing banker. Bank notes are but paper—paper tools—not the property or capital itself. Interest does not depend on more or fewer tools of paper being used, but on wealth available for lending.

Banking, with all its machinery of bank notes, checks, bills, and the like, is only intermediate agency; the only thing it does is—not to create property, but simply to place it in different hands. There is only one case in which an issue of bank notes might tell on interest, and that is in a particular spot, at a special time, and under stated circumstances—in a panic in the money market.

Therefore, drawing the conclusion that by increasing the forms of bank notes there is no increased range of prices. Is that statement true?

Mr. A. J. WARNER. There is no increase in the price of gold.

Mr. HALL. I did not speak of gold. I am speaking of commodities.

Mr. A. J. WARNER. It is not true at all.

Mr. HALL. You have taken the position that any increase in the forms of bank notes is the same as an increase of what you call primary money?

Mr. A. J. WARNER. If the bank notes perform the same work as primary money, and if they go into circulation the same, then their effect is the same; but the effect of bank notes and of primary money is not always quite equal.

Mr. HALL. John Stuart Mill lays down the principle that any increase in the forms of money increases the prices of commodities, and that any decrease in the forms of money decreases the prices of commodities. Is that so?

Mr. A. J. WARNER. Yes; that is the law.

Mr. HALL. Do you maintain that this principle applies to bank notes?

Mr. A. J. WARNER. Precisely the same as any other form of money.

Mr. HALL. I read that to show how far you differ from Bonamy Price.

Mr. A. J. WARNER. I differ from him almost in toto. I could have told you that in the beginning. Bonamy Price is sound on almost nothing.

Mr. SPERRY. I want to inquire once more about your statement that an increase of money in any country increases the prices of commodities.

Mr. A. J. WARNER. The prices of everything bought and sold.

Mr. SPERRY. Would it increase the price of labor?

Mr. A. J. WARNER. Very little; at first, not. The rise in the wages of labor will follow a rise in prices, but the wages do not go up usually until after a rise in prices, and they do not fall until after a fall in prices.

Mr. SPERRY. According to the reports of the Secretary of the Treasury, the total amount of money in the country was 774 millions. The actual amount outstanding (outside of the United States Treasury) was 751 millions. In 1892 the actual amount of gold money in the country was 2,219 millions, or an increase of 200 per cent. Now, predicating my inquiry on the facts as stated by the Secretary of the Treasury, that there had been an increase of 200 per cent from 1873 to 1892, how do you account for the fact of the fall in prices in the presence of a great increase in the amount of money in the country?

Mr. A. J. WARNER. In the first place, I challenge the correctness of that statement as to the 2,200,000,000. Coin and currency and certificates are counted twice over to make that up.

Mr. SPERRY. I assume that the condition stated in 1873 was precisely as stated in 1893?

Mr. A. J. WARNER. No; I beg pardon. They were not the same. We had no silver in 1873; no silver coin on which certificates were issued. We had no gold in circulation in the country, and no estimates of gold in the country. We had no subsidiary silver in circulation, and no estimates of subsidiary silver. I think that that statement of the currency is excessive.

The estimate of gold in the country is without any data. There is no data on which to found an estimate of 625,000,000 of gold in this country outside of the Treasury, and the Treasury does not pretend to have any. The estimate as given, would require over 400,000,000 in the pockets of the people outside of the banks this side of the Missouri River. Does anybody believe that? That estimate is based, in the first instance, on the guess of Mr. Burchard, when he was Director of the Mint, and it has been added to and taken from as coin and bullion have come in or gone out from the Treasury, without counting what has been taken out of the country by private individuals, or which has been consumed in the arts. I therefore say that this estimate of the volume of gold in the country is excessive by not less than 200,000,000.

That estimate of currency, too, takes no account of the loss of legal-tender notes or bank notes by fire, by wear and tear, or in any other way for thirty years. When you have equated them, and taken the proportion of actual currency at that time and now, I think that gentleman will find that the law I have stated holds good.

Mr. SPERRY. The Government can not control bank credits, so that that element does not come into this discussion. I understood you to say that, under your plan, an increase of money in the country increases the price of commodities, and that a decrease of the circulating medium decreases prices.

Mr. A. J. WARNER. Always.

Mr. SPERRY. I hold before me an estimate of the Secretary of the

Treasury. It is not stated in gold nor in silver, but, from such information as is accesible to him, he has estimated that the money of all kinds in the country outstanding, outside of the Treasury, in 1873, was 175,000,000, and that in 1892 it was 1,600,000,000. Now, you can strike off 100,000,000 for inaccuracies, if you want to, and still there is an increase of 100 per cent in the forms of circulating mediums, and there is a fall in prices.

Mr. A. J. WARNER. There had been a larger volume of money up to that time. There was a collapse following the panic, when prices went down to where they had not been at any time before.

Mr. SPERRY. You assume in your answer that there had been more coin in circulation previous to that time. The figures of the Secretary of the Treasury indicate that there never was so much money previous to that time.

Mr. A. J. WARNER. From what statement do you read?

Mr. SPERRY. From a statement of the Secretary of the Treasury showing the amount of money in the United States in the Treasury and in circulation on the dates specified.

Mr. A. J. WARNER. All that I have to say of that is, that if that statement is true then all the Secretaries of the Treasury (including Chase, McCullough, and Boutwell, and all who occupied that office immediately after the war), did not tell the truth, for they stated the volume of currency following the war as averaging more than $50 per capita.

Mr. SPERRY. The stability of your theories depends on your impeachment of the accuracy of the Treasury figures; is that it?

Mr. A. J. WARNER. The stability of my theories does not depend on that at all, but I do say that the statement given of the volume of money at the close of the war is not correct.

Mr. SPERRY. In 1873?

Mr. A. J. WARNER. Before that?

Mr. SPERRY. I am not asking anything before that. I am taking the data for 1873.

Mr. A. J. WARNER. I do not challenge the statement as to 1873, but as to the volume of currency before that.

Mr. SPERRY. Never mind that; I do not care about it. It is not in this case. I am speaking of the range of prices. Since 1873 they have been constantly downward, while the money outstanding has been constantly upward. Now, I want you to reconcile that fact with your theory that an increase of money meant increased prices.

Mr. A. J. WARNER. We have had an increase of population. The population has increased about 66 per cent over that of 1873. And as early as 1873 the circulation had not become very widely spread over the whole country; that is, not in the South. That was soon after the war. The first expansion of the currency had to go to the South.

Mr. SPERRY. I do not want to wander down South.

Mr. A. J. WARNER. You must do it. Then there has been, of course, an increase of wealth in this country, an increase faster than the increase of population. The census reports show that things to be bought and sold have more than doubled in the United States in that time. Now, we compare the volume of currency with population and wealth.

Mr. SPERRY. Compare it with population, but never mind wealth.

Mr. A. J. WARNER. We must take wealth into the count.

Mr. SPERRY. The per capita circulation in this country in 1873 was $18, and in 1892 it was over $24.

Mr. A. J. WARNER. That assumes that there is 625,000,000 of gold in circulation, and that there has been no loss of paper currency.

Mr. SPERRY. It assumes nothing; it states facts.

Mr. A. J. WARNER. I know; but it is based on the supposed circulation of gold which I do not think exists, and it takes no account of the increase of wealth. The two elements which determine prices are the quantity of commodities and the number of people to make exchanges; that is, the things to be bought and sold and the number of people to carry on trade.

Mr. SPERRY. When you stated to this committee that an increase of money would increase prices, did you take into account the increase of wealth?

Mr. A. J. WARNER. That is, of commodities. Certainly; I spoke of an increase of currency as compared with commodities or wealth.

Mr. WARNER. Do you include in currency bank deposits?

Mr. A. J. WARNER. I did not take deposits into account.

Mr. WARNER. Did we not have to take them into account to straighten out France and England a few minutes ago?

Mr. A. J. WARNER. When you take it into account in that way you assume that it will vary always in the same country pretty nearly as the volume of currency varies.

Mr. WARNER. Were you not explaining a few minutes ago that its failure to do so is what made this great difference between bank credits and actual money?

Mr. A. J. WARNER. Yes; it affects prices, undoubtedly.

Mr. WARNER. Is your theory anything more than this, that under similar circumstances similar causes will produce similar results?

Mr. A. J. WARNER. I have stated that if there is an expansion of credit it will have its effect on prices for the time being, but I say it is generally assumed that credits will expand and contract with the currency.

Mr. WARNER. You have explained it as a matter of fact that that is not what they do at all.

Mr. A. J. WARNER. And they affect prices.

Mr. WARNER. So that the prices which are modified by these varying figures need have no necessary connection with the amount of actual currency in the country?

Mr. A. J. WARNER. Credit may vary one way or the other more rapidly than the currency. It will affect prices, but it is so difficult to measure the effect that it is seldom taken into account, it being assumed that there always will be about the same proportion between money and credit.

Mr. SPERRY. You have stated that an increase of money in the country would increase prices and also increase wages.

Mr. A. J. WARNER. It will increase prices, and ultimately increase wages.

Mr. SPERRY. Now, I will read to you from the report of the Finance Committee of the Senate in the Fifty-second Congress an estimate made of wages in this country from 1840 to 1891. The committee took the year 1860 as the year to start from, and ascertained what the wages were, calling the wages of this year 100. From that they went backward to 1840, estimating the percentage of loss, and then forward to 1891, estimating the percentage of increase. In 1873, on that basis, the wages were $1.48, and in 1891, $1.60.

Mr. A. J. WARNER. The wages given there are wages in organized industries, but that does not include wages in agriculture or the wages of those that depend directly on the price of what they produce. It includes only wages in organized industries, and there it is true that through labor organizations wages were raised by combinations and strikes. Wages were raised for the time being even while prices were falling, but there was more idle labor and less time was made and earnings were less. But the law will assert itself, and wages must, in the end, obey that law and come down. Half the people working for $1 a day can not buy what the other half produces at $2 a day.

Mr. BROSIUS. Would you not, for the convenience of your statement that an increase in the volume of currency increase prices, qualify it with the words, "other things remaining the same?"

Mr. A. J. WARNER. The increase in the volume of money relative to population and commodities increases prices, that means other things remaining the same.

Mr. JOHNSON, of Ohio. When you speak of currency being loaned to banks on security, you would prefer Government bonds, of course?

Mr. A. J. WARNER. I would prefer Government bonds.

Mr. JOHNSON, of Ohio. You believe that Government bonds, in a time of panic, should be changed into legal tender currency?

Mr. A. J. WARNER. Yes; I think that would be a good provision in time of panic for the Government to issue a certain amount of currency on interest and to take as security Government bonds first and then perhaps other securities.

Mr. JOHNSON, of Ohio. Would you lend that money to any bank?

Mr. A. J. WARNER. I do not like the term "lending." I would issue it as currency.

Mr. JOHNSON, of Ohio. But that is the fact.

Mr. A. J. WARNER. I think you have done enough when you provide to supply the great centers with currency.

Mr. JOHNSON, of Ohio. Would you lend to State banks as well as to national banks?

Mr. A. J. WARNER. I do not see any reason why we should not lend to State banks as well as to national.

Mr. JOHNSON, of Ohio. Would you lend to manufacturers?

Mr. A. J. WARNER. No.

Mr. JOHNSON, of Ohio. You would draw the line there?

Mr. A. J. WARNER. I should draw the line there, because it is through bank deposits that the trouble comes, and I would provide the currency for the banks so that they could supply their depositors with currency.

Mr. JOHNSON, of Ohio. Would you lend to farmers?

Mr. A. J. WARNER. I would not.

Mr. JOHNSON, of Ohio. I wanted to get you on record.

Mr. A. J. WARNER. That is right. I should want it to be used as currency to the bank depositors. In the last panic depositors could not get their money. There was scarcely a bank in the Eastern States that could pay the checks of their depositors. I would supply the means of paying them so as not to stop the wheels of trade and commerce in the country.

Mr. COX. And you would not let the farmer have it although he might have deposits in the bank?

Mr. A. J. WARNER. The object is not to lend capital; it is not as capital but as currency. I would not have the Government lend capital. That is banking business. But I would have the Government create currency temporarily to supply the place of a credit destroyed.

Mr. JOHNSON, of Ohio. Would you have the currency a legal-tender money?

Mr. A. J. WARNER. Yes; make it legal tender.

Mr. JOHNSON, of Ohio. And you would not lend it to the laborers?

Mr. A. J. WARNER. I would not lend it as capital at all. I would issue it as currency to stop panic; nothing else.

Mr. JOHNSON, of Ohio. You know, Mr. Warner, that you and I may stump together some time, and I may want to quote you on this subject.

Mr. A. J. WARNER. I would put it out as an augmentation of currency. I would not lend it as capital to anybody, not to banks.

Mr. JOHNSON, of Ohio. Would you lend it as legal-tender money to banks?

Mr. A. J. WARNER. I would supply a currency to fill the place of credit currency destroyed.

Mr. COX. Let me see if I understand you. In case of emergency you would provide a board consisting of officers of the Government, and you would have the banks go and place securities there for the purpose of establishing what I would call an emergency circulation?

Mr. A. J. WARNER. That is a very good term, an emergency currency.

Mr. COX. A bank takes that emergency fund and puts it in its vaults, the object being to meet all checks that may be drawn on deposits, but you do not mean to say that you want the bank, when it has got the emergency fund, to meet the checks of manufacturers any more than it meets the checks of farmers?

Mr. A. J. WARNER. No; certainly not.

Mr. COX. And you do not mean to say that a laborer should be denied the payment of his check any less than the manufacturer or the farmer?

Mr. A. J. WARNER. I have said nothing to indicate anything of the kind. I am not for supplying capital, but an emergency currency.

Mr. JOHNSON, of Indiana. That is like recognizing the principle of an elastic currency.

Mr. A. J. WARNER. It takes the place of collapsed credit.

Mr. WARNER. Does not that put us all in the hands of the banks?

Mr. A. J. WARNER. I think not.

Mr. WARNER. It does if you lend only to the banks.

Mr. A. J. WARNER. It is not capital at all, but currency that I am for providing.

(The committee took a recess until 2.15 p. m.)

The CHAIRMAN. The chair desires to state to the committee that the venerable Mr. Pratt, of Baltimore, is now present, and the chair suggests he make his statement now, and Mr. Warner can be recalled at any time hereafter if any questions are desired to be asked of him by members of the committee.

Mr. ELLIS (to Mr. Warner): Will you remain?

Mr. WARNER. Yes, sir.

The CHAIRMAN. Mr. Enoch Pratt, of Baltimore, a gentleman well known in financial circles, is present, and will take the stand. I will state to the members of the committee that Mr. Pratt is hard of hearing, and they will be governed in that respect by that fact. This is Mr. Pratt, gentlemen.

STATEMENT OF MR. ENOCH PRATT, OF BALTIMORE, MD.

Mr. PRATT said: I did not wish to come here to discuss this question. The matter of the Baltimore plan is laid before you here and it has been perfectly illustrated.

The CHAIRMAN. The committee desires to have your views in regard to that plan, and also any other views in regard to the currency question which you might desire to submit.

Mr. PRATT. The documents sent here from the Clearing-House Association are my sentiments and wishes, and they have been fully explained here by our Mr. Homer, two days ago, I believe. That was in perfect accord with my views. I am president of the Clearing-House Association of Baltimore, and the matter has been discussed, there, and we have very clearly in accord with the plan which we have set forth, and I can add nothing to that that I know of. I did not know that the desire of the committee was to have any further information on that point. I think it is very clear. I had understood that the committee would desire to hear something about the action of the State banks in issuing their notes. The State-bank currency was the currency of the country up to the time of the establishment of the national banks, and the gentlemen here are all of them familiar with it, no doubt; but my information, I believe, looking around here, goes beyond the age of any of the people here.

I commenced work as a clerk in Boston in 1823, at the age of 15 years. At that time we had nothing but local banks, and the currency of the country was, of course, the issues of those banks of promise, which were seldom fulfilled. The notes of a bank 10 miles from Boston were at a discount, and all the currency of the country was at a discount of from a half to 10 per cent. My business as a young clerk was to go to the brokers and sell instantly all bank notes we got, as we did not desire to keep them in our possession a great while, not knowing their security. The evil became so great that the strong banks in Boston and others resolved upon adopting a principle that was incorporated in our national-bank law, making the banks responsible for the redemption of their money that they put out, and they formed an association and appointed the Suffolk Bank, in Boston, as the exchange. Every bank was obliged to put up a certain amount for the redemption of their notes which would be redeemed by that bank. That system created a very great revolution, and made the money, for a time being, a secure currency for the business of the country. A bank which failed to keep its deposits in that Suffolk Bank to redeem their notes was thrown out and considered to have failed.

I came to Baltimore in 1830, and I found the same uncurrent money prevailing there, and through a large part of my business life, up to 1860, I had to deal with this uncurrent money which was circulated. Right here in Virginia the State Bank of Virginia, a large bank, established its branches around the country, and they would make their notes redeemable in some inaccessible point in the Allegheny Mountains, where people were obliged to go to have their money redeemed. I recollect one broker who collected about $5,000 and went over there to have it redeemed, but it got circulated about that he had come there to get that money out of the bank, and he had to take out of town very quickly, and he did not get his money. The merchants, in paying our bills would buy this Virginia money, which was at a discount of from 1½ to 3 per cent all the time. They would buy that money and bring it there and tender it to us in payment of debts, when we had trusted them for goods for twelve months, and we had to take that or get nothing.

Those were the evils of an irredeemable bank-note system with which, of course, most of you gentlemen are familiar as much as I am. As for our Baltimore plan here for the preservation and perpetuation of the national-bank system it is the best system the world has ever seen, there is no question about it. We have had a currency that is perfectly current all over the country, whereas, under the old banking system, we could not buy a ticket to go anywhere out of the State. I think the plan the Baltimore clearing-house has perpetrated, if put into operation, would serve our purpose to continue this bank-note system, which is likely to come to an end in consequence of securities which we have to put up to perpetuate the banks.

We are obliged to have Government bonds, and when the 4 per cent bonds of the Government, which is the longest bond now in existence, are paid off, why the banks will cease; but it is our desire that some plan should be adopted; that this is a perfect plan of security in bank notes, and it should be preserved. We do not care whether a national bank fails or not; we have no anxiety about it. Our notes pass just as well. It is only for the local stockholders to look out for their own interest, and this Baltimore plan, I think, will meet that case. I do not think I can add anything more to it.

Mr. ELLIS. What have you to say about the fifth section in the bill submitted by the Secretary of the Treasury, which provides for the ultimate liability of all the banks of the country for every other bank which goes into the system?

Mr. PRATT. Well, I think the security would be good, but I do not think you can force the banks into that arrangement. I confess I have not considered it very carefully, but it strikes me you can hardly force a strong bank into this. I doubt whether you could force them into it. It would be very well if you could. I consider my bank a very strong bank, and it would be a matter for us to very seriously consider whether we would. I have been connected with my bank about fifty-five years and have a very great desire to keep it strong as long as the Lord preserves me for the rest of my short life.

Mr. BROSIUS. I would like to ask, if you please, whether the Suffolk Bank system, to which you have alluded, recognized the principle of joint liability of banks in any sense?

Mr. PRATT. None whatever. It was a forced measure of those banks there to force those people to keep their deposit there. If they did not do it they would throw them out and consider them failed.

Mr. BROSIUS. Each bank supplied its own means to redeem the notes?

Mr. PRATT. Yes, sir; it was a strong pressure brought to bear upon them, and that system worked admirably. That system lasted up to the commencement of the national bank system, say from before 1830—I do not recollect the exact year; but it was in existence clear up to the time this national-bank system went into operation, and they kept their currency strong.

Mr. BROSIUS. Do you think it practical now to establish a bank system in which each bank supplies its own means of redeeming its notes?

Mr. PRATT. No; they could not do that; the country is getting too big; we have too many States and cities.

The CHAIRMAN. I do not think you understood Mr. Brosius's question.

Mr. PRATT. Yes; I say I answered that by saying I thought no. I do not think you can force them to do it.

Mr. WALKER. I would like to ask, did that system, practically compelled by the joint banks through the Suffolk bank, work any injustice to any one of the other banks?

Mr. PRATT. No, sir; it was an advantage to them.

Mr. WALKER. It kept them strong, all of them?

Mr. PRATT. It kept them strong all the time. They were obliged to be strong. A bank could not afford to do otherwise, for if they did not keep up their deposit they were thrown out and adjudged bankrupt.

Mr. WALKER. Do you think it is possible to compose the general finances of the country and establish the confidence that existed in New England by the Suffolk Bank system all over the country to-day without retiring the greenbacks and treasury notes?

Mr. PRATT. I do not think they could; the country is too large. The greenbacks would have nothing to do with it. A bank that undertakes to put out notes must be responsible and take them in. A bank that puts notes out must pay them, and the national-bank notes would have nothing to do with that.

Mr. WALKER. That is entirely clear, but you do not understand my question. My question is, whether we can have a proper banking system and cheap money, as cheap as it was under the Suffolk system, where the United States Government is responsible for the redemption practically of all the notes, currency notes, in the country, as it is now, in gold?

Mr. PRATT. Well, that would be a very strong feature.

Mr. WALKER. It would be a strong feature, but——

Mr. PRATT. Would the Government do it?

Mr. WALKER. Well, the Government is doing it now or attempting to do it?

Mr. PRATT. Under the Suffolk system, yes.

Mr. WALKER. Well, now, what is the primary and fundamentally necessary thing to be first done to give us sound banks and a sound banking system of sound finances?

Mr. PRATT. I could not point that out to you. That would require a good deal of calculation, and I would not answer that question.

The CHAIRMAN. What he desires to know was, whether the retirement of the greenbacks from circulation would facilitate a sound banking currency?

Mr. PRATT. Well, now, I do not think it would. I do not think you are going to get any sound banking system under a State-bank system. I am utterly opposed to having any old State-bank systems.

Mr. HENDERSON. Do you think it is desirable to retire the greenback circulation?

Mr. PRATT. No; I do not; I would like to have the Government increase it, because I know it is safe and I would like to have them altogether. I would like to go in for safety. I think the Government is doing a right thing in putting currency out.

The CHAIRMAN. Mr. Cobb here says "Are you willing to put your age in the record?"

Mr. PRATT. Yes, sir; I am four months over 86 years old. I have always been a Republican and a strong Union man, and I thank God for it. My sentiments have been known all my life and I have never put my candle under a bushel. I did not do so in 1861 when the country was in the midst of a war, and I have not veiled my sentiments up to to-day. My father was the same before me and transmitted my sentiments to me. One of my great-grandfathers cast the first cannon that was ever cast in this country in the Revolutionary war. [Applause.]

The CHAIRMAN. Mr. Johnson, of Ohio, desires to ask whether you put a limit upon the amount of greenback circulation the Government should admit?

Mr. PRATT. Not a cent of limit in the world. Let them put out all they can get paid for. But I am utterly opposed to their putting out so much currency and piling up silver in their vaults, for I do not see what they are going to do with it.

The CHAIRMAN. We are very much obliged to you.

Mr. PRATT. I think you will find I have talked too much.

AFTER RECESS.

STATEMENT OF MR. ALFRED L. RIPLEY.

The CHAIRMAN. The chair has invited two gentlemen from Boston, Mr. Ripley, vice-president of the Hide and Leather Bank, and Mr. C. C. Jackson. These gentlemen are now present and will address the committee. Mr. Ripley will first take the stand.

Mr. RIPLEY. Mr. Chairman and gentlemen of the Committee on Banking and Currency, I appreciate it a high honor to be allowed to come and address your honorable committee on this subject. I realize, too, I trust, that your labors have already been long, arduous, and diligent, and I will endeavor to detain you but briefly. What I wish to do is this: I wish to set forth certain considerations that show to my mind conclusively that the issue of the demand notes by our Government, as s done at present, is vicious.

In the second place, I wish to show what should be the safeguards under which another form of currency, much better and much safer, may be issued by the banks.

And then I desire briefly to call attention to certain points in the bill produced by the honorable Secretary of the Treasury with which I have the honor to differ.

No civilized country desires, needs, and understands the use and advantages of a good paper currency for home circulation so well as the United States. By a good paper currency is meant, of course, a convertible one. While the "Greenbackers" are not all dead by any means, no one whose judgment in such matters is worth anything wishes to go back to the ante-resumption days and a gold premium. And any proposition looking to such an end needs no discussion; reason and experience condemn it utterly. Now, our paper currency comes from two sources: first, the Government, which issues, or has issued, gold certificates, silver certificates, certificates of deposits for legal tenders—a form of paper currency seen only in banks—old legal tenders of 1862, or "greenbacks," and legal tenders of 1890, or coin certificates; and second, the national banks, which issue their own notes in accordance with the United States law. The total amount of the Government issues outstanding is approximately as follows: Gold certificates, $65,000,000; silver certificates, $338,000,000; old legal tenders, or "greenbacks," $346,000,000; legal tenders of 1890, $152,000,000, a total of $901,000,000. (The certificates of deposit for legal tenders need not and must not be counted, as they simply represent an equal amount of "greenbacks" stored in the vaults of the United States subtreasuries.)

Here, then, is at first sight an apparently enormous economy in the use of bullion. But there are items on the other side of the account. Every dollar represented by the outstanding gold certificates lies idle in the Treasury, either as coin or bullion; every dollar represented by silver certificates has a coined silver dollar in the Treasury to meet it; every dollar of the legal tenders of 1890 represents bullion lying in the Treasury vaults whose cost in dollars equaled the amount of these legal tenders at the time they were issued. In other words, the portion of our paper currency represented by the gold certificates, silver certificates, and legal tenders of 1890 represents no economic gain—barring, of course, the fact that the silver is not worth as much as the paper issued against it; in other words, the collateral is not good for the notes. The addition to the apparent stock of money in the country is counterbalanced by the hoarded metal in the Treasury; the community gains in convenience and ease of handling, but there is no real economy.

The old legal tenders, or greenbacks, on the contrary, represent a real economy of capital, and the function of the Government in issuing them is totally different from its function in issuing the other forms of paper currency already described. In the latter case its part is essentially that of a warehouseman, issuing a negotiable receipt for goods deliverable to bearer; a warehouseman pure and simple in the case of the gold certificates, but with an all-important requirement in the case of the silver certificates and legal tenders of 1890, that of the act of Congress, 1890, which at the close of section 2 declares it to be "the established policy of the United States to maintain the two metals on a parity with each other upon the present legal ratio, or such ratio as may be provided by law."

In the case of the greenbacks, on the other hand, the Government becomes a banker, having borrowed money or services of its citizens and given in return therefor its own notes payable on demand. It must in so far, therefore, be guided by sound banking principles and employ sound methods; all the more so because its liabilities are so tremendous, and its creditors take its notes under compulsion. Hence the need of an idle reserve of gold, and for no other reason; withdraw the cause and the Treasury needs only the funds to meet current expenses.

It is perhaps outside the limit of the present paper to discuss at length whether it is sound and wise public economy for the Government thus to continue in the banking business. But a few facts may be noted, and all bear in one direction. In the first place, no first-class power has seen fit to follow our example. The note issues of England, France, and Germany are made by banks, not by the Government; even if the Government have, as in France, a voice in the management of the bank of issue, the bank's affairs are in the hands of trained financiers, not of a cabinet officer or legislative body. Again, the system under which the Government conducts its banking business is as badly adapted to the purpose as any that could be devised. Good banking calls for sagacious, experienced, and prudent managers, carefully selected, armed with most ample discretionary powers, and able to act promptly and decisively in an emergency. Does our present system of Government banking meet any of these requirements? The history of the past two years gives convincing answer.

Again, the Government has no means of adjusting the amount of its banking reserve to the demands of the time. It can not call in and cancel its notes when the supply is abundant, but must pile up idle reserve; it has no quick assets which it can convert speedily to meet gold withdrawals, but must see its reserve dwindle at the very time when it should be strong. Its only way of getting rid of a surplus is by lavish expenditure, of increasing low reserves by selling bonds—borrowing in another form—or by increased taxation. And all these remedies have two cardinal defects: They require the sanction of the legislative body, and they are slow of execution. The reserve held by the Government under the existing system is, therefore, almost sure to be either too large or too small. In the one case the economic waste is out of all proportion to any possible advantage; in the other the people pay far more for the anxiety and dread which the diminished reserve inspires than they can save in taxes by lending the Government some three hundred millions without interest. The Treasury becomes a possible and potent factor in the market; what that may mean is best shown by such scandals as the gold scandal of Black Friday, in October of 1869*. And to-day it is both possible and easy for a body of speculators for the fall to work havoc in the market by withdrawing gold for shipment, playing upon the fears already aroused by the notoriously weak position of the Government's reserves.

But even were it advisable that the Government should continue its banking business, there is a grave defect in the currency thus issued. The supply is, under existing laws, absolutely inelastic, understanding by elasticity the capacity to expand and contract in accordance with the demands of trade. This is obviously true of the gold and silver certificates; they can be canceled only on the release of the same amount of coin to take their place; they can be issued only upon deposit of coin to be hoarded in the Treasury; in fact, no new gold certificates are at present issued. The legal tenders of 1890 may be paid in coin and canceled, but can not be increased. The issue of greenbacks is by law (approved May 31, 1878) kept at a fixed amount, and when redeemed they must be reissued. But whether needed or not, the Government notes must be kept alive, and can not be retired when the commercial demand is over; they become in dull times a clog and a menace in rendering gold exports so much the easier.

And in point of elasticity our national-bank notes are but very little better than the Government paper issues. True, they may be and are presented for redemption in large amounts. But the conditions of their issue preclude the issuing bank from either withdrawing them freely or increasing their number. No bank cares to run the risk involved in constant purchases and sales of Government bonds; for even if the price fluctuates but slightly, a very small change is enough to convert a profit on the circulation into a loss. And when money is close the banks, as a rule, have no funds to spare to lock up in Government bonds for the sake of getting a reduced amount of currency. It is true that the national-bank note circulation was enormously increased during the months of August and September, 1893. But two things must be borne in mind in that connection: First, that it was done at an expense which would have been prohibitory except in a time of panic; and second, that it could never have been done at all had the banks had to pay cash for the bonds; in other words, had the banks at the time settled their clearings in cash. Only clearing-house loan certificates made bond purchases possible at all.

To sum up, therefore, our Government paper issues furnish us an absolutely inelastic currency, with very small economy of metal and with very grave risks and dangers to the whole country, which form a necessary and inevitable defect in the system. Our national-bank note issues, while possessing the essential requisite of security, are almost equally inelastic, and call for a tremendous locking up of capital in a form of assets which must be sold to be liquidated.

The prime requisite for a circulating note should be that it is secure, and all the cries of "wildcat" and "red-dog" currency, which were so loudly heard from the opponents of repeal, sprang from a fear, either real or feigned, that we were in grave danger of going back to antebellum conditions. The cries were really a gross injustice to the business sense of the community, a vastly different thing from its political sense; as if we had progressed so marvelously the past forty years, and yet learned nothing of banking. A reason for the outcry was sought for in argument like this: The note holder is now secured by

* See Yale Review, vol. 3, p. 8, May 1894.

the obligation of the Government at 90 per cent of its par value. What better security can the note holder, what better asset can the bank have than this? But in just this point consists our progress—we have learned that a bank can have better assets than Government bonds, which will make the note holder as certain of ultimate and more certain of immediate repayment. A note-issuing bank's best assets are its good business notes, falling due and paid each day. So long as the makers are solvent a bank is in far better position to pay circulating notes from its bills receivable than from any kind of bonds for which it must find a market.

And the same objection holds true, only with far greater force, of all the divers substitutes proposed for the Government bond as security for circulating notes, whether State, county, city, or railroad bonds. All these forms of security lack in greater or less measure the wide credit and steady market which the obligations of our Government enjoy.

But it may properly be urged that under our present system the security for the holder of national-bank notes is in the hands of a third party, the Government, whereas were notes issued by the banks on the security of their own assets it might well happen that, in case of any trouble in the issuing bank, the security would be found to have disappeared, bad assets having taken the place of good ones. Granting the objection, let us see how the difficulty is to be avoided.

Any system of note issue must be a national one. By that is meant that the laws governing the issue of circulating notes must be made by Congress, and not by the several State legislatures; that all the conditions and regulations as to issue, redemption, and withdrawal should be defined and controlled by a department of the National Government, and that the notes themselves should be printed and furnished by the Government alone.

These matters can not, with any safety, be left to the several States. For, in the first place, it is indispensable that the currency should be uniform in quality, not varying from good to bad. We have been so long free from the necessity of having to scrutinize and value each bank bill that a return to such conditions would be intolerable. And such uniformity can only be attained under United States laws. In the various States at present we find great diversity in the banking laws as to payment of capital in full; as to the additional liability of stockholders for an amount equal to the amount of their capital; as to the amount which any bank may loan to directors and to individuals; as to cash reserve; as to loans on mortgage of real estate; as to public reports of condition, examinations, and inspections; as to treatment of the assets in insolvency. But for note-issuing banks at least the laws governing these matters must be uniform and made by Congress, else the differences in the note security will be so great as to give us, from the very outset, good notes and bad notes, which only the expert can distinguish. One of the most potent factors in building up our present national banking system has been the fact that they are all chartered and operated under the same laws. The word "national," as applied to a bank, gives some clue to its organization and management, and our whole vast system of internal exchanges would never have grown so rapidly or attained such enormous proportions without this.

A speedy and uniform system of redemption is also a prime requisite for any system of circulating notes, and this must be furnished by the National Government, as is done at present in the case of the national-bank notes. And the notes must be printed and issued to the banks by the Government. In no other way can we secure uniformity of design, execution, and general appearance; and in no other way can we guard against the possibility of overissue or illegal issue on the part of some bank, and reduce the danger of counterfeiting to a minimum.

An issue of uncovered notes, that is, of notes for the redemption of which no specific security is pledged, would unquestionably be safe, so far as the public is concerned, if made under national legislation embodying the above conditions. The privilege should be granted to no banks of less than $50,000 capital, or whose capital is not fully paid up; to no banks whose stockholders are not liable for an additional amount equal to their share of the bank's capital; to no banks which loan on mortgage security or for a length of time greater than six months; it is of vital importance that the assets of a note-issuing bank be kept quick.

Such notes must further be an unquestioned first lien on all the assets of a bank in case of insolvency. The issuing bank must further undergo thorough and frequent examinations by a Government examiner, and publish full reports of its condition. And as an additional and complete security, the issuing banks must be taxed at the outset to establish a guarantee fund, out of which the Government should pay the notes of a failed bank, supposing—what would rarely be the case—that the assets of the bank and the sum derived from the shareholders on account of their double liability should prove inadequate to do so. Experience in the past has shown conclusively that a guarantee fund of 5 per cent of the total outstanding circulation would be amply sufficient for this purpose; and when once the fund had reached that point, the tax might be suspended until the fund should need replenishing.

Another important point must be considered: The question of taxation of such note issues. The national banks at present pay a tax of 1 per cent per annum on their outstanding circulation; and this tax, coupled with the premium on the bonds which must be deposited before circulation can be taken out, reduces the profit on any such circulation to such a low point that many conservative banks prefer to take out no circulation at all. And no bank can be expected to issue notes unless it sees a profit in so doing. A bank which puts out notes must be ready to redeem them, and to do so must carry idle reserve and keep its assets quick and well in hand. All this means a diminished return to the bank, which can only be made good by the profit to be derived from its circulation. A fair return must be had for the loss thus incurred and the risk run; else the conservative bank will decline to issue notes, and leave this business to the very banks which should not be encouraged to go into it.

But, on the other hand, the privilege of note issue should not be made a monopoly which brings in extravagant profit to those enjoying it. Much wild and foolish talk has been indulged in as to the value of this privilege to our national banks, and a reason for the prejudice which exists against the national-banking system is doubtless to be found in the current belief that it has been a source of great profit to the banks. But it is certain that a far greater profit was derived by the banks from the appreciation of the bonds on which the circulation was based than from the circulation itself; and, in buying these bonds, the banks took the same risk and ran the same chance as the individual purchaser. And, whatever may have been the profit derived from circulation in the fifteen years following the war, it is safe to say that the present generation of bankers for the past twenty years have known little or nothing of it.

This subject can not be left without noticing a popular and widespread delusion which must be energetically combatted and denied, viz, the per capita theory as to the necessary amount of currency. Even the simplest and most plausible statement of this belief, that a certain determinable minimum amount of currency per capita is necessary for the country's business can not be assented to in this form. It is quite conceivable that population and business may increase and yet the need for and use of currency decrease. Suppose a small town without banking facilities; each inhabitant must carry an idle sum of money (greater or less) and settle most of his daily transactions with it. But suppose that with the advent of more settlers a bank is started and gathers in as deposits the cash which has been previously hoarded by individuals. The bank carries, as cash reserve, adequate for its business, only 10 to 20 per cent of the total deposits; the people settle their transactions largely by checks, and the result is that more business is done, and better done, with less money than before. The same holds true of the country at large. Few who understand the subject at all will hesitate to say that the growth of banks and the spread of banking intelligence throughout the people has nearly if not quite kept pace with the increased need for currency which might arise from a larger population and greater business.

I have submitted certain considerations, as I said in the first place, showing the viciousness of the issue of Government notes.

In the second place, I have endeavored to state what I believe to be safeguards, and requisite safeguards, in the event of any legislation which shall allow the banks to issue notes against their own assets held in their own possession.

As to the bill submitted by the honorable Secretary of the Treasury, I wish to briefly call attention to two or three points in connection with it.

Sections 10 and 11, dealing with the question of State banks, seem to me faulty, and I can not approve the bill it those sections shall remain in it in their present form.

In the first place, it seems to me that the opportunity afforded for counterfeiting will be extremely great, and that the door will be thrown very wide open. The state of the case is this: The eleventh section of the Secretary's bill says that Government paper may be furnished to State banks for their use in printing notes under such regulations as the Secretary may see fit to impose, but there is no requirement that such paper shall be furnished. Therefore, a State bank may apparently print a perfectly valid note in any form and on any kind of paper it may select. That being the case, I have no hesitation in saying or maintaining that, in my opinion, it would be exceedingly easy for counterfeit notes to be printed in one section of the country to be put in circulation in other sections, or for notes of wildcat banks to be organized for no other purpose than to put out such notes, and the authors escape with their funds before the matter be found out. In other words, it will allow an opportunity for a return to the worst form of wildcat banks, as we knew them in the days before the war. I do not mean to say that such frauds could not be much more easily detected and run to earth than they then were, because communication is much more direct and rapid, and intelligence is much greater. Yet, at the same time, I consider that a possibility which is very serious and which to my mind entirely vitiates this section.

I have a further matter to bring up in connection with that.

Mr. BLACK. Would it meet your objection on that point to make that requirement compulsory?

Mr. RIPLEY. What requirement?

Mr. BLACK. That they shall take that paper from the Government.

Mr. RIPLEY. Not wholly, I think. The bill must be made over, if I may be allowed the remark, because, apart from this small permissive feature of the bill, there is the additional requirement that the notes shall not be like those of the national banks; in other words, that we shall have a varied currency, in many hands, like that of our national banks, with no one to look to see who issues it.

Mr. JOHNSON, of Indiana. Is it the character of the paper upon which the notes are printed that makes them difficult to counterfeit, or is it the character of the engraving?

Mr. RIPLEY. I am not sufficiently an expert to answer. I understand that the officials of the Bank of England think that from their experience the only safeguard is distinctive paper, and they have that supplied. On the contrary, in this country, we believe that the best protection is secured by the geometric lathe and by the design.

I think we shall have a vastly greater number of objections made to the provisions of that section.

It further seems to me that the notes issued by the State banks, if there be no further requirements made of them than are proposed in this section, will be from the outset discredited. The notes of a national bank, under an earlier section of the proposed bill, will be secured by the 30 per cent guarantee fund of the bank itself, and by the 5 per cent safety fund to which all the other banks must contribute, and by the liability on the part of the stockholders to make good any deficit. In other words, a note of a national bank has behind it the guarantee of the safety fund of all the banks, and of the 30 per cent guarantee fund of itself. A note of a State bank issued under this proposed section, so far as I can see, would have solely the guarantee of the 30 per cent deposit made by the State bank and of the assets and double liability of the stockholders of the bank. There is no provision for a 5 per cent safety fund, though that may be required by the State law, and there is no grouping of the banks to sustain one another.

I consider, as I have said, that this law will give rise at the outset to a discrimination between the two classes of notes, and I consider that principle faulty and objectionable.

The provision of the fourth section of the Secretary's bill also does not commend itself to me as it stands. That is a section which has to do with the question of the redemption of notes. The provision is that the national banks shall redeem the notes issued as therein provided, at home, or at home and at some agency. There is no requirement there that the banks shall keep an agency. The banks may elect to redeem solely at home. It seems to me that this is going back to a method in banking which the banks have been doing their best for many years past to discard. We have come to adopt a system of clearings so far as possible, and we use every opportunity to extend that system. For years we have been operating under the system of clearing our bank notes through the central agency at Washington, the department for the redemption of national currency This section, it seems to me, asks us to go back to the old plan—to illustrate by the subject of checks—whereby, instead of presenting our checks at one place (the clearing house) and there settling with all the banks at once, we shall have to take each check around to the bank on which it was drawn. The possibility is that in the case of these notes we may have to do the same; in other words, send the notes around to the bank by which they are put out in order to have them redeemed. It seems to me that that is going back to an antiquated method and that it is going to necessitate an increased cost to the banks and to the people, and that the people will be exceedingly intolerant of it. That feature, looked at from the point of view of the future, I feel is an objectionable one.

There is one further point that I have not seen raised in any of the discussions, so far as I have followed them in the papers, and that is this: At present the national-bank notes are legal tender between the banks; that is, a national bank must accept from me national-bank notes in discharge of my liability, and I say with perfect frankness that I have no objection to doing so. But suppose this law shall be passed in the form in which it is presented in the bill before us. I have not noticed—it may be that I have overlooked it—any provision for repealing that provision of the law making national-bank notes a legal tender between national banks. At the same time I consider that it would be distinctly questionable to continue that feature of the law with a circulation based on so entirely different a theory as the one proposed in the Secretary's plan. I understand that at present a national-bank note is perfectly secure. I understand that I have the promise of the Government behind me at 90 cents on the dollar. But here it is proposed to allow banks to issue notes based on their own assets. As this proposition is now it will be a serious question whether the banks can be got to go into the system largely.

Mr. COX. As I understand you, you think this system of legal-tender notes continually running into the Treasury for the purpose of drawing out gold is vicious?

Mr. RIPLEY. Essentially vicious.

Mr. COX. What would you do about it?

Mr. RIPLEY. I should get the greenbacks out of the way.

Mr. COX. How?

Mr. RIPLEY. I ought to say honestly that I came here rather to criticise than to lay down any definite system.

Mr. COX. We are in a different fix, however.

Mr. RIPLEY. I admit that; but I do not feel myself competent to answer that.

Mr. COX. So you have not provided any way for doing anything with the greenbacks?

Mr. RIPLEY. The greenbacks are the nation's debt.

Mr. COX. I understand that; but I say you have not matured any plan for doing that?

Mr. RIPLEY. I should like to see the Government pay its greenbacks.

Mr. COX. Had we the money there would be no trouble about that. But, passing from that point, let me put this question to you in regard to State banks: If the note of a State bank is made absolutely good, as good as the note of a national bank, have you any objection to it?

Mr. RIPLEY. Not the slightest. I would say amen heartily to that provision.

Mr. COX. Now, we have got together on one point.

Mr. RIPLEY. The only objection I would have to such a proposition is that it seems to me to be unfair to the State banks.

Mr. COX. Wait a moment. We agree, and when we agree that ends it. Do you think it possible that a State bank could put out its notes in competition with the notes of a national bank, which we assume to be good, and ever be able to pass its notes over its counter unless they were as good as national-bank notes? How could that be done?

Mr. RIPLEY. Let me see if I understand that.

Mr. COX. I will repeat it.

Mr. RIPLEY. If you please.

Mr. COX. I will make it as plain as I can.

Mr. RIPLEY. Thank you.

Mr. COX. You have a national bank in your city, and by your door a State bank. Now, assume an issue of notes of doubtful value from that State bank. You know that your national-bank note is good. How would it be possible for me to pay anybody that I owed with a note of that State bank, which is a depreciated note, when he knows that he could just as well have a note issued by the national bank next door?

Mr. RIPLEY. You can not do it if the man understands it. That is the trouble.

Mr. COX. It has to go to the ignorance of the man to whom I offered to pay it.

Mr. RIPLEY. So far as I understand it. If people are enlightened there is no trouble, but the difficulty is that people are ignorant about such matters.

Mr. COX. Do you really think that the Government of the United States has to take care of the intelligence of its people?

Mr. RIPLEY. That is a wide question.

Mr. COX. Well, let us pass from that, then, and let us come back a moment. The Secretary's bill provides that the State bank shall deposit 30 per cent of its capital stock in legal-tender notes; that is the first requirement. The next one is that the note holder shall have a first lien upon all the assets of the bank; that is the second one. The third is that the stockholders shall be liable individually to the extent of their stock. Now, I ask you as a banker, would not that secure the note of any bank of issue in the world if the proposed law were honestly administered? And there is a limitation of circulation, too.

Mr. RIPLEY. I think I understand that now.

Mr. COX. Let me go over it again. I will put it in a different shape. The State bank has a circulation of 70 per cent. It deposits to secure that circulation 30 per cent in legal-tender notes of the United States in the hands of a Federal officer. It then has a first lien upon all the assets of the bank. It then has the liability of the stockholders. Now, I ask you as a banker, would not any note issued under such conditions as that be absolutely good?

Mr. RIPLEY. I will be very frank to answer that. In the first place, I am not sure whether the Secretary's definition of "a corporation doing exclusively a banking business" may not be held to include a corporation that loans money on land security. I hold that any corporation doing a banking business on real-estate security should not be allowed to issue notes. In themselves, loans on real estate are very good, and I have no objection to them. In our State we encourage savings banks to lend money on real-estate security. At the same time, for a note-issuing bank, I think that is the last thing it should do.

Mr. COX. That answer necessarily goes to the administration of the bank and the character of its loans, does it not?

Mr. RIPLEY. Yes, sir.

Mr. COX. Now, come back with me again. You have no doubt heard of clearing-house certificates in New York during the panic. They were good, were they not?

Mr. RIPLEY. I should have taken them if I had been in New York.

Mr. COX. There was no express statute for the issuing of those notes?

Mr. RIPLEY. No, sir.

Mr. COX. Do you think a banking association in the city of New York or in the city of Boston is safer, for the issuance of currency, than a State?

Mr. RIPLEY. I do not understand just what you refer to by "State."

Mr. COX. Take any 10, 20, or 30 banks in the city of New York, taking out a circulation of the same kind, call it clearing-house certificates or whatever you please. You say they are good. Do you not think that, if you intrust that power to banking associations, you can very well intrust the very same power to a State legislature?

Mr. RIPLEY. Pardon me. There is this difference, which is very important: The clearing-house certificates were issued only on the specific pledge of approved assets for an amount considerably more than the par value of the notes.

Mr. COX. There is no doubt of that, but do you think that any State legislature in the United States would authorize a corporation to go out and practice a fraud in the issue of notes?

Mr. RIPLEY. No, sir; I hope not.

Mr. COX. Then does it not come back to the matter of legislation at last?

Mr. RIPLEY. It is not a question of fraud, so much as it is a question of wisdom, and in the matter of wisdom I think the States are different.

Mr. COX. Your city is a very rich one?

Mr. RIPLEY. There have been some losses recently in the city of Boston.

Mr. COX. Boston is not alone in that, by a good deal. But take an agricultural community where the principal wealth consists of real estate. It has no bonds, it has no stocks, it has no collaterals to use as you do in your city. If a bank organizes in such a country as that, and puts itself under the restrictions contained in the bill introduced by the Secretary, do you not think such a bank, with such restrictions upon it, would be of vast importance and utility to such a country as that?

Mr. RIPLEY. Doubtless of importance and utility, but I am not prepared to grant that the notes would be good.

Mr. COX. Wait a moment. Suppose you establish such a bank as that with these kinds of restrictions and limitations upon it; does not that come in competition with the great money centers of this country to the extent of the money it uses in its own locality?

Mr. RIPLEY. I do not quite apprehend.

Mr. COX. We borrow money of you every year. Now, if we can furnish that money at home, money that suits us for circulation, that comes in competition with you, does it not?

Mr. RIPLEY. I doubt if our money would go out there, except through people we know.

Mr. COX. Suppose we furnish ourselves with a currency that we ourselves are satisfied with, then that destroys the use of yours?

Mr. RIPLEY. I beg pardon. I do not understand.

Mr. COX. I say, that if we establish a currency in our country, always assuming that the note is good and will be redeemed——

Mr. WALKER. Finally redeemed, or immediately?

Mr. COX. Any way; I do not care anything about that, so it is good. Then we use that note. That destroys the necessity for us to borrow your money as long as we have money of our own to borrow, does it not?

Mr. RIPLEY. I should say that if the notes are good——

Mr. COX. I have assumed the notes to be good.

Mr. RIPLEY. Yes; I say——

Mr. COX. Do we not come in competition with your money in such a case? Do we not come in competition with the money of the great money centers of the country?

Mr. RIPLEY. Yes, sir; I think so.

Mr. COX. Then there would be a personal interest in opposition to establishing such banks with good circulation?

Mr. RIPLEY. I think not, sir.

Mr. COX. None in the world?

Mr. RIPLEY. No, sir.

Mr. COX. So your interest is not controlling the great money centers at all?

Mr. RIPLEY. I do not speak for the great money centers; I simply speak as an individual.

Mr. COX. Now, coming back to the first proposition: If we can make our notes, under proper restrictions, as good as your national-bank notes, so that they will circulate side by side in the transaction of business, can there be any objection to them whatever?

Mr. RIPLEY. No, sir; but I think you beg the question that I raise.

Mr. COX. I assume that we can do it, and you assume that we can not?

Mr. RIPLEY. Yes, sir; I do, under existing conditions.

Mr. COX. You do not think, then, that a State can make a State-bank note good?

Mr. RIPLEY. Pardon me, that is not my point at all. My point is this: The bank notes, to be good, should be of uniform quality, issued under uniform regulations. At present, as I understand it, the laws of States governing banks differ widely as to their capital being paid in.

Mr. COX. Then they would have to change their laws?

Mr. RIPLEY. Then I go to the point I raised, as to whether they would lend money on real estate security.

Mr. COX. I do not care to go into that. But do you not know, as a matter of history before the war, that the best security in the United States was real estate?

Mr. RIPLEY. I do not know that, sir.

Mr. COX. That nine-tenths of the capital of banks was loaned on real-estate security?

Mr. RIPLEY. I do not consider it good banking to make loans upon notes secured by real estate.

Mr. COX. Would you create a banking system that discriminates against real estate as a security and say that it is not good security for loaning money upon, but that stocks and bonds are?

Mr. RIPLEY. Pardon me a moment, if you please. I have not intended to say that at all. I have said that in my opinion a bank that issues notes should not loan on land.

Mr. COX. In other words, it is not good for the banks?

Mr. RIPLEY. I did not say that, sir; I beg your pardon.

Mr. COX. Now to my point. If you discriminate in your national banking system and say you will not loan on real estate, whether it is for the interest of the bank or not good policy to do it, but go upon the plan and pursue that plan of loaning your money upon quick commercial paper or collateral bonds and stocks, have you not discriminated against real estate as security?

Mr. RIPLEY. Not as a note-issuing bank must.

Mr. COX. Do you not depreciate the value of real estate and appreciate the value of collaterals?

Mr. RIPLEY. Do not understand that that is my business at all.

Mr. WALKER. You said it was an objection, if I understood you, to the Carlisle plan that it compelled the State-bank notes to differ in appearance from the national-bank notes.

Mr. RIPLEY. That is a minor objection, and one that I did not mean to raise.

Mr. WALKER. I did not ask whether it was a minor or major objection.

Mr. RIPLEY. Pardon me, I was discussing the probability of counterfeiting; that was the point. I was making the point that, under the bill as I read it, counterfeiting would be possible and likely; and that was one of the points of the discussion in connection with it—that it allowed of a multitudinous variety of notes. Instead of notes that are similar in appearance, it would allow notes of so many different kinds that the public would not be able to discriminate between the good and the bad.

Mr. WALKER. Would your objections to State banks be at all modified if their bills were as little likely to be counterfeited as those of national banks?

Mr. RIPLEY. That would remove a difficulty. I am not prepared to say that it would remove all objections.

Mr. WALKER. Would it remove any material difficulty?

Mr. RIPLEY. Yes, sir; I think so. If there were no more possibility of counterfeiting under the proposed plan than there is under the present law, I think that would remove a material difficulty.

Mr. WALKER. Then, if I understand you, as a banker the first thing that strikes your mind as an objection to a State bank is not that it might locate in the woods a thousand miles from anywhere, and redeem its note over its counter only, but it is on the ground of the liability of counterfeiting its bills?

Mr. RIPLEY. I did not mean to give that impression, sir.

Mr. WALKER. What is the principal objection to State-bank bills, if there is any other than counterfeiting?

Mr. RIPLEY. I endeavored to bring out a further objection along the line that you have just raised, that the bills will come out under varying laws governing security, governing the character of the bank's loans, and therefore differing very markedly from the bank notes which are issued by banks enjoying a uniform law.

Mr. WALKER. I understood you, in reply to a question asked by the honorable gentleman from Tennessee (Mr. Cox), to say that you could not make a man who knew his business take an inferior money in payment of a debt.

Mr. RIPLEY. Did you understand that those were my words?

Mr. WALKER. Very nearly those; equivalent. Though you may put it in any language you choose.

Mr. RIPLEY. I did not mean to give as broad an answer as that, possibly. A man will frequently take 50 per cent on the dollar because he can not get the other 50. But if he had a choice, and could enforce that choice, he would want his pay in the best.

Mr. WALKER. You change the conditions by your answer.

Mr. RIPLEY. If I have made any answer in the form you indicate, I am certainly very glad to have had an opportunity to correct it.

Mr. WALKER. Is it not a fact that if a man offers you money for goods, you can accept or decline the money? But if you had any experience before the war, such as I have had, when a man owes you money on an obligation, in ninety-nine cases out of a hundred you would be obliged to take the money he offers, or sue him, and it might be the case of suing a beggar and catching a louse. Do you know anything about our experience in the East before the war, or have you heard it?

Mr. RIPLEY. I do not. I do not think I have heard enough to know positively, and I have had no experience of my own.

Mr. WALKER. Is it not a fact that when a man holds a note against another, to whom he has sold goods, he is practically obliged to take the money that is offered, or make a discount on his note? Does it not come down to practical insolvency of the man who owes the money, else that the man who owes it must be allowed to pay in whatever money he has?

Mr. RIPLEY. I should not be willing to make any general statement on that line.

Mr. WALKER. You were asked by Mr. Cox also whether it is safer for a bank to issue notes than for a State to issue notes? You did not reply directly to that.

Mr. RIPLEY. There would be a point as to whether you refer to ultimate payment or immediate payment. A bank, I take it, is an institution——

Mr. WALKER. Wait a moment. Do we talk about ultimate payment in talking about whether a bank note is good or bad? If it is not instantly redeemable in coin it is a bad note, is it not?

Mr. RIPLEY. Yes, sir.

Mr. WALKER. Keeping that in mind, I will ask this question that Mr. Cox asked you: Is a bank safer to issue notes than a State to issue notes?

Mr. RIPLEY. That depends entirely on the bank. I should say a well-managed bank could issue and pay demand notes more easily than a State can, unless the State finances are run for the purpose of paying notes.

Mr. WALKER. What do you mean by "more easily?"

Mr. RIPLEY. Pay them immediately on presentation.

Mr. WALKER. The moment a bank note is not paid immediately on presentation it ceases to be money, does it not, and becomes an obligation like an individual note?

Mr. RIPLEY. We used the legal tenders for some years, and they were not paid immediately on presentation.

Mr. WALKER. And that put gold at a premium. They were poor money, were they not?

Mr. RIPLEY. Yes, sir.

Mr. WALKER. Then a bank note that can not be redeemed in coin at once is poor money, bad money?

Mr. RIPLEY. In my opinion it is.

Mr. WALKER. Then I will ask the question again. I want to get down to that, if I can. Is a bank safer to issue notes than a State to issue currency notes?

Mr. RIPLEY. I do not think I understand what is meant there by the word "safer."

Mr. WALKER. You spoke about local State money competing with Eastern money. As I understood you, you said that if they issued local State money it would compete with Eastern money. Would it not always be at a discount, and must it not necessarily be so?

Mr. RIPLEY. If it got into the East it would doubtless be subject to the expense of collection and loss of interest during transit, but at the same time it might be good.

Mr. WALKER. What do you mean by good?

Mr. RIPLEY. Payable on presentation.

Mr. WALKER. Do you mean payable at the counter, or at some other point?

Mr. RIPLEY. It makes no difference where it is paid, so long as it costs nothing to get it paid.

Mr. WALKER. Does it cost any more to get a note paid a thousand miles from Galveston, Tex., than it does to get it paid in the case of a bank in Boston?

Mr. RIPLEY. Pardon me; that is exactly what I had reference to—express charges and loss of interest in transit.

Mr. WALKER. Then instead of sending it for collection you would be apt to take it to a broker and sell it at a discount, and he would send it home for redemption. Is not that the policy always pursued by banks?

Mr. RIPLEY We have had none of that kind in my experience.

Mr. WARNER. The Secretary's plan provides for a 30 per cent greenback deposit. Do you consider that necessary for the safety of the notes proposed?

Mr. RIPLEY. My opinion is that the theory of a safety fund in banking would be much better met by requiring no deposits whatever of greenbacks. At the same time, we are going from one theory to another quite the reverse, and it means a considerable change in the public mind. A considerable educational process has got to be gone through with. There is no doubt, I think, that the public would feel safer knowing that there was an actual deposit of cash covering bank notes issued. In so far. I do not at present object to that. As a lasting provision I should probably, but at present I do not object to it.

Mr. WARNER. As a banker you do not consider it logical, though in view of public opinion it may be desirable?

Mr. RIPLEY. I think so. That expresses it.

Mr. WARNER. You made a suggestion, I believe, that it was desirable to have a better provision for redemption than that which you understood was proposed in the Secretary's bill. Do I understand you that you imagine that any considerable number of banks in themselves, or any considerable bank in itself, would not arrange for better redemption of their notes than that?

Mr. RIPLEY. I think they would have to.

Mr. WARNER. Or the notes would not go out?

Mr. RIPLEY. Exactly.

Mr. WARNER. Then, is it a serious objection that the law does not require it?

Mr. RIPLEY. Always providing, Mr. Warner, that the bank notes issued under the proposed act be not legal tender as between banks.

Mr. WARNER. That is what I was coming to in the next point. Then, in your opinion, in case that provision were eliminated the banks would be likely. of themselves and without reference to the law, in order to keep their notes out, to provide very much greater redemption facilities than are required by the Carlisle plan?

Mr. RIPLEY. I can not conceive of redemptions being made under the bald requirements of that plan.

Mr. WARNER. You can not conceive that a bank could otherwise keep its circulation out or would try to?

Mr. RIPLEY. It is not possible. No bank that issued its notes in good faith would try to.

Mr. WARNER. So that in all probability we would have very much more extended facilities, whether required by law or not?

Mr. RIPLEY. In the course of time; yes. How long the process would be I can not say.

Mr. WARNER. You referred to that one feature of our present national-bank circulation by which the notes are made legal tender as between the banks and in payments to them. What effect has that upon the elasticity of the currency? Does it not greatly reduce it, if not entirely?

Mr. RIPLEY. I do not think our national-bank note currency at present could be called really elastic at all.

Mr. WARNER. How would it be if that provision were eliminated?

Mr. RIPLEY. It would make all the change in the world.

Mr. WARNER. Would it not make it more elastic?

Mr. RIPLEY. Unquestionably so.

Mr. WARNER. Without regard to the redemption provisions?

Mr. RIPLEY. If I have the privilege of refusing a national-bank note, it has got to go home a great deal faster than if I have not that privilege.

Mr. WARNER. Of how great comparative importance do you regard the provision in regard to greenback withdrawal? In other words, is it worth while for us to consider a currency plan without providing for it, or do you believe that we can provide a currency plan and then take up the other issue?

Mr. RIPLEY. In my opinion, the retirement of the greenback is by all odds the important problem. I look on the question of providing currency as secondary to that in importance.

Mr. WARNER. As to the mutual-unlimited-liability provision of the Carlisle plan—you understand that?

Mr. RIPLEY. I understand it.

Mr. WARNER. Do you think that is necessary for the safety of the notes?

Mr. RIPLEY. With the 30 per cent guaranty, I believe not. At the same time, it is asking for a prophecy that I feel is a little more than I want to give dogmatically.

Mr. WARNER. Do you consider that it would be much of a deterrent to banks that were considering whether they should come in under this system?

Mr. RIPLEY. Undoubtedly. As I understand it, under the Baltimore plan the proposal is that the banks should be taxed at a certain specified rate to make good a deficit in the safety fund; in other words, if a bank issues circulation under that plan it knows how much it has to contribute per annum, while under the Secretary's plan we do not know that. There would be some years when there would be no contribution required, and there would be other years, such as the year 1893, when we might be called upon to contribute 5 per cent.

Mr. WARNER. Is the difficulty so much with regard to the probable amount of the contribution, or as to the vague character of the requirement?

Mr. RIPLEY. It is the vagueness of the requirement. My opinion is that banks would be far more willing to pay the higher tax, if they knew its certainty, but they would dread to make an uncertain jump into the dark.

Mr. WARNER. Then your idea would be to eliminate that?

Mr. RIPLEY. I have not been prepared to make that suggestion of elimination.

Mr. WARNER. What are your Boston banks going to do; are they going to stay out, or will they come in? And how are we going to induce them to come in?

Mr. RIPLEY. I can not speak for the Boston banks, but I can say that I do not believe the banks in any city to-day are ready to say whether they will come in or not.

Mr. WARNER. Do you think this would bother them but little, or is it something to take into serious account?

Mr. RIPLEY. It is something that is to be taken into serious account in the two cities of Boston and New York, to go no further.

Mr. BLACK. Would your bank hold out against it on that account?

Mr. RIPLEY. I can not say. That is a matter for further canvass.

Mr. SPERRY. What would be your present judgment about it?

Mr. RIPLEY. I am a younger man than some of the directors, but personally I think I should be willing to do it. At the same time, I think the older men among the directors of my bank will hesitate.

Mr. JOHNSON, of Indiana. You were asked by Mr. Cox whether or not you thought it possible that a State-bank note could be gotten over the counter if it were not as good as a national-bank note. Along the line of that question I want to ask you if the necessities of men and the exigencies of business are not such that very frequently they are compelled to take, and do take, in the course of business, depreciated bank notes when there are good bank notes in existence in the same neighborhood?

Mr. RIPLEY. I must answer yes to the question in that form. Beyond doubt, we take punched silver pieces and Canada coins.

Mr. JOHNSON, of Indiana. The laborer, for instance, is very frequently compelled to take the kind of paper in which his employer may want to pay him, although it may not be the very best; or a man seeking labor may be required, as a matter of necessity, to accept depreciated paper in payment. Am I not right about that?

Mr. RIPLEY. But all our money is about on a level, is it not?

Mr. JOHNSON, of Indiana. I know that. But was it not the case, during the State-bank régime in this country, when depreciated paper circulated along with paper that was not depreciated; that one class of creditors was obliged to accept the one and another class obtained the other?

Mr. RIPLEY. I have no doubt that was the case.

Mr. JOHNSON, of Indiana. For instance, a creditor might be obliged to accept depreciated currency in payment of his debt if he knew he could not get anything else from his debtor. Am I right?

Mr. RIPLEY. I think that case might have arisen.

Mr. JOHNSON, of Indiana. If bad currency did not exist, then of course he would obtain good.

Mr. RIPLEY. There is no doubt about that—if he obtained any.

Mr. JOHNSON, of Indiana. There is a very large scope, is there not, within which as to State-bank paper, as authorized by this bill of Mr. Carlisle, we omit restrictions which are put by his bill upon national-bank paper? There are many provisions of the national-bank law which apply to national banks in Mr. Carlisle's bill, and which are not applicable to State banks.

Mr. RIPLEY. I think I have said that. There are provisions which national banks must observe and which are not in the bill here.

Mr. JOHNSON, of Indiana. You think that might cause a preference?

Mr. RIPLEY. I endeavored to state that, that I thought there might be two classes of notes.

Mr. JOHNSON, of Indiana. A preference begets inequality in the payment of money, does it not?

Mr. RIPLEY. Yes.

Mr. JOHNSON, of Indiana. Then, under a State-bank system the provisions of the laws of the various States with respect to bank issues might vary very greatly, might they not?

Mr. RIPLEY. I have not read the laws of the different States, but they do vary; how much I do not know.

Mr. JOHNSON, of Indiana. That would be likely to create a preference among the various kinds of State-bank bills, would it not?

Mr. RIPLEY. Issued under the proposed bill, do you mean?

Mr. JOHNSON, of Indiana. Yes.

Mr. RIPLEY. Yes, sir.

Mr. JOHNSON, of Indiana. Your point, as I understand it, is that it is safer to have circulating notes issued under the exclusive control of one set of authorities than it would be to have them issued, even with certain governmental restrictions, under the authority of a number of independent sovereigns?

Mr. RIPLEY. I believe that the fundamental laws governing the circulation should be prescribed by the National Government, as I said in the paper I read.

Mr. JOHNSON, of Indiana. It is much easier, I presume, for the business world to familiarize itself with one law under which a currency is issued for the whole country than it would be to familiarize itself with the laws of a number of independent States.

Mr. RIPLEY. There is no question about that. I think that, for that reason, we may explain why the national banking system has spread so largely—because it was known under what conditions the banks were organized and operated.

Mr. JOHNSON, of Indiana. Mr. Cox used the expression in his questions, "money to suit us," referring to money to suit the individuals in some particular State. Can you conceive of any benefit which a State banking system would confer upon the people of any particular locality that could not be just as well conferred upon them by a properly devised national issue of money?

Mr. RIPLEY. I think gentlemen are apt to overrate the value of currency issue, anyway. As I understand it, there are a large number of sections of the country which call for more currency, but it has always seemed to me that that call was defective; that it was not currency that was wanted, so much as capital, and that the incoming of capital was to be encouraged by sound banking as well as by other considerations.

Mr. JOHNSON, of Indiana. Possibly you do not catch my question, or maybe I have not been very fortunate in my method of expression. Can you conceive of the want of the people living in any State in this Union which could not be supplied just as well by a national currency as it could by a currency under State law?

Mr. RIPLEY. You mean a currency issued under laws laid down by the National Government?

Mr. JOHNSON, of Indiana. Yes.

Mr. RIPLEY. I believe that is the preferable way; not merely as good, but better.

Mr. BROSIUS. Suppose you establish in Boston a bank with $100,000 capital, under the Secretary's plan; you take out circulation up to the limit of $75,000; you make a deposit of 30 per cent on that, which is $25,500. That reduces your capital stock to $74,500. Then your circulation of $75,000, added, makes $149,500. You have the liability of 30 per cent, and the double liability of your stockholders. Suppose your bank negotiates a great many very bad loans; many of the debtors of your bank become insolvent; a number of your stockholders become insolvent; and your cashier runs away with half of the capital. What becomes of the holders of your notes?

Mr. RIPLEY. Under the conditions laid down, the holders of the notes, it appears to me, would have a hard time.

Mr. BROSIUS. Under the existing conditions of our present national banking system, do you think they would have a hard time?

Mr. RIPLEY. No, sir.

Mr. BROSIUS. Then there is a liability here as to note holders losing the value of their notes in individual instances, such as have occurred within your knowledge in the last few years, unless there is either a Government liability behind these notes or a joint liability on the part of the banks?

Mr. RIPLEY. Yes, sir. It may come to pass that, unless the safety fund be called upon, the individual bank issuing the notes may not have assets enough to meet them.

Mr. BROSIUS. Then you must have security to cover such a case, must you not, in order to make every note holder in the United States feel sure that we will sustain no loss by reason of having such notes?

Mr. RIPLEY. If we wish to introduce a system, or to continue our system, absolutely secure, so that the notes shall be absolutely secure beyond peradventure, by pledge of assets with somebody else, the proposed system is wrong.

Mr. WALKER. That answer is all wrong, so far as national-bank notes are concerned. Let the answer be read.

The reporter read the answer, as follows:

If we wish to introduce a system, or to continue our system, absolutely secure, so that the notes shall be absolutely secure beyond peradventure, by pledge of assets with somebody else, the proposed system is wrong.

Mr. WARNER. And the present system is all right?

Mr. RIPLEY. Yes, sir.

Mr. SPERRY. If I correctly understand you, it is your opinion that the banks would not operate under the Carlisle system, for the several reasons you have specified?

Mr. RIPLEY. May I correct? I have endeavored to give you my individual opinion, but I dare not form an opinion as to what the banks will do.

Mr. SPERRY. I understood that you thought they would not, for the several reasons you specified.

Mr. RIPLEY. I said that in my opinion the difficulties in the bill, which I tried to specify, would operate against it, but I do not wish to go on record here as predicting positively the action of banks.

Mr. SPERRY. You are giving us your opinion of its probable effect, are you not?

Mr. RIPLEY. Yes, sir.

Mr. SPERRY. That is all I wanted. Suppose, as a matter of fact, the banks should operate under it and put out circulation; what would be the effect of that circulation on the legal-tender paper money of the Government? Would it tend to return that legal-tender money to the Treasury for redemption?

Mr. RIPLEY. Let me get that clear. If the banks issue notes as proposed, obviously a considerable part—how many we can not say until the result—a considerable part of the greenbacks will be locked up in the Treasury.

Mr. SPERRY. That is assumed by the Secretary.

Mr. RIPLEY. Your question has to do with the remainder?

Mr. SPERRY. Certainly.

Mr. RIPLEY. I have no question that when there is a call for gold shipment, legal tenders will be likely to be presented in order to secure gold, so long as the Government agrees, and carries out its agreement, to pay gold on demand.

Mr. SPERRY. You do not get the idea in my question. It has been suggested by some banking men that banks would make an effort to circulate their own bills as distinguished from other money. Now, you think that is a fact?

Mr. RIPLEY. I think that is a fact, sir.

Mr. SPERRY. Then, if that is a fact, would not the effect of that be to cause the greenbacks to flow back to the Treasury for redemption?

Mr. RIPLEY. I think not; I think the banks would hold greenbacks, inasmuch as they are lawful money, for the redemption of their own notes. They would be a part of their reserve.

Mr. SPERRY. You think they would rather hold them than to hold gold coin?

Mr. RIPLEY. I think they would rather hold paper than gold, so long as there is no question about payment. This is what I mean by it. Four years ago, in the settlement of clearing-house balances, gold certificates were used very largely. At present, I think I am not wrong in saying that in the settlement of clearing-house balances, both in Boston and New York, very little or any gold is used at all. The legal tenders are used instead. In other words, the banks have had a tendency to cling to their gold. But if, under the conditions you propose, there were that same preference, existing banks would undoubtedly prefer to hold gold rather than greenbacks. Otherwise I can see no reason for it.

Mr. SPERRY. Would not that drive gold out of the Treasury at once?

Mr. RIPLEY. I should not say it would have that tendency, to withdraw gold at once.

Mr. WARNER. If the number of greenbacks outstanding were decreased as you propose, would it not make the banks have a greater tendency not to present greenbacks than they have now?

Mr. RIPLEY. I am inclined to think so. As I say, the greenbacks are lawful money for the purpose of redemption, and on that ground it seems to me they would be gathered in the banks. In other words, the banks would hold reserves of greenbacks and gold. If the question of export comes up, in case their stock of gold is large and in case they have no question but that they can get their legal tenders paid in gold, they would give up the gold. If, on the contrary, they have a shadow of doubt about that, the tendency would be to give up the legal tenders.

Mr. RUSSELL. Kindly give your opinion on this: Would the enactment of Secretary Carlisle's bill, with its provisions as now drafted, be more favorable to State-bank issue than to national-bank currency?

Mr. RIPLEY. In my opinion, as I tried to set it forth, as I read the provisions of the bill affecting State-bank notes, the difference between them and national-bank notes very obviously would be so marked that the State-bank notes would enjoy very little or any circulation under it.

Mr. JOHNSON, of Ohio. Because of the character of the notes themselves?

Mr. RUSSELL. You misunderstand my question.

Mr. JOHNSON, of Ohio. I beg your pardon.

Mr. RUSSELL. Take the provisions of the Carlisle bill now under consideration by us, without any change of its provisions. I am not speaking about the character of the bills issued under the proposed law. But are not those provisions of the Carlisle bill more favorable to the issue of State-bank currency than they are to the issue of national-bank currency?

Mr. WALKER. On the face of them.

Mr. RUSSELL. In other words, are there not fewer restrictions in this measure of Secretary Carlisle's affecting State-bank currency than there are for national-bank currency?

Mr. RIPLEY. Allow me to answer in this way: In case of the desire of banks to issue notes, and the willingness of the public to take the notes, I think under this bill the banks themselves would be tempted to try and put their notes out. But the main contention I make is that under the terms of the bill it seems to me that the public would at once discriminate between the two, and discriminate in favor of the national-bank notes. I beg to be allowed to repeat that.

Mr. RUSSELL. Then, in other words, a State currency under this bill would not circulate?

Mr. RIPLEY. I doubt it very much. I beg to repeat that point. The national-bank notes issued under this bill are secured apart from the 30 per cent fund (in which case they are on a level with the State-bank notes), apart from the first lien on the assets (in which they are also on a level with the State banks), and apart from the double liability of the stockholders (in which also they are on a level with the State-bank notes). The national-bank notes participate in the security afforded by the 5 per cent fund which is levied on all the banks. There is no such requirement affecting State-bank notes.

Mr. JOHNSON, of Ohio. Each national bank has to take the notes of other national banks?

Mr. RIPLEY. That is the present law.

Mr. JOHNSON, of Ohio. Internal-revenue taxes are paid in them?

Mr. RIPLEY. I do not know what the present practice is in that respect.

Mr. RUSSELL. That is, the requirements of the national-bank notes, under Secretary Carlisle's bill, are more exacting than they are for the issuance of State-bank currency.

Mr. RIPLEY. I do not quite apprehend.

Mr. JOHNSON, of Indiana. The question is easy if you think a moment.

The CHAIRMAN. The answer is, that it does exact one more condition; that is all.

Mr. RUSSELL. Let the gentleman answer for himself.

Mr. JOHNSON, of Indiana. The question is, which is the easiest banking law under which to issue notes?

Mr. RIPLEY. I think it is easier for the national banks. If, by issuing notes, you mean by putting them out, I think the national bank gets them out.

Mr. JOHNSON, of Ohio. People take them more quickly.

STATEMENT OF C. C. JACKSON.

The CHAIRMAN. Mr. C. C. Jackson, of Boston, is present and will address the committee.

Mr. JACKSON. Mr. Chairman and gentlemen of the committee, I feel very much gratified to be allowed to come before you to say a word upon this matter. I am not a banker. I am a stockbroker. It would be absurd for me to attempt to say anything about the details of currency after the excellent expert testimony you have had on that subject. But I do want to urge that you will put one particular clause in whatever bill you report for the reform of the currency, namely: One directing the Secretary of the Treasury to begin in January, 1895, to cancel each month $4,000,000 United States Government legal-tender notes now used as currency, either greenbacks or Treasury notes, as he finds most convenient; to use the sinking fund for this purpose so far as it will serve; and to sell bonds to raise the required cash, if necessary, and to continue this process till the legal-tender notes are all canceled.

It would be absurd for me to give suggestions about the details of a currency system when you have experts like Mr. Hepburn on the subject before you. But the effect on the investing public produced by anxiety about Government notes I have had a good chance to observe and good reason to carefully study.

It is now generally admitted that the use of these Government notes is harmful, and the favorite plan seems to be to get some of them out of the market into the hands of the Government, and to allow the Secretary, if he pleases, to buy up and cancel others of them when he gets surplus revenue. It does not seem to me to be wise to confine legislative action to these steps. If the notes are kept alive and only held by the Government, instead of by the public, the world will not feel sure that they may not any day be ordered into the market again by Congress. And as for the cancellation by the Secretary of the Treasury with surplus revenue, who knows when we shall begin to have surplus revenue, or how long we shall continue to have it after we have begun; and who knows what may be the desires as to cancellation of the gentlemen who will hereafter be Secretaries of the Treasury? I think the case demands much more certain and immediate treatment. We want to immediately convince the financial world that we see clearly the harm which the use of Government notes as currency is doing us, and that we are going to cancel them just as fast as prudence may allow so great a change to be made.

For more than two years, now, every day when we have come to breakfast we have all looked to see how the gold reserve of the Treasury stood. And not only we, but all Europeans who are seriously interested in financial questions have for that two years watched with anxiety lest our Government should fail to keep its promises and should break down in its effort to redeem its notes in gold. The strain on the nerves and the distraction from business produced by this anxiety has been very serious. But I think the disgrace to our country is still more important. Why should we make it possible for anybody to doubt whether we will keep our promises as to a duty so light and so entirely within our power to certainly perform? The constant prompt redemption of $500,000,000 of paper by a great nation of 70,000,000 of people left uncertain! Why, it is only $7 per head for the total amount. We had far better tax ourselves this $7 per head at once and pay the whole amount off than suffer this disgrace and anxiety.

Think of the humiliation involved in the last sale of bonds. The Treasury evidently had to make a special bargain with a strong syndicate, because it feared that no other buyers of the bonds would furnish it with the needed gold. I think the Treasury officials were right in making this bargain under the circumstances; but how clearly it proved the weakness of our system. Our system depends for its success on favorable conditions of business and on the favor of strong money syndicates. The Treasury is debarred from getting the money it wants—that is, gold—by popular subscription, because it is pledged to give gold always at its own counter for its own paper. Who knows how this money syndicate will be disposed to act as to gold when the Treasury comes begging again? It is really an instance of poetic justice. It is dishonorable in our Government to force creditors by legal-tender laws now, in time of peace, when there is no emergency, to force creditors now to accept in satisfaction of debts paper which we know is not quite so good as gold, because at the best these people on whom it has been forced can not use it to pay any debts they may have abroad. And the obvious distrust of this paper by our importers and banks has lately made its inferiority and the injustice of this Government, action still greater. It is poetic justice, therefore, that our Government should find its unjust laws recoiling on itself, and forcing it to beg from some people and to bully others in order to get its needed supply of the standard money of the civilized world.

And we hesitate to grapple boldly with this evil and to promptly root it out. Why? Because we should be substituting an interest-bearing for a noninterest-bearing security. We know that we ought to gradually cancel $500,000,000 Government demand notes. If bonds were sold to raise the $500,000,000 needed for this purpose at a rate of interest a little under 3 per cent, and with the advantage of some saving in expenses of redemption, etc., the added annual cost to the Government might be $14,000,000. This is the whole story, and the work would then be complete.

We should no longer be ridiculous in the eyes of the world; we should not again have to humiliate ourselves before money syndicates; we should no longer cause our own and foreign capitalists to hesitate about investing here; and we should make it much easier to get the consent of conservative people, who wisely fear inflation, to the adoption of more liberal laws for the issue of currency by banks.

How can we strike a balance between the gain and loss here? How can we compare an outgo of $14,000,000 per year with the great annoyance caused by lack of currency in the sparsely settled districts and the humiliation and dishonor of our Government, and all the misery and anxiety which it causes watchful citizens? We can not make this comparison, because, if for no other reason, the importance of dishonor can not be expressed in money.

But there is one comparison which we can make, and it is a suggestive one. The best statisticians consider, I believe, that the average income of each of our inhabitants is somewhere about $200 per year. Perhaps it is not quite so much as this, but this is near enough to the fact. Suppose that the decrease in incomes caused by the timidity in expenditure and hesitation in business, arising from fear about the gold reserve, has amounted to 5 per cent during the last two years. This would be $10 per head each year, or $700,000,000 in the whole country each year, or $1,400,000,000 in the two years. Now, of this the $14,000,000 added annual interest, which is so feared, is only 1 per cent. It is only one-tenth of 1 per cent of the annual income of our citizens. It is, of course, very easy to make startling figures by adding a few zeros, and so to prove almost anything. But am I at all at fault in this computation? I beg you to go over it carefully yourselves. The statement that $14,000,000,000 is the aggregate amount of the annual incomes of all the people of the country often puzzles men, because they know that the total annual products of the country do not amount to nearly as much as this. A very large part of the incomes of our people, however, are derived from services rendered to each other, and the incomes are none the less fairly earned and none the less important to the earners merely because they do not represent the production of solid things, like potatoes and iron.

Take, for instance, the fees and salaries of lawyers, ministers, painters, and singers. We know that many of such people have had their incomes sadly curtailed during these two years. And among those of not so great capacity, who act as brokers, or teachers in the schools, or accountants, etc., how many instances of great suffering we have heard of lately! Sometimes the depression does tell strongly even on the production of solid things—as when, for a most striking case, the rate of production of iron fell for some months in 1893 to 40 per cent of what it had been before.

Besides the hesitation and timidity in this country we must take into the account the withdrawal of capital by foreigners, which caused an excess of exports over imports of $279,000,000 in the year August 1, 1893, to August 1, 1894, and say one-half that amount in the current year.

It seems to me that to attribute a decrease of 5 per cent in incomes during the last two years, a loss of $1,400,000,000, to anxiety at home and abroad about the gold reserve is thoroughly reasonable. And we must remember that this anxiety and loss is by no means ended yet, and also that it began to some extent back in 1885, and has been more or less active almost ever since then.

And I have taken no account here of the frightful wreck of health and life and property in the panic of 1893. We all know instances of sad loss of health, and most of us, probably, of one or more cases of death among our own friends, which were obviously caused by that panic.

Now, it would be absurd to attribute the panic wholly to the vicious character of our currency. Panics pretty regularly recur about ten years apart. But unquestionably our bad currency was one of several causes of this panic, and it increased the sharpness and intensity of it enormously. It is only necessary to compare our experience in this panic with our experience in former ones, and with the experience of England during the last twenty years, in order to feel sure that our vicious currency doubled our sufferings.

And we consider an annual interest charge of $14,000,000 as more important than the lowering of the honor of our country plus a loss of $700,000,000 in a single year, with nobody knows how many more losses to follow.

We brokers have the same kind of question constantly facing us that the Government has. We, of course, can not borrow on call without interest, as the Government can, but we can almost always borrow much cheaper on call than on time. We do not dare, however, to have more than a moderate share of our loans on call, although we always have good convertible quick assets backing up every loan. The Government has almost no quick assets beyond its working balance, and has $500,000,000 out on call, but it is not willing to fund this call loan, because it would force the inhabitants of the country to pay an additional 20 cents apiece each year, even though this funding would save it from humiliation, and would save these inhabitants from losses of hundreds of millions each year.

Was there ever such indifference to reputation or such bad business judgment? Putting aside all consideration of honor, the fear of a charge of $14,000,000 per year, at the most, distributed among 70,000,000 of people. prevents our putting our finances in proper order, and prevents our sharing as we might in the revival of enterprise which is now springing up in Europe.

On this latter point let me read you a paragraph from the financial column of the New York Evening Post of last Wednesday:

It is not improbable that the railway shares may later on reflect further the expectations roused by the interstate amendment, especially if the bill goes promptly through the Senate. But the hesitation of the market to-day, taken in connection with its action since October. is evidence enough that the trouble now existing lies much deeper. Europe's view of our currency situation, reflected in the foreign sales, even after the election and the bond issue, and expressed with little reservation in the best-informed foreign newspapers, is shared in no small degree by home-investing interests. It does not excite alarm, but it prompts the utmost caution and checks all efforts to anticipate returning prosperity. The gold movement's continuance will depend largely upon how far the conduct of our legislators justifies or belies these honest misgivings. But for this doubt over the possibility of currency-reform legislation, a foreign buying movement in American securities would now be almost certain. The spread of the investment movement in London is shown by the fact that subscriptions to new security issues in that city have risen from a weekly average of $3,500,000 in September and $6,500,000 in October to $15,000,000 since November's opening. But little or nothing of this new capital comes to the United States. Of the fifty-million Federal loan of November, hardly more than a million passed into foreign keeping.

The world is watching to see whether Congress will allow our Treasury to drift along in its present helpless condition—appealing more and more frequently and weakly to the money powers—or whether Congress will do boldly, promptly, what it has evidently decided to do eventually. and root out the evil immediately. The cancellation can be as slow as we please. What is needed to restore our good standing and peace is the adoption of a plan which will surely, without fail, effect this cancellation within a definite period of time. Capital is much wanted in the newer parts of the country and can much more easily be got if the greenbacks and Treasury notes are once canceled.

This seems to me to be of vastly more importance than is generally appreciated. It is about two years and a half since people began to be anxious about the Treasury position. I suppose we people in the street—as we say—feel it more than most people. But certainly it has been our experience that it has been the cause of great anxiety and worry to every business man of the country. The $14,000,000 charged is the largest element at the very worst, and it would not be as much as that.

The Carlisle bill or the Eckles bill, taken alone without anything further, will not, so far as I can judge, give confidence either to home investors or to European investors.

Mr. JOHNSON, of Ohio. Your reason for wanting to retire greenbacks is to avoid the necessity of carrying a gold reserve?

Mr. JACKSON. In a general way, but I want to say another thing. if you go into details. I think that very soon after a great many greenbacks were canceled we should be compelled to make the silver dollars convertible into gold on demand. I do not think it would increase the strain on the Treasury to-day.

Mr. JOHNSON, of Ohio. You want to retire the greenbacks so that there will be no call loans for gold?

Mr. JACKSON. Exactly.

Mr. JOHNSON, of Ohio. And then you want to propose a step further—that is. to make every silver dollar or silver certificate redeemable by the Government in gold.

Mr. JACKSON. Every one of them.

Mr. JOHNSON, of Ohio. So you would still have to carry gold

Mr. JACKSON. Yes, sir.

Mr. JOHNSON, of Ohio. Until what point should be reached?

Mr. JACKSON. I do not know exactly how I would treat the silver dollars eventually; I have not thought of that. The Treasury would need a much smaller reserve in the future if the greenbacks or Treasury notes were out of the way. In fact, I think the need would be almost next to nothing.

Mr. JOHNSON, of Ohio. You would have to have a small reserve for that.

Mr. JACKSON. Undoubtedly.

Mr. JOHNSON, of Ohio. You would reissue the silver dollars after they have gone into the Treasury, would you?

Mr. JACKSON. It is enough to begin. I should like to retire the silver dollars by and by, but we have got to protect the Treasury notes and greenbacks first.

Mr. JOHNSON, of Ohio. The amount of greenbacks and Treasury notes is about $500,000,000?

Mr. JACKSON. I think so.

Mr. JOHNSON, of Ohio. And the amount of silver and silver certificates?

Mr. JACKSON. I think the amount of silver certificates is about $340,000,000 additional, and about $56,000,000 of silver dollars.

Mr. JOHNSON, of Ohio. Ultimately you want to retire all those with gold?

Mr. JACKSON. That is what I should prefer.

Mr. JOHNSON, of Ohio. Is that the feeling of the "street," as you express it?

Mr. JACKSON. I think without doubt that is the feeling of men who have really given thought to it. Of course, I know men do not really think much about it. But there is no question about it at all, and it is perfectly impossible to make many people believe that we are not going upon a silver basis, and that soon. I have talked with many who thought so. I have talked with one gentleman whose father is in the Bank of England, in London, and he says: "You are going to silver in three years, as a matter of course." They take it as a matter of course. We have got to change that if we want to get on a proper footing with the rest of the nations of the world.

Mr. JOHNSON, of Ohio. After destroying the belief of the people in further silver, as you think ought to be done, you think the next step would be to retire greenbacks and finally to retire all the silver in circulation?

Mr. JACKSON. That is it.

Mr. JOHNSON, of Ohio. And that is the feeling among the people of New York City?

Mr. JACKSON. I live in Boston, but I should say it is, decidedly.

Mr. SPERRY. Would you circulate any silver at all?

Mr. JACKSON. As subsidiary coinage, of course; halves and quarters. I do not think a little silver could do any great harm. But this matter of passing silver as a legal tender when it is only intrinsically worth 50 cents on the dollar is, of course, vitally wrong and must do harm.

Mr. SPERRY. Do you think we shall ever be able to redeem our obligations in gold?

Mr. JACKSON. I do not think there is the slightest question of it. I think this notion about the scarcity of gold is an entire mistake.

Mr. SPERRY. Our circulation is how much larger than our gold?

Mr. JACKSON. Five hundred million dollars in greenbacks and Treasury notes together, as near as I can estimate; I would not pretend to be accurate; $340,000,000 of silver certificates and $56,000,000 of silver.

Mr. SPERRY. How long, in your judgment, would it require the United States to redeem its obligations in gold?

Mr. JACKSON. I think to cancel greenbacks at the rate of about $50,000,000 a year would not only be perfectly easy, but would be moderate enough. It is not a question of redeeming and canceling in gold particularly. All the Secretary has to do is to sell $500,000,000 in bonds, and destroy the greenbacks received in payment.

Mr. SPERRY. What would you issue, if anything, in place of the Treasury notes taken in and destroyed?

Mr. JACKSON. When you say "you" do you mean the Government, or do you mean the banks?

Mr. SPERRY. The Government. When the Government takes in the United States Treasury notes, greenbacks, and notes issued under the act of 1890, and destroys them, what would you issue in place of them, if anything?

Mr. JACKSON. I should not properly call it issuing at all. But what I should do would be to coin the gold brought to the mint into standard dollars and eagles and subsidiary coinage.

Mr. SPERRY. Would you substitute for the destroyed currency any other paper currency?

Mr. JACKSON. I would let the banks take care of themselves, just as I would let an apothecary take care of medicine, and let shoemakers take care of shoes. It is a great deal worse for the Government to enter into the business of banking than it is for an apothecary; there is much greater difference in the avocation.

Mr. WALKER. Do you understand that there are $346,000,000 of greenbacks?

Mr. JACKSON. I think so. I may not be accurate, but I think so.

Mr. WALKER. Suppose we had a banking system which required the banks to keep their bank reserve, half in gold and you might keep the other half in silver. Assume $400,000,000 altogether, then there would be $200,000,000 of each. Suppose $246,000,000 of the greenbacks out were destroyed after being purchased by bonds or by the banks assuming the greenbacks for their own notes; and then suppose the Treasury redeemed the remaining $100,000,000 out for the other $100,000,000. That would clean up the greenbacks?

Mr. JACKSON. Yes; that would clean them up. They would still be in existence.

Mr. WALKER. No.

Mr. JACKSON. I thought you said they would be held against the bank notes.

Mr. WALKER. No, sir. You will please mark my question as I put it.

Mr. JACKSON. I misunderstood you.

Mr. WALKER. If the Government took up $246,000,000 of greenbacks and destroyed them, and the banks put their own notes in place of them, provided the Government would agree when they went out of existence to pay them with good money, that being the condition on which they took them; then the Treasury had the $100,000,000 to pay the other $100,000,000 of greenbacks. That would destroy the whole, so far as the Treasury is concerned, in current redemption?

Mr. JACKSON. Yes.

Mr. WALKER. That being the case, would there then be the slightest idea in Europe, in this country, or anywhere else, that there is the least danger of our coming to a silver basis if the Government would say, "We will pay no more gold; you can go to the banks for your gold?"

Mr. JACKSON. I understand that that is your bill——

Mr. WALKER. I did not ask that.

Mr. JACKSON. No, sir; I say I think that is a good deal better. I think your notion of paying greenbacks is vastly better than Eckels's or Carlisle's plan of holding them. But what I want to say is this: I do not think that would establish confidence so much as going ahead on a definite plan to burn up all that is taken in. That is what would establish confidence. Sometime ago, after the war, at any rate, we had a certain number of greenbacks out. Then we got some more out, and got some back, and so on.

Mr. WALKER. You are not answering the question.

Mr. JACKSON. Yes, I am; I want to show you why it would not establish confidence, as you think it would—at least in my opinion, if you want my opinion. My opinion is that it would not, and for this reason, if you please, sir.

SEVERAL MEMBERS OF THE COMMITTEE. Go ahead.

Mr. JACKSON. I say that confidence by the action of the Government has been seriously impaired. When we had $346,000,000 of greenbacks everybody said that would never increase. But silver certificates were issued which were apparently receivable for dues, and were held by the banks as reserves (very nearly as bad as if they were absolutely redeemable in gold); then, in addition, there were the silver certificates amounting to nearly $350,000,000, and $150,000,000 more of Treasury notes, making altogether about $840,000,000 of this wretched stuff, when we should have had but $346,000,000. I think that Mr. Walker's plan, along with the plan of Mr. Carlisle or Mr. Eckels, is defective in that way. It will not restore confidence. We have got to turn a sharp angle. We can not slide along easily. We have got to turn sharply around and adopt a plan which will cancel all these notes and show a perfect change of heart, I think. I have tried to answer you.

Mr. WALKER. I believe you have said that about three times; I hope you will not say it again.

Mr. JACKSON. I do not know that that is necessary. Still, if that is your method in here, of course I shall respect it.

The CHAIRMAN. I believe the witness is entirely respectful.

Mr. WALKER. I suppose members of the committee have some rights.

Mr. JACKSON. And I suppose a witness has. I agree with you very decidedly financially, but I do not wish——

Mr. WALKER. I was asking you a question, and I want to say here that since Mr. Carlisle has brought in his bill it has seemed out of order to speak of any other bill, and I believe you are the first gentleman who has spoken of any other bill.

Mr. JACKSON. I was not aware of it. I am very sorry.

Mr. WALKER. You are the first man who has introduced my name.

Mr. JACKSON. I apologize most humbly. I was not aware that it was improper.

Mr. WALKER. I only say that I was asking questions for information, and you have chosen to answer them as you have. I think I will ask no more.

Mr. BROSIUS. Suppose all the greenbacks and Treasury notes are out of the way, and that all of our paper money consists of notes under the banking system. Would you consider it practicable to have those notes all redeemed in gold at the Treasury of the United States, instead of having them redeemed over the counters of the banks? In other words, having a single place for one redemption instead of having three or four thousand, as the case may be, according to the number of banks.

Mr. JACKSON. That is a thing I have not thought of. I should think it would be extremely inconvenient for many people. The notes are now redeemable at the banks and at the Treasury, and sometimes at other places, and I think that has worked very well.

Mr. BROSIUS. Some publicists advocate having a single place to keep gold to be used for purposes of redemption, on the ground that it is very much more economical to do so; that it requires more gold to be held in reserve if divided up into 4,000 parcels than to keep it all together.

Mr. JACKSON. I do not believe that is the case. That same notion was held by these large industrial concerns. They thought because they were big they could have a large floating indebtedness, but it turned out that large concerns can not have nearly so large indebtedness as a smaller concern. In the long run it is my impression that the Government would have the same experience. Of course I do not know.

Mr. HAUGEN. Do you think this large gold reserve would always be the object of attack?

Mr. JACKSON. I should not like that method.

The CHAIRMAN. If there are no other questions to be asked this gentleman, the Chair will state that to-morrow Mr. St. John, of New York, and Mr. Williams, the president of the Chemical Bank, of New York City, will be here, and the committee will meet at 10 o'clock unless there be some other order.

Mr. WALKER. I move that we go into executive session for a few minutes.

The motion to go into executive session was agreed to at 4 o'clock and 20 minutes p. m. After a short executive session the committee adjourned, to meet at 10 o'clock to-morrow morning.

COMMITTEE ON BANKING AND CURRENCY,
Saturday, December 15, 1891.

The Committee met at 10 a. m.

There were present Mr. Springer (chairman); Mr. Sperry; Mr. Cox; Mr. Cobb, of Missouri; Mr. Culberson; Mr. Ellis; Mr. Cobb, of Alabama; Mr. Warner; Mr. Johnson, of Ohio; Mr. Black; Mr. Hall; Mr. Walker; Mr. Brosius; Mr. Henderson; Mr. Russell; Mr. Haugen; and Mr. Johnson, of Indiana.

The CHAIRMAN. The committee will please come to order. The chair has received the following letter, which he desires to submit to the committee. It is from York, Nebr.

Mr. JOHNSON, of Indiana. What is the name?

The CHAIRMAN. George W. Post, president of the York National Bank.

The chairman proceeded to read the letter.

Mr. JOHNSON, of Indiana. Does the chair desire that to go in the record?

The CHAIRMAN. Yes.

Mr. JOHNSON, of Indiana. Has the chair received letters from people throughout the country in regard to the bill, letters of a general character addressed to the chair?

The CHAIRMAN. Some of that character, yes.

Mr. JOHNSON, of Indiana. By what method does the chair determine which to present and have incorporated in the record and which to keep back?

The CHAIRMAN. The chair has heretofore presented letters only addressed to the committee from those who have been invited to appear before the committee, and the reason this letter was presented here was, it came from a region of country from which we had not been able to get persons.

Mr. JOHNSON, of Indiana. It seems to me if we are going to put into the record individual letters from those people who favor this bill, it would be a pretty good idea to put in letters generally on this subject, so we will have a general consensus of the opinion of the country.

The CHAIRMAN. If there is any objection, I will withdraw the letter.

Mr. JOHNSON, of Indiana. I would like to ask the chairman a question first. I would like to ask the chairman if this is the only letter of that kind indorsing the Carlisle plan.

The CHAIRMAN. This is the only one from a national banker.

Mr. JOHNSON. I would suggest that they all be put in or that this one be withdrawn.

The CHAIRMAN. The chair will withdraw the letter.

Mr. HALL. I got a letter from a Populist this morning in which he denounced the bill.

The CHAIRMAN. The chair desires to state that he has received a letter from Mr. John W. Stewart, of New York, who regrets that he can not be present, he having been invited to be present. The gentlemen present to-day are Mr. St. John, of the Mercantile National Bank, and Mr. Williams, of the Chemical National Bank of New York. Mr. Williams will first address the committee.

STATEMENT OF MR. GEORGE G. WILLIAMS, PRESIDENT CHEMICAL NATIONAL BANK, NEW YORK.

Mr. Williams addressed the committee, as follows:

Mr. Chairman and gentlemen of the committee: Invited to present my views before this committee, they shall be as brief as the subjects in hand will permit.

The situation is one requiring but firmness and common sense. The first problem in our clumsy and conglomerated financial system is the disposition to be made of the legal-tender notes. Coming into being during the war, they performed their functions admirably as a war measure, but we now wake up and find that the war is over and that the notes are in the way and are not wanted. No financial scheme can be permanently successful without providing for the elimination of these notes from our fiscal system. Provision should be made at once for the funding of a part of them, say $250,000,000, in amounts of perhaps $50,000,000 at a time, at the discretion of the Secretary of the Treasury.

United States bonds bearing a rate of interest not over 3 per cent—and my idea would be that a 3 per cent bond would be the most advisable to issue, as it would never go below par—and that these bonds should be received as security for circulating notes of national banks on a basis of par for the bonds, the Government having a first lien also on the assets of the banks as additional security. No further margin need be required, as the security would be ample. These notes should be redeemable in the city of New York, and when issued in sufficient volume and being readily convertible would furnish adequate elasticity to the currency, which is so much desired, but in no event should be made subordinate to that of security.

The tax on the circulation of national banks should at once be removed, and it will be readily seen that with a 3 per cent bond at par and no tax to be paid on the circulation there will be some inducement for national banks as a matter of profit to take out circulating notes.

I might say one word in regard to the Baltimore plan, and it is this: That the security would be ample for notes issued by banks conducted in as conservative a manner as are those of the banks of that city, but it is to be remembered that this system would apply to nearly 4,000 banks, many of them very small, and located in all parts of the country, and that it is presumable that very many mushroom banks would be started, merely with a view of issuing circulating notes; and it seems hardly possible that loss can be avoided to the whole system, arising from the failure of such banks. As to the proposed issue of notes secured by a sinking fund and a tax to be levied on solvent banks, to secure the circulation of any number of mushroom banks which would undoubtedly spring up, it will be readily seen that conservative and well-managed institutions would absolutely refuse to join hands in making good losses sure to arise from failed banks.

Providing in this manner for the funding of the legal-tender notes, and for a new issue of national-bank notes, there still remains to be dealt with the question of the silver certificates and of the Sherman notes. With reference to the latter, the reserve of $100,000,000 in the Treasury would seem to be ample for their protection; and as for the silver certificates, I would say that it would be wise to pass an act of Congress allowing them to be redeemed in silver bullion at its market value, at the discretion of the Secretary of the Treasury; and I do not know but that it might be well enough to include in such an act the Sherman notes also.

With these few changes in the law, our financial system would be upon a sound basis, without which it is impossible to do business with confidence, and the efficiency of our banking system, the most perfect which has ever been devised, would be increased and strengthened.

Mr. WARNER. Do you think that the plan you propose would give sufficient elasticity to the currency?

Mr. WILLIAMS. I think that the national-bank notes would take the place of the legal-tender notes, and when they are not wanted, as at present, they would be redeemed. That would give sufficient elasticity to the currency. If $250,000,000 of legal-tender notes were withdrawn and an equal amount of national-bank notes substituted which would be readily redeemed, I think it would afford sufficient elasticity to the currency. The details of this can be worked out by the Treasury Department having on hand ready printed and ready to be issued at any moment a sufficient quantity of these notes in reserve, which would afford relief in case of emergency.

Mr. WARNER. To what elasticity do you especially refer; the elasticity which will keep the general volume of notes in accord with the general development of business, or the elasticity which will provide a large excess in one month, for example, over what might be necessary in the next month?

Mr. WILLIAMS. There are times when there is too much money, and times again when money is scarce. When money is a plethora in the market, as it is at present, and can not be used it will be taken in, and national-bank notes will remain locked up in the vaults of the national banks. When a demand comes they would go out by discounts.

Mr. WARNER. Your idea is this would provide elasticity to meet the varying demands of business week by week and month by month?

Mr. WILLIAMS. I do.

Mr. WARNER. And your term "elasticity" refers to that and not to a general expansion to meet all the developments of business, by years, for example?

Mr. WILLIAMS. I think that will provide for itself.

Mr. WARNER. I understand you. You speak about redemption facilities. Do you consider that would have enough of elasticity unless we had better redemption facilities than we have now?

Mr. WILLIAMS. The better the redemption facilities the more elastic is the currency.

Mr. WARNER. Do you think, for example, that provision of our present law which makes the national-bank notes a practical legal tender between banks were repealed, our currency would be more elastic?

Mr. WILLIAMS. I do not know that I get your idea.

Mr. WARNER. As I understand, our present national-bank law practically makes the notes of national banks legal tenders in transactions between banks?

Mr. WILLIAMS. Yes; among themselves.

Mr. WARNER. And that takes away what might, under some circumstances, be an inducement for the banks to send each other's notes promptly in for redemption, does it not?

Mr. WILLIAMS. We never have found in our experience that provision was objectionable.

Mr. WARNER. You think it has little or no effect?

Mr. WILLIAMS. It has not with us. These notes are redeemable readily at a central point, and when they are not wanted they are taken in, and when they are wanted they quickly go out.

Mr. WARNER. So that in regard to that special feature you suggest no change?

Mr. WILLIAMS. I suggest no change.

Mr. WARNER. But, generally speaking, additional redemption facilities would assist elasticity?

Mr. WILLIAMS. Redemption in the city of New York would be more desirable than in Washington, simply because of the cost of transporting notes by express from New York and different cities to Washington.

Mr. WARNER. The greater the redemption facilities the greater the elasticity?

Mr. WILLIAMS. Yes.

Mr. WARNER. Now, I am about to ask you a few questions; but it is not my intention to go into the business of your bank to any extent which is not now published, so if I should inadvertently ask any question which you think goes beyond that, I trust you will stop me. I want to show the position of your bank and the conservatism of that position. What is the capital of your bank?

Mr. WILLIAMS. Three hundred thousand dollars.

Mr. WARNER. What is the present quotation of its stock?

Mr. WILLIAMS. About forty-three hundred.

Mr. WARNER. So that the capital of your bank now represents how many millions of dollars?

Mr. WILLIAMS. Our capital is $300,000 and our surplus is about $7,000,000.

Mr. WARNER. Your stock is worth about $4,300 a share?

Mr. WILLIAMS. Yes, sir; it sells for that. It sells for more than it is worth.

Mr. WARNER. Forty-three times as much as its par. What is the amount of your bond deposit?

Mr. WILLIAMS. The Chemical Bank has never taken out any circulation whatever. Our bond deposit is $50,000; but we have never circulated any notes.

Mr. WARNER. You think the Baltimore plan is not sufficiently conservative?

Mr. WILLIAMS. My idea is—I have no confidence in the circulation. We tried it in the city of New York and State of New York, and it was not successful; and the Baltimore plan, as I have stated in the paper I have presented, would be all very well for the institutions where there has not a failure occurred in a bank for about sixty years, and where there is a correct public sentiment and nothing mushroom would be tolerated; but it is to be presumed, if the bond security is taken away, that any number of banks will spring up in great numbers at every crossroad town in the West, and let the Comptroller of the Currency do the best he can, those banks will get ahead of him and there will be lots of little failures.

Mr. WARNER. You are referring now to the national banks?

Mr. WILLIAMS. Yes, sir.

Mr. WALKER. I want to get at under what conditions he announces these mushroom banks would spring up?

Mr. WILLIAMS. In the event of being allowed to issue circulating notes without every one of them being absolutely secured.

Mr. WARNER. That is under the Baltimore plan, for example.

Mr. WILLIAMS. Now, I am talking about the Baltimore plan.

Mr. WARNER. What is the reason, may I ask, that you have not taken out circulation?

Mr. WILLIAMS. We were under the State-bank system and issued circulating notes up to the breaking out of the war, and at that time we had about $300,000 of notes in circulation, and we redeemed every one of them in gold—and we did not care, as a matter of pride, and a little profit in it too; but we did not care, as a matter of pride, to issue notes which could not be redeemed in gold.

Mr. WALKER. As I understand, you see no necessity for funding but $250,000,000 of the $500,000,000 of Treasury notes, etc.?

Mr. WILLIAMS. I meant to have added to my remarks the remaining legal tenders could be provided for in due time by the surplus revenues. I would like to add that. I meant to have done so. I would like to add to this statement that the remainder of the legal tenders should be provided for in due time by the surplus revenues of the Government.

Mr. WALKER. How are they to be redeemed by the surplus revenues of the Government when the revenues are $6,000,000 or $8,000,000 a month less than the current expenses of the Government?

Mr. WILLIAMS. Well, I take it for granted some time or other there will be money enough in the Treasury to redeem these legal-tender notes at par instead of buying 4 per cent bonds at 130, as the Government did at one time.

Mr. WALKER. Why should you assume that under present conditions?

Mr. WILLIAMS. Only from the history of the past.

Mr. WALKER. Well, are we not under very different laws from what we had in the past, revenue laws of all kinds?

Mr. WILLIAMS. That may all be, but the Government has reduced its debt from the time of the close of the war over $2,000,000,000, and I do not believe we are going to be a bankrupt treasury either.

Mr. WALKER. Do you think the experiment thus far under present revenue laws and conditions would justify our expecting the revenues will soon exceed the expenditures?

Mr. WILLIAMS. I think they will in the course of ten or fifteen years.

Mr. WALKER. Then in due time you mean ten or fifteen years?

Mr. WILLIAMS. Yes; I do not say in six months.

Mr. WALKER. Then for ten or fifteen years, according to your testimony——

Mr. WILLIAMS. Excuse me. I am jumping at that.

Mr. WALKER. I understand that. Then for ten or fifteen years there will be $250,000,000——

Mr. WILLIAMS. There will be $146,000,000. The legal tender notes now——

Mr. WALKER. And the Treasury notes; do not the Treasury notes threaten the gold in the Treasury just to the same extent?

Mr. WILLIAMS. I have provided for this.

Mr. WALKER. But I haven't asked my question yet. Do not they threaten the gold of the Treasury just as much as the greenbacks?

Mr. WILLIAMS. Quite as much.

Mr. WALKER. What answer do you give to that?

Mr. WILLIAMS. Fund the legal tenders and then the $100,000,000 of gold in the Treasury would be as a reserve for the Treasury notes.

Mr. WALKER. Well, but you are only funding $250,000,000, and you leave $100,000,000 of greenbacks and $150,000,000——

Mr. WILLIAMS. We leave those greenbacks; many are destroyed and a great many are out of sight and not in circulation, hoarded up, and they will hardly come to the surface—will hardly be felt.

Mr. WALKER. Do you think if $250,000,000 of the $500,000,000 of greenbacks and Treasury notes all equally payable in gold by the Treasury were taken out of circulation and bank notes substituted, that the other $250,000,000 would not be sought and used to take gold out of the Treasury by those who export gold?

Mr. WILLIAMS. If it were needed; but I think the contraction which would result to a moderate extent in funding $250,000,000 of legal tenders, and the redemption facilities of redeeming national-bank notes would inspire confidence in our currency and would relieve the Treasury there would not be so large an amount of gold wanted in export, and and foreign capital would be invested here.

Mr. WALKER: Will not you explain to the committee how substituting $250,000,000 of national-bank currency for $250,000,000 of Treasury notes and greenbacks is going to relieve the Treasury from current redemption? The demand would then be just as big as it is to-day; how are you going to lessen the demand for gold with still $250,000,000 notes to use to get it?

Mr. WILLIAMS: The funding of $250,000,000 of legal tenders leaves the Treasury notes to be provided for by the $100,000,000 gold in the Treasury.

MR. WALKER: Is not that being taken out to-day, and has it not been for the last year or two?

Mr. WILLIAMS. I think the facilities for redeeming the national-bank notes and the elasticity which would result from the legal tenders being changed to national-bank notes, the legal tender being a fiat currency, whereas the national-bank notes can be redeemed, every one of them, would so tone up the money markets that the rates of interest would be improved and foreign capital would be utilized in the New York market.

Mr. WALKER. Will you give the committee, so far as you know, the class of persons and their business who have taken gold from the Treasury in the last twenty-four months. Are they not brokers and those who furnish the money for the importers to pay for their goods, etc.?

Mr. WILLIAMS. There is always a large amount of foreign money used in New York if the rate of interest would justify its being left there. The Canadian banks always use a large amount in the New York markets, provided they can get interest enough to make it an object to be left there. Money can always be borrowed in New York of the foreign bankers, or rather, foreign money can always be borrowed in New York by those doing business abroad, collateral being left with the bankers here and the money being drawn for by the lenders on the other side.

Mr. WALKER. What you said is interesting, but I want, if you please, to fix your mind on my question. How will the minds or habits of persons who need gold, and they do need it constantly, be affected by the changing of $250,000,000 of greenbacks and Treasury notes into national-bank notes; how will it lessen the demand for gold? We do not know how it is going to do it. How is it going to relieve the Treasury from this constant drain of gold, in view of the fact they keep wanting but a very few millions of dollars on a given day or week?

Mr. WILLIAMS. The Secretary of the Treasury, in his report, if you remember, states that about $243,000,000 of the balance of trade has been in our favor, and yet we have exported gold. A large part of that $243,000,000 is foreign capital, which has been removed from this country, and most of it would have remained here provided it could have been utilized, but with the rate of interest at 1 per cent in New York for call money, and the rate of interest at 2 per cent in Paris and 3 per cent in Berlin, money is sure to be taken from our market, and it has in that way. There has been also a fear of our currency. There has been a fear on the part of foreigners that we would go to a silver basis and they would be caught with their investments here, which would make them silver investments. For that reason timid people—and capital is always timid—have taken their money largely away from America.

Mr. WALKER. I am despairing of an answer?

Mr. WILLIAMS. Give it to me again.

Mr. WALKER. I have given it five or six times, and as there are quite a number of gentlemen here who would like to ask questions I will drop that. Are you aware of a prejudice in the country against the use of United States bonds to secure circulation, and that it is said on nearly every stump in political addresses that the bankers get the interest of the bonds and then change the bonds for substantially smaller bonds, which they loan to the people in the shape of money and then get additional interest on that? That is to say, throughout the whole of this country where interest is high they claim that bankers get 3 per cent on the bonds and then they get money for the bonds and then they get anywhere from 6 to 10 per cent on that money, making from 10 to 13 per cent. That is the way it lays in the public mind. Now, in view of that fact, what reason have you to believe Congress will issue a 3 per cent bond and provide any arrangement to keep it at par to secure notes and then repeal the tax on banks?

Mr. WILLIAMS. I have nothing to say as to what Congress will do; but I simply say what is the wise thing to do. This proposition of mine is a wise thing, and that is all I can say.

Mr. WALKER. How are they to keep this 3 per cent bond at par so the banks can get them at par?

Mr. WILLIAMS. I do not think they would get par; I think they would be at a little premium, but I think the 3 per cent bond is the best bond to issue because they would never go below par in tight times.

Mr. WALKER. Would you advise the Government to issue bonds to bankers at 3 per cent at par continuously, so they might have the banks——

Mr. WILLIAMS. No, sir; I would advise them to offer them to the public and get the best price they can.

Mr. WALKER. How are you to make the use of money any cheaper and make it any more for the advantage of banks to issue money than there has been up to the present time, and the testimony of every banker, I think, who has come here is that with bonds at a premium there is no profit. How are you going to get the banks to issue money if there is no profit in it?

Mr. WILLIAMS. I have stated there it will be advisable to take off the tax of 1 per cent on circulation.

Mr. WALKER. You would advise the Government to still pay interest on the bonds, give its money out, and then to take the tax off the banks?

Mr. WILLIAMS. I would. Observe the Chemical Bank issues no circulation and we do not intend to, but I think the Government ought to go out of the banking business, and it is no more part of their business to issue legal-tender notes than it is for them to issue, as during the war, the 3-cent pieces. I have now in my possession a 3-cent piece issued by the Government of the United States. It is pretty close quarters when they get to doing that.

Mr. WALKER. In paper, you mean?

Mr. WILLIAMS. I do not think it is the business of the Government to issue notes at all, and especially for a great Goverment like this that ought to have the best credit of any government in the whole world.

Mr. WALKER. What are the express charges per $1,000, nominal value, on currency from New York to Washington for redemption?

Mr. WILLIAMS. I really can not tell you.

Mr. ST. JOHN. Twenty-five cents a thousand.

Mr. WALKER. How would you get the national-bank notes back to the vaults of the banks promptly, so that each bank would issue its own notes, and no other?

Mr. WILLIAMS. I do not mean they should be redeemed by different banks in the city of New York, but I mean they should be redeemed in the case of New York the same as they are redeemed now in Washington and sent home.

Mr. WALKER. I did not ask you what should be done. That is interesting, but my point was, What legal restriction or what device of any form would you put in the statute so as to induce or compel each bank to promptly redeem its circulation? There is nothing in them now. In fact, the law is rather against it by making them a legal tender between banks. What device do you suggest?

Mr. WILLIAMS. If we get a surplus of bank notes all we have to do is to send them to Washington and the Government sends legal tender to you.

Mr. WALKER. I understand that. You talked about that. Do you mean to say that custom in all national banks is going to make each national bank redeem its notes at some central agency? It is not done at the present time. It is only $20,000,000 redeemed last year out of $175,000,000; are you not aware, with currency thus forced back to the banks, there ought to be a billion or two redeemed? Do you know what the custom was in the old Suffolk system?

Mr. WILLIAMS. Yes, sir.

Mr. WALKER. Do you know the proportion of notes issued which were redeemed?

Mr. WILLIAMS. No, sir; I do not.

Mr. WALKER. Why does not your bank capitalize some of the immense surplus it has?

Mr. WILLIAMS. Our surplus profits have all been earned by the bank itself, and we have thought it was best for us to let well enough alone. We have never considered the question of making our surplus into capital.

Mr. WALKER. You have not considered the question? What dividend has been declared?

Mr. WILLIAMS. We pay now at the rate of 150 per cent per annum on the stock, and let the rest accumulate.

Mr. WALKER. How much did you accumulate the last two or three years?

Mr. WILLIAMS. The last two or three years—we had the silver panic in 1893, and we did not accumulate so much, but ordinarily we add about $300,000 to our surplus profits annually, beside our dividend of $450,000.

Mr. WALKER. You spoke about banks springing up at the cross-roads or Western settlements and issuing notes, etc. Do you think that would be a disadvantage to the country?

Mr. WILLIAMS. I do.

Mr. WALKER. Do you think it a disadvantage to the neighbors to have a bank located there?

Mr. WILLIAMS. I do.

Mr. WALKER. Do you think it is a disadvantage to small towns and farmers of the district to have banks in them?

Mr. WILLIAMS. I think they may have too many.

Mr. WALKER. If you will excuse me, the question is what I want answered. Do you think it is a disadvantage to these neighbors and small towns and the farmers of the district to have banks in them?

Mr. WILLIAMS. I think every bank is a disadvantage which is not conservatively managed for the safety of the public, no matter where it is located. I think there may be too many banks.

Mr. WALKER. Do you think these banks in the country maybe as safely managed as banks in a city?

Mr. WILLIAMS. Oh, yes; they maybe, but I think they are not.

Mr. WALKER. Do you think the failures of banks in the country with a capital of from $50,000 to $100,000 each will show, their aggregated capital and liabilities, larger than the failed banks in the cities?

Mr. WILLIAMS. I think they are more numerous.

Mr. WALKER. I knew that before. They may be more numerous, but that is not the question.

Mr. WILLIAMS. They could not necessarily be larger in volume, because they do not have as large deposits.

Mr. WALKER. My question was, whether the country banks of $50,000 to $100,000 capital, in the aggregate sum involved in their failures, and the aggregate liabilities involved in their failures, are more than the aggregate liabilities of the large banks which have failed in cities?

Mr. WILLIAMS. Well, I could not say. That would be a matter of statistics altogether.

Mr. WALKER. If it is not larger, where is the damage to the community any more in these failures than the failures of city banks?

Mr. WILLIAMS. I think that the failures would be more numerous.

Mr. WALKER. It is not the question of being more numerous. If any fifty merchants fail for $20,000 each it is no worse than one merchant failing with an aggregate liability of that?

Mr. WILLIAMS. The bank could not fail——

Mr. WALKER. I asked you the question; what do you say in regard to that?

Mr. WILLIAMS. What is the question?

Mr. WALKER. My question is, if 50 merchants fail for $20,000 each is it worse for the public than it would be if any one merchant should fail owing the same amount?

Mr. WILLIAMS. Yes, it might be, because the assets——

Mr. WALKER. Assuming the assets be the same?

Mr. WILLIAMS. If the liabilities were scattered among poorer people then it would be worse.

Mr. WALKER. Would not their assets be more scattered and be more equitably divided?

Mr. WILLIAMS. The liabilities of a bank of $50,000 capital would be likely to strike poorer people.

Mr. WALKER. You do not think, then, it is for the interest of the country to have a banking system that would induce or permit bankers to organize smaller banks throughout the country, as in Scotland, but you would prefer to keep them concentrated, as in Paris, one great bank?

Mr. WILLIAMS. Yes, sir; I would not have the banking system too diffuse—too many of them.

The CHAIRMAN. Mr. Williams, some members of the committee desire to understand exactly the condition of your bank. What did you state the capital was?

Mr. WILLIAMS. Three hundred thousand dollars.

The CHAIRMAN. And the surplus?

Mr. WILLIAMS. The surplus and undivided profits are about $7,000,000. The surplus is $6,000,000 and the undivided profits a little over a million dollars, making a little over $7,000,000 of surplus and undivided profits.

The CHAIRMAN. And how much deposits?

Mr. WILLIAMS. Thirty million dollars.

The CHAIRMAN. What dividend do you pay per annum on your stock?

Mr. WILLIAMS. We pay now 150 per cent per annum.

The CHAIRMAN. How long has your bank been in existence?

Mr. WILLIAMS. It was originally chartered in 1823; became that from a special charter which expired in 1844. We then reorganized under the State banking law, the general banking law of the State of New York, and remained so until 1862 or 1863, I think it was, when we came under the national-banking system. I forget the year.

The CHAIRMAN. You stated the dividend last year was 150 per cent.

Mr. WILLIAMS. Yes, sir.

The CHAIRMAN. What were the undivided profits of that year?

Mr. WILLIAMS. Well, I have not it in mind; but owing to the panic our profits last year were not as large as usual. Usually we expect to add to our surplus 100 per cent besides the dividend we pay of 150 per cent.

The CHAIRMAN. That is $300,000 a year?

Mr. WILLIAMS. Yes, sir.

The CHAIRMAN. And a dividend of 150 per cent besides?

Mr. WILLIAMS. Yes, sir.

The CHAIRMAN. Will you state how much of your profits are due to the fact that you are organized as a national bank, and what would be your probable condition if you were simply operating as a State bank under the laws of New York?

Mr. WILLIAMS. I do not think that could be readily told, for the reason the only advantage we derive from being organized under the laws of the United States is that we are permitted to receive national-bank deposits, or rather that the deposits of national banks counts as their reserve when they are with us. If we were a State bank the deposits of national banks out of New York could not count with us as a part of their reserve, and I think the national-bank deposits are somewhere between $3,000,000 and $4,000,000, but I am not certain.

The CHAIRMAN. Do you pay interest on your deposits?

Mr. WILLIAMS. We pay no interest whatever on our deposits.

The CHAIRMAN. Neither national banks nor private individuals?

Mr. WILLIAMS. No interest whatever to any one under any circumstance.

The CHAIRMAN. Your profit would principally be made out of their deposits?

Mr. WILLIAMS. Our business comes from confidence. People have confidence in us and deposit their money with us.

The CHAIRMAN. It is money which brings——

Mr. WILLIAMS. It is money which makes money.

The CHAIRMAN. Which brings interest upon your investment?

Mr. WILLIAMS. Yes, sir.

Mr. JOHNSON, of Indiana. Mr. Williams, are you familiar with the provisions of the bill prepared by Mr. Carlisle and introduced by Mr. Springer, and now pending before this committee?

Mr. WILLIAMS. I have read it; yes.

Mr. JOHNSON, of Indiana. I wish you would take that bill up and go through with it as briefly as you reasonably can and tell us what you think of its provisions.

Mr. WILLIAMS. I have briefly stated here, if you will allow me to call your attention to it, "as to the proposed issue of notes secured by a sinking fund and a tax to be levied on solvent banks to secure the circulation of any number of mushroom banks which would undoubtedly spring up, it will be readily seen that conservative and well-managed institutions would absolutely refuse to join hands in making good losses sure to rise from such failed banks."

Mr. JOHNSON, of Indiana. Then you are opposed to the theory of protecting the noteholder by a safety fund in place of bond security as provided in the existing law?

Mr. WILLIAMS. I am, most heartily. I think the national-banking system of the United States is the best system which has ever been devised by the ingenuity of man, and all it wants is some few amendments to make it almost perfect.

Mr. JOHNSON, of Indiana. But there are other provisions in the Springer bill than the one to which you referred in the answer which you have just made me, and I would like to have you take these up in detail and give your opinion on them. Here is a copy of the bill if you desire to look it over, and time will be afforded you.

Mr. WILLIAMS. The bill itself is most skillfully and ably devised; if we were to have circulation under any system in which the notes are not fully secured it would be a very good system indeed, but I do not believe that conservative institutions would join hands in being jointly responsible for the circulation of 3,000 or 4,000 banks.

Mr. JOHNSON, of Indiana. Well, take now, if you please, what is known as the tenth section of the bill which in effect provides for State bank issues under certain restrictions to be imposed by the Federal Government. What do you think of that feature of the bill?

Mr. WILLIAMS. I think it would be almost impossible to make the circulation safe to be issued under such a bill as that.

Mr. JOHNSON, of Indiana. What is your opinion, aside from the kind of State-bank issue provided for in Mr. Carlisle's bill, as to the relative merits of a national system of note issue and a State-bank system of note issue? Do you get my idea?

Mr. WILLIAMS. No; repeat that, if you please.

Mr. JOHNSON, of Indiana. Which system do you think preferable for circulating notes in this country, a system under Federal control or a system exclusively under State control, or a system under joint Federal and State control?

Mr. WILLIAMS. Federal control, absolutely. This country has now had a circulation in which there has not been a dollar lost for thirty years. Prior to that time I have seen the circulation of Illinois State banks, secured by the stock of the State of Illinois, as good a State now as anywhere, and I have seen that currency discounted 10 per cent.

Mr. JOHNSON, of Indiana. But it is argued by those in favor of a State-bank system that these defects in the State-bank system occurred when there were fewer people and less means of communication, etc., and that now it would not be subject to the defects of the old system. What have you to say as to that?

Mr. WILLIAMS. There is no system equal to the national-bank system, and there never will be, only improve it up to the times, as it is hardly up. The law has hardly been changed for thirty years. Alter it a little and it will go all right. Paper money is like dynamite. It is worse than powder; sometimes it is like self-righteousness—the more you have of it the worse off you are. It is the most dangerous thing in the hands of irresponsible men that can be, and therefore I would not put it into the hands of irresponsible men. Where paper money is issued by banks which have large capital and large means behind it and responsible men who have character and capital and reputation, they will keep things straight, as they would in Baltimore under this Baltimore plan before your committee. But thousands of institutions would spring up with a view of getting a little extra circulation, and there would be losses under it just as certain as the sun rises.

Mr. JOHNSON, of Indiana. It is your idea then in devising a general system of banking and currency that the national-bank law should be the nucleus and its defects should be amended and its infirmities made whole?

Mr. WILLIAMS. Absolutely so.

Mr. JOHNSON, of Indiana. What do you consider the greatest defect in the present national-banking law?

Mr. WILLIAMS. Well, that is pretty hard. I ought to study on that a little.

Mr. JOHNSON, of Indiana. It furnishes a safe and sound currency?

Mr. WILLIAMS. Yes, sir.

Mr. JOHNSON, of Indiana. In what material particular essential to a good currency would you amend it?

Mr. WILLIAMS. The tax ought to be taken off, that is one thing.

Mr. JOHNSON, of Indiana. Why?

Mr. WILLIAMS. To enable the banks to make a little profit out of the circulation.

Mr. JOHNSON, of Indiana. It is your belief that the reason why we have not more extended circulation of the national-bank notes is because there is no profit in the circulation?

Mr. WILLIAMS. That is the great reason.

Mr. JOHNSON, of Indiana. And that it is impossible to get bankers to issue circulating notes unless there is some profit on the notes?

Mr. WILLIAMS. That is it.

Mr. JOHNSON, of Indiana. The act of the bankers making a profit on circulation does not necessarily mean that the people are oppressed thereby?

Mr. WILLIAMS. Not at all.

Mr. JOHNSON of Indiana. The bankers might make a profit and yet the welfare of the people might still be subserved?

Mr. WILLIAMS. Most certainly.

Mr. JOHNSON of Indiana. You take it then that the interest of the bankers and the interest of the people in this particular are identical and not hostile?

Mr. WILLIAMS. Certainly.

Mr. JOHNSON of Indiana. What would you say of a system for national banking which would put the control of banks, so far as the deposit and discount feature is concerned, under the control of one jurisdiction, and the issue of circulating notes under an entirely different jurisdiction?

Mr. WILLIAMS. Well, I suppose you refer to there being no supervision, no law as to reserve for deposits?

Mr. JOHNSON of Indiana. No.

Mr. WALKER. As provided in the Carlisle bill.

Mr. JOHNSON, of Indiana. What I mean is this, are the functions of a bank, so far as it being a bank of discount and deposit upon the one hand and a bank for issuing circulating notes upon the other, so susceptible of separation that the bank may be successfully operated under two tribunals, one regulating it as a bank of discount and deposit and the other regulating it as a bank for issuing circulating notes?

Mr. WILLIAMS. That can be done but I would not advise it. I think it is a great deal better that all banks should be under surpervision. The national bank system of examination by examiners is a wonderful check on insecure banking.

Mr. COX. Mr. Williams, in giving the reason why gold flows from this country, as I understand, you assign two reasons. One was the rate of interest in the United States being lower than it was in foreign countries it naturally made the gold seek a higher rate of interest. That was one?

Mr. WILLIAMS. That was one; yes, sir.

Mr. COX. Another reason you assigned was fear of the foreign investors in this country that their property would be brought to a silver basis?

Mr. WILLIAMS. Yes, sir; the fear of it.

Mr. COX. Those are the words I used, "the fear." Now then I understand you to say as a matter of fact that money in New York was at a lower rate of interest than it was in foreign countries?

Mr. WILLIAMS. Some of them; yes.

Mr. COX. And that is the reason gold went out?

Mr. WILLIAMS. That is one reason.

Mr. COX. That is a thing to which I wish to direct your attention for a moment. Now, if there is a lower rate of interest in New York than there is in foreign countries under any system would not gold go out? Would not the same law govern under any system, provided that the rate of interest in New York is lower than in foreign countries?

Mr. WILLIAMS. Money will go where it can be used most profitably.

Mr. COX. Certainly; that is what money is for, to make money.

Mr. WILLIAMS. And the rates of interest in the New York market have been abnormally low for very nearly a year past.

Mr. COX. Now let me call your mind to this point. That is enough to bring out all I want on that point. Now you say the rate of interest in the city of New York has been very low. Will you tell me about what is the rate of interest in New York?

Mr. WILLIAMS. The rate of interest for the past summer has been on call money almost uniformly 1 per cent.

Mr. COX. That is exceedingly low, Mr. Williams?

Mr. WILLIAMS. Wonderfully low for money. It is now about 1½ per cent.

Mr. COX. Now, suppose I give you a section in the West——

Mr. ELLIS. At the rate of 1 per cent per annum, do you mean? You mean the rate of interest has been at the rate of 1 per cent per annum?

Mr. WILLIAMS. Yes, sir; on demand money. Time money has been 2½ to 3 per cent, depending upon the length of time. Loans have been negotiated for six months at 3 per cent, some of them perhaps on fancy securities, on very gilt-edge securities, at little less perhaps than that.

Mr. ELLIS. At a rate of 3 per cent per annum?

Mr. WILLIAMS. Yes, sir.

Mr. COX. Now, you think it advisable, while money is at 1 per cent on demand in the city of New York, that the Government should issue a number of bonds to take up the greenback circulation and pay interest on those bonds at 3 per cent? You think that this is advisable?

Mr. WILLIAMS. Yes, I do; but I would have them sell the bonds in the market at the very best price they can get for them.

Mr. COX. But the rate of interest would be 3 per cent?

Mr. WILLIAMS. I think it would be well for the Government to issue 3 per cent bonds, for the reason sometimes in a panic Government bonds fall off and then they might go below 3 per cent.

Mr. COX. I want to get some facts, not the reasoning about it. Now, if I gave you a section of country involving almost the entire country west of the Mississippi River and almost the entire country south of the Ohio, when on demand loans the rate of interest is 8 to 15 per cent, and in New York it is 1 per cent, how do you account for that?

Mr. WILLIAMS. Because the securities of those sections are not known in the city of New York, and also because such loans as you speak of at such a high rate of interest are not really call loans. You can not get your money when you call for it, and if the transaction is liquidated it might take years for you to get your money back.

Mr. COX. Your securities you have in New York consist generally of stocks, bonds, and securities which you can sell on the exchange there at once?

Mr. WILLIAMS. Yes.

Mr. COX. Now take a country where there are no such things as that apparently, no stocks, no bonds, no collateral, and where they have nothing, substantially, but real estate and personal credit. Now, do you think those countries ought to be excluded from having banks?

Mr. WILLIAMS. Not at all. But I would not have a bank at every crossroad.

Mr. COX. But suppose we have one at every crossroad?

Mr. WILLIAMS. Where are they going to get the money?

Mr. COX. That is the point they look up. You will have them wherever the community wants them. You will have as a money deposit 30 per cent in greenbacks to secure that circulation; you then give a first lien upon all the assets of the bank; you then make every stockholder liable to the extent of his stock. Now, I ask you, with such security as that, is there any danger in the issue?

Mr. WILLIAMS. My dear sir, the first thing, before you get a bank at all, is that you have got to get the capital stock subscribed, and nine out of ten of such banks would whip the devil around the stump in getting the capital stock subscribed and deposit——

Mr. COX. Do they ever whip the devil around the stump in large cities?

Mr. WILLIAMS. I do not say they do not.

Mr. COX. Then if they do——

Mr. WILLIAMS. But they will whip him around the stump anywhere that they can turn a penny.

Mr. COX. Is not the same restraint upon the man in the rural country to prevent whipping the devil around the stump as there is in the city?

Mr. WILLIAMS. Yes, sir.

Mr. COX. I do not see then the force of your argument?

Mr. WILLIAMS. You try and see it, and you will see it is more easy to whip the devil around the stump in the cross corners than in a large community.

Mr. COX. You think you can whip him better in the country than in the city?

Mr. WILLIAMS. I mean those fellows in the city will go to the country and whip him around the stump.

Mr. COX. Now, one word; did you ever accept any paper from the Southern or Western country?

Mr. WILLIAMS. Lots of it.

Mr. COX. Wait a moment, you have not heard my question—upon the personal credit of an individual?

Mr. WILLIAMS. Lots of it.

Mr. COX. On the personal standing of an individual?

Mr. WILLIAMS. Lots of it.

Mr. COX. Is not it your rule that when a rural bank applies to your bank for rediscount, that the rural bank has to indorse the paper?

Mr. WILLIAMS. Yes, sir.

Mr. COX. So, then, you charge a rate of discount for the paper; then the rural bank takes it back home, lets its customer have it, and charges 8 to 10 per cent. That is the way it works, is it not?

Mr. WILLIAMS. I presume it is.

Mr. COX. So that whenever there is a scarcity of money in the South or West they are forced to the necessity of coming to the great money centers to get it; is that true?

Mr. WILLIAMS. Yes.

Mr. COX. That has no impression or influence on your mind——

Mr. WILLIAMS. Hold on. That is a fact. I will say that it is a fact.

Mr. COX. There is no doubt about that fact.

Mr. JOHNSON, of Indiana. But I did not understand the witness to say that that makes no impression upon his mind.

Mr. WILLIAMS. No.

Mr. COX. I did not finish the question. I am going to ask him that. Has your attention ever been called to a system somewhat in the nature of banking that prevails in some of the Southern States in regard to crops, where they mortgage the crops, before the seed is planted, to the commission merchants?

Mr. WILLIAMS. Yes, sir.

Mr. COX. And storekeepers?

Mr. WILLIAMS. Yes, sir.

Mr. COX. That is rather an expensive kind of banking, is it not?

Mr. WILLIAMS. Yes.

Mr. COX. But you think it is better than to put up banks and make the issue good in such rural districts?

Mr. WILLIAMS. No, I do not say that.

Mr. COX. And let the bank do the business?

Mr. WILLIAMS. I do not say that.

Mr. COX. Do not you think——

Mr. WILLIAMS. If the bank is started I want it to be started on a right basis. Let them get the capital subscribed. Credit is not capital, or at least capital is one thing and credit is another, but if a bank is started let them get the absolute cash capital subscribed honestly and not let them borrow on the capital stock. Let us have a good bank if you have any.

Mr. COX. I agree with you there. The only point of difference is I think that can be done anywhere in the country, if we have the proper laws. Now there is only one more question which I desire to ask you in regard to the matter. If these rural banks, assuming they are organized honestly, assuming their capital stock is paid, and assuming they are well secured and it is all done honestly and fairly and frankly, and they are organized all over the country under that system, does not that detract from the business of the great money centers in the loaning of money?

Mr. WILLIAMS. I do not think so.

Mr. COX. You do not think it would?

Mr. WILLIAMS. No, sir.

Mr. COX. Then it could not hurt them if the bank is the worst sort of a bank?

Mr. WILLIAMS. There is no objection to them if they are good, honest banks. There is no objection whatever if they are good, honest banks.

Mr. COX. Well, you would have an objection to a dishonest bank anywhere?

Mr. WILLIAMS. Certainly.

Mr. COX. So at least the only objection you have to such banks rests on the fact you are afraid of dishonest banks?

Mr. WILLIAMS. I would not have a bank where it is really not needed.

Mr. COX. But if a man puts money in honestly where it is not needed, he is the one who suffers?

Mr. WILLIAMS. Yes, I agree with you.

Mr. COX. Ought not he to have the liberty of doing it?

Mr. WILLIAMS. Certainly.

Mr. COX. So your whole objection reaches down to the one point in regard to smaller banks, and that is you are fearful there will be frauds practiced by them?

Mr. WILLIAMS. Exactly.

Mr. COX. And that they will not be good?

Mr. WILLIAMS. That is it.

Mr. COX. Now, let me ask you, as a banker, with capital stock paid in, 30 per cent deposited of legal-tender notes, and liability of stockholders, honestly executed, would not the issue based on that be as good as any money?

Mr. WILLIAMS. It probably would be in the long run. It probably would be, but it would not be equal to the security of United States bonds behind the circulation.

Mr. COX. One word more. You took out your circulation in your bank and you charge 1 per cent on demand loans. That is a low rate, of course. You draw interest upon your bonds every quarter, do you not? That will substantially give you 5 or 6 per cent on your investment from 4 to 6 per cent?

Mr. WILLIAMS. No.

Mr. COX. How much will it give you?

Mr. WILLIAMS. How is that?

Mr. COX. You deposited bonds and the Government pays interest. They are 4 per cent bonds?

Mr. WILLIAMS. But you can not buy at par, you buy at a premium.

Mr. COX. That is like every other investment?

Mr. WILLIAMS. Yes.

Mr. COX. I am talking about what you realize, not what it cost. You get 4 per cent from the Government and you loan at 1 per cent on demand. Will not that make your money, assuming the bond was bought at par, make from 4 to 6 per cent?

Mr. WILLIAMS. If you assume the bonds were bought at par; but you can not assume it. You can not buy United States bonds at par, except the 2 per cent bonds, and of the 2 per cent bonds the Government have outstanding about $25,000,000, and they sell for a little under par, but you can not talk about getting 4 per cent bonds at par, or 5 per cent bonds at par, or 6 per cent bonds at par.

Mr. COX. If you will permit me to ask you, what did your bonds cost you when you bought for your bank?

Mr. WILLIAMS. We bought them twenty years ago.

Mr. COX. Well, I know, but what did they cost you, Mr. Williams?

Mr. WILLIAMS. Our bond deposit with the Government is $50,000 and they are currency sixes, and I think they cost a little under par, but I am not certain.

Mr. ELLIS. I would like to get you to state, if you will, what, in your judgment, has conspired to bring about the low rate of interest which you say has prevailed for a year or more in New York?

Mr. WILLIAMS. Diminution of business—stagnation in business, I might probably say—reduction in the prices of all kinds of merchandise and produce, such as cotton, wheat, and manufactured goods. Say, for instance, Clafflins, who have sold 20 per cent more in goods during the first six months of the year than the last, 20 per cent more in quantity but in value vastly less. The reduction in the rate of interest is stagnation and diminution in business, the low price of produce, and the low price of manufactured goods. That is largely it.

Mr. ELLIS. You have stated now, as far as it occurs to you at present, the chief causes which have brought about the result you have indicated?

Mr. WILLIAMS. Yes, sir.

Mr. ELLIS. Let me ask this question. Take, for instance, my State, Kentucky—the city of Louisville, which is the largest city in that State. Now the rate of interest in the last year and year and a half has been 8, 9, and 10 per cent, and during the panic of last August and September we could not get money at 15 per cent on Government bonds or anything else. How do you account for these widely varying rates of interest, for instance, in the city of New York and the State of Kentucky, in one and the same time?

Mr. WILLIAMS. The money which is loaned in New York is money which is largely of depositors, and banks having it on deposit must be prepared to pay it out at any moment, and consequently they loan large amounts on call, and they keep a large amount of cash on hand. My own bank has had long back from $12,000,000 to $15,000,000 in cash to go toward paying its depositors. The money is largely the money of depositors, and the banks must be prepared to pay that money on call at any moment when it is called for. They can not go and loan that on call at Louisville no matter how good the security is with a view of getting it back at any moment, consequently they can not loan money there on call. They must loan money so that they can get it and have it on hand to pay depositors when they call for it.

Mr. ELLIS. Does this make the difference in the rate of interest in your judgment?

Mr. WILLIAMS. Yes, that makes it largely. The deposits of the banks of the city of New York are $500,000,000, all of it payable on demand. How are the banks going to pay depositors on demand? The banks of New York are loaning largely their deposited money, as I observed, and they have got to be prepared to pay it, and they keep, first, a large amount of cash on hand. Then they keep a large amount of collateral on hand, then they keep a large amount of bills receivable running at maturity, and this enables them to always be prepared to cash their deposits when called for.

Mr. ELLIS. That will account perhaps for the difference as far as it relates to call loans, but let us take the commercial loan of ninety days or four months' loan. How would you account for this vastly different rate of interest in New York and Kentucky and the South generally?

Mr. WILLIAMS. I have been buying paper—I buy a large amount of commercial paper, and I buy the notes of the best houses in the different cities, but I want something fireproof, that is ironclad, and I have been buying such paper, and such paper was selling last summer at 4 and 4½ per cent, and the bankers in Louisville they can not make any money unless they get 6 per cent, and when money is tight they probably loan to their custumors at 6 to 8 per cent, and when money is easier they expect their customers to respond to that and pay a good round rate, but I have been buying paper all the summer at 4 to 4½ per cent of the best houses in the different cities in the country.

Mr. WALKER. South and West?

Mr. WILLIAMS. South and West.

Mr. ELLIS. Would you suggest, Mr. Williams, any amendment to the present currency law which would obviate or tend to obviate this disparity in the rate of interest throughout the country on first-class loans?

Mr. WILLIAMS. The first and most essential thing in all kinds of business is confidence. Let your bank have the unlimited confidence of the people in their section, and they will bring out their money from their stocking feet and will put it in the banks, and that will give the bank deposits with which to loan money, but I have no method of making money. This fiat money is all moonshine. If we have got any money we want it to be money. The populace and peer who have got a dollar in their pockets want a good dollar, and they always will want a good dollar. A bank, to be successful, must have the confidence of the community in which it is placed, and it must not overdo in business and loan too much. Merchants do too much and go to the banks and make their wants known and make the banks loan too much, and there is a good deal of business which is overdone that is to be avoided.

Mr. ELLIS. Well, will you state now all the remedies which you would propose to obviate this evil?

Mr. WILLIAMS. Well, I do not know; it is a thing to obviate itself. We are not going to put our money—the Chemical Bank or other banks in New York are not going to put their money where it can not come back. We want confidence, and to know we are going to get our money back.

Mr. BROSIUS. Mr. Williams, the chief complaint made against the present national banking system is its lack of elasticity. I want to ask you what may seem to be a trite question. What constitutes elasticity in a bank currency?

Mr. WILLIAMS. Its facility of redemption and its facility for being called forth by legitimate business when it is wanted.

Mr. BROSIUS. In other words, always having on hand the currency to pay out if an increase is needed at any time?

Mr. WILLIAMS. Yes, sir.

Mr. BROSIUS. Now, does that principle or that quality of currency concern itself about the source from which the notes emanate or the security which is behind the notes? Do you understand me?

Mr. WILLIAMS. The people will not take the notes, or, if they take them, they will not keep them unless the notes are secure, unless they have confidence in the notes.

Mr. BROSIUS. I understand that; that is very true, but the principle or quality of elasticity does not depend upon whether the note was issued by the Government of the United States or issued by the bank itself, provided it is there to go out when the need requires?

Mr. WILLIAMS. That would seem to be true.

Mr. BROSIUS. Now, if a bank has issued a circulation upon the basis of Government security and they can afford to hold bonds of sufficient amount to supply themselves with all the currency that they need to meet the demand, that currency would be elastic, would it not?

Mr. WILLIAMS. So far as that kind of circulation could make it elastic, but I have said nothing about bank checks, and the great business of the country is done by bank checks.

Mr. BROSIUS. I understand that, but we can not legislate as to the checks. Then, essentially, a currency based upon Government bonds may be as elastic as currency issued against the bank's assets alone?

Mr. WILLIAMS. Well, with this difference, that issued on Government bonds it would be restricted, while issued by the bank itself without restriction, it would put out this currency, and keep it out as fast as it could. It could discount the notes of Tom, Dick, or Harry with the agreement that these notes should be taken off into Montana and issued as circulation there.

Mr. BROSIUS. I never thought of any kind issued without any limit. I am assuming the limit is the same in both instances, say 90 per cent of the capital stock in both instances. The point I make is that the currency issued by the bank, based on Government security, is just as elastic as the same amount of currency issued against the assets of a bank without the Government security?

Mr. WILLIAMS. Just as elastic? Well, it is hardly elasticity. There is rather more restriction where the Government bonds are behind it.

Mr. BROSIUS. To what restriction do you refer?

Mr. WILLIAMS. They can only be issued up to the bonds which are behind.

Mr. BROSIUS. Well, I take that limit into consideration in all my inquiries.

Mr. WILLIAMS. And your other supposition, where they could issue notes against a certain part of their capital, why they would discount notes and pay for them in these notes of their own up to a certain part of their capital.

Mr. BROSIUS. Oh, certainly it has to be within limits, say 75 per cent. Say they can issue 75 per cent of the capital stock in bank notes, secured by Government bonds as under the present law. Now, I am assuming they may have one kind of currency or the other. If they have the national-bank currency as they now have, and have enough of it, that is if they can afford to have enough ot it, will not they be as elastic as currency issued against the bank's assets?

Mr. WILLIAMS. It seems to me it would be sufficiently elastic.

Mr. BROSIUS. Then there is not anything, as I understand you, inherent in the present system of bank currency that makes it necessarily unelastic?

Mr. WILLIAMS. No, sir.

Mr. BROSIUS. Just one more question and I will not detain you any further. I did not quite understand how you proposed to supply the bonds to be used as a basis of the circulation.

Mr. WILLIAMS. By funding the legal tenders.

Mr. BROSIUS. You would fund the legal tenders?

Mr. WILLIAMS. I would get them out of the way.

Mr. BROSIUS. That is a matter I did not understand. You did allude to another mode of disposing of the greenbacks by paying them off out of the surplus——

Mr. WILLIAMS. I would advise the funding of $250,000,000 of legal tenders, and the remainder to be redeemed out of the surplus revenues when we have any.

Mr. BROSIUS. That is the very point I was bringing out. You would advise paying half of the legal tenders by issuing bonds and rely upon the surplus for the payment of the balance?

Mr. WILLIAMS. That is what I would do for the present.

Mr. BROSIUS. Then you would continue the national-banking system substantially as it is now?

Mr. WILLIAMS. I would.

Mr. BLACK. You spoke of what you denominated a call loan on which money has been loaned in New York at 1 per cent. Have not you a loan there known as a demand loan?

Mr. WILLIAMS. Demand loans and call loans are synonymous.

Mr. BLACK. I had information you had loans beside the call loans on which you had to give a day or two's notice?

Mr. WILLIAMS. That may be stipulated in the notice, on demand after one day or eight days.

Mr. BLACK. You have such loans?

Mr. WILLIAMS. Oh, yes.

Mr. BLACK. Do you give any notice on a call loan?

Mr. WILLIAMS. On what is called a sharp-call loan there is no notice at all. The understanding in Wall street is that the demand must be made before 11 o'clock.

Mr. BLACK. Then you have another loan on which you do give notice where it is stipulated in the note?

Mr. WILLIAMS. Yes.

Mr. BLACK. What difference is the rate of interest between those two?

Mr. WILLIAMS. Well, it is a matter of negotiation, and usually in the market as it has been during the past few months there is very little difference. Usually a little notice of eight days is simply for the convenience of the borrower.

Mr. BLACK. Did not you speak about a loan here at 4½ per cent?

Mr. WILLIAMS. I spoke of purchasing commercial paper issued by merchants in different parts of the country, in the different cities of the country, first-class notes made by merchants in different parts of the country, at 4½ per cent.

Mr. BLACK. Was not some paper last summer down to 2 per cent?

Mr. WILLIAMS. No, sir. The only loans which were negotiated at 2 per cent as a rule were those which are call or nearly call, thirty days, or something like that.

Mr. BLACK. We will get away from these call loans and go to loans which you make with your merchants at sixty or ninety days—I do not know exactly your time—what is the rate of interest on those loans?

Mr. WILLIAMS. There are very few loans of merchants at less than four months. It is usually four-months' paper.

Mr. BLACK. What is the rate of interest on those?

Mr. WILLIAMS. Last summer the rate has been from 3 to 4 per cent. It is now from a half to 1 cent better.

Mr. BLACK. Well, on what security; what security do they furnish their own paper?

Mr. WILLIAMS. This is single-name paper.

Mr. BLACK. Without any collaterals?

Mr. WILLIAMS. And without any collateral.

Mr. BLACK. I would like to direct your attention to this condition of things somewhat in the line of what Mr. Cox suggested. In large sections of the country these transactions demand a rate of interest, say a minimum rate of 8 per cent. Can you suggest any remedy for that condition of things?

Mr. WILLIAMS. These notes are not so well known.

Mr. BLACK. They are not known in New York, but they are known in the locality where they are offered. They are known to the local bank; they are leading merchants and responsible houses. Here is the condition: In New York, when one of your merchants goes to your bank or some other bank he gets a four months' loan on his individual paper at 3 or 4 per cent. The merchants in other localities, a large section of the country, who have the same relative standing in that locality as your merchant has in New York, just as good, just as reliable and solvent, has to pay from 8 to 10 per cent. I do not mean to get the money from New York, but there at home.

Mr. WILLIAMS. But he can not expect New York to be placed at his own door. He must make his credit known in New York if he wants to borrow money in New York. These transactions regulate themselves; I do not think that is a matter of legislation.

Mr. BLACK. I just wanted to get your opinion about it, but perhaps I have not made myself clear?

Mr. WILLIAMS. I think I understand it.

Mr. BLACK. He is not asking for money in New York, but he is asking for money at home, and the banks have money, and they will not loan it out for less than 8 per cent, and sometimes more than that?

Mr. WILLIAMS. Well, they have the right to get whatever they can. I do not think it is a matter for legislation to step in and correct.

Mr. BLACK. You do not think we ought to legislate on that line?

Mr. WILLIAMS. No; I do not.

Mr. BLACK. Now, Mr. Williams, how long was your bank a State bank—just approximately?

Mr. WILLIAMS. Oh, for nearly forty years.

Mr. BLACK. Was it a bank of issue?

Mr. WILLIAMS. Yes, sir.

Mr. BLACK. Will you please state what its career was during that period, as to whether it was successful or not?

Mr. WILLIAMS. The success of the Chemical Bank depended upon the individuals who managed it. It started in 1824, and it was not a very great success until 1844, when new men came in charge of it, and then its success began by conservative management, and I do not know—I do not think it depended at all upon the State or national system as to its success.

Mr. BLACK. From 1824 until 1862 or 1863 it was a State bank?

Mr. WILLIAMS. A State bank.

Mr. BLACK. A State bank of issue?

Mr. WILLIAMS. A State bank of issue.

Mr. BLACK. And a successful State bank of issue?

Mr. WILLIAMS. Yes.

Mr. BLACK. Commanding the confidence of the community and yielding a reasonable profit to those who were interested in it?

Mr. WILLIAMS. Yes.

Mr. BLACK. Well, if a bank could be organized and managed by such gentlemen as composed that, men of integrity and conservatism, and all these other qualifications, do you see any reason why such a bank could not be made such a success now?

Mr. WILLIAMS. Not the slightest. I have every reason to believe it could. I might say, in regard to circulation, that in New York State in 1824, when the Chemical Bank was first started, the circulation was not even registered. It was redeemable by each bank by itself and only at its own counter. It gave no security for anything, and the circulation was not registered at Albany, and it was only after the act of 1838 was passed notes issued by the banks were registered, and the national-bank act was molded after that act of 1838.

Mr. BLACK. The national-bank act, then, is molded after the State-bank system?

Mr. WILLIAMS. Molded to a certain extent after the State law of 1838 in the State of New York.

Mr. BLACK. Do you know the persons who have recently been the purchasers of these Government bonds and who have drawn gold out of the Treasury for that purpose?

Mr. WILLIAMS. If you name them perhaps I can tell you.

Mr. BLACK. Will you look at that list and kindly say whether they are the persons?

Mr. COX. Put that in the record.

New York Life Insurance Company	$2,000,000
Bank of America	1,330,000
Bank of the Manhattan Company	1,000,000
Union Trust Company	1,000,000
I. & S. Wormser	700,000
National Bank of Commerce	1,977,000
American Exchange National Bank	1,289,000
Fourth National Bank	1,878,000
United States Trust Company	618,000
Bank of New York National Banking Association	588,875
J. & W. Seligman	500,000
Corn Exchange Bank	870,000
Kuhn, Loeb & Co	600,000
New York Security and Trust Company	600,000
Bank State of New York	500,000

Mr. WILLIAMS. The New York Life Insurance Company. I think I have seen this list. It is a list of the institutions which drew money out of the Treasury when the first $50,000,000 of bonds were issued, and not of institutions which have drawn money out of the Treasury to pay for this last issue of $50,000,000. The New York Life Insurance Company have here $2,000,000. Those were the first $50,000,000 of Government bonds issued, and it was pretty difficult work in New York to make up the amount of $50,000,000. I know we worked pretty hard at it and I did missionary work myself to get this subscribed to. Colonel Strong, who is now our mayor, is a director of the New York Life, and I think he was instrumental in getting that subscription taken. I know I went to see him and urged the thing upon him and he urged it upon the New York Life. It is a life company and they had the money to invest but had no gold, and consequently had to draw the gold from the Treasury to subscribe to the first $50,000,000. I presume that the Bank of America did not have the gold. The Union Trust Company, they had no gold. They used their legal tenders to buy bonds; they had to buy the gold to pay for them. I presume that is the same thing with the rest of them.

Mr. BLACK. You think this is a list of the purchasers of the first issue and not of the last?

Mr. WILLIAMS. I know it absolutely.

Mr. BLACK. Well, were you part of that syndicate who purchased the bonds, your bank?

Mr. WILLIAMS. Not the last; no, sir.

Mr. BLACK. The first?

Mr. WILLIAMS. We helped along. I took $1,000,000. I did not want them; I took them to make the thing go.

Mr. BLACK. Did you use the greenbacks?

Mr. WILLIAMS. No, sir, we used the gold; paid it in honest gold. For the first $50,000,000 we paid in about $2,800,000. We did not buy a cent of gold from the Treasury. For this last loan we paid $4,000,000 of gold. We paid over $4,000,000 of our own stock of gold and have not drawn a single cent from the Treasury.

Mr. BLACK. One of the grave difficulties which seems to bring about the present condition is the ability of these holders of notes to go to the Treasury and demand gold for them. That can be done by what are commonly called the Sherman notes, as well as the greenbacks, can it not?

Mr. WILLIAMS. Yes.

Mr. BLACK. As far as the Sherman notes are concerned, can we not rid ourselves of that trouble by having the Treasury pay them in silver?

Mr. WILLIAMS. It could be done, of course, but to the ruin of the whole of our banking system.

Mr. BLACK. Would there be any violation of law in it?

Mr. WILLIAMS. That you can judge better than I, because you know more about the law than I do.

Mr. BLACK. Would there be any violation of faith in it?

Mr. WILLIAMS. I think there would be, most unquestionably. When the bonds of the United States were made payable in coin there was no coin used but gold.

Mr. BLACK. We are not speaking now about bonds, but about the Sherman notes issued under the act of 1890, which authorized the purchase of silver bullion and the deposit of the bullion as security against these notes.

Mr. WILLIAMS. If you remember, I suggested in the paper which I read that those notes might be made redeemable in silver bullion at its market value, and that would make them secure and inspire confidence in them, but the Government would have to stand the loss, as it ought to.

Mr. BLACK. You say that it might be done in that way?

Mr. WILLIAMS. Yes, by a change in the law.

Mr. BLACK. I am speaking now of existing law, and of the very law under which those notes were issued.

Mr. WILLIAMS. You can judge of the law better than I can, but I think that it would be one of the greatest disasters that could befall the country.

Mr. BLACK. Why?

Mr. WILLIAMS. For this reason. The loss to the country by the silver panic last year was worth more than all the silver. If the silver mined in the United States had been taken and dumped into the ocean it would have been less loss than the loss to the whole country by the depression of business and by the fall in prices which occurred in consequence of the panic of 1893.

Mr. BLACK. I am not speaking of all the silver. I am calling your attention to this particular act of 1890 and to the redemption of the particular notes issued under that act. Now, it is no violation of good faith for an individual or a Government to pay debts in accordance with a contract.

Mr. WILLIAMS. These notes were issued under a law which provided that gold and silver should circulate on a parity. When they cease to circulate on a parity by the action of the Government then that law is broken and the notes are not redeemed according to the spirit of the law.

Mr. BLACK. There is another provision in the law besides the one declaring the policy of the Government to maintain parity. Besides the provision which declares the public policy of the Government as to parity, there is a third section of the act which requires the Secretary of the Treasury to coin so much of the bullion up to the 1st of July, 1891, and after that time to coin of the silver bullion purchased under the provisions of that act as much as may be necessary to provide for the redemption of the Treasury notes as therein provided for. Now, if the Secretary coins that and pays it out on these notes in the very terms of the contract, is there any violation of public faith in that?

Mr. WILLIAMS. Suppose he does, and suppose he coins these dollars and pays them out, they will be paid in again for customs.

Mr. BLACK. Why, what will be paid in for customs?

Mr. WILLIAMS. The silver notes. They will be paid for customs, and then what is the Secretary going to do with them? They can take these standard dollars and demand silver certificates for them at the Treasury, and then the Secretary has to receive these silver certificates for customs.

Mr. BLACK. Well, suppose he has?

Mr. WILLIAMS. Then he has not got nothing else to pay out but the silver certificates.

Mr. BLACK. Has he got anything else now?

Mr. WILLIAMS. He is getting rapidly down to that.

Mr. BLACK. Have we not already got down to it under your construction of this law, and of how it ought to be enforced?

Mr. WILLIAMS. I think not.

Mr. COBB, of Alabama. You spoke a moment ago in answer to a question by Mr. Black about the different rates of interest. Now I want to ask you this question—whether legislation to a large extent makes a difference in the rate of interest between New York and other sections of the country to which your attention has been directed? Does not the difference in the interest for money in Wall street and the interest for money in the South and West originate largely from the law, and is it not produced by the law of the land?

Mr. WILLIAMS. I think not. The usury law of the State of New York is most barbarous. Under it a man can be sent to State prison for taking more than the legal rate of interest, which is 6 per cent, and yet we see hardly anything passing at 6 per cent.

Mr. COBB, of Alabama. If it is the usury law which makes the difference, then it does grow out of the law at last.

Mr. WILLIAMS. I do not think that has much to do with it in times like the present. But I believe that there should be no usury law at all. I think that the whole thing if left to itself would regulate itself.

Mr. COBB, of Alabama. Do you suppose that it is the business conditions of the country, independent of law, that make the difference in the rates of interest in New York and, say, in Augusta, Ga? Has the law nothing to do with it?

Mr. WILLIAMS. I do not think the law has much to do with it. Money now flows to those centers where it can be recalled at any moment.

Mr. COBB, of Alabama. Assuming that the banks are properly organized under laws which make the bill holder secure, is it not true that the more banks the country has and the more widely they are diffused the better it is for the people, provided always that the system of relying on banks for currency is adopted.

Mr. WILLIAMS. No; I do not think that it is better for the people.

Mr. COBB, of Alabama. Would not that condition bring the banks and the people together so that money can be borrowed at a low interest?

Mr. WILLIAMS. I do not think it would.

Mr. COBB, of Alabama. Why? You have said that one reason for low interest in New York is that the banks are there and the people are there who want the money. Now, if you bring the banks and the people together in the South and the West would you not have the same conditions?

Mr. WILLIAMS. There is no use in talking about making money.

Mr. COBB, of Alabama. I am not talking about making money, but about making banks. Are not the banks a mode of supplying people with money?

Mr. WILLIAMS. The bank note is good for nothing unless it is redeemable in cash on demand.

Mr. COBB, of Alabama. Is it not true that the banks of the country are the agencies through which the people borrow money?

Mr. WILLIAMS. Yes.

Mr. COBB, of Alabama. And is it not also true that the farther the bank is removed from the people who want the money, the greater the burden on the people who borrow it? Is it not true that the high rate of interest in the South, and the depressed condition of things in the South and West, from the want of money, originate largely from the fact that the banks in New York are so far removed from the people who want the use of money—so far removed from the people who want to borrow money?

Mr. WILLIAMS. Money centers in New York—how are you going to get it out?

Mr. COBB, of Alabama. I am asking you the question. I want to know of you as a banker whether it is not true that the interests of the people would be subserved if you carried banks right among them.

Mr. WILLIAMS. And have a bank at every man's back door?

Mr. COBB, of Alabama. Yes, if the interests of the country demand it.

Mr. WILLIAMS. I do not object to banks if they are honestly organized, if they are well organized and are in honest hands.

Mr. COBB, of Alabama. Assuming that they are well organized and are in honest hands, would it not be to the interest of the people to have banks generally established throughout the country?

Mr. WILLIAMS. They would not be well managed. The privilege would be abused. A bank has got to be a conservative institution. It can not do business properly on cats and dogs. It can only do business properly when in the hands of upright people and when it is confined to upright transactions.

Mr. COBB, of Alabama. Do you believe it possible for any bank to do business on a cat and dog security, if the law under which that bank is organized is of such a character as to make such a thing impossible?

Mr. WILLIAMS. I do not believe you could make it impossible.

Mr. COBB, of Alabama. Why? The two points made by you are that the rate of interest in the South and West has been increased and the burden of supplying the people with money made more difficult because of the fact that in those sections they have not banks, but have to resort to New York and other commercial centers in order to get money. The question that I ask you under that assumption is whether if, such a condition of affairs is made by law as that they can have safe and secure banks among the people who desire to borrow money—I mean good banks with sufficient capital and honestly and properly managed—it would not be better?

Mr. WILLIAMS. Yes, if the bank is in a place where there is business enough to warrant it.

Mr. COBB, of Alabama. Would a bank go where there is no business to warrant it?

Mr. WILLIAMS. I am afraid it would not.

Mr. COBB, of Alabama. Do you agree with gentlemen who have been before the committee in the opinion that in the Carlisle bill abundant security is given to banks that contribute to pay the bills of failed banks?

Mr. WILLIAMS. I am opposed to that feature of the Carlisle bill.

Mr. COBB, of Alabama. Do you agree that under the Carlisle system the contributing banks are amply secured, so that there is no chance of loss to them?

Mr. WILLIAMS. I do not believe that good sound banks would take out a dollar of circulation under that clause.

Mr. COBB, of Alabama. Why?

Mr. WILLIAMS. Because they would be unwilling to be bound up with other banks.

Mr. COBB, of Alabama. But if they are amply secured?

Mr. WILLIAMS. The question of ample security is a question of opinion. Some banks might think the security ample and others not.

Mr. COBB, of Alabama. Every banker who has been before the committee, except you, has expressed the opinion that the security is ample.

Mr. WILLIAMS. It is ample if no more banks fail than have failed so far under the national banking system, but I think there would be more failures.

Mr. COBB, of Alabama. You do not think, then, that the security is ample?

Mr. WILLIAMS. I do not know; I would not go into it.

Mr. RUSSELL. Relative to the two recent bond issues by the Government (as brought out by questions of Mr. Black) I wish to ask you one or two questions. Did not the banks or financial institutions (in New York City, for example) feel it incumbent upon themselves to subscribe to those issues, or to see to their being subscribed to, in order to continue the gold redemption by the United States Treasury?

Mr. WILLIAMS. They did.

Mr. RUSSELL. I am asking now in relation to the placing of the first issue?

Mr. WILLIAMS. Yes.

Mr. RUSSELL. Did they have the same feeling in regard to the placing of the second issue?

Mr. WILLIAMS. Not quite so much, because there was a better feeling in relation to this last loan, and it was readily seen that it would be oversubscribed. But the same desire was manifested.

Mr. RUSSELL. Taking the two issues together in this last analysis, has not the continuance of the gold redemption by the United States Treasury been dependent upon banks and financiers?

Mr. WILLIAMS. I think it has been.

Mr. BLACK. Assuming, as you seem to have done, that under this act of 1890, which requires the parity to be maintained when these Sherman notes were presented, they ought to have been redeemed in gold, do you think it is a wise financial policy to reissue them and continue that so as to make them a perpetual drain upon the gold reserve?

Mr. WILLIAMS. The Secretary has got do so under the present law.

Mr. BLACK. He has got to reissue these Sherman notes?

Mr. WILLIAMS. Yes.

Mr. BLACK. If the law did not require him to do so, do you think that it would be a wise financial policy?

Mr. WILLIAMS. What should he do? He is to redeem these notes.

Mr. BLACK. What does a private individual do when he redeems his obligations.

Mr. WILLIAMS. The Treasury is one of the greatest banks in the world and it has not got a sufficient reserve. If it had a reserve as the Bank of France has, if it had a reserve of $200,000,000 or $300,000,000 instead of $100,000,000, then this whole subject would not be thought of and we would not be here. But the Secretary of the Treasury is hampered by law. No bank could carry on business if it were hampered as the Secretary of the Treasury is. He has not got authority to go and make a temporary loan if his revenues are run down. He ought to have power enough to carry on his business because, as I say, he is one of the greatest bankers in the world. We find that we have in our business to keep a large reserve. The Treasury should maintain a large reserve, but it has not got it, and there is where the trouble comes in.

Mr. William St. John was permitted by the committee to ask Mr. Williams a question. He said: In the summer prior to the first issue of the $50,000,000 bonds there was a period of extreme dullness in the money market, and I want to refresh Mr. Williams's memory about it because it is important to some things that I want to say. Time loans were made in the city of New York at 2 per cent per annum, and sixty-day notes of business men were sold at 1½ per cent discount per annum. I want to remind Mr. Williams about that, because I can prove it and he can prove it by his own books. And (turning to Mr. Hendrix) your books will confirm it also. There is no dispute between Mr. Williams and myself on any matter of fact. We are the best of friends. But that one thing I want confirmed, that is, that money at 1½ per cent per annum was secured on sixty-day notes by merchants.

Mr. WILLIAMS. I would not dispute that at all. At the same time I should say that these were exceptional transactions, because I have taken none under 2 per cent.

Mr. ST. JOHN. But you believe that what I state is true?

Mr. WILLIAMS. Oh, unquestionably so; but I think that these were rather exceptions.

STATEMENT OF WILLIAM P. ST. JOHN.

Mr. William P. St. John, president of the Mercantile National Bank, of New York, addressed the committee.

He said: Mr. Chairman, you will remember that I declined your first invitation to be heard on the topic pending. My apology was, and I repeat as my explanation and excuse for what I shall say, that at this juncture, while our primary money is so undetermined, I deem any new creation of bank notes, State or national, perilous to the prosperity of the United States.

There is a very widespread unrest of opinion on this topic and the allied topic, called the "silver question," even in New York and New England. Public opinion is under a newspaper terrorism in New York. Men who agree with me fully, and I know many of them of considerable wealth, prefer to keep silent for the present. Any nobody who will write at length a lot of nothingness adverse to silver money will be accorded certain newspaper's space and be dignified into great authorities. Rejoinder, if complete, and the more complete the more certainly is denied even a limited space. Again, other men believe that until a change of administration here approaches it will merely cost them influence to speak their conclusions favorable to silver money. Then, too, certain newspapers shield their readers against intelligence and cow them out of any timid convictions they might indulge.

As an instance, Mr. Horace White's Evening Post a few weeks ago quoted at length from the London Economist one Rawlinson's criticism of Manchester's complaint of England's gold monometallism as relating Manchester to India. The complete rejoinder of two weeks later in the Economist, a compilation of facts that refuted Rawlinson totally, has never even been mentioned by the Evening Post. The Evening Post spreads at length in several columns a reprint of a recent paper of Mr. McLeod, nine-tenths of which matter is as acceptable to myself, as an independent bimetallist, as to anybody else. The real truth which is so universally acceptable is a pad of dignity to the conclusions which they do not, in the slightest degree, warrant. And so it goes.

But conditions current here and elsewhere are forcing the truth upon general attention, and a rebellion against this tyranny and concealment of facts will manifest itself ere long in New York as elsewhere. I have recently been urged by commercial bodies of two important Eastern cities to address them at length upon my convictions. I declined on the ground that I have talked so much that I deem it unwise to be heard again on the topic until invited to speak by my immediate associates in the city of New York.

The paper that I now ask the privilege of reading was prepared for a monthly magazine of importance. I asked the space at first but afterwards withdrew the request. The editor urged my carrying out my first intention. His private secretary heard the matter in the rough and urged me the more to complete it for his magazine. I learn this morning that more acceptable matter will crowd me out, which is only another evidence of what you gentlemen, aiming to serve your country, are entitled to complain of in the Eastern press.

I would like to explain in advance a term I use for the sake of brevity and without intending offense to anyone, namely, "goldites." The "goldites" are that infinitesimally small but prodigiously influential coterie in the United States who believe that no one nation, not only, but not all the commercial nations combined in a concert of laws, could provide unlimited coinage for gold and silver on one ratio, and attract thereby the gold and silver coins, or certificates for them, into concurrent circulation as money.

Mr. St. John then read the following paper:

GOLD MONOMETALLISM THE PERIL OF THE UNITED STATES.—BIMETALLISM ATTEMPTED INDEPENDENTLY, TO ACHIEVE BIMETALLISM IN EUROPE BY THE EQUIVALENT OF A CONCERT OF LAWS.

Under official dictation, tutored by the one most aggressive of all our handful of "goldites" in the United States, Congress fiddles with bank notes while the burning issue is our primary money.

Identically tutored, our Chief Executive has required his Secretary to abandon the option conferred by law upon the United States and grant to holders of the United States notes the right to exact gold always, silver never, as their redeeming coin. Had the option to redeem in silver dollars been exercised boldly at the time when only 3,000,000 silver dollars were owned by the United States, with an ownership of $116,000,000 gold, any possible alarm could have been laughed to scorn. To attempt to seize upon and exercise the option now, or under immediately prospective conditions of our Treasury, would be to court all the perils of disaster.

Identically tutored, the demand appears, "one step at a time," to substitute bank promises of money for $907,000,000 of the primary and secondary money which they promise. Were the scheme adopted and successful, the result achieved would be $907,000,000 of new bank promises, $207,000,000 of existing bank promises, and $1,700,000,000 of promises called deposits, an aggregate of $2,854,000,000 of national-bank liabilities payable on demand, resting or wrangling on our available supplies of gold. The pretense of the tuition is that this is "sound finance."

Redundant bank notes have invaribly banished gold and silver. They never were suspected of enticing either into money. And national banks can not hope for popular consent to their redeeming their circulating notes in officially discarded silver dollars.

LAW THE LIFE PRINCIPLE IN MONEY.

Money is the creature of law. Money is all domestic. Our $10 gold piece is accounted 258 grains of nine-tenths fine gold when beyond the jurisdiction of the United States.

Money and the yardstick have nothing in common. The yardstick is an exact, unvarying measure of length. Money is an uncertain, variable measure of varying values. The yardstick is not bartered for commodities. Money is the means of acquisition and momentarily the measure of value of the thing acquired. The yardstick is a unit of length. The dollar as a "unit of value" is preposterous. Our Hamilton-Jefferson statute, founding the mint, provided a dollar as our "unit of account." That dollar of 1792 and the dollar of 1894 contain identically 371.25 grains of silver.

AGGREGATE OF MONEY DETERMINES PRICES.

The aggregate of all money afloat and in bank in the United States, is our true measure of normal value of commodities here. The aggregate of money of all nations trading internationally is the measure of normal value of all commodities consumed by all. Therefore, to enlarge the aggregate of money in the trading world, is to raise normal prices of commodities everywhere. To enlarge the aggregate of money in the United States is to raise normal prices for home and internationally consumed commodities here. Per contra, to diminish the aggregate of money in the United States is to lower all normal prices here; and to diminish the world's aggregate of money is to lower all normal prices of internationally moving commodities in all the trading world.

PERFECTION IN MONEY IMPRACTICABLE.

Omniscience and infinite integrity in law making, but nothing short of these, would yield perfection in money. Perfection in money, thus provided, would involve the use of neither gold nor silver, nor any other commodity.

Now, if my caution against it will be quoted along with my description of it, I will describe perfect money, to wit:

Any convenient substance of about the "intrinsic" properties of silk-ribbed paper prepared to defy the counterfeiter, issued by authority of the law of the United States, and promise no redemption whatever, except acceptance for all dues to the United States and also made receivable and payable for all dues and debts, public and private, within the jurisdiction of the United States. But my caution against any attempt at such perfection in money of the United States is that imperfect humanity has not been more safe to handle any near approach to it, nor with any other than commodity money, than children are to toy with keen-edged tools. The peril is the reasonable certainty of over-issue and collapse.

If United States notes of 1862 and Treasury notes of 1890, together

$497,000,000, were retired, they might all be replaced with logically perfect money as described, provided silver dollars and certificates and bank notes were also all retired. The success of the issue would insure overissue, and then collapse.

Bank notes differ only in degree from Treasury notes, for this same peril lurking in them. The wary can escape a degree of peril in the bank note, refusing it as not a legal tender. But the peril is in the bank note, nevertheless, as Jefferson and Andrew Jackson knew. Nature's restrictions upon the world's supplies of gold and silver, and the burden of the art and industrial uses for these commodities, make these safer than irredeemable paper as our tool of trade.

MINT PRICE MAKES MARKET PRICE.

Gold bullion and United States gold coin enter Europe with one and the same right conferred by law, the right of transition into Europe's money. By law gold carries the right of transition into English money at the price of £3 17s. 10½d. per Troy ounce, eleven-twelfths and 1 pennyweight fine. By law, France, Germany, and the other important continental states similarly endow gold. And, by virtue of our law, gold carries the right of transition into the money of the United States at the fixed price of 23.22 grains pure, or 25.8 grains nine-tenths fine, for a dollar.

Thus, by law, the market price and mint price of gold are one and the same, so long as there is gold produced each year more than the arts and industries and India absorb. For so long, gold in the lump, its weight and fineness being known, is the equivalent of coin in Europe and the United States, for the reason that the possessors of gold will accept no lower price while the mint price is offered in lawful money at the mint; and artisans will not pay more for gold because it is obtainable at the mint price by melting the coin.

IMAGINE SILVER MONOMETALLISM SUBSTITUTED.

Imagine all these mints of Europe and the United States to deprive gold of all further right of transition into money. Imagine the law of each of all these nations to grant to silver exclusively the right of transition into the money of each, at one price, equivalent to 371.25 grains pure (412.5 grains nine-tenths fine) for a dollar. Thenceforth the "price of silver" in Europe and the United States would be this one mint price. Silver in the lump then, as gold now, its weight and fineness being known, would be the equivalent of coin. Possessors of silver then would not accept less than this one mint price for it, for the reason that lawful money could be had for it, at this price, at the mint; and the artisan would pay no more for silver because he could obtain it at this mint price by melting silver coin.

LAW DICTATES THE PRICE OF GOLD.

But, with the support of mints withdrawn from gold and provided there is, as some economists aver, a yearly production of gold neighboring $25,000,000 more than the arts, industries, and India absorb, the market price of gold would fall rapidly until the price attained would permit the lower arts, in utensils and the like, to absorb the surplus gold. Exactly this result is evident in the world's withdrawal of mint support from silver, but much less rapidly attained.

BIMETALLISM BY CONCERT OF LAWS EXPLAINED.

Next, imagine all these mints of Europe and the United States to grant alike to gold and silver the right of transition into their money at the will of the possessor, at one price for gold, equivalent to 23.22 grains for a dollar; and at one price for silver, equivalent to 371.25 grains for a dollar, all the coins resulting to be unlimited legal tender within the territory of the nation coining them. If gold is produced each year more than the arts, industries, and India absorb, the one only use for it is employment as money. If there were silver produced each year other than is likewise absorbed, and no one doubts it, the only use for such surplus silver would be employment as money. Hence, for so long as there continued to be any surplus of gold and any surplus of silver over the said absorption of each, and provided the surplus of neither metal were sufficient alone for the world's entire need of money, for so long the mint price and market price would be one for gold, and the mint price and market price would be one for silver. Which would mean that the one mint price for gold and the one mint price for silver would be the universal market price for each; and would mean universal parity of the gold and silver coins at the ratio established by these mints.

This is bimetallism by a concert of laws. It does not seem akin to the attempts which our "goldites" would thrust upon us; as, for instance, the setting up of a universal price for each of all commodities, or for any one of them so abundant everywhere as iron.

RESPECTABLE "SILVER LUNATICS."

Among other "silver lunatics" sanctioning the confidence that bimetallism thus attempted could not fail, are the learned professors of political economy in the colleges of London, Oxford, Cambridge, and Edinburg, and the late De Laveleye with others of the profession on the Continent, and a host of men of other callings eminent throughout Europe and in the United States.

STATECRAFT COST THE WORLD BIMETALLISM.

The aforesaid self-same tutor, to the contrary notwithstanding, the abandonment of silver and substitution of gold alone as the primary money of unlimited coinage is not the "natural selection of commerce," but the ignorant or vicious achievement of statecraft.

The subjects of England were deprived of their right to convert silver into money—temporarily first in 1798 and finally in 1816—under conditions of little public concern, for the reason that irredeemable bank notes were England's full substitute for money. Precisely similarly the people of the United States were deprived of their right to convert silver into money, a right enjoyed for eighty years, while irredeemable paper of sundry kinds and excessive volume supplanted gold and silver money in the United States.

[Extract of note of Sir David Barbour (British finance secretary to India) October 20, 1887.]

In no portion of Lord Liverpool's "Treatise on the coins of the realm" is there any allusion to: (1) The treasury order of 25th October, 1697, directing that guineas should be taken at 22s. each; (2) the council order of 8th September, 1698, referring the question of the high rate of the guinea to the council of trade; (3) the report of the council of trade, dated 22d September, 1698; (4) the resolution of the House of Commons on that report; (5) the orders of the treasury to receive the guineas on public account at 21s. 6d. each, "and not otherwise."

With the publication of these documents falls Lord Liverpool's statement that the English people, by general consent and without any interposition of public authority, attached a higher value to the guinea after the great recoinage than the market value of gold would justify; and with the fall of the alleged fact must disappear the conclusion drawn from it, namely, that with the increase of wealth and commerce the English people in 1698 had come to prefer gold to silver. And with the disappearance of this hypothesis there disappears the only evidence brought forward in support of the theory regarding the progress of wealthy countries from silver to gold, which Lord Liverpool invented in order to overthrow Locke's opinion that "gold is not the money of the world, or measure of commerce, nor fit to be so."

Lord Liverpool's theory may, of course, be sound, though the facts on which he relied in 1805 were imaginary; on the other hand, it may fairly be said that it was the acceptance of the theory on the authority of Lord Liverpool which brought about in the nineteenth century that state of affairs which is now held to prove the soundness of the theory. * * *

How Lord Liverpool, or those who acted under his orders, came to overlook the existence of the documents which I have quoted, and which at that time would have destroyed the basis of his argument, is unaccountable.

SILVER MONOMETALLISM SAFER THAN GOLD MONOMETALLISM.

But if any attempt of ours to achieve bimetallism independently is to yield silver as our only money, my conviction is the conviction of Robert Morris, namely, that silver is preferable to gold if either is to be the only current money of the United States. The present Secretary of the Treasury of the United States and his associates of the President's Cabinet have lately shared a well-advertised effort to heap posthumous honors on Robert Morris.

THE WORLD'S BLIND EXPERIMENT.

The repeal of our "Sherman Act," November 1, 1893, following the closing of India's mints in June against the further coining of silver on private account, severed the last link that coupled silver to its crippled right of transition into the money of the Western world. Hence, just thirteen months ago, for the first time in history, the commercial world began a free concert of absolutely blind experiment in money.

The latest estimates of Soetbeer, in his almost posthumous publication of 1892, accorded little, if any, new gold from the mines each year to the world's increase of money. Note, then, that while the population of the United States enlarges at a rate equivalent to adding the population of Mexico to ours within seven years, or of adding the population of Canada and all other British possessions in North America within three years, this absolutely blind experiment which the United States shares demands that whoever would increase the world's aggregate of money by the equivalent of $1,000 must provide 4.03 pounds Troy of gold.

RESULTS AND PERILS OF GOLD MONOMETALLISM.

Within the last half of the brief period succeeding 1873, 10 cents a pound was a sentimental price for cotton and "dollar wheat" was a sentimental term. Recently, 5 cents a pound in towns and 4¼ cents on the plantation, 50 cents in towns and "hog feed" on the farm were prices current. The dollar of the United States, half an inch in width and a thirty-second thick, is thus become $2 with which to buy the sweat and toil and anxieties of a season, at the very head and front of prosperity in the United States. While thus the dollar of the United States is worth 2 bushels of wheat or 20 pounds of cotton, it gauges the prosperity of the United States at 1½ cents a year, if invested for the period of sixty days in strictly prime commercial paper of New York.

The flood of our prosperity can not rise higher than its source. The font is where the nourished earth yields her own increase and for toil returns a hundred-fold. It follows that the conditions contemplated must alter presently, or the want of a traveling public and the lack of sufficiently liberal movements of freight, at profitable rates, will shrink the earnings of certain of our main trunk lines of railway into a deficiency of any dividends and, later, into default of interest on their bonds. Unless relief of law ensues without delay, choice parcels of real estate in New York City will manifest declines in prices, exceeding 20 per cent, between sales in January, 1893, and December, 1896.

I am well aware that moderate demand upon liberal supplies of commodities produced at low cost and distributed cheaply will yield low prices. On these terms, low prices stimulate moderate demand into a liberal demand upon the same supplies, and so tend to recover prices. On this basis, low prices of our staple necessities are desirable. In such variations of demand relative to such supplies, the producer may gather amid the fluctuations of prices, his fair share of the advantages conferred on all by his abundance.

EXPERIENCE SAFER THAN EXPERIMENT.

But, for the reason that the producer does not share the general advantages of the abundance of his supplies, the United States at large is sufferer. Relief must be provided, and for that achievement we propose that, at all hazards, the United States shall abandon experiment.

We ask the Congress now sitting to restore our Hamilton-Jefferson coinage system, founded with the mint, maintained for eighty years without complaint, and overthrown unobservedly at a time when neither gold nor silver was our current money.

On December 6 I submitted to the Chamber of Commerce a developed plan to restore, or attempt, bimetallism independently, the plan providing the modern convenience of paper substitutes for coin and providing ample means to stifle any possible money panic arising with the enactment. No moment could be more propitious than the present for any such attempt. Idle accumulations of money in our important money centers, like the present, are rare.

"GOLDITE" OBJECTION COMMENDS INDEPENDENT BIMETALLISM.

Our "goldites" antagonize every such proposal with two objections, to wit:

(1) That such legislation is superfluous because "if there is not gold enough for all, there is gold enough for us. * * * We can command gold in competition with all nations. * * * The United States is the largest and best source of supply of the commodities that the world most needs—cotton, wheat, provisions, petroleum, and the like."

(2) That to reopen our mints to silver without limit while offering coinage to gold without limit, will merely substitute silver monometallism for gold monometallism in the United States. They mean that the proposed enactment will yield silver dollars and paper redeemable in silver dollars as our only money, and for the reason that it will banish gold from money and expel it from the United States.

We adopt both of their predictions as the assurance of our safety in making the attempt.

Our ability to command gold in competition with nations striving for the meager supply of gold available to money would depend upon the further sacrifice of our producers of petroleum, provisions, wheat, cotton, and the like. Lower and lower prices for these elementary essentials of our prosperity must pursue a foreign market, and every drain of Europe's gold to us as our return for them would further lower Europe's prices for all commodities, including any more of these she buys.

By our proposal, on the contrary, the United States provides itself the convenient ability to part with gold composedly. Instead of our present restriction to gold alone as our tremulous necessity, we propose to be able to loan our gold to Europe for our own sakes, selfishly. If, as our Mint Director estimates, we have $600,000,000 of gold and $20,000,000 annually produced in excess of our needs in the arts and industries, to spare a liberal portion to Europe, having a convenient abundance of domestic money at home, is to loan Europe the vehicle with which to carry our prosperity. To increase thereby Europe's aggregate of money is to raise normal prices of all commodities in Europe, including those for which the United States is Europe's "best source of supply." Therefore, diametrically the opposite in achievement to what our "goldites" urge, we would enlarge Europe's demand for our surplus petroleum, provisions, cotton, and wheat, and upon a higher plane of prices for them as she buys.

SILVER BASIS ONLY TEMPORARY.

Imagine, as the immediate achievement of our proposed enactment silver dollars and paper redeemable in silver dollars to be the only money of the United States. The tendency first evident will be its restriction upon our importations of European products. This is evident under India's silver monometallism in her relation to the outside world. But a home experience may be recalled:

During the period of plethoric State bank notes in the United States, when a New York merchant had sold to Western and Southern merchants and bills were due, his collector obtaining local bank notes in a Western city would invest in grain or flour, in a Southern city would invest in cotton. Shipping the flour and cotton to New York. the sales would realize New York bank notes. The operation was thus equivalent to shipping New York bank notes from the Western or Southern cities to New York. The like operation between the United States and Europe for our international trade settlements would take the place of gold shipments, if gold were hoarded for a high premium, as feared. Each such operation would swell the volume of our exports of commodities and benefit, primarily, those for whom we must be most concerned.

But the likelihood of any need of such an operation as a part of the contemplation of the New York merchant in selling to the West and South tended to make him indisposed to sell there. To such extent the Southern and Western importations from New York were lessened. To the like extent our foreign importations will be lessened under our silver-money regime, to the advantage of our home manufacturers as against the foreign manufacturers all the time. But in our experience, when the New York merchant or manufacturer found his home market not broad enough for all his wares, as was frequently the case, his surplus was sold West and South at as low price and sometimes even lower prices than to customers at home. The home price being for the greater portion of their merchandise was maintained, at a sacrifice of profit on the moderate surplus sold elsewhere. Similarly Manchester, Lyons, and German manufacturers would experience the restriction of our silver money upon them. Our importations of Europe's products are to some extent a surplus which she must sell. To that extent our importations of foreign products will continue to foreign disadvantage and our gain.

But, because we are Europe's "best source of supply" for our great surplus of staple commodities, Europe will buy of us, even though we do not buy of her. As, for instance, we buy from Cuba $75,000,000 worth of goods a year and sell to Cuba $12,000,000 to $25,000,000 only; or as Brazil finds a market here for $70,000,000 of her commodities and buys $40,000,000 only of our commodities in return; and finally as England, on the contrary, is debtor to the United States for an excess of $100,000,000 a year by average in our mutual barter of commodities with her.

OUR SILVER DOLLAR AT A PREMIUM.

Therefore, with our silver money restriction upon importations setting all our spindles turning, employing operatives at full time and these operatives made thereby to enlarge our aggregate of home consumers of all home products; with our trade settlements in merchandise serving to enlarge the exportations of our spare products; with Europe's prices for our products enhanced by our enlargement of Europe's aggregate of money, our achievement next evident will be a credit balance of trade established in Europe for the merchants of the United States. At that point exchange on London would sell in Wall street at a discount. This means a draft on gold payable seven days from date offered at a discount in standard silver dollars—the despised, stigmatized 50-cent-silver piece in Wall street, held at a premium over gold in London. It means our silver dollars and our gold coin at par; bimetallism a reality in the United States. Our prosperity as her example, and to such a degree at her expense, is likely to enforce the influence of Manchester's opinion of English monometallism, the result of which may mean the abandonment of England's vicious monetary system soon.

Europe's only silver is her money. Europe's silver coin is valued from 3.06 cents to over 13.33 cents per dollar more than ours. Her "silver pots and spoons" carry the additional price of labor in them. She will ship us gold, therefore, rather than silver, at a minimum preference of 3 per cent.

GOLD DESPISED IN 1853.

Our "goldites" would dismiss all this on the ground of an overabundance of silver. Had the most influential doctrinaire in money in Europe been as influential with lawmakers in 1853, as our aforesaid tutor was influential with law dictators in 1893, France would have closed her mints to gold. Silver monometallism would have been the coinage system of the world. Chevalier threatened France with an abundance of gold as cheap and overwhelming as iron. Silver is the overabundant prediction of our influential doctrinaires. Note, however, that $5,000,000 worth of silver bullion is at this moment an overestimate for the world's distributing-markets' supplies of silver.

INDEPENDENT BIMETALLISM ACHIEVED.

Finally, our "goldites," and in particular our tutor aforesaid, distort history for proof that bimetallism has proved itself a failure; and that independent bimetallism in the United States during eighty years, furnished the experience for the certainty of failure if attempted now. The facts, justly handled, refute both assertions flatly.

The world's great mints were never open to gold and silver without limit on a single price among them for each metal. In consequence, every seeming divergence between a market price and a mint price for either metal was invariably a difference between mint prices. Divergence between one mint price and another, or other mint prices, has to answer in history for every annoying flight of gold or of silver internationally. By undervaluing gold relative to silver, compared with the French mint's valuation of gold relative to silver, our coinage act of 1792 caused our merchants to choose gold preferably to silver for their foreign settlements, following 1792. By undervaluing silver relative to gold, compared with the French mint's relative valuation of the two, in our coinage act of 1834, we made our merchants choose silver preferably to gold for foreign settlements thereafter. This divergence between mint prices—not divergence between our mint price and any market price—cost us gold in one period and cost us silver in the other, for the reason only that during most of both periods we were usually the debtors in balancing our foreign trade.

UNITED STATES' INDEPENDENT BIMETALLISM EXPERIENCED.

Our "goldite" assertion that our said act of 1792 effectually demonetized gold by expelling it from the country, and that our act of 1834 effectually demonetized silver by expelling it, are alike refuted by indisputable records, not made for argument butreporting facts. Thus for the twelve years ending 1805, our gold coinage exceeded our silver coinage. In the eighteen years following, our gold coinage was half our silver coinage. In the nine years ending 1833 our gold coinage was one-fourth our silver coinage. And in this same period of "banished gold" (?) our trade movements of both metals were usually in one direction, usually export in excess of import of both until ending 1823. In 1824 the net movement of the two was import in excess of export. 1825 refutes this gold banishing theory flatly by a net import of gold and a net export of silver. In the five years following, both metals moved together again, import in excess of export. In 1831 our "goldites" are again refuted flatly by the net import of gold with a net export of silver. Thereafter gold and silver both show import in excess of export until 1834.

And in the period following 1834, while "banished silver" (?) is the assumption of our "goldites," our silver coinage in the first eight years equaled our silver coinage of the eight years prior. Our silver coinage in these first eight years exceeded by $3,000,000 our coinage of gold. In the second eight years ending 1850 we coined $18,000,000 of silver, although we were not producing silver, but were producing gold in amounts more vast than the world had known. And in the first four years of this "silver banished" (?) period our imports of silver exceeded our exports of silver by $6,000,000 more than our imports exceeded our exports of gold. For the three years ending 1842 the net movement of both metals was together, export in excess of import. And nine years after this act of 1834 our net movement was import in excess of export for gold and silver both. Our "goldites" are refuted notably and finally in the fact that prior to our civil war no single important movement of the one metal inward and the other metal outward is the record of a year.

And note also in this connection and at this particular moment, besides the considerable sum in coins of foreign nations, circulating as our legal tender until 1857, and besides the unlimited legal tender function of half dollars, quarters, and dimes until 1853, and besides the fact that 80 per cent of all the silver dollars coined were coined after 1834, this fact, namely, that redundant bank notes which increased by more than $200,000,000 in a period of ten years, were tending all the time to house both gold and silver in quiet bank reserves.

FRANCE A SAFE CRITERION.

Finally, I regret profoundly that space forbids the mention of independent bimetallism in France and the record of her mint dictation of the world's market price for gold and silver during a period of seventy years. On the closing of her mints against silver in 1874 France had $900,000,000 of gold and $700,000,000 of silver circulating side by side as money. Her population barely exceeded 35,000,000. Our present population exceeds 65,000,000, with a promise of exceeding the aggregate population of Great Britain and France within ten years; and our use for gold and silver is for a circulation over a territory seventeen times the area of France.

I will append a portion of her record and a table for the printed report.

[Appended as follows.]

INDEPENDENT BIMETALLISM OF FRANCE.

By act of her Corps Legislatif, March 28, 1803, "5 grams of silver, nine-tenths fine, constitute the money unit, which retains the name of franc."

The articles prescribed the same fineness for gold coin, and direct the coining of 20-franc and 40-franc gold pieces, as well as 5-franc and smaller silver pieces. A thousand grams of gold, nine-tenths fine, are to yield 3,100 francs; and at the rate of 5 grams to the franc, 1,000 grams of silver are to yield 200 francs—the mint price of gold, therefore, being 15.5 times the mint price of silver; the 1-franc silver pieces being, as absolutely as gold pieces, the unlimited legal-tender coin of France, and they continued to be until the founding of the Latin Union in 1865. As already noted, the 5-franc silver piece continues to be unlimited legal tender in France, and, therefore, the full equivalent of gold in France, although no longer coined, and at the relative price for gold of 15.5 times silver in the existing coins.

Appended hereto are tables C D, reporting in dollars the gold and silver coinage of France during the seventy years in which her mints were open to the unlimited coining of both gold and silver, at a moderate charge, into unlimited primary moneys. And there will appear the world's production of gold and silver during this period, showing astounding variations in quantities of each produced, and yet as notable an approach to fixity in the relative market price of gold and silver during the period.

The coinage of either metal being by the voluntary act of its owner all the time, the coinage shows that conversion into French money was as good a use as any other to which the owner could put it, or the charge for coining would not have been paid.

In 1806, with the year's production of silver fifty and one-quarter times the year's production of gold, we see the coinage of nearly

$200,000 worth more of gold than of silver for the year. In 1818, with the year's production of silver forty-six times the production of gold, the coinage of gold is seven times the coinage of silver for the year. In 1852, when the production of silver had fallen to four and one-half times the year's production of gold, the coinage of silver is five times the coinage of gold for the year. And when in 1806, the gold and silver coinage of France was so nearly equal for the year, with the production of silver fifty and one-quarter times the year's production of gold, we see the average market price of gold at 15.6 times silver, governed, we infer, by this effectual mint price of 15.5. In 1818 with the coinage of gold seven times the coinage of silver, and the production of silver forty-six times the year's production of gold, the world's market price averages 15.4, as governed by this mint price, 15.5.

And notwithstanding the timid scream of Chevalier and others in 1853 against the further admission of gold into money, gold seeming then to threaten to rival iron in its abundance, the mints of France continued to accept all tenders of gold and silver, and continued to govern the world's market price composedly until 1871, when war with Germany interfered. And the result, which finally appeared after the closing of her mints in 1874, reported to the Paris conference 1878, was a stock of gold and silver money afloat and in bank in France, exceeding $700,000,000 worth of silver money and $900,000,000 worth of gold.

The late De Laveleye, in his "La Monnaie et le Bimétallisme," 1891, makes plain that all the divergence between the French mint price and the London and Hamburg prices for gold or silver, from time to time during the seventy years, was within the aggregate of the costs of a shipment of the momentarily cheaper metal to Paris and the charge for coining there. And, as observed already, the mints of France had little appreciable assistance in their governance of the world's market price for gold or silver during any consecutive important period of years.

Note once more that the population of France did not exceed 35,000,000 and that their employment of money was within an area of 203,000 square miles; and that the present population of the United States approaches 67,000,000, whose demand for money is for a circulation over an area of territory exceeding 3,600,000 square miles. And recollect that her mint price for silver, the value of silver in her existing 5-franc pieces, is at the rate of 3.06 cents on a dollar higher than ours. This means that if the mints of the United States were open to unlimited coinage for our silver dollars, the French would prefer by over 3 per cent, to ship their gold rather than their silver money in any bullion settlement with us as our debtor in trade. The same preference to ship gold rather than their silver money to our equally open mints would appear in the case of any of the European nations except England. England's preference to ship us gold in trade settlements due us, rather than her silver money, would exceed 13 cents on the dollar.

And note finally as to France, that while her unrestricted mints accepted and coined gold and silver without limit during periods when the year's production of silver was only four and one-half times the year's production of gold, and when the production of silver was fifty and one-fourth times the production of gold, governing the price of both metals in all markets the while, the year's production of silver was only twenty-three and one-half times the year's production of gold in the world in 1892, and is proportionately less just now—twenty-one and one-fourth times for 1893.

TABLE C D.

The world's production of gold and silver in periods from 1493 to 1890: Soetbeer. The same for the calendar year 1891: United States Director of the Mint.

The proportions of gold and silver relative to the sum of the two, for each period; and these proportions according to value, at the French mint valuation of 1 to 15.50.

The relative weight of the gold and the silver produced in each period; in other words, the "ratio of production," i. e., the "intrinsic value" (?) of either measured by the other, if production determines value.

Average "market-price" for each period, i. e., average relative value of gold and silver in the open market—London and Hamburgh: Soetbeer, and United States Director of the Mint.

Coinage of France during seventy years to 1873, while her law allowed equally unlimited access for gold and silver to her mints on private account, at a valuation of 1 to 15.50, for emission in unlimited legal-tender coins.

Period.	Pounds avoirdupois.		Proportion of the total.				Relative production gold to silver. (weight).	Relative market value gold to silver.
			By weight.		At value.			
	Gold.	Silver.	Gold.	Silver.	Gold.	Silver.		
1493-1520	357,280	2,895,200	11	89	66	34	1 to 8.10	1 to 10.5-11.1
1521-44	378,048	4,762,560	7	93	55	45	12.59	11.25
1545-60	299,552	10,968,320	3	97	30	70	36.61	11.30
1561-80	300,960	13,178,000	2	98	26	74	43.78	11.50
1581-1600	324,720	18,431,600	2	98	21	79	56.70	12.00
1601-20	374,880	18,607,000	2	98	24	76	49.63	12.50
1621-40	365,200	17,318,400	2	98	25	75	47.42	14.00
1641-60	385,880	16,117,200	2	98	27	73	41.77	14.50
1661-80	407,440	14,828,000	3	97	30	70	36.39	15.00
1681-1700	473,660	15,043,000	3	97	33	67	31.76	14.96
1701-20	564,080	15,646,400	3	97	36	64	27.74	15.21
1721-40	839,520	18,972,800	4	96	41	59	22.60	15.09
1741-60	1,082,840	23,458,380	4	96	42	58	21.66	14.74
1761-80	911,020	28,720,560	3	97	33	67	31.52	14.72
1781-1800	782,760	38,678,040	2	98	24	76	49.41	15.09
1801-10 [1]	391,116	19,671,300	2	98	24	76	50.29	15.61
1811-20	251,790	11,896,940	2	98	25	75	47.25	15.49
1821-30	312,752	10,132,320	3	97	33	67	32.39	15.76
1831-40	446,358	13,121,900	3	97	35	65	29.40	15.70
1841-50	1,204,698	17,169,130	7	93	52	48	14.25	15.81
1851-55	2,172,665	9,747,265	18	82	78	22	4.49	15.42
1856-60	2,266,638	9,954,890	19	81	78	22	4.39	15.30
1861-65	2,036,353	12,112,650	14	86	74	26	5.95	15.41
1866-70	2,110,900	14,729,935	13	87	69	31	6.98	15.55
1871-75	1,877,425	21,663,675	8	92	57	43	11.54	15.97
1876-80	1,881,726	24,200,088	7	93	54	46	13.21	17.89
1881-85	1,694,258	29,333,894	5	95	47	53	17.31	18.59
1886-90	1,863,700	37,962,785	5	95	43	57	20.37	21.15
1891	415,710	9,847,300	5	95	41	59	23.68	20.92

[1] Mints of France from 1803 to 1873 equally open to gold and silver on the valuation of 1 to 15.50. See coinage table annexed.

Coinage at the mints of France, from 1803 to 1870 in said periods, valuing the franc roughly at 5 to the United States dollar.

Period.	Gold.	5 francs silver.	Period.	Gold.	5 francs silver.
1803-10	$33,504,964	$53,865,244	1851-55	$310,766,198	$34,252,910
1811-20	110,907,676	149,752,376	1856-60	505,494,552	9,279,042
1821-30	15,031,752	208,757,061	1861-65	179,491,304	194,216
1831-40	29,198,152	233,834,909	1866-70	227,777,130	51,954,842
1841-50	35,157,480	175,845,263			
			Total	1,447,329,208	917,735,863

Years of noteworthy coinages, in better evidence of the automatic regulation of the "market price" of gold and silver, by the mints of France.

Year.	Coinage of the mints of France.		Relative production gold to silver (weight).	Relative market value gold to silver.
	Gold.	5 francs silver.		
1803	$233,048	$4,565,400		
1806	4,607,800	4,485,649	1 to 50.29	1 to 15.61
1807	3,357,776	804,423		
1809	2,880,440	7,985,445		
1811	16,282,372	48,947,496		
1812	13,883,190	31,045,613		
1813	12,148,216	26,002,853		
1814	13,908,914	12,157,747	1 to 47.25	1 to 15.49
1816	2,560,424	6,836,669		
1818	16,171,404	2,419,939		
1820	5,712,376	3,612,292		
1841	2,475,012	14,659,936		
1842	370,544	13,175,982		
1845	23,828	16,780,658	1 to 14.25	1 to 15.81
1849	5,421,912	40,766,309		
1850	15,854,376	16,120,678		
1851	53,941,904	11,409,200		
1852	2,776,260	13,990,200	1 to 4.49	1 to 15.42
1854	101,743,432	10,615		
1855	85,898,300	4,861,173		
1859	131,316,076	3,365		
1860	79,937,648	....	1 to 4.40	1 to 15.30
1861	17,150,224	22,098		
1865	30,658,000	97,134	1 to 6.00	1 to 15.44
1866	68,872,548	37,893		
1867	36,858,604	10,810,312		
1868	65,506,130	18,724,110	1 to 6.98	1 to 15.55
1869	45,670,088	11,652,857		
1870	10,869,760	10,729,670		
1871 [1]	10,033,976	942,181		
1872	....	77,838		
1873 [2]	....	30,929,809	1 to 11.54	1 to 15.97
1874	4,863,940	11,999,202		
1875	46,982,400	15,000,000		
1876 [3]	35,298,632	10,532,263	1 to 12.90	1 to 17.88

[1] In 1871 Franco-Prussian war was waged, followed by French payments of indemnity to Germany.
[2] In 1873 Germany's sales of silver began, the United States having demonetized silver by act of February 12, 1873.
[3] The full legal-tender silver coinage restricted, by Latin Union agreement of 1874; stopped finally by agreement of 1878.

LATIN MONETARY UNION.

The Latin Union did not appreciably enlarge the ability of France to maintain the parity of her gold and silver coins; that is, did not add to the ability of France to maintain bimetallism independently. The coins of all gravitated to France.

France compacted with Belgium, Italy, Switzerland, and later with Greece also, a union whose purpose was "to rid their several people of annoying conditions of intercourse and business transactions resulting from differing valuations of silver in the subsidiary silver moneys of these several States, and with the purpose also to achieve a uniformity of weights, measures, and moneys among them."

This Latin Union was formed December 23, 1865. It provided unlimited coinage and the unlimited legal-tender function for gold and for silver 5-franc pieces, thus exceeding its first aforesaid intent. The union was maintained with this unlimited 5-franc piece included until 1874 (under Germany's sales), and thereafter with a continuance of subsidiary silver coining under restrictions until 1878. Except that coining silver has ceased, the union remains in force effectually. Each State made the authorized gold and silver coins of all receivable and payable at its public treasury. Each State contracted to redeem its own issues of subsidiary silver in gold or the 5-franc pieces of the State asking the redemption.

The evidence of the independence of France in her bimetallism, her independence of her associates in her maintenance of the parity of gold and silver money, is easily made manifest. Much of all their gold and silver money gravitated to France, and for the reason that in Switzerland the rate of exchange on Paris was so frequently and so continuously at a premium; for the reason that the same was painfully true of Belgium, as the late De Laveleye records; and for the reason that the like was glaringly true of Italy, whose only currency became irredeemable paper.

The population of France barely reached 36,000,000, and the territory over which her money circulated was less in area than 202,600 square miles, before 1865. The combined territory of Belgium, Italy, Switzerland and Greece and their combined population, were respectively, 166,500 square miles and 37,500,000 people. The aggregate population of all the Latin-Union States, therefore, did not exceed 73,000,000 and their combined area was less than 370,000 square miles.

The present population of the United States approaches 67,000,000 and promises to exceed 85,000,000 within ten years, whose employment for circulating money is over an area of 3,600,000 square miles.

AUSTRIA'S MONEY.

As for Austria-Hungary, while at heavy cost incurred in the purchase of $100,000,000 of gold at a premium, her stock of that metal may have been increased to that extent. Nevertheless, in no right sense of the word can it be justly asserted that the monetary system of that Empire has been established on a gold basis, even approximately. If her mints have been coining gold every week during the last year, so, too, have they been coining silver to a material extent, and thus increasing the volume of its silver currency as well as that of her gold. As recently indeed as the 15th of March, 1894, the monetary situation of the Austro-Hungarian Bank was as follows:

Gold	$50, 268, 363, or	39 per cent.
Silver	79, 261, 480, or	61 per cent.
Making a total of	129, 529, 843, or	100 per cent.

Note circulation, $194,228,000; that is no less than 61 per cent of the present stock of specie in the Austro-Hungarian Bank as recently as the 15th March, 1894, was of silver.

Gold commands a premium in Austria thus far still. She does not redeem her paper in gold as yet, and will not if she abandons silver. Her already burdensome debt of nearly $2,000,000,000 increases almost every year.

AFTER RECESS.

The CHAIRMAN. Does any member of the committee desire to submit any further questions to Mr. St. John?

Mr. CULBERSON. I want to ask him a question. In view of present conditions, Mr. St. John, what would you have this Congress do?

Mr. ST. JOHN. Shall I offer a bill? Shall I give you a bill to offer in the House if you approve it?

Mr. CULBERSON. You can answer that question just as you think proper.

The CHAIRMAN. Your answer is that you would like to have the following bill enacted?

Mr. St. JOHN. That is it.

Mr. WARNER. Let it be read.

Mr. CULBERSON. He need not read it; he can briefly state the effect of it.

Mr. JOHNSON, of Indiana. Let him briefly explain its contents.

Mr. ST. JOHN. I find a wide difference between explaining a thing and giving the thing itself.

Mr CULBERSON. I think you had better read it.

Mr. ST. JOHN. I should like to read it. I think I can take it up by paragraphs, which I believe to be the method of legislation.

The CHAIRMAN. Read it and then make your explanation.

Mr. St. John read his proposed bill as follows:

A BILL to restore the bimetallic coinage system of the United States, and for other purposes.

Be it enacted, etc., That upon the terms and conditions and charges prescribed by law for the like deposits of gold, owners of silver not too base for the operations of the mint may deposit the same, in amounts of not less value than $100, at any mint of the United States and receive therefor silver dollars containing each 412½ grains Troy of standard silver.

SEC. 2. The standard silver dollars of the United States are hereby required to be received for all dues to the United States and are made receivable and payable for all dues and debts, public and private, within the United States.

SEC. 3. Depositors of gold and depositors of silver as aforesaid, at any mint of the United States, shall receive therefor on their request, instead of the coin to which they shall be entitled, coin certificates of the United States which shall be redeemed on demand in coin. And depositors of gold coin and of silver coin, other than subsidiary coins, at the Treasury or any subtreasury of the United States, in sums of not less than $20, may receive the herein-provided coin certificates therefor. And no gold certificates and no silver certificates and no Treasury notes authorized by act of July 14, 1890, entitled "An act directing the purchase of silver bullion and the issue of Treasury notes thereon, and for other purposes," shall hereafter be issued.

SEC. 4. The herein-provided coin certificates shall be redeemed in gold or silver coin, at the convenience of the United States; and the Secretary of the Treasury is hereby authorized, in his discretion, to redeem the same on request in gold or silver standard bars, at the like convenience of the United States.

SEC. 5. The Secretary of the Treasury is hereby required to reserve on hand, in coin and standard bars, an aggregate sum of gold and silver equal to the aggregate sum of the herein-provided coin certificates outstanding, except as hereinafter provided.

SEC. 6. The Secretary of the Treasury is hereby authorized, in his discretion and under regulations which he may prescribe, to direct the Treasurer of the United States, from time to time, to receive, at the Treasury or any subtreasury of the United States, interest-bearing bonds of the United States, duly hypothecated to the Treasurer, and issue therefor safe amounts of the herein-provided coin certificates as loans at interest. The rate of interest to be required on such loans of coin certificates shall be in every case the same as the rate of interest payable by the United States on the bonds hypothecated therefor: *Provided always*, That the aggregate sum of coin certificates issued for deposits of interest-bearing bonds of the United States shall not reduce the aggregate sum of coin and standard bars reserved for the redemption of coin certificates below 60 per cent of the aggregate sum of all coin certificates outstanding.

SEC. 7. The coin certificates provided in this act shall be received for all dues to the United States, and shall be receivable and payable for all dues and debts, public and private, except where otherwise expressly stipulated in the contract.

SEC. 8. All authority of law for the transportation of standard silver dollars for private account at public expense, in exchange for other lawful money of the United States, and all other acts and parts of acts in conflict with this act, are hereby repealed.

Mr. ST. JOHN. I should like to explain sections six and seven before any question is asked me, while I think of what I want to say.

The suggestion to make these coin certificates a legal tender with the limit proposed, silver dollars being made as unlimited legal tender as gold coin, is in order that the New York Clearing House banks shall accept these coin certificates as it does the Treasury notes of 1890, which are exactly thus limited tender, in settlements of daily balances.

The proposed section 6 is an emergency issue, and would be availed of in real emergencies only, for two reasons:

(1) Because owners of bonds would not accept long-time loans at a cost of all the interest on their investment; and

(2) Borrowers of 4 per cent and 5 per cent United States bonds, hired to hypothecate for such loans, would only appear when a real emergency made high rates for money in the open market.

If a money-market panic threatened the proposed enactment with a sharp contraction of our aggregate of money, this provision (section 6) would empower the Secretary of the Treasury to issue over $200,000,000 of United States coin certificates against silver coin and bullion already in the Treasury, and loan them at 4 per cent and 5 per cent per annum against United States interest-bearing bonds. This issue would reduce the aggregate reserve against silver certificates and Treasury notes to about 62 per cent.

If lack of engraved coin certificates threaten the Secretary's immediate convenience, I suggest that boldness equaling the recent issuing of interest-bearing bonds will momentarily substitute silver certificates, with some distinguishing stamp on them, therefor.

The bill merely proposes in effect: "That the Congress restore immediately the coinage system of the United States founded with the mint in 1792, maintained for eighty years thereafter and overthrown, unobservedly, when neither gold nor silver was our current money. It provides the modern convenience of paper substitute for coin, on the choice of the depositors of gold and of silver at the mint, one and the same coin certificate redeemable on demand in coin; and redeems these coin certificates in gold or silver, at the option and convenience of the United States. It provides an 'emergency issue' of these coin certificates, additionally, with 'elasticity' unquestionable and with redemptions on demand assured, and the means in the Secretary's hands to stifle any panic in Wall street instanter."

Mr. BROSIUS. What limitation would you put upon the legal-tender quality of the certificates you have descirbed?

Mr. ST. JOHN. The coin certificates?

Mr. BROSIUS. Yes.

Mr. ST. JOHN. Only the limitation that you and I might be able to contract against receiving them, if we desire, exactly as the Treasury note of 1890 is limited in its legal-tender function, and exactly as the silver dollar is now limited. But I propose to remove the limitation from the silver dollar. Let our gold and silver coins stand alike before the law, as in France; and then the United States Supreme Court will not permit the enforcement of contracts in gold coin only. Such discrimination then would be "against good public policy" to enforce.

Mr. BROSIUS. You have spoken of the limited legal-tender quality, but you have not yet stated what the limit was.

Mr. ST. JOHN. The limit only that you would have a right to contract against them, as you have in the Treasury note of 1890.

Mr. ELLIS. I came into the room after you had read part of your bill. I will ask you whether your bill provides for the repeal of the law of 1873 making the gold dollar the unit of value?

Mr. ST. JOHN. You gentlemen are lawyers, and I need not give you the law. But as I understand statute law to-day, each new statute supersedes any prior act that conflicts with it. The provisions of my proposed bill conflict with that law of 1873, and my final clause provides that all acts and parts of acts in conflict herewith are hereby repealed.

Mr. ELLIS. Do you propose to establish the silver dollar as the unit of value—if that is a good term?

Mr. St. John. I do not think it is a good term. I presume you mean the unit of account.

Mr. Ellis. The unit of account?

Mr. St. John. No, sir; my bill recognizes the dollar of the United States as the unit of account; it does not distinguish between the gold dollar and the silver dollar.

Mr. Ellis. Does it provide any ratio at which the metals shall be coined—if that is a good term?

Mr. St. John. You did not hear the bill read?

Mr. Ellis. No, sir.

Mr. St. John. The first portion is explicit on that point. It simply provides that the silver dollar now existing shall be coinable, without limit in amount, on producing the bullion for it, and on the same terms as are now prescribed for gold.

Mr. Ellis. Would your theory put this country on a silver basis?

Mr. St. John. Momentarily, it might—I think it would, immediately.

Mr. Ellis. How long would that condition, in your judgment, prevail?

Mr. St. John. I read you a paper this morning in which I tried to answer that. I shall have to refer you to that for my complete answer. I would not predict the achievement of actual bimetallism in the United States under the bill earlier than two years; that is, two years at the outside. I should expect it earlier, if conditions now existing abroad, existing outside of France, prevail; I would expect it to be accomplished within one year. There is no business prosperity anywhere in the world to-day, outside of France.

Mr. Ellis. To what do you attribute the prosperity of France?

Mr. St. John. To an abundance of good, sound money; that is, primary money that can not be refused, money that the financiers of that country handle on a scientific basis, France being the only nation of financiers.

Mr. Ellis. I was criticised the other day for asking some witness something about primary money. I was asked what I meant by primary money. Now, I wish you would give a definition of that term.

Mr. St. John. Primus, I think, means first, or nothing ahead of it. It is absolute money—unconditional, primary money. Secondary money is the greenback which, although a limited legal tender, is a promise of money. Gold coin does not promise any redemption. It is not the stamp on the coin that makes it money. It is the law behind it. You can not refuse it, and the condition all over the world to-day is, practically, that all you have to do is to present gold bullion, and lawful money is returned to you for it under the mint laws of all the commercial nations.

Mr. Ellis. You have examined the Baltimore plan and the plan submitted by the Secretary of the Treasury, I presume?

Mr. St. John. I have.

Mr. Ellis. If either one of those plans were adopted, state whether or not, in your opinion, the volume of paper money would be increased or decreased.

Mr. St. John. I do not look upon a bank note as money, but a promise of money, and therefore I do not quite get your question.

Mr. Ellis. I will ask it in this form: If either of those plans were adopted would the volume of paper currency be increased or decreased?

Mr. St. John. You mean now, money and substitutes for money. Will you confine me to one plan, because I would treat these plans on different bases.

Mr. Ellis. Answer in your own way.

Mr. ST. JOHN. Suppose you confine me to one; otherwise you give me large ground to cover.

Mr. ELLIS. Then I will confine you first to paper currency. Would the volume of paper currency be increased?

Mr. ST. JOHN. To which of the bills shall I confine myself?

Mr. ELLIS. We have the Baltimore plan, already spoken of, and the other plan submitted by the Secretary of the Treasury.

Mr. ST. JOHN. Confining myself for the time to the last named, if the Secretary's bill were enacted as introduced it would fall absolutely flat; not a note would be taken out under it.

Mr. ELLIS. Why?

Mr. ST. JOHN. For the reason that Mr. Williams and several other gentlemen have given you, as I understand their testimony.

Mr. ELLIS. You seem to have overlooked the fact that there is a mandatory provision in one of these plans.

Mr. ST. JOHN. On the contrary, that panic-assuring provision will be resisted and the panic ensue concurrently. All I have to do under the statutes of New York is to make application one day and the next day I can become a State bank. We are not obliged to be a national bank, although we prefer it. We will not continue under national charter and guarantee the liabilities of other banks. We are more experienced than to do that.

Mr. ELLIS. I wish you would follow the bill in detail as far as you like.

Mr. ST. JOHN. I could follow it to criticise it.

Mr. ELLIS. I should like you to do it.

The CHAIRMAN. Would the currency issued under that be safe?

Mr. ST. JOHN. There would not be any currency issued under it as it now stands, but there would be the greatest panic that this country has ever seen.

The CHAIRMAN. What would cause the panic if the banks did not issue currency?

Mr. ST. JOHN. The fact that conservative banks would abandon their national charters rather than guarantee the liabilities of others, and such abandonment would throw upon an unresponsive market $200,000,000 worth of United States bonds, of which $21,000,000 are 2 per cents, not now salable at par. These withdrawals of bonds by national banks would mean surrenders of the circulation secured by them. That would mean, in the aggregate, a "contraction of the currency" of the United States by $180,000,000 in the period between the enactment of the law and July, 1895. This burdening of the bond market, under antagonism of the national banks, would make it impossible for the Treasury to sell its next $50,000,000 of bonds to recoup its gold reserve, and chaos would reign supreme.

In February of 1881, when I had been only one month in the Mercantile National Bank, and without previous bank experience, there came out in the New York papers a mistaken notion that between January and July the national banks must replace all the bonds they possessed by the substitution of new 3 per cents. The President was induced to veto the bill by the panic occasioned by an $18,000,000 contraction of the currency which ensued. There are only three concerns in New York City buying and selling Government bonds. They make the market, practically, and sometimes are quite arbitrary about it. There is sometimes a difference of 1 per cent between their buying and selling prices for United States bonds, the best of securities in the world. Therefore it was thought by the national banks then that they had better sell promptly. Hence the contraction and the panic. If section 7 of the Secretary's bill is passed we would have to find a market for $200,000,000 United States bonds between the date of its passage and July next. We would prefer to sell ours forthwith.

The national-bank note is guaranteed by the United States, for the reason that the national bank, as a creature of the United States, is an arm of the Government. The national banks, with their note-issue system, were created as a means of providing a ready market for United States bonds by a method yielding acceptable substitutes in moderate amount for money, and for no other reason. That means of providing such market ought to be preserved by the United States. If the United States desired the Mercantile National Bank of New York to take $900,000 of their 3 per cent bonds at par to-day, or their 5 per cent bonds on a 3 per cent basis, and did not exact gold for it, but would let us pay for the bonds with our notes which the Comptroller would issue on them, we would do so promptly. We did not buy any of the first or second $50,000,000 of United States bonds lately issued, because I did not believe any existing law provided for the issue. I think necessity rather exceeded the law, as it usually does, and I find no fault. There was nothing else to do under the circumstances. The circumstances could have been prohibited, however. We made a direct contribution of $500,000 of gold coin to the Treasury reserve "in exchange for any lawful money;" but the newspapers were not told of it.

A copy of the Secretary's bill has been handed me. Suppose I take it up by paragraphs. I shall not consume much time.

Mr. Ellis. Consume all the time that is necessary.

Mr. St. John. In the first place, under this proposed bill of the Secretary's a sum of "greenbacks" or Treasury notes of 1890 are to be impounded. This effects an immediate contraction of the currency. To procure and deposit these notes you contract the currency existing. There is a period of time, involving from fifteen to forty days, before a national bank can get its notes from the Comptroller, under existing law, put them into shape, and get them into circulation. It is not always easy to float national-bank notes. We took out $800,000 of national-bank notes some three or four years ago and it took us nearly two months to get them out. They were nothing but chips—I do not mean poker chips, but chips of wood—until we could get them into circulation. This element of temporary contraction is an element of danger in the Secretary's bill.

Now we come to the provision that the notes are a first lien upon all the assets of the association issuing the same. That might be open to this question: Whether they are a lien also on the stockholders' additional liability. That liability of shareholders is perhaps not an asset of the bank.

The Secretary's third section provides: "That in lieu of all existing taxes" one-fourth of 1 per cent per annum is payable as a duty for each half year upon the average amount of the bank notes in circulation. That is to pay for the Government's interest in the matter. But there are two quarters to be paid under section 5, as a means of establishing a safety fund. That means one half of 1 per cent per annum.

The Chairman. Until the 5 per cent is reached.

Mr. St. John. That means a period of ten years before the safety fund is established. What would happen to your banks during that ten years preceding the establishment of a safety fund? In the meantime there is only dubious safety. That is logical, if it is not true; and I think it is true.

There is particularly no safety for the good banks that would be liable to demands upon them, during ten years, to pay failed banks' notes and take the chance of any assets of these failed banks to reimburse them. At least the Osawatomie People's National Bank can not have this right to jeopardize the Mercantile National Bank of the city of New York if we have to surrender our national charter to prevent it.

Each association hereafter organized and each association applying for additional circulation shall pay its pro rata share into the said fund before receiving notes.

I suppose that means that if 5 per cent has been contributed by banks already issuing, any new bank must contribute 5 per cent as a starter. That is another deterrent; but it ought to be required if the rest of the bill is enacted, of course.

The underlying proposal pertaining to all these bills, the Secretary's indirectly and all, under the recommendations of Mr. Horace White and associates, whom you have heard, is the retirement of the greenbacks and Treasury notes; and Mr. White wants the silver dollars and certificates retired also. The proposal amounts to a demand that the United States abandon a profit to the people at large and confer a profit on the banks instead.

Mr. COBB, of Alabama. Will you please explain how it is, if this bill becomes a law, that the United States would guarantee a profit to the national banks?

Mr. ST. JOHN. I do not say that. I have said that the Secretary's bill would fall flat, and if section 7 is enacted will create a panic. I say the underlying demand of the gentlemen who have been here to testify in behalf of any of these bills is that the greenbacks shall be retired. That is basal in their demands. Profit to the issuing banks is the first requisite of any creation of bank notes.

Mr. COBB, of Alabama. Are you opposed to the retirement of greenbacks? If so, state why; and if you are not, state why not.

Mr. ST. JOHN. I am opposed to asking any sacrifice of the people at large in order to provide profit to banks. I do not dare ask any such thing. I never did and I never will. I would not so sacrifice the popularity that the national banks of the United States have legitimately earned. The great popularity to which they are entitled is being sacrificed by well-meaning doctrinaires, outsiders, who know little about banking. Think of it, the United States issues $100,000,000 of bonds, on which interest is to be paid for ten years at 5 per cent per annum. At the same time it is proposed that $346,000,000 greenbacks, a debt which does not bear interest, and therefore is saving (at 5 per cent per annum) $17,300,000 a year to the people at large, shall be retired. More interest-bearing debt to issue to retire them. And as a feature of the proposal is that bank notes, yielding profit to banks as the first essential of their existence, shall supersede them! It is preposterous!

Mr. JOHNSON, of Indiana. What is your opinion of section 10 of the Carlisle bill?

Mr. ST. JOHN. My opinion of that is just what I said when I came here, that it is absolutely impossible for the banks of the United States to redeem a liberal issue of bank notes in gold. The possibility does not exist.

The CHAIRMAN. Section 10 is in regard to State banks.

Mr. JOHNSON, of Indiana. Section 10 is the one which provides for the issue by State banks, under certain conditions therein imposed.

The CHAIRMAN. Take our printed copy of the bill. That is the only bill to which we refer.

Mr. ST. JOHN. Section 10 provides, I see, that the use of circulating notes issued by a banking corporation duly organized under the laws of any State, and which transacts no other than a banking business, shall be exempt from taxation under the laws of the United States under certain conditions. That section is the State-bank feature. What I would have to say about that is two things: First of all, the Secretary introduces a bill based on his timidity as to a sufficient gold reserve. He says that he is asked to pay gold for greenbacks and Treasury notes, and he wants to put that burden upon the banks. He proposes to allow a State bank to issue notes if the State bank will first lodge with some State officer a certain number of dollars' worth of greenbacks or Treasury notes. He does not provide that the State officer must withhold these greenbacks or Treasury notes from circulating, and is without any right in the Constitution of the United States to compel such State officer to do so. He is simply furnishing a means of issuing State-bank notes and leaving those greenbacks or Treasury notes in circulation also. He is not reducing by a dollar the demand on the Treasury for greenback and Treasury-note redemptions.

Mr. JOHNSON, of Indiana. You said there were two reasons; you have given one.

Mr. ST. JOHN. I meant to couple that with the fact that I think that the national-bank-note system ought to be preserved, so far as it is to the public interest to preserve it, and so far as it is to the public interest to create or preserve any banks of issue. The national-bank-note system of note issue ought to be preserved as the means of assuring market for United States bonds when the Government needs to issue interest-bearing bonds.

Mr. JOHNSON, of Indiana. You contemplate, of course, the continued use of paper money?

Mr. ST. JOHN. I propose to create coin certificates of the United States secured by a reserve of 100 per cent in coin and standard bars in lieu of the Treasury notes of 1890 and other paper, excepting the greenbacks and excepting national-bank notes, as now issued, also. The greenback is a note that did not promise anything but money; it did not say what money, and it did not promise coin until by act of 1874, which said it should be paid in coin. That act says gold or silver, explicitly.

Mr. JOHNSON, of Indiana. What is your opinion as to the relative merits of a system of paper money under direct Federal control, as compared with a system of paper money under the control of the various States?

Mr. ST. JOHN. With no Federal control attempted?

Mr. JOHNSON, of Indiana. Yes.

Mr. ST. JOHN. Well, we have had a history in this country that was exceedinly expensive; very costly. Uncertainty caused a difference in exchange between cities, which varied from a tenth of 1 per cent to 3 per cent quite commonly, and sometimes exceeded 5 per cent. That difference in exchange was the price of that system to the producing sections, whose products were exchanged by means of State-bank notes for products hailing from the money centers.

Mr. JOHNSON, of Indiana. Do you believe that conditions have so changed in the interval that there is now no danger of the evils from which we then suffered under the old State-bank system?

Mr. ST. JOHN. Has anybody furnished any fact to verify that statement? I do not admit it.

Mr. JOHNSON, of Indiana. I want to develop your views.

Mr. ST. JOHN. I am willing to be converted by facts, but I have not seen any facts to warrant even a suspicion of such a change.

Mr. JOHNSON, of Indiana. If we are to have a system of circulating notes issued by banks, which system do you think is preferable and would best subserve public interest—a system under exclusive Federal control, or a system partially under Federal control and partially under the control of the States?

Mr. ST. JOHN. I do not believe it would be possible to maintain a system under two controls under the Constitution of the United States as I read it.

Mr. JOHNSON, of Indiana. But let us assume the constitutionality.

Mr. ST. JOHN. I can not assume it, because I do not believe it is possible. I think the Constitution would interfere. I think that is an absurdity, and I do not think you want to ask me to assume an absurdity.

Mr. JOHNSON, of Indiana. But as there might be a difference of opinion on the legal aspect of the question, assume that it is possible from a legal standpoint; as a practical business man what would you say as to the desirability?

Mr. ST. JOHN. I have had no experience to justify any opinion whatever, and I do not think anybody else has. I do not respect opinions that are based on imagination only. I will not ask you to do so.

Mr. JOHNSON, of Indiana. Are the functions of a bank, so far as its discounts and deposits are concerned, so entirely separable from its functions as a bank of issue of circulating notes that, in your opinion, as a practical business man, and leaving out of view the constitutional aspect of the question, that the discount and deposit functions could be subjected to one jurisdiction and the note-issuing functions to another jurisdiction?

Mr. ST. JOHN. There is nothing but imagination that could answer that question. I do not know. I have no suspicion that such a disjunctive conjunction could survive the first strain upon the money market.

Mr. JOHNSON, of Indiana. The witness who was on the stand just before you came was asked by the gentleman from Kentucky (Mr. Ellis) to explain why it was that no money could be borrowed on short time by the merchant in New York on personal security at a low rate of interest, whereas a merchant in a city like Louisville, Ky., who was unquestionably solvent, could not obtain money from the banks there on the same time at so low a rate of interest. Can you give us a solution of that problem?

Mr. ST. JOHN. I can mention one of the causes.

Mr. JOHNSON, of Indiana. What is your explanation? Does that condition exist?

Mr. ST. JOHN. It does.

Mr. JOHNSON, of Indiana. Why?

Mr. ST. JOHN. I will give you one reason. There are many, doubtless, but one is this: The statutes of the United States establish a requirement of reserves of money in national banks In the country banks—banks out of the main cities—it is 15 per cent of their deposits; in the larger cities it is 25 per cent of their deposits. Banks of those cities of the 25 per cent class which are not designated "reserve cities" and banks of the cities that are in the 15 per cent class are allowed by law to carry a portion of what is called their "cash reserve" on cash deposit in the city of New York. Thus, in law, a deposit in New York subject to check is a portion of the cash reserve required of the Ossawatomie National Bank. The money is in the city of New York and is employed in New York. The banks in New York, competing with each other, invite such deposits, sometimes at a small rate of interest. The result is an accumulation of money in the banks of New York. One of the effects is a competition to employ it safely. There are too many lenders at times and low rates. Great demoralization in the money market in New York ensues. The effect has been evident in the condition for a year past until the last bond issue reduced funds, the prime New York borrower being able to get money on his own terms.

Mr. JOHNSON, of Indiana. There are accumulations of money in New York?

Mr. ST. JOHN. There are, frequently.

Mr. JOHNSON, of Indiana. That is your answer boiled down?

Mr. ST. JOHN. Yes, with this addition: The peril of these accumulations is what your section appreciates in your disadvantage in rates, which you ask me to explain. New York banks lend the money on an average calculation of demands upon them. If they lend too much of the money intrusted to them they are in danger. Hence, when their habit of thought is accustomed to the accumulation they dread the first evidence of its diminishing. To forestall this dread they lend to New York merchants of certainty to pay and whose paper will sell everywhere, in preference to lending to Louisville, when just as certain of payment, but not certain that Louisville paper will sell if money is drawn and must be provided.

Mr. JOHNSON, of Indiana. Is that in your opinion sufficient to explain this discrepancy in the rates of interest between Louisville and New York?

Mr. ST. JOHN. Here is another thing: The Mercantile National Bank of New York has to-day some $10,000,000 to $11,000,000 of other people's money on deposit, and some $5,000,000 of idle money in our vaults, part of which latter ought to be earning interest. But the times are uncertain; there is a threatened alarm on the gold shipment question, and there are other disturbing elements in prospect, so that we do not dare lend as closely as we would like. Under present conditions I would rather buy a prime New York merchant's note for $100,000 at a discount of 3 per cent per annum than Louisville paper at 6 per cent per annum, four months to run.

Mr. JOHNSON, of Indiana. If you will be kind enough to make your answers a little more concise it will perhaps better serve our purpose.

Mr. ST. JOHN. If that is not pertinent it may be stricken out. It is pertinent to remind ourselves that as communities grow in wealth they keep more and more of their money at home. Every government's bonds that sell at par and over are practically all at home.

Mr. JOHNSON, of Indiana. You feel certain that the reason why you could loan money at a low rate of interest is because of the superior character of the paper?

Mr. ST. JOHN. In times like these there is no security except in the most strictly prime paper known to be such, and available to sell as such.

Mr. JOHNSON, of Indiana. I am assuming that the primest security is offered in Louisville.

Mr. ST. JOHN. I know banks in Louisville that are prime, and I know one that can get $200,000 from me whenever it wants it. They can get money from me at 4 per cent and lend it at 6.

Mr. JOHNSON, of Indiana. Do you think it is the selfishness of the banks that causes this difference in the rate of interest?

Mr. ST. JOHN. No, sir; it is due to timidity, in view of the general lack of prosperity in the producing sections, or belief that producers are suffering generally.

Mr. JOHNSON, of Indiana. Does not that timidity obtain in New York as well as in Louisville?

Mr. ST. JOHN. It does indeed.

Mr. JOHNSON, of Indiana. Then how would that effect the difference in interest complained of?

Mr. ST. JOHN. It is not quite the same in New York. In New York we have a very large clientage of men who are worth a million dollars or more each and known to be. That condition does not obtain in the smaller cities. I can take paper of Louisville merchants with entire confidence, because I know them. But I can not be certain of getting cash for it if my depositors draw on me heavily.

Mr. JOHNSON, of Indiana. Are there not men of unquestioned financial standing in Louisville as well as in New York? How could that create the difference?

Mr. ST. JOHN. I answered before that there are accumulations in New York such as are not in Louisville, those accumulations being partly the result of statute law. I explained our competition in New York as lenders, and our required caution as to amount to lend.

Mr. JOHNSON, of Indiana. But I understood that there were other reasons, and it is with respect to the additional reasons that I was inquiring. Something has also been said in the course of the examinations we have had here about the scarcity of money in the agricultural sections of the country at what is known as the crop-moving time, and about the high rate of interest charged for money with which to move the crops. Can you explain the reason for the scarcity of the money and why it is that it costs the people living in those sections so much to get it? Describe the process whereby money is made high to them in order to move their crops.

Mr. ST. JOHN. Primarily and underlying the whole thing is the fact that the aggregate sum of money in the United States is not sufficient. If there were a general business revival in the United States we would have a painfully stringent money market within ninety days. That is one answer to the question.

Mr. JOHNSON, of Indiana. Is it not a fact that at the very time that these people in the agricultural sections are complaining about the scarcity of money there are large quantities of money lying idle and congested in the money centers?

Mr. ST. JOHN. Undoubtedly so, as I thought I had explained.

Mr. JOHNSON, of Indiana. Then would you say that the reason why this complaint exists is that there is not sufficient money for the purpose of moving the crops?

Mr. ST. JOHN. I would, undoubtedly. When I find an accumulation in every bank of Europe greater this year than for years past, I know there is a reason for it. The increase of the aggregate money of the world is stopped, except as one can provide 4.03 pounds of gold when he wants to add a thousand dollars to it. Distrust is the concomitant and distress the achievement.

Mr. JOHNSON, of Indiana. Is the reason why money can not be had in agricultural districts in sufficient quantities to enable the crops to be moved, because of the fear among lenders that there is no security for the money?

Mr. ST. JOHN. It is one and a sufficient reason for bank caution. The people who are making these complaints, and justly too, I think, are not prosperous. They are mortgaged to death to their factors and stores and country merchants. What they mortgage their homes and crops for is dollars. If their product will not yield dollars they can not pay their debts. Cheap overcoats do not concern the planter and farmer unless dollars are the outcome of their crops.

I have said that the aggregate of all our money is our measure of all values. It follows that the aggregate of money must increase with the aggregate of the commodity considered if the price of that commodity is to remain unchanged. Large volume of wheat, low price for it; large volume of dollars, low value of dollars. I don't mean interest value of dollars. I mean relative value of wheat and dollars. High prices for flour and high rates of interest are found together. We see this conjunction in mining districts. To be brief, it is the fact that the world's growing abundance of the necessaries and luxuries is surpassing the world's sufficiency of money. The prime sufferer is the producer of the abundance. Reflectively and painfully all elements suffer on account of him.

When crops move from the producing sections they move East and North and out of the country. The Western or Southern draft follows the merchandise to New York, is cashed in New York, and the money for which the merchandise sells is there. Now, to get the actual money to the West or South it has to be shipped there. That process of shipping is expensive in two ways. First, the express charges. Second, the alarm it nearly always causes the money-center banks who are asked to ship; it raises their rates of interest.

Mr. JOHNSON, of Indiana. That is what I am trying to get at. The items that go to form the dearness of currency at the time it reaches the crop moving section is due to what, do you say?

Mr. ST. JOHN. It is because it has to be shipped from the money centers to the crop-producing localities. That is a process demanding money. The insufficiency of our aggregate of money in the United States appears at such times glaringly to the unprejudiced. When crops move from the producer he wants actual money. Checks, drafts, and like credit substitutes for money do not content him. Money is the measure of his sales.

Mr. JOHNSON, of Indiana. Let us stick to the question. You have stated one reason why money is so scarce and high, and that is because of the cost of transportation. You stated that there was another reason. What is that?

Mr. ST. JOHN. I thought I said that the cost of transportation was one element. I meant to say that the timidity element mentioned is the chief cause.

Mr. JOHNSON, of Indiana. The feeling that the security offered for the money will not be sufficient if the people are not sufficiently prosperous?

Mr. ST. JOHN. Only partly that. More importantly, the money-center banks are timid at once upon every large drain upon their cash resources.

Mr. JOHNSON, of Indiana. Are they afraid to realize on idle money with which the money centers are loaded?

Mr. ST. JOHN. I would rather say cautious. If cash reserves run down, we become a little more conservative of what remains.

Mr. JOHNSON, of Indiana. Can you think of any other reason?

Mr. ST. JOHN. I do not think of any other reason. I am sorry to be so verbose in these. I was not expecting these inquiries.

Mr. HAUGEN. Would not that timidity that you refer to, and the demand for money, exist in New York as well as elsewhere?

Mr. ST. JOHN. It always does. If checks are drawn upon a bank the money must be there to meet them, or must be raised instanter.

Mr. HAUGEN. What rate of interest did you charge during the panic a year ago?

Mr. ST. JOHN. The Mercantile National Bank of New York never exacts more than 6 per cent from its dealers, under the present administration of thirteen years. There was one instance during that panic of 1893 in which we did exact 8 per cent, I think. We had been badly abused, and might have exacted 20 per cent if we had wanted to.

Mr. HAUGEN. What was the current rate about?

Mr. ST. JOHN. There was no current rate. Lenders got anything they chose to exact.

Mr. HAUGEN. It was much higher than it is now?

Mr. ST. JOHN. Yes; brokers paid on prime security three-fourths per cent per day and 6 per cent per annum; 276 per cent per annum for some days.

Mr. JOHNSON, of Indiana. Can you give us, in a succinct form, your explanation as to how there can be a remedy for the high price and scarcity of money in the agricultural districts in crop-moving times?

Mr. ST. JOHN. If there were a larger aggregate of money in the United States it could circulate over our vast territory without occasioning alarm. If I knew that the world believed that Louisville is absolutely prosperous, I would like to lend much of my money in Louisville. I would do so with the same certainty that I have mentioned as pertaining to New York. I merely take Louisville as the illustration, because you mention it.

Mr. JOHNSON, of Indiana. Take any other prosperous Western city where rates are higher on good security than with you.

Mr. ST. JOHN. I regard Louisville as one of the most prosperous cities of the West and South. I did not mean to reflect on Louisville. But there is no general prosperity in the United States to-day. That is what I meant to say.

Mr. JOHNSON, of Indiana. The rates of interest throughout New England have been a good deal less than in other sections of the country, have they not?

Mr. ST. JOHN. Yes.

Mr. COBB, of Alabama. Is it not a fact that it is because of this vast accumulation of money in New York, and a number of other cities, that the country is not generally prosperous?

Mr. ST. JOHN. These accumulations are not the cause; they are one evidence of the lack of prosperity.

Mr. COBB, of Alabama. Have you any opinion as to what causes this want of general prosperity, whether it is from natural conditions, or from the result of operations of law, or what is your idea?

Mr. ST. JOHN. My opinion is that the aggregate sum of money in the United States is insufficient to establish confidence in its ability to meet the demands upon it under ordinary prosperity. Also, our money has a scarcity value proportionate to our abundance of the commodities which it values. "Prices," or dollar valuation of commodities, is ruinous to those who provide prosperity when we have any.

Mr. COBB, of Alabama. What remedy can you suggest?

Mr. ST. JOHN. Enlarging the primary money of the United States.

Mr. COBB, of Alabama. How?

Mr. ST. JOHN. Abandon experiment and go back to eighty years of our own experience and the world's experience in money.

Mr. COBB, of Alabama. In your opinion, would that give us a more general dissemination of the volume of money in the country?

Mr. St. John. It would decidedly. May I read my answer to that inquiry on another occasion? I assume that I may.

At this present moment a dollar, as the means of acquisition and measure of value, is more efficient than in any other period of recent years, prices of staple commodities being ruinously low. And yet at this same time money seeking wages, entitled interest, seeks employment vainly, or at rates that barely pay. Under these conditions fixed capital suffers in the failure of investments, the banker suffers as a lender, the merchant in the restricted distribution of commodities, the manufacturer and other producer in the current low prices, and labor in want of employment starves. In the mutual relations between these elements of the people, accumulated wealth loses in the reduction of its income, but regains a portion in the increased efficiency of the remainder as related to the commodities which he consumes. No other one of these elements, as such other, has profited at all. Labor has lost everything in losing its employment. The enduring fact, therefore, if these functions in money were the only ones to be be preserved, would be "the rich made relatively richer at the expense of the poor made poorer," as one achievement of statute law.

Mr. Johnson, of Ohio. Do you consider that the enactment of Secretary Carlisle's plan into law will produce a great panic?

Mr. St. John. It will, if the seventh requirement is included, that banks must, in order to stay under national charter, not only guarantee each other's notes, but sell their $200,000,000 of bonds before July, 1895. And if they will not guarantee, but prefer to abandon national charter, this sale of their bonds will contract the currency by $180,000,000. It can not help creating panic.

Mr. Johnson, of Ohio. The forcing of United States bonds on the market is one element?

Mr. St. John. That is the primal cause; and then if the Government has to issue more bonds to recoup its gold reserve the timidity aroused in Wall street as to prices for Government bonds would manifest itself in the lack of any market for them, and prove perilous.

Mr. Johnson, of Ohio. You do not believe in bank currency as a substitute for greenbacks and national currency?

Mr. St. John. What do you mean by "national currency?"

Mr. Johnson, of Ohio. There are two or three forms. There is the Treasury note, which is really a legal tender, and there are the silver certificates and gold certificates. Those are national currencey, and they are proposing now to substitute the national-bank note for that. Do you believe in that plan?

Mr. St. John. I believe that if additional national-bank notes, or any other bank notes, were issued in liberal amount while our primary money is chaotic we would go to pieces for a time.

Mr. Johnson, of Ohio. Are you opposed on principle to this change that so many bankers have favored. of the Government going out ot the note issuing business and the banks going into it?

Mr. St. John. I am opposed to the substitution.

Mr. Johnson, of Ohio. You are not as wise as some who are in favor of redeeming and destroying greenbacks. You do not object to them as they do?

Mr. St. John. The only timidity I have with reference to the greenback—and I have that timidity, I am bound to confess—is that it is so good a money, so nearly perfect money, and yet not money, that you gentlemen will provide more and more to excess of it. The greenback is perilously good money, as suggesting more and more of it until collapse.

Mr. Johnson, of Ohio. Your practical suggestion is not to take in the notes by the Government?

Mr. St. John. I would not disturb the greenbacks.

Mr. JOHNSON, of Ohio. You propose in your plan, if I understand it, a dollar-for-dollar reserve in coin against these coin certificates. How much do you propose in order to provide for times of stringency?

Mr. ST. JOHN. Forty per cent of coin-certificates additional.

Mr. JOHNSON, of Ohio. An increase on the amount of what you have of $66\frac{2}{3}$ per cent.

Mr. ST. JOHN. Forty per cent reduction in the reserve.

Mr. JOHNSON, of Ohio. I beg pardon. You are wrong in the calculation.

Mr. ST. JOHN. I see what you mean. Your statement is correct mathematically, but I do not believe it would be intelligible after my other statement.

Mr. JOHNSON, of Ohio. That is, in extraordinary times you propose that the coin certificates out shall not be increased beyond the point of a 40 per cent reserve, which amounts to an increase of $66\frac{2}{3}$ per cent?

Mr. ST. JOHN. I mean that until bimetallism is the actual achievement of my bill, if it be enacted, that the usual reserve against the coin certificates shall be 100 per cent. But emergency issues may be made against deposits of United States bonds, but only reducing the reserve to 60 per cent at lowest.

Mr. JOHNSON, of Ohio. Does that afford an elastic currency?

Mr. ST. JOHN. It is the only really elastic currency that has been mentioned to your committee.

Mr. JOHNSON, of Ohio. I am inclined to agree with you.

Mr. ST. JOHN. There has been no elastic currency mentioned before in the course of these hearings, so far as I have read. This would be an elastic currency, and I have given you the reasons for it.

Mr. JOHNSON, of Ohio. You propose to convert the various Government bonds indirectly from bonds into currency?

Mr. ST. JOHN. Stopping the interest that the Government has to pay for the time the owners or borrowers use the money which the Treasury thus provides, and for no longer.

Mr. JOHNSON, of Ohio. It is really an interconvertible plan?

Mr. ST. JOHN. It is a temporarily convertible bond of the United States.

Mr. JOHNSON, of Ohio. It will contract?

Mr. ST. JOHN. The coin certificates will contract in amount as soon as the unusual demand for money ceases.

Mr. BLACK. Did I understand you to say this morning that, under existing circumstances, you would favor a bond issue?

Mr. ST. JOHN. What I said was this: That the business community of the United States to-day is in grave peril; that necessity knows no law but the law of self-preservation. I say that the United States to-day must redeem its notes in gold, even in defiance of law if necessary, for the sake of your prosperity and mine. But I say also that this ought not to be so.

Mr. BLACK. As I understand, the mistake of the Government has been made, but your idea is that we can not adopt any other plan?

Mr. ST. JOHN. The Government can not adopt any other course until it is strong enough in gold and silver both to make alarm ridiculous. A giant can do things that a child can not do. The United States was able to redeem greenbacks and Treasury notes in silver and laugh at such consequences as could have ensued. It is not able to do so to-day.

Mr. BLACK. That is what I understand. Then, under existing conditions, you would favor an issue of bonds?

Mr. ST. JOHN. I hope, but my judgment is against the hope, that we need not issue bonds. But until you furnish a statute which will enable the United States to create money in a way to stifle panic, I say yes, issue bonds to maintain a gold reserve, although I say we are at fault officially for this need.

Mr Cox. In regard to the plan suggested by the Secretary, you seem to have a very serious objection to the requirement that the banks shall guarantee the notes of each other. It seems that that is based, to a certain extent, upon the idea that liability would be unknown. Suppose the law were so amended as to provide that the banks should pay up to the extent of 5 per cent of their circulation, and that they should then be released; would not that relieve the difficulty?

Mr. St. John. That would take away the negotiability of the note. People would be afraid of the notes.

Mr. Cox. I do not think you have my idea.

Mr. St. John. Then I misunderstood you. The people to whom you offer a note would say: "Is that a note of the Chemical Bank? If it is, all right. If it is a note of the Osawotomie Bank, I don't want it."

Mr. Cox. The guarantee fund is raised to 5 per cent.

Mr. St. John. But it is to take ten years to raise it. What may happen meanwhile? Suppose it is exhausted in the first panic. It would take a second ten years to restore this 5 per cent "safety fund."

Mr. Sperry. The country is now on a gold basis, I take it?

Mr. St. John. The country is decidedly on a gold basis.

Mr. Sperry. If I understood you correctly this morning, you said that the proposed scheme would put us immediately upon a silver basis, and that in about two years we should come back again to the gold basis.

Mr. St. John. No, sir; I allowed the conclusion that we reach a silver basis at once. If we did, then I said we would achieve a bimetallic basis within two years, when both our dollars, gold and silver, would be at par.

Mr. Sperry. Then what basis would we be on?

Mr. St. John. A bimetallic basis, with the option to every debtor to pay in either coin, one coin being as good as another in the United States, and practically everywhere else in the world.

Mr. Sperry. In case we should go on a silver basis, under your proposed scheme, what effect would that have on the prices of labor and commodities?

Mr. St. John. It would enhance them materially, but not at once. The theory that we would jump into some region of excessively high prices is ridiculous. It is not historical. Everything that is readily negotiable would advance promptly. It would take real estate in New York City two years to begin to show the advance notably. Government bonds would not advance for the reason that they are already high-priced for the income they yield. But securities in general, railroad securities, would advance, because railroads would promise to be prosperous. There would not be any large immediate rise in normal prices of commodities for the reason that there is no great amount of silver bullion available to the United States to convert into money. I said this morning that about $5,000,000 is a liberal estimate for supplies on hand in distributing markets, and as soon as present owners saw that our mint would fix the price at $1.29 per ounce, they would not sell at less. India's supplies would go to her at $1.29 per ounce, as they now go at 62 cents an ounce.

Mr. Sperry. Then the immediate effect of reaching a silver basis would reduce the prices of commodities?

Mr. St. John. I said just the reverse. I said the immediate effect would be to raise the prices of everything, but that the rise would not be so rapid as some people imagine.

Mr. Sperry. Would there be any immediate effect?

Mr. St. John. There would be, decidedly.

Mr. Sperry. Then either I do not understand you or you do not understand me. What would be the immediate effect?

Mr. St. John. If the Secretary be the bold man I think him to be, and determine to carry out the law in spirit as in letter proposed, he would say, "Gentlemen of the United States, if anybody wants any part of $200,000,000 at 4 per cent or 5 per cent per annum, let him lodge United States bonds therefor and he can have it." Otherwise, the immediate effect would be a panic. This provision of my bill would stifle any panic that threatened to arise.

Mr. Sperry. Suppose we leave the bravery of the Secretary of the Treasury out of the account, and I will put it in this way: Under your proposed scheme we should go upon a silver basis?

Mr. St. John. I say I would not dispute that; I would admit it by way of argument. Practically I think that is not true. The demand for money, and no silver immediately available for money, would attract gold into use, at interest, just as soon as all alarm was seen to be ridiculous.

Mr. Sperry. What would be the immediate effect upon prices of labor?

Mr. St. John. The immediate effect, so far as felt at all, would be to raise the prices of everything, including labor.

Mr. Sperry. Immediately?

Mr. St. John. That would be the immediate tendency. "Immediate" is a vague term.

Mr. Sperry. There would be no effect downward?

Mr. St. John. No, sir.

Mr. Sperry. Would there be a panic?

Mr. St. John. No, sir; panic would be stifled, as I propose.

Mr. Sperry. I am asking for the immediate effect, not the final effect. I had thought that if we go on the silver basis the effect might be a panic.

Mr. St. John. If the means were not at hand to allay it there would be a panic. No business man gets panicky if he can see the means to allay it right at hand certain to be used.

Mr. Sperry. I am speaking of the condition of affairs, which I understand would result from your bill, if we should go immediately upon a silver basis. In that case would not the immediate effect be a panic?

Mr. St. John. No, sir; the sight of the means at immediate command to allay panic would prevent a panic.

Mr. Sperry. There would not be a panic if there was not any panic. I understand that.

Mr. St. John. I mean to answer you with entire frankness, and I do not mean to be captious. As I understand it, a panic could arise only from a shrinkage, or fear of shrinkage, in the volume of money. Now, I propose to meet that with $200,000,000 of coin certificates of the United States of America—as good a certificate for money as can be made.

Mr. Sperry. In other words, $600,000,000 of gold would go out?

Mr. St. John. I did not say that; I do not admit it. My bank has $1,400,000 of gold on hand as part of its reserve. Not a dollar of it would be disturbed. It would all lie there as now, in reserve against our $10,000,000 or $11,000,000 of deposits.

Mr. SPERRY. Would you cash checks with that gold?

Mr. ST. JOHN. We would not. We do not do so now except as a favor.

Mr. SPERRY. It does not circulate?

Mr. ST. JOHN. No.

Mr SPERRY. You prefer it as a reserve?

Mr. ST. JOHN. I do, decidedly, under the statutes as they exist. For large transactions gold is preferable to sixteen times its weight in silver, and doubtless always will be.

Mr. SPERRY. Then there would be no immediate panic?

Mr. ST. JOHN. None whatever, if the provision proposed is included in the act. Men are not children. We are not doing business on that basis in New York or elsewhere.

Mr. SPERRY. What are the means you speak of, that you think would allay what is generally considered to be an immediate effect of going off a gold basis?

Mr. St. JOHN. I think if anybody has the United States bonds, or if he can hire them, as has frequently been done, he could lodge them in any subtreasury or in the Treasury, and obtain any part of the $200,000,000 coin-certificates. These coin-certificates are to be a limited legal tender; as such, unless contracted against, they are money. There will be no objections to them if the money market is stringent. Clearing-house certificates are good enough for money in dread of panics: the United States certificate is their superior.

Mr. SPERRY. Those coin certificates would be redeemable, how?

Mr. ST. JOHN. In coin, at the Treasury's option as to whether gold or silver coin.

Mr. SPERRY. And if the condition of the Treasury were such as to force the Treasury to redeem those coin certificates in silver, then what?

Mr. ST. JOHN. The Treasury would not be asked to redeem any, that is all. It would not now be asked to redeem greenbacks or Treasury notes, had the like option been availed of when it ought to have been.

Mr. SPERRY. Then should we not be on a silver basis?

Mr. ST. JOHN. I said so; or on a paper basis, because the Treasury only owns a few million silver dollars at present.

Mr. SPERRY. Then the means you propose to allay the panic would not come into operation, would they?

Mr. ST. JOHN. I do not know why not. I never a saw a silver dollar at a discount, and I have bought them at 3 per cent premium. I offered in large type in every New York daily paper, for two days, three-quarters of 1 per cent premium for silver dollars to be paid for in clearing-house checks at the height of the panic of 1893.

Mr. SPERRY. In your judgment, if we go immediately upon a silver basis and the Government bonds are brought in and transferred into coin certificates, possibly in silver, no panic would result?

Mr. ST. JOHN. Not if my proposition of relief is adopted in the shape discussed.

Mr. SPERRY. What would be its effect on foreign exchange?

Mr. ST. JOHN. I told you this morning what the first effect would be if we were on a silver basis; it would depend entirely upon how much silver was offered at our mints. If a stringent demand for money appeared I would not be surprised to see dollars of the United States, of whatever composed, worth a premium as money in New York, over exchange on anywhere, right off. If scarcity of money were caused by the fulfillment of your idea that we would be immediately upon a silver basis, the demand upon gold for use as money would be superior to any promise of a premium on the gold in hoarding. If scarcity of money did not ensue the point of your inquiry is removed.

Mr. SPERRY. If you now draw exchange on London it calls for gold, does it not?

Mr. ST. JOHN. It means gold on the other side, or Bank of England notes.

Mr. SPERRY. Those are the equivalent of gold always.

Mr. ST. JOHN. Not always, but means that now.

Mr. SPERRY. If at the present time you draw exchange from London on New York that means gold?

Mr. ST. JOHN. Nobody ever does that.

Mr. SPERRY. Are not remittances made if there is a balance in our favor?

Mr. ST. JOHN. That is the other way. There are no remittances to us in that shape, in sums worth mentioning. Dealings in money between Europe and the United States are by drafts always on London, or elsewhere over there.

Mr. SPERRY. If I wanted to remit to New York, would I draw a draft?

Mr. ST. JOHN. No, sir; actual money would be shipped, unless you made a deposit in London to the credit of your creditors. If exchange on London were at a discount in New York, they would ship gold this way; it is the only acceptable thing they have to ship.

Mr. SPERRY. Are there times when exchange on London is at a discount in New York?

Mr. ST. JOHN. Many times. As, for instance, while the "Sherman Act" repeal bill was pending, and the New York papers had told alarmingly of our exportations of $71,000,000 between February and June, there came a day in June, 1893, when gold began to return. In the course of the four months ending with September, $55,000,000 of gold returned from Europe to New York. Would you believe that the New York papers forgot to direct public attention the fact? The "Sherman law" was not repealed until November 1. The reason that gold came back, the continuing "Sherman Act" to the contrary notwithstanding, was because exchange on London was at a discount in New York.

Mr. SPERRY. What would be the rate of exchange between New York and London if we were on a silver basis?

Mr. ST. JOHN. That would be a mere guess at present; there is nothing to base an opinion upon.

Mr. SPERRY. What would it represent?

Mr. ST. JOHN. It would represent the then present value of the money of the United States; which I think will be as good money, and as attractive to other nations, as an example, as any money in the world. It will be the very best if it restores our own and their prosperity.

Mr. SPERRY. That is the bullion value?

Mr. ST. JOHN. No, sir.

Mr. SPERRY. Would it represent the bullion value of gold and silver money?

Mr. ST. JOHN. It would represent what was then the relative bullion values of our gold and silver coins.

Mr. SPERRY. At the present time a merchant buying $1,000 worth of goods in London pays $1,000 in New York, within a range of 1 or 2 per cent for exchange, I take it?

Mr. ST. JOHN. I think I understand you, and if I do, that is about correct.

Mr. SPERRY. Suppose we were on a silver basis and that a New York merchant buys $1,000 worth of goods in London; how much will his draft cost him?

Mr. St. John. That will be taken into the account in the price of the goods when buying, and he will not remit such money as you imagine. I will explain: The silver dollar of the United States, if it were in London to-day, would sell there at a discount of about five-eighths of 1 per cent. That is par, less freight, insurance, and interest to New York. It would not sell at the value of the bullion composing it, as you are sometimes told here. If the mints of the United States were wide open to silver, as they are to gold, the market price of silver, for a time at least—and this will commend itself to anybody—would be the coining price of silver at our mint.

Mr. Sperry. What does the Mexican dollar sell for in London?

Mr. St. John. It sells for its bullion value without regard to the law of Mexico. Let me explain.

Mr. Sperry. Answer it now.

Mr. St. John. I will answer it now. I object, first of all, to Mexico as a criterion for the United States. Mexico's population does not exceed the aggregate population of Pennsylvania and New York. Mexico's little internal-trade employment for her money may be imagined from the fact that her entire railroad system embraces about one-third the direct track mileage of the Erie Railway, only one-sixth of the direct and side-track mileage of that single one of the railroad systems of the United States; and Mexico imports of commodities, which are her mere comforts, together with her luxuries, an aggregate of more than she has anything else, but her silver product to give for them. Therefore, as a seller of silver necessarily at any price obtainable, her silver coin and bullion stand practically alike in the markets of the world.

Mr. Sperry. What is the relative bullion value of the Mexican dollar and the American dollar?

Mr. St. John. One is about 420 grains and the other about 412½, nine-tenths fine.

Mr. Sperry. The bullion value of the Mexican dollar is worth more than the bullion value of the American dollar?

Mr. St. John. Yes; and our trade-dollar's bullion value was the same as that of Mexico when we had trade dollars. When our trade dollars were deprived of their legal-tender function they sold like bullion, at a discount, while our ordinary 412.50-grain silver dollar was at par.

Mr. Sperry. Have you stated the price of the Mexican dollar in London?

Mr. St. John. It is whatever the price of silver bullion is, and a little more. They fetch anywhere from one-half of 1 per cent to 1 per cent more than bullion, because available for exportations to China as money.

Mr. Sperry. It sells as bullion?

Mr. St. John. At a moderate premium over bullion.

Mr. Sperry. The American dollar does not sell as bullion?

Mr. St. John. It would sell to-day in London for 100 cents in gold, less about five-eighths of 1 per cent, the cost of transportation to New York.

Mr. Sperry. Just on a par with the greenback?

Mr. St. John. Or the gold dollar when exchange on London is at a premium as now.

Mr. Sperry. These two kinds of dollars, Mexican and American, being of substantially the same bullion value, can you explain why it is that in London the Mexican sells for about 50 cents in gold and the American for about 100 cents in gold?

Mr. St. John. Because the aggregate of American dollars (gold, silver, and paper) is not greater than our aggregate employment for them all as money. Our gold, silver, and paper dollars, as long as they are equivalent legal tenders and as long as the aggregate of them does not exceed our use for them as money, will always be at par at home and abroad. Demand for dollars here relative to the supply of dollars here will comprehend the whole question.

Mr. Sperry. Would it be true to say in answer to the question I put to you that the American dollar sells at par, so to speak, because the American Government maintains a parity between the two metals?

Mr. St. John. Not a bit of it. The Government does not do it. Neither the Treasurer of the United States nor any assistant treasurer would dare to-day to redeem 10,000,000 of silver dollars in gold. He would have a storm of popular indignation upon him over night.

Mr. Sperry. Then you think the Government does not maintain a parity?

Mr. St. John. I know that the Government does not maintain the parity between our silver dollars and our gold coin. The business demand for dollars, whatever composes dollars, maintains this parity in their use as money. The Government does not, and could not just now.

Mr. Sperry. The parity is maintained, is it?

Mr. St. John. It is, in spite of the pitiable condition of our Treasury.

Mr. Sperry. Then I will put the question in that way: Do you think the American silver dollar sells at par in London because the parity of the two metals is maintained in the United States?

Mr. St. John. Yes, sir; that is it exactly. You mean the coins, of course.

Mr. Sperry. Of course I meant gold and silver coin. If we go on a silver basis, that ends the maintenance of the parity between the two metals?

Mr. St. John. I did not admit it for a moment; and I do not believe it, though I assented to it, provided it suited you. I said, to begin with, that there is not $5,000,000 worth of silver bullion available at once to the United States, if our mints were reopened to silver. Can you imagine the United States unable to add $5,000,000 to its aggregate of money at par? Until the volume of silver brought to our mints becomes so great that we can not use the money into which we convert it, $1.29 per ounce pure will be the world's price for silver bullion everywhere.

Mr. Sperry. Then, in your judgment, if we should go upon the silver basis, the parity being destroyed by whomsoever destroyed, a merchant in New York buying $1,000 worth of goods in London would merely remit $1,000 without regard to the difference in value between gold and silver coin?

Mr. St. John. You surely would not attribute any such impression to an intelligent man. I did not say anything like that.

Mr. Sperry. I understood you to say so.

Mr. St. John. No, sir.

Mr. Sperry. Then what would be the effect, the parity being broken down or lost, if a New York merchant wants to settle a $1,000 account in London? How much will it cost him in American money?

Mr. St. John. That would depend upon relative prices in New York and London, ascertained daily by cable, for wheat, cotton, pretroleum, and the like. The difference and a margin for safety would determine practically the rate of sterling exchange.

Mr. Sperry. He would speculate in the wheat market?

Mr. St. John. He would decidedly not speculate. Such transactions proceed daily now. The buying here and selling over there are practically done at a single moment. The movement of commodities from the United States determines whether exchange on London is at par, or a premium, or a discount in New York.

Mr. Sperry. Suppose he did not want to go into the wheat market?

Mr. St. John. He would not need to go into the wheat market. I told you the way in which the price of exchange is fixed. But if the movement of commodities left us debtors in the balancing of trade, then the rate of exchange on London would be fixed at once and for so long at the difference between London's price for the gold bullion and silver bullion in our dollars.

Mr. Sperry. Suppose he did not want his banker in London to speculate in the wheat market. Suppose he should go to his New York banker and ask for a London draft to pay $1,000 in London; how much would he have to pay his New York bank for the London draft after the parity is lost?

Mr. St. John. The difference in exchange would equal the difference in the parity, as just explained, under the conditions mentioned.

Mr. Sperry. That is exactly what I am trying to get at. That would be the difference between the bullion value of gold and silver coinage of the United States, would it?

Mr. St. John. At the time when the transaction is made, our mints being open without limit to both metals, our trade relations with Europe would answer your inquiry. I predicted this morning our relations to become the creditor in trade with Europe.

Mr. Sperry. Then if the silver dollar were worth 50 cents, and we were on a silver basis so that all the New York checks would be cashed in silver, he would have to draw a draft for how much—$2,000?

Mr. St. John. I could not suppose any such thing. That could not exist. The supposition is an impossibility in itself, when the United States stands ready to coin at 1.29 per ounce.

Mr. Sperry. Now, you are assuming.

Mr. St. John. But you must not put upon me an assumption that I regard ridiculous.

Mr. Sperry. But you are assuming that the United States comes in to establish the parity, are you not?

Mr. St. John. I am not; not to establish the parity as you mean; but if the United States proposes to coin into our money without limit all the silver that is offered, and if all that can be offered, for years at least, can not be more than we can use acceptably as money, your assumption is not reasonable.

Mr. Sperry. Is it an answer to the question to assume that the United States comes to the assistance of the New York merchant and establishes a parity?

Mr. St. John. That would seem, on its face, to be an offensive way of putting your inquiry.

Mr. Sperry. I do not wish to be offensive, but if you can answer my question I will put it over again, and give you another opportunity. Whatever you say goes. The question is this: Assume that we have lost the parity. Under your answer I take it I had a right to assume that. New York checks are cashed in silver dollars, the bullion value of which is 50 cents of their face, in round numbers. A New York merchant wants to settle a $1,000 account in London which calls for gold. He goes to his New York banker and asks for a draft on London. How much will he have to pay for that draft in order to settle that account in London?

Mr. ST. JOHN. Unless the chairman insists upon my answering that question "yes or no," which would be grossly unfair to me, I will restate all there is of a question in what you ask, and answer it. Whatever is the difference in price between 371.25 grains of silver bullion in New York and 23.22 grains of gold bullion in New York, that difference will be the premium on exchange on London in New York, unquestionably.

Mr. SPERRY. That is exactly what I supposed.

Mr. ST. JOHN. I will not assume for a moment that 50 cents will be the price of the silver bullion in our dollar anywhere, when our mint values it at a hundred cents. I would not sanction that statement for a moment, so long as India continues her vast demands upon the world's supplies of silver, and there is not the slightest prospect that it will cease.

Mr. SPERRY. What is the bullion value of a silver dollar to-day?

Mr. ST. JOHN. About forty-nine and odd cents. I have not seen the quotations for two or three days. But our own and every other mint in the world are practically closed against silver, excepting that of India. Indian princes are coining; and the Government is coining rupees on Government account, and will continue to.

Mr. SPERRY. We have to deal in legislation with existing conditions.

Mr. ST. JOHN. Oh, no; not at all. We create conditions by law. We govern sixty odd millions of people, occupying 3,000,000 square miles of as productive territory as the face of the globe could provide, under one dictation of enlightened law.

The CHAIRMAN. Are there any other questions?

Mr. ST. JOHN. I should like to place myself on record by saying two or three things, if it will not take up too much time.

I object to the conclusions of the Comptroller of the Currency, in his report for the present year. On page 33 of that report, at the bottom of the page, he says:

> Under the existing laws, the Government standing responsible for the redemption of the circulation of failed national banks, up to January 1 last, had there been no bond deposit whatever, the loss to it would have been but $1,139,253, and of this amount $958,247 represents the loss by banks whose trusts are still open and will pay further dividends, thus reducing the amount last named.

My comment on this is that no one knows what would have happened "if." We do know that the safety-fund system of the Baltimore plan failed disastrously in New York, that the Suffolk system failed expensively in emergency, and that every other but the one national-banking system of note issue has been costly to the people of the United States.

I desire to ask if I may submit this paper with reference to the experience of France that I referred to this morning.

The CHAIRMAN. Certainly.

Mr. HAUGEN. It is understood that he may offer anything he desires.

The CHAIRMAN. Certainly.

Mr. ST. JOHN. With your permission, then, I will append this matter in proper sequence for the printer, following the paper read this morning.

Mr. JOHNSON, of Indiana. Pardon me. Mr. Chairman, I believe a meeting for the committee has been appointed for to-night. It will be very inconvenient for members to come up here, and I desire to move that we now go into executive session, with a view of seeing if we can not attend to our business and avoid a night meeting. We are all tired. Mr. St. John has been heard at length, and it seems to me that he might have made these attacks or refutations in the time he has occupied, instead of going so extensively into a discussion of the silver question. I think he should be allowed to put himself on record without testifying.

Mr. St. John. I only desire to refer to two or three other matters.

The Chairman. Mr. St. John can state briefly what he desires.

Mr. St. John. Mr. Horace White, on page 85 of the report of these hearings, said, in commending the safety-fund system of bank notes:

Both systems (the New York safety-fund and Suffolk systems) aim to secure note-holders, and both are adequate to that end.

I beg to offer, in rebuttal, Hon. John J. Knox, in his report as Comptroller for 1876. On page xxiii he reports regarding the New York safety-fund experience that:

Contributions to the fund were first made in 1831. In 1841 to 1842 eleven of the safety-fund banks failed, with an aggregate capital of $3,150,000. The sum which had been paid into the fund by these banks was about $86,274, while the amount required for the redemption of their circulation was $1,548,588.

Mr. Walker. In a subsequent report Mr. Knox changed his opinion.

Mr. St. John. This is no part of his opinion. I do not offer anyone's opinions. Facts only interest me in this perilous controvesy. I will offer in rebuttal again of Mr. Horace White, and these points cover all he offered you as facts to base your opinions on, the following as to the Suffolk system. It went to pieces on more than one occasion, and it did not aim to maintain bank notes at par. It bought bank notes at a discount. The people have learned the value of money at par. They won't approve of any other. Here is the rebuttal of Mr. Horace White:

[The Suffolk Bank, by D. R. Whitney, president of the Suffolk Bank, Riverside Press, Cambridge Mass., 1878.]

The business man of to-day knows little by experience of the inconvenience and loss suffered by the merchant of sixty years ago arising from the currency in which debts were then paid (p. 1). Suffolk Bank's charter was granted February 10, 1818. There were only six banks in Boston (p. 3). If any bank deposits with Suffolk Bank $5,000 permanently, and more as needed from time to time, such bank shall have the privilege of receiving its own bills at the same discount at which they are purchased (p. 7). About this time, May, 1825 (p. 16), the Phœnix and Pacific banks of Nantucket failed to redeem their bills. * * * After a delay of two months a settlement was made (p. 17). Between 1831 and 1833 a great increase took place in the number of banks in New England. * * * The Suffolk Bank became overloaded with bills (p. 23).

During the winter of 1835-36 thirty-two new banks were chartered. * * * Many of these banks with little or no real capital; specie was borrowed one day to be counted by the bank commissioner and replaced next day by the notes of stockholders; the bills of these banks, loaned in violation of the usury law at high rates of interest, were used in the wildest speculations. * * * These bills poured in upon the Suffolk Bank until forty-four banks were overdrawn $664,000, and Suffolk Bank rebelled (p. 25). * * * The threatening storm now broke (May, 1837); Suffolk Bank, in common with other banks, suspended specie payments (p. 28). * * * Suffolk Bank's total losses by Eastern banks was very great (p. 30). * * * About this time (1844) arrangement was made with bankers and others in New York to receive New England bills at one-tenth of 1 per cent discount (p. 38). * * * In December, 1855, the difficulties attending the business had become so great that the propriety of giving it up was discussed. It was decided to continue it (p. 52). During the five years preceding 1857 a large increase of banks took place in New England. * * * Speculation was rampant, * * * specie reserve was low, * * * loans had increased, so that the banks were in a very poor position to withstand the panic which then took place (p. 55). On October 14, in common with other banks and on recommendation of the clearing house, the Suffolk Bank suspended specie payments (p. 56).

Mr. Johnson, of Indiana. What went to pieces?

Mr. St. John. The Suffolk redemption system, not the Suffolk Bank. That is a prime national bank to-day; and we are one of its correspondents in New York. That note-redemption system was utterly inadequate. It was a disastrous failure at three distinctly separate times.

Mr. JOHNSON, of Indiana. What broke down?

Mr. ST. JOHN. The whole system known as the Suffolk Bank note-redeeming system. The whole thing broke down because too much work was put upon it. It was not adequate to the occasion. There was not specie available with which to fulfill obligations created and floated. Nothing similar would fare better to-day.

Mr. JOHNSON, of Indiana. The distinguishing feature of that system was the redemption of bank notes?

Mr. ST. JOHN. Yes: they did not always have the means to redeem the notes.

Mr. JOHNSON, of Indiana. I do not want to seem to be discourteous to Mr. St. John, but much he has said, in my opinion, has not been relevant. If he desires to make a direct reference that will occupy but a few moments, I have no objection to his doing so, or to his inserting in the record some quotation that he thinks desirable. But I do not believe that it is necessary for us to hear these matters in extenso.

The CHAIRMAN. How much time do you desire, Mr. St. John?

Mr. ST. JOHN. If I can have five minutes I can say all I desire.

The CHAIRMAN. Proceed.

Mr. WARNER. I understand that Mr. St. John is at liberty also to extend his remarks and put them in the shape he wishes to have them appear in the record.

Mr. ST. JOHN. After the stenographer's notes are sent me I can make my revision?

Mr. WARNER. Yes.

Mr. ST. JOHN. With regard to the testimony of Mr. Butler, of New Haven, I will say that he is my personal friend, and knows that I esteem him highly. We differ in our notions as to money. He seems to have said that if free coinage of silver were to be provided he would sell out everything and invest in real estate, "because I could raise my rentals and get a fair return for my money." I would rejoin that if there were no prosperity accompanying free coinage his tenants could not stand a rise in rent, if they could pay any rent at all.

A similar prediction was attributed by the New York papers to my warm personal friend, Mr. George S. Coe. president of the American Exchange National Bank of New York, and chairman of the finance committee of the Chamber of Commerce, in connection with the Bland-Allison act of 1878, as that enactment might affect specie payments in 1879. Our newspapers attributed to Mr. Coe the assertion that he would give $50,000 to purchase first place on the line at the subtreasury in New York to demand gold for greenbacks on January 1, 1879, if the Bland-Allison act were not vetoed by the President. The act became a law over the veto, and against the predictions of the New York papers of a cataclysm if it should. In 1880, while the Bland act was in execution, and 75,000,000 of silver dollars were already coined, the United States imported $75,000,000 more than it exported of gold that year; and in 1881, after $105,000,000 of silver dollars had been coined, the United States imported $97,000,000 more of gold than it exported that year. And remember that $55,000,000 of gold was imported after $71,000,000 had been exported, while the Sherman Act repeal was still pending and uncertain in 1893.

I desire to say also that I object to the conclusions of Mr. Hepburn, when Comptroller of the Currency, on page 32 of his report for 1892.

Mr. Hepburn is now president of the Third National Bank of New York. On that page 32 he said:

> Over 90 per cent of all business transactions are done by means of credit. When the public lose confidence and credit is impaired and refused, over 90 per cent of all business transactions are directly affected. It is easy to realize how impossible it is for the remaining 10 per cent of money to carry on the business of the country without monetary stringency and financial distress.

Ninety per cent of the banking business may be conducted in credit substitutes for money, but the banking business is only a portion of all the business of the United States. The buying of cotton and of grain from first hands, called the "first movement of the crops," is done mostly with actual money. Railroad fares and city travel are paid for in actual money. Much of the retail business of the country of all kinds and pay rolls, etc., employ actual money, as Comptroller Eckels in his recent report shows. The aggregate of all other than the banking business, therefore, is vast, and employs a vast aggregate of money.

I desire further to object to Canada as a criterion for the United States, as advanced by Mr. Horace White and Mr. Cornwell.

Canada will be a criterion for the United States when the eagle takes dictation from the humming bird.

The total population of all the provinces composing Canada is less than 4,850,000; the population of the State of New York alone is 5,900,000; population of the United States, 67,000,000. The circulating notes of all the chartered banks of Canada are less than $40,000,000; the gold coin in the clearing-house banks of New York City, November 25, 1894, was $96,000,000. The aggregate resources of all the chartered banks of Canada was less than $315,000,000; the aggregate resources of the clearing-house banks of New York City alone exceeds $1,434,000,000; the aggregate resources of the State and national banks of the United States exceeds $7,340,000,000.

Canada's bank act was "assented" to May 16, 1890. It has had no strain upon it. Thirty-nine banks compose the system which it governs. The United States statutes, on the lines proposed by Secretary Carlisle, would govern 8,000 banks (State and national).

I desire, finally, to submit for the consideration of the committee the following concurrent resolution intoduced in the Senate by Senator Matthews December 6, 1877, which passed the Senate January 25, 1878, and passed the House promptly thereafter:

> *Therefore, be it resolved by the Senate (the House of Representatives concurring therein),* That all the bonds of the United States issued or authorized to be issued under the said act of Congress hereinbefore recited are payable, principal and interest, at the option of the Government of the United States, in silver dollars, of the coinage of the United States, containing 412½ grains each of standard silver: and that to restore to its coinage such silver coins as a legal tender in payment of said bonds, principal and interest, is not in violation of the public faith, nor in derogation of the rights of the public creditor.

Mr. Stanley Matthews died a justice of the Supreme Court of the United States.

Mr. Chairman and gentlemen, I hope you will overlook the defects of my statements. My nervousness is due to my severe cold, which kept me coughing half the night. I apologized for it in advance; and I thank the committee for its kind attention.

Mr. JOHNSON, of Ohio. I move that the hearings be now closed.

The motion was agreed to.

Mr. JOHNSON, of Indiana. I move that the committee go into executive session.

The motion was agreed to; and at 3.54 o'clock p. m. the committee went into executive session.

The CHAIRMAN. Mr. William B. Dana, editor of the Commercial and Financial Chronicle, of New York, who was invited to address the committee, has forwarded the following letter, transmitting an article from his journal, giving his views as to the adjustability and safety of bank notes:

NEW YORK, *December 15, 1894.*

DEAR SIR: I have written a short article in the Chronicle issued to-day on what seems to be the most important feature of a new bank-note system. As you desired my views on the questions now before your committee, I take the liberty of sending you a copy of the paper, and have also sent a copy to each member of your committee.

Yours, very truly,

WILLIAM B. DANA.

Hon. WILLIAM M. SPRINGER.

The article is as follows:

"THE ADJUSTABILITY AND SAFETY OF BANK NOTES.

"As the week closes the indications are that the Banking and Currency Committee will report Mr. Carlisle's currency measure to the House on Monday or soon thereafter. We think this step is taken not because the majority favor the bill as it now is, but in deference to the Administration and to hasten the progress of the subject-matter for legislative action. There are obvious defects in the bill as it stands, needing amendment, and yet it has also some admirable features which can be utilized, so that altogether a good system and a rectification of our Government issues may be put into operation speedily, if the sentiment of the Senate and House on currency matters has been sufficiently progressed by the events of the past few months.

"It is impossible to say much in one short article on so broad a subject. There is, however, a point in this discussion with reference to a new bank-note system at which the advocates of reform divide and separate into two distinct bodies, getting farther and farther apart as the details of any plan are unfolded. By fixing the attention on that feature and analyzing the existing differences of opinion in that particular between men equally earnest and honest, it may be that a more perfect union of sentiment can be obtained. An effort for such a union is highly desirable, for the views held now are so antagonistic—not as apparent in the general purpose as in the arrangement of the details—that both can not be right; one or the other position must be abandoned in formulating a new system.

"The difference referred to grows out of a preference between the choice of methods suggested by the alternative whether, in providing a bank-note system, elasticity or safety is the prime consideration. That is, should the aim first be to devise a note that is safe—"as good as gold," as one writer has expressed it—and then try to make the system responsive to commerce, or should we first make it elastic, that is, responsive to commerce, and then make the note as safe as it can be made consistent with perfect elasticity. A very considerable body of our people start with a firm belief that the present national-bank note system is a perfect model, claiming that since no man ever lost a dollar from the use of these notes, that it has been and is what we must have again. On the other hand, a large number say that the use of bank notes is to facilitate commercial transactions, and as there are tides in those transactions, periods in each year and periods among the years, when the body of merchandise to be moved and the body of exchanges occurring vary greatly, so there should be corresponding currency tides. In other words, the system ought to be so planned that the quantity of the notes outstanding will always and automatically adjust itself to the varying extent of the commercial requirements. These words express in brief two classes of thought, one or the other of which, as already said, must control in the formation of a bank-note plan, for both conditions can not be brought to perfection in the same contrivance.

"We say the two can not be in perfection in the same system, because what is intended by "perfect safety," or "as good as gold," is the conferring upon a commercial instrument—upon a mere promise to pay, which is all that a bank note can be—the quality of passing everywhere like gold, being hoarded like that metal, never consequently seeking its issuer, but enjoying a grade of confidence that public credit alone enjoys. This position can be secured only when no easy and quick method of redemption is adopted, and when the Government in some form is made sponsor to the promise—a situation which, if created, will ever after prevent the note from being in touch with commerce, that is, from going into and out of the issuer's vaults in response to the varying degrees of commercial activity, such as call for an increase or decrease of the volume of currency afloat.

"If we were to subject the Baltimore plan and Mr. Carlisle's plan to this test we should say that neither of them was satisfactory; in one feature Mr. Carlisle's plan is the better though not perfect, but in the other the two are alike lacking. The point in which the Secretary's arrangement is preferable is with respect to the Government indorsement; his scheme does not provide any such liability. On the other hand, the Baltimore plan states that "the notes of insolvent banks shall be redeemed by the Treasurer of the United States out of the guaranty fund if it shall be sufficient, and if not sufficient then out of any money in the Treasury, the same to be reimbursed to the Treasury out of the guaranty fund when replenished either from the assets of the failed banks or from the tax aforesaid." This provision we consider is objectionable, both because it puts the Government into the banking business, and also because no currency can be responsive to commerce which circulates on and enjoys the credit of the Government.

"No matter in what way the Government responsibility may be attached to the promise, it takes from the mobility of the note. That, of course, is the more obvious when the method of securing this responsibility is by the use of a United States bond, as is the case at present with our national-bank notes. Mr. Hepburn remarked upon this point at the bankers' convention when the Baltimore plan was under discussion. He stated that no bank-note device secured by stocks or bonds could possess elasticity. "A currency to be elastic must be issued against credit." "In no other way can it meet the wants of commerce." Mr. Homer on the same occasion said: "Our currency must be supplied by the banks, not by the Government. * * * The banks are the arteries of commerce, feeling instantly the changes of commercial activity and intimately acquainted with its volume and requirements. * * * Hence the currency must be elastic, stretching out over the broad expanse of business activity, able to supply its fullest wants, and contracting again as the strain of commercial vitality relaxes." Mr. Carlisle, in his recent report, made much the same assertions, showing how unsuitable the present bank-note device is for meeting great exigencies, that is occasions when commerce needs quick currency expansion, and, he might also have added, when it calls for corresponding temporary retirement. We have ourselves several times referred to the same defect; the last two occasions were about two months ago (October 13, p. 622, and October 27, p. 719), when we specified some of the difficulties interposed to the automatic expansion and contraction of a bank currency based upon stocks or bonds or the credit of the Government.

"Both of these plans are also defective in the matter of redeeming agencies for the note. The Baltimore scheme, instead of providing a method with as little friction and as much within the lines of commerce as possible, makes the redemption the same as now exists under the national banking law. Consequently Washington, the capital of the country, and in no sense a commercial center, becomes the axis around which this "flexible currency, responsive to the demands of commerce," must revolve. We can do no better than to quote the words of Mr. George A. Butler, of New Haven, on this point, who gave his views the current week to Chairman Springer and the members of the Banking and Currency Committee:

"'One thing [he said] he would insist upon, and that was that a central redemption bureau should be maintained in New York, since banking, being a purely commercial and not a political business, should be centered in the commercial rather than the political capital of the country. By having redemption conducted at the point to which nearly all the notes of banks all over the country were attracted, the redemption process would be made quick and easy and the profit and the security of the circulation of all the banks thereby promoted.'

"This feature of quick, easy, and natural redemption in place of the artificial and circuitous affair maintained at Washington is so essential to the keeping of any bank-note currency subject to and its quantity under the influence of commerce, we should think it would commend itself to every experienced banker desiring to make the new note system safe and to put it beyond the power of deranging our industries.

"If, then, the bankers who prepared the Baltimore plan really meant what they said, will it not be necessary for them before they can attain the ends they are seeking (1) to take out the clause which makes the Government sponsor for the note and (2) to change the method of redemption?"

ADDENDUM.

On page 49 of the hearings, at the close of the second paragraph, the Secretary of the Treasury submitted a table showing the comparative profits of circulation under the proposed plan and under the existing law. This table was prepared in the office of the Comptroller of the Currency, and is as follows:

Statement showing profit accruing to a bank issuing circulation upon the plan proposed by the Secretary of the Treasury.

[Prepared by the Comptroller of the Currency.]

Under plan proposed by the Secretary:
A bank with $100,000 capital could receive $75,000 in notes, but must deposit $22,500 in legal tenders.

$75,000 loaned at 6 per cent would yield		$4,500.00
Deduct expenses, etc., viz:		
Loss of interest on $22,500 investedin "legal tenders" deposited (at 6 per cent)	$1,350.00	
Annual cost redemption of $75,000 circulation	37.50	
Express charges on $75,000 circulation	2.50	
Cost of plates for $75,000 circulation	6.25	
Agents' fees on $75,000 circulation	5.82	
(This charge is based on cost of present plan of redemption.)		
One-fourth of 1 per cent tax on $75,000 for "safety fund"	187.50	
One-fourth of 1 per cent tax on $75,000, bureau expenses	187.50	
	1,777.07	
1 per cent tax on $75,000 for "safety fund," first year	750.00	
		2,527.07
Net profit on $75,000 first year		1,972.93
Net profit on $75,000 after first year		2,722.93

Statement showing profit accruing to a bank issuing circulation based upon a deposit of United States 2 per cent bonds, October 31, 1894.

Amount of bonds necessary to secure $75,000 circulation		$86,805.55
Interest on $86,805.55 bonds (costing, at 96 per cent, $83,333.33), at 2 per cent		1,736.11
Interest on $75,000 circulation, at 6 per cent		4,500.00
Gross profits		6,236.11
Deduct:		
1 per cent tax on $75,000 circulation	$750.00	
Annual cost of redemption	37.50	
Express charges	2.50	
Cost of plates for circulation	6.00	
Agent's fees	5.83	
		801.83
Net profits		5,434.28
$83,333⅓ (cost of bonds) would yield, at 6 per cent		5,000.00
Net profit in favor of circulation		434.28

Statement showing profit accruing to a bank issuing circulation based upon a deposit of United States 4 per cent bonds, October 31, 1894.

Interest on $83,333.33 bonds (worth, a t115, $95,833.33), at 4 per cent		$3,333.33
Interest on $75,000 circulation, at 6 per cent		4,500.00
Gross profits		7,833.33
Deduct:		
1 per cent tax on $75,000 circulation	$750.00	
Annual cost of redemption	37.50	
Express charges	2.50	
Cost of plates for circulation	6.00	
Agent's fees	5.83	
Sinking fund (reinvested quarterly) to liquidate premium	670.00	
		1,471.83
Net profits		6,361.50
$95,833.33 (cost of bonds) would yield, at 6 per cent		5,750.00
Net profit in favor of circulation		611.50

Statement showing profit accruing to a bank issuing circulation based upon a deposit of United States 5 per cent bonds, October 31, 1894.

Interest on $83,333.33 bonds (worth at 119 $99,166.66) at 5 per cent		$4,166.66
Interest on $75,000 circulation at 6 per cent		4,500.00
Gross profits		8,666.66
Deduct:		
1 per cent tax on $75,000 circulation	$750.00	
Annual cost of redemption	37.50	
Express charges	2.50	
Cost of plates for circulation	6.00	
Agent's fees	5.83	
Sinking fund (reinvested quarterly) to liquidate premium	1,355.00	
		2,156.83
Net profits		6,509.83
$99,166.66 (cost of bonds) would yield, at 6 per cent		5,950.00
Net profit in favor of circulation		559.83

Statement showing profit accruing to a bank issuing circulation based upon a deposit of United States 6 per cent bonds, October 31, 1894.

Interest on $83,333.33 bonds (worth at 108 $90,000) at 6 per cent		$5,000.00
Interest on $75,000 circulation at 6 per cent		4,500.00
Gross profits		9,500.00
Deduct:		
1 per cent tax on $75,000 circulation	$750.00	
Annual cost of redemption	37.50	
Express charges	2.50	
Cost of plates for circulation	6.00	
Agent's fees	5.83	
Sinking fund (reinvested quarterly) to liquidate premium	1,650.00	
		2,451.83
Net profits		7,048.
$90,000 (cost of bonds) would yield, at 6 per cent		5,400.
Net profit in favor of circulation		1,648.

BANKING AND CURRENCY HEARINGS, 1894.

FIFTY-THIRD CONGRESS, THIRD SESSION.

INDEX.

www.ingramcontent.com/pod-product-compliance
Lightning Source LLC
Chambersburg PA
CBHW030902270326
41929CB00008B/531
* 9 7 8 3 3 3 7 1 1 9 5 6 0 *